Western Civilizations

Their History & Their Culture

Joshua Cole

Carol Symes

Western Civilizations

Their History & Their Culture

EIGHTEENTH EDITION

VOLUME 2

W. W. Norton & Company ▪ NEW YORK ▪ LONDON

W. W. Norton & Company has been independent since its founding in 1923, when William Warder Norton and Mary D. Herter Norton first published lectures delivered at the People's Institute, the adult education division of New York City's Cooper Union. The firm soon expanded its program beyond the Institute, publishing books by celebrated academics from America and abroad. By midcentury, the two major pillars of Norton's publishing program—trade books and college texts—were firmly established. In the 1950s, the Norton family transferred control of the company to its employees, and today—with a staff of four hundred and a comparable number of trade, college, and professional titles published each year—W. W. Norton & Company stands as the largest and oldest publishing house owned wholly by its employees.

Copyright © 2014, 2011, 2008, 2005, 2002, 1998, 1993, 1988, 1984, 1980, 1973, 1968, 1963, 1958, 1954, 1949, 1947, 1941 by W. W. Norton & Company, Inc.

Editor: Jon Durbin
Associate editor: Justin Cahill
Editorial assistant: Penelope Lin
Project editor: Melissa Atkin
Managing editor, College: Marian Johnson
Copyeditor: Jude Grant
E-media editors: Steve Hoge, Tacy Quinn
Ancillary editor: Lorraine Klimowich
Assistant editor, E-media: Stefani Wallace
Photo editor: Evan Luberger
Photo research: Rona Tucillo
Marketing manager, History: Sarah England
Production manager, College: Sean Mintus
Design director: Rubina Yeh
Book designer: Judith Abbate / Abbate Design
Composition: Jouve
Cartographers: Mapping Specialists
Manufacturing: Transcontinental

Library of Congress has catalogued the one-volume edition as follows:

Cole, Joshua, 1961–
    Western civilizations : their history & their culture / Joshua Cole and Carol Symes. —Eighteenth edition.
        pages cm
    Includes bibliographical references and index.
    ISBN 978-0-393-92213-4 (hardcover)
    1. Civilization, Western—Textbooks.   2. Europe—Civilization—Textbooks.   I. Symes, Carol.   II. Title.
    CB245.C56 2013
    909'.09821—dc23
                                                                2013029952

This edition:
ISBN: 978-0-393-92215-8 (pbk.)

W. W. Norton & Company, Inc., 500 Fifth Avenue, New York, N. Y. 10110
wwnorton.com

W. W. Norton & Company Ltd., Castle House, 75/76 Wells Street, London W1T 3QT

1 2 3 4 5 6 7 8 9 0

To our families:

Kate Tremel, Lucas and Ruby Cole
Tom, Erin, and Connor Wilson

with love and gratitude for their support.
And to all our students, who have also been
our teachers.

About the Authors

JOSHUA COLE (Ph.D., University of California, Berkeley) is Associate Professor of History at the University of Michigan, Ann Arbor. His publications include work on gender and the history of the population sciences, colonial violence, and the politics of memory in nineteenth- and twentieth-century France, Germany, and Algeria. His first book was *The Power of Large Numbers: Population, Politics, and Gender in Nineteenth-Century France* (Ithaca, NY: Cornell University Press, 2000).

CAROL SYMES (Ph.D., Harvard University) is Associate Professor of History and Director of Undergraduate Studies in the history department at the University of Illinois, Urbana-Champaign, where she has won the top teaching award in the College of Liberal Arts and Sciences. Her main areas of study include medieval Europe, the history of information media and communication technologies, and the history of theater. Her first book was *A Common Stage: Theater and Public Life in Medieval Arras* (Ithaca: Cornell University Press, 2007).

Brief Contents

Chapter 16 ▪ THE NEW SCIENCE OF THE SEVENTEENTH CENTURY   519

Chapter 17 ▪ EUROPE DURING THE ENLIGHTENMENT   547

Maps

Primary Sources

This new edition of *Western Civilizations* sharpens and expands the set of tools we have developed to empower students—our own and yours—to engage effectively with the themes, sources, and challenges of history. It presents a clear and vigorous narrative, supplemented by a compelling selection of primary sources and striking images. At the same time, as the authors of this book's previous edition, we have worked to develop a unified program of pedagogical elements that guide students toward a more thorough understanding of the past, and of the ways that historians reconstruct that past. This framework helps students to analyze and interpret historical evidence on their own, encouraging them to become active participants in the learning process.

Moreover, the wide chronological scope of this book offers an unusual opportunity to trace central human developments (population movements, intellectual currents, economic trends, the formation of political institutions, the power of religious belief, the role of the arts and of technologies) in a region of the world whose cultural diversity has been constantly invigorated and renewed by its interactions with peoples living in other places. Students today have a wide selection of introductory history courses to choose from, thanks to the welcome availability of introductory surveys in Latin American, African, and Asian history, alongside both traditional and innovative offerings in the history of the United States and Europe. Global history has also come into its own in recent years. But our increasing awareness that no region's history can be isolated from global processes and connections has merely heightened the need for a richly contextualized and broad-based history such as that represented in *Western Civilizations*.

As in previous editions, we have attempted to balance the coverage of political, social, economic, and cultural phenomena with extensive treatment of material culture, daily life, gender, sexuality, art, science, and popular culture. And following the path laid out by the book's previous authors, Judith Coffin and Robert Stacey, we have insisted that the history of European peoples must be understood through their interactions with peoples in other parts of the world. Our treatment of this history is accordingly both deep and dynamic, attentive to the latest developments in historical scholarship.

Given the importance of placing human history in a global context, those of us who study the histories of ancient, medieval, and modern Europe are actively changing the ways that we teach this history. For good reasons reflected in the title of this book, few historians today would uphold a monolithic vision of a single and enduring "Western civilization" whose inevitable march to domination can be traced chapter by chapter through time. This older paradigm, strongly associated with the curriculum of early twentieth-century American colleges and universities, no longer conforms to what we know about the human past. Neither the "West" nor "Europe" can be seen as distinct, unified entities in space or time; the meanings attributed to these geographical expressions have changed in significant ways. Moreover, historians now agree that a linear notion of any civilization persisting unchanged over the centuries was made coherent only by leaving out the intense conflicts, extraordinary ruptures, and dynamic changes that took place at the heart of the societies we call "Western." Smoothing out the rough edges of the past does students no favors; even an introductory text such as this one should present the past as it appears to the historians who study it—that is, as complex panorama of human effort, filled with possibility and achievement but also fraught with discord, uncertainty, accident, and tragedy.

We know that current and future users of our text will be enthusiastic to see the efforts made in this new edition to update and reorganize the Late Medieval and Early Modern periods in order to place them in a larger Atlantic World context. The major highlight of this reorganization is a brand new chapter, entitled "Europe in the Atlantic World, 1550–1650." It places the newly integrated space of the Atlantic at the center of the story, exploring the ways, that religious warfare, economic developments, population movements, and cultural trends shaped—and were shaped by—historical actors on this dynamic frontier. Another significant result of the reorganization of these two periods is to provide a clearer chronological framework for the narrative, so that the students can better see how major topics and events emerge from their historical contexts. This, of course, was part of a larger effort begun across the entire text in the previous edition. These revisions demonstrate our dual commitment to keep the book current and up-to-date, while striving to integrate strong pedagogical features that help students build their study and history skills.

New and Revised Pedagogical Features

In our ongoing effort to shape students' engagement with history, this book is designed to reinforce your course objectives by helping students to master core content while challenging them to think critically about the past. In order to achieve these aims, our previous edition augmented the traditional strengths of *Western Civilizations* by introducing several exciting new features. These have since been refined and revised in accordance with feedback from student readers and teachers of the book. The most important and revolutionary feature is the pedagogical structure that supports each chapter. As we know from long experience, many students in introductory survey courses find the sheer quantity of information overwhelming, and so we have provided guidance to help them navigate through the material and to read in meaningful ways.

At the outset of each chapter, the **Before You Read This Chapter** feature offers three preliminary windows onto the material to be covered: *Story Lines*, *Chronology*, and *Core Objectives*. *Story Lines* allow the student to become familiar with the primary narrative threads that tie the chapter's elements together, and the *Chronology* grounds these *Story Lines* in the period under study. *Core Objectives* provide a checklist to ensure that the student is aware of the primary teaching points in the chapter. The student is then reminded of these teaching points upon completing the chapter, in the **After You Read This Chapter** section, which prompts the student to revisit the chapter in three ways. The first, *Reviewing the Core Objectives*, asks the reader to reconsider core objectives by answering a pointed question about each one. The second, *People, Ideas, and Events in Context*, summarizes some of the particulars that students should retain from their reading, through questions that allow them to relate individual terms to the major objectives and story

lines. Finally, *Thinking about Connections*, new to this edition, allow for more open-ended reflection on the significance of the chapter's material, drawing students' attention to issues that connect it to previous chapters and giving them insight into what comes next. As a package, the pedagogical features at the beginning and end of each chapter work together to enhance the student's learning experience, by breaking down the process of reading and analysis into manageable tasks.

A second package of pedagogical features is designed to capture students' interest and to compel them to think about what is at stake in the construction and use of historical narratives. Each chapter opens with a vignette that showcases a particular person or event representative of the era as a whole. Within each chapter, an expanded program of illustrations and maps has been enhanced by the addition of **Guiding Questions** (following these illustrations' and maps' captions) that urge the reader to explore the historical contexts and significance of these features in a more analytical way. The historical value of images, artifacts, and material culture is further emphasized in another feature we introduced in our previous edition, **Interpreting Visual Evidence**. This section provides discussion leaders with a provocative departure point for conversations about the key issues raised by visual sources, which students often find more approachable than texts. Once this conversation has begun, students can further develop their skills by **Analyzing Primary Sources**, through close readings of primary texts accompanied by cogent interpretive questions. The dynamism and diversity of Western civilizations are also illuminated through a look at **Competing Viewpoints** in each chapter, in which specific debates are presented through paired primary-source texts. The bibliographical **Further Readings**, located at the end of the book, has also been edited and brought up-to-date.

In addition to these features, which have proven successful, we are delighted to introduce an entirely new segment with this eighteenth edition. The new **Past and Present** features in the main text prompt students to connect events unfolding in the past with the breaking news of our own time, by taking one episode from each chapter and comparing it with a phenomenon that resonates more immediately with our students. To bring this new feature to life for students, we have also created a new series of **Author Videos**, in which we describe and analyze these connections across time and place. There are a number of illuminating discussions, including, "Spectator Sports," which compares the Roman gladiatorial games with NFL Football; "The Reputation of Richard III," which shows how modern forensics like those we see used on numerous TV shows were recently used to identify the remains of Richard III;

"The Persistence of Monarchies in a Democratic Age," which explains the origins and evolution of our ongoing fascination with royals like Louis XIV and Princess Diana; and "The Internet and the Enlightenment Public Sphere," which compares the kinds of public networks that helped spread Enlightenment ideas to the way the Internet can be used today to spread political ideas in movements such as the Arab Spring and Occupy Wall Street. Through this new feature, not only do we want to encourage students to recognize the continuing relevance of seemingly distant historical moments, but also we want to encourage historically-minded habits that will be useful for a lifetime. If students learn to see the connections among their world and the past, they will be more apt to place unfolding developments and debates in a more informed and complex historical context.

A Tour of New Chapters and Revisions

Our previous edition of *Western Civilizations* featured significant changes to each of the book's first five chapters, and this process of revision has continued in the present edition. In Chapter 1, the challenge of locating and interpreting historical evidence drawn from nontextual sources (archaeological, environmental, anthropological, mythic) is a special focus. Chapter 2 further underscores the degree to which recent archeological discoveries and new historical techniques have revolutionized our understanding of ancient history, and have also corroborated ancient peoples' own understandings of their past. Chapter 3 offers expanded coverage of the diverse polities that emerged in ancient Greece, and of Athens' closely related political, documentary, artistic, and intellectual achievements. Chapter 4's exploration of the Hellenistic world includes an unusually wide-ranging discussion of the scientific revolution powered by this first cosmopolitan civilization. Chapter 5 emphasizes the ways that the unique values and institutions of the Roman Republic are transformed through imperial expansion under the Principate.

With Chapter 6, a more extensive series of revisions has resulted in some significant reshaping and reorganization, so that the book's narrative reflects recent scholarship. The story of Rome's transformative encounter with early Christianity has been rewritten to ensure clarity and also to emphasize the fundamental ways that Christianity itself changed through the Roman Empire and in contact with peoples from northwestern Europe. Chapter 7, which examines Rome's three distinctive successor civilizations, now offers more extensive coverage of the reign of Justinian

and emergence of Islam. Balanced attention to the interlocking histories of Byzantium, the Muslim caliphates, and western Europe has carried forward in subsequent chapters. Chapters 8 contains an entirely new section, "A Tour of Europe around the Year 1000," with coverage of the Viking diaspora, the formation of Scandinavian kingdoms and the empire of Cnute, early medieval Rus' and eastern Europe, and the relationship among Mediterranean microcosms. It also features greatly expanded coverage of economy, trade, and the events leading up to the First Crusade. Chapter 9, which now covers the period 1000–1250, features a new segment on the Crusader States and crusading movements within Europe.

Chapter 10's treatment of the medieval world between 1250 and 1350 is almost wholly new, reflecting cutting-edge scholarship on this era. It includes a fresh look at the consolidation of the Mongol Khanates, new images and maps, some new sources, and a new *Interpreting Visual Evidence* segment on seals and their users. Chapters 11 and 12 have been thoroughly reorganized and rewritten to ensure that the narrative of medieval Europeans' colonial ventures (from the western Mediterranean to the eastern Atlantic and Africa, and beyond) is integrated with the story of the Black Death's effects on the medieval world and the impetus for the intellectual and artistic innovations of the Renaissance. In previous editions of the book, these concurrent phenomena were treated as separate, as though they took place in three separate periods (the later Middle Ages, the Renaissance, and the Age of Exploration). This made the connections among them almost impossible to explain or appreciate. In this eighteenth edition, therefore, the voyages of Columbus are firmly rooted in their historical contexts while the religious, social, and cultural upheavals of the Reformation (Chapter 13) are more clearly placed against a backdrop of political and economic competition in Europe and the Americas.

This program of revisions sets the stage for the most significant new chapter in the book: Chapter 14, "Europe in the Atlantic World, 1550–1650." This chapter, the hinge between the book's first and second halves, resulted from a close collaboration between us. It is designed to function either as the satisfying culmination of a course that surveys the history of Western civilizations up to the middle of the seventeenth century (like that taught by Carol Symes) or to provide a foundation for a course on the history of the modern West (like that taught by Joshua Cole). The chapter illuminates the changing nature of Europe as it becomes fully integrated into the larger Atlantic world that dramatically impacts all of its internal political, social, cultural, and economic development. In addition to greatly enhanced treatment of the transatlantic slave trade and the Columbian

Exchange, it also features new sections on the different models of colonial settlement in the Caribbean and the Americas, as well as expanded coverage of the Thirty Years' War.

The new emphasis on the emergence of the Atlantic world carries over to Chapter 15, which covers the emergence of powerful absolutist regimes on the continent and the evolution of wealthy European trading empires in the Americas, Africa, and Asia. This material has now been reorganized to clarify developments over time, as the early successes of the Spanish empire are gradually eclipsed by the successes of the Dutch, the French, and the British empires. A new document on the Streltsy rebellion, meanwhile, allows students to better understand the contested nature of power under the Russian tsars during the absolutist period. We have retained the emphasis on intellectual and cultural history in Chapter 16, on the Scientific Revolution, and in Chapter 17, on the Enlightenment. In Chapter 16 we have enhanced our treatment of the relationship between Christian faith and the new sciences of observation with a new primary-source document by Pierre Gassendi. In Chapter 17, meanwhile, we have sought to set the Enlightenment more clearly in its social and political context, connecting it more explicitly to the theme of European expansion into the Americas and the Pacific. This helps, for example, in connecting a document like the American Declaration of Independence with the ideas of European Enlightenment thinkers.

Chapters 18–19 cover the political and economic revolutions of the late eighteenth and early nineteenth centuries. Chapter 18 covers the French Revolution and the Napoleonic empires in depth, while also drawing attention to the way that these central episodes were rooted in a larger pattern of revolutionary political change that engulfed the Atlantic world. Chapter 19 emphasizes both the economic growth and the technological innovations that were a part of the Industrial Revolution, while also exploring the social and cultural consequences of industrialization for men and women in Europe's new industrial societies. The *Interpreting Visual Evidence* feature in Chapter 19 allows students to explore the ways that industrialization created new perceptions of the global economy in Europe, changing the way people thought of their place in the world.

Chapters 20–21 explore the successive struggles between conservative reaction and radicals in Europe, as the dynamic forces of nationalism unleashed by the French Revolution redrew the map of Europe and threatened the dynastic regimes that had ruled for centuries. Here, however, we have sought to clarify the periodization of the post-Napoleonic decades by focusing Chapter 20 more clearly on the conservative reaction in Europe after 1815, and the ideologies of conservatism, liberalism, republicanism, socialism,

and nationalism. By setting the 1848 revolutions entirely in Chapter 21 (rather than split between the two chapters as in previous editions) instructors should be able to demonstrate more easily the connection between these political movements and the history of national unification in Germany and Italy in subsequent decades. While making these changes in the organization of the chapters, we have retained our treatment of the important cultural movements of the first half of the nineteenth century, especially Romanticism.

Chapter 22 takes on the history of nineteenth-century colonialism, exploring both its political and economic origins and its consequences for the peoples of Africa and Asia. The chapter gives new emphasis to the significance of colonial conquest for European culture, as colonial power became increasingly associated with national greatness, both in conservative monarchies and in more democratic regimes. Meanwhile, Chapter 23 brings the narrative back to the heart of Europe, covering the long-term consequences of industrialization and the consolidation of a conservative form of nationalism in many European nations even as the electorate was being expanded. The chapter emphasizes the varied nature of the new forms of political dissent, from the feminists who claimed the right to vote to the newly organized socialist movements that proved so enduring in many European countries.

Chapters 24 and 25 bring new vividness to the history of the First World War and the intense conflicts of the interwar period, while Chapter 26 uses the history of the Second World War as a hinge for understanding European and global developments in the second half of the twentieth century. The *Interpreting Visual Evidence* feature in Chapter 24 allows for a special focus on the role of propaganda among the belligerent nations in 1914–1918; and the chapter's section on the diplomatic crisis that preceded the First World War has been streamlined to allow students to more easily comprehend the essential issues at the heart of the conflict. In Chapter 25 the *Interpreting Visual Evidence* feature continues to explore the theme touched on in earlier chapters, political representations of "the people," this time in the context of fascist spectacles in Germany and Italy in the 1930s. These visual sources help students to understand the vulnerability of Europe's democratic regimes during these years as they faced the dual assault from fascists on the right and Bolsheviks on the left.

Chapters 27–29 bring the volumes to a close in a thorough exploration of the Cold War, decolonization, the collapse of the Soviet Union and the Eastern Bloc in 1989–1991, and the roots of the multifaceted global conflicts that beset the world in the first decade of the twenty-first century. Chapter 27 juxtaposes the Cold War with decolonization, showing how this combination sharply diminished the ability of European nations to control events in the international arena, even as they succeeded in rebuilding their economies at home. Chapter 28 explores the vibrancy of European culture in the crucial period of the 1960s to the early 1990s, bringing new attention to the significance of 1989 as a turning point in European history. Finally, extensive revisions to Chapter 29, add to the issues covered in our treatment of Europe's place in the contemporary globalized world. The chapter now includes a new section on efforts to deal with climate change, as well as expanded discussion of the impact of global terrorism, and recent developments in the Arab-Israeli conflict. The discussion on the financial crisis of 2008 and the presidency of Barack Obama has been brought up to date, and two new sections have been added to allow students to think about the Arab Spring of 2011 and the European debt crisis of recent years in connection with the broader history of European democracy, nation-building, and colonialism in the modern period.

Media Resources for Instructors and Students

LMS COURSEPACKS WITH STRONG ASSESSMENT AND LECTURE TOOLS

- **Dynamic Author Videos (55 total)** in which the authors discuss two of the main topics or themes in each chapter. New to this edition, illustrations, maps, and other types of media are integrated into the interviews to make them richer and more dynamic. These segments can serve as lecture launchers or as a preview tool for students before and after they read a chapter. (Available in PowerPoint and on Norton StudySpace.)
- **NEW *Past and Present* Author Videos (29 total)** that connect topics across time and place and show why history is relevant to understanding our world today (see further explanation above). Examples include "Spectator Sports," "Medieval Plots and Modern Movies," "Global Pandemics," and "The Atlantic Revolutions and Human Rights" (Available in PowerPoint and on Norton StudySpace.)
- **NEW Guided Reading Exercises** by Scott Corbett (Ventura College) are designed to help students learn how to effectively read a textbook. The reading exercises, which are keyed to each chapter's *People, Ideas, and Events in Context*

questions, instill a three-step Note-Summarize-Assess pedagogy. Exercises are based on actual passages from the textbook (three exercises per chapter). Feedback will provide model responses with direct page references. (Available only in the Norton Coursepack.)
- **NEW 36 Map Exercises** can be assigned for assessment. These activities ask students a series of questions about historical events that must be answered by clicking on the map to record the answer. (Available only in the Norton Coursepack.)
- **NEW Chrono-Quiz** improving on the ever-popular Chrono-Sequencer, the Chrono-Quiz is now available as an assessment activity that will report to the school's native LMS. (Available only in the Norton Coursepack.)
- **NEW *StoryMaps*** break complex maps into a sequence of four to five annotated screens that focus on the *story* behind the *geography*. There are ten StoryMaps that include such topics as The Silk Road, The Spread of the Black Death, and Nineteenth-Century Imperialism. (Available only on wwnorton.com/web/westernciv18/instructors.)

INSTRUCTOR'S MANUAL

Bob Brennan (Cape Fear Community College)
Bruce Delfini (Rockland Community College)
Christopher Laney (Berkshire Community College)
Alice Roberti (Santa Rosa Community College)

The Instructor's Manual for *Western Civilizations*, Eighteenth edition, is designed to help instructors prepare lectures and exams. The Instructor's Manual contains detailed chapter outlines, general discussion questions, document discussion questions, lecture objectives, interdisciplinary discussion topics, and recommended reading and film lists. **This edition has been revised to include sample answers to all of the student-facing comprehension questions in the text.**

TEST BANK

Geoffrey Clark (SUNY Potsdam)
Donna Trembinski (St. Francis Xavier University)

The Test Bank contains over 2,000 multiple-choice, true/false, and essay questions. This edition of the Test Bank has been completely revised for content and accuracy. All test questions are now aligned to Bloom's Taxonomy for greater ease and effectiveness of assessment.

FOR STUDENTS

⊚ wwnorton.com/web/westerncivl8
Free and open to all students, Norton StudySpace includes

- **Author Videos (over 80 in all)** for every chapter, including the new *Past and Present* segments that connect topics. Examples include
  - "Medieval Plots and Modern Movies"
  - "Controlling Consumption" (the legalization of controlled substances, from sixteenth-century regulations to contemporary marijuana policy)
  - "The Internet and the Enlightenment Public Sphere"
- **Chapter Outlines and Quizzes.** Quiz feedback is aligned to student learning outcomes and core objectives, along with page references.
- **World History Tours,** powered by Google Earth™, now operate from within the browser, eliminating the need to download third-party applications or files.
- **iMaps** allow students to view layers of information on each map.
- **Map Worksheets** provide each map without labels for offline re-labeling and quizzing.
- **Flashcards** align key terms and events with brief descriptions and definitions.
- Over **400 primary-source documents and images**
- **Ebook links** tie the online text to all study and review materials.

A FEW WORDS OF THANKS

Our first edition as members of *Western Civilizations'* authorial team was a challenging and rewarding one. Our second edition has been equally rewarding in that we have been able to implement a number of useful and engaging changes in the content and structure of the book, which we hope will make it even more student- and classroom-friendly. We are very grateful for the expert assistance and support of the Norton team, especially that of our editor, Jon Durbin. Melissa Atkin, our fabulous project editor, has driven the book beautifully through the manuscript process. Justin Cahill has provided good critiques of the illustrations and the new *Past and Present* features in addition to all the other parts of the project he has handled so skillfully. Evan Luberger and Rona Tucillo did an excellent job finding many of the exact images we specified. Lorraine Klimowich did an expert job developing the print ancillaries. Sean Mintus has efficiently marched

us through the production process. Steve Hoge has done a great job developing the book's fantastic emedia, particularly the new *Past and Present* Author Videos, the new Guided Reading Exercises, and the new StoryMaps. Jude Grant and John Gould were terrific in skillfully guiding the manuscript through the copyediting and proofreading stages. Finally, we want to thank Sarah England for spearheading the marketing campaign for the new edition. We are also indebted to the numerous expert readers who commented on various chapters and who thereby strengthened the book as a whole. We are thankful to our families, for their patience and advice, and to our students, whose questions and comments over the years have been essential to the framing of this book. And we extend a special thanks to, and hope to hear from, all the teachers and students we might never meet—their engagement with this book will frame new understandings of our shared past and its bearing on our future.

REVIEWERS

17ᵗʰ Edition Consultants
Paul Freedman, Yale University
Sheryl Kroen, University of Florida
Michael Kulikowski, Pennsylvania State University
Harry Liebersohn, University of Illinois, Urbana-Champaign
Helmut Smith, Vanderbilt University

17ᵗʰ Edition Reviewers
Donna Allen, Glendale Community College
Ken Bartlett, University of Toronto
Volker Benkert, Arizona State University
Dean Bennett, Schenectady City Community College
Patrick Brennan, Gulf Coast Community College
Neil Brooks, Community College of Baltimore County, Essex
James Brophy, University of Delaware
Kevin Caldwell, Blue Ridge Community College
Keith Chu, Bergen Community College
Alex D'Erizans, Borough of Manhattan Community College, CUNY
Hilary Earl, Nipissing University
Kirk Ford, Mississippi College
Michael Gattis, Gulf Coast Community College
David M. Gallo, College of Mount Saint Vincent
Jamie Gruring, Arizona State University
Tim Hack, Salem Community College
Bernard Hagerty, University of Pittsburg
Paul T. Hietter, Mesa Community College

Paul Hughes, Sussex County Community College
Kyle Irvin, Jefferson State Community College
Llana Krug, York College of Pennsylvania
Guy Lalande, St. Francis Xavier University
Chris Laney, Berkshire Community College
Charles Levine, Mesa Community College
Michael McKeown, Daytona State University
Dan Puckett, Troy State University
Dan Robinson, Troy State University
Craig Saucier, Southeastern Louisiana University
Aletia Seaborn, Southern Union State College
Victoria Thompson, Arizona State University
Donna Trembinski, St. Francis Xavier University
Pamela West, Jefferson State Community College
Julianna Wilson, Pima Community College

18th Edition Reviewers
Matthew Barlow, John Abbott College
Ken Bartlett, University of Toronto
Bob Brennan, Cape Fear Community College
Jim Brophy, University of Delaware
Keith Chu, Bergen Community College

Geoffrey Clark, SUNY Potsdam
Bill Donovan, Loyola University Maryland
Jeff Ewen, Sussex County Community College
Peter Goddard, University of Guelph
Paul Hughes, Sussex County Community
    College
Michael Kulikowski, Penn State University
Chris Laney, Berkshire Community College
James Martin, Campbell University
Derrick McKisick, Fairfield University
Dan Puckett, Troy University
Major Ben Richards, US Military Academy
Bo Riley, Columbus State Community College
Kimlisa Salazar, Pima Community College
Sara Scalenghe, Loyola University Maryland
Suzanne Smith, Cape Fear Community College
Bobbi Sutherland, Dordt College
David Tengwall, Anne Arundel Community
    College
Pam West, Jefferson State Community College
Julianna Wilson, Pima Community College
Margarita Youngo, Pima Community College

Western Civilizations

Their History & Their Culture

Before You Read This Chapter

STORY LINES

- The Mongol Empire widened channels of communication, commerce, and cultural exchange between Europe and the Far East. At the same time, Europeans were extending their reach into the Atlantic Ocean.

- Western civilizations' integration with this wider medieval world led to new ways of mapping, measuring, and describing that world.

- Despite these broadening horizons, most Europeans' lives were bounded by their communities and focused on the parish church.

- Meanwhile, the growing strength of the kings of France and England drew them into terminal disputes that led to the Hundred Years' War.

- As global climate change affected the ecosystems of Europe and caused years of famine, the integrated networks of the medieval world facilitated the rapid transmission of the Black Death.

CHRONOLOGY

1206–1260	Rapid expansion of the Mongol Empire under Genghis Khan and his heirs
1240	Kievan Rus' is taken by the Mongols; Khanate of the Golden Horde established
1260–1294	Reign of Kublai Khan, Great Khan and emperor of China
1271–1295	Travels of Marco Polo
1309	"Babylonian Captivity" of the papacy in Avignon begins
1315–1322	The Great Famine in Europe
1320	The Declaration of Arbroath proclaims Scotland's independence from England
1326–1354	The travels of Ibn Battuta
1337	Beginning of the Hundred Years' War
1347–1353	Spread of the Black Death
1352	Mandeville's *Book of Marvels* is in circulation

The Medieval World, 1250–1350

CORE OBJECTIVES

- **DESCRIBE** the effects of the Mongol conquests.

- **IDENTIFY** the key characteristics of the medieval world system and the responses to it.

- **DEFINE** the concept of sovereignty and its importance in this era.

- **UNDERSTAND** the reasons for the papacy's loss of prestige.

- **EXPLAIN** the rapid spread of the Black Death in this historical context.

When Christopher Columbus set out to find a new trade route to the East, he carried with him two influential travel narratives written centuries before his voyage. One was *The Book of Marvels*, composed around 1350 and attributed to John de Mandeville, an English adventurer (writing in French) who claimed to have reached the far horizons of the globe. The other was Marco Polo's *Description of the World*, an account of that Venetian merchant's journey through the vast Eurasian realm of the Mongol Empire to the court of the Great Khan in China. He had dictated it to an author of popular romances around 1298, when both men (Marco Polo and his ghostwriter) were in prison—in Columbus's own city of Genoa, coincidentally. Both of these books were the product of an extraordinary era of unprecedented interactions among the peoples of Europe, Asia, and the interconnected Mediterranean world. And both became extraordinarily influential, inspiring generations of mercantile adventurers, ambitious pilgrims, and armchair travelers. Eventually, they would fuel the imaginations of those future mariners who launched a further age of discovery (see Chapter 12).

In many ways, these narratives were as fantastical as they were factual. That makes them problematic sources for historians to use, but it also makes them representative of an era that seemed wide open to every sort of influence. This was a time when ease of communication and commercial exchange made Western civilizations part of an interlocking network that potentially spanned the globe. Although this network would prove fragile in the face of a large-scale demographic crisis, the Black Death, it created a lasting impression of infinite possibilities. Indeed, it was only *because* of this network's connective channels that the Black Death was able to wreak such devastation in the years around 1350. Looking back, we can see the century leading up to this near-global crisis as the beginning of a new global age.

Europeans' integration with this widening world not only put them into contact with unfamiliar cultures and commodities, it opened up new ways of looking at the world they already knew. New artistic and intellectual responses are discernible in this era, as are a host of new inventions and technologies. At the same time, involvement in this wider world placed new pressures on long-term developments within Europe: notably the growing tensions among large territorial monarchies, and between these secular powers and the authority of the papacy. By the early fourteenth century, the papal court would literally be held hostage by the king of France. A few decades later, the king of England would openly declare his own claim to the French throne. The ensuing struggles for sovereignty would have a profound impact on the balance of power in Europe, and further complicate Europeans' relationships with one another and with their far-flung neighbors.

THE MONGOL EMPIRE AND THE REORIENTATION OF THE WEST

In our long-term survey of Western civilizations, we have frequently noted the existence of strong links between the Mediterranean world and the Far East. Trade along the network of trails known as the Silk Road can be traced far back into antiquity, and we have seen that such overland networks were extended by Europe's waterways and by the sea. But it was not until the late thirteenth century that Europeans were able to establish direct connections with India, China, and the so-called Spice Islands of the Indonesian archipelago. For Europeans, these connections would prove profoundly important, as much for their impact on the European imagination as for their economic significance. For the peoples of Asia, however, the more

frequent appearance of Europeans was less consequential than the events that made these journeys possible: the rise of a new empire that encompassed the entire continent.

The Expansion of the Mongol Empire

The Mongols were one of many nomadic peoples inhabiting the vast steppes of Central Asia. Although closely connected with the Turkish populations with whom they frequently intermarried, the Mongols spoke their own distinctive language and had their own homeland, located to the north of the Gobi Desert in what is now known as Mongolia. Essentially, the Mongols were herdsmen whose daily lives and wealth depended on the sheep that provided shelter (sheepskin tents), woolen clothing, milk, and meat. But the Mongols were also highly accomplished horsemen and raiders. Indeed, it was to curtail their raiding ventures that the Chinese had fortified their Great Wall, many centuries before. Primarily, though, China defended itself from the Mongols by attempting to ensure that they remained internally divided, with their energies turned against each other.

In the late twelfth century, however, a Mongol chief named Temujin (c. 1162–1227) began to unite the various tribes under his rule. He did so by incorporating the warriors of each defeated tribe into his own army, gradually building up a large and terrifyingly effective military force. In 1206, his supremacy over all these tribes was reflected in his new title: Genghis Khan, from the Mongol words meaning "universal ruler." This new name also revealed wider ambitions, and in 1209 Genghis Khan began to direct his enormous army against the Mongols' neighbors. Taking advantage of the fact that China was then divided into three warring states, he launched an attack on the Chin Empire of the north, managing to penetrate deep into its interior by 1211. These initial attacks were probably looting expeditions rather than deliberate attempts at conquest, but the Mongols' aims were soon sharpened under Genghis Khan's successors. Shortly after his death in 1227, a full-scale invasion of both northern and western China was under way. In 1234, these regions also fell to the Mongols. By 1279, one of Genghis Khan's numerous grandsons, Kublai Khan, would complete the conquest by adding southern China to this empire.

For the first time in centuries, China was reunited, and under Mongol rule. It was also connected to western and central Asia in ways unprecedented in its long history, since Genghis Khan had brought crucial commercial cities and Silk Road trading posts (Tashkent, Samarkand, and Bukhara) into his empire. One of his sons, Ögedei (*EHRG-*

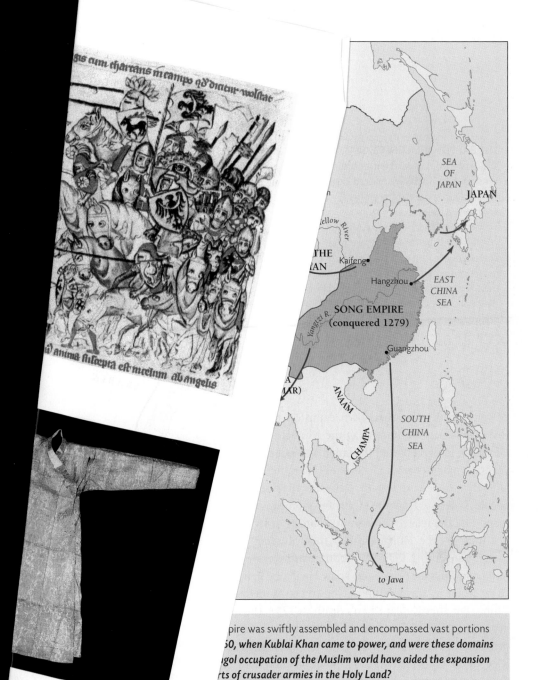

gis cum thartaris in campo qd dicitur wolstac

In anima suscepta est micelum ab angelis

...GOLD. The majestic term
...oth the power and the splendor
...d Rus' and many other lands. The
...e thirteenth or early fourteenth
...old: silk woven with gold (and
...t surprisingly durable material
...tents. A robe similar to this one
...quarter of a million dollars.

...atched relations between
...st deteriorate drastically
...e openly hostile to west-
...ple was captured and
...hapter 9), an event that
...as the last remaining

SEA OF JAPAN

JAPAN

ellow River

THE ...AN

Kaifeng

Hangzhou

EAST CHINA SEA

Yangzi R.

SONG EMPIRE
(conquered 1279)

Guangzhou

...A ...AR)

ANAM

CHAMPA

SOUTH CHINA SEA

to Java

...pire was swiftly assembled and encompassed vast portions
...50, when Kublai Khan came to power, and were these domains
...gol occupation of the Muslim world have aided the expansion
...ts of crusader armies in the Holy Land?

...ajo. It could have moved even deeper into Europe after
...his important victory, but it withdrew when Ögedei Khan
died in December of that same year.

Muscovy and the Mongol Khanate

As we have seen in previous chapters, the Russian capital
at Kiev had fostered crucial diplomatic and trading relations with both western Europe and Byzantium, and with
the Islamic Caliphate at Baghdad. That dynamic changed
with the arrival of the Mongols, who shifted the locus of

THE BATTLE OF LIEGNITZ, 1241.
This image from a fourteenth-century chronicle shows heavily armored knights from Poland and Germany (at right) confronting the swift-moving mounted archers of the Mongol cavalry. Mongol warriors often had the advantage over Europeans because their smaller, faster horses carried lighter loads and because the warriors themselves could shoot down their opponents at long range. ▪ *Which army appears to be gaining the upper hand here?*

power from Kiev to their own camp on the lower Volga River. This became known as the Khanate of the Golden Horde, an integral part of the larger Mongol Empire for 150 years. Its magnificent name evokes the impression made by tents that shone with wealth, some literally hung with cloth of gold. It derives from the Mongol word meaning "encampment" and the related Turkish word *ordu* ("army").

Initially, the Mongols ruled their Russian territories directly, installing their own administrative officials and requiring Russian princes to show their obedience to the Great Khan by traveling in person to the Mongol court in China. But after Kublai Khan's death in 1294, the Mongols began to tolerate the existence of several semi-independent principalities from which they demanded regular tribute. Kiev never recovered its dominant position, but one of these newer principalities would eventually form the core of a Russian state called Muscovy, centered on the duchy of Moscow. As the tribute-collecting center for the Mongol Khanate, Moscow received some protection against attack. Its dukes were even encouraged to absorb neighboring territories in this region, in order to increase Moscow's security. But this also meant that the Muscovite dukes could extend their powers even further without attracting too much attention from their Mongol overlords, whose power base was far away.

Compared to Kiev, Moscow's location was less advantageous for forging commercial contacts with the Baltic and Black Sea regions. Its direct ties with western Europe were also less developed, but this had little to do with geography. The Moscovites were staunchly loyal to the Orthodox

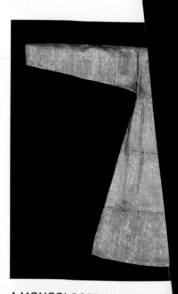

A MONGOL ROBE IN CLOTH OF
Khanate of the Golden Horde captures
of the Mongol warriors who conquer
robe depicted here dates from the late
century and was made from cloth of g
sometimes silver) thread, a precious b
that was also used for banners and eve
was sold at auction in 2011, for nearly a

Church of Byzantium and had w
the Latin West and the Greek E
during the Crusades. They becam
ern Europeans after Constantin
sacked by crusaders in 1204 (see C
led Moscovites to see themselves

protectors of the Orthodox Roman Church. Eventually, as we shall see in Chapter 12, they would claim to be the rightful heirs of Roman imperial power.

The Making of the Mongol Ilkhanate

As Ögedei Khan moved into the lands of Rus' and eastern Europe, Mongol armies were also sent to subdue the vast territory that had been encompassed by the former Persian Empire, then by the empires of Alexander and Rome. Indeed, the strongest state in this region was known as the sultanate of Rûm, the Arabic word for "Rome." This was a Sunni Muslim sultanate that had been founded by the Seljuq Turks in 1077, just prior to the launching of the First Crusade, and which consisted of Anatolian provinces formerly belonging to the eastern Roman Empire. It had

successfully withstood waves of crusading aggression from Latin Christendom while capitalizing on the further misfortunes of Byzantium, taking over several key ports on the Mediterranean and the Black Sea while cultivating a flourishing overland trade as well. But in 1243, the Seljuqs of Rûm were forced to surrender to the Mongols, who had already succeeded in occupying what is now Iraq, Iran, portions of Pakistan and Afghanistan, and the Christian kingdoms of Georgia and Armenia.

Thereafter, the Mongols easily found their way into regions weakened by centuries of Muslim infighting and Christian crusading movements. Byzantium, as we noted in Chapter 9, had been fatally weakened by the Fourth Crusade: Constantinople was now controlled by the Venetians, and Byzantine successor states centered on Nicaea (in Anatolia) and Epirus (in northern Greece) were hanging on by their fingertips. The capitulation of Rûm left

THE MONGOL RULER OF MUSLIM PERSIA, HIS CHRISTIAN QUEEN, AND HIS JEWISH HISTORIAN. The *Compendium of Chronicles* by the Jewish-born Muslim polymath Rashid al-Din (1247–1318) exemplifies the pluralistic culture encouraged by Mongol rule: written in Persian (and often translated into Arabic), it celebrates the achievements of Hulagu Khan (1217–1265), a grandson of Genghis and brother of Kublai, who consolidated Persia and its neighboring regions into the Ilkhanate. But it also embeds those achievements within the long history of Islam. This image depicts Hulagu with his wife, Dokuz Khatun, who was a Turkic princess and a Christian. ▪ *Why would Rashid al-Din have wanted to place the new Mongol dynasty in this historical context?*

remaining Byzantine possessions in Anatolia without a buffer, and most of these were absorbed by the Mongols. In 1261, the emperor Michael VIII Peleologus (r. 1259–82) managed to regain control of Constantinople and its immediate hinterland, but the depleted empire he ruled was ringed about by hostile neighbors. The crusader principality of Antioch, which had been founded in 1098, finally succumbed to the Mongols in 1268. The Mongols themselves were only halted in their drive toward Palestine by the Mamluk Sultanate of Egypt, established in 1250 and ruled by a powerful military caste of non-Arab Muslims.

All of these disparate territories came to be called the Ilkhanate, the "subordinate khanate," meaning that its Mongol rulers paid deference to the Great Khan. The first Ilkhan was Hulagu, brother of China's Kublai Khan. His descendants would rule this realm for another eighty years, eventually converting to Islam but remaining hostile toward the Mamluk Muslims, who remained their chief rivals.

The Pax Mongolica *and Its Price*

Although the Mongols' expansion of power into Europe had been checked in 1241, their combined conquests made them masters of territories that stretched from the Black Sea to the Pacific Ocean: one-fifth of the earth's surface, the largest land empire in history. Within this domain, no single Mongol ruler's power was absolute. Kublai Khan (1260–1294), who took the additional title *khagan*, or "Great Khan," never claimed to rule all Mongol khanates directly. In his own domain of China and Mongolia, his power was highly centralized and built on the intricate (and ancient) imperial bureaucracy of China; but elsewhere, Mongol governance was directed at securing a steady payment of tribute from subject peoples, which meant that local rulers could retain much of their power.

This distribution of authority made Mongol rule flexible and adaptable to local conditions—in this, it resembled the Persian Empire (see Chapter 3) and could also be regarded as building on Hellenistic and Roman examples. But if their empire resembled those of antiquity in some respects, the Mongol khans differed from most contemporary Western rulers in being highly tolerant of all religious beliefs. This was an advantage in governing peoples who observed an array of Buddhist, Christian, and Muslim practices, not to mention Hindus, Jews, and the many itinerant groups and individuals whose languages and beliefs reflect a melding of many cultures.

This acceptance of cultural and religious difference, alongside the Mongols' encouragement of trade and love of rich things, created ideal conditions for some merchants and artists. Hence, the term *Pax Mongolica* ("Mongol Peace") is often used to describe the century from 1250 to 1350, a period in many ways analogous to that fostered by the Roman Empire at its greatest extent (see Chapter 5). No such term should be taken at face value, however: this peace was bought at a great price. Indeed, the artists whose varied talents created the gorgeous textiles, utensils, and illuminated books prized by the Mongols were not all willing participants in a peaceful process. Many were captives or slaves subject to ruthless relocation. During more settled years, the Mongols would often transfer entire families and communities of craftsmen from one part of the empire to another, encouraging a fantastic blend of artistic techniques, materials, and motifs. The result was an intensive period of cultural exchange that might combine Chinese, Persian, Venetian, and Russian influences (among many others) in a single work of art. These objects encapsulate the many conflicting legacies of the Mongols' empire.

The Mongol Peace was also achieved at the expense of many flourishing Muslim cities that had preserved the heritage of even older civilizations and that were devastated or crippled during the bloody process of Mongol expansion. The city of Heràt, situated in one of Afghanistan's few fertile valleys and described by the Persian poet Rumi as "the pearl in the oyster," was entirely destroyed by Genghis Khan in 1221 and did not fully recover for centuries. Baghdad, the splendid capital of the Abbasid Caliphate and a haven for artists and intellectuals since the eighth century (Chapter 8), was savagely besieged and sacked by the Mongols in 1258. Amid many other atrocities, the capture of the city resulted in the destruction of the House of Wisdom, a library and research center where Muslim scientists, philosophers, and translators preserved classical knowledge (including the works of Plato and Aristotle) and advanced cutting-edge scholarship in such fields as mathematics, engineering, and medicine. Baghdad's destruction is held to mark the end of Islam's golden age, since the establishment of the Mongol Ilkhanate in Persia eradicated a continuous zone of Muslim influence that had blended cultures stretching from southern Spain and North Africa to India.

Bridging East and West

To facilitate the movement of people and goods within their empire, the Mongols began to control the caravan routes that led from the Mediterranean and the Black Sea through Central Asia and into China, policing bandits and making conditions safer for travelers. They also encouraged and streamlined trade by funneling many exchanges through the Persian city of Tabriz, on which both land and sea routes from China converged. These measures accelerated and intensified the contacts possible between the Far East and the West. Prior to Mongol control, such commercial networks had been inaccessible to most European merchants. The Silk Road was not so much a highway as a tangle of trails and trading posts, and there were few outsiders who understood its workings. Now travelers at both ends of the route found their way smoothed.

Among the first travelers from the West were Franciscan missionaries whose journeys were bankrolled by European rulers. In 1253, William of Rubruck was sent by King Louis IX of France as his ambassador to the Mongol court, with letters of introduction and instructions to make a full report of his findings. Merchants quickly followed. The most famous of these are three Venetians: the brothers Niccolò and Matteo Polo, and Niccolò's son, Marco (1254–1324). Marco Polo's account of his travels (which began when he was sev-

enteen) includes a report of his twenty-year sojourn in the service of Kublai Khan and the story of his journey home through the Spice Islands, India, and Persia. As we noted above, this book had an enormous effect on the European imagination; Christopher Columbus's copy still survives.

Even more impressive in scope than Marco's travels are those of the Muslim adventurer Ibn Battuta (1304–1368), who left his native Morocco in 1326 to go on the sacred pilgrimage to Mecca—but then kept going. By the time he returned home in 1354, he had been to China and sub-Saharan Africa as well as to the ends of both the Muslim and Mongolian worlds: a journey of over 75,000 miles.

Yet the window of opportunity that made such journeys possible was relatively narrow. By the middle of the fourteenth century, hostilities among and within various components of the Mongol Empire were making travel along the Silk Road perilous. The Mongols of the Ilkhanate, who dominated the ancient trade routes that ran through

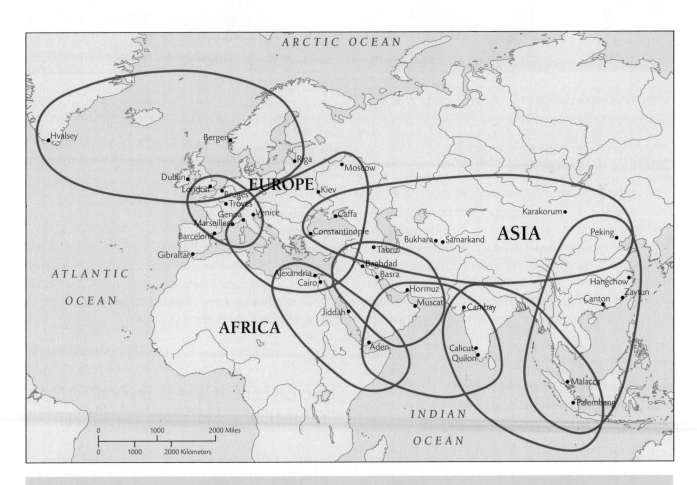

THE MEDIEVAL WORLD SYSTEM, c. 1300. At the turn of the fourteenth century, Western civilizations were more closely connected to one another and to the rest of the world than ever before: waterways and overland routes stretched from Greenland to the Pacific coast of Southeast Asia. ▪ *How has Europe's relationship with its neighbors changed as a result of its integration into this wider world?* ▪ *How might we need to see seemingly marginal territories (like Rus' or Hungary, Scotland or Norway) as central to one or more interlocking components of this system?*

VENETIAN AMBASSADORS TO THE GREAT KHAN. Around 1270, the Venetian merchants Niccolò and Matteo Polo returned to Europe after their first prolonged journey through the empire of the Great Khan, bearing with them an official letter to the Roman pope. This image, from a manuscript of Marco Polo's *Description of the World*, shows his father and uncle at the moment of their arrival in the Great Khan's court, to which they have seemingly brought a Christian cross and a Bible. ▪ *Based on what you've learned about the Mongols and the medieval world, is it plausible that the Polo brothers would have carried these items with them?*

Persia, came into conflict with merchants from Genoa who controlled trade at the western ends of the Silk Road, especially in the transport depot of Tabriz. Mounting pressures finally forced the Genoese to abandon Tabriz, thereby breaking one of the major links in the commercial chain forged by the Mongol Peace. Then, in 1346, the Mongols of the Golden Horde besieged the Genoese colony at Caffa on the Black Sea. This event simultaneously disrupted trade while serving as a conduit for the Black Death, which passed from the Mongol army to the Genoese defenders, who returned with it to Italy (see below).

Over the next few decades, the European economy would struggle to overcome the devastating effects of the massive depopulation caused by plague, which made recovery from these setbacks slower and harder. In the meantime, in 1368, the last Mongol rulers of China were overthrown. Most Westerners were now denied access to its borders, while the remaining Mongol warriors were restricted to cavalry service in the imperial armies of the new Ming dynasty. The conditions that had fostered an integrated trans-Eurasian cultural and commercial network were

no longer sustainable. Yet the view of the world that had been fostered by Mongol rule continued to exercise a lasting influence. European memories of the Far East would be preserved and embroidered, and the dream of reestablishing close connections between Europe and China would survive to influence a new round of commercial and imperial expansion in the centuries to come.

THE EXTENSION OF EUROPEAN COMMERCE AND SETTLEMENT

Western civilizations' increased access to the riches of the Far East during the period of the Pax Mongolica ran parallel to a number of ventures that were extending Europeans' presence in the Mediterranean and beyond it. These endeavors were both mercantile and colonial, and in many cases resulted in the control of strategic trade routes or islands by representatives of a single adventurous state.

The language of crusading, with which we have become familiar, now came to be applied to these economic and political initiatives, whose often violent methods could be justified on the grounds that they were supporting papally sanctioned Christian causes. To take one prominent example, the strategic goal of the Crusades that targeted North Africa in this era was to cut the economic lifelines that supported Muslim settlements in the Holy Land. Yet the only people who stood to gain from this were the merchants who dreamed of controlling the commercial routes that ran through Egypt, not only those that connected North Africa to the Silk Road but the conduits of the sub-Saharan gold trade.

The Quest for African Gold

The European trade in African gold was not new. It had been going on for centuries, facilitated by Muslim middlemen whose caravans brought a steady supply from the Niger River to the North African ports of Algiers and Tunis. In the early thirteenth century, rival bands of merchants from Catalonia and Genoa had established trading colonies in Tunis to expedite this process, exchanging woolen cloth from northern Europe for both North African grain and sub-Saharan gold.

But the medieval demand for gold accelerated during the late thirteenth and fourteenth centuries and could not be satisfied by these established trading relationships. The luxuries coveted by Europeans were now too costly to be bought solely with bulk goods, which were in any case a cumbersome medium of exchange. Although precious textiles (usually silk) were a form of wealth valued by the Mongols, the burgeoning economy of the medieval world demanded a reliable and abundant supply of more portable currency. Silver production, which had enabled the circulation of coinage in Europe, fell markedly during the 1340s as Europeans reached the limits of their technological capacity to extract silver ore from deep mines. This shortfall would lead to a serious cash-flow problem, since more European silver was moving east than could now be replenished from extant sources.

Gold therefore represented an obvious alternative currency for large transactions, and in the thirteenth century some European rulers began minting gold coins. But Europe itself had few natural gold reserves. To maintain and expand these currencies, new sources of gold were needed. The most obvious source was Africa, especially Mali and Ghana—which was called "the Land of Gold" by Muslim geographers.

Models of Mediterranean Colonization: Catalonia, Genoa, and Venice

The heightened European interest in the African gold trade, which engaged the seafaring merchants of Genoa and Catalonia in particular, coincided with these merchants' creation of entrepreneurial empires in the western Mediterranean. During the thirteenth century, Catalan adventurers conquered and colonized a series of western Mediterranean islands, including Majorca, Ibiza, Minorca, Sardinia, and Sicily. Except in Sicily, which already had a large and diverse population that included many Christians (see Chapter 8), the pattern of Catalan conquest was largely the same on all these islands: expulsion or extermination of the existing population, usually Muslim; the extension of economic concessions to attract new settlers; and a heavy reliance on slave labor to produce foodstuffs and raw materials for export.

These Catalan colonial efforts were mainly carried out by private individuals or companies operating under royal charters; they were not actively sponsored by the state. They therefore contrast strongly with the established colonial practices of the Venetian maritime empire, whose strategic ventures were focused mainly on the eastern Mediterranean, where the Venetians dominated the trade in spices and silks. Venetian colonies were administered directly by the city's rulers or their appointed colonial governors. These colonies included long-settled civilizations like Greece, Cyprus, and the cities of the Dalmatian coast, meaning that Venetian administration laid just another layer on top of many other economic, cultural, and political structures.

The Genoese, to take yet another case, also had extensive interests in the western Mediterranean, where they traded bulk goods such as cloth, hides, grain, timber, and sugar. They too established trading colonies, but these tended to consist of family networks that were closely integrated with the peoples among whom they lived, whether in North Africa, Spain, or the shores of the Black Sea.

From the Mediterranean to the Atlantic

For centuries, European maritime commerce had been divided between this Mediterranean world and a very different northeastern Atlantic world, which encompassed northern France, the Low Countries, the British Isles, and Scandinavia. Starting around 1270, however, Italian merchants began to sail through the Straits of Gibraltar and

Competing Viewpoints

Two Travel Accounts

> Two of the books that influenced Columbus and his contemporaries were travel narratives describing the exotic worlds that lay beyond Europe: worlds that may or may not have existed as they are described. The first excerpt below is taken from the account dictated by Marco Polo of Venice in 1298. The young Marco had traveled overland from Constantinople to the court of Kublai Khan in the early 1270s, together with his father and uncle. He became a gifted linguist, and remained at the Mongol court until the early 1290s, when he returned to Europe after a journey through Southeast Asia, Indonesia, and the Indian Ocean. The second excerpt is from the Book of Marvels attributed to John de Mandeville. This is an almost entirely fictional account of wonders that also became a source for European ideas about Southeast Asia. This particular passage concerns a legendary Christian figure called Prester ("Priest") John, who is alleged to have traveled to the East and become a great ruler.

Marco Polo's Description of Java

Departing from Ziamba, and steering between south and south-east, fifteen hundred miles, you reach an island of very great size, named Java. According to the reports of some well-informed navigators, it is the greatest in the world, and has a compass above three thousand miles. It is under the dominion of one king only, nor do the inhabitants pay tribute to any other power. They are worshipers of idols.

The country abounds with rich commodities. Pepper, nutmegs, spikenard, galangal, cubebs, cloves and all the other valuable spices and drugs, are the produce of the island; which occasion it to be visited by many ships laden with merchandise, that yields to the owners considerable profit.

The quantity of gold collected there exceeds all calculation and belief. From thence it is that . . . merchants . . . have imported, and to this day import, that metal to a great amount, and from thence also is obtained the greatest part of the spices that are distributed throughout the world. That the Great Khan [Kublai] has not brought the island under subjection to him, must be attributed to the length of the voyage and the dangers of the navigation.

Source: *The Travels of Marco Polo*, trans. William Marsden, rev. and ed. Manuel Komroff (New York: 1926), pp. 267–68.

John de Mandeville's Description of Prester John

This emperor Prester John has great lands and has many noble cities and good towns in his realm and many great, large islands. For all the country of India is separated into islands by the great floods that come from Paradise, that divide the land into many parts. And also in the sea he has many islands. . . .

on up to the wool-producing regions of England and the Low Countries. This was a step toward the extension of Mediterranean patterns of commerce and colonization into the Atlantic Ocean. Another step was the discovery (or possibly the rediscovery) of the Atlantic island chains known as the Canaries and the Azores, which Genoese sailors reached in the fourteenth century.

Efforts to colonize the Canary Islands, and to convert and enslave their inhabitants, began almost immediately. Eventually, the Canaries would become the focus of a new wave of colonial settlement sponsored by the Portuguese, and the base for Portuguese voyages down the west coast of Africa. They would also be the jumping-off point from which Christopher Columbus would sail

This Prester John has under him many kings and many islands and many varied people of various conditions. And this land is full good and rich, but not so rich as is the land of the Great Khan. For the merchants do not come there so commonly to buy merchandise as they do in the land of the Great Khan, for it is too far to travel to. . . .

[Mandeville then goes on to describe the difficulties of reaching Prester John's lands by sea.]

This emperor Prester John always takes as his wife the daughter of the Great Khan, and the Great Khan in the same way takes to wife the daughter of Prester John. For these two are the greatest lords under the heavens.

In the land of Prester John there are many diverse things, and many precious stones so great and so large that men make them into vessels such as platters, dishes, and cups. And there are many other marvels there that it would be too cumbrous and too long to put into the writing of books. But of the principal islands and of his estate and of his law I shall tell you some part.

This emperor Prester John is Christian and a great part of his country is Christian also, although they do not hold to all the articles of our faith as we do. . . .

And he has under him 72 provinces, and in every province there is a king. And these kings have kings under them, and all are tributaries to Prester John.

And he has in his lordships many great marvels. For in his country is the sea that men call the Gravelly Sea, that is all gravel and sand without any drop of water. And it ebbs and flows in great waves as other seas do, and it is never still. . . . And a three-day journey from that sea there are great mountains out of which flows a great flood that comes out of Paradise. And it is full of precious stones without any drop of water. . . .

He dwells usually in the city of Susa [in Persia]. And there is his principal palace, which is so rich and so noble that no one will believe the report unless he has seen it. And above the chief tower of the palace there are two round pommels of gold and in each of them are two great, large rubies that shine full brightly upon the night. And the principal gates of his palace are of a precious stone that men call sardonyxes [a type of onyx], and the frames and the bars are made of ivory.

And the windows of the halls and chambers are of crystal. And the tables upon which men eat, some are made of emeralds, some of amethyst, and some of gold full of precious stones. And the legs that hold up the tables are made of the same precious stones. . . .

Source: *Mandeville's Travels*, ed. M. C. Seymour (Oxford: 1967), pp. 195–99 (language modernized from Middle English by R. C. Stacey).

Questions for Analysis

1. What does Marco Polo want his readers to know about Java, and why? What does this suggest about the interests of these intended readers?

2. What does Mandeville want his readers to know about Prester John and his domains? Why are these details so important?

3. Which of these accounts seems more trustworthy, and why? Even if we cannot accept one or both at face value, what insight do they give us into the expectations of Columbus and the other European adventurers who relied on these accounts?

westward across the Atlantic Ocean in the hope of reaching Asia (see Chapter 12).

There was also a significant European colonial presence in the northern Atlantic, and had been for centuries. Viking settlers had begun to colonize Greenland in the late tenth century, and around 1000 had established a settlement in a place they called Vinland: the coast of Newfoundland in present-day Canada. According to the sagas that tell the story of these explorations, written down in the late twelfth and thirteenth centuries, a band of adventurers led by Leif Eiriksson had intended to set up a permanent colony there. Numerous expeditions resulted in the construction of houses, a fortification, and even attempts to domesticate livestock transported from Scandinavia. Yet North America

THE CHURCH AT HVALSEY, GREENLAND. Located on the southern tip of Greenland, Hvalsey was originally a farmstead established in the late tenth century by the uncle of Eirik the Red, father of the explorer Leif. The church at Hvalsey, pictured here, was built in the twelfth century and would have been roofed with turf. It was the site of the last documented event in the history of Norse settlement on the island, a wedding that took place in 1408. By that time, the population had largely died out due to starvation and disease.

Economic Tools: Balance Sheets, Banks, Charts, and Clocks

The economic boom that resulted from the integration of European and Asian commerce called for the refinement of existing business models and accounting techniques. New forms of partnership and the development of insurance contracts helped to minimize the risks associated with long-distance trading. Double-entry bookkeeping, widely used in Italy by the mid-fourteenth century, gave merchants a much clearer picture of their profits and losses by ensuring that both credits and debits were clearly laid out in parallel columns, a practice that facilitated the balancing of accounts. The Medici family of Florence established branches of their bank in each of the major cities of Europe and were careful that the failure of one would not bankrupt the entire firm, as earlier branch-banking arrangements had done. Banks also experimented with advanced credit techniques borrowed from Muslim and Jewish financiers,

did not become home to a permanent European population at this time; the sagas report that relations with indigenous peoples were fraught, and there may have been other factors hindering settlement.

However, Norse settlers did build a viable community on Greenland, which eventually formed part of the kingdom of Norway. This was facilitated by the warming of the earth's climate between 800 and 1300—the same phenomenon that partly enabled the agricultural revolution discussed in Chapter 8. For several centuries, these favorable climatic conditions made it possible to sustain some farming activities on the southern coastline of that huge island, supplemented by fishing, hunting, and foraging. But with the gradual cooling of the climate in the fourteenth century, which caused famines even in the rich farmlands of Europe, this fragile ecosystem was gradually eroded and the Greenlanders died out.

WAYS OF KNOWING AND DESCRIBING THE WORLD

The success of European commercial and colonial expansion in this era both drove and depended on significant innovations in measuring and mapping. It also coincided with intellectual, literary, and artistic initiatives that aimed to capture and describe the workings of this wider world, and to imagine its celestial (or infernal) counterparts.

DEVIL WITH EYEGLASSES. Spectacles were most commonly worn by those who made a living by reading and writing, notably bureaucrats and lawyers. In this conceptualization of hell, the devil charged with keeping track of human sin wears eyeglasses.
■ *What might this image reveal about popular attitudes toward record-keeping and the growing legal and administrative bureaucracies of the later Middle Ages?*

allowing their clients to transfer funds without any real money changing hands—and without endangering their capital by carrying it with them. Such transfers were carried out by written receipts: the direct ancestors of the check, the money order, and the currency transfer.

Other late medieval technologies kept pace in different ways with the demands for increased efficiency and accuracy. Eyeglasses, first invented in the 1280s, were perfected in the fourteenth century, extending the careers of those who made a living by reading, writing, and accounting. The use of the magnetic compass helped ships sail farther away from land, making longer-distance Atlantic voyages possible for the first time. And as more and more mariners began to sail waters less familiar to them, pilots began to make and use special charts that mapped the locations of ports. Called *portolani*, these charts also took note of prevailing winds, potential routes, good harbors, and known perils.

Among the many implements of modern daily life invented in this era, the most familiar are clocks. Mechanical clocks came into use shortly before 1300 and proliferated immediately thereafter. They were too large and expensive for private purchase, but towns vied with one another to install them in prominent public buildings, thus advertising municipal wealth and good governance. Mechanical timekeeping had two profound effects. One was the further stimulation of interest in complex machinery of all sorts, an interest already awakened by the widespread use of mills in the eleventh and twelfth centuries (see Chapter 8).

More significant was the way that clocks regulated daily life. Until the advent of clocks, time was flexible. Although days had been *theoretically* divided into hours, minutes, and seconds since the time of the Sumerians (see Chapter 1),

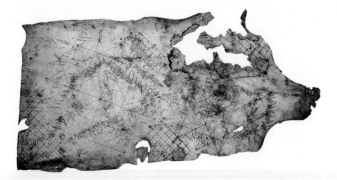

PORTOLAN CHART. Accurate mapping was essential to the success of maritime colonial ventures in the thirteenth and fourteenth centuries. The chart shown here is the oldest surviving example of a map used by mariners to navigate between Mediterranean ports. (The word *portolan* is used to describe such charts.) It dates from the end of the thirteenth century, and its shape clearly indicates that it was made from an animal hide. Although parchment was extremely durable, it would have slowly worn away owing to prolonged exposure to salt water and other elements—hence the rarity of this early example.

there had never been a way of mapping these temporal measurements onto an actual day. Now, clocks relentlessly divided time into exact units, giving rise to new expectations about labor and productivity. People were expected to start and end work "on time," to make the most of the time spent at work, and even to equate time with money. Like the improvements in bookkeeping, timekeeping made some kinds of work more efficient, but it also created new tensions and obsessions.

Knowledge of the World and of God

In the mid-thirteenth century, Thomas Aquinas had constructed a theological view of the world as rational, organized, and comprehensible to the inquiring human mind (see Chapter 9). Confidence in this picture began to wane in the fourteenth century, even before the Black Death posed a new challenge to it. Philosophers such as William of Ockham (d.c. 1348), an English member of the Franciscan order, denied that human reason could prove fundamental theological truths such as the existence of God. He argued that human knowledge of God, and hence salvation, depends entirely on what God himself has chosen to reveal through scripture. Instead, Ockham urged humans to investigate the natural world and to better understand its laws—without positing any necessary connection between the observable properties of nature and the unknowable essence of divinity.

This philosophical position, known as nominalism, had its roots in the philosophy of Plato (see Chapter 4) and has had an enormous impact on modern thought. The nominalists' distinction between the rational comprehensibility of the real world and the spiritual incomprehensibility of God encourages investigation of nature without reference to supernatural explanations: one of the most important foundations of the modern scientific method (see Chapter 16). Nominalism also encourages empirical observation, since it posits that knowledge of the world should rest on sensory experience rather than abstract theories. The philosophical principles laid down by these observers of the medieval world are thus fundamental to modern science.

Creating God's World in Art

Just as a fascination with the natural world informed developments in medieval science, the artists of this era were paying close attention to the way plants, animals, and human beings really looked. Carvings of leaves and flowers were increasingly made from direct observation and are clearly recognizable to modern botanists as distinct

Analyzing Primary Sources

Vikings Encounter the Natives of North America

Although Norse voyagers had explored and settled the coast of Newfoundland around the year 1000, written accounts of these exploits were not made or widely circulated until the thirteenth century. The excerpt below comes from one of these narrative histories, the Grænlendinga Saga *("Greenlanders' Saga"). Its hero is Thorfinn Karlsefni, a Norwegian adventurer who arrives in Greenland and marries Gudrid, the twice-widowed sister-in-law of the explorer Leif Eiriksson. Leif had established the original colony of Vinland, but had since returned to Greenland.*

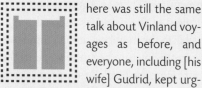 here was still the same talk about Vinland voyages as before, and everyone, including [his wife] Gudrid, kept urging Karlsefni to make the voyage. In the end he decided to sail and gathered a company of sixty men and five women. He made an agreement with his crew that everyone should share equally in whatever profits the expedition might yield. The took livestock of all kinds, for they intended to make a permanent settlement there if possible.

Karlsefni asked Leif if he could have the houses in Vinland; Leif said that he was willing to lend them, but not to give them away.

They put to sea and arrived safe and sound at Leif's Houses and carried their hammocks ashore. Soon they had plenty of good supplies, for a fine big rorqual* was driven ashore; they went down and cut it up, and so there was no shortage of food.

The livestock were put out to grass, and soon the male beasts became very frisky and difficult to manage. They had brought a bull with them.

Karlsefni ordered timber to be felled and cut into lengths for a cargo for the ship, and it was left out on a rock to season. They made use of all the natural resources of the country that were available, grapes and game of all kinds and other produce.

The first winter passed into summer, and then they had their first encounter with Skrælings,† when a great number of them came out of the wood one day. The cattle were grazing near by and the bull began to bellow and roar with great vehemence. This terrified the Skrælings and they fled, carrying their packs which contained furs and sables and pelts of all kinds. They made for Karlsefni's houses and tried to get inside, but Karlsefni had the doors barred against them. Neither side could understand the other's language.

Then the Skrælings put down their packs and opened them up and offered their contents, preferably in exchange for weapons; but Karlsefni forbade his men to sell arms. Then he hit on the idea of telling the women to carry milk out to the Skrælings, and when the Skrælings saw the milk they wanted to buy nothing else. And so the outcome of their trading expedition was that the Skrælings carried their purchases away in their bellies, and left their packs and furs with Karlsefni and his men.

After that, Karlsefni ordered a strong wooden palisade to be erected round the houses, and they settled in.

species. Statues of humans also became more realistic in their portrayals of facial expressions and bodily proportions. According to a story in circulation around 1290, a sculptor working on a likeness of the German emperor allegedly made a hurried return trip to study his subject's face a second time, because he'd heard that a new wrinkle had appeared on the emperor's brow.

This trend toward naturalism extended to manuscript illumination and painting. The latter was, to a large extent, a new art. As we saw in Chapter 1, wall paintings are among the oldest forms of artistic expression in human history, and throughout antiquity and the Middle Ages artists had decorated the walls of public and private buildings with frescoes (paintings executed on "fresh"—wet—plaster). But in addition to frescoes, Italian artists in the thirteenth century began to adapt the techniques used by icon painters in Byzantium, making freestanding pictures on pieces of wood or canvas using tempera (pigments mixed with water and natural gums). Because these altarpieces, devotional images, and portraits were portable, they were also more commercial. As long as artists could afford the necessary materials, they did not have to wait for specific commissions. This meant that they had more freedom to choose their subject matter and to put an individual stamp on their

About this time Karlsefni's wife, Gudrid, gave birth to a son, and he was named Snorri.

Early next winter the Skrælings returned, in much greater numbers this time, bringing with them the same kind of wares as before. Karlsefni told the women, 'You must carry out to them the same produce that was most in demand last time, and nothing else.' . . .

[B]ut a Skræling was killed by one of Karlsefni's men for trying to steal some weapons. The Skrælings fled as fast as they could, leaving their clothing and wares behind . . .

'Now we must devise a plan,' said Karlsefni, 'for I expect they will pay us a third visit, and this time with hostility and in greater numbers. This is what we must do: ten men are to go out on the headland here and make themselves conspicuous, and the rest of us are to go into the wood and make a clearing there, where we can keep our cattle when the Skrælings come out of the forest. We shall take our bull and keep him to the fore.'

The place where they intended to have their encounter with the Skrælings had the lake on one side and the woods on the other.

Karlsefni's plan was put into effect, and the Skrælings came right to the place that Karlsefni had chosen for the battle. The fighting began, and many of the Skrælings were killed. There was one tall and handsome man among the Skrælings and Karlsefni reckoned that he must be their leader. One of the Skrælings had picked up an axe, and after examining it for a moment he swung it at a man standing beside him, who fell dead at once. The tall man then took hold of the axe, looked at it for a moment, and then threw it as far as he could out into the water. Then the Skrælings fled into the forest as fast as they could, and that was the end of the encounter.

Karlsefni and his men spent the whole winter there, but in the spring he announced that he had no wish to stay there any longer and wanted to return to Greenland. They made ready for the voyage and took with them much valuable produce, vines and grapes and pelts. They put to sea and reached Eiriksfjord safely and spent the winter there.

*A kind of whale, the largest species of which is a blue whale.

†A Norse word meaning "savages," applied to the different indigenous peoples of Greenland and of North America.

Questions for Analysis

1. What policies do the Norse settlers adopt toward the native peoples they encounter on the coast of Newfoundland? How effective are they?

2. Given their extensive preparations for colonization and the success of their early efforts, why do you think that Karlsefni and his companions abandoned their settlement in North America? Are there clues discernible in the text?

3. Compare this encounter to the sources describing other interactions between Europeans and the indigenous inhabitants of the New World after 1492 (see Chapters 12 and 14). How do you account for any similarities? What are some key differences?

work—one of the reasons why we know the names of many more artists from this era.

One of these, Giotto di Bondone of Florence (c. 1267–1337), painted both walls and portable wooden panels. Like some of his contemporaries, Giotto (gee-OHT-toh) was preeminently an imitator of nature. Not only do his human beings and animals look lifelike, they seem to do natural things. When Christ enters Jerusalem on Palm Sunday, boys climb trees to get a better view; when Saint Francis is laid out in death, someone checks to see whether he has really received the *stigmata*, the marks of Christ's wounds; and when the Virgin's parents, Joachim and Anna, meet after a long separation, they embrace and kiss one another tenderly. Although many of the artists who came after Giotto moved away from naturalism, this style would become the norm by 1400. It is for this reason that Giotto is often regarded as the first painter of the Renaissance (see Chapter 11).

A Vision of the World We Cannot See

One of Giotto's exact contemporaries had a different way of capturing the spiritual world in a naturalistic way, and he worked in a different medium. Dante Alighieri (1265–1321)

claimed the right to appoint bishops and priests to vacant offices anywhere in Christendom, directly, therefore bypassing the rights of individual dioceses and allowing the papacy to collect huge fees from successful appointees.

By these and other measures, the Avignon popes further strengthened administrative control over the Church. But they also further weakened the papacy's moral authority. Stories of the court's unseemly luxury circulated widely, especially during the reign of the notoriously corrupt Clement VI (r. 1342–52), who openly sold spiritual benefits for money (boasting that he would appoint a jackass to a bishopric if he thought it would turn a profit) and insisted that his sexual transgressions were therapeutic. His reign coincided with the Black Death, whose terrifying and demoralizing effects were not alleviated by the quality of his leadership.

Uniting the Faithful: The Power of Sacraments

Despite the centralizing power of the papacy, which came to fruition under Innocent III, most medieval Christians accessed the Church at a local level, within their communities. Somewhat paradoxically, this was another of Innocent III's legacies: because he had insisted that all people should have direct access to religious instruction, nearly all of Europe was covered by a network of parish churches by the end of the thirteenth century. In these churches, parish priests not only taught the elements of Christian doctrine, they administered the sacraments ("holy rites") that conveyed the grace of God to individual Christians, marking significant moments in the life cycle of every person and significant times in the Christian calendar.

Medieval piety came to revolve around these seven sacraments: baptism, confirmation, confession (or penance), communion, marriage, extreme unction (last rites for the dying), and ordination (of priests). Baptism, a ceremony of initiation administered in the early centuries of Christianity to adults (see Chapter 6), had become a sacrament administered to infants as soon as possible after birth, to safeguard their souls in case of an early death. The confirmation of adolescents reaffirmed the promises made on a child's behalf at baptism by parents and godparents. Periodic confession of sins to a priest guaranteed forgiveness by God; for if a sinner did not perform appropriate acts of penance, atonement for sins would have to be completed in purgatory—that netherworld between heaven and hell explored by Dante, whose existence was made a matter of Church doctrine

for the first time in 1274 (though its existence had been posited by Pope Gregory the Great centuries earlier—see Chapter 7).

Marriage was a relatively new sacrament, increasingly emphasized but very seldom practiced as a ceremony; in reality, marriage in this period required only the exchange of solemn promises and was often formed simply by an act of sexual intercourse or the fact of cohabitation. Extreme unction refers to the holy oil with which the priest anointed the forehead of a dying person, signifying the final absolution of all sins and thus offering a final assurance of salvation. Like baptism, this rite could, in an emergency, be administered by any Christian believer. The other sacraments, however, could be administered only by a properly ordained priest—or, in the case of confirmation and ordination, by a bishop. Ordination was therefore the only sacrament reserved for the small percentage of Christians who became priests, and it conveyed to the priest the special authority to share God's grace through the sacraments: a power that could never be lost, even by a priest who led an immoral life.

This sacramental system was the foundation on which the practices of medieval popular piety rested. Pilgrimages, for example, were a form of penance and could lessen one's time in purgatory. Crusading was a kind of extreme pilgrimage that promised the complete fulfillment of all penances the crusader might owe for all the sins of his (or her) life. Many other pious acts—saying the prayers of the rosary, for example, or giving alms to the poor—could also serve as penance for one's sins while constituting good works that would help the believer in his or her journey toward salvation.

The Miracle of the Eucharist

Of these sacraments, the one was most central to the religious lives of medieval Christians was the communion ceremony of the Mass, also known as the Eucharist. As we noted in Chapter 9, the ritual power of the Mass was greatly enhanced in the twelfth century, when the Church began promoting the doctrine of transubstantiation. Christians attending Mass were taught that when the priest spoke the ritual words "This is my body" and "This is my blood," the substances of bread and wine on the altar were miraculously transformed into the body and blood of Jesus Christ. To consume one or both of these substances was to ingest holiness; and so powerful was this idea that most Christians received the sacramental bread just once a year, at Easter. Some holy women, however, attempted to sustain themselves by consuming only the single morsel of bread consecrated at daily Mass.

"THIS IS MY BODY": THE ELEVATION OF THE HOST.
This fresco from a chapel in Assisi was painted by Simone Martini in the 1320s. It shows the moment in the Mass when the priest raises the eucharistic host so that it can be seen by the faithful. The Latin phrase spoken at this moment, *Hoc est corpus meum* ("This is my body"), came to be regarded as a magical formula because it could transform one substance into another: *hocus pocus*. ▪ *Since medieval Christians believed that the sight of the host was just as powerful as ingesting it, how would they have responded to this life-size image of the elevation?* ▪ *What does the appearance of angels (above the altar) signify?*

Yet, to share in the miracle of the Eucharist, one did not have to consume it. One had only to witness the elevation of the host, the wafer of bread raised up by the priest, which "hosted" the real presence of Jesus Christ. Daily attendance at Mass simply to view the consecration of the host was therefore a common form of devotion, and this was facilitated by the practice of displaying a consecrated wafer in a special reliquary called a monstrance ("showcase"), which could be set up on an altar or carried through the streets. Believers sometimes attributed astonishing properties to the eucharistic host, feeding it to sick animals or rushing from church to church to see the consecrated bread as many times as possible in a day. Some of these practices were criticized as superstitious. But, by and large, these expressions of popular piety were encouraged and fervently practiced by many.

The Pursuit of Holiness

The fundamental theme of preachers in this era, that salvation lay open to any Christian who strove for it, helps to explain the central place of the Mass and other sacraments in daily life. It also led many to seek out new paths that could lead to God. As we noted in Chapter 9, some believers who sought to achieve a mystical union with God (through rigorous prayer, penance, and personal sacrifice) were ultimately condemned for heresy because they did not subordinate themselves to the authority of the Church. But even less radical figures might find themselves treading on dangerous ground, especially if they published their ideas. For example, the German preacher Master Eckhart (c. 1260–1327), a Dominican friar, taught that there is a "spark" deep within every human soul and that God lives in this spark. Through prayer and self-renunciation, any person could therefore retreat into the inner recesses of her being and access divinity. This conveyed the message that a layperson might attain salvation through her own efforts, without the intervention of a priest or any of the sacraments he alone could perform. As a result, many of Eckhart's teachings were condemned. But views like these would find support in the teachings of popular preachers after the Black Death, when close-knit communities revolving around the parish church were broken up or weakened (see Chapter 11).

STRUGGLES FOR SOVEREIGNTY

When the French king Philip IV transplanted the papal court from Rome to Avignon, he was not just responding to previous popes' abuse of power: he was bolstering his own. By the middle of the thirteenth century, the growth of strong territorial monarchies, combined with the increasing sophistication of royal justice, taxation, and propaganda, had given some secular rulers a higher degree of power than any western European ruler had wielded since the time of Charlemagne (see Chapter 7).

Meanwhile, monarchs' willingness to support the Church's crusading efforts not only yielded distinct economic and political advantages, it also allowed them to assert their commitment to the moral and spiritual improvement of their realms. Although a king still needed to be anointed with holy oil at the time of his coronation in order to claim that he ruled "by the grace of God"—a rite that required a bishop and, by extension, papal support—a king's authority in his own realm rested on the acquiescence of the aristocracy and on popular perceptions of his reputation for justice, piety, and regard for his subjects' prosperity. On the wider stage of the medieval world, it also rested on his successful assertion of his kingdom's sovereignty.

The Problem of Sovereignty

Sovereignty can be defined as inviolable authority over a defined territory. In Chapter 9, we noted that Philip Augustus was the first monarch to call himself "king of France" and not "king of the French." In other words, he was defining his kingship in geographical terms, claiming that there was an entity called France and that he was king within that area.

But what was France? Was it the tiny "island" (Île-de-France) around Paris, which had been his father's domain? If so, then France was very small—and very vulnerable, which would make it hard to maintain a claim to sovereignty. Was it, rather, any region whose lord was willing to do homage to the French king, like Champagne or Normandy? In that case, the king would need to enforce these rights of lordship constantly and, if necessary, exert his rule directly—as Philip did when he took Normandy away from England's King John in 1214.

But what if some of France's neighboring lords ruled in their own right, as did the independent counts of Flanders, thus threatening the security of France's borders? In that case, the king would either need to forge an alliance with these borderlands or negate their independence. He would need to assert his sovereignty by absorbing these regions into an ever-growing kingdom.

This is the problem: a claim to sovereignty is only credible if it can be backed up with real power, and a state's or ruler's power must never seem stagnant or passive. The problem of sovereignty, then, is a zero-sum game: one state's sovereignty is won and maintained by diminishing that of other states. Although many French citizens today would assert that France has, in some mystical way, always existed in its present form, the fact is that France and every other modern European state was being cobbled together in the medieval period through a process of annexation and colonization—just as the United States was assembled at the expense of the empires that had colonized North America (the British, French, and Spanish), not to mention the killing or displacement of autonomous native peoples.

The process of achieving sovereignty is thus an aggressive and often violent one, affecting not only the rulers of territories but their peoples, too. In Spain, the "Reconquest" of Muslim lands, which had accelerated in the twelfth century, continued apace in the thirteenth and fourteenth, to the detriment of these regions' Muslim and Jewish inhabitants. German princes continued to push northward into the Baltic, where native peoples'

resistance to colonizing efforts was met with brutal force. Meanwhile, the Scandinavian kingdoms that had been forming in the eleventh and twelfth centuries were warring among themselves and their neighbors for the control of contested regions and resources. Italy and the Mediterranean became a constant battleground, as we have observed. Among all these emerging states, the two most strident and successful in their assertion of sovereignty were France and England.

The Prestige of France: The Saintly Kingship of Louis IX

After the death of Philip Augustus in 1223, the heirs to the French throne continued to pursue an expansionist policy, pushing the boundaries of their influence out to the east and south. There were significant pockets of resistance, though, notably from the southwestern lands that the kings of England had inherited from Eleanor of Aquitaine (see Chapter 9) and from the independent towns of Flanders that had escaped conquest under Philip Augustus. In 1302, citizen militias from several of these towns, fighting on foot with farming implements and other unconventional weapons, even managed to defeat a heavily armed French cavalry. This victory at the Battle of Courtrai (Kortrijk) is still celebrated as a national holiday in Belgium (although, ironically, its ultimate meaning is currently at the center of a divisive controversy between French- and Flemish-speaking Belgians).

This defeat was a setback for Philip IV of France, but we have already observed that Philip had other ways of asserting the power of French sovereignty. Much of that power derived from his grandfather, Louis IX (r. 1226–70), who would probably have been horrified by the ways his grandson used it. Louis was famous for his piety and for his conscientious exercise of his kingly duties. Unlike most of his fellow princes, he not only pledged to go on crusade—he actually went. And while both of his campaigns were notorious failures (he died on the second, in 1270) they cemented Louis's saintly reputation and political clout.

First, Louis's willingness to risk his life (and that of his brothers) in the service of the Church would give him tremendous influence in papal affairs—a key factor in making his youngest brother, Charles of Anjou, the king of Naples and Sicily. Second, the necessity of ensuring the good governance of his kingdom during his years of absence prompted Louis to reform or invent many key aspects of royal governance, which made France the bureaucratic rival of England for the first time. Third, Louis's first crusading venture was

A CONTAINER FOR THE CROWN OF THORNS. The Sainte-Chapelle, built by Louis IX, was a giant reliquary for the display of this potent artifact and symbol that Christ's divine majesty, which increased the prestige of king of France.

seen as confirmation that the king of France had inherited the mantle of Charlemagne as the protector of the Church and the representative of Christ on earth. Although it was a military fiasco, this crusade found lasting artistic expression in the Sainte-Chapelle (Holy Chapel), a gorgeous jewel box of a church that Louis built in Paris for his collection of Passion relics—that is, artifacts thought to have been used for the torture and crucifixion of Christ. The most important of these was the Crown of Thorns, intended by Pilate as a mocking reference to "the king of the Jews" (see Chapter 6). Now that this holy crown belonged to Louis and was housed in Paris, it could be taken as a sign that Paris was the new Jerusalem.

Widely regarded as a saint in his lifetime, Louis was formally canonized in 1297—by the same Pope Boniface VIII brought down by Philip IV. Indeed, Boniface partly intended this gesture as a rebuke to the saint's grandson. Philip himself, however, turned it to his advantage. He even used his grandfather's pious reputation as a cloak for his frankly rapacious treatment of the Knights Templar, whose military order he suppressed in 1314 so that he could confiscate its extensive property and dissolve his own debts to the order. He had expelled the Jews from his realm in 1306 for similar reasons.

Castles and Control: Edward I and the Expansion of English Rule

The expulsion of Jews who depended on a king's personal protection had actually been a precedent set by Philip's contemporary and kinsman, Edward I of England

(r. 1272–1307). Unlike Philip, Edward had to build up the sovereignty of his state almost from scratch. His father, Henry III (1216–1272), had a long but troubled reign. Inheriting the throne as a young boy, shortly after his father John's loss of Normandy and capitulation to Magna Carta (see Chapter 9), Henry had to contend with factions among his regents and, later, the restive barons of his realm who rose against him on several occasions. His son Edward even sided with the rebels at one point, but later worked alongside his father to suppress them. When Edward himself became king in 1272, he took steps toward ensuring that there would be no further revolts on his watch, tightening his control on the aristocracy and their lands, diffusing their power by strengthening that of Parliament, reforming the administration of the realm, and clarifying its laws.

Having seen to the internal affairs of England, Edward looked to its borders. Since Welsh chieftains had been major backers of the barons who had rebelled against his father, Edward was determined to clean up the border region and bring "wild Wales" within the orbit of English sovereignty. He initially attempted to do this by making treaties with various Welsh princes, but none of these arrangements were stable or gave Edward the type of control he wanted. He accordingly embarked on an ambitious and ruthless campaign of castle-building, ringing the hilly country with enormous fortifications on a scale not seen in most of Europe; they were more

CAERNARVON CASTLE. One of many massive fortifications built by Edward I, this castle was the birthplace of the first English "Prince of Wales" and the site where the current Prince of Wales, Charles, was formally invested with that title in 1969. ■ *Castles of this size and strength had been constructed in the Crusader States and on the disputed frontiers of Muslim and Christian Spain but never before in Britain (see the photos on pages 292 and 295 of Chapter 9).* ■ *What does their construction reveal about Edward's attitude toward the Welsh?*

A Declaration of Scottish Independence

In April of 1320, a group of powerful Scottish lords gathered at the abbey of Arbroath to draft a letter to Pope John XII in Avignon. The resulting "Declaration of Arbroath" petitioned the exiled pope (a Frenchman loyal to the French king) to recognize the Scots as a sovereign nation and to support their right to an independent kingdom that would be free from encroachment by the English. The Scots' elected king, Robert the Bruce, had been excommunicated by a previous pope, who had also upheld English claims to lordship in Scotland. The letter therefore makes a number of different arguments for the recognition of the Scots' right to self-governance.

We know, most holy father and lord, and have gathered from the deeds and books about men in the past, that . . . the nation of the Scots has been outstanding for its many distinctions. It journeyed from the lands of Greece and Egypt by the Tyrrhenian Sea and the Pillars of Hercules, . . . but could not be subdued anywhere by any peoples however barbaric. . . . It took possession of the settlements in the west which it now desires, after first driving out the Britons and totally destroying the Picts, and although often attacked by the Norwegians, Danes and English. Many were its victories and innumerable its efforts. It has held these places always free of all servitude, as the old histories testify.

One hundred and thirteen kings of their royal lineage have reigned in their kingdom, with no intrusion by a foreigner.

If the noble qualities and merits of these men were not obvious for other reasons, they shine forth clearly enough in that they were almost the first to be called to his most holy faith by the King of Kings and Lord of Lords, our Lord Jesus Christ, after his Passion and Resurrection, even though they were settled on the most distant boundaries of the earth. . . .

Thus our people lived until now in freedom and peace . . . , until that mighty prince Edward [I] king of England (the father of the present king) in the guise of a friend and ally attacked our kingdom in hostile fashion, when it had no head and the people were not harbouring any evil treachery, nor were they accustomed to

wars or attacks. His unjust acts, killings, acts of violence, pillagings, burnings, imprisonments of prelates, burnings of monasteries, robbings and killings of regular clergy, and also innumerable other outrages, which he committed against the said people, sparing none on account of age or sex, religion or order—no one could write about them or fully comprehend them who had not been instructed by experience.

From these countless ills we have been set free, with the help of Him who follows up wounds with healing and cures, by our most energetic prince, king and lord Sir Robert [the Bruce, r. 1306–29]. . . . By divine providence his succession to his right according to our laws and customs which we intend to maintain to the death, together with the due consent

like crusader castles, and Edward certainly treated the Welsh (who were actually his fellow Christians) as infidels. Indeed, he treated conquered Wales like a crusader state, making it a settler colony and subjecting the Welsh to the overlordship of his own men. When his son, the future Edward II, was born in 1284 at the great castle he had built at Caernarvon, he gave the infant the title "Prince of Wales," a title usually borne by a Welsh chieftain.

Edward then turned to Scotland, England's final frontier. Until now, control of Scotland had not been an English concern: the Scottish border had been peaceful for many years, and the Scottish kings did homage to the English king for some of their lands. In 1290, however, the succession to the Scottish throne was disputed among many rival

claimants, none of whom had enough backing to secure election. Edward intervened, pressing his own claim to the kingdom and seemingly prepared to take Scotland by conquest. To avoid this, the Scots forged an alliance with the French, but this did not prevent Edward's army from fighting its way through to Scone Abbey in 1296.

Scone was a symbolic target: the site of the Stone of Destiny on which Scottish kings were traditionally enthroned. So Edward seized this potent symbol, brought it back to Westminster Abbey in London, and embedded it in the coronation chair of his namesake, Edward the Confessor, the last Anglo-Saxon king of England (see Chapter 8). Save for a brief hiatus in 1950 (when the stone was stolen from the abbey by Scottish nationalists, students and assent of us all, have made him our prince and king.... But if he should give up what he has begun, seeking to subject us or our kingdom to the king of the English, ... we would immediately strive to expel him as our enemy and a subverter of his right and ours, and we would make someone else our king, who is capable of seeing to our defence. For as long as a hundred of us remain alive, we intend never to be subjected to the lordship of the English, in any way. For it is not for glory in war, riches or honours that we fight, but only for the laws of our fathers and for freedom, which no good man loses except along with his life.

Therefore, most holy father and lord, we implore your holiness with all vehemence in our prayers that you ... look with paternal eyes on the troubles and difficulties brought upon us and the church of God by the English. And that you deign to admonish and exhort the king of the English, who ought to be satisfied with what he has (since England was formerly enough for seven kings or more), to leave us Scots in peace, living as we do in the poor country of Scotland beyond which there is no dwelling place, and desiring nothing but our own....

It is important for you, holy father, to do this, since you see the savagery of the heathen raging against Christians (as the sins of Christians require), and the frontiers of Christendom are being curtailed day by day, and you have seen how much it detracts from your holiness's reputation if (God forbid!) the church suffers eclipse or scandal in any part of it during your time. Let it then rouse the Christian princes who are covering up their true motivation when they pretend that they cannot go to the assistance of the Holy Land on account of wars with their neighbours. The real reason that holds them back is that in warring with their smaller neighbours they anticipate greater advantage to themselves and weaker resistance....

But if your Holiness too credulously trusts the tales of the English fully, or does not leave off favouring the English to our confusion, then we believe that the Most High will blame you for the slaughter of bodies.... Dated at our monastery at Arbroath in Scotland 6 April 1320 in the fifteenth year of our said king's reign.

Questions for Analysis

1. On what grounds does this letter justify the political independence of the Scots? What different arguments does it make? Which, in your view, is the most compelling one?

2. Why does this letter mention crusading? What are the Scottish lords implying about the relationship between Europe's internal conflicts and the ongoing wars with external adversaries?

3. Imagine that you are an adviser to the pope. Based on your knowledge of the papacy's situation at this time, would you advise him to do as this letter asks? Why or why not?

at the University of Glasgow) it would remain there until 1996, as a sign that the sovereignty of Scotland had yielded to that of England. (It will be temporarily returned to London when the next English monarch is crowned.)

Edward considered the subjugation of Scotland to be England's manifest destiny: he called himself "the Hammer of the Scots," and when he died he charged his son Edward II (r. 1307–1327) with the completion of his task. But Edward, unlike his father, was not a ruthless and efficient advocate of English expansion. And he had to contend with a rebellion led by his own queen, Isabella of France, who also engineered his abdication and murder. Their son, Edward III (r. 1327–1377), would eventually renew his grandfather's expansionist policies—but his main target would be France, not Scotland. He would thus launch Europe's two strongest monarchies into a war that lasted over a hundred years.

The Outbreak of the Hundred Years' War

The Hundred Years' War was the largest, longest, and most wide-ranging military conflict since Rome's wars with Carthage in the third and second centuries B.C.E. (see Chapter 5). Although England and France were its principal antagonists, almost all of the major European powers became involved in it at some stage. Active hostilities began in 1337 and lasted until 1453, interrupted by truces of varying lengths.

The most fundamental source of conflict, and the most difficult to resolve, was the fact that the kings of England held the duchy of Gascony as vassals of the French king; this had been part of Eleanor of Aquitaine's domain, added to the Anglo-Norman Empire in 1154 (see Chapter 9). In the twelfth and thirteenth centuries, when the French kings had not yet absorbed this region into their domain, this fact had seemed less of an anomaly. But as Europe's territorial monarchies began to claim sovereignty based on the free exercise of power within the "natural" boundaries of their domains, the English presence in "French" Gascony became more and more problematic. That England also had close commercial links, through the wool trade, with Flanders—which consistently resisted French imperialism—added fuel to the fire. So did the French alliance with the Scots, who continued to resist English imperialism.

Complicating this volatile situation was the disputed succession of the French crown. In 1328, the last of Philip IV's three sons died without leaving a son to succeed him: the Capetian dynasty, founded by the Frankish warlord Hugh Capet in 987 (see Chapter 8), had finally exhausted itself. A new dynasty, the Valois, came to the throne—but only by insisting that women could neither inherit royal power nor pass it on. For otherwise, the heir to France was Edward III of England, whose ambitious mother, Isabella, was Philip IV's only daughter. When his claim was initially passed over, Edward was only fifteen and in no position to protest. In 1337, however, when the disputes over Gascony and Scotland erupted into war, Edward raised the stakes by claiming to be the rightful king of France, a claim that subsequent English kings would maintain until the eighteenth century.

Although France was richer and more populous than England by a factor of at least three to one, the English crown was more effective in mobilizing the entire population, for reasons that we discussed in Chapter 9. Edward III was therefore able to levy and maintain a professional army of seasoned and well-disciplined soldiers, cavalry, and archers. The huge but virtually leaderless armies assembled by the French proved no match for the tactical superiority of these smaller English forces. English armies pillaged the French countryside at will, while civil wars broke out between embattled French lords. A decade after the declaration of war, French knights were defeated in two humiliating battles, at Crécy (1346) and Calais (1347). The English seemed invincible. Yet they were no match for an adversary approaching from the Far East.

FROM THE GREAT FAMINE TO THE BLACK DEATH

By 1300, Europe was connected to Asia and the lands in between by an intricate network that fostered commerce, communication, and connections of all kinds. Yet Europe was also reaching its own ecological limits. Between 1000 and 1300, the population had tripled, and a sea of grain

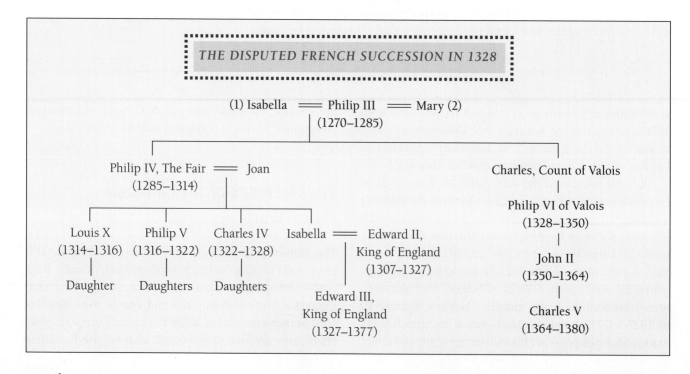

THE DISPUTED FRENCH SUCCESSION IN 1328

(1) Isabella ⚌ Philip III ⚌ Mary (2)
(1270–1285)

Philip IV, The Fair ⚌ Joan
(1285–1314)

Charles, Count of Valois

Philip VI of Valois
(1328–1350)

Louis X
(1314–1316)

Philip V
(1316–1322)

Charles IV
(1322–1328)

Isabella ⚌ Edward II,
King of England
(1307–1327)

John II
(1350–1364)

Daughter

Daughters

Daughters

Edward III,
King of England
(1327–1377)

Charles V
(1364–1380)

Past and Present

Global Pandemics

Although advances in medical science have made the causes of disease less mysterious, the rapid spread of new viruses is still terrifying and the variety of human responses to the possibility of sudden infection have changed little over time. The image on the left shows monks receiving the blessings of a priest at a special service in honor of St. Sebastian, who was regarded as a healer to those stricken with plague. On the right, citizens of Mumbai wear masks as they wait to receive testing for the swine flu virus.

 Watch related author interview on StudySpace
wwnorton.com/web/westernciv18

fields stretched, almost unbroken, from Ireland to the Ukraine. Forests had been cleared, marshes drained, and pastureland reduced by generations of peasants performing lifetimes of backbreaking labor. But still, Europe was barely able to feed its people. At the same time, the warming trend that had begun in the late eighth century reversed itself. Even a reduction of one or two degrees centigrade is enough to cause substantial changes in rainfall patterns, shorten growing seasons, and lessen agricultural productivity. So it did in Europe, with disastrous consequences.

Evil Times: The Seven Years' Famine

Between the years 1315 to 1322, the cooling climate caused nearly continuous adverse weather conditions in northern Europe. Winters were extraordinarily severe: in 1316, the Baltic Sea froze over and ships were trapped in the ice. Rains

prevented planting in spring or summer, and when a crop did manage to struggle through it would be dashed by rain and hail in autumn. In the midst of these natural calamities, dynastic warfare continued in the sodden wheatfields, as the princes of Scandinavia and the Holy Roman Empire fought for supremacy and succession. In the once-fertile fields of Flanders, French armies slogged through mud in continued efforts to subdue the Flemish population. On the Scottish and Welsh borders, uprisings were ruthlessly suppressed and the paltry storehouses of the natives were pillaged to feed the English raiders.

The result was human suffering more devastating than that caused by any famine affecting Europe since that time: hence the acceptance of the name "Great Famine" to describe this terrible crisis. Weakened by years of malnutrition and relentless efforts to counteract the climactic effects on the landscape, between 10 and 15 percent of the population of northern Europe perished. Many starved, and others

The Code of Chivalry: Putting Honor before Plunder

The Hundred Years' War between England and France pitted these two countries' warrior aristocracies against one another. Yet these knights had a great deal in common: they all spoke French, many were closely related, and they were supposed to share a common set of values. The following excerpt is taken from The Book of Chivalry *written in French by Geoffroi de Charny, a French nobleman and veteran of this war's first major battles who ultimately died in combat at Poitiers in 1356. Because the war was fought almost entirely on French soil, Geoffroi was keenly aware of the toll it took on the land and its people. In the following passage, he addresses the problem of how a knight can sustain his honor when he is driven to acquire booty for himself through the theft of others' property.*

Those Who Are Brave but Too Eager for Plunder

 now need to consider yet another category of men-at-arms, who deserve praise, who are strong and skillful, bold and sparing no effort, some of whom always want to be at the forefront, riding as foragers to win booty or prisoners or other profit from the enemies of those on whose side they fight. And they know well how to do it skillfully and cleverly; and because they are so intent on plunder, it often happens that on the entry into a town won by force, those who are so greedy for plunder dash hither and thither and find themselves separated from those of their companions who have no thought for gain but only for completing their military undertaking. And it often happens that such men, those who ride after and hunt for great booty, are killed in the process—frequently it is not known how, sometimes by their enemies, sometimes through quarrels in which greed for plunder sets one man against another. It often occurs that through lack of those who chase after plunder before the battle is over, that which is thought to be already won can be lost again and lives or reputations as well. It can also happen in relation to such people who are very eager for booty that when there is action on the battlefield, there are a number of men who pay more attention to taking prisoners and other profit, and when they have seized them and other winnings, they are more anxious to safeguard their captives and their booty than to help to bring the battle to a good conclusion. And it may well be that a battle can be lost in this way. And one ought instead to be wary of the booty which results in the loss of honor, life, and possessions. In this vocation one should therefore set one's heart and mind on winning honor, which endures for ever, rather than on winning profit and booty, which one can lose within one single hour. And yet one should praise and value those men-at-arms who are able to make war on, inflict damage on, and win profit from their enemies, for they cannot do it without strenuous effort and great courage. But again I shall repeat: he who does best is most worthy.

Questions for Analysis

1. How does Geoffroi justify the act of plundering? What insights into contemporary military tactics does this passage provide?

2. Given that Geoffroi would have seen Englishmen pillaging French lands, do you find his justification of this activity surprising? Why or why not?

---

fell victim to epidemic diseases that affected both animals and people. In southern Europe, around the shores of the Mediterranean, the effects of climate change were more muted, and there were also different channels through which food could be distributed. Nonetheless, the overall health of this region suffered from the disruption of trade and the shortage of some staple goods, as well as from the highly unstable political situation we have already discussed.

As food grew scarcer, prices climbed unpredictably. Plans for future crops, which kept hope alive, would be dashed when spring arrived and flooded fields prevented seeds from germinating. Cold summers and autumns were spent foraging for food. Hunting was restricted to the nobility, but even those who risked the death penalty for poaching found little game. Wages did not keep pace with rising costs, and so those who lived in towns

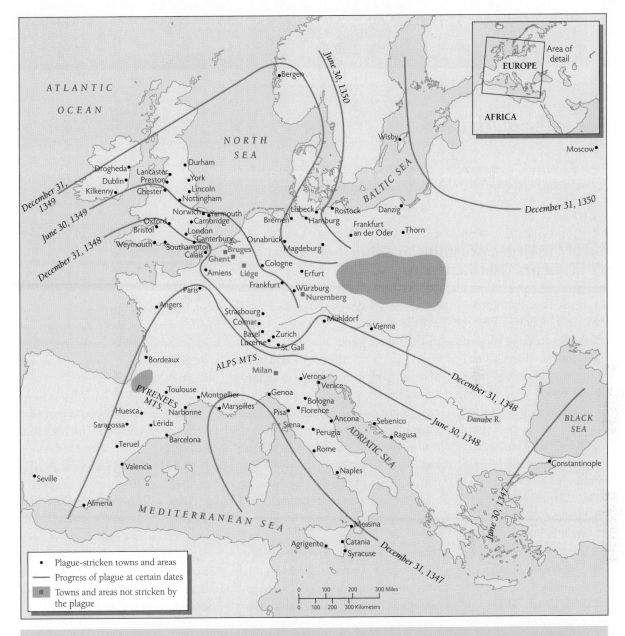

THE PROGRESS OF THE BLACK DEATH, FOURTEENTH CENTURY. ▪ *What trajectories did the Black Death follow once it was introduced into Europe?* ▪ *How might the growth of towns, trade, and travel have contributed to the spread of the Black Death?* ▪ *Would such a rapid advance have been likely during the early Middle Ages or even in the ancient world?*

and depended on markets had less to spend on scarce provisions. Only a year after the famine began, townspeople were dying of ailments that would not have been fatal in good years.

The effects of the famine were especially devastating for children, since even those who survived would be highly susceptible to disease, owing to the severe impairment of their immune systems. It may have been the Great Famine, then, that paved the way for the more transient (if more horrific) destruction of the Black Death.

A Crisis of Connectivity: Tracking the Black Death

The Black Death is the name given to a deadly pandemic that spread from China to Mongolia, northern India, and the Middle East during the 1330s and 1340s. By 1346, the plague had reached the Black Sea, where it was transmitted to the Genoese colonists at Caffa (as we noted above). From there, in 1347, Genoese ships inadvertently

Responses to the Black Death

Many chroniclers, intellectuals, and private individuals have left accounts of the plague in which they attempt to understand why it had occurred, how it spread, and how communities should respond to it.

The Spread of the Plague According to Gabriele de' Mussi (d. 1356), a Lawyer in Piacenza (Northern Italy)

Oh God! See how the heathen Tartar races, pouring together from all sides, suddenly infested the city of Caffa [on the Black Sea] and besieged the trapped Christians there for almost three years.... But behold, [in 1346] the whole army was affected by a disease which overran the Tartars and killed thousands upon thousands every day. It was as though arrows were raining down from heaven to strike and crush the Tartars' arrogance. All medical advice and attention was useless; the Tartars died as soon as the signs of disease appeared on their bodies: swellings in the armpit or groin caused by coagulating humours, followed by a putrid fever.

The dying Tartars, stunned and stupefied by the immensity of the disaster brought about by the disease, and realising that they had no hope of escape, lost interest in the siege. But they ordered corpses to be placed in catapults and lobbed into the city in the hope that the intolerable stench would kill every-

one inside. What seemed like mountains of dead were thrown into the city, and the Christians could not hide or flee or escape from them, although they dumped as many of the bodies as they could in the sea. And soon the rotting corpses tainted the air and poisoned the water supply.... Moreover one infected man could carry the poison to others, and infect people and places with the disease by look alone. No one knew, or could discover, a means of defence.

Thus almost everyone who had been in the East... fell victim... through the bitter events of 1346 to 1348—the Chinese, Indians, Persians, Medes, Kurds, Armenians, Cilicians, Georgians, Mesopotamians, Nubians, Ethiopians, Turks, Egyptians, Arabs, Saracens and Greeks....

* * *

As it happened, among those who escaped from Caffa by boat were a few sailors who had been infected with the poisonous disease. Some boats were

bound for Genoa, others went to Venice and to other Christian areas. When the sailors reached these places and mixed with the people there, it was as if they had brought evil spirits with them....

* * *

Scarcely one in seven of the Genoese survived. In Venice, where an inquiry was held into the mortality, it was found that more than 70 percent of the people had died.... The rest of Italy, Sicily and Apulia and the neighbouring regions maintain that they have been virtually emptied of inhabitants.... The Roman Curia at Avignon, the provinces on both sides of the Rhône, Spain, France, and the Empire cry up their griefs....

* * *

Everyone has a responsibility to keep some record of the disease and the deaths, and because I am myself from Piacenza I have been urged to write more about what happened there in 1348....

brought it to Sicily and northern Italy. From Italy, it spread westward along trade routes, first striking seaports, then turning inland with the travelers who carried it. It moved with astonishing rapidity, advancing about two miles per day, summer or winter. By 1350, it had reached Scandinavia and northern Russia, then spread southward again until it linked up with the original waves of infection that had brought it from Central Asia to the Black Sea. It continued to erupt in local epidemics for the next 300 years; some localities could expect a renewed outbreak every decade. The last Europe-wide instance occurred between 1661 and 1669, although there were

I don't know where to begin. Cries and laments arise on all sides. Day after day one sees the Cross and the Host being carried about the city, and countless dead being buried.... The living made preparations for their [own] burial, and because there was not enough room for individual graves, pits had to be dug in colonnades and piazzas, where nobody had ever been buried before. It often happened that man and wife, father and son, mother and daughter, and soon the whole household and many neighbours, were buried together in one place....

A Letter from the Town Council of Cologne to the Town Council of Strasbourg (Germany), 12 January 1349

Very dear friends, all sorts of rumours are now flying about against Judaism and the Jews prompted by this unexpected and unparalleled mortality of Christians.... Throughout our city, as in yours, many-winged Fame clamours that this mortality was initially caused, and is still being spread, by the poisoning of springs and wells, and that the Jews must have dropped poisonous substances into them. When it came to our knowledge that serious charges had been made against the Jews in several small towns and villages on the basis of this mortality, we sent numerous letters to you and to other cities and towns to uncover the truth behind these rumours, and set a thorough investigation in train....

If a massacre of the Jews were to be allowed in the major cities (something which we are determined to prevent in our city, if we can, as long as the Jews are found to be innocent of these or similar actions) it could lead to the sort of outrages and disturbances which would whip up a popular revolt among the common people—and such revolts have in the past brought cities to misery and desolation. In any case we are still of the opinion that this mortality and its attendant circumstances are caused by divine vengeance and nothing else. Accordingly we intend to forbid any harassment of the Jews in our city because of these flying rumours, but to defend them faithfully and keep them safe, as our predecessors did—and we are convinced that you ought to do the same....

Source: From Rosemary Horrox, ed. and trans., *The Black Death* (Manchester: 1994), pp. 16–21, 219–20.

Questions for Analysis

1. How does Gabriele de' Mussi initially explain the causes of the plague? How does his understanding of it change as he traces its movements from East to West—and closer to Italy?

2. Why does the Council of Cologne wish to quell violence against the Jews? How does this reasoning complement or challenge what we have learned so far about the treatment of Jews in medieval Europe?

3. In your view, do these two perspectives display a rational approach to the horrors of the Black Death? Why or why not?

---

sporadic outbreaks in Poland and Russia until the end of the eighteenth century.

What caused the Black Death? In 2011, scientists were able to confirm that it can be traced to the deadly microbe *Yersinia pestis*, and that it did indeed originate in China. *Y. pestis* actually causes three different kinds of contagion: bubonic plague and its even deadlier cousins, septicemic plague and pneumonic plague. In its bubonic form, this microbe is carried by fleas that travel on the backs of rats; humans catch it only if they are bitten by an infected flea or rat. Bubonic plague attacks the lymphatic system, producing enormous swellings (buboes) of the lymph nodes in the groin, neck,

a revolution, and it partly succeeded. Although the leaders were eventually captured and executed, the rebellion had made the strength of the common people known to all.

The fourteenth century is often seen as a time of crisis in the history of Western civilizations. Famine and plague cut fearful swaths through the population; war was a brutally recurrent fact of life; and the papacy spent seventy years in continuous exile from Italy, only to see its prestige decline further after its return to Rome. But this was also a time of extraordinary opportunity and achievement. The exhausted land of Europe recovered from centuries of overfarming, while workers gained the economic edge; eventually, some even gained social and political power. Meanwhile, popular and intellectual movements sought to reform the Church. A host of intellectual, artistic, and scientific innovations contributed to all of these phenomena.

This era of rebirth and unrest has been called by two different names: the later Middle Ages and the Renaissance. The latter refers to an intellectual and artistic movement that began in northern Italy, where the citizens of warring city-states desperately sought new models of governance and cultural cohesion by looking back to the older civilizations of Greece and Rome. But these are not two separate historical periods; rather they reflect two different ways of looking back at an era that is considered to be the immediate precursor of modernity. To understand it, we need to study it holistically. And we need to begin with a survey of Western civilizations after the Black Death.

THE PLAGUE CLAIMS A VICTIM. A priest gives last rites to a bedridden plague victim as a smiling devil pierces the dying man with a spear and as Christ looks mercifully down from heaven.
▪ *What are the possible meanings of this image?* ▪ *What does it reveal about contemporary attitudes toward death by plague?*

LIFE AFTER THE BLACK DEATH

By 1353, when the bubonic plague began to loosen its death grip on Europe, the Continent had lost nearly half of its population. This happened suddenly, within a half century, owing to a combination of famine and disease (see Chapter 10). In the following century, recurring outbreaks of the plague and frequent warfare in some regions would result in further drastic reductions. In Germany, some 400,000 villages disappeared. Around Paris, more than half of the farmland formerly under cultivation became pastureland. Elsewhere, abandoned fields returned to woodland, increasing the forested areas of Europe by about a third.

Life after the Black Death would therefore be radically different for those who survived it, because this massive depopulation would affect every aspect of existence, from nutrition to social mobility to spirituality.

First and foremost, it meant a relative abundance of food. The price of grain fell, which made it more affordable.

At the same time, the scarcity of workers made peasant labor more valuable: wages rose and work became easily obtainable. With wages high and food prices low, ordinary people could now afford more bread and could also spend their surplus cash on dairy products, meat, fish, fruits, and wine. As a result, the people of Europe were better nourished than they had ever been—better than many are today. A recent study of fifteenth-century rubbish dumps has concluded that the people of Glasgow (Scotland) ate a healthier diet in 1405 than they did in 2005.

The Rural Impact

In the countryside, a healthier ecological balance was almost immediately reestablished in the wake of the plague. And gradually, with the lessened demand for fuel and building materials, forests that had almost disappeared began to recover and expand. Meanwhile, the declining demand for grain allowed many farmers to expand their livestock herds. By turning arable land into pastureland, farmers reduced the need to hire so many workers and they also improved the fertility of the soil through manuring. Some farmers were even able to enlarge their holdings, because so much land had been abandoned.

Most of these innovations were made by small farmers because many great lords—individuals as well as monasteries—were slower to adjust to the changing circumstances. But some large landholders were quick to seize the advantage, responding to the shortage of workers and the rising cost of wages by forcing their tenants to perform additional unpaid labor. In parts of eastern Europe, many free peasants became serfs for the first time as a result. In Castile, Poland, and Germany, too, lords succeeded in imposing new forms of servitude.

In France and the Low Countries, by contrast, peasants remained relatively free, although many were forced to pay a variety of new fees and taxes to their lords or to the king. In England, where peasant bondage had been more common than in France, serfdom eventually disappeared altogether. Although the Peasants' Revolt of 1381 was ultimately unsuccessful, increased economic opportunity allowed English serfs to vote with their feet, either by moving to town or to the lands of a lord who offered more favorable terms: lower rents, more animals, fewer work requirements, and greater personal freedoms. Geographical mobility and social mobility are, as we have often noted, intertwined.

The Urban Impact

Mortality rates were high in the crowded cities and towns of Europe, but not all cities were equally affected by the plague and many recovered quickly. In London and Paris, for example, large-scale immigration from the countryside reversed the short-term declines caused by the plague. Many of these newcomers were women, whose economic opportunities (usually very limited) were greatly enhanced by urban labor shortages. Other urban areas suffered more from internal violence or warfare than from disease. In Florence, for example, the population rebounded quickly after the Black Death but was eventually depleted by civil unrest: by 1427, it had dropped from around 300,000 to about 100,000. In Toulouse (southwestern France), the population remained fairly stable until 1430, when it was reduced by a staggering 75 percent as a result of the ravages of the Hundred Years' War.

So while the overall population of Europe declined drastically because of the plague, it is noteworthy that a far larger percentage of all people were living in towns by 1500: approximately 20 percent as opposed to 10 or 15 percent prior to the Black Death. Fueling this urban growth was the increasing specialization of the late-medieval economy. With farmers under less pressure to produce grain in bulk, land could be devoted to livestock, dairy farming, and the production of a more diverse array of fruits and vegetables; and these could now be exchanged more efficiently on the open market.

Towns with links to extant trading networks benefited accordingly. In northern Germany, a group of entrepreneurial cities formed a coalition to build an entirely new mercantile corporation, the Hanseatic League, whose members came to control commerce from Britain and Scandinavia to the Baltic. In northern Italy, the increased demand for luxury goods—which even some peasants and urban laborers could now afford—brought renewed wealth to the spice- and silk-trading city of Venice and also to the fine-cloth manufacturers of Milan and the jewelers of Florence. Milan's armaments industry also prospered, supplying its warring neighbors and the armies of Europe.

Of course, not all urban areas flourished. The Franco-Flemish cities that had played such a large role in economic and cultural life since the eleventh century suffered a serious economic depression, exacerbated by incessant wars in the region. But, on the whole, surviving Europeans profited from the plague. A century afterward, they were poised to extend their commercial networks farther into Africa, Asia, and (ultimately) the Americas (see Chapter 12).

Popular Revolts and Rebellions

Although the consequences of the Black Death were ultimately beneficial for many, Europeans did not adjust easily to this new world; established elites, in particular, resisted the demands of newly powerful workers. When these demands were not met, violence erupted. Between 1350 and 1425, hundreds of popular rebellions challenged the status quo in many regions of Europe. In 1358, peasants in northeastern France rose up violently against their lords, destroying property, burning buildings and crops, and even murdering targeted individuals. This incident is known as the Jacquerie Rebellion, because all French peasants were caricatured by the aristocracy as "Jacques" ("Jack").

In England, as we have already noted, a very different uprising occurred in June of 1381, far more organized and involving a much wider segment of society. Thousands of people marched on London, targeting the bureaucracies of the royal government and the Church, capturing and killing the archbishop of Canterbury, and meeting personally with the fourteen-year-old king, Richard II, to demand an end to serfdom and taxation and to call for the redistribution of property. It ended with the arrest and execution of the ringleaders. In Florence, workers in the cloth industry—known as the Ciompi (*chee-OHM-pee*)—protested high unemployment and mistreatment by the manufacturers who also ran the Florentine government. They seized control of the city, demanding relief from taxes, full employment, and political representation. They maintained power for a remarkable six weeks before their reforms were revoked.

The local circumstances that lay behind each of these revolts were unique, but all of them exhibit certain common features. First of all, they were not bread riots spurred by destitution: those who took part in them were not protesting starvation wages, they were empowered by the new economic conditions and wanted to leverage their position in order to enact even larger changes. Some rebellions, like the English Peasants' Revolt, were touched off by resistance to new and higher taxes. Others, like the Jacquerie and the revolt of the Ciompi, took place at moments when unpopular governments were weakened by factionalism and military defeat. The English revolt was also fueled by the widespread perception of corruption within the Church and the royal administration.

Behind this social and political unrest, therefore, lies not poverty and hunger but the growing prosperity and self-confidence of village communities and urban laborers who were taking advantage of the changed economic circumstances that arose from the plague. For the most part, the rebels' hopes that they could fundamentally alter the conditions of their lives were frustrated. Kings, aristocrats, and urban oligarchs sometimes lost their nerve in the middle of an uprising, but they were almost always successful, after a time, in reasserting dominance. Yet this tradition of popular rebellion would remain an important feature of Western civilizations. It would eventually fuel the American War of Independence and the French Revolution (see Chapter 18), and it continues to this day.

Aristocratic Life in the Wake of the Plague

Although the urban elites and rural aristocracies of Europe did not adapt easily to "the world turned upside down" by the plague, this was hardly a period of crisis for those in power. Quite the contrary: many great families became far wealthier than their ancestors had ever been. Nor did the plague undermine the dominant position they had established. It did, however, make their situations substantially more complex and uncertain, at a time when the costs of maintaining a fashionable lifestyle were escalating rapidly.

Across Europe, most noble families continued to derive much of their revenue from vast land holdings. Many also tried to increase their sources of income through investment in trading ventures. In Catalonia, Italy, Germany, and England, this became common practice. In France and Castile, however, direct involvement in commerce was regarded as socially demeaning and was, therefore, avoided by established families. Commerce could still be a route to ennoblement in these kingdoms; but once aristocratic rank was achieved, one was expected to abandon these employments and adopt an appropriate way of life: living in a rural

A HUNTING PARTY. This fifteenth-century illustration shows an elaborately dressed group of noblemen and noblewomen setting out with falcons, accompanied by their servants and their dogs. Hunting, an activity restricted to the aristocracy, was an occasion for conspicuous consumption and display.

castle or urban palace surrounded by a lavish household, embracing the values and conventions of chivalry (engaging in the hunt, commissioning a family coat of arms), and serving the ruler at court and in war.

What it meant to be "noble" became, as a result, even more difficult to define than it had been during the twelfth and thirteenth centuries. In countries where noble rank entailed clearly defined legal privileges—such as the right to be tried only in special courts—proven descent from noble ancestors might be sufficient to qualify a family as noble in the eyes of the law. Legal nobility of this sort was, however, a somewhat less exclusive distinction than one might expect. In fifteenth-century Castile and Navarre, 10 to 15 percent of the total population had claims to be recognized as noble on these terms. In Poland, Hungary, and Scotland, the legally privileged nobility was closer to 5 percent, whereas in England and France fewer than 2 percent could plausibly claim the legal privileges of noble status.

Fundamentally, however, nobility was expressed and epitomized by an individual's lifestyle. Hereditary land ownership, political influence, deference from social inferiors, courtly manners, and the ostentatious display of wealth—these combined to constitute a family's honor and hence to mark it as noble. This means that, in practice, the social distinctions between noble and non-noble families were very hard to discern. And even on the battlefield, where the mark of nobility was to fight on horseback, the supremacy of the mounted knight was being threatened by the growing importance of professional soldiers, archers, crossbowmen, and artillery experts. There were even hints of a more radical critique of the aristocracy's claims to innate superiority. As the English rebels put it in 1381: "When Adam dug and Eve spun, Who then was a gentleman?" In other words, all social distinctions are entirely artificial.

Precisely because nobility was contested, those who claimed it took elaborate measures to assert their exclusive right to this status through conspicuous consumption. This accounts, in part, for the extraordinary number, variety, and richness of the artifacts and artworks that survive from this period. Aristocrats—or those who wanted to be classed as such—vied with one another in hosting lavish banquets, which required numerous costly utensils, specially decorated dining chambers, legions of servants, and the most exotic foods attainable. They dressed in rich and extravagant clothing: close-fitting doublets and hose with long pointed shoes for men, multilayered silk dresses with ornately festooned headdresses for women. They maintained enormous households: in France, around 1400, the Duke of Berry had 400 matched pairs of hunting dogs and 1,000 servants. They took part in elaborately ritualized tournaments and pageants, in which the participants pretended to be the heroes of chivalric romances. Aristocrats also emphasized their tastes and refinement by supporting authors and artists and some-

A NOBLE BANQUET. Uncle of the mad king Charles VI, the Duke of Berry left politics to his brothers, the Duke of Burgundy and the Duke of Anjou. In return, he received enormous subsidies from the royal government, which he spent on sumptuous buildings, festivals, and artworks, including the famous Book of Hours (prayer book), which includes this image. Here, the duke (seated at right, in blue) gives a New Year's Day banquet for his household, who exchange gifts while his hunting dogs dine on scraps from the table. In the background, knights confront one another in a tournament.

times by becoming accomplished artists themselves. Nobility existed only if it was recognized, and to be recognized noble status had to be constantly reasserted and displayed.

Rulers contributed to this process; indeed, they were among its principal supporters and patrons. Kings and princes across Europe competed in founding chivalric orders such as the Knights of the Garter in England and the Order of the Star in France. These orders honored men who had demonstrated the idealized virtues of knighthood, virtues celebrated as characteristic of the nobility as a whole. By exalting the nobility as a class, then, chivalric orders helped cement the links that bound the nobility to their kings and princes. These bonds were further strengthened by the gifts, pensions, offices, and marriage prospects that kings and princes could bestow on their noble followers.

Given the decline in the agricultural revenues of many noble estates, such rewards of princely service were critically important to maintaining noble fortunes. Indeed, the alliance that was forged in the fifteenth century between kings and their noble supporters would become one of the most characteristic features of Europe's ruling class. In France, this "Old Regime" (*ancien régime*) alliance lasted until the French Revolution of 1789. In Germany, Austria, and Russia, it would last until the outbreak of World War I. In England, it persisted in some respects until World War II.

Capturing Reality in Writing

The writings of literary artists who survived the Black Death, or who grew up in the decades immediately following it, are characterized by intense observations of the real world—and by appeals to a far larger and more diverse audience than their predecessors. We have noted that vernacular languages were becoming powerful vehicles for poetry and narrative in the twelfth century (see Chapter 9). Now they were being used to express some of the most innovative and critical perspectives on changing social mores, political developments, and philosophical outlooks. Behind this phenomenon lie three interrelated developments: the growing identification between vernacular language and the community of a realm, the still-increasing accessibility of education, and the emergence of a substantial reading public for literature in these languages. We can see these influences at work in three of the major authors who flourished during this period: Giovanni Boccaccio, Geoffrey Chaucer, and Christine de Pisan.

Boccaccio (*bohk-KAHT-chee-oh*, 1313–1375) is best known for *The Decameron*, a collection of prose tales about sex, adventure, and trickery. He presents these stories as being told over a period of ten days (hence the title of the book, which means "work of ten days"), by and for a sophisticated party of young women and men who have taken up residence in a country villa outside Florence in order to escape the ravages of the Black Death. Boccaccio borrowed the outlines of many of these tales from earlier sources, especially the fabliaux discussed in Chapter 9, but he couched them in a freely colloquial Italian. Whereas Dante had used the same Florentine dialect to evoke the awesome landscape of sacred history in the exquisite verse of his *Divine Comedy* (Chapter 10), Boccaccio used it to capture the foibles of human beings and their often graphic sexual exploits in plainspoken prose.

The English poet Geoffrey Chaucer (c. 1340–1400) is similar in many ways to Boccaccio, whose influence on him was profound. Chaucer was among the first generation of English authors whose compositions can be understood by modern readers of that language with relatively little effort. By the late fourteenth century, the Anglo-Saxon (Old English) tongue of England's preconquest inhabitants had mixed with the French dialect spoken by their Norman conquerors, to create the language which is the ancestor of our own: Middle English.

Chaucer's masterpiece is *The Canterbury Tales*. Like *The Decameron*, this is a collection of stories held together by a framing narrative. In this case, the stories are told by an array of people traveling together on a pilgrimage from London to the shrine of Saint Thomas Becket at Canterbury. But there are also significant differences between *The Decameron* and *The Canterbury Tales*. Chaucer's stories are in verse, for the most part, and they are recounted by people of all different classes—from a high-minded knight to a poor university student to a lusty widow. Each character tells a story that is particularly illustrative of his or her own occupation and outlook on the world, forming a kaleidoscopic human comedy.

This period, a generation or so after the Black Death, also saw the emergence of professional authors who made their living through the patronage of the aristocracy and the publication of their works. One of the first was a woman, Christine de Pisan (c. 1365–c. 1434). Although born in northern Italy, Christine spent her adult life in France, where her husband was a member of the king's household. When he died, the widowed Christine wrote to support herself and her children. She mastered a wide variety of literary genres, including treatises on chivalry and warfare, which she dedicated to King Charles VI of France. She also wrote for a larger and more popular audience. For example, her imaginative *Book of the City of Ladies* is an extended defense of the character, capacities, and history of women, designed to help female readers refute their male detractors. Christine also took part in a vigorous pamphlet campaign that condemned the misogynistic claims made by influential (male) authors like Boccaccio. This debate was ongoing for several hundred years and became so famous that it was given a name: the *querelle des femmes*, "the debate over women." Remarkably, Christine also wrote a song in praise of Joan of Arc. Sadly, she probably lived long enough to learn that this other extraordinary woman had been put to death for behaving in a way that was considered dangerously unwomanly (see below).

Visualizing Reality

Just as the desire to capture real experiences and convey real emotions was a dominant trait of the literature produced after the Black Death, so it was in the visual arts. This is evident both in the older arts of manuscript illumination and also in the new kinds of sculpture we discussed in Chapter 10.

CHRISTINE DE PISAN. One of the most prolific authors of the Middle Ages, Pisan used her influence to uphold the dignity of women and to celebrate their history and achievements. Here she is seen describing the prowess of an Amazon warrior who could defeat men effortlessly in armed combat.

A further innovation in the fifteenth century was the technique of painting in oils, a medium pioneered in Flanders, where artists found a ready market for their works among the nobility and wealthy merchants.

Oil paints were a revolutionary development: because they do not dry as quickly as water-based pigments, a painter can work more slowly and carefully, taking time with more difficult aspects of the work and making corrections as needed. Masterful practitioners of this technique include Rogier van der Weyden (c. 1400–1464), who excelled at communicating both deep spiritual messages and the minute details of everyday life (see **Interpreting Visual Evidence** on page 366). Just as contemporary saints saw divinity in material objects, so too an artist could portray the Virgin and Child against a background vista of ordinary life, with people going about their business or a man urinating against a wall. This was not blasphemous. To the contrary, it conveyed the message that the events of the Bible are constantly present, here and now: Christ is our companion, such artworks suggest, not some distant figure whose life and outlook are irrelevant to us.

The same immediacy is also evident in medieval drama. Plays were often devotional exercises that involved the efforts of an entire community, but they also celebrated that community. In the English city of York, for example, an annual series of pageants reenacted the entire history of human salvation from the Creation to the Last Judgment in a single summer day, beginning at dawn and ending late at night. Each pageant was produced by a particular craft guild and showcased that guild's special talents: "The Last Supper" was performed by the bakers, whose bread was a key element in their reenactment of the first Eucharist, while "The Crucifixion" was performed by the nail makers and painters, whose wares were thereby put on prominent display in the depiction of Christ's bloody death on the cross. In Italy, confraternities competed with one another to honor the saints with songs and processions. In Catalonia and many regions of Spain, there were elaborate dramas celebrating the life and miracles of the Virgin, one of which is still performed every year in the Basque town of Elche: it is the oldest European play in continuous production. In northern France, the Low Countries, and German-speaking lands, civic spectacles were performed over a period of several days, celebrating local history or the place of the community in the sacred history of the Bible. But not all plays were pious. Some honored visiting kings and princes. Others celebrated the flouting of social conventions, featuring cross-dressing and the reversal of hierarchies. They were further expressions of the topsy-turvy world created by the Black Death.

Why a Woman Can Write about Warfare

Christine de Pisan (c. 1365–c. 1434) was one of the West's first professional writers, best known today for her Book of the City of Ladies *and* The Treasure of the City of Ladies, *works that aimed to provide women with an honorable and rich history and to combat generations of institutionalized misogyny. But in her own time, Christine was probably best known for the work excerpted here,* The Book of the Deeds of Arms and of Chivalry, *a manual of military strategy and conduct written at the height of the Hundred Years' War, in 1410.*

 s boldness is essential for great undertakings, and without it nothing should be risked, I think it is proper in this present work to set forth my unworthiness to treat such exalted matter. I should not have dared even to think about it, but although boldness is blameworthy when it is foolhardy, I should state that I have not been inspired by arrogance or foolish presumption, but rather by true affection and a genuine desire for the welfare of noble men engaging in the profession of arms. I am encouraged, in the light of my other writings, to undertake to speak in this book of the most honorable office of arms and chivalry. . . . So to this end I have gathered together facts and subject matter from various books to produce this present volume. But inasmuch as it is fitting for this matter to be discussed factually, diligently, and sensibly . . . and also in consideration of the fact that military and lay experts in the aforesaid art of chivalry are not usually clerks or writers who are expert in language, I intend to treat the matter in the plainest possible language. . . .

As this is unusual for women, who generally are occupied in weaving, spinning, and household duties, I humbly invoke . . . the wise lady Minerva [Athena], born in the land of Greece, whom the ancients esteemed highly for her great wisdom. Likewise the poet Boccaccio praises her in his *Book of Famous Women*, as do other writers praise her art and manner of making trappings of iron and steel, so let it not be held against me if I, as a woman, take it upon myself to treat of military matters. . . .

O Minerva! goddess of arms and of chivalry, who, by understanding beyond that of other women, did find and initiate among the other noble arts and sciences the custom of forging iron and steel armaments and harness both proper and suitable for covering and protecting men's bodies against arrows slung in battle—helmets, shields, and protective covering having come first from you—you instituted and gave directions for drawing up a battle order, how to begin an assault and to engage in proper combat. . . . In the aforementioned country of Greece, you provided the usage of this office, and insofar as it may please you to be favorably disposed, and I in no way appear to be against the nation from which you came, the country beyond the Alps that is now called Apulia and Calabria in Italy, where you were born, let me say that like you I am an Italian woman.

Source: From *The Book of the Deeds of Arms and of Chivalry*, ed. Charity Cannon Willard and trans. Sumner Willard (University Park, PA: 1999), pp. 11–13.

Questions for Analysis

1. Christine very cleverly deflects potential criticism for her "boldness" in writing about warfare. What tactics does she use?

2. The Greco-Roman goddess Athena (Minerva) was the goddess of wisdom, weaving, and warfare. Why does Christine invoke her aid? What parallels does she draw between her own attributes and those of Minerva's?

THE BEGINNINGS OF THE RENAISSANCE IN ITALY

Rummaging through some old books in a cathedral library, an Italian bureaucrat attached to the papal court at Avignon was surprised to find a manuscript of Cicero's letters—letters that no living person had known to exist. They had probably been copied in the time of Charlemagne, but had then been forgotten for hundreds of years. How many other works of this great Roman orator had been lost to posterity? Clearly, thought Francesco Petrarca (1304–1374), he was living in an age of ignorance. A great gulf seemed to open up between his own time and

PETRARCH'S COPY OF VIRGIL. Petrarch's devotion to the classics of Roman literature prompted him to commission this new frontispiece for his treasured volume of Virgil's poetry. It was painted by the Sienese artist Simone Martini, who (like Petrarch) was attached to the papal court at Avignon. It is an allegorical depiction of Virgil (top right) and his poetic creations: the hero Aeneas (top left, wearing armor) and the farmer and shepherd whose humble labors are celebrated in Virgil's lesser-known works. The figure next to Aeneas is the fourth-century scholar Servius, who wrote a famous commentary on Virgil. He is shown drawing aside a curtain to reveal the poet in a creative trance. The two scrolls proclaim (in Latin) that Italy was the country that nourished famous poets and that Virgil helped it to achieve the glories of classical Greece. ▪ *How does this image encapsulate and express Petrarch's devotion to the classical past?*

have written to you long ago," he said in a Latin letter to the Greek poet Homer (dead for over 2,000 years), "had it not been for the fact that we lack a common language."

Petrarch was famous in his own day as an Italian poet, a Latin stylist, and a tireless advocate for the resuscitation of the classical past. The values that he and his followers began to espouse would give rise to a new intellectual and artistic movement in Italy, a movement strongly critical of the present and admiring of a past that had disappeared with the fragmentation of Rome's empire and the end of Italy's greatness. We know this movement as the Renaissance, from the French word for "rebirth" that was applied to it in the eighteenth century and popularized in the nineteenth, when the term *medieval* was also invented. It has since become shorthand for the epoch *following* the Middle Ages—but it was really part of that same era.

Renaissance Classicism

Talking about "the Renaissance," then, is a way of talking about some significant changes in education and artistic outlook that transformed the culture of northern Italy from the late fourteenth to the early sixteenth centuries and that eventually influenced the rest of Europe in important ways. The term has often been taken literally, as though the cultural accomplishments of antiquity had ceased to be appreciated and therefore needed to be "reborn." Yet we have been tracing the enduring influence of classical civilization for many chapters, and we have constantly noted the reverence accorded to the heritage of antiquity, not to mention the persistence of Roman law and Roman institutions.

That said, one can certainly find distinguishing traits that make the concept of "renaissance" newly meaningful in this era. For example, there was a significant quantitative difference between the ancient texts available to scholars in the first thousand years after Rome's fragmentation and those that became accessible in the fourteenth and fifteenth centuries. The discovery of "new" works by Livy, Tacitus, and Lucretius expanded the classical canon considerably, supplementing the well-studied works of Virgil, Ovid, and Cicero. More important was the expanded access to ancient Greek literature in western Europe. In the twelfth and thirteenth centuries, as we have seen in Chapters 8 and 9, Greek scientific and philosophical works became available to western Europeans thanks to increased contact with Islam, via Latin translations of Arabic translations of the original Greek.

Still, no Greek poems or plays were yet available in Latin translations, and neither were the major dialogues of Plato. Moreover, only a handful of western Europeans could

that of the ancients: a middle age that separated him from those well-loved models.

For centuries, Christian intellectuals had regarded "the dark ages" as the time between Adam's expulsion from Eden and the birth of Christ. But now, Petrarch (the name by which English-speakers call Petrarca) redefined that concept and applied it to his own era. According to him, the Middle Ages was not the pagan past but the time that separated him from direct communion with the classics. Yet this did not stop him from trying to bridge the gap. "I would

Realizing Devotion

These two paintings by the Flemish artist Rogier van der Weyden (*FAN-der-VIE-den*, c. 1400–1464) capture some of the most compelling characteristics of late medieval art, particularly the trend toward realistic representations of holy figures and sacred stories. On the left (image A), the artist depicts himself as the evangelist Luke, regarded in Christian tradition as a painter of portraits; he sketches the Virgin nursing the infant Jesus in a town house overlooking a Flemish city. On the right (image B), van der Weyden imagines the entombment of the dead Christ by his followers, including the Virgin (left), Mary Magdalene (kneeling), and the disciple John (right). Here, he makes use of a motif that became increasingly prominent in the later Middle Ages: Christ as the Man of Sorrows, displaying his wounds and inviting the viewer to share in his suffering. In both paintings, van der Weyden emphasizes the humanity of his subjects rather than their iconic status (see Chapter 7), and he places them in the urban and rural landscapes of his own world.

Questions for Analysis

1. How are these paintings different from the sacred images of the earlier Middle Ages (see, for example, pages 214 and 217)? What messages does the artist convey by setting these events in his own immediate present?

2. In what ways do these paintings reflect broad changes in popular piety and medieval devotional practices? Why, for example, would the artist display the dead and wounded body of Christ—rather than depicting him as resurrected and triumphant, or as an all-seeing creator and judge?

3. In general, how would you use these images as evidence of the worldview of the fifteenth century? What do they tell us about people's attitudes, emotions, and values?

A. Saint Luke drawing the portrait of the Virgin.

B. The Deposition.

read the language of classical Greece. But as the Mongols and, after them, the Ottoman Turks put increasing pressure on the shrinking borders of Byzantium (see below), more and more Greek-speaking intellectuals fled to Italy, bringing their books and their knowledge with them.

Thanks to these developments, some Italian intellectuals not only had increased access to more classical texts, they also used these texts in new ways. For centuries, Christian scholars had worked to bring ancient writings and values into line with their own beliefs (see Chapter 6). By contrast, the new reading methods pioneered by Petrarch and others fostered an increased awareness of the conceptual gap that separated the contemporary world from that of antiquity. This awakened a determination to recapture truly ancient worldviews and value systems, and it would eventually be expressed in visual terms, too. In the second half of the fifteenth century, especially, classical models contributed strikingly to the distinctive artistic style that is most strongly associated with the Renaissance (something we will address in Chapter 12).

Another distinguishing feature of this new perspective on the classical past was the way that it became overtly materialistic and commercialized. The competition among and within Italian city-states fostered a culture of display that used the symbols and artifacts of ancient Rome as pawns in an endless power game. Meanwhile, the relative weakness of the Church contributed to the growth of claims to power based on classical models—even by Italian bishops and Church-sponsored universities. When the papacy was eventually restored to Rome, it too had to compete in this Renaissance arena, by patronizing the artists and intellectuals who espoused these aesthetic and political ideals.

Renaissance Humanism

The most basic feature of this new intellectual and political agenda is summarized in the term *humanism*. This was a program of study that aimed to replace the scholastic emphasis on logic and theology—which would continue to be central to the curriculum of medieval universities like Paris and Oxford—with the study of ancient literature, rhetoric, history, and ethics. That is, the goal of a humanist education was the understanding of the human experience as viewed through the lenses of the classical past, and devoted to the fulfillment of human potential in the present. By contrast, a scholastic education filtered human experience through the teachings of scripture and the Church fathers, with human salvation as the ultimate goal.

Moreover, some intellectuals like Petrarch believed that the university curriculum concentrated too much on abstract speculation, rather than the achievement of virtue and ethical conduct in the here-and-now. He felt that the true Christian thinker must cultivate literary eloquence and so inspire others to do good through the pursuit of beauty and truth. And according to him, the best models of eloquence were to be found in the classics of Latin literature, which were also filled with ethical wisdom. Petrarch dedicated himself, therefore, to rediscovering such texts and to writing his own poems and moral treatises in a Latin style modeled on classical authors.

Humanists accordingly preferred ancient writings to those of more recent authors, including their own contemporaries. And although some humanists wrote in Italian as well as Latin, most regarded vernacular literature as a lesser diversion suitable only for the uneducated; serious scholarship and praiseworthy poetry could be written only in Latin or Greek. Proper Latin, moreover, had to be the classical Latin of Cicero and Virgil (Chapter 5), not the evolving language common to universities, international diplomacy, the law, and the Church. Renaissance humanists therefore condemned the living Latin of their day as a barbarous departure from classical (and therefore "correct") standards of Latin style. And ironically, their determination to revive this older language actually killed the lively Latin that had continued to flourish in Europe. By insisting on outmoded standards of grammar, syntax, and diction, they turned Latin into a fossilized discourse that ceased to have any direct relevance to daily life. They thus contributed, unwittingly, to the ultimate triumph of the various European vernaculars they despised, as well as to the demise of Latin as a common medium of communication.

Because humanism was an educational program designed to produce virtuous citizens and able public officials, it largely excluded women because women were largely excluded from Italian political life. Here again there is a paradox: as more and more Italian city-states fell into the hands of autocratic rulers, the humanist educational curriculum lost its immediate connection to the republican ideals of ancient Rome. Nevertheless, humanists never lost their conviction that the study of the "humanities" (as the humanist curriculum came to be known) was the best way to produce political leaders.

Why Italy?

These new attitudes toward education and the ancient past were fostered in a northern Italy for historically specific reasons. After the Black Death, this region was the most densely populated part of Europe; other urban areas, notably northeastern France and Flanders, had been decimated by the Great Famine as well as the plague. This region also differed from the rest of urbanized Europe because aristocratic families customarily lived in cities rather than in rural castles and consequently became more fully involved in public affairs than their counterparts north of the Alps. Moreover, many town-dwelling aristocrats were engaged in banking or mercantile enterprises, while many rich mercantile families imitated the manners of the aristocracy. The Florentine ruling family, the Medici, originally made their fortune in banking and commerce and yet were able to assimilate into the nobility.

These developments help to explain the emergence of the humanist ideals described above. Newly wealthy families were not content to have their sons learn only the skills necessary to becoming successful businessmen; they sought teachers who would impart the knowledge and finesse that would enable them to cut a figure in society, mix with their noble neighbors, and speak with authority on public affairs. Consequently, Italy produced and attracted a large number of independent intellectuals who were not affiliated with monasteries, cathedral schools, or universities—many of whom served as schoolmasters for wealthy young men while acting as cultural consultants and secretaries for their families. These intellectuals advertised their learning by producing political and ethical treatises and works of literature that would attract the attention of wealthy patrons or reflect well on the patrons they already had. As a result, Italian schools and private tutors turned out the best-educated laymen in all of Europe, men who constituted a new generation of wealthy, knowledgeable patrons ready to invest in the cultivation of new ideas and new forms of literary and artistic expression.

A second reason why late-medieval Italy was the birthplace of the Renaissance movement has to do with its vexed political situation. Unlike France and England, or the kingdoms of Spain, Scandinavia, and eastern Europe, Italy had no unifying political institutions. Italians therefore looked to the classical past for their time of glory, dreaming of a day when Rome would be, again, the center of the world. They boasted that ancient Roman monuments were omnipresent in their landscape and that classical Latin literature referred to cities and sites they recognized as their own.

Italians were particularly intent on reappropriating their classical heritage because they were seeking to establish an independent cultural identity that could help them oppose the intellectual and political supremacy of France. The removal of the papacy to Avignon had heightened antagonism between the city-states of Italy and the burgeoning nation-state beyond the Alps. This also explains the Italians' rejection of the scholasticism taught in northern Europe's universities and their embrace of intellectual alternatives. As Roman literature and learning took hold in the imaginations of Italy's intellectuals, so too did Roman art and architecture, for Roman models could help Italians create an artistic alternative to the dominant French school of Gothic architecture, just as Roman learning offered an intellectual alternative to the scholasticism of Paris.

Finally, this Italian Renaissance could not have occurred without the underpinning of Italian wealth gained through the commercial ventures described in Chapter 10. This wealth meant that talented men seeking employment and patronage were more likely to stay at home, fueling the artistic and intellectual competition that arose from the intensification of urban pride and the concentration of individual and family wealth in urban areas. Cities themselves became the primary patrons of art and learning in the fourteenth century.

The Renaissance of Civic Ideals

Petrarch's personal goal was a solitary life of contemplation and asceticism. But subsequent Italian intellectuals, especially those of Florence, developed a different vision of life's true purpose. For them, the goal of classical education was civic enrichment. Humanists such as Leonardo Bruni (c. 1370–1444) and Leon Battista Alberti (1404–1472) agreed with Petrarch on the importance of eloquence and the value of classical literature, but they also taught that man's nature equips him for action, for usefulness to his family and society, and for serving the state—ideally a city-state after the Florentine model. In their view, ambition and the quest for glory are noble impulses that ought to be encouraged and channeled toward these ends. They also refused to condemn the accumulation of material possessions, arguing that the history of human progress is inseparable from the human dominion of the earth and its resources.

Many of the humanists' civic ideals are expressed in Alberti's treatise *On the Family* (1443), in which the nuclear family is presented as the fundamental unit of the city-state and, as such, to be governed in such a way as to further the city-state's political and economic goals. Alberti accordingly argued that the family should mirror the city-state's organization. He therefore consigned women—who, in reality, governed the household—to childbearing, child rearing, and subservience to men even within this domestic realm. He asserted, furthermore, that women should play no role whatsoever in the public sphere. Although such dismissals of women's abilities were fiercely resisted by actual women, the humanism of the Renaissance was characterized by a pervasive denigration of them—a

A Renaissance Attitude toward Women

Italian society in the fourteenth and fifteenth centuries was characterized by marriage patterns in which men in their late twenties or thirties customarily married women in their mid- to late teens. This demographic fact probably contributed to the widely shared belief that wives were essentially children, who could not be trusted with important matters and who were best trained by being beaten. Renaissance humanism did little to change such attitudes. In some cases, it even reinforced them.

 fter my wife had been settled in my house a few days, and after her first pangs of longing for her mother and family had begun to fade, I took her by the hand and showed her around the whole house. I explained that the loft was the place for grain and that the stores of wine and wood were kept in the cellar. I showed her where things needed for the table were kept, and so on, through the whole house. At the end there were no household goods of which my wife had not learned both the place and the purpose. . . .

Only my books and records and those of my ancestors did I determine to keep well sealed. . . . These my wife not only could not read, she could not even lay hands on them. I kept my records at all times . . . locked up and arranged in order in my study, almost like sacred and religious objects. I never gave my wife permission to enter that place, with me or alone. . . .

[Husbands] who take counsel with their wives . . . are madmen if they think true prudence or good counsel lies in the female brain. . . . For this very reason I have always tried carefully not to let any secret of mine be known to a woman. I did not doubt that my wife was most loving, and more discreet and modest in her ways than any, but I still considered it safer to have her unable, and not merely unwilling, to harm me. . . . Furthermore, I made it a rule never to speak with her of anything but household matters or questions of conduct, or of the children.

Source: Leon Battista Alberti, "On the Family," in *The Family in Renaissance Florence*, ed. and trans. Renée N. Watkins (Columbia, SC: 1969), pp. 208–13, as abridged in Julie O'Faolain and Lauro Martines, eds., *Not in God's Image: Women in History from the Greeks to the Victorians* (New York: 1973), pp. 187–88.

Questions for Analysis

1. For what reasons did Alberti argue that a wife should have no access to books or records?

2. Would you have expected humanism to make attitudes to women more liberal and "modern"? How do views like Alberti's challenge such assumptions?

3. Compare Alberti's view of women to that of Christine de Pisan (page 364). How do you think Christine would have responded to this passage?

denigration often mirrored in the works of classical literature that these humanists so much admired.

The Emergence of Textual Criticism

The humanists of Florence eventually surpassed Petrarch in their knowledge of classical literature and philosophy, especially that of ancient Greece. In this, they were aided by a number of Byzantine scholars who had migrated to Italy in the first half of the fifteenth century and who gave instruction in the ancient form of their own native language. Wealthy, well-connected Florentines increasingly aspired to acquire Greek masterpieces for themselves, which often involved journeys back to Constantinople. In 1423, one adventurous bibliophile managed to bring back 238 manuscript books, among them rare works of Sophocles, Euripides, and Thucydides. These were quickly paraphrased in Latin and thus made accessible to western Europeans for the first time.

This influx of new classical texts spurred a new interest in textual criticism. A pioneer in this activity was Lorenzo Valla (1407–1457). Born in Rome and active primarily as a secretary to the king of Naples and Sicily, Valla had no allegiance to the republican ideals of the Florentine humanists. Instead, he turned his skills to the painstaking analysis of Greek and Latin writings in order to show how the historical study of language could discredit old assumptions and even unmask some texts as forgeries. For example, some papal propagandists argued that the papacy's claim to secular power in Europe derived from rights granted to the bishop of Rome by the emperor Constantine in the fourth century, enshrined in a document known as "The Donation of Constantine." By analyzing the language of this spurious text, Valla proved that it could not have been written in the time of Constantine because it contained more recent Latin usages and vocabulary.

This demonstration not only discredited more traditional scholarly methods, it made the concept of anachronism central to all subsequent textual study and historical thought. Indeed, Valla even applied his expert knowledge of Greek to elucidating the meaning of Saint Paul's letters, which he believed had been obscured by Jerome's Latin translation (see Chapter 6). This work was to prove an important link between Italian Renaissance scholarship and the subsequent Christian humanism of the north, which in turn fed into the Reformation (see Chapter 13).

THE END OF THE EASTERN ROMAN EMPIRE

The Greek-speaking refugees who arrived in Italy after the Black Death were self-appointed exiles. They were responding to the succession of calamities that had reduced the once-proud eastern Roman Empire to a scattering of embattled provinces. As we've noted, when Constantinople fell to western crusaders in 1204, the surrounding territories of Byzantium were severed from the capital that had held them together as constituent parts of that empire (see Chapter 9). When the Latin presence in Constantinople was finally expelled in 1261, imperial power had been so weakened that it extended only into the immediate hinterlands of the city and to parts of the Greek Peloponnese. The rest of the empire had become a collection of small principalities that existed in precarious alliance with the Mongols and indeed depended on the Pax Mongolica for survival (see Chapter 10). Then, with the coming of the Black Death, the imperial capital suffered the loss of half of its inhabitants and

shrunk still further. Meanwhile, the disintegration of the Mongol Empire laid the larger region of Anatolia open to a new set of invaders.

The Rise of the Ottoman Turks

Like the Mongols, the Turks were originally a nomadic people whose economy depended on raiding. When the Mongols arrived in northwestern Anatolia, the Turks were already established there and were being converted to Islam by the resident Muslim powers of the region: the Seljuq Sultanate of Rûm and the Abbasid Caliphate of Baghdad. But when the Mongols toppled these older powers, they eliminated the two traditional authorities that had kept Turkish border chieftains in check. Now they were free to raid, unhindered, along the soft frontiers of Byzantium. At the same time, they remained far enough from the centers of Mongol authority to avoid being destroyed themselves. One of their chieftains, Osman Gazi (1258–1326), established his own independent kingdom. Eventually, his name would characterize the Turkish dynasty that controlled the most ancient lands of Western civilizations for six centuries: the Ottomans.

By the mid-fourteenth century, Osman's successors had solidified their preeminence by capturing a number of important cities. These successes brought the Ottomans to the attention of the Byzantine emperor, who hired a contingent of them as mercenaries in 1345. They were extraordinarily successful—so much so that the eastern Roman Empire could not control their movements. They struck out on their own and began to extend their control westward. By 1370, their holdings stretched all the way to the Danube. In 1389, they defeated a powerful coalition of Serbian forces at the battle of Kosovo, which enabled them to begin subduing Bulgaria, the Balkans, and eventually Greece. In 1396, the Ottoman army even attacked Constantinople itself, although it withdrew to repel an ineffectual crusading force that had been hastily sent by the papacy.

In 1402, another attack on Constantinople was deflected—this time, by a more potent foe who had ambitions to match those of the Ottomans. Timur the Lame (Tamerlane, as he was called by European admirers) was born to a family of small landholders in the Mongol Khanate of Chagatai (named for its first ruler, the second son of Genghis Khan). Although Timur may have been a Turk himself, he acted as the spiritual heir of the Mongol Empire. While still a young man, he rose to prominence as a military leader and gained a reputation for tactical genius. He was no politician, though, and never officially assumed the title of khan in any of the territories he dominated. Instead, he moved ceaselessly from conquest to conquest, becoming the master of lands stretching

THE HEAD OF TIMUR THE LAME. This bust of the Mongol leader known in the West as Tamerlane is based on a forensic reconstruction of his exhumed skull.

from the Caspian Sea to the Volga River, as well as most of Persia. For a time, it looked briefly as if the Mongol Empire might be reunited under his reign. But Timur died in 1405, on his way to invade China, and his various conquests fell into the hands of local rulers. Mongol influence continued in the Mughal Empire of India, whose rulers claimed descent from the followers of Genghis Khan. But in Anatolia, the Ottoman Turks were once again on the rise.

The Fall of Constantinople

After the death of Timur, Ottoman pressure on Constantinople resumed and escalated. During the 1420s and 1430s, monasteries and schools that had been established since the fourth century found themselves in the path of an advancing army, and a steady stream of fleeing scholars strove to salvage a millennium's worth of Byzantine books—many of them preserving the heritage of ancient Greece and the Hellenistic

world. Then, in 1451, the Ottoman sultan Mehmet II turned his full attention to the conquest of the imperial city. In 1453, after a brilliantly executed siege, his army succeeded in breaching its walls. The Byzantine emperor was killed in the assault, the city itself was plundered, and its remaining population was sold into slavery. The Ottomans then settled down to rule their new capital in a style reminiscent of their Byzantine predecessors.

The Ottoman conquest of Constantinople administered an enormous shock to European rulers and intellectuals—and, indeed, the latter would profit mightily from this event. Yet its actual political and economic impact was minor. Ottoman control may have reduced European access to the Black Sea, but the bulk of the Far Eastern luxury trade with Europe had never passed through Black Sea ports in the first place. Europeans got most of their spices and silks through Venice, which imported them from Alexandria and Beirut, and these two cities did not fall to the Ottomans until the 1520s. Moreover, as we saw in Chapter 10, Europeans already had colonial ambitions and significant trading interests in Africa and the Atlantic that connected them to far-reaching networks.

But if the practical effects of the Ottoman conquest were modest where western Europe was concerned, the effects on the Turks themselves were transformative. Vast new wealth poured into Anatolia, which the Ottomans increased by carefully tending to the industrial and commercial interests of their new capital city, Constantinople, which they also called Istanbul—the Turkish pronunciation of the Greek phrase *eis tan polin* "in (or to) the city." Trade routes were redirected to feed the capital, and the Ottomans became a naval power in the eastern Mediterranean as well as in the Black Sea. As a result, Constantinople's population grew rapidly, from fewer than 100,000 in 1453 to more than 500,000. By 1600, it was the largest city in the world outside of China.

Slavery and Social Advancement in the Ottoman Empire

Despite the Ottomans' careful attention to commerce, their empire continued to rest on the spoils of conquest. To manage its continual expansion, the size of the Ottoman army and administration grew exponentially, drawing more and more manpower from conquered territories. And because both army and bureaucracy were largely composed of slaves, the demand for more soldiers and administrators could best be met through further conquests that would capture yet more slaves. Those conquests, however, required a still larger army and an even more extensive bureaucracy—and so the cycle continued. It mirrors, in many respects, the

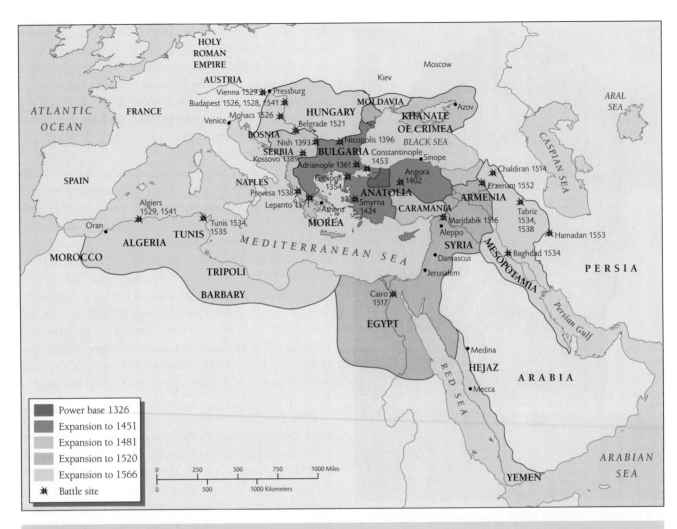

THE GROWTH OF THE OTTOMAN EMPIRE. Consider the patterns of Ottoman expansion revealed in this map. ▪ *Where is Constantinople, and how might the capture of Constantinople in 1453 have facilitated further conquests?* ▪ *Compare the extent of the Ottoman Empire in 1566 with that of the Byzantine Empire under Justinian (see the map on page 212). How would you account for their similarities?*

dilemma of the Roman Empire in the centuries of its rapid expansion beyond Italy (see Chapter 5), which created an insatiable demand for slaves.

Not only were slaves the backbone of Ottoman government, they were also critical to the lives of the Turkish upper class. One of the important measures of status in Ottoman society was the number of slaves in one's household. After the capture of Constantinople, new wealth would permit some elites to maintain households in the thousands. By the sixteenth century, the sultan alone possessed more than 20,000 slave attendants, not including his bodyguard and elite infantry units, both of which also comprised slaves.

Where did all of these slaves come from? Many were captured in war. Many others were taken on raiding forays into Poland and Ukraine and sold to Crimean slave merchants, who shipped their captives to the slave markets of Constantinople. But slaves were also recruited (some willingly, some by coercion) from rural areas of the Otto-

man Empire itself. Because the vast majority of slaves were household servants and administrators rather than laborers, some men willingly accepted enslavement, believing that they would be better off as slaves in Constantinople than as impoverished peasants in the countryside. In the Balkans especially, many people were enslaved as children, handed over by their families to pay the "child tax" the Ottomans imposed on rural areas too poor to pay a monetary tribute. Although an excruciating experience for families, this practice did open up opportunities for social advancement. Special academies were created at Constantinople to train the most able of the enslaved male children to act as administrators and soldiers, some of whom rose to become powerful figures in the Ottoman Empire.

For this reason, slavery carried relatively little social stigma. Even the sultan himself was most often the son of an enslaved woman. And because Muslims were not permitted to enslave other Muslims, the vast majority of Ottoman welcome refuge from the persecutions and expulsions that had characterized Jewish life in late-medieval Europe. After their expulsion from Spain in 1492 (see Chapter 12), more than 100,000 Spanish (Sephardic) Jews ultimately immigrated to the territories of the Ottoman Empire.

Because the Ottoman sultans were Sunni Muslims, they often dealt harshly with other Muslim sects. But they were extremely tolerant of non-Muslims. They organized the major religious groups of their empire into legally recognized units and permitted them considerable rights of self-government. They were especially careful to protect and promote the authority of the Greek Orthodox patriarch of Constantinople over the Orthodox Christians of their empire. As a result, the Ottomans enjoyed staunch support from their Orthodox Christian subjects during their wars with the Christians of western Europe.

Russia: "The Third Rome"

The Orthodox Church also received staunch support from the Russian people, whose own Church had been founded by Byzantine missionaries in the tenth century (see Chapter 8) and whose written language was based on the Greek alphabet and Greek grammar. Indeed, the emerging duchy of Muscovy (see Chapter 10) saw itself as the natural protector and ally of the eastern Roman Empire, and its alienation from western Europe increased as Byzantium grew weaker and the responsibility for defending Orthodox Christianity devolved onto the Russian Church.

But when the patriarch of Constantinople agreed to submit to the authority of Rome in 1438, in the desperate hope that the papacy would rally military support for the besieged city, Russian clergy refused to follow suit. After Constantinople fell to the Turks—predictably, without any help from Latin Christendom—the Russian Church emerged as the only surviving proponent of Orthodox Christianity.

Its sense of isolation was increased by developments on its western borders. In the thirteenth century, the small kingdom of Poland had struggled to defend itself from absorption by German princes. But when the Holy Roman Empire's strength waned after the death of Frederick the Great (see Chapter 9), Poland's situation grew more secure. In 1386, its reigning queen, Jadwiga, subsequently enabled its dramatic expansion when she married Jagiello, the duke of neighboring Lithuania, thus doubling the size of her kingdom. Lithuania had begun to carve out an extensive territory stretching from the Baltic to modern-day Belarus and Ukraine, and this expansionist momentum increased after its union with Poland. In 1410, a combined Polish and Lithuanian force defeated the Teutonic Knights at the Battle of Tannenberg,

SULTAN MEHMET II, "THE CONQUEROR" (r. 1451–81). This portrait, executed by the Ottoman artist Siblizade Ahmed, exhibits features characteristic of both Central Asia and Europe. The sultan's pose—his aesthetic appreciation of the rose, his elegant handkerchief—are indicative of the former, as is the fact that he wears the white turban of a scholar and the thumb ring of an archer. But the subdued coloring and three-quarter profile may reflect the influence of Italian portraits. ▪ *What did the artist achieve through this blending of styles and symbols?* ▪ *What messages does this portrait convey?*

slaves were Christian—although many eventually converted to Islam. And because so many of the elite positions within Ottoman government were held by these slaves, the paradoxical result was that Muslims, including the Turks themselves, were effectively excluded from the main avenues of social and political influence in the Ottoman Empire. Avenues to power were therefore remarkably open to men of ability and talent, most of them non-Muslim slaves.

Nor was this power limited to the government and the army. Commerce and business also remained largely in the hands of non-Muslims, most frequently Greeks, Syrians, and Jews. Jews in particular found in the Ottoman Empire a crushing the military order that controlled a crucial region lying between the allied kingdoms. Thereafter, Poland-Lithuania began to push eastward toward Muscovy.

Although many of Lithuania's aristocratic families were Orthodox Christians, the established church in Poland was loyal to Rome. Thus, when the inhabitants of Muscovy started to feel threatened by Poland-Lithuania, one way of constructing a shared Muscovite identity was to direct hostility toward Latin Christendom. Another was to take up the imperial mantle that had been abandoned when Constantinople fell, and to declare the Muscovite state the divinely appointed successor to Rome. To drive the point home, Muscovite dukes began to take the title of tsar, "caesar." "Two Romes have fallen," said a Muscovite chronicler, "the third is still standing, and a fourth there shall not be."

WARFARE AND NATION-BUILDING IN EUROPE

War has always been an engine for the development of new technologies. This is something we have noted since Chapter 1, but in the era after the Black Death the pace and scale of warfare was escalated to an unprecedented degree—and so was the deployment of new weapons. Although explosives had been invented in China, and originally used in displays of fireworks, they were first put to devastating and destructive effect in Europe. In fact, the earliest cannons were as dangerous to those who fired them as to those who were targeted. But by the middle of the fifteenth century, they were reliable enough to revolutionize the nature of warfare. In 1453, heavy artillery played a leading role in the outcomes of two crucial conflicts: the Ottoman Turks breached the ancient defenses of Constantinople with cannon fire and the French captured the English-held city of Bordeaux, bringing an end to the attenuated conflict known as the Hundred Years' War.

Thereafter, cannons made it more difficult for rebellious aristocrats to hole up in their stone castles and so consequently aided in the consolidation of national monarchies. Cannons placed aboard ships made Europe's developing navies more effective. A handheld firearm, the pistol, was also invented in the fourteenth century, and around 1500 the musket ended forever the military dominance of heavily armored cavalry, giving the advantage to foot soldiers recruited from the ranks of average citizens.

This suggests that there is a symbiotic relationship between warfare and nation-building as well as between warfare and technology. Because Europeans were almost constantly at war from the fourteenth century to the middle

of the twentieth, governments claimed new powers to tax their subjects and to control their subjects' lives. Armies became larger, military technology deadlier. Wars became more destructive, society more militarized. As a result of these developments, the most successful European states were aggressively expansionist and aggressively engaged in creating an idea of national identity that would bind people together against a common enemy.

The Hundred Years' War Resumes

The hostilities that make up the Hundred Years' War can be divided into three main phases (see the maps on page 000). The first phase dates from the initial declaration of war in 1337 (see Chapter 10), after which the English won a series of startling military victories before the Black Death put a temporary halt to the hostilities. The war then resumed in 1356, with another English victory at Poitiers. Four years later, in 1360, Edward III decided to leverage his strong position: he renounced his larger claim to the French throne, and in return he was to be guaranteed full sovereignty over a greatly enlarged duchy of Gascony and the promise of a huge ransom for the king of France, whom he held captive.

But the terms of the treaty were never honored, nor did it resolve the underlying issues that had led to the war itself, namely the problem of making good on any claim to sovereignty in contested territory and the question of the English king's place in the French royal succession. The French king continued to treat the English king as his vassal, while Edward and his heirs quickly renewed their claim to the throne of France.

Although there were no pitched battles in France itself for two decades after this, a destabilizing proxy war developed during the 1360s and 1370s, which spread violence to neighboring regions. Both the English troops (posted in Gascony) and the French troops (eager to avenge their losses) were reluctant to settle down. Many organized into "Free Companies" of mercenaries and hired themselves out in the service of hostile factions in Castile and competing city-states in northern Italy. By 1376, when the conflict between England and France was reignited, the Hundred Years' War had become a Europe-wide phenomenon.

England's Disputed Throne and the Brief Victory of Henry V

In this second phase of the war, the tide quickly shifted in favor of France. The new king, Charles V (r. 1364–80), imposed a series of taxes to fund the raising of an army,

A FIFTEENTH-CENTURY SIEGE WITH CANNONS. Cannons were an essential element in siege warfare during the Hundred Years' War.

restored order by disbanding the Free Companies, and hired the leader of one of these bands as the commander of his army. He thereby created a professional military that could match the English in discipline and tactics. By 1380, English territories in France had been reduced to a core area around the southwestern city of Bordeaux and the port of Calais in the extreme northeast.

Meanwhile, the aging Edward III has been succeeded by his nine-year-old grandson, Richard II (r. 1377–99), who was too young to prosecute a claim to the French crown. This was problematic, because the war had been extremely popular in England. Indeed, its mismanagement by Richard's advisers was one of the issues that triggered the Peasants' Revolt in 1381. And when Richard came of age and showed no signs of martial ambition, many of his own aristocratic relatives turned against him. Richard retaliated against the ringleader of this faction, his cousin Henry of Lancaster, by sending him into exile and confiscating his property. Henry's supporters used this as pretext for rebellion. In 1399, Richard was deposed by Henry and eventually murdered.

As a usurper whose legitimacy was always in doubt, Henry IV (r. 1399–1413) struggled to maintain his authority in the face of retaliatory rebellions and other challenges to his kingship. The best way to unite the country would have been to renew the war against France, but Henry was frequently ill and in no position to lead an army into combat. But when his son Henry V succeeded him in 1413, the new king immediately began to prepare for an invasion. His timing was excellent: the French royal government was foundering owing to the insanity of the reigning king, Charles VI (r. 1380–1422). A brilliant diplomat as well as a capable soldier, Henry V sealed an alliance with the powerful Duke of Burgundy, who was allegedly loyal to France but stood to gain from its defeat at the hands of the English. Henry also made a treaty with the German emperor, who agreed not to come to France's aid.

When he crossed the Channel in the autumn of 1415, Henry V's troops thus faced a much-depleted French army that could not rely on reinforcements. Although it was still vastly larger and boasted hundreds of mounted knights, it was undisciplined. It was also severely hampered by bad weather and deep mud when the two armies clashed at Agincourt on October 25 of that year—conditions that favored the lighter English infantry. Henry's men managed to win a crushing victory.

Then, over the next five years, Henry conquered most of northern France. In 1420, the ailing Charles VI was forced to recognize him as heir to the throne of France, thereby disinheriting his own son. (This prince bore the ceremonial title of *dauphin*, "the dolphin," from the heraldic device of the borderland province he inherited.) Henry sealed the deal by marrying the French princess, Catherine, and fathering an heir to the joint kingdom of England and France.

Joan of Arc's Betrayal and Legacy

Unlike his great-grandfather Edward III, who used his claim to the French throne largely as a bargaining chip to secure sovereignty over Gascony (see Chapter 10), Henry V honestly believed himself to be the rightful king of France. And his astonishing success in capturing the kingdom seemed to put the stamp of divine approval on that claim. But Henry's successes in France also transformed the nature of the war, turning it from a profitable war of conquest and plunder into an extended and expensive military occupation. It might have been sustainable had Henry been as long-lived as many of his predecessors. But he died early in 1422, just short of his thirty-sixth birthday. King Charles VI died only a few months later.

The new king of England and France, Henry VI (r. 1422–61), was only an infant, and yet the English armies under the command of his regents continued to press southward into territories held by the dauphin. Although it seemed unlikely that English forces would ever succeed

JOAN OF ARC. A contemporary sketch of Joan was drawn in the margin of this register documenting official proceedings at the Parlement of Paris in 1429.

in dislodging him, confidence in the dauphin's right to the throne had been shattered by his own mother's declaration that he was illegitimate. It might have happened that England would once again rule an empire comprising much of northern France, as it had for a century and a half after the Norman conquest.

But this scenario fails to reckon with Joan of Arc. In 1429, a peasant girl from Lorraine (a territory only nominally part of France) made her way to the dauphin's court and announced that an angel had told her that he, Charles, was the rightful king, and that she, Joan, should drive the English out of France. The fact that she even got a hearing underscores the hopelessness of the dauphin's position, as does the extraordinary fact that he gave her a contingent of troops. With this force, Joan liberated the strategic city of Orléans, then under siege by the English, after which a series of victories culminated in Charles's coronation in the cathedral of Reims, the traditional site for the crowning of French kings.

But, despite her miraculous success, Joan was an embarrassment whose very charisma made her dangerous: a peasant leading aristocrats, a woman leading men, and a commoner who claimed to have been commissioned by God. When, a few months later, the Burgundians captured her in battle and handed her over to the English, the king she had helped to crown did nothing to save her. Accused of witchcraft, condemned by the theologians of Paris, and tried for heresy by an English ecclesiastical court, Joan was burned to death in the market square at Rouen in 1431. She was nineteen years old.

The French forces whom Joan had inspired, however, continued on the offensive. In 1435, the duke of Burgundy withdrew from his alliance with England, and when the young English king, Henry VI, proved first incompetent and then insane, a series of French military victories brought hostilities to an end with the capture of Bordeaux in 1453. English kings would threaten to renew the war for another century, and Anglo-French hostility would last until the defeat of Napoleon in 1815. But after 1453, English control over French territory would be limited to the port of Calais, which eventually fell in 1558.

The Long Shadow of the Hundred Years' War

The Hundred Years' War challenged the very existence of France. The disintegration of that kingdom, first during the 1350s and 1360s, and again between 1415 and 1435, glaringly revealed the fragility of the bonds that tied the king to the nobility, and the royal capital Paris to the kingdom's

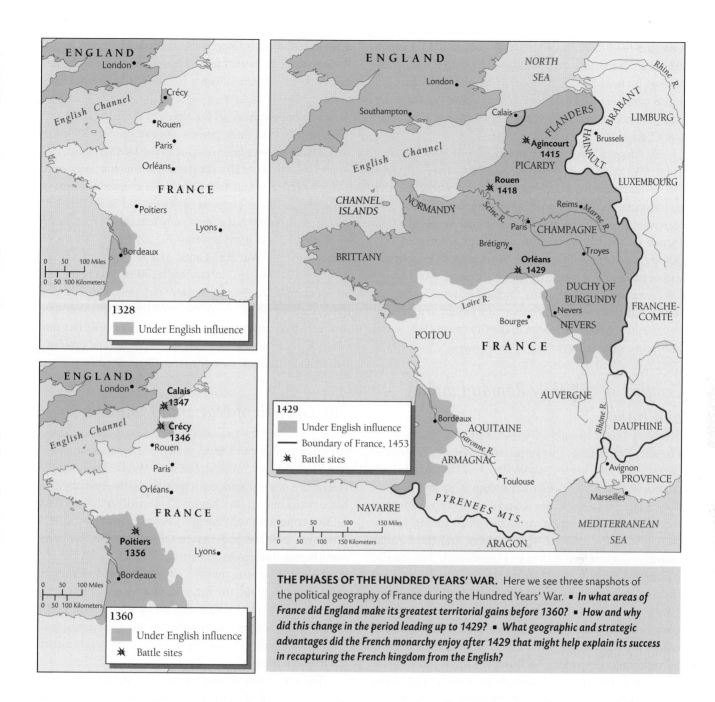

THE PHASES OF THE HUNDRED YEARS' WAR. Here we see three snapshots of the political geography of France during the Hundred Years' War. ▪ *In what areas of France did England make its greatest territorial gains before 1360?* ▪ *How and why did this change in the period leading up to 1429?* ▪ *What geographic and strategic advantages did the French monarchy enjoy after 1429 that might help explain its success in recapturing the French kingdom from the English?*

outlying regions. Nonetheless, the king's power was actually increased by the war's end, laying the foundations on which the power of early modern France would be built.

The Hundred Years' War also had dramatic effects on the English monarchy. When English armies in France were successful, the king rode a wave of popularity that fueled an emerging sense of English identity. When the war turned against the English, however, defeats abroad undermined support for the monarch at home. Of the nine English kings who ruled England between 1307 and 1485, five were deposed and murdered by factions.

This was a consequence of England's peculiar form of kingship, whose strength depended on the king's ability to

mobilize popular support through Parliament while maintaining the support of his nobility through successful wars. Failure to maintain this balance was even more destabilizing in England than it would have been elsewhere, precisely because royal power was so centralized. In France, the nobility could endure the insanity of Charles VI because his government was not powerful enough to threaten them. In England, neither the nobility nor the nation could afford the weak kingship of Henry VI. The result was an aristocratic rebellion against the king that led to a full-blown civil war: the Wars of the Roses, so called—by the novelist Sir Walter Scott (1771–1832)—because of the floral emblems, red and white, adopted by the two competing noble families

Lancaster and York. It ended only when a Lancastrian claimant, Henry Tudor (r. 1485–1509), resolved the dynastic feud by marrying Elizabeth of York, ruling as Henry VII and establishing a new Tudor dynasty whose symbol was a rose with both white and red petals. His son was Henry VIII (see Chapter 13).

So, despite England's ultimate defeat, the Hundred Years' War strengthened English identity in several ways. First, it equated national identity with the power of the state and its king. Second, it fomented a strong anti-French sentiment that led to the triumph of the English vernacular over French for the first time since the Norman conquest over 300 years earlier: the first English court to speak English was that of Richard II, a patron of Geoffrey Chaucer. And having lost its continental possessions, England became, for the first time, a self-contained island nation that looked to the sea for defense and opportunity—not to the Continent. This would later prove to be an advantage in many ways.

Conflict in the Holy Roman Empire and Italy

Elsewhere in Europe, the perpetual warfare that began to characterize the history of Western civilizations in this period was even more destructive than it proved to be in the struggle between England and France. In the lands of the Holy Roman Empire, armed conflict among territorial princes, and between these princes and the German emperor, weakened all combatants significantly. Periodically, a powerful emperor would emerge to play a major role, but the dominant trend was toward the continuing dissolution of power, with German princes dividing their territories among their heirs while free cities and local lords strove to shake off the princes' rule. Between 1350 and 1450, near anarchy prevailed in many regions. Only in the eastern regions of the empire were the rulers of Bavaria, Austria, and Brandenburg-Prussia able to strengthen their authority, mostly by supporting the efforts of the nobility to subject their peasants to serfdom and by conquering and colonizing new territories on their eastern frontiers.

In northern and central Italy, the last half of the fourteenth century was also marked by incessant conflict. With the papacy based in Avignon, the Papal States collapsed and Rome itself was riven by factional violence. Warfare among northern city-states added to the violence caused by urban rebellions in the wake of the plague. But around 1400, Venice, Milan, and Florence had succeeded in stabilizing their differing forms of government. Venice was now ruled by an oligarchy of merchants; Milan by a family of despots; and Florence was ruled as a republic but dominated by the influence of a few wealthy clans, especially the Medici banking family. Having settled their internal problems, these three cities then began to expand their influence by subordinating other cities to their rule.

Eventually, almost all the towns of northern Italy were allied with one of these powers. An exception was Genoa, which had its own trading empire in the Mediterranean and Atlantic (see Chapter 10). The papacy, meanwhile, reasserted its control over central Italy when it was restored to Rome in 1377. The southern kingdom of Naples and Sicily persisted as a separate entity but a constantly unstable one, riven by local warfare and poor government. After 1453, when the Hundred Years' War had ended and Ottoman expansion had been checked at Constantinople, an uneasy peace was achieved in Italy. But diplomacy and frequently shifting alliances did little to check the ambitions of any one state for further expansion, and it could not change the fact that none of these small-scale states could oppose the powerful national monarchies or empires that surrounded Italy.

The Growth of National Monarchies

In France and England, then, as well as in smaller kingdoms like Scotland and Portugal, the later Middle Ages saw the emergence of European states more cohesive than any that had existed before. (In Chapter 12, we will see how powerful this cohesion made the new united kingdom of Spain.) The basic political patterns established in the formative twelfth and thirteenth centuries had made this possible, yet the active construction of a sense of national identity in these territories, and the fusion of that identity with kingship, were new phenomena. Forged by war and fueled by the growing cultural importance of vernacular languages, this fusion produced a new type of political organization: the national monarchy.

The advantages of these national monarchies when compared to older forms of political organization—such as the empire, the principality, or the city-state—would become very evident. When the armies of France or Spain invaded the Italian peninsula at the end of the fifteenth century, neither the militias of the city-states nor the far-flung resources of Venice were a match for them. Germany and the Low Countries would suffer similar invasions only a few generations later and, along with Italy, would remain battlegrounds for competing armies until the middle of the nineteenth century. But the new national monarchies brought significant disadvantages, too. They guaranteed the prevalence of warfare in Europe as they continued their struggle for sovereignty and territory, and they would eventually transport their rivalry to every corner of the globe in the late nineteenth and early twentieth centuries.

The Condemnation of Joan of Arc by the University of Paris, 1431

After Joan's capture by the Burgundians, she was handed over to the English and tried for heresy at an ecclesiastical court set up in Rouen. It was on this occasion that the theology faculty of Paris pronounced the following verdict on her actions.

You, Joan, have said that, since the age of thirteen, you have experienced revelations and the appearance of angels, of St. Catherine and St. Margaret, and that you have very often seen them with your bodily eyes, and that they have spoken to you. As for the first point, the clerks of the University of Paris have considered the manner of the said revelations and appearances . . . Having considered all . . . they have declared that all the things mentioned above are lies, falsenesses, misleading and pernicious things and that such revelations are superstitions, proceeding from wicked and diabolical spirits.

Item: You have said that your king had a sign by which he knew that you were sent by God, for St. Michael, accompanied by several angels, some of which having wings, the others crowns, with St. Catherine and St. Margaret, came to you at the chateau of Chinon. All the company ascended through the floors of the castle until they came to the room of your king, before whom the angel bearing the crown bowed. . . .

As for this matter, the clerks say that it is not in the least probable, but it is rather a presumptuous lie, misleading and pernicious, a false statement, derogatory of the dignity of the Church and of the angels. . . .

Item: you have said that, at God's command, you have continually worn men's clothes, and that you have put on a short robe, doublet, shoes attached by points, also that you have had short hair, cut around above the ears, without retaining anything on your person which shows that you are a woman, and that several times you have received the body of Our Lord dressed in this fashion, despite having been admonished to give it up several times, the which you would not do. You have said that you would rather die than abandon the said clothing, if it were not at God's command, and that if you were wearing those clothes and were with the king, and those of your party, it would be one of the greatest benefits for the kingdom of France. You have also said that not for anything would you swear an oath not to wear the said clothing and carry arms any longer. And all these things you say you

have done for the good and at the command of God. As for these things, the clerics say that you blaspheme God and hold him in contempt in his sacraments; you transgress Divine Law, Holy Scripture, and canon law. You err in the faith. You boast in vanity. You are suspected of idolatry and you have condemned yourself in not wishing to wear clothing suitable to your sex, but you follow the custom of Gentiles and Saracens.

Source: Carolyne Larrington, ed. and trans., *Women and Writing in Medieval Europe* (New York: 1995), pp. 183–84.

Questions for Analysis

1. Paris was in the hands of the English when this condemnation was issued. Is there any evidence that its authors were coerced into making this pronouncement?

2. On what grounds was Joan condemned for heresy?

3. In what ways does Joan's behavior highlight larger trends in late medieval spirituality and popular piety?

THE TRIALS OF THE ROMAN CHURCH

Although the century after the Black Death would witness the papacy's return to Rome, it would also witness changes in the Church that would have far-reaching consequences in the centuries to come. Like other large landowners, the monasteries of Europe suffered from the economic changes brought about by the new world order, as did the Church's bishops, who confronted the same dilemmas as the secular nobility. But no ecclesiastical institution suffered more severe trials than the papacy, which endured almost seventy years of exile from Rome followed by a debilitating forty-year schism. It then faced a protracted battle with reformers who sought to reduce the pope's role

Competing Viewpoints

Council or Pope?

> The Great Schism spurred a fundamental and far-reaching debate about the nature of authority within the Church. Arguments for papal supremacy rested on traditional claims that the popes were the successors of Saint Peter, to whom Jesus Christ had delegated his own authority. Arguments for the supremacy of a general council had been advanced by many intellectuals throughout the fourteenth century, but it was only in the circumstances of the schism that these arguments found a wide audience. The following documents trace the history of the controversy, from the declaration of conciliar supremacy at the Council of Constance (Haec Sancta), to the council's efforts to guarantee regular meetings of general councils thereafter (Frequens), to the papal condemnation of appeals to the authority of general councils issued in 1460 (Execrabilis).

Haec Sancta Synodus (1415)

This holy synod of Constance . . . declares that being lawfully assembled in the Holy Spirit, constituting a general council and representing the Catholic Church Militant, it has its power directly from Christ, and that all persons of whatever rank or dignity, even a Pope, are bound to obey it in matters relating to faith and the end of the Schism and the general reformation of the church of God in head and members.

Further, it declares that any person of whatever position, rank, or dignity, even a Pope, who contumaciously refuses to obey the mandates, statutes, ordinances, or regulations enacted or to be enacted by this holy synod, or by any other general council lawfully assembled, relating to the matters aforesaid or to other matters involved with them, shall, unless he repents, be . . . duly punished. . . .

Source: R. L. Loomis, ed. and trans., *The Council of Constance* (New York: 1961), p. 229.

Frequens (1417)

The frequent holding of general councils is the best method of cultivating the field of the Lord, for they root out the briars, thorns, and thistles of heresies, errors, and schisms, correct abuses, make crooked things straight, and prepare the Lord's vineyard for fruitfulness and rich fertility. Neglect of general councils sows the seeds of these evils and encourages their growth. This truth is borne in upon us as we recall times past and survey the present.

Therefore by perpetual edict we . . . ordain that henceforth general councils shall be held as follows: the first within the five years immediately following the end of the present council, the second within seven years from the end of the council next after this, and subsequently

younger contemporary, the housewife Margery Kempe (c. 1372–c. 1439), resented the fact that she had a husband, several children, and a household to support, and thus could not take such a step. In later life, she renounced her wifely duties and devoted her life to performing acts of histrionic piety, which alienated many of those who came into contact with her. For example, she was so moved by the contemplation of Jesus's sufferings on the cross that she would cry hysterically for hours, disrupting the Mass. When on pilgrimage in Rome, she cried at the sight of babies that reminded her of the infant Jesus, or young men whom she thought resembled him.

The extraordinary piety of such individuals could be inspiring, but it could also threaten the Church's control over religious life and the links that bound individuals to their communities. It could, therefore, be dangerous. More safely orthodox was the practical mysticism preached by Thomas à Kempis, whose *Imitation of Christ* (c. 1427) taught readers how to appreciate aspects of the divine in their everyday lives. Originally written in Latin, *The Imitation* was quickly

every ten years forever.... Thus there will always be a certain continuity. Either a council will be in session or one will be expected at the end of a fixed period. . . .

Source: R. L. Loomis, ed. and trans., *The Council of Constance* (New York: 1961), pp. 246–47.

Execrabilis (1460)

An execrable abuse, unheard of in earlier times, has sprung up in our period. Some men, imbued with a spirit of rebellion and moved not by a desire for sound decisions but rather by a desire to escape the punishment for sin, suppose that they can appeal from the Pope, Vicar of Jesus Christ—from the Pope, to whom in the person of blessed Peter it was said, "Feed my sheep" and "whatever you bind on earth will be bound in heaven"—from this Pope to a future council. How harmful this is to the Christian republic, as well as how contrary to canon law, anyone who is not ignorant of the law can understand. For . . . who would not consider it ridiculous to appeal to something which does not now exist anywhere nor does anyone know when it will exist? The poor are heavily oppressed by the powerful, offenses remain unpunished, rebellion against the Holy See is encouraged, license for sin is granted, and all ecclesiastical discipline and hierarchical ranking of the Church are turned upside down.

Wishing therefore to expel this deadly poison from the Church of Christ, and concerned with the salvation of the sheep committed to us . . . with the counsel and assent of our venerable brothers, the Cardinals of the Holy Roman Church, together with the counsel and assent of all those prelates who have been trained in canon and civil law who follow our Court, and with our own certain knowledge, we condemn appeals of this kind, reject them as erroneous and abominable, and declare them to be completely null and void. And we lay down that from now on, no one should dare . . . to make such an appeal from our decisions, be they legal or theological, or from any commands at all from us or our successors. . . .

Source: Reprinted by permission of the publisher from Gabriel Biel, *Defensorium Obedientiae Apostolicae et Alia Documenta*, ed. and trans. Heiko A. Oberman, Daniel E. Zerfoss, and William J. Courtenay (Cambridge, MA: 1968), pp. 224–27. Copyright © 1968 by the President and Fellows of Harvard College.

Questions for Analysis

1. On what grounds does *Haec Sancta* establish the authority of a council? Why would this be considered a threat to papal power?

2. Why was it considered necessary for councils to meet regularly (*Frequens*)? What might have been the logical consequences of such regular meetings?

3. On what grounds does *Execrabilis* condemn the appeals to future councils that have no specified meeting date? Why would it not have condemned the conciliar movement altogether?

translated into many vernacular languages and is now more widely read than any other Christian book except the Bible.

Popular Reform Movements

For the most part, the threat of heretical movements was less dangerous to the Church than the corruption of the papacy. But in the kingdoms of England and Bohemia (the modern Czech Republic), some popular movements did pose serious challenges. The key figure in both cases was John Wycliffe (c. 1330–1384), an Oxford theologian and powerful critic of the Church. A survivor of the Black Death, Wycliffe lived at a time when the authority and integrity of the papacy were at a particularly low ebb. Indeed, he concluded that the empty sacraments of a corrupt Church could not save anyone. He therefore urged the English king to confiscate ecclesiastical wealth and to replace corrupt priests and bishops with men who would live according to apostolic standards of poverty and piety.

THE GREAT SCHISM, 1378–1417. During the Great Western Schism, the various territories of Europe were divided in their allegiances.
▪ *According to the map key, who were they choosing between?* ▪ *What common interests would have united the supporters of the Avignon pope or of the Roman pope?* ▪ *Why would areas like Portugal and Austria waver in their support?*

Some of Wycliffe's followers, known to their detractors as Lollards (from a word meaning "mumblers" or "beggars"), went even further, dismissing the sacraments as fraudulent attempts to extort money from the faithful. Lollard preachers also advocated for direct access to the scriptures and promoted an English translation of the Bible sponsored by Wycliffe himself.

Wycliffe's teachings played an important role in the Peasants' Revolt of 1381, and Lollardy gained numerous adherents in the decades after his death. The movement

was even supported by a number of aristocratic families; certainly the idea of dissolving the Church's wealth would have been attractive to many of those who stood to gain from it. But, after a failed Lollard uprising in 1414, both the movement and its supporters went underground in England.

In Bohemia and eastern Europe, however, Wycliffe's ideas lived on and struck even deeper roots. They were adopted by Jan Hus (c. 1373–1415), a charismatic teacher at the royal university in Prague. In contrast to the Lollards,

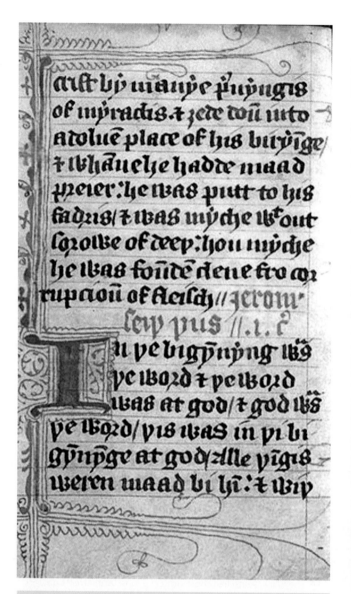

THE TEACHINGS OF JAN HUS. An eloquent religious reformer, Jan Hus was burned at the stake in 1415 after having been found guilty of heresy at the Council of Constance. This lavishly illustrated booklet of his teachings was published over a century later in his native Bohemia and includes texts in the Czech vernacular and in Latin. ▪ *What does its later publication suggest about the uses to which Hus's image and theology were put during the Protestant Reformation?*

WYCLIFFE'S ENGLISH BIBLE. Although John Wycliffe was not directly responsible for this translation of the Bible, it was made in the later fourteenth century by his followers. Written in the same Middle English vernacular used by Geoffrey Chaucer for his popular works, it was designed to be accessible to lay readers who did not understand Latin. This page shows the beginning of the Gospel of John: "In ye bigynnyng was / ye word & ye word / was at god & god was the word. Yis was in ye bi / gynninge at god, all yingis weren maad bi him. . . ." ▪ *Compare this translation to a modern one. How different (or not) is this version of English?* ▪ *What might have been the impact of this language on readers and listeners in the late fifteenth century?* ▪ *How would translation have helped to further the reforming efforts of Wycliffe and his disciples?*

who had scornfully dismissed the Mass and thereby lost much popular support, Hus emphasized the centrality of the Eucharist to Christian piety. Indeed, he demanded that the laity be allowed to receive not only the conse-crated bread but also the consecrated wine, which was usually reserved solely for priests. This demand became a rallying cry for the Hussite movement. Influential nobles also supported Hus, partly in the hope that the reforms he demanded might restore revenues they had lost to the Church over the previous century.

Accordingly, most of Bohemia was behind him when Hus traveled to the Council of Constance to publish his views and to urge the assembled delegates to undertake sweeping reforms. But rather than giving him a hearing, the other delegates to the council convicted Hus of heresy and had him burned at the stake. Back home, Hus's supporters raised the banner of open revolt, and the aristocracy took advantage of the situation to seize Church property. Between 1420 and 1424, armed bands of fervent Hussites resoundingly defeated several armies, as priests, artisans, and peasants rallied to pursue Hus's goals of religious reform and social justice.

These victories increased popular fervor, but they also made radical reformers increasingly volatile. In 1434, accordingly, a more conservative arm of the Hussite movement was able to negotiate a settlement with the Bohemian church. By the terms of this settlement, Bohemians could receive both the bread and wine of the Mass, which thus placed them beyond the pale of Latin orthodoxy and effectively separated the Bohemian national church from the Church of Rome.

Lollardy and Hussitism exhibit a number of striking similarities. Both began in the university and then spread to the countryside. Both called for the clergy to live in simplicity and poverty, and both attracted noble support, especially in their early days. Both movements were also strongly nationalistic, employing their own vernacular languages (English and Czech) and identifying themselves with the English or Czech people in opposition to a "foreign" Church. They also relied on vernacular preaching and social activism. In all these respects, they established patterns that would emerge again in the vastly larger currents of the Protestant Reformation (see Chapter 13).

CONCLUSION

The century after the Black Death was a period of tremendous creativity and revolutionary change. The effects of the plague were catastrophic, but the resulting food surpluses, opportunities for expansion, and labor shortages encouraged experimentation and opened up broad avenues for enrichment. Europe's economy diversified and expanded, and increasing wealth and access to education produced new forms of art and new ways of looking at the world. Hundreds and perhaps thousands of new schools were

After You Read This Chapter

Visit StudySpace for quizzes, additional review materials, and multimedia documents. wwnorton.com/web/westernciv18

REVIEWING THE OBJECTIVES

- The Black Death had short-term and long-term effects on the economy and societies of Europe. What were some of the most important changes?
- The later "Middle Ages" and "the Renaissance" are often perceived to be two different periods, but the latter was actually part of the former. Explain why.
- What were some of the intellectual, cultural, and artistic innovations of this era in Italy and elsewhere in Europe?
- How were some European kingdoms becoming stronger and more centralized during this period? What are some examples of national monarchies?
- The conciliar movement sought to limit the power of the papacy. How? Why was this movement unsuccessful?

established, and scores of new universities would emerge as a result. Women were still excluded from formal schooling but nevertheless became active—and in many cases dominant—participants in literary endeavors, cultural life, and religious movements. Average men and women not only became more active in cultivating their own worldly goals, they also took control of their spiritual destinies at a time when the institutional Church provided little inspiring leadership.

Meanwhile, some states were growing stronger and more competitive while other regions remained deeply divided. The rise of the Ottoman Empire eventually absorbed many of the oldest territories of Western civilizations, including the venerable Muslim caliphate at Baghdad, the Near Eastern portions of the former Mongolian Empire, the Christian Balkans and Greece, and—above all—the surviving core of the eastern Roman Empire at Constantinople. Greek-speaking refugees streamed into Italy, many bringing with them classics of Greek philosophy and literature hitherto unknown in Europe. Fueled by new ideas and a fervid nostalgia for the ancient past, Italians began to experiment with new ways of reading ancient texts, advocating a return to classical models while at the same time trying to counter the political and artistic authority of the more powerful kingdoms north of the Alps.

In contrast to Italy, these emerging national monarchies cultivated group identity through the promotion of a shared vernacular language and allegiance to a strong, more centralized state. These tactics would allow smaller kingdoms like Poland and Scotland to increase their territories and their influence and would lead France and England into an epic battle for sovereignty and hegemony. The result, in all cases, was the escalation of armed conflict as incessant warfare drove more powerful governments to harvest a larger percentage of their subjects' wealth through taxation, which they proceeded to invest in ships, guns, and the standing armies made possible by new technologies and more effective administration.

In short, the generations who survived the calamities of famine, plague, and warfare seized the opportunities their new world presented to them. In the latter half of the fifteenth century, they stood on the verge of an extraordinary period of expansion and conquest that enabled them to dominate the globe.

PEOPLE, IDEAS, AND EVENTS IN CONTEXT

- Compare and contrast the **BLACK DEATH**'s effects on rural and urban areas.
- In what ways do rebellions like the **ENGLISH PEASANTS' REVOLT** reflect the changes brought about by the plague? How do the works of **GIOVANNI BOCCACCIO**, **GEOFFREY CHAUCER**, and **CHRISTINE DE PISAN** exemplify the culture of this era?
- What was **HUMANISM**? How was it related to the artistic and intellectual movement known as the **RENAISSANCE**?
- How did the **OTTOMAN EMPIRE** come to power? What were some consequences of its rise?
- On what grounds did **MUSCOVY** claim to be "the third Rome"? What is the significance of the title **TSAR**?
- What new military technologies were in use during the **HUNDRED YEARS' WAR**? How did this conflict affect other parts of Europe, beyond England and France? What role did **JOAN OF ARC** play?
- How did the **COUNCIL OF CONSTANCE** respond to the crisis of the **GREAT SCHISM**?
- Why did **CONCILIARISM** fail? How did **JOHN WYCLIFFE** and **JAN HUS** seek to reform the Church?

THINKING ABOUT CONNECTIONS

- In the year 2000, a group of historians was asked to identify the most significant historical figure of the past millennium. Rather than selecting a person (e.g., Martin Luther, Shakespeare, Napoleon, Adolf Hitler), they chose the microbe *Yersinia pestis,* which had caused the Black Death. Do you agree with this assessment? Why or why not?
- In your view, which was more crucial to the formation of the modern state: the political and legal developments we surveyed in Chapter 9 or the emergence of national identities we discussed in this chapter? Why?
- Was the conciliar movement doomed to failure, given what we have learned about the history of the Roman Church? How far back does one need to go, in order to trace the development of disputes over ecclesiastical governance?

Before
You
Read
This
Chapter

Innovation and Exploration, 1453–1533

CORE OBJECTIVES

- **UNDERSTAND** the relationship between Renaissance ideals and the political and economic realities of Italy.

- **IDENTIFY** the key characteristics of Renaissance arts and learning during this period.

- **DEFINE** the term *Reconquista* and its meaning in Spain.

- **DESCRIBE** the methods and motives of European colonization during this period.

- **EXPLAIN** why Europeans were able to dominate the peoples of the New World.

W hat if exact copies of an idea could circulate quickly, all over the world? What if the same could be done for the latest news, the oldest beliefs, the most beautiful poems, the most exciting—and deadly—discoveries? It would be doing for knowledge what the invention of coinage did for wealth: making it portable, easier to use and disseminate. Indeed, it's no accident that the man who developed such a technology, Johannes Gutenberg of Mainz (c. 1398–1468), was the son of a goldsmith who made coins for the bishop of that German city. Both crafts were based on the same principle and used the same basic tools. Coins are metal disks that have each been stamped with identical words and images, impressed on them with a reusable matrix. The pages of the first printed books—and later newspapers, leaflets, and pamphlets—were stamped with ink spread on rows of movable type (lead or cast-iron letter forms and punctuation marks) slotted into frames to form lines of words. Once a set of pages was ready, a press could make hundreds of copies in a matter of hours, many hundreds of times faster than the same page could be copied by hand. Afterward, the type could be reused.

389

A major stimulus for this invention was the more widespread availability of paper, a trend that had begun in the late thirteenth century. Parchment, northern Europe's chief writing material since the advent of the codex (see Chapter 6), was extremely expensive to manufacture and required special training on the part of those who used it—one reason why writing remained a specialized skill for much of the Middle Ages, while the ability to read was common. Paper, made from rags turned into pulp by mills, was both cheaper and far easier to use; accordingly, books became cheaper and written communication became easier and more widespread. Growing levels of literacy led to a growing demand for books, which in turn led to experimentation with different methods of book production—and to Gutenberg's breakthrough of the 1450s. By 1455, his workshop had printed multiple copies of the Latin Bible, of which forty-eight complete or partial volumes survive. Although printing never entirely replaced traditional modes of publication via manuscript, it made the cost of books affordable and revolutionized the spread of information.

In fact, the printing press played a crucial role in many of the developments that we will study in this chapter. The artistic and intellectual experiments that contributed to an Italian Renaissance were rapidly exported to other parts of Europe, and specifications for innovative weapons would be printed on the same presses that churned out humanist biographies. News of Columbus's first voyage and the subsequent conquests of the Americas would spread via the same media as critiques of European imperialism there. Printing not only increased the volume and rapidity of communication, it made it more difficult for those in power to censor dissenting opinions.

But at the same time as it created new forms of agency, the printing press also become an indispensable tool of more traditional powers, making it possible for rulers to govern growing empires abroad and increasingly centralized states at home. The "reconquest" of Spain and the extension of Spanish imperialism to the New World were both facilitated by the circulation of printed propaganda. The widespread availability of reading materials even helped to standardize national languages, by enabling governments to promote one official printed dialect over others. Hence the "king's English," the variety of the language spoken around London, was imposed as the only acceptable literary and bureaucratic language throughout the English realm, contributing to the growth of a common linguistic identity among readers. For these reasons, among others, many historians consider the advent of print to be both the defining event and the driving engine of modernity, and

it coincided with another essentially modern development: the discovery of a "New World."

RENAISSANCE IDEALS— AND REALITIES

The intellectual and artistic movement that had begun in Italy during the fourteenth century was, as we noted in Chapter 11, characterized by an intense interest in the classical past and by a new type of educational program known as humanism. These Renaissance ideals—and the realities that both undergirded and complicated them—would be extended and diversified in the later fifteenth century through the medium of the printing press. By the time the Ottoman conquest of Constantinople was complete, just a year before Gutenberg's workshop began to produce pages of the Bible, decades of uncertainty and warfare had propelled hundreds of refugees from the eastern Roman Empire into Italy. Many carried with them precious manuscripts of Greek texts that had long been unavailable in western Europe: the epics of Homer, the major surviving works of Athenian dramatists, the dialogues of Plato. Prior to the invention of print, such manuscripts could be owned and studied by only a very few, very privileged men. Now printers in Venice and other European cities rushed to produce cheap editions of these texts as well as Greek grammars and glossaries that could facilitate reading them.

Within a few decades, so many men were engaged in the study of Plato that an informal "Platonic Academy" had formed in Florence. There, the work of intellectuals like Marsilio Ficino (1433–1499) and Giovanni Pico della Mirandola (1463–1494) was fostered by the patronage of the wealthy Cosimo de' Medici. Based on his reading of Plato, Ficino's philosophy moved away from the focus on ethics and civic life that had been such a feature of earlier humanist thought. He taught instead that the individual should look primarily to the salvation of his immortal soul, to free it from its "always miserable" mortal body: a very Platonic idea that was also compatible with much late-medieval Christian piety. His disciple Pico likewise rejected the everyday world of public affairs but took a more exalted view of man's intellectual and artistic capacities, arguing that man (but not woman) can aspire to union with God through the exercise of his unique talents. Ficino's great achievement was his translation of Plato's works into Latin, which made them widely accessible in Europe for the first time—again, thanks to the medium of print.

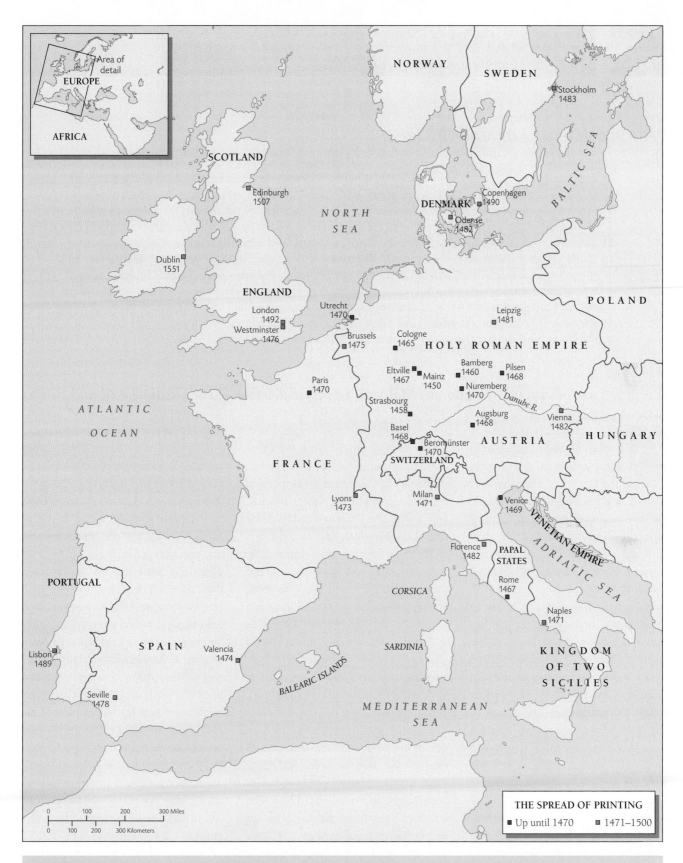

THE SPREAD OF PRINTING

■ Up until 1470   ■ 1471–1500

THE SPREAD OF PRINTING. This map shows how quickly the technology of printing spread throughout Europe between 1470 and 1500. ■ *In what regions were printing presses most heavily concentrated?* ■ *What factors would have led to their proliferation in the Low Countries, northern Italy, and Germany—as compared to France, Spain, and England?* ■ *Why would so many have been located along waterways?*

Competing Viewpoints

Printing, Patriotism, and the Past

The printing press helped to create new communities of readers by standardizing national languages and even promoting patriotism. And while it enabled authors of new works to reach larger audiences, it also allowed printers to popularize older writings that had previously circulated in manuscript. The two sources presented here exemplify two aspects of this trend. The first is the preface to a version of the legend of King Arthur, which was originally written by an English soldier called Sir Thomas Malory, who completed it in 1470. It was printed for the first time in 1485, when it quickly became a best seller. The author of this preface was also the printer, William Caxton of London, who specialized in publishing books that glorified England's history and heritage. The second excerpt is from the concluding chapter of Machiavelli's treatise The Prince. *Like the book itself, these remarks were originally addressed to Lorenzo de' Medici, head of Florence's most powerful family. But when* The Prince *was printed in 1532, five years after Machiavelli's death, the author's passionate denunciation of foreign "barbarians" and lament for Italy's lost glory would have resonated with a wider Italian-speaking public.*

William Caxton's preface to Thomas Malory's *Le Morte d'Arthur* ("The Death of Arthur"), 1485

AFTER I had accomplished and finished diverse histories, both of contemplation and of other historical and worldly acts of great conquerors and princes, . . . many noble and diverse gentlemen of this realm of England came and demanded why I had not made and imprinted the noble history of the Holy Grail, and of the most renowned Christian king and worthy, King Arthur, which ought most to be remembered among us Englishmen before all other Christian kings. . . . The said noble gentlemen instantly required me to imprint the history of the said noble king and conqueror King Arthur, and of his knights, with the history of the Holy Grail . . . considering that he was a man born within this realm, and king and emperor of the same: and that there be, in French, diverse and many noble volumes of his acts, and also of his knights. To whom I answered that diverse men hold opinion that there was no such Arthur, and that all such books as have been made of him be feigned and fables, because some chronicles make of him no mention. . . . Whereto

they answered, and one in special said, that in him that should say or think that there was never such a king called Arthur might well be accounted great folly and blindness. . . . For in all places, Christian and heathen, he is reputed and taken for one of the Nine Worthies, and the first of the three Christian men. And also, he is more spoken of beyond the sea, and there are more books made of his noble acts than there be in England, as well in Dutch, Italian, Spanish, and Greek, as in French. . . . Wherefore it is a marvel why he is no more renowned in his own country. . . .

Then all these things aforesaid alleged, I could not well deny but that there was such a noble king named Arthur, reputed one of the Nine Worthies, and first and chief of the Christian men. And many noble volumes be made of him and of his noble knights in French, which I have seen and read beyond the sea, which be not had in our maternal tongue. . . . Wherefore, among all such [manuscript] books as have late been drawn out briefly into English I have . . . undertaken to imprint a book of the noble histories of the said

King Arthur, and of certain of his knights, after a copy unto me delivered—which copy Sir Thomas Malory did take out of certain books of French, and reduced it into English. And I, according to my copy, have done set it in print, to the intent that noble men may see and learn the noble acts of chivalry, the gentle and virtuous deeds that some knights used in those days, by which they came to honor, and how they that were vicious were punished and oft put to shame and rebuke; humbly beseeching all noble lords and ladies (with all other estates of what estate or degree they be) that shall see and read in this said book and work, that they take the good and honest acts to their remembrance, and follow the same. . . . For herein may be seen noble chivalry, courtesy, humanity, friendliness, hardiness, love, friendship, cowardice, murder, hate, virtue, and sin. Do after the good and leave the evil, and it shall bring you to good fame and renown.

Source: Sir Thomas Malory, *Le Morte d'Arthur* (London: 1485), (text and spelling slightly modernized).

From the conclusion of Niccolò Machiavelli's *The Prince* (completed 1513, printed 1533)

Reflecting in the matters set forth above and considering within myself where the times were propitious in Italy at present to honor a new prince and whether there is at hand the matter suitable for a prudent and virtuous leader to mold in a new form, giving honor to himself and benefit to the citizens of the country, I have arrived at the opinion that all circumstances now favor such a prince, and I cannot think of a time more propitious for him than the present. If, as I said, it was necessary in order to make apparent the virtue of Moses, that the people of Israel should be enslaved in Egypt, and that the Persians should be oppressed by the Medes to provide an opportunity to illustrate the greatness and the spirit of Cyrus, and that the Athenians should be scattered in order to show the excellence of Theseus, thus at the present time, in order to reveal the valor of an Italian spirit, it was essential that Italy should fall to her present low estate, more enslaved than the Hebrews, more servile than the Persians, more disunited than the Athenians, leaderless and lawless, beaten, despoiled, lacerated, overrun and crushed under every kind of misfortune. . . . So Italy now, left almost lifeless, awaits the coming of one who will heal her wounds, putting an end to the sacking and looting in Lombardy and the spoliation and extortions in the Realm of Naples and Tuscany, and cleanse her sores that have been so long festering. Behold how she prays God to send her some one to redeem her from the cruelty and insolence of the barbarians. See how she is ready and willing to follow any banner so long as there be someone to take it up. Nor has she at present any hope of finding her redeemer save only in your illustrious house [the Medici] which has been so highly exalted both by its own merits and by fortune and which has been favored by God and the church, of which it is now ruler. . . .

This opportunity, therefore, should not be allowed to pass, and Italy, after such a long wait, must be allowed to behold her redeemer. I cannot describe the joy with which he will be received in all these provinces which have suffered so much from the foreign deluge, nor with what thirst for vengeance, nor with what firm devotion, what solemn delight, what tears! What gates could be closed to him, what people could deny him obedience, what envy could withstand him, what Italian could withhold allegiance from him? THIS BARBARIAN OCCUPATION STINKS IN THE NOSTRILS OF ALL OF US. Let your illustrious house then take up this cause with the spirit and the hope with which one undertakes a truly just enterprise. . . .

Source: Niccolò Machiavelli, *The Prince,* ed. and trans. Thomas G. Bergin (Arlington Heights, IL: 1947), pp. 75–76, 78.

Questions for Analysis

1. What do these two sources reveal about the relationship between patriotism and the awareness of a nation's past? Why do you think that Caxton looks back to a legendary medieval king, whereas Machiavelli's references are all to ancient examples? What do both excerpts reveal about the value placed on history in the popular imagination?

2. How does Caxton describe the process of printing a book? What larger conclusions can we draw from this about the market for printed books in general?

3. Why might Machiavelli's treatise have been made available in a printed version, nearly twenty years after its original appearance in manuscript? How might his new audience have responded to its message?

The Politics of Italy and the Philosophy of Machiavelli

But not all Florentines were galvanized by Platonic ideals. Indeed, the most influential philosopher of this era—and one of the most widely read authors of all time—was a thoroughgoing realist who spent more time studying Roman history than Greek philosophy: Niccolò Machiavelli (1469–1527). Machiavelli's political writings reflect the unstable political situation of his home city as well as his wider aspirations for a unified Italy that could revive the glory of ancient Rome. We have observed that Italy had been in political disarray for centuries, a situation exacerbated by the "Babylonian Captivity" of the papacy and the controversies raging after its return to Rome (see Chapters 10 and 11). Now Italy was becoming the arena in which bloody international struggles were being played out. The kings of France and Spain both had imperial ambitions, and both claimed to be the rightful champions of the papacy. Accordingly, both sent invading armies into the peninsula while they busily competed for the allegiance of the various city-states, which in turn were torn by internal dissension.

In 1498, Machiavelli became a prominent official in the government of a new Florentine republic, set up four years earlier when a French invasion of the region had led to the expulsion of the ruling Medici family. His duties largely involved diplomatic missions to other Italian city-states. While in Rome, he became fascinated with the attempt of Cesare Borgia, son of Pope Alexander VI, to create his own principality in central Italy. He noted with approval Cesare's ruthlessness and his complete subordination of personal ethics to political ends. He remembered this example in 1512, when the Medici returned to overthrow the Florentine republic and Machiavelli was deprived of his position, imprisoned, tortured, and exiled. He now devoted his energies to the articulation of a political philosophy suited to the times and to the tastes of the family that had ousted him from his job.

On the surface, Machiavelli's two great works of political analysis appear to contradict each other. In his *Discourses on Livy*, which drew on the works of that Roman historian (see Chapter 5), he praised the ancient Roman Republic as a model for his own contemporaries, lauding constitutional government, equality among citizens, and the subordination of religion to the service of the state. There is little doubt, in fact, that Machiavelli was a committed believer in the free city-state as the ideal form of human government. But Machiavelli also wrote *The Prince*, "a handbook for tyrants" in the eyes of his critics, and he dedicated this work to Lorenzo, son of Piero de' Medici, whose family had overthrown the Florentine republic that Machiavelli had served.

THE STATES OF ITALY, C. 1494. This map shows the divisions of Italy on the eve of the French invasion in 1494. Contemporary observers often described Italy as being divided among five great powers: Milan, Venice, Florence, the Papal States, and the united Kingdoms of Naples and Sicily. ▪ *Which of these powers would have been most capable of expanding their territories?* ▪ *Which neighboring states would have been most threatened by such attempts at expansion?* ▪ *Why would Florence and the Papal States so often find themselves in conflict with each other?*

Because *The Prince* has been so much more widely read than *Discourses*, it has often been interpreted as an endorsement of power for its own sake. Machiavelli's real position was quite different. In the political chaos of early-sixteenth-century Italy, he saw the likes of Cesare Borgia as the only hope for revitalizing the spirit of independence among his contemporaries, and so making Italy fit, eventually, for self-governance. However dark his vision of human nature, Machiavelli never ceased to hope that his contemporaries would rise up, expel French and Spanish occupying forces, and restore ancient traditions of liberty and equality. He regarded a period of despotism as a necessary step toward that end, not as a permanently desirable form of government.

Machiavelli continues to be a controversial figure. Some modern scholars, like many of his own contemporaries, represent him as disdainful of conventional morality, interested solely in the acquisition and exercise of power. Others see him as an Italian patriot. Still others see him as a realist influenced by Saint Augustine (see Chapter 6), who understood that, in a fallen world populated by sinful people, a ruler's good intentions do not guarantee that his policies will have good results. Accordingly, Machiavelli insisted that a prince's actions must be judged by their consequences and not by their intrinsic moral quality. He argued that "the necessity of preserving the state will often compel a prince to take actions which are opposed to loyalty, charity, humanity, and religion." As we shall see in later chapters, many subsequent political philosophers would go even further than Machiavelli in arguing that the preservation of the state—and the avoidance of political chaos—does indeed warrant the exercise of absolute power on the part of the ruler (see Chapters 14 and 15).

The Ideal of the Courtier

Machiavelli's political theories were informed by years of diplomatic service in the courts of Italy, and so was his engaging literary style. Indeed, he never abandoned his interest in the literary arts of the court and continued to write poems, plays, and adaptations of classical comedies. In this he resembled another poet-courtier, Ludovico Ariosto (1474–1533), who undertook diplomatic missions for the Duke of Ferrara and some of Rome's most powerful prelates. His lengthy verse narrative, *Orlando Furioso* (The Madness of Roland), was a retelling of the heroic exploits celebrated in the French *Song of Roland* (see Chapter 8)—but without the heroism. Although very different in form and tone from *The Prince*, it shared that work's skepticism of political or chivalric ideals. Instead, it emphasized the comedy of its lovers' passionate exploits and sought to charm an audience who sought consolation in pleasure and beauty.

Thus a new Renaissance ideal was born, one that promoted the arts of pleasing the powerful secular and ecclesiastical princes who were in a position to employ clever men like Machiavelli and Ariosto: the ideal of the courtier. The components of this ideal were embodied by their contemporary, the diplomat and nobleman Baldassare Castiglione (1478–1529), who would later write a manual for those who aspired to acquire these skills. If *The Prince* was a forerunner of modern self-help books, *The Book of the Courtier* was an early handbook of etiquette; and both stand in sharp contrast to the treatises on public virtue composed in the previous century. Whereas Bruni and Alberti (see Chapter 11) had taught the sober virtues of strenuous service on behalf of the city-state, Castiglione taught how to attain the elegant and seemingly effortless skills necessary for advancement in princely courts.

More than anyone else, Castiglione articulated and popularized the set of talents still associated with the "Renaissance man": one accomplished in many different pursuits, witty, cultured, and stylish. And in many ways, this new ideal actually represents a *rejection* of the older ideals associated with the Renaissance as a rebirth of classical education for public men. Castiglione even rejected the misogyny of the humanists by stressing the ways in which court ladies could rise to influence and prominence through the graceful exercise of their womanly powers. Widely read throughout Western civilizations, his *Courtier* set the standard for polite behavior until the First World War.

The Dilemma of the Artist

Without question, the most enduring legacy of the Italian Renaissance has been the contributions of its artists, particularly those who embraced new media and new attitudes toward the human body. We have already noted (see Chapter 11) the creative and economic opportunities afforded by painting on canvas or wood, which freed artists from having to work on site and entirely on commission: such paintings are portable—unlike wall paintings—and can be displayed in different settings, reach different markets, and be more widely distributed. We also saw that the use of oil paints, pioneered in Flanders, further revolutionized painting styles. To these benefits, the artists of Italy added an important technical ingredient: mastery of a vanishing (one-point) perspective that gave to painting an illusion of three-dimensional space. They also experimented with effects of light and shade, and studied intently the anatomy and proportions of the human body. These techniques also influenced the sculptors of this age.

New Illusions and the Career of Leonardo

For much of the fifteenth century, the majority of the great painters were Florentines who followed in the footsteps of the precocious Masaccio (1401–1428), who had died prematurely at the age of twenty-seven. His lasting legacy was the pioneering use of one-point perspective and dramatic lighting effects. Both are evident in his painting of the Trinity, where the body of the crucified Christ appears to be thrust forward by the impassive figure of God the Father, while the Virgin's gaze directly engages the viewer. Masaccio's most obvious successor was Sandro Botticelli (1445–1510), who excelled in depicting graceful motion and the sensuous pleasures of nature. He is most famous today for paintings that evoke classical mythology and that seem to be devoid of any Christian frame of reference.

The most adventurous and versatile artist of this period was Leonardo da Vinci (1452–1519). Leonardo personifies the Renaissance ideal: he was a painter, architect, musician, mathematician, engineer, and inventor. The illegitimate son of a notary, he set up an artist's shop in Florence by the time he was twenty-five and gained the patronage of the Medici ruler, Lorenzo the Magnificent. Yet Leonardo had a weakness: he worked slowly, and he had difficulty finishing anything. This naturally displeased Lorenzo and other Florentine patrons, who regarded artists as craftsmen who worked on specific projects, and on their patrons' time—not their own. Leonardo, however, strongly objected to this view; he considered himself to be an inspired, independent innovator. He therefore left Florence in 1482 and went to work for the of Sforza dictators Milan, whose favor he courted by emphasizing his skills as a maker of bombs, heavy ordinance, and siege engines. He remained there until the French invasion of 1499; he then wandered about, finally accepting the patronage of the French king, under whose auspices he lived and worked until his death.

Paradoxically, considering his skill in fashioning deadly weapons, Leonardo was convinced of the essential divinity of all living things. He was a vegetarian—unusual at the time—and when he went to the marketplace to buy caged birds he released them to their native habitat when he had finished observing them. His approach to painting was that it should be the most accurate possible imitation of nature. He made careful studies: blades of grass, cloud formations, a waterfall. He obtained human corpses for dissection and reconstructed in drawing the minutest features of anatomy, carrying this knowledge over to his paintings. *The Virgin of the Rocks* typifies not only his technical skill but also his passion for science and his belief in the universe as a well-ordered place.

THE IMPACT OF PERSPECTIVE. Masaccio's painting *The Trinity with the Virgin* illustrates the startling sense of depth made possible by observing the rules of one-point perspective.

Behind all of the beautiful artworks created in this era, which led to the glorification of the artist as a new type of hero, lie the harsh political and economic realities within which these artists worked. Increasing private wealth and the growth of lay patronage opened up new markets and created a huge demand for buildings and objects that could increase those grappling for prestige. Portraiture was a direct result of this trend, since princes and merchants alike sought to glorify themselves and their families and to compete with their neighbors and rivals. An artist therefore had to study the techniques of the courtier as well as the new artistic techniques in order to succeed in winning a patron. He also had to be ready to perform other services for which he had to cultivate other talents: overseeing the building and decoration of palaces; designing tableware, furniture, fanciful liveries for servants and soldiers; and even decorating guns. Some artists, like Leonardo da Vinci, were prized as much for their capacity to invent deadly weapons as for their paintings and sculptures.

THE BIRTH OF VENUS. This painting was executed by Sandro Botticelli in Florence, and represents the artist's imaginative treatment of stories from ancient mythology. Here, he depicts the moment when Aphrodite, goddess of love, was spontaneously engendered from the foam of the sea by Chronos, the god of time.

THE VIRGIN OF THE ROCKS. This painting reveals Leonardo's interest in the variety of human faces and facial expressions and in natural settings.

The figures are arranged geometrically, with every stone and plant depicted in accurate detail. In *The Last Supper*, painted on the refectory walls of a monastery in Milan (and now in an advanced state of decay), he displayed his equally keen studies of human psychology. In this image, a serene Christ has just announced to his disciples that one of them will betray him. The artist succeeds in portraying the mingled emotions of surprise, horror, and guilt on the faces of the disciples as they gradually perceive the meaning of their master's statement. He also implicates the painting's viewers in this dramatic scene, since they too dine alongside Christ, in the very same room.

Renaissance Arts in Venice and Rome

The innovations of Florentine artists were widely imitated. By the end of the fifteenth century, they had influenced a group of painters active in the wealthy city of Venice, among them Tiziano Vecellio, better known as Titian (c. 1490–1576). Many of Titian's paintings evoke the luxurious, pleasure-loving life of this thriving commercial center; for although they copied Florentine techniques,

statues became figures "in the round" rather than sculptural elements incorporated into buildings or featured as effigies on tombs. By freeing sculpture from its bondage to architecture, the Renaissance reestablished it as a separate art form.

The first great master of Renaissance sculpture was Donatello (c. 1386–1466). His bronze statue of David, triumphant over the head of the slain Goliath, is the first free-standing nude of the period. Yet this *David* is clearly an agile adolescent rather than a muscular Greek athlete like that of Michelangelo's *David*, executed in 1501, as a public expression of Florentine civic life: not merely graceful but heroic. Michelangelo regarded sculpture as the most exalted of the arts because it allowed the artist to imitate God most fully in re-creating human forms. Furthermore, in Michelangelo's view,

THE POWER AND VULNERABILITY OF THE MALE BODY. Donatello's *David* (left) was the first freestanding nude executed since antiquity. It shows the Hebrew leader as an adolescent youth and is a little over five feet tall. The *David* by Michelangelo (center) stands thirteen feet high and was placed prominently in front of Florence's city hall to proclaim the city's power and humanistic values. Michelangelo's *Descent from the Cross* (right), which shows Christ's broken body in the arms of the elderly Nicodemus, was made by the sculptor for his own tomb. (The Gospels describe Nicodemus as a Pharisee who became a follower of Jesus and who was present at his death.) ▪ *Why would Michelangelo choose this figure to represent himself?* ▪ *How does his representation of David—and the context in which this figure was displayed—compare to that of Donatello?*

the most God-like sculptor disdained slavish naturalism; anyone could make a plaster cast of a human figure, but only an inspired creative genius could endow his sculpted figures with a sense of life. Accordingly, Michelangelo's sculpture subordinated reality to the force of his imagination and sought to express his ideals in ever more astonishing forms. He also insisted on working in marble—the "noblest" sculptural material—and by creating figures twice as large as life. By sculpting a serenely confident young man at the peak of physical fitness, Michelangelo celebrated the Florentine republic's own determination in resisting tyrants and upholding ideals of civic justice.

Yet the serenity seen in *David* is no longer prominent in the works of Michelangelo's later life when, as in his painting, he began to explore the use of anatomical distortion to create effects of emotional intensity. While his statues remained awesome in scale, they also communicate rage, depression, and sorrow. The culmination of this trend is his unfinished but intensely moving *Descent from the Cross*, a depiction of an old man (the sculptor himself) grieving over the distorted, slumping body of the dead Christ.

ST. PETER'S BASILICA, ROME. This eighteenth-century painting shows the massive interior of the Renaissance building. But were it not for the perspective provided by the tiny human figures, the human eye would be fooled into thinking this a much smaller space.

Renaissance Architecture

To a much greater extent than either sculpture or painting, Renaissance architecture had its roots in the classical past. The Gothic style pioneered in northern France (see Chapter 9) had not found a welcome reception in Italy; most of the buildings constructed there were Romanesque in style, and the great architects influenced by the Renaissance movement generally adopted their building plans from these structures—some of which they believed (mistakenly) to be ancient. They also copied decorative devices from the authentic ruins of ancient Rome. But above all, they derived their influence from the writings of Vitruvius (fl. c. 60–15 B.C.E.), a Roman architect and engineer whose multivolume *On Architecture* was among the humanists' rediscovered ancient texts. The governing principles laid out by Vitruvius were popularized by Leon Battista Alberti in his own book, *On the Art of Building*, which began to circulate in manuscript around 1450.

In keeping with these classical models, Renaissance buildings emphasize geometrical proportion. These aesthetic values were also reinforced by the interest in Pla-tonic philosophy, which taught that certain mathematical ratios reflect the harmony of the universe. For example, the proportions of the human body serve as the basis for the proportions of the quintessential Renaissance building: St. Peter's Basilica in Rome. Designed by some of the most celebrated architects of the time, including Bramante and Michelangelo, it is still one of the largest buildings in the world. Yet it seems smaller than a Gothic cathedral because it is built to human scale. The same artful proportions are evident in smaller-scale buildings too, as in the aristocratic country houses later designed by the northern Italian architect Andrea Palladio (1508–1580), who created secular miniatures of ancient temples (such as the Roman Pantheon) to glorify the aristocrats who dwelled within them.

THE RENAISSANCE NORTH OF THE ALPS

Despite Italian resentment of the political encroachment of foreign monarchs, contacts between Italy and northern Europe were close throughout this period. Italian merchants and financiers were familiar figures at northern courts; students from all over Europe studied at Italian universities such as Bologna or Padua; northern poets (including Geoffrey Chaucer; see Chapter 11) and their works traveled to and from Italy; and northern soldiers were frequent; combattants in Italian wars. Yet only at the very end of the fifteenth century did the innovative artistry and learning of Italy begin to be exported across the Alps into northern Europe and across the eastern Mediterranean into Spain.

A variety of explanations have been offered for this delay. Northern European intellectual life in the later Middle Ages was dominated by universities such as those of Paris, Oxford, and Prague, whose curricula focused on the study of philosophical logic, Christian theology, and (to a lesser extent) medicine. These rigorous courses of study left little room for the study of classical literature. In Italy, by contrast, universities were more often professional schools specializing in law and medicine and were more integrally tied to the nonacademic intellectual lives of the cities in which they were situated. As a result, a more secular, urban-oriented educational tradition took shape in Italy, as we saw in our previous discussion of humanism. In northern Europe, by contrast, those scholars who *were* influenced by Italian ideas usually worked outside the university system under the private patronage of kings and princes.

Before the turn of the sixteenth century, northern rulers were also less committed to patronizing artists and intellectuals than were the city-states and princes of Italy. In Italy, as we may have seen, such patronage was an important arena for competition between political rivals. In northern Europe, however, political units were larger and political rivals were fewer. It was therefore less necessary to use art for political purposes in a kingdom than it was in a city-state—a major exception being the independent duchy of Burgundy, which surpassed even the French court in its magnificence. A statue erected in a central square of Florence would be seen by all the city's residents. In Paris, such a statue would be seen by only a tiny minority of the French king's subjects. But as royal courts became more firmly established in royal capitals and so became showcases for royal power, kings needed to impress townspeople, courtiers, and visitors—and they consequently relied more and more on artists and intellectuals to advertise their wealth and taste.

Christian Humanism and the Career of Erasmus

In general, then, the Renaissance movement of northern Europe differed from that of Italy because it grafted certain Italian ideals onto preexisting traditions, rather than sweeping away older forms of knowledge. This can be seen very clearly in the case of the intellectual development known as Christian humanism. Although Christian humanists shared the Italian humanists' scorn for scholasticism's limitations, northern humanists were more committed to seeking ethical guidance from biblical and religious precepts, as well as from Cicero or Virgil. Like their Italian counterparts, they embraced the wisdom of antiquity, but the antiquity they favored was Christian as well as classical—the antiquity of the New Testament and the early Church. Similarly, northern artists were inspired by the accomplishments of Italian masters and copied their techniques, but they depicted classical subjects less frequently and almost never portrayed completely nude human figures.

Any discussion of Christian humanism must begin with the career of Desiderius Erasmus (c. 1469–1536). The illegitimate son of a priest, Erasmus was born near Rotterdam in the Netherlands. Later, as a result of his wide travels, he became a virtual citizen of all Europe. Forced into a monastery against his will when he was a teenager, the young Erasmus found little formal instruction there—but plenty of freedom to read what he liked. He devoured all the classics he could get his hands on, alongside the writings of the church fathers (see Chapter 6). When he

ERASMUS BY HANS HOLBEIN THE YOUNGER. This is generally regarded as the most evocative portrait of the preeminent Christian humanist.

The Reputation of Richard III

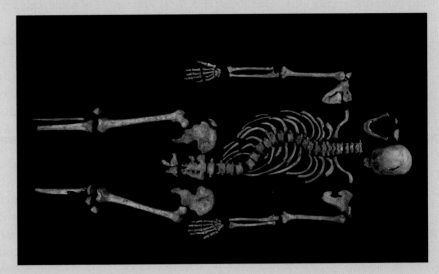

England's King Richard III (r. 1483–1485) has been a byword for villainy since the time of his death, when Sir Thomas More and other propagandists working for his successor, Henry VII, alleged that his physically deformed body was matched by the depravity of his actions. For centuries, historians have debated the truth of both claims. Was Richard really a hunchback—and a murderer, too? In 2012, the stunning discovery of Richard's body (under a parking lot near the medieval battlefield where he died) confirmed that he had indeed suffered from severe scoliosis. The other claim has yet to be proven.

 Watch related author interview on StudySpace
wwnorton.com/web/westernciv18

was about thirty years old, he obtained permission to leave the monastery and enroll in the University of Paris, where he completed the requirements for a bachelor's degree in divinity.

But Erasmus subsequently rebelled against what he considered the arid learning of Parisian academe. Nor did he ever serve actively as a priest. Instead, he made his living from teaching, writing, and the proceeds of various ecclesiastical offices that required no pastoral duties. Ever on the lookout for new patrons, he traveled often to England, stayed for three years in Italy, and resided in several different cities in Germany and the Low Countries before settling finally, toward the end of his life, in Basel (Switzerland). By means of a voluminous correspondence with learned friends, Erasmus became the leader of a humanist coterie. And through the popularity of his numerous publications, he also became the arbiter of northern European cultural tastes during his lifetime.

Erasmus's many-sided intellectual activity may be assessed from two different points of view: the literary and the doctrinal. As a Latin prose stylist, Erasmus was unequaled since the days of Cicero. Extraordinarily eloquent and witty, he reveled in tailoring his mode of discourse to fit his subject, creating dazzling verbal effects and coining puns that took on added meaning if the reader knew Greek as well as Latin. Above all, Erasmus excelled in the deft use of irony, poking fun at everything, including himself. For example, in his *Colloquies* (Discussions) he has a fictional character lament the evils of the times: "Kings make war, priests strive to line their pockets, theologians invent syllogisms, monks roam outside their cloisters, the commons riot, and Erasmus writes colloquies."

But although Erasmus's urbane Latin style and humor earned him a wide audience on those grounds alone, he intended everything he wrote to promote what he called the "philosophy of Christ." Erasmus believed that the society of his day had lost sight of the Gospels' teachings. Accordingly, he offered his contemporaries three different kinds of writings: clever satires in which people could recognize their own foibles, serious moral treatises meant to offer guidance toward proper Christian behavior, and scholarly editions of basic Christian texts.

In the first category belong the works of Erasmus that are still widely read today: *The Praise of Folly* (1509), in which he ridiculed pedantry and dogmatism, ignorance and gullibility—even within the Church; and the *Colloquies* (1518), in which he held up contemporary religious practices for examination, couching a serious message in the ironic tone we just noted. In these books, Erasmus let fictional characters do the talking so his own views on any given topic can only be determined by inference. But in his second mode, Erasmus spoke clearly in his own voice. In the *Handbook of the Christian Knight* (1503), he used the popular language of chivalry as a means to encourage a life of inward piety; in the *Complaint of Peace* (1517), he argued movingly for Christian pacifism. Erasmus's pacifism was one of his most deeply held values, and he returned to it again and again in his published works.

Despite the success of these writings, Erasmus considered textual scholarship his greatest achievement. Revering the authority of the earliest church fathers, he brought out reliable printed editions of works by Saints Augustine, Jerome, and Ambrose. He also used his extraordinary command of Latin and Greek to produce a more accurate edition of the New Testament. For after reading Lorenzo Valla's *Notes on the New Testament* in 1504, Erasmus became convinced that nothing was more imperative than divesting the Christian scriptures of myriad errors in transcription and translation that had piled up over the course of preceding centuries. He therefore spent ten years comparing all the early Greek biblical manuscripts he could find in order to establish an authoritative text. When it finally appeared in 1516, Erasmus's Greek New Testament, published together with explanatory notes and his own new Latin translation, became one of the most important scholarly landmarks of all time. In the hands of Martin Luther, it would play a critical role in the early stages of the Reformation (see Chapter 13).

The Influence of Erasmus

One of Erasmus's closest friends, and a close second to him in distinction among Christian humanists, was the Englishman Sir Thomas More (1478–1535). In later life, following a successful career as a lawyer and speaker of the House of Commons, More was appointed lord chancellor of England in 1529. He was not long in this position, however, before he opposed King Henry VIII's plan to establish a national church under royal control that would deny the supremacy of the pope (see Chapter 13). (He was eventually executed and is now revered as a Catholic martyr.) Much earlier, however, in 1516, More published his most famous book, *Utopia* (No Place).

Purporting to describe an ideal community on an imaginary island, the book is really an Erasmian critique of contemporary culture: disparities between poverty and wealth, drastic punishments, religious persecution, and the senseless slaughter of war. In contrast to Europeans, the inhabitants of the fictional Utopia hold all their goods in common, work only six hours a day (so that all may have leisure for intellectual pursuits), and practice the natural virtues of wisdom, moderation, fortitude, and justice. Although More advanced no explicit arguments here in favor of Christianity, he might have meant to imply that if the Utopians could manage their society so well without the benefit of Christian revelation, Europeans who knew the Gospels ought to be able to do even better.

Erasmus and More head a long list of energetic and eloquent northern humanists who made signal contributions to the collective enterprise of revolutionizing the

SIR THOMAS MORE BY HANS HOLBEIN THE YOUNGER. Holbein's skill in rendering the gravity and interiority of his subject is matched by his masterful representation of the sumptuous chain of office, furred mantle, and velvet sleeves that indicate the political and professional status of Henry VIII's lord chancellor.

study of early Christianity, and their achievements had a direct influence on Protestant reformers—as we shall see in the next chapter. Yet very few of them were willing to join Luther and other Protestant leaders in rejecting the fundamental principles on which the power of the Roman Church was based. Most tried to remain within its fold while still espousing an ideal of inward piety and scholarly inquiry. But as the leaders of the Church grew less and less tolerant of dissent, even mild criticism came to seem like heresy. Erasmus himself died early enough to escape persecution, but several of his less fortunate followers did not.

The Literature of the Northern Renaissance

Although Christian humanism would be severely challenged by the Reformation, the artistic Renaissance in the North would flourish. Poets in France and England vied with one another to adapt the elegant lyric forms pioneered by Petrarch (Chapter 11) and popularized by many subsequent poets, including Michelangelo. The sonnet was particularly influential and would become one of the verse forms embraced by William Shakespeare (1554–1616; see chapter 14). Another English poet, Edmund Spenser (c. 1552–1599), drew on the literary innovation of Ariosto's *Orlando Furioso*: his *Faerie Queene* is a similarly long chivalric romance that revels in sensuous imagery. Meanwhile, the more satirical side of Renaissance humanism was embraced by the French writer François Rabelais (*RA-beh-lay*, c. 1494–1553).

Like Erasmus, whom he greatly admired, Rabelais began his career in the Church; but he soon left the cloister to study medicine. A practicing physician, Rabelais interspersed his professional activities with literary endeavors, the most enduring of these are the twin books *Gargantua* and *Pantagruel*, a series of "chronicles" describing the lives and times of giants whose fabulous size and gross appetites serve as vehicles for much lusty humor. Also like Erasmus, Rabelais also satirized religious hypocrisy, scholasticism, superstition, and bigotry. But unlike Erasmus, who wrote in a highly cultivated classical Latin style comprehensible only to learned readers, Rabelais chose to address a different audience by writing in extremely crude French and by glorifying every human appetite as natural and healthy.

Northern Architecture and Art

Although many architects in northern Europe continued to build in the flamboyant Gothic style of the later Middle Ages, the classical values of Italian architects can be seen in some of the splendid new castles constructed in France's Loire valley—châteaux too elegant to be defensible—and in the royal palace (now museum) of the Louvre in Paris, which replaced an old twelfth-century fortress. The influence of Renaissance ideals are also visible in the work of the German artist Albrecht Dürer (*DIRR-er*, 1471–1528). Dürer was the first northerner to master the techniques of proportion and perspective, and he shared with contemporary Italians a fascination with nature and the human body. He also took advantage of the printing press to circulate his work to a wide audience, making his delicate pencil drawings into engravings that could be mass produced.

But Dürer never really embraced classical subject, drawing inspiration instead from more traditional Christian legends and from the Christian humanism of Erasmus. For example, Dürer's serenely radiant engraving of Saint Jerome seems to express the scholarly absorption that Erasmus would have enjoyed while working quietly in his study. Indeed, Dürer aspired to immortalize Erasmus himself in a major portrait, but the paths of the two men crossed only once. Instead, the accomplishment of capturing Erasmus's pensive spirit in oils was left to another northern artist, the German Hans Holbein the Younger (1497–1543). Holbein also painted an acute portrait of Erasmus's friend and kindred spirit, Sir Thomas More. These two portraits, in themselves, exemplify a Renaissance emphasis on the making of naturalistic likenesses that express human individuality.

Tradition and Innovation in Music

Like the visual arts, the gorgeous music produced during this era was nourished by patrons' desire to surround themselves with beauty. Yet unlike painting and sculpture, musical practice did not reach back to classical antiquity but drew instead on well-established medieval conventions. Even before the Black Death, a musical movement called *ars nova* ("new art") was already flourishing in France, and it had spread to Italy during the lifetime of Petrarch. Its outstanding composers had been Guillaume de Machaut (c. 1300–1377) and Francesco Landini (c. 1325–1397).

The madrigals (part-songs) and ballads composed by these musicians and their successors expanded on earlier genres of secular music, but their greatest achievement was a highly complicated yet delicate contrapuntal style adapted for the liturgy of the Church. Machaut was the first-known composer to provide a polyphonic (harmonized) version of the major sections of the Mass. In the fifteenth century, the dissemination of this new musical aesthetic combined with a host of French, Flemish, and Italian elements in the multicultural courts of Europe, particularly that of Burgundy.

SAINT JEROME IN HIS STUDY BY DÜRER. Jerome, the biblical translator of the fourth century (see Chapter 6), was a hero to both Dürer and Erasmus: the paragon of inspired Christian scholarship. Note how the scene exudes contentment, even down to the sleeping lion, which seems more like an overgrown tabby cat than a symbol of Christ.

By the beginning of the sixteenth century, Franco-Flemish composers came to dominate many important courts and cathedrals, creating a variety of new forms and styles that bear a close affinity to Renaissance art and poetry.

Throughout Europe, the general level of musical proficiency in this era was very high. The singing of part-songs was a popular pastime in homes and at informal social gatherings, and the ability to read a part at sight was expected of the educated elite. Aristocratic women, in particular, were expected to display mastery of the new musical instruments that had been developed to add nuance and texture to existing musical forms, including the lute, the viol, the violin, and a variety of woodwind and keyboard instruments like the harpsichord.

Although most composers of this period were men trained in the service of the Church, they rarely made sharp distinctions between sacred and secular music. Like sculpture, music was coming into its own as a serious independent art. As such, it would become an important medium for the expression of both Catholic and Protestant ideals during the Reformation and also one of the few art forms equally acceptable to all.

THE POLITICS OF CHRISTIAN EUROPE

We have already observed how the intellectual and artistic activity of the Renaissance movement was both fueled and hindered by the political developments of the later fifteenth century—within Italy, and throughout Europe. In 1453, France had emerged victorious in the Hundred Years' War, while England plunged into a further three decades of bloody civil conflict that touched every corner of that kingdom. The French monarchy was therefore able to rebuild its power and prestige while at the same time extending its control over regions that had long been controlled by the English crown and that were now part of an enlarged kingdom of France.

In 1494, the French king Charles VIII acted on a plan to expand his reach even further, into Italy. Leading an army of 30,000 well-trained troops across the Alps, he intended to press ancestral claims to the duchy of Milan and the kingdom of Naples. This effort yielded only a tenuous hold on Naples by the time Charles left a year later, and it solidified Italian opposition to French occupation, as we noted above; in our discussion of Machiavelli.

The rulers of Spain, whose territorial claims on Sicily also extended to Naples, were spurred by this to forge an uneasy alliance among the Papal States, some principalities of the Holy Roman Empire, Milan, and Venice. But the respite was brief. Charles's successor, Louis XII, launched a second invasion in 1499. For over a generation, until 1529, warfare in Italy was virtually uninterrupted. Alliances and counteralliances among city-states became further catalysts for violence and made Italy a magnet for mercenaries who could barely be kept in check by the generals who employed them.

Meanwhile, northern Italian city-states' virtual monopoly of trade with Asia, which had been one of the chief economic underpinnings of artistic and intellectual patronage, was being gradually eroded by the shifting of trade routes from the Mediterranean to the Atlantic (Chapters 10 and 11). It was also hampered by the increasing power of the Ottoman Empire, and even by the imperial pretensions of a new Russian ruler.

The Imperial Power of Ivan the Great

In previous chapters, we noted that the Russian duchy of Muscovy had become the champion of the Greek Orthodox Church and, as such, considered itself a true heir of Rome. After the fall of Constantinople to the Ottomans, the Muscovite grand duke even assumed the imperial title *tsar* (caesar)

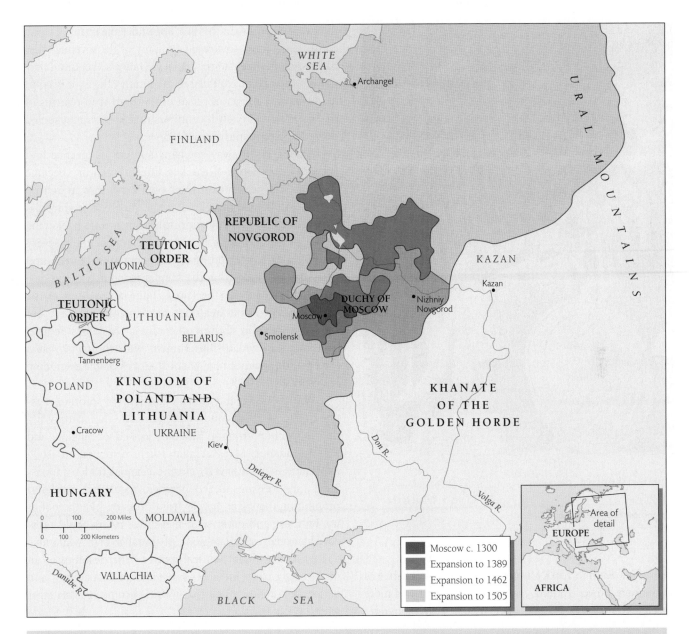

THE EXPANSION OF MUSCOVITE RUSSIA TO 1505. The grand duchy of Moscow was the heart of what would soon become the Russian Empire. ▪ *With what other empires and polities did the Muscovites have to compete during this period of expansion?* ▪ *How did the relative isolation of Moscow, compared with early Kiev, allow for the growth of Muscovite power, on the one hand, and Moscow's distinctively non-Western culture, on the other?* ▪ *How might the natural direction of the expansion of Muscovite power until 1505 help to encourage attitudes often at odds with those of western European civilization?*

and borrowed the Byzantine ideology of the ruler's divine election. These claims would eventually undergird the sacred position later ascribed to the tsars. But ideology alone could not have built the Russian Empire. Behind its growth lay the steadily growing power of its rulers, especially that of Grand Duke Ivan III (1462–1505), known as Ivan the Great, the first to lay down a distinctive imperial agenda.

Ivan launched a series of conquests that annexed all the independent principalities lying between Moscow and the border of Poland-Lithuania. After invading Lithuania in 1492 and 1501, Ivan even succeeded in bringing parts of that domain (portions of modern Belarus and Ukraine) under his control. Meanwhile, he married the niece of the last Byzantine emperor, giving real substance to the claim that Muscovy was New Rome. He also rebuilt his fortified Moscow residence, known as the Kremlin, in magnificent Italianate style. He would later adopt, as his imperial insignia, the double-headed eagle of Rome and its legions. By the

IVAN THE GREAT. This modern tribute to Ivan III prominently displays the two-headed eagle of imperial Rome. ■ *What is the significance of this symbolic choice?*

that were emerging in this era. For under the terms of these concordats, kings now received many of the revenues that had previously gone to the papacy. They also acquired new powers to appoint candidates to church offices. It was, in many ways, a drastic reversal of the hard-won reforms of the eleventh and twelfth centuries that had created such a powerful papacy in the first place.

Having given away so many sources of revenue and authority, the popes of the late fifteenth century became even more dependent on their own territories in central Italy. But to tighten their hold on the Papal States, they had to rule like other Italian princes: leading armies, jockeying for alliances, and undermining their opponents by every possible means—including covert operations, murder, and assassination. Judged by the secular standards of the day, these efforts paid off: the Papal States became one of the better-governed and wealthier principalities in Italy. But such methods did nothing to increase the popes' reputation for piety, and disillusionment with the papacy as a force for the advancement of spirituality became even more widespread.

With both papal authority and Rome's spiritual prestige in decline, kings and princes became the primary figures to whom both clergy and laity looked for religious and moral guidance. Many secular rulers responded to such expectations aggressively, closing scandal-ridden monasteries, suppressing alleged heretics, regulating vice, and prohibiting the lower classes from dressing like the nobility. By these and other such measures, rulers could present themselves as champions of moral reform while also strengthening their political power. The result was an increasingly close link between national monarchies and national churches, a link that would become even stronger after the Reformation.

time of his death in 1505, Muscovy was firmly established as a dominant power. Indeed, the power of the tsar was more absolute in this period than that of any European monarch.

The Growth of National Churches

Meanwhile, as Muscovy laid claim to the mantle of Roman imperial power, the papacy was pouring resources into the glorification of the original Rome and the aggrandizement of the papal office. But neither the city nor its rulers could keep pace with their political and religious rivals. Following the Council of Constance (see Chapter 11), the papacy's victory over the conciliarists was a costly one. To win the support of Europe's kings and princes, various popes negotiated a series of religious treaties known as "concordats," which granted these rulers extensive authority over churches within their domains. The papacy thus secured its theoretical supremacy at the expense of its real power. Reigning popes also strengthened the national monarchies

The Triumph of the "Reconquista"

The kingdoms of the Iberian Peninsula were also in constant conflict during this period. In Castile, civil war and incompetent governance allowed the Castilian nobility to gain greater control over the peasantry and greater independence from the monarchy. In Aragon, royal government benefited from the extended commercial influence of Catalonia, which was under Aragonese authority. But after 1458, Aragon too became enmeshed in a civil war, a war in which both France and Castile became involved.

A solution to the disputed succession that had caused the war in Aragon would ultimately lie in the blending of powerful royal families. In 1469, Prince Ferdinand of Aragon was recognized as the undisputed heir to that throne

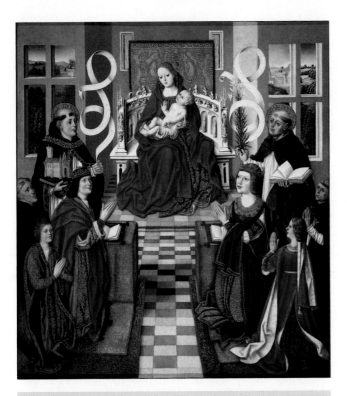

FERDINAND AND ISABELLA HONORING THE VIRGIN. In this contemporary Spanish painting, the royal couple are shown with two of their children and two household chaplains and in the company of the Blessed Virgin, the Christ Child, and saints from the Dominican order (the Dominicans were instrumental in conducting the affairs of the Spanish Inquisition). ▪ *How clear is the distinction between these holy figures and the royal family?* ▪ *What message is conveyed by their proximity?*

and, in the same year, secured this position by marrying Isabella, the heiress to Castile. Isabella became a queen in 1474, Ferdinand a king in 1479; and although Castile and Aragon continued to be ruled as separate kingdoms until 1714—there are tensions between the two former kingdoms even now—the marriage of Ferdinand and Isabella enabled the pursuit of several ambitious policies. In particular, their union allowed them to spend their combined resources on the creation of Europe's most powerful army, which was initially employed to conquer the last remaining principality of what had been al-Andalus: Muslim Spain. That principality, Granada, fell in 1492.

The End of the Convivencia and the Expulsion of the Jews

For more than seven relatively centuries, Spain's Jewish communities had enjoyed the many privileges extended by their Muslim rulers, who were also relatively tolerant of their Christian subjects. Indeed, scholars often refer to this period of Spain's history as a time of *convivencia*, a word that means "living together" or "harmonious coexistence." While relations among various religious and ethnic groups were not always uniformly peaceful or positive, the policies of Muslim rulers in al-Andalus had enabled an extraordinary hybrid culture to flourish there.

The aims of the Spanish Reconquista were diametrically opposed to those of "living together." The crusading ideology of "reconquest" sought instead to forge a single, homogenous community, based on the fiction that Spain had once been entirely Christian and should be restored to its former purity. The year 1492 therefore marks not only the end of Muslim rule in medieval Spain but also the culmination of a process of Jewish exclusion that had accelerated in the late thirteenth century (see Chapter 9). Within this history, the Spanish expulsion of the Jews stands out for the staggering scope of the displacements and destruction it entailed: at least 100,000 and possibly as many as 200,000 men, women, and children were deprived of their homes and livelihoods.

The Christian monarchs' motives for ordering this expulsion are still debated. Tens of thousands of Spanish Jews had converted to Christianity between 1391 and 1420, many as a result of coercion but some from sincere religious conviction. And for a generation or so, it seemed possible that these converts, known as *conversos*, might successfully assimilate into Christian society. But the same civil wars that led to the union of Ferdinand and Isabella made the *conversos* targets of discriminatory legislation. Conflict may also have fueled popular suspicions that these converts remained Jews in secret. To make "proper" Christians out of the *conversos*, the "Most Catholic" monarchs—as they were now called—may have concluded that they needed to remove any potentially seditious influences that might stem from the continuing presence of a Jewish community in Spain.

What became of the Spanish Jews? Some traveled north, to the Rhineland towns of Germany or to eastern Europe, but most settled in Muslim regions of the Mediterranean and Middle East. Many found a haven in the Ottoman Empire. As we already noted, there were many opportunities for advancement in the Ottoman imperial bureaucracy, while the Ottoman economy benefited from the highly skilled labor of Jewish artisans and the vast trading networks of Jewish merchants. In time, new forms and expressions of Jewish culture would emerge, and new communities would form. And although the extraordinary opportunities afforded by the *Convivencia* could never be revived, the descendants of these Spanish Jews—known as

Sephardi Jews, or Sephardim—still treasure the traditions and customs formed in Spain over a thousand years ago.

The Extension of the Reconquista

Although the Christian kingdoms of Iberia had been devoted, for centuries, to the reconquest of territory, the victory over the Muslims of Granada and the expulsion of the Jews in 1492 were watershed events. They mark the beginning of a sweeping initiative to construct a new basis for the precariously united kingdoms of Aragon and Castile, one that could transcend rival regional identities. Like other contemporary monarchs, Ferdinand and Isabella sought to strengthen their emerging nation-state by constructing an exclusively Christian identity for its people and by attaching that new identity to the crown and promoting a single national language, Castilian Spanish. They also succeeded in capturing and redirecting another language: the rhetoric of crusade.

The problem with the crusading ethos, as we have seen, is that it always seeks new outlets. Having created a new exclusively Christian Spanish kingdom through the defeat of all external enemies and internal threats, where were the energies harnessed by the Reconquista to be directed? The answer came from an unexpected quarter and had very unexpected consequences. Just a few months after Ferdinand and Isabella marched victoriously into Granada, the queen granted three ships to a Genoese adventurer who promised to reach India by sailing westward across the Atlantic Ocean, claiming any new lands he found for Spain. Columbus never reached India, but he did help to extend the tradition of reconquest to the New World—with far-reaching consequences.

NEW TARGETS AND TECHNOLOGIES OF CONQUEST

The Spanish monarchs' decision to underwrite a voyage of exploration was spurred by their desire to counter the successful Portuguese ventures of the past half century. For it was becoming clear that a tiny kingdom on the northwestern tip of the Iberian Peninsula would soon dominate the sea-lanes if rival entrepreneurs did not attempt to find alternate routes and establish equally lucrative colonies. This competition with Portugal was another reason why Isabella turned to a Genoese sea captain when she sought

to expand Spain's wealth and global influence—not to a Portuguese one.

Prince Henry the Navigator and Portuguese Colonial Initiatives

Although Portugal had been an independent Christian kingdom since the twelfth century (see Chapter 9), it was never able to compete effectively with its more powerful neighbors (Muslim or Christian) on land. But when the focus of European economic expansion began to shift toward the Atlantic (see Chapter 10), Portuguese mariners were well placed to take advantage of the trend. A central figure in the history of Portuguese maritime imperialism is Prince Henry, later called "the Navigator" (1394–1460), a son of King João I of Portugal and his English queen, Philippa of Lancaster (sister of England's Henry IV).

Prince Henry was fascinated by the sciences of cartography and navigation, and he helped to ensure that Portuguese sailors had access to the latest charts and navigational instruments. He was also inspired by the stories told by John de Mandeville and Marco Polo—particularly the legend of Prester John, a mythical Christian king dwelling somewhere at the end of the earth, whom Europeans believed would be their ally against the Muslims if only they could locate him. More concretely, Prince Henry had ambitions to extend Portuguese control into the Atlantic, to tap into the burgeoning market for slaves in the Ottoman Empire and to establish direct links with the sources of African gold.

Prince Henry played an important part in organizing the Portuguese colonization of Madeira, the Canary Islands, and the Azores—and in the process he pioneered the Portuguese slave trade, which almost entirely eradicated the population of the Canaries before targeting Africa. By the 1440s, Portuguese explorers had reached the Cape Verde Islands. In 1444, they landed on the African mainland in the area that became known as the Gold Coast, where they began to collect cargoes of gold and slaves for export back to Portugal. Prince Henry personally directed eight of the thirty-five Portuguese voyages to Africa that occurred during his lifetime. And in order to outflank the cross-Saharan gold trade, largely controlled by the Muslims of North Africa and mediated by the Genoese, he decided to intercept this trade at its source by building a series of forts along the African coastline. This was also his main reason for colonizing the Canary

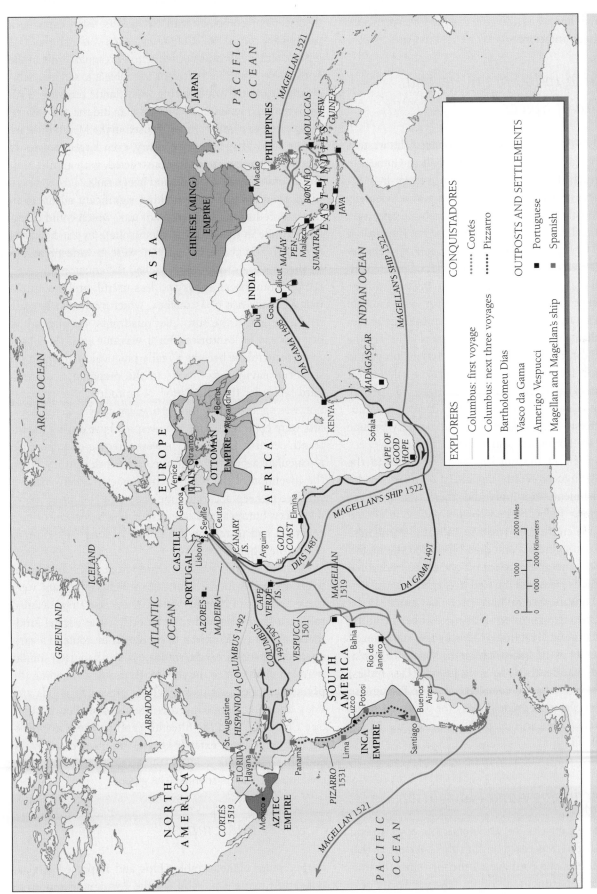

OVERSEAS EXPLORATION IN THE FIFTEENTH AND SIXTEENTH CENTURIES. ▪ *What were the major routes taken by European explorers of the fifteenth and sixteenth centuries?* ▪ *What appear to be the explorers' main goals?* ▪ *How might the establishment of outposts in Africa, America, and the East Indies have radically altered the balance of power in the Old World, and why?*

Islands, which he saw as a staging ground for expeditions into the African interior.

From Africa to India and Beyond: An Empire of Spices

By the 1470s, Portuguese sailors had rounded the western coast of Africa and were exploring the Gulf of Guinea. In 1483, they reached the mouth of the Congo River. In 1488, the Portuguese captain Bartholomeu Dias was accidentally blown around the southern tip of Africa by a gale, after which he named the point "Cape of Storms." But King João II (r. 1481–95) took a more optimistic view of Dias's achievement: he renamed it the Cape of Good Hope and began planning a naval expedition to India. In 1497–98, accordingly, Vasco da Gama rounded the cape, and then, with the help of a Muslim navigator named Ibn Majid, crossed the Indian Ocean to Calicut, on the southwestern coast of India. For the first time, this opened a viable sea route between Europe and the Far Eastern spice trade. Although Gama lost half his fleet and one-third of his men on his two-year voyage, his cargo of spices was so valuable that his losses were deemed insignificant. His heroism became legendary, and his story became the basis for the Portuguese national epic, the *Lusiads*.

Now masters of the quickest route to riches in the world, the Portuguese swiftly capitalized on their decades of accomplishment. Not only did their trading fleets sail regularly to India, there were Portuguese efforts to monopolize the entire spice trade: in 1509, the Portuguese defeated an Ottoman fleet and then blockaded the mouth of the Red Sea, attempting to cut off one of the traditional routes by which spices had traveled to Alexandria and Beirut. By 1510, Portuguese military forces had established a series of forts along the western Indian coastline, including their headquarters at Goa. In 1511, Portuguese ships seized Malacca, a center of the spice trade on the Malay Peninsula. By 1515, they had reached the Spice Islands (East Indies) and the coast of China. So completely did the Portuguese now dominate the spice trade that by the 1520s even the Venetians were forced to buy their pepper in the Portuguese capital of Lisbon.

Naval Technology and Navigation

The Portuguese caravel—the workhorse ship of those first voyages to Africa—was based on ship and sail designs that had been in use among Portuguese fishermen since the thirteenth century. Starting in the 1440s, however, Portuguese shipwrights began building larger caravels of about 50 tons

displacement equipped with two masts, each carrying a triangular (lateen) sail. Columbus's *Niña* was a ship of this design, although it was refitted with two square sails in the Portuguese-held Canary Islands to enable it to sail more efficiently before the wind during the Atlantic crossing. Such ships required much smaller crews than did the multi-oared galleys that were still commonly used in the Mediterranean. By the end of the fifteenth century, even larger caravels of around 200 tons were being constructed, with a third mast and a combination of square and lateen sails.

Europeans were also making significant advances in navigation during this era. Quadrants, which could calculate latitude in the Northern Hemisphere by the height of the North Star above the horizon, were in widespread use by the 1450s. As sailors approached the equator, however, the quadrant became less and less useful, and navigators instead made use of astrolabes, which reckoned latitude by the height of the sun. Like quadrants, astrolabes had been in use for centuries. But it was not until the 1480s that the astrolabe became a really practical instrument for seaborne navigation, thanks to the preparation of standard tables for the calculation of latitude whose preparation was sponsored by the Portuguese crown. Compasses, too, were coming into more widespread use during the fifteenth century. Longitude, however, remained impossible to calculate accurately until the eighteenth century, when the invention of the marine chronometer finally made it possible to keep accurate time at sea. In this prior age of discovery, Europeans sailing east or west across the oceans generally had to rely on their skill at dead reckoning to determine where they were.

European sailors also benefited from a new interest in maps and navigational charts. Especially important were books known as *rutters* or *routiers*. These contained detailed sailing instructions and descriptions of the coastal landmarks a pilot could expect to encounter en route to a variety of destinations. Mediterranean sailors had used similar portolan charts since the thirteenth century, mapping the ports along the coastlines, tracking prevailing winds and tides, and indicating dangerous reefs and shallow harbors (see Chapter 10). In the fifteenth century, these mapmaking techniques were extended to the Atlantic Ocean; by the end of the sixteenth century, the accumulated knowledge contained in rutters spanned the globe.

Artillery and Empire

Larger, more maneuverable ships and improved navigational aids made it possible for the Portuguese and other European mariners to reach Africa, Asia, and—eventually—

SPANISH GALLEON. The larger, full-bottomed ships that came into use during the fifteenth century would become engines of imperial conquest and the vessels that brought the riches of those conquests back to Europe. This wooden model was made for the Museo Storico Navale di Venezia (Naval History Museum) in Venice, Italy.

into the Indian Ocean in 1498, but the Portuguese did not gain control of that ocean until 1509, when they defeated combined Ottoman and Indian naval forces. Portuguese trading outposts in Africa and Asia were essentially fortifications, built not so much to guard against the attacks of native peoples as to ward off assaults from other Europeans. Without this essential military component, the European maritime empires that were emerging in this period could not have existed.

Atlantic Colonization and a New Kind of Slavery

Although slavery had effectively disappeared in much of northwestern Europe by the early twelfth century, it continued in parts of the Mediterranean world and had been introduced into some regions of eastern Europe after the Black Death. But this slavery existed on a very small scale. There were no slave-powered factories or large-scale agricultural systems in this period. The only major slave markets and slave economies were in the Ottoman Empire, and there slaves ran the vast Ottoman bureaucracy and staffed the army. And in all these cases, as in antiquity, no aspect of slavery was racially based. In Italy and elsewhere in the medieval Mediterranean world, slaves were often captives from an array of locales. In eastern Europe, they were functionally serfs. Most Ottoman slaves were European Christians, predominantly Poles, Ukrainians, Greeks, and Bulgarians. In the early Middle Ages, Germanic and Celtic peoples had been widely enslaved. Under the Roman Empire, slaves had come from every part of the known (and unknown) world.

What was new about the slavery of the late fifteenth century was its increasing racialization—an aspect of modern slavery that has made an indelible impact on our own society. To Europeans, African slaves were visible in ways that other slaves were not, and it became convenient for those who dealt in them to justify the mass deportation of entire populations by claiming their racial inferiority and their "natural" fitness for a life of bondage. This nefarious practice, too, has had long-lasting and tragic consequences that still afflict the civilizations of our own world.

In Lisbon, which became a significant market for enslaved Africans during Prince Henry's lifetime, something on the order of 15,000 to 20,000 African captives were sold within a twenty-year period. In the following half century, by about 1505, the numbers amounted to 150,000. For the most part, the purchasers of these slaves regarded them as

the Americas. But fundamentally, these European commercial empires were military achievements that capitalized on what Europeans had learned in their wars against each other. Perhaps the most critical military advance was the increasing sophistication of artillery, a development made possible not only by gunpowder but also by improved metallurgical techniques for casting cannon barrels. By the middle of the fifteenth century, as we observed in Chapter 11, the use of artillery pieces had rendered the stone walls of medieval castles and towns obsolete, a fact brought home in 1453 by the successful French siege of Bordeaux (which ended the Hundred Years' War), and by the Ottoman siege of Constantinople (which ended the Byzantine Empire).

Indeed, the new ship designs (first caravels, and then the heavier galleons) were important in part because their larger size made it possible to mount more effective artillery pieces on them. European vessels were now conceived as floating artillery platforms, with scores of guns mounted in fixed positions along their sides and swivel guns mounted fore and aft. These guns were vastly expensive, as were the ships that carried them, but for those rulers who could afford them, such ships made it possible to back mercantile ventures with military power. As we already noted, Vasco da Gama had been able to sail

Analyzing Primary Sources

The Ottomans' Army of Slaves

Although the growing African slave trade was creating a newly racialized idea of slavery in the Caribbean and the Americas, slavery in Europe was not tied to race. Indeed, slavery could be a path to upward mobility in the Ottoman Empire. The following account is from a memoir written by Konstantin Mihailovic, a Serbian Christian who was captured as a youth by the army of Sultan Mehmet II. For eight years, he served in the Ottoman janissary ("gate-keeper") corps. In 1463, the fortress he was defending for the sultan was captured by the Hungarians, after which he recorded his experiences for a Christian audience.

 henever the Turks invade foreign lands and capture their people, an imperial scribe follows immediately behind them, and whatever boys there are, he takes them all into the janissaries and gives five gold pieces for each one and sends them across the sea [to Anatolia]. There are about two thousand of these boys. If, however, the number of them from enemy peoples does not suffice, then he takes from the Christians in every village in his land who have boys, having established what is the most every village can give so that the quota will always be full. And the boys whom he takes in his own land are called *cilik*. Each one of them can leave his property to whomever he wants after his death. And those whom he takes among the enemies are called *pendik*. These latter after their deaths can leave nothing; rather, it goes to the emperor, except that if someone comports himself well and is so deserving that he be freed, he may leave it to whomever he wants. And on the boys who are across the sea the emperor spends nothing; rather, those to whom they are entrusted must maintain them and send them where he orders. Then they take those who are suited for it on ships and there they study and train to skirmish in battle. There the emperor already provides for them and gives them a wage. From there he chooses for his own court those who are trained and then raises their wages.

Source: Konstantin Mihailovic, *Memoirs of a Janissary* (Michigan Slavic Translations 3), trans. Benjamin Stolz (Ann Arbor, MI: 1975), pp. 157–59.

Questions for Analysis

1. Why might the Ottoman emperor have established this system for "recruiting" and training janissaries? What are its strengths and weaknesses?

2. Based on your knowledge of Western civilizations, how unusual would you deem this method of raising troops? How does it compare to the strategies of other rulers we have studied?

---

status symbols; it became fashionable to have African footmen, page boys, and ladies' maids. In the Atlantic colonies—Madeira, the Canaries, and the Azores—land was still worked mainly by European settlers and sharecroppers. Slave labor, if it was employed at all, was generally used only in sugar mills. On Madeira and the Canaries, where sugar became the predominant cash crop during the last quarter of the fifteenth century, some slaves were introduced as agricultural laborers. But even sugar production did not lead to the widespread introduction of slavery on these islands.

However, a new kind of slave-based sugar plantation began to emerge in Portugal's eastern Atlantic colonies in the 1460s, starting on the Cape Verde Islands and then extending southward into the Gulf of Guinea. These islands were not populated when the Portuguese began to settle them, and their climate generally discouraged most Europeans from living there. They were ideally located, however, along the routes of slave traders venturing outward from the nearby West African coast. It was this plantation model that would be exported to Brazil by the Portuguese and to the Caribbean islands of the Americas by their Spanish conquerors, with incalculable consequences for the peoples of Africa, the Americas, and Europe (see Chapter 14).

EUROPEANS IN A NEW WORLD

Like his contemporaries, Christopher Columbus (1451–1506) understood that the world was a sphere. But like them, he also thought it was much smaller than it actually is. (As we saw in Chapter 4, the accurate calculation of the globe's circumference made in ancient Alexandria had been suppressed centuries later by Roman geographers.) Furthermore, it had long been accepted that there were only three continents, Europe, Asia, and Africa—hence Columbus's decision to reach Asia by sailing west, a plan that seemed even more plausible after the discovery and colonization of the Canary Islands and the Azores. The existence of these islands reinforced a new hypothesis that the Atlantic was dotted with similar lands all the way to Japan. This emboldened Columbus's royal patrons, who became convinced that the Genoese mariner could reach China in about a month, after a stop for provisions on the Canaries. This turned out to be a kind of self-fulfilling prophecy, for when Columbus reached the Bahamas and the island of Hispaniola after only a month's sailing, he reported that he had reached the outer islands of Asia.

The Shock of Discovery

Of course, Columbus was not the first European to set foot on the American continents. As we have already learned, Viking sailors briefly settled present-day Newfoundland, Labrador, and perhaps even portions of New England around the year 1000 (see Chapter 8). But knowledge of these Viking landings had been forgotten or ignored outside of Iceland for hundreds of years. It wasn't until the 1960s that the stories of these expeditions were corroborated by archaeological evidence. Moreover, the tiny Norwegian colony on Greenland—technically part of the North American landmass—had been abandoned in the fifteenth century, when the cooling of the climate (see Chapter 10) destroyed the fragile ecosystems that had barely sustained the lives of Norse settlers there.

Although Columbus brought back no spices to prove that he had found an alternate route to Asia, he did return with some small samples of gold and a few indigenous people—whose existence gave promise of entire tribes that might be "saved" by conversion to Christianity and whose lands could provide homes for Spanish settlers seeking new frontiers after the Reconquista. This provided sufficient incentive for the "Most Catholic" monarchs to finance three further expeditions by Columbus, and many more by other adventurers, missionaries, and colonists.

Meanwhile, the Portuguese, who had already obtained a papal bull granting them (hypothetical) ownership of all lands south of the Canaries, rushed to establish their own claims. After two years of wrangling and conflicting papal pronouncements, the Treaty of Tordesillas (1494) sought to demarcate Spanish and Portuguese possession of as-yet-undiscovered lands. The Spanish would ultimately emerge as the big winners in this gambling match. Within a decade, the coasts of two hitherto unknown continents were identified, as were clusters of new islands, most on the Spanish side of the (still disputed) meridian.

Gradually, Europeans reached the conclusion that the voyages of Columbus and his immediate successors had revealed an entirely "New World." And—shockingly—this world had not been foretold either by the teachings of Christianity or the wisdom of the ancients. Among the first to champion the fact of two new continents' existence was the Italian explorer and geographer Amerigo Vespucci (1454–1512), whose name was soon adopted as a descriptor for them. Eventually, those who came to accept this fact were forced to question the reliability of the key sources of knowledge on which Western civilizations had hitherto hinged (see Chapter 14).

At first, the realization that the Americas (as they were now called) were not an outpost of Asia came as a disappointment to the Spanish: two major land masses and two vast oceans disrupted their plans to beat the Portuguese to the Spice Islands. But new possibilities gradually became clear. In 1513, the Spanish explorer Vasco Núñez de Balboa first viewed the Pacific Ocean from the Isthmus of Panama, and news of the narrow divide between two vast oceans prompted Ferdinand and Isabella's grandson to renew their dream. This young monarch, Charles V (1500–1556), ruled not only Spain but the huge patchwork of territories encompassed by the Holy Roman Empire. In 1519, he accepted Ferdinand Magellan's proposal to see whether a route to Asia could be found by sailing around South America.

But Magellan's voyage demonstrated beyond question that the world was simply too large for any such plan to be feasible at that time. Of the five ships that left Spain under his command, only one returned, three years later, having been forced to circumnavigate the globe. Out of a crew of 265 sailors, only 18 survived. Most had died of scurvy or starvation; Magellan himself had been killed in a skirmish with native peoples in the Philippines.

This fiasco ended all hope of discovering an easy southwest passage to Asia—although the deadly dream

America as an Object of Desire

Under the influence of popular travel narratives that had circulated in Europe for centuries, Columbus and his fellow voyagers were prepared to find the New World full of cannibals. They also assumed that the indigenous peoples' custom of wearing little or no clothing—not to mention their "savagery"—would render their women sexually available. In a letter sent back home in 1495, one of Columbus's men recounted a notable encounter with a "cannibal girl" whom he had taken captive in his tent and whose naked body aroused his desire. He was surprised to find that she resisted his advances so fiercely that he had to tie her up—which of course made it easier for him to "subdue" her. In the end, he cheerfully reports, the girl's sexual performance was so satisfying that she might have been trained, as he put it, in a "school for whores."

The Flemish artist Jan van der Straet (1523–1605) would have heard many such reports of the encounters between (mostly male) Europeans and the peoples of the New World. This engraving, based on one of his drawings, is among the thousands of mass-produced images that circulated widely in Europe, thanks to the invention of printing. It imagines the first encounter between a male "Americus" (like Columbus or Amerigo Vespucci himself) and the New World, "America," depicted as a voluptuous, available woman. The Latin caption reads: "America rises to meet Americus; and whenever he calls her, she will always be aroused."

Questions for Analysis

1. Study the details of this image carefully. What does each symbolize, and how do they work together as an allegory of conquest and colonization?

2. On what stereotypes of indigenous peoples does this image draw? Notice, for example, the cannibalistic campfire of the group in the background or the posture of "America."

3. The New World itself—America—is imagined as female in this image. Why is this? What messages might this—and the suggestive caption—have conveyed to a European viewer?

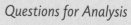

Americen Americus retexit, AMERICA. *Semel vocauit inde ſemper excitam.*

of a northwest passage survived and motivated many European explorers of North America into the twentieth century. It has been revived today: in our age of global warming, the retreat of Arctic pack ice has led to the opening of new shipping lanes, and in 2008 the first commercial voyage successfully traversed the Arctic Ocean.

The Dream of Gold and the Downfall of Empires

Although the unforeseen size of the globe made a westward passage to Asia untenable, given the technologies then available, Europeans were quick to capitalize on the sources of wealth that the New World itself could offer. What chiefly fired the imagination were those small samples of gold that Columbus had initially brought back to Spain. While rather paltry in themselves, they nurtured hopes that gold might lie piled in ingots somewhere in these vast new lands, ready to enrich any adventurer who discovered them. Rumor fed rumor, until a few freelance Spanish soldiers really did strike it rich beyond their most avaricious imaginings.

Their success, though, had little to do with their own efforts. Within a generation after the landing of the first ships under Columbus's command, European diseases had spread rapidly among the indigenous peoples of the Caribbean and the coastlines of the Americas. These diseases—especially measles and smallpox—were not fatal to those who carried them, because Europeans had developed immunities over many generations. But to the peoples of this New World, they were deadly in the extreme. For example, there were probably 250,000 people living on Hispaniola when Columbus arrived; within thirty years—a single generation—70 percent had perished from disease.

Moreover, the new waves of *conquistadores* (conquerors) were assisted by the complex political, economic, and military rivalries that already existed among the highly sophisticated societies they encountered. The Aztec Empire of Mexico rivaled any European state in its power, culture, and wealth—and like any successful empire it had subsumed many neighboring territories in the course of its own conquests. Its capital, Tenochtitlán (*ten-och-tit-LAN*, now Mexico City), amazed its European assailants, who had never seen anything like the height and grandeur of its buildings or the splendor of its public works. This splendor was itself evidence of the Aztecs' imperial might, which was resisted by many of the peoples from whom they demanded tribute.

The Aztecs' eventual conqueror, Hernán Cortés (1485–1547), had arrived in Hispaniola as a young man, in the wake of Columbus's initial landing. He had received a land grant from the Spanish crown and acted as magistrate of one of the first towns established there. In 1519, he headed an expedition to the mainland, which had been the target of some earlier exploratory missions that had not resulted in any permanent settlements—owing largely to the tight control of the Aztecs, whose imperial domain extended far beyond Tenochtitlán.

When Cortés arrived on the coast of the Aztec realm, he formed an intimate relationship with a native woman known as La Malinche. She became his consort and interpreter in the Nahua language, which was a lingua franca among the many different ethnic groups within the empire. With her help, he discovered that some peoples subjugated by the Aztecs were rebellious, and so he began to form stra-

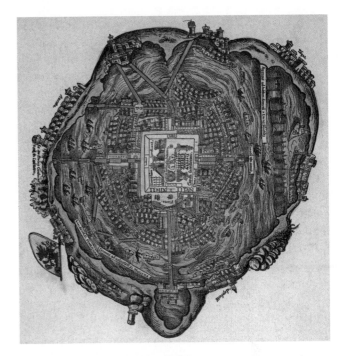

THE AZTEC CITY OF TENOCHTITLÁN. The Spanish conquistador Bernal Díaz del Castillo (1492–1585) took part in the conquest of the Aztec Empire and later wrote a historical account of his adventures. His admiring description of the Aztec capital at Tenochtitlán records that the Spaniards were amazed to see such a huge city built in the midst of a vast lake, with gigantic buildings arranged in a meticulous urban plan around a central square and broad causeways linking the city to the mainland. This hand-colored woodcut was included in an early edition of Hernán Cortés's letters to Emperor Charles V, printed at Nuremberg (Germany) in 1524.

tegic alliances with their leaders. Cortés himself could only muster a force of a few hundred men, but his native allies numbered in the thousands.

These strategic alliances were crucial: although Cortés and his men had potentially superior weapons—guns and horses—these were more effective for their novelty than their utility. In fact, the rifles were of inferior quality, while gunpowder dampened by the humid climate had a tendency to misfire or fail to ignite altogether. So Cortés adopted the tactics and weaponry of his native allies in his dealings with the Aztec king, Montezuma II (r. 1502–1520), and in his final assaults upon the fortification of Tenochtitlán. In the end, though, it was European bacteria (not European technology or cunning) that led to his victory: the Aztecs were devastated by an outbreak of the plague virus that had arrived along with Cortés and his men. In 1521, their empire fell.

In 1533, another lucky conquistador, Francisco Pizarro, would manage to topple the highly centralized empire of the Incas, based in what is now Peru, by similar voluntary and involuntary means. In this case, he took advantage of an ongoing civil war that had weakened the reigning dynasty. He was also assisted by an epidemic of smallpox. Like Cortés, Pizarro promised his native allies liberation from an oppressive regime. Those formerly subject to the Aztecs and Incas would soon be able to judge how partial these promises were.

The Price of Conquest

The astonishing conquests of Mexico and Peru gave the conquistadors access to hoards of gold and silver that had been accumulated for centuries by Aztec and Inca rulers. Almost immediately, however, a search for the sources of these precious metals was launched by agents of the Spanish crown. The first gold deposits were discovered in Hispaniola, where surface mines were speedily established using native laborers, who were already dying in appalling numbers from disease and were now further decimated by brutality and overwork. The population dwindled further, to a mere 10 percent of its Pre-Columbian strength.

The loss of so many workers made the mines of Hispaniola uneconomical to operate, so European colonists turned instead to cattle raising and sugar production. Modeling their sugarcane plantations on those of the Cape Verde Islands and St. Thomas (São Tomé) in the Gulf of Guinea, colonists began to import thousands of African slaves to labor in the new industry. Sugar production was, by its nature, a capital-intensive undertaking. The need to import slave labor added further to its costs, guaranteeing that control over the new industry would fall into the hands of a few extremely wealthy planters and financiers.

Despite the establishment of sugar production in the Caribbean and cattle ranching on the Mexican mainland—whose devastating effects on the fragile ecosystem of Central America will be discussed in Chapter 14—it was mining that would shape the Spanish colonies most fundamentally in this period. If gold was the lure that had initially inspired the conquest, silver became its most lucrative export. Even before the discovery of vast silver deposits, the Spanish crown had taken steps to assume direct control over all colonial exports. It was therefore to the Spanish crown that the profits of empire were channeled. Europe's silver

SPANISH CONQUISTADORS IN MEXICO. This sixteenth-century drawing of conquistadors slaughtering the Aztec aristocracy emphasizes the advantages that plate armor and steel swords gave to the Spanish soldiers.

A Spanish Critique of New World Conquest

Not all Europeans approved of European imperialism or its "civilizing" effects on the peoples of the New World. One of the most influential contemporary critics was Bartolomé de las Casas (1484–1566). In 1502, when Bartolomé was eighteen years old, he and his father joined an expedition to Hispaniola. In 1510, he became the first ordained priest in the Americas and eventually became bishop of Chiapas (Mexico). Although he was a product of his times—he owned many slaves—he was also prescient in discerning the devastating effects of European settlement in the West Indies and Central America, and he particularly deplored the exploitation and extermination of indigenous populations. The following excerpt is from one of the many eloquent manifestos he published in an attempt to gain the sympathies of the Spanish crown and to reach a wide readership. It was printed in 1542 but draws on the impressions and opinions he had formed since his arrival in New Spain as a young man.

God made all the peoples of this area, many and varied as they are, as open and as innocent as can be imagined. The simplest people in the world—unassuming, long-suffering, unassertive, and submissive—they are without malice or guile, and are utterly faithful and obedient both to their own native lords and to the Spaniards in whose service they now find themselves.... They are innocent and pure in mind and have a lively intelligence, all of which makes them particularly receptive to learning and understanding the truths of our Catholic faith and to being instructed in virtue; indeed, God has invested them with fewer impediments in this regard than any other people on earth....

It was upon these gentle lambs... that from the very first day they clapped eyes on them the Spanish fell like ravening wolves upon the fold, or like tigers and savage lions who have not eaten meat for days. The pattern established at the outset has remained unchanged to this day, and the Spaniards still do nothing save tear the natives to shreds, murder them and inflict upon them untold misery, suffering and distress, tormenting, harrying and persecuting them mercilessly....

When the Spanish first journeyed there, the indigenous population of the island of Hispaniola stood at some three million; today only two hundred survive. The island of Cuba, which extends for a distance almost as great as that separating Valladolid from Rome, is now to all intents and purposes uninhabited; and two other large, beautiful and fertile islands, Puerto Rico and Jamaica, have been similarly devastated. Not a living soul remains today on any of the islands of the Bahamas... even though every single one of the sixty or so islands in the group... is more fertile and more beautiful than the Royal Gardens in Seville and the climate is as healthy as anywhere on earth. The native population, which once numbered some five hundred thousand, was wiped out by forcible expatriation to the island of Hispaniola, a policy adopted by the Spaniards in an endeavour to make up losses among the indigenous population of that island....

At a conservative estimate, the despotic and diabolical behaviour of the Christians has, over the last forty years, led to the unjust and totally unwarranted deaths of more than twelve million souls, women and children among them....

The reason the Christians have murdered on such a vast scale and killed anyone and everyone in their way is purely and simply greed.... The Spaniards have shown not the slightest consideration for these people, treating them (and I speak from first-hand experience, having been there from the outset) not as brute animals—indeed, I would to God they had done and had shown them the consideration they afford their animals—so much as piles of dung in the middle of the road. They have had as little concern for their souls as for their bodies, all the millions that have perished having gone to their deaths with no knowledge of God and without the benefit of the Sacraments. One fact in all this is widely known and beyond dispute, for even the tyrannical murderers themselves acknowledge the truth of it: the indigenous peoples never did the Europeans any harm whatever....

Source: Bartolomé de las Casas, *A Short Account of the Destruction of the Indies*, trans. Nigel Griffin (Harmondsworth, UK: 1992), pp. 9–12.

Questions for Analysis

1. Given his perspective on the behavior of his countrymen, how might Bartolomé de las Casas have justified his own presence in New Spain (Mexico)? What do you think he may have hoped to achieve by publishing this account?

2. What comparisons does the author make between New Spain (Mexico) and the Old, and between indigenous peoples and Europeans? What is he trying to convey?

3. Compare this account with the contemporary engraving on page 000. What new light does this excerpt throw on that visual allegory? How might a reader-viewer of the time have reconciled these two very different pictures of European imperialism?

shortage, which had been acute for centuries, therefore came to an end.

Yet this massive infusion of silver into the European economy created more problems than it solved, because it accelerated an inflation that had already begun in the late fifteenth century. Initially, inflation had been driven by the renewed growth of the European population, an expanding colonial economy, and a relatively fixed supply of food. Thereafter, thanks to the influx of New World silver, inflation was driven by the hugely increased supply of coinage. As we shall see, this abundance of coinage led to the doubling and quadrupling of prices in the course of the sixteenth century and the collapse of this inflated economy—paradoxically driving a wave of impoverished Europeans to settle in the New World in ever greater numbers.

CONCLUSION

The expansion of the Mediterranean world into the Atlantic, which had been ongoing since the thirteenth century, was the essential preliminary to Columbus's voyages and to the rise of European empires in Africa, India, the Caribbean, and the Americas. Other events and innovations that we have surveyed in this chapter played a key role, too: the relatively rapid communications facilitated by the printing press; the tussle for power in Italy that led to the development of ever deadlier weapons; the navigational and colonial initiatives of the Portuguese; and the success of the Spanish Reconquista, which displaced Spain's venerable Jewish community and enabled Spanish rulers and adventurers to seek their fortunes overseas.

After You Read This Chapter

(S) Visit StudySpace for quizzes, additional review materials, and multimedia documents. **wwnorton.com/web/westernciv18**

REVIEWING THE OBJECTIVES

- The artists of Italy were closely tied to those with political and military power. How did this relationship affect the kinds of work these artists produced?
- What aspects of Renaissance artistry and learning were adopted in northern Europe?
- What was the Reconquista, and how did it lead to a new way of thinking about Spanish identity?
- Europeans, especially the Portuguese, were developing new technologies and techniques that enabled exploration and colonial ventures in this period. What were they?
- The "discovery" of the New World had profound effects on the indigenous peoples and environment of the Americas. Describe some of these effects.

For the indigenous peoples and empires of the Americas, the results were cataclysmic. Within a century of Europeans' arrival, between 50 and 90 percent of some native populations had perished from disease, massacre, and enslavement. Moreover, Europeans' capacity to further their imperial ambitions wherever ships could sail and guns could penetrate profoundly destabilized Europe and its neighbors, sharpening the divisions among competing kingdoms and empires.

The ideals of the humanists and the artistry associated with the Renaissance often stand in sharp contrast to the harsh realities alongside which they coexisted and in which they were rooted. Artists could thrive in the atmosphere of competition and one-upmanship that characterized this period, but they could also find themselves reduced to the status of servants in the households of the wealthy and powerful—or forced to subordinate their artistry to the demands of warfare and espionage. Meanwhile, intellectuals and statesmen looked for inspiration to the precedents and glories of the past. But to which aspects of the past? Some humanists may have wanted to revive the principles of the Roman Republic, but many of them worked for ambitious despots who modeled themselves on Rome's dictators. The theories that undergirded European politics and colonial expansion were being used to legitimize many different kinds of power, including that of the papacy. All of these trends would be carried forward in the sixteenth century and would have a role to play in the upheaval that shattered Europe's fragile religious unity. It is to this upheaval, the Reformation, that we turn in Chapter 13.

PEOPLE, IDEAS, AND EVENTS IN CONTEXT

- Why was **GUTENBERG**'s invention of the **PRINTING PRESS** such a significant development?
- How did **NICCOLÒ MACHIAVELLI** respond to Italy's political situation within Europe? In what ways do artists like **LEONARDO DA VINCI** and **MICHELANGELO BUONARROTI** exemplify the ideals and realities of the Renaissance?
- How did northern European scholars like **DESIDERIUS ERASMUS** and **THOMAS MORE** apply humanist ideas to Christianity? How were these ideas expressed in art?
- What is significant about **IVAN THE GREAT**'s use of the title **TSAR**? In what other ways did the Russian emperor claim to be the heir of Rome?
- How did **ISABELLA OF CASTILE** and **FERDINAND OF ARAGON** succeed in creating a unified Spain through the **RECONQUISTA**?
- How does **PRINCE HENRY THE NAVIGATOR** exemplify the motives for pursuing overseas expansion? Why were the Portuguese so successful in establishing colonies in this period?
- What were the expectations that launched **COLUMBUS**'s voyage? What enabled the Spanish **CONQUISTADORS** to subjugate the peoples of the **AMERICAS**?

THINKING ABOUT CONNECTIONS

- Phrases like "Renaissance man" and "a Renaissance education" are still part of our common vocabulary. Given what you have learned in this chapter, how has your understanding of such phrases changed? How would you explain their true meaning to others?
- How do the patterns of conquest and colonization discussed in this chapter compare to those of earlier periods, for example the era of the Crusades or the empires of antiquity? How many of these developments were new?
- Although the growth of the African slave trade would result in a new racialization of slavery in the Atlantic world, the justifications for slavery had very old roots. How might Europeans have used Greek and Roman precedents in defense of these new ventures? (See Chapters 4 and 5.)

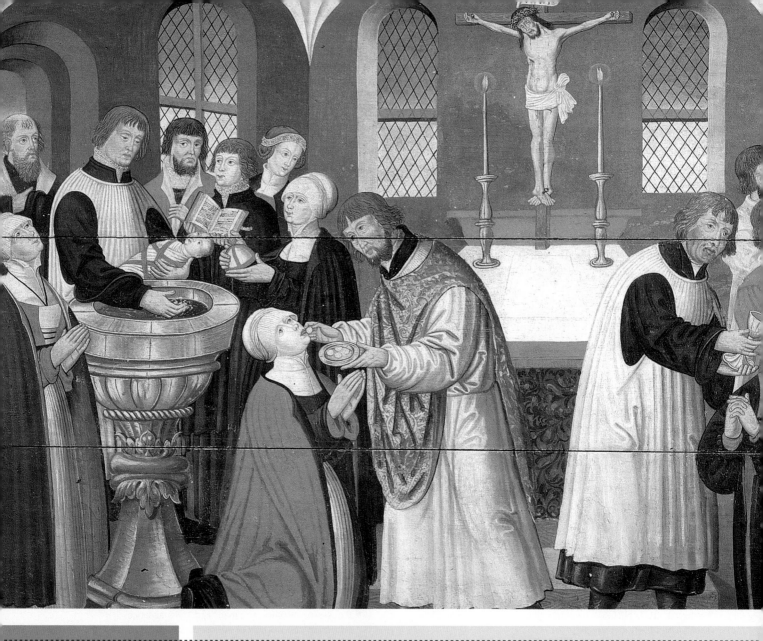

Before
You
Read
This
Chapter

The Age of Dissent and Division, 1500–1564

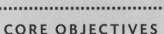

CORE OBJECTIVES

- **DEFINE** the main premises of Lutheranism.

- **EXPLAIN** why Switzerland emerged as an important Protestant center.

- **IDENTIFY** the ways in which family structures and values changed during the Reformation.

- **UNDERSTAND** the reasons behind England's unusual brand of Protestantism.

- **DESCRIBE** the Catholic Church's response to the challenge of Protestantism.

n 1517, on the night before the Feast of All Saints—All Hallows' Eve, or Halloween—a professor of theology at a small university in northern Germany published a series of debating points on the door of Wittenberg's All Saints' Church, which served as the university's chapel. (It was also known as "Castle church," because it formed part of the princely palace recently built for the local ruler, the elector of Saxony.) This was not a prank; it was the usual method of announcing a scholarly disputation, and the door of the church had been used for this purpose since the university's founding in 1502. Yet there was something peculiarly appropriate in Martin Luther's choice of an evening traditionally associated with mischief-making. Although he cannot have anticipated the magnitude of mischief it would cause, the posting of ninety-five theses was a subversive act. For one thing, the sheer number of propositions that Dr. Luther offered to debate was unusual. But what really caught the attention of his fellow scholars was their unifying theme— the corruption of the Church and, in particular, the office of the pope—and the rational yet passionate manner in which that theme was expounded. It was a topic very much in vogue at the time, but it had seldom been dissected so clearly by a licensed theologian who was also a monk, an ordained priest, a charismatic teacher, and a man of strong convictions.

Thanks to Luther's well-placed correspondents, this document and the debate it stimulated soon found audiences well beyond Wittenberg. By the time the papacy formally retaliated, in 1520, dissent was widespread—and not only among academics. Many of Europe's kings and princes saw the political advantages of either defying or defending the pope, and they chose sides accordingly. Luther's own lord, Frederick III of Saxony, would spend the rest of his life shielding the man who had first expounded those theses in his own Castle church.

Luther had grown up in a largely peaceful Europe. After two centuries of economic, social, and political turmoil, its economy was expanding, its cities were growing, and its major monarchies were secure. Indeed, governments at every level were extending and deepening their control over people's lives, and the population itself was increasing. Europeans had also embarked on a new period of colonial expansion. Meanwhile, the Church had weathered the storms of the Avignon captivity and the Great Schism. Heresies had been suppressed or contained. In the struggle over conciliarism, the papacy had won the support of all major European rulers, which effectively relegated the conciliarists to academic isolation at the University of Paris. At the local level, the devotion of ordinary Christians was strong and the parish a crucial site of community identity. To be sure, there were some problems. The educational standards of parish clergy were higher than they had ever been, but reformers noted that too many priests were ignorant or neglectful of their spiritual duties. Monasticism, by and large, seemed to have lost its spiritual fire. Religious enthusiasm sometimes led to superstition. Yet, on the whole, these problems were manageable.

No one could have predicted that Europe's religious and political coherence would be irreparably shattered in the course of a generation, or that the next century would witness an appallingly destructive series of wars. Nor could anyone have foreseen that the catalyst for these extraordinary events would be a university professor. The debate ignited by Martin Luther (1483–1546) would set off the chain reaction we know as the Reformation. Initially intended as a call for another phase in the Church's long history of internal reforms, Luther's teachings instead launched a religious revolution that would splinter western Christendom into a variety of Protestant ("dissenting") faiths, while prompting the Roman Church to reaffirm its status as the only true Catholic ("universal") faith through a parallel revolution. At the same time, these movements deepened existing divisions among peoples, rulers, and states. The result was a profound transformation of the religious, social, and political landscape that affected the lives of everyone in Europe—and everyone in the new European colonies, then and now.

MARTIN LUTHER'S CHALLENGE

To explain the impact of Martin Luther's ideas, we must answer three central questions:

1. Why did Luther's theology lead him to break with Rome?
2. Why did large numbers of people rally to his cause?
3. Why did so many German princes and towns impose the new Protestant religion within their territories?

As we shall see, those who followed Luther found his message appealing for different reasons. Many peasants hoped that the new religion would free them from the exactions of their lords; towns and princes thought it would allow them to consolidate their political independence; national-

MARTIN LUTHER. This late portrait is by Lucas Cranach the Elder (1472–1553), court painter to the electors of Brandenburg and a friend of Luther.

ists thought it would liberate Germany from the demands of foreign popes bent on feathering their own nests in central Italy.

But what Luther's followers shared was a conviction that their new understanding of Christianity would lead to spiritual salvation, whereas the traditional religion of Rome would not. For this reason, *reformation* is a misleading term for the movement they initiated. Although Luther himself began as a reformer seeking to change the Church from within, he quickly developed into an uncompromising opponent of its principles and practices. Many of his followers were even more radical. The movement that began with Luther therefore went beyond "reformation." It was a frontal assault on religious, political, and social institutions that had been in place for a thousand years.

Luther's Quest for Justice

Although Martin Luther became an inspiration to millions, he was a terrible disappointment to his father. The elder Luther was a Thuringian peasant who had prospered through some in business ventures. Eager to see his clever son rise still further, he sent young Luther to the University of Erfurt to study law. In 1505, however, Martin shattered his hopes by becoming a monk of the Augustinian order. In some sense, though, Luther was a chip off the old block. Throughout his life, he lived simply and expressed himself in the vigorous, earthy vernacular of the German peasantry.

Luther arrived at his personal understanding of religious truth through a dramatic conversion experience. As a monk, he zealously pursued all the traditional means for achieving holiness. Not only did he fast and pray continuously, but also he reportedly confessed his sins so often that his exhausted confessor would sometimes jokingly suggest that he should do something really bad if he wanted to do penance. Yet, try as he might, Luther could find no spiritual peace; he feared that he could never perform enough good deeds to deserve so great a gift as salvation. But an insight then led to a new understanding of God's justice.

For years, Luther had worried that it seemed unfair for God to issue commandments that he knew humans could not observe—and then to punish them with eternal damnation. But after becoming a professor of theology at the University of Wittenberg, Luther's further study of the Bible suggested to him that God's justice lay not in his power to punish but rather in his mercy. As Luther later wrote, "I began to understand the justice of God as that by which God makes us just, in his mercy and through faith . . . and at this I felt as though I had been born again, and had gone through open gates into paradise." Since this realization came to Luther in the tower room of his monastery, it is often termed his "tower experience."

Lecturing at Wittenberg in the years immediately following this incident, which occurred around 1515, Luther pondered a passage in Saint Paul's Letter to the Romans—"[T]he just shall live by faith" (1:17)—until he reached his central doctrine of "justification by faith alone." Luther

LUTHER'S TRANSLATION OF THE BIBLE. The printing press was instrumental to the rapid dissemination of Luther's messages, as well as those of his supporters and challengers. Also essential was the fact that Luther addressed his audience in plain language, in their native German, and that pamphlets and vernacular Bibles like this one could be rapidly and cheaply mass produced.

concluded that God's justice does not demand endless good works and religious rituals for salvation, because humans can never be saved by their own weak efforts. Rather, humans are saved by God's grace alone, which God offers as an utterly undeserved gift to those whom he has predestined for salvation. Because this grace comes to humans through the gift of faith, men and women are "justified" (i.e., made worthy of salvation) by faith alone. Those whom God has justified through faith will manifest that fact by performing works of piety and charity; but such works are not what saves them. Piety and charity are merely visible signs of each believer's invisible spiritual state, which is known to God alone.

SAINT PETER'S BASILICA, ROME. The construction of a new papal palace and monumental church was begun in 1506. This enormous complex replaced a modest, dilapidated Romanesque basilica that had replaced an even older church built on the site of the apostle Peter's tomb. ▪ *How might this building project have been interpreted in different ways, depending on one's attitude toward the papacy?*

The essence of this doctrine was not original to Luther. It had been central to the thought of Augustine (see Chapter 6), the patron saint of Luther's own monastic order. During the twelfth and thirteenth centuries, however, theologians such as Peter Lombard and Thomas Aquinas (see Chapter 9) had developed a very different understanding of salvation. They emphasized the role that the Church itself (through its sacraments) and the individual believer (through acts of piety and charity) could play in the process of salvation. None of these theologians claimed that a human being could earn his or her way to heaven by good works alone, but the late medieval Church had encouraged this misunderstanding by presenting the process of salvation in increasingly quantitative terms—declaring, for example, that by performing a specific action (such as a pilgrimage or a pious donation), a believer could reduce the penance she or he owed to God by a specific number of days.

Since the fourteenth century, popes had claimed to dispense such special grace from the so-called Treasury of Merits, a storehouse of surplus good works piled up by Christ and the saints in heaven. By the late fifteenth century, when Luther was a child, the papacy began to claim that the dead could receive this grace, too, and so speed their way through purgatory. In both cases, grace was withdrawn from this "Treasury" through indulgences: special remissions of penitential obligations. When indulgences were first conceived in the eleventh and twelfth centuries, they could be earned only by demanding spiritual exercises, such as joining a crusade. By the end of the fifteenth century, however, indulgences were for sale.

To many, this looked like heresy, specifically simony: the sin of exchanging God's grace for cash. It had been a practice loudly condemned by Wyclif and his followers (see Chapter 11), and it was even more widely criticized by reformers like Erasmus (see Chapter 12). But Luther's objections to indulgences had much more radical consequences, because they rested on a set of theological premises that, taken to their logical conclusion, resulted in dismantling much of contemporary religious practice, not to mention the authority and sanctity of the Church. Luther himself does not appear to have realized this at first. But as the implications of his ideas became clear, he did not withdraw them. Instead, he pressed on.

The Scandal of Indulgences

Luther developed his ideas in an academic setting, but in 1517 he was provoked by a local abuse of spiritual power into attacking actual practice. The worldly bishop

POPE LEO X. Raphael's portrait shows the pope with his nephews: Giulio de' Medici (who would succeed him as pope in 1523) and Cardinal de Rossi.

Albert of Hohenzollern, youngest brother of the elector of Brandenburg, had sunk into debt and paid a large sum for papal permission to hold the lucrative bishoprics of Magdeburg and Halberstadt concurrently—even though, at twenty-three, he was not old enough to be a bishop at all. Moreover, when the prestigious archbishopric of Mainz fell vacant in the next year, Albert bought that, too. Obtaining the necessary funds by taking out loans from a German banking firm, he then struck a bargain with Pope Leo X (r. 1513–21): Leo would authorize the sale of indulgences in Albert's ecclesiastical territories—where Luther lived—with the understanding that half of the income would go to Rome for the building of St. Peter's Basilica, the other half to Albert.

Luther did not know the sordid details of Albert's bargain, but he did know that a Dominican friar named Tetzel was soon hawking indulgences throughout much of the region and that Tetzel was deliberately giving people the impression that an indulgence was an automatic ticket to heaven for oneself or one's loved ones in purgatory. For Luther, this was doubly offensive: not only was Tetzel violating Luther's conviction that people are saved by God's grace, not the purchase of papal favors; he was also misleading people into thinking that if they purchased an indulgence, they no longer needed to confess their sins to a priest. Tetzel was thus putting innocent souls at risk. So Luther's ninety-five theses were focused on dismantling the doctrine of indulgences.

Luther wrote up these points for debate in Latin, not German, but they were soon translated and published even more widely, and the hitherto obscure academic suddenly gained widespread notoriety. Tetzel and his allies demanded that Luther withdraw his theses. Rather than backing down, however, Luther became even bolder in his attacks. In 1519, at a public disputation held in Leipzig and attended by throngs of people, Luther defiantly maintained that the pope and all clerics were merely fallible men and that the highest authority for an individual's conscience was the truth of scripture.

Luther's year of greatest activity came in 1520, when he composed a series of pamphlets setting forth his three primary premises: justification by faith, the authority of scripture, and "the priesthood of all believers." We have already examined the meaning of the first premise. By the second, he meant that the reading of scripture took precedence over Church traditions—including the teachings of all theologians—and that beliefs (such as purgatory) or practices (such as prayers to the saints) not explicitly grounded in scripture should be rejected as human inventions. Luther also declared that Christian believers were spiritually equal before God, which meant denying that priests, monks, and nuns had any special qualities by virtue of their vocations: hence "the priesthood of all believers."

From these premises, a host of practical consequences logically followed. Because works could not lead to salvation, Luther declared fasts, pilgrimages, and the veneration of relics to be spiritually valueless. He also called for the dissolution of all monasteries and convents. He advocated a demystification of religious rites, proposing the substitution of German and other vernaculars for Latin and calling for a reduction in the number of sacraments from seven to two. In his view, the only true sacraments were baptism and the Eucharist, both of which had been instituted by Christ. (Later, he included penance.) Although Luther continued to believe that Christ was really present in the consecrated bread and wine of the Lord's Supper, he insisted that it was only through the faith of each individual believer that this sacrament could lead anyone to God; it was not a magical act performed by a priest.

To further emphasize that those who served the Church had no supernatural authority, Luther insisted on calling them "ministers" or "pastors" rather than priests. He also

Decoding Printed Propaganda

The printing press has been credited with helping to spread the teachings of Martin Luther, and so securing the success of the Protestant Reformation. But even before Luther's critiques were published, reformers were using the new technology to disseminate images that attacked the corruption of the Church.

After Luther rose to prominence, both his supporters and detractors vied with one another in disseminating propaganda that appealed, visually, to a lay audience and that could be understood even by those who were unable to read.

The first pair of images below is really a single printed artifact datable to around 1500: an early example of a "pop-up" card. It shows Pope Alexander VI (r. 1492–1503) as stately pontiff (image A) whose true identity is concealed by a flap. When the flap is raised (image B), he is revealed as a devil. The Latin texts read: "Alexander VI, *pontifex maximus*" (image A) and "I am the pope" (image B).

The other two examples represent two sides of the debate as it had developed by 1530, and both do so with reference to the same image: the seven-headed

A. Alexander as pontiff.

B. Alexander as a devil.

beast mentioned in the Bible's Book of Revelation. On the left (image C), a Lutheran engraving shows the papacy as the beast, with seven heads representing seven orders of Catholic clergy. The sign on the cross (referring to the sign hung over the head of the crucified Christ) reads, in German: "For money, a sack full of indulgences." The Latin words on either side say "Reign of the Devil." On the right (image D), a Catholic engraving produced in Germany shows Luther as Revelation's beast, with its seven heads labeled: "Doctor–Martin–Luther–Heretic–Hypocrite–Fanatic–Barabbas," the last alluding to the thief who should have been executed instead of Jesus, according to the Gospels.

Questions for Analysis

1. Given that this attack on Pope Alexander VI precedes Martin Luther's critique of the Church by nearly two decades, what can you conclude about its intended audience? To what extent can it be read as a barometer of popular disapproval? What might have been the reason(s) for the use of the concealing flap?

2. What do you make of the fact that both Catholic and Protestant propagandists were using the same imagery? What do you make of key differences: for example, the fact that the seven-headed beast representing the papacy sprouts out of an altar in which a Eucharistic chalice is displayed, while the seven-headed Martin Luther is reading a book?

3. All of these printed images also make use of words. Would the message of each image be clear without the use of texts? Why or why not?

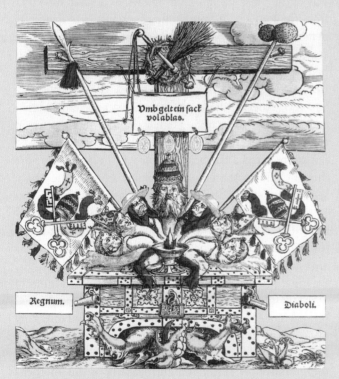

C. The seven-headed papal beast.

D. The seven-headed Martin Luther.

proposed to abolish the entire ecclesiastical hierarchy from popes to bishops on down. Finally, on the principle that no spiritual distinction existed between clergy and laity, Luther argued that ministers could and should marry. In 1525, he himself took a wife, Katharina von Bora, one of a dozen nuns he had helped escape from a Cistercian convent.

The Break with Rome

Widely disseminated by means of the printing press, Luther's polemical pamphlets of 1520 electrified much of Germany, gaining him passionate popular support and touching off a national religious revolt against the papacy. In highly colloquial German, Luther declared that "if the pope's court were reduced ninety-nine percent it would still be large enough to give decisions on matters of faith"; that "the cardinals have sucked Italy dry and now turn to Germany"; and that, given Rome's corruption, "the reign of Antichrist could not be worse." As word of Luther's defiance spread, his pamphlets became a publishing sensation. Whereas the average press run of a printed book before 1520 had been 1,000 copies, the first run of *To the Christian Nobility* (1520) was 4,000—and it sold out in a few days. Many thousands of copies quickly followed. Even more popular were woodcut illustrations mocking the papacy and exalting Luther. These sold in the tens of thousands and could be readily understood even by those who could not read. (See **Interpreting Visual Evidence** on pages 428–29.)

Luther's denunciations reflected widespread public dissatisfaction with the conduct and corruption of the papacy. Pope Alexander VI (r. 1492–1503) had bribed cardinals to gain his office and had then used the money raised from the papal jubilee of 1500 to support the military campaigns of his illegitimate son. Julius II (r. 1503–13) devoted his reign to enlarging the Papal States in a series of wars; a contemporary remarked that he would have deserved the glory he won—if only he had been a secular prince. Leo X (r. 1513–21), Luther's opponent, was a member of the Medici family of Florence. Although an able administrator, he was also a self-indulgent aesthete. In *The Praise of Folly*, first published in 1511 and frequently reprinted (see Chapter 12), Erasmus had declared that if the popes of his day were ever forced to lead Christlike lives, as their office surely required, they would be incapable of it. In *Julius Excluded*, published anonymously in 1517, he went even further, imagining a conversation at the gates of heaven between Saint Peter and Julius II, in which Peter refuses to admit the pope because he cannot believe that this armored, vainglorious figure could possibly be his own earthly representative.

In Germany, resentment of the papacy ran especially high because there were no special agreements (concordats) limiting papal authority in its principalities, as there were in Spain, France, and England (see Chapter 12). As a result, German princes complained that papal taxes were so high that the country was drained of its wealth. And yet Germans had almost no influence over papal policy. Frenchmen, Spaniards, and Italians dominated the College of Cardinals and the papal bureaucracy, and the popes were almost invariably Italian—as they would continue to be until 1978 and the election of Pope John Paul II. As a result, graduates from the rapidly growing German universities almost never found employment in Rome. Instead, many joined the throngs of Luther's supporters to become leaders of the new religious movement.

Emperor Charles V and the Condemnation at Worms

In the year 1520, Pope Leo X issued a papal edict condemning Luther's publications as heretical and threatening him with excommunication if he did not recant. This edict was of the most solemn kind, known as a *bulla,* or "bull," from the lead seal it bore. Luther's reponse was flagrantly defiant: rather than acquiescing to the pope's demand, he staged a public burning of the document. Thereafter, his heresy confirmed, he was formally given over for punishment to his lay overlord, Frederick III "the Wise" of Saxony. Frederick, however, proved a supporter of Luther and a critic of the papacy. Rather than burning Luther at the stake for heresy, Frederick declared that Luther had not yet received a fair hearing. Early in 1521, he therefore brought him to the city of Worms to be examined by a select representative assembly known as a "diet."

At Worms, the diet's presiding officer was the newly elected Holy Roman Emperor, Charles V. As a member of the Habsburg family, he had been born and bred in his ancestral holding of Flanders, then part of the Netherlands. By 1521, however, through the unpredictable workings of dynastic inheritance, marriage, election, and luck, he had become not only the ruler of the Netherlands but also king of Germany and Holy Roman emperor, duke of Austria, duke of Milan, and ruler of the Franche-Comté. And as the grandson of Ferdinand and Isabella on his mother's side, he was also king of Spain; king of Naples, Sicily, and Sardinia; and ruler of all the Spanish possessions in the New World. Governing such an extraordinary combination

THE EUROPEAN EMPIRE OF CHARLES V, c. 1526. Charles V ruled a vast variety of widely dispersed territories in Europe and the New World, and as Holy Roman emperor he was also the titular ruler of Germany. ■ *What were the main countries and kingdoms under his control?* ■ *Which regions would have been most threatened by Charles's extraordinary power, and where might the rulers of these regions turn for allies?* ■ *How might the expansion of the Ottoman Empire have complicated political and religious struggles within Christian Europe?*

of territories posed enormous challenges. Charles's empire had no capital and no centralized administrative institutions; it shared no common language, no common culture, and no geographically contiguous borders. It thus stood completely apart from the growing nationalism that was shaping late medieval states.

Charles recognized the diversity of his empire and tried wherever possible to rule it through local officials and institutions. But he could not tolerate threats to the two fundamental forces that held his empire together: himself as emperor and Catholicism—as the religion of Rome was coming to be called. Beyond such political calculations,

THE WARTBURG, EISENACH (GERMANY). This medieval stronghold became the refuge of Martin Luther after his condemnation at the Diet of Worms in 1520. His room in the castle has since been preserved.

THE EMPEROR CHARLES V. This portrait by the Venetian painter Titian depicts Europe's most powerful ruler sitting quietly in a chair, dressed in simple clothing of the kind worn by judges or bureaucrats. ▪ *Why might Charles have chosen to represent himself in this way—rather than in the regalia of his many royal, imperial, and princely offices?*

however, Charles was also a faithful and committed servant of the Church, and he was deeply disturbed by the prospect of heresy within his empire. There was therefore little doubt that the Diet of Worms would condemn Martin Luther for heresy. And when Luther refused to back down, thereby endangering his life, his lord Frederick the Wise once more intervened, this time arranging for Luther to be "kidnapped" and hidden for a year at the elector's castle of the Wartburg, where he was kept out of harm's way.

Thereafter, Luther was never again in mortal danger. Although the Diet of Worms proclaimed him an outlaw, this edict was never enforced. Instead, Charles V left Germany in order to conduct a war with France, and in 1522 Luther returned in triumph to Wittenberg, to find that the changes he had called for had already been put into practice by his university supporters. When several German princes formally converted to Lutheranism, they brought their territories with them. In a little over a decade, a new form of Christianity had been established.

The German Princes and the Lutheran Church

At this point, the last of our three major questions must be addressed: Why did some German princes, secure in their own powers, nonetheless establish Lutheran religious practices within their territories? This is a crucial development, because popular support for Luther would not have been enough to ensure the success of his teachings had they not been embraced by a number of powerful rulers and free cities. Indeed, it was only in those territories where Lutheranism was formally established that the new religion prevailed. Elsewhere in Germany, Luther's sympathizers were forced to flee, face death, or conform to Catholicism.

The power of individual rulers to control the practice of religion in their own territories reflects developments we have noted in previous chapters. Rulers had long sought to control appointments to Church offices in their own realms, to restrict the flow of money to Rome and to limit the independence of ecclesiastical courts. The monarchs of Europe—primarily the kings of France and Spain—had already taken advantage of the continuing struggles between the papacy and the conciliarists to extract many concessions from the embattled popes during the fifteenth century (see Chapters 11 and 12). But in Germany, as noted above, neither the emperor nor the princes were strong enough to secure special treatment.

This changed as a result of Luther's initiatives. As early as 1520, the papacy's fiery challenger had recognized

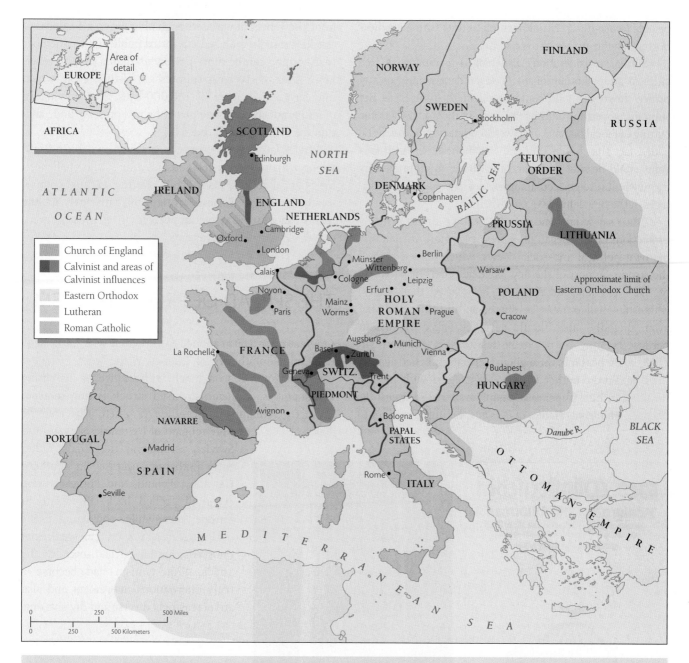

CONFESSIONAL DIFFERENCES, c. 1560. The religious affiliations (confessions) of Europe's territories had become very complicated by the year 1560, roughly a generation after the adoption of Lutheranism in some areas. ▪ *What major countries and kingdoms had embraced Protestantism by 1560?* ▪ *To what extent do these divisions conform to political boundaries, and to what extent would they have complicated the political situation?* ▪ *Why might Lutheranism have spread north into Scandinavia but not south into Bavaria or west across the Rhine?*

that he could never hope to institute new religious practices without the strong arms of princes, so he explicitly encouraged them to confiscate the wealth of the Church as an incentive. At first the princes bided their time, but when they realized that Luther had enormous public support and that Charles V could not act swiftly enough, several moved to introduce Lutheranism into their territories. Personal piety surely played a role in

individual cases, but political and economic considerations were generally more decisive. Protestant princes could consolidate authority by naming their own religious officials, cutting off fees to Rome, and curtailing the jurisdiction of Church courts. They could also guarantee that the political and religious boundaries of their territories would now coincide. No longer would a rival ecclesiastical prince (such as a bishop or archbishop) be able to use his spiritual position to undermine a neighboring secular prince's sovereignty.

Similar considerations also moved a number of free cities to adopt Lutheranism. Acting independently of any prince, town councils could establish themselves as the supreme governing authorities within their jurisdictions, cutting out local bishops or powerful monasteries. Given the added fact that under Lutheranism monasteries and convents could be shut down and their lands appropriated by the newly sovereign secular authorities, the practical advantages of the new faith were overwhelming.

Once safely ensconced in Wittenberg under princely protection, Luther began to express ever more vehemently his own political and social views, which tended toward the strong support of the new political order. In a treatise of 1523, *On Temporal Authority*, he insisted that "godly" (Protestant) rulers must be obeyed in all things and that even "ungodly" ones should never be targets of dissent because tyranny "is not to be resisted but endured." In 1525, when peasants throughout Germany rebelled against their landlords, Luther therefore responded with intense hostility. In his vituperative pamphlet of 1525, *Against the Thievish, Murderous Hordes of Peasants*, he urged readers to hunt the rebels down as though they were mad dogs: to "strike, strangle, stab secretly or in public, and remember that nothing can be more poisonous than a man in rebellion." After the ruthless suppression of this revolt, which may have cost as many as 100,000 lives, the firm alliance of Lutheranism with state power helped preserve and sanction the existing social order.

In his later years, Luther concentrated on debating with younger, more radical religious reformers who challenged his political conservatism, while offering spiritual counsel to all who sought it. Never tiring in his amazingly prolific literary activity, he wrote an average of one treatise every two weeks for twenty-five years.

THE SPREAD OF PROTESTANTISM

Originating as a term applied to Lutherans who "protested" the Catholic authority of Charles V, the word *Protestant* was soon applied to a much wider range of dissenting Christianities. Lutheranism itself struck lasting roots in northern Germany and Scandinavia, where it became the state religion of Denmark, Norway, and Sweden as soon as the 1520s. Other early Lutheran successes in southern Germany, Poland, and Hungary were eventually rolled back. Elsewhere in Europe, meanwhile, competing forms of Protestantism soon emerged from the seeds that Luther had sown. By the 1550s, Protestantism had become a truly international movement and also an increasingly diverse and divisive one.

Protestantism in Switzerland

In the early sixteenth century, Switzerland was ruled neither by kings nor by territorial princes; instead, prosperous Swiss cities were either independent or on the verge of becoming so. Hence, when the leading citizens of a Swiss municipality decided to adopt Protestant reforms, no one could stop them. Although religious arrangements varied from city to city, three main forms

THE ANABAPTISTS' CAGES, THEN AND NOW. After the three Anabaptist leaders of Münster were executed in 1535, their corpses were prominently displayed in cages hung from a tower of the marketplace church. As can be seen from the photo on the right, the bones are gone but the iron cages remain. ▪ *What would be the purpose of keeping these cages on display? What different meanings might this sight convey?*

of Protestantism emerged in Switzerland between 1520 to 1550: Zwinglianism, Anabaptism, and Calvinism.

Zwinglianism, founded by Ulrich Zwingli (*TSVING-lee*, 1484–1531) in Zürich, was the most theologically moderate form of the three. Zwingli had just begun his career as a Catholic priest when his humanist-inspired study of the Bible convinced him that Catholic theology and practice conflicted with the Gospels. His biblical studies eventually led him to condemn religious images and hierarchical authority within the Church. Yet he did not speak out publicly until Luther set a precedent. In 1522, accordingly, Zwingli began attacking the authority of the Catholic Church in Zürich. Soon much of northern Switzerland had accepted his religious leadership.

Although Zwingli's reforms closely resembled those of the Lutherans in Germany, Zwingli differed from Luther as to the theology of the Eucharist. Whereas Luther believed in the real presence of Christ's body in the sacrament, for Zwingli the Eucharist conferred no grace at all; it was simply a reminder and celebration of Christ's historical sacrifice on the cross. This fundamental disagreement prevented Lutherans and Zwinglians from uniting in a common Protestant front. When Zwingli died in battle against Catholic forces in 1531, his movement was absorbed by the more systematic Protestantism of John Calvin (see below).

Before Calvinism prevailed, however, an even more radical form of Protestantism arose in Switzerland and parts of Germany. The first Anabaptists were members of Zwingli's circle in Zürich, but they broke with him around 1525 on the issue of infant baptism. Because Anabaptists were convinced that the sacrament of baptism was only effective if administered to willing adults who understood its significance, they required followers who had been baptized as infants to be baptized again as adults (the term *Anabaptism* means "rebaptism"). This doctrine reflected the Anabaptists' fundamental belief that the true church was a small community of believers whose members had to make a deliberate, inspired decision to join it.

No other Protestant groups were prepared to go so far in rejecting the medieval Christian view of the Church as a single vast body to which all members of society belonged from birth. And in an age when almost everyone assumed that religious and secular authority were inextricably connected, Anabaptism was bound to be anathema to all established powers, both Protestant and Catholic. It was a movement that appealed to sincere religious piety in calling for pacifism, strict personal morality, and extreme simplicity of worship.

This changed when a group of Anabaptist extremists managed to gain control of the German city of Münster in 1534. These zealots were driven by millenarianism, the belief that God intends to institute a completely new order of justice and spirituality throughout the world before the end of time. Determined to help God bring about this goal, the extremists attempted to turn Münster into a new Jerusalem. A former tailor named John of Leyden assumed the title "king of the New Temple" and proclaimed himself the successor of the Hebrew king David. Under his leadership, Anabaptist religious practices were made obligatory, private property was abolished, and even polygamy was permitted on the grounds of Old Testament precedents. Such practices were deeply shocking to Protestants and Catholics alike. Accordingly, Münster was besieged and captured by Catholic forces little more than a year after the Anabaptist takeover. The new "David," together with two of his lieutenants, was put to death by torture, and the three bodies were displayed in iron cases in the town square.

Thereafter, Anabaptists throughout Europe were ruthlessly persecuted on all sides. The few who survived banded together in the Mennonite sect, named for its founder, the Dutchman Menno Simons (c. 1496–1561). This sect, dedicated to pacifism and the simple "religion of the heart" of original Anabaptism, is still particularly strong in the central United States.

John Calvin's Reformed Theology

A year after the events in Münster, a twenty-six-year-old Frenchman named John Calvin (1509–1564), published the first version of his *Institutes of the Christian Religion*, the most influential formulation of Protestant theology ever written. Born in Noyon, in northern France, Calvin had originally trained for the law; but by 1533, he was studying the Greek and Latin classics while living off the income from a priestly benefice. As he later wrote, he was "obstinately devoted to the superstitions of popery" until he experienced a miraculous conversion. He became a Protestant theologian and propagandist, evenually fleeing the Swiss city of Basel to escape persecution.

Although some aspects of Calvin's early career resemble those of Luther's, the two men were very different. Luther was an emotionally volatile personality and a lover of controversy. He responded to theological problems as they arose or as the impulse struck him; he never attempted to systematize his beliefs. Calvin, however, was a coolly analytical legalist, who resolved in his *Institutes* to set forth all the principles of Protestantism comprehensively, logically, and systematically. As a result, after several revisions and enlargements (the definitive edition appeared in 1559), Calvin's *Institutes* became the Protestant equivalent of Thomas Aquinas's *Summa Theologiae* (see Chapter 9).

JOHN CALVIN. This recently discovered portrait by an anonymous artist shows the young Protestant reformer as a serene and authoritative figure. It places the grotesque caricature of Calvin (right) in perspective.

CALVIN AS SEEN BY HIS ENEMIES. In this image, which circulated among Calvin's Catholic detractors, the reformer's facial features are a disturbing composite of fish, toad, and chicken.

Calvin's austere and stoical theology started with the omnipotence of God. For Calvin, the entire universe depends utterly on the will of the Almighty, who created all things for his greater glory and who knows all things present and to come. Because of man's original fall from grace, all human beings are sinners by nature, bound to an evil inheritance they cannot escape. Yet God (for reasons of his own) has predestined some for eternal salvation and damned all the rest to the torments of hell. Nothing that individual humans may do can alter fate; all souls are stamped with God's blessing or curse before they are born. Nevertheless, Christians cannot be indifferent to their conduct on earth. If they are among the elect, God will implant in them the desire to live according to his laws. Upright conduct is thus a sign, though not an infallible one, that an individual has been chosen to sit at the throne of glory. Membership in the Reformed Church (as Calvinist churches are more properly known) is another presumptive sign of election to salvation. But most of all, Calvin urged Christians to conceive of themselves as chosen instruments of God, charged to work actively to fulfill God's purposes on earth. Because sin offends God, Christians should do all they can to prevent it, not because their actions will lead to anyone's salvation (they will not), but simply because God's glory is diminished if sin is allowed to flourish unchecked by the efforts of those whom he has chosen for salvation.

Calvin always acknowledged a great theological debt to Luther, but his religious teachings diverged from those of the Wittenberg reformer in several essentials. First of all, Luther's attitude toward proper Christian conduct in the world was much more passive than Calvin's. For Luther, a Christian should endure the trials of this life through suffering, whereas for Calvin the world was to be mastered in unceasing labor for God's sake. Calvin's religion was also more controlling than Luther's. Luther, for example, insisted that his followers attend church on Sunday, but he did not demand that during the remainder of the day they refrain from all pleasure or work. Calvin, however, issued stern strictures against worldliness of any sort on the Sabbath and forbade all sorts of minor self-indulgences, even on non-Sabbath days.

The two men also differed on fundamental matters of church governance and worship. Although Luther broke with the Catholic system of hierarchical church government, Lutheran district superintendents exercised some of the same powers as bishops, including supervision of parish clergy. Luther also retained many features of traditional Christian worship, including altars, music, and ritual. Calvin, however, rejected everything that smacked to him of "popery." He argued for the elimination of all traces of hierarchy within any church. Instead, each congregation should elect its own ministers, and assemblies of ministers and "elders" (laymen responsible for maintaining proper religious conduct among the faithful) were to govern the Reformed Church as a whole. Calvin also insisted on the utmost simplicity in worship, prohibiting (among much else) vestments, processions, instrumental music, and religious images of any sort, including stained-glass windows. He also dispensed with all remaining vestiges of Catholic sacramental theology by making the sermon, rather than the Eucharist, the centerpiece of reformed worship.

Calvinism in Geneva

Consistent with his theological convictions, Calvin was intent on putting his religious teachings into practice. Sensing an opportunity in the French-speaking Swiss city of Geneva—then in the throes of political and religious upheaval—he moved there late in 1536 and immediately began preaching and organizing. In 1538, his activities caused him to be expelled by the city council, but in 1541 he returned and brought the city under his sway.

With Calvin's guidance, Geneva's government became a theocracy. Supreme authority was vested in a "consistory" composed of twelve lay elders and between ten and twenty pastors, whose weekly meetings Calvin dominated. In addition to passing legislation proposed by a congregation of ministers, the consistory's main function was to supervise morality, both public and private. To this end, Geneva was divided into districts, and a committee of the consistory visited every household, without prior warning, to check on the behavior of its members. Dancing, card playing, attending the theater, and working or playing on the Sabbath: all were outlawed as works of the devil. Innkeepers were forbidden to allow anyone to consume food or drink without first saying grace, or to permit any patron to stay up after nine o'clock. Adultery, witchcraft, blasphemy, and heresy all became capital crimes. Even penalties for lesser crimes were severe. During the first four years after Calvin gained control in Geneva, there were no fewer than fifty-eight executions in this city with a total population of only 16,000.

As rigid as such a regime may seem today, Calvin's Geneva was a beacon of light to thousands of Protestants throughout Europe in the mid-sixteenth century. Calvin's disciple John Knox (c. 1514–1572), who brought the reformed religion to Scotland, declared Geneva "the most perfect school of Christ that ever was on earth since the days of the Apostles." Converts such as Knox flocked to Geneva for refuge or instruction and then returned home to become ardent proselytizers for the new religion. Geneva thus became the center of an international movement dedicated to spreading reformed religion to France and the rest of Europe through organized missionary activity and propaganda.

These efforts were remarkably successful. By the end of the sixteenth century, Calvinists were a majority in Scotland (where they were known as Presbyterians) and Holland (where they founded the Dutch Reformed Church). They were also influential in England, although the Church of England adopted reformed theology but not reformed worship (Calvinists who sought further reforms in worship were known as Puritans). There were also substantial Calvinist minorities in France (where they were called Huguenots), Germany, Hungary, Lithuania, and Poland. By the end of the sixteenth century, Calvinism would spread to the New World.

The Beginnings of Religious Warfare

Less than a generation after Luther's challenge to the Church, wars between Catholic and Protestant rulers began. In Germany, Charles V attempted to establish Catholic unity by launching a military campaign against several German princes who had instituted Lutheran worship in their territories. But despite several notable victories, his efforts to defeat the Protestant princes failed. In part, this was because Charles was also involved in wars against France; but primarily, it was because the Catholic princes of Germany worked against him, fearing that any suppression of Protestant princes might also diminish their own independence. As a result, the Catholic princes' support for the foreign-born Charles was only lukewarm; at times, they even joined with Protestants in battle against him.

This regional warfare sputtered on and off until a compromise settlement was reached via the Peace of Augsburg in 1555. Its governing principle was *cuius regio, eius religio,* "as the ruler, so the religion." This meant that in those principalities where Lutherans ruled, Lutheranism would be the sole state religion; but where Catholic princes ruled, the people of their territories would also be Catholic. For better and for worse, the Peace of Augsburg was a historical milestone. For the first time since Luther had been excommunicated, Catholic rulers were forced to acknowledge the legality of Protestantism. Yet the peace also set a dangerous precedent because it established the principle that no sovereign state can tolerate religious diversity. Moreover, it excluded Calvinism entirely and thus spurred German Calvinists to become aggressive opponents of the status quo. As a result, Europe would be riven by religious warfare for another century and would export sectarian violence to the New World (see Chapter 14).

THE DOMESTICATION OF REFORM

Within two decades, Protestantism had become a diverse revolutionary movement whose radical claims for the spiritual equality of all Christians had the potential to undermine the political, social, and even gender hierarchies on which European society rested. Luther himself did not anticipate that his ideas might have such implications, and he was genuinely shocked when the rebellious German peasants and the radical Anabaptists at Münster interpreted his teachings in this way. And Luther was by no means the only staunchly conservative Protestant. None of the prominent early Protestants were social or political radicals; most depended on the support of existing elites: territorial princes, of course, but also the ruling elites of towns. As a result, the Reformation movement was speedily "domesticated" in two senses. Its revolutionary potential was muffled—Luther himself rarely spoke about "the priesthood of all believers" after 1525—and there was an increasing emphasis on the patriarchal family as the central institution of reformed life.

Reform and Discipline

As we have seen, injunctions to lead a more disciplined and godly life had been a frequent message of religious reform movements since the Black Death (see Chapter 11). Many of these efforts were actively promoted by princes and town councils, most famously perhaps in Florence, where the Dominican preacher Girolamo Savonarola led the city on an extraordinary but short-lived campaign of puritanism and moral reform between 1494 and 1498. And there are numerous other examples of rulers legislating against sin. When Desiderius Erasmus called on secular authorities to think of themselves as abbots and of their territories as giant monasteries, he was sounding an already-familiar theme.

Protestant rulers, however, took the need to enforce godly discipline with particular seriousness, because the depravity of human nature was a fundamental tenet of Protestant belief. Like Saint Augustine at the end of the fourth century (see Chapter 6), Protestants believed that people would inevitably turn out bad unless they were compelled to be good. It was therefore the responsibility of secular and religious leaders to control and punish the behavior of their people, because otherwise their evil deeds would anger God and destroy human society.

Protestant godliness began with the discipline of children. Luther himself wrote two catechisms (instructional tracts) designed to teach children the tenets of their faith and the obligations—toward parents, masters, and rulers—that God imposed on them. Luther also insisted that all children, boys and girls alike, be taught to read the Bible in their own languages. Schooling thus became a characteristically Protestant preoccupation and rallying cry. Even the Protestant family was designated a "school of godliness," in which fathers were expected to instruct and discipline their wives, their children, and their household servants.

But family life in the early sixteenth century still left much to be desired in the eyes of Protestant reformers. Drunkenness, domestic violence, illicit sexual relations, lewd dancing, and the blasphemous swearing of oaths were frequent topics of reforming discourse. Various methods of discipline were attempted, including private counseling, public confessions of wrongdoing, public penances and shamings, exclusion from church services, and even imprisonment. All these efforts met with varying, but generally modest, success. Creating godly Protestant families, and enforcing godly discipline on entire communities, was going to require the active cooperation of godly authorities.

Protestantism, Government, and the Family

The domestication of the Reformation in this sense took place principally in the free towns of Germany, Switzerland, and the Netherlands—and from there spread westward to North America. Protestant attacks on monasticism and clerical celibacy found a receptive audience among townsmen who resented the immunity of monastic houses from taxation and regarded clerical celibacy as a subterfuge for the seduction of their own wives and daughters. Protestant emphasis on the depravity of the human will and the consequent need for that will to be disciplined by authority also resonated powerfully with guilds and town governments, which were anxious to maintain and increase the control exercised by urban elites (mainly merchants and master craftsmen) over the apprentices and journeymen who made up the majority of the male population. By eliminating the competing jurisdictional authority of the Catholic Church, Protestantism allowed town governments to consolidate all authority within the city into their own hands.

Competing Viewpoints

Marriage and Celibacy: Two Views

These two selections illustrate the strongly contrasting views on the spiritual value of marriage versus celibacy that came to be embraced by Protestant and Catholic religious authorities. The first selection is part of Martin Luther's more general attack on monasticism, which emphasizes his contention that marriage is the natural and divinely intended state for all human beings. The second selection, from the decrees of the Council of Trent (1545–63), restates traditional Catholic teaching on the holiness of marriage but also emphasizes the spiritual superiority of virginity to marriage as well as the necessity of clerical celibacy.

Luther's Views on Celibacy (1535)

Listen! In all my days I have not heard the confession of a nun, but in the light of Scripture I shall hit upon how matters fare with her and know I shall not be lying. If a girl is not sustained by great and exceptional grace, she can live without a man as little as she can without eating, drinking, sleeping, and other natural necessities.

Nor, on the other hand, can a man dispense with a wife. The reason for this is that procreating children is an urge planted as deeply in human nature as eating and drinking. That is why God has given and put into the body the organs, arteries, fluxes, and everything that serves it. Therefore what is he doing who would check this process and keep

nature from running its desired and intended course? He is attempting to keep nature from being nature, fire from burning, water from wetting, and a man from eating, drinking, and sleeping.

Source: E. M. Plass, ed., *What Luther Says,* vol. 2 (St. Louis, MO: 1959), pp. 888–89.

Canons on the Sacrament of Matrimony (1563)

Canon 1. If anyone says that matrimony is not truly and properly one of the seven sacraments . . . instituted by Christ the Lord, but has been devised by men in the Church and does not confer grace, let him be anathema [cursed].

Canon 9. If anyone says that clerics constituted in sacred orders or regulars [monks and nuns] who have made solemn profession of chastity can contract marriage . . . and that all who feel that they have not the gift of chastity, even though they have made such a vow, can

contract marriage, let him be anathema, since God does not refuse that gift to those who ask for it rightly, neither does *he suffer us to be tempted above that which we are able.*

Canon 10: If anyone says that the married state excels the state of virginity or celibacy, and that it is better and happier to be united in matrimony than to remain in virginity or celibacy, let him be anathema.

Source: H. J. Schroeder, *Canons and Decrees of the Council of Trent* (St. Louis, MO: 1941), pp. 181–82.

Questions for Analysis

1. On what grounds does Luther attack the practice of celibacy? Do you agree with his basic premise?

2. How do the later canons of the Catholic Church respond to Protestant views like Luther's? What appears to be at stake in this defense of marriage and celibacy?

Meanwhile, Protestantism reinforced the control of individual men over their own households by emphasizing the family as the basic unit of religious education. In place of a priest, an all-powerful father figure was expected to assume responsibility for instructing and disciplining his household according to the precepts of reformed religion. At the same time, Protestantism introduced a new religious ideal for women. No longer was the original nun the exemplar of female holiness; in her place now stood the married and obedient Protestant "goodwife." As one Lutheran prince wrote in 1527: "Those who bear children please God better than all the monks and nuns singing and praying." To this extent, Protestantism resolved the tensions between piety and sexuality that had long characterized Christian teachings, by declaring the holiness of marital sex.

But this did not promote a new view of women's spiritual potential, nor did it elevate their social and political status. Quite the contrary: Luther regarded women as more sexually driven than men and less capable of controlling their sexual desires—reflecting the fact that Luther confessed himself incapable of celibacy. His opposition to convents allegedly rested on his belief that it was impossible for women to remain chaste, so sequestering them simply made illicit behavior inevitable. To prevent sin, it was necessary that all women should be married, preferably at a young age, and so placed under the governance of a godly husband.

For the most part, Protestant town governments were happy to cooperate in shutting down female monasteries. The convent's property went to the town, after all. But conflicts did arise between Protestant reformers and town fathers over marriage and sexuality, especially over the reformers' insistence that both men and women should marry young as a restraint on lust. In many towns, men were traditionally expected to delay marriage until they had achieved the status of master craftsman—a requirement that had become increasingly difficult to enforce as guilds sought to restrict the number of journeymen permitted to become masters. In theory, then, apprentices and journeymen were not supposed to marry. Instead, they were expected to frequent brothels and taverns, a legally sanctioned outlet for extramarital sexuality long viewed as necessary to men's physical well-being, but that Protestant reformers now deemed morally abhorrent.

Towns responded in a variety of ways to these opposing pressures. Some instituted special committees to police public morals, of the sort we have noted in Calvin's Geneva. Some abandoned Protestantism altogether. Others, like the German town of Augsburg, alternated between Protestantism and Catholicism for several decades. Yet regardless of a town's final choice of religious allegiance, by the end of the sixteenth century a revolution had taken place with respect to governments' attitudes toward public morality. In their competition with each other, neither Catholics nor Protestants wished to be seen as soft on sin. The result was the widespread abolition of publicly licensed brothels, the outlawing of prostitution, and far stricter governmental supervision of many other aspects of private life than had ever been the case in any Western civilization.

The Control of Marriage

Protestantism also increased parents' control over their children's choice of marital partners. The medieval Church had defined marriage as a sacrament that did not require the involvement of a priest. The mutual free consent of two individuals, even if given without witnesses or parental approval, was enough to constitute a legally valid marriage in the eyes of the Church. Opposition to this doctrine came from many quarters, especially from families who stood to lose from this liberal doctrine. Because marriage involved rights of inheritance to property, it was regarded as too important a matter to be left to the choice of adolescents. Instead, parents wanted the power to prevent unsuitable matches and, in some cases, to force their children to accept the marriage arrangements their families might negotiate on their behalf. Protestantism offered an opportunity to achieve such control. Luther had declared marriage to be a purely secular matter, not a sacrament at all, and one that could be regulated however the governing authorities thought best. Calvin largely followed suit, although Calvinist theocracy drew less of a distinction than did Lutheranism between the powers of church and state.

Even the Catholic Church was eventually forced to give way. Although it never abandoned its insistence that both members of a couple must freely consent to their marriage, by the end of the sixteenth century the Church's new doctrine required formal public notice of intent to marry and insisted on the presence of a priest at the actual wedding ceremony. Both were efforts to prevent elopements, allowing families time to intervene before an unsuitable marriage was concluded. Individual Catholic countries sometimes went even further in trying to assert parental control over their children's choice of marital partners. In France, for example, although couples might still marry without parental consent, those who did so now forfeited all of their rights to inherit their families' property. In somewhat different ways, both Protestantism and Catholicism thus moved to strengthen the control that parents could exercise over their children—and, in the case of Protestantism, that husbands could exercise over their wives.

THE REFORMATION OF ENGLAND

In England, the Reformation took a rather different course than it did in continental Europe. Although a long tradition of popular reform survived into the sixteenth century, the number of dissidents was too small and their influence too limited to play a significant role there. Nor was England particularly oppressed by the papal exactions and abuses that roiled Germany. When the sixteenth century began, English monarchs already exercised close control over Church appointments within the kingdom; they also received the lion's share of the papal taxation collected from England. Nor did ecclesiastical courts inspire any particular resentments. On the contrary, these courts would continue to function in Protestant England until the eighteenth century. Why, then, did sixteenth-century England become a Protestant country at all?

"The King's Great Matter"

In 1527, King Henry VIII of England had been married to Ferdinand and Isabella's daughter, Catherine of Aragon, for eighteen years. Yet all the offspring of this union had died

HENRY VIII OF ENGLAND. Hans Holbein the Younger executed several portraits of the English king. This one represents him in middle age, confident of his powers.

in infancy, with the exception of a daughter, Mary. Because Henry needed a male heir to preserve the peaceful succession to the throne and because Catherine was now past childbearing age, Henry had political reasons to propose a change of wife. He also had more personal motives, having become infatuated with a lady-in-waiting named Anne Boleyn.

Henry therefore appealed to Rome to annul his marriage to Catherine, arguing that because she had previously been married to his older brother Arthur (who had died in adolescence), Henry's marriage to Catherine had been invalid from the beginning. As Henry's representatives pointed out, the Bible pronounced it "an unclean thing" for a man to take his brother's wife and cursed such a marriage with childlessness (Leviticus 20:31). Even a papal dispensation, which Henry and Catherine had long before obtained for their marriage, could not exempt them from such a clear prohibition—as the marriage's childlessness proved.

Henry's petition put Pope Clement VII (r. 1523–34) in an awkward position. Both Henry and Clement knew that popes in the past had granted annulments to reigning monarchs on far weaker grounds than the ones Henry was alleging. If, however, the pope granted Henry's annulment, he would cast doubt on the validity of all papal dispensations. More seriously, he would provoke the wrath of the emperor Charles V, Catherine of Aragon's nephew, whose armies were in firm command of Rome and who at that moment held the pope himself in captivity. Clement was trapped; all he could do was procrastinate and hope that the matter would resolve itself. For two years, he allowed Henry's case to proceed in England without ever reaching a verdict. Then, suddenly, he transferred the case to Rome, where the legal process began all over again.

Exasperated by these delays, Henry began to increase the pressure on the pope. In 1531, he compelled an assembly of English clergy to declare him "protector and only supreme head" of the Church in England. In 1532, he encouraged Parliament to produce an inflammatory list of grievances against the English clergy and used this threat to force them to concede his right, as king, to approve or deny all Church legislation. In January 1533, Henry married Anne Boleyn (already pregnant) even though his marriage to Queen Catherine had still not been annulled. The new archbishop of Canterbury, Thomas Cranmer, later provided the required annulment in May, acting on his own authority.

In September, Princess Elizabeth was born; her father, disappointed again in his hopes for a son, refused to attend her christening. Nevertheless, Parliament settled the succession to the throne on the children of Henry and Anne,

The Six Articles of the English Church

Although Henry VIII withdrew the Church of England from obedience to the papacy, he continued to reject most Protestant theology. Some of his advisers, most notably Thomas Cromwell, were committed Protestants; and the king allowed his son and heir, Edward VI, to be raised as a Protestant. But even after several years of rapid (and mostly Protestant) change in the English Church, Henry reasserted a set of traditional Catholic doctrines in the Six Articles of 1539. These would remain binding on the Church of England until the king's death in 1547.

 irst, that in the most blessed sacrament of the altar, by the strength and efficacy of Christ's mighty word, it being spoken by the priest, is present really, under the form of bread and wine, the natural body and blood of our Savior Jesus Christ, conceived of the Virgin Mary, and that after the consecration there remains no substance of bread or wine, nor any other substance but the substance of Christ, God and man;

Secondly, that communion in both kinds is not necessary for salvation, by the law of God, to all persons, and that it is to be believed and not doubted . . . that in the flesh, under the form of bread, is the very blood, and with the blood, under the form of wine, is the very flesh, as well apart as though they were both together;

Thirdly, that priests, after the order of priesthood received as afore, may not marry by the law of God;

Fourthly, that vows of chastity or widowhood by man or woman made to God advisedly ought to be observed by the law of God. . . .

Fifthly, that it is right and necessary that private masses be continued and admitted in this the king's English Church and congregation . . . whereby good Christian people . . . do receive both godly and goodly consolations and benefits; and it is agreeable also to God's law;

Sixthly, that oral, private confession is expedient and necessary to be retained and continued, used and frequented in the church of God.

Source: *Statutes of the Realm,* vol. 3 (London: 1810–28), p. 739 (modernized).

Questions for Analysis

1. Three of these six articles focus on the sacrament of the Eucharist (the Mass). Given what you have learned in this chapter, why would Henry have been so concerned about this sacrament? What does this reveal about his values and those of his contemporaries?

2. Given Henry's insistence on these articles, why might he have allowed his son to be raised a Protestant? What does this suggest about the political situation in England?

redirected all papal revenues from England into the king's hands, prohibited appeals to the papal court, and formally declared "the King's highness to be Supreme Head of the Church of England." In 1536, Henry executed his former tutor and chancellor Sir Thomas More (see Chapter 12) for his refusal to endorse this declaration of supremacy, and took the first steps toward dissolving England's many monasteries. By the end of 1539, the monasteries and convents were gone and their lands and wealth confiscated by the king, who distributed them to his supporters.

These measures, largely masterminded and engineered by Henry's Protestant adviser, Thomas Cromwell (c. 1485–1540), broke the bonds that linked the English Church to Rome. But they did not make England a Protestant country.

Although certain traditional practices (such as pilgrimages and the veneration of relics) were prohibited, the English Church remained overwhelmingly Catholic in organization, doctrine, ritual, and language. The Six Articles promulgated by Parliament in 1539 at Henry VIII's behest left no room for doubt as to official orthodoxy: oral confession to priests, masses for the dead, and clerical celibacy were all confirmed; the Latin Mass continued; and Catholic Eucharistic doctrine was not only confirmed but its denial made punishable by death. To most English people, only the disappearance of the monasteries and the king's own continuing matrimonial adventures (he married six wives in all) were evidence that their Church was no longer in communion with Rome.

The Reign of Edward VI

For truly committed Protestants, and especially those who had visited Calvin's Geneva, the changes Henry VIII enforced on the English Church did not go nearly far enough. In 1547, the accession of the nine-year-old king Edward VI (Henry's son by his third wife, Jane Seymour) gave them the opportunity to finish the task of reform. Encouraged by the apparent sympaties of the young king, Edward's government moved quickly to reform the doctrine and ceremonies of the English Church. Priests were permitted to marry; English services replaced Latin ones; the veneration of images was discouraged, and the images themselves were defaced or destroyed; prayers for the dead were declared useless, and endowments for such prayers were confiscated; and new articles of belief were drawn up, repudiating all sacraments except baptism and communion and affirming the Protestant creed of justification by faith alone. Most important, *The Book of Common Prayer*, authored by Archbishop Cranmer and considered one of the great landmarks of English literature, was published to define precisely how the new English-language services of the church were to be conducted. Much remained unsettled with respect to both doctrine and worship; but by 1553, when the youthful Edward died, the English Church appeared to have become a distinctly Protestant institution.

Mary Tudor and the Restoration of Catholicism

Edward's successor, however, was his pious and much older half sister Mary (r. 1553–58), granddaughter of "the most Catholic monarchs" of Spain, Ferdinand and Isabella (see Chapter 11). Mary speedily reversed her half brother's religious policies, restoring the Latin Mass and requiring married priests to give up their wives. She even prevailed on Parliament to vote a return to papal allegiance. Hundreds of Protestant leaders fled abroad, many to Geneva; others, including Archbishop Thomas Cranmer, were burned at the stake for refusing to abjure their Protestantism. News of the martyrdoms spread like wildfire through Protestant Europe. In England, however, Mary's policies sparked relatively little resistance. After two decades of religious upheaval, most English men and women were probably

QUEEN MARY AND QUEEN ELIZABETH. The two daughters of Henry VIII were the first two queens regnant of England: the first women to rule in their own right. Despite the similar challenges they faced, they had strikingly different fates and have been treated very differently in popular histories. ▪ *How do these two portraits suggest differences in their personalities and their self-representation as rulers?*

hoping that Mary's reign would bring some stability to their lives.

This, however, Mary could not do. The executions she ordered were insufficient to wipe out religious resistance—instead, Protestant propaganda about "Bloody Mary" caused widespread unease, even among those who welcomed the return of traditional religious forms. Nor could Mary do anything to restore monasticism: too many leading families had profited from Henry VIII's dissolution of the monasteries for this to be reversed. Mary's marriage to her cousin Philip, Charles V's son and heir to the Spanish throne, was another miscalculation. Although the marriage treaty stipulated that Philip could not succeed her in the event of her death, her English subjects never trusted him. When the queen allowed herself to be drawn by Philip into a war with France on Spain's behalf—in which England lost Calais, its last foothold on the European continent—many people became highly disaffected. Ultimately, however, what doomed Mary's policies was simply the accident of biology: Mary was unable to conceive an heir. When she died after only five years of rule, her throne passed to her Protestant sister, Elizabeth.

The Elizabethan Compromise

The daughter of Henry VIII and Anne Boleyn, Elizabeth (r. 1558–1603) was predisposed in favor of Protestantism by the circumstances of her parents' marriage as well as by her upbringing. But Elizabeth was no zealot and wisely recognized that supporting radical Protestantism in England might provoke bitter sectarian strife. Accordingly, she presided over what is often known as "the Elizabethan settlement." By a new Act of Supremacy (1559), Elizabeth repealed Mary's Catholic legislation, prohibiting foreign religious powers (i.e., the pope) from exercising any authority within England and declaring herself "supreme governor" of the English church—a more Protestant title than Henry VIII's "supreme head," since most Protestants believed that Christ alone was the head of the Church. She also adopted many of the Protestant liturgical reforms instituted by her half-brother, Edward, including Cranmer's revised version of *The Book of Common Prayer*. But she retained vestiges of Catholic practice, too, including bishops, church courts, and vestments for the clergy. On most doctrinal matters, including predestination and free will, Elizabeth's Thirty-nine Articles of Faith (approved in 1562) struck a decidedly Protestant, even Calvinist, tone. But the prayer book was more moderate and, on the critical issue of the Eucharist, deliberately ambiguous. By combining Catholic and Protestant interpretations ("This is my body. . . . Do this in remembrance of me") into a single declaration, the prayer book permitted an enormous latitude for competing interpretations of the service by priests and parishioners alike.

Yet religious tensions persisted in Elizabethan England, not only between Protestants and Catholics but also between moderate and more extreme Protestants. The queen's artful fudging of these competing Christianities was by no means a recipe for success. Rather, what preserved "the Elizabethan settlement" and ultimately made England a Protestant country was the extraordinary length of Queen Elizabeth's reign, combined with the fact that for much of that time Protestant England was at war with Catholic Spain. Under Elizabeth, Protestantism and English nationalism gradually fused together into a potent conviction that God himself had chosen England for greatness. After 1588, when English naval forces won an improbable victory over a Spanish Armada (see Chapter 14), Protestantism and Englishness became nearly indistinguishable to most of Queen Elizabeth's subjects. Laws against Catholic practices became increasingly severe, and although an English Catholic tradition did survive, its adherents were a persecuted minority. Significant, too, was the situation in Ireland, where the vast majority of the population remained Catholic despite the government's efforts to impose Protestantism on them. As a result, Irishness would be as firmly identified with Catholicism as was Englishness with Protestantism; but it was the Protestants who were in power in both countries.

THE REBIRTH OF THE CATHOLIC CHURCH

So far, our emphasis on the spread of Protestantism has cast the spotlight on dissident reformers such as Luther and Calvin. But there was also a powerful internal reform movement within the Church in these same decades, which resulted in the birth (or rebirth) of a Catholic ("universal") faith. For some, this movement is the "Catholic Reformation"; for others, it is the "Counter-Reformation." Those who prefer the former term emphasize that the Church was continuing significant reforming movements that can be traced back to the eleventh century (see Chapter 8) and which gained new momentum in the wake of the Great Schism (see Chapter 11). Others insist that most Catholic reformers of this period were reactionary, inspired primarily by the urgent need to resist Protestantism and to strengthen the power of the Roman Church in opposition to it.

Past and Present

Controlling Consumption

Although laws regulating the conspicuous consumption of expensive commodities—especially status-conscious clothing—were common during the later Middle Ages, it was not until after the Reformation that both Protestant and Catholic leaders began to criminalize formerly acceptable bodily practices and substances. New theories of sensory perception, the availability of new products like coffee and tobacco, and a new concern to internalize reform led some authorities to outlaw prostitution (hitherto legal) and to ban normal social practices like drinking and dancing. The image on the left shows the militant Catholic League founded in sixteenth-century France, which combatted Protestantism and promoted strict religious observance. The image on the right shows Czech protesters calling for the decriminalization of marijuana.

 Watch related author interview on StudySpace
wwnorton.com/web/westernciv18

Catholic Reforms

Even before Luther's challenge to the Church, as we have seen, there was a movement for moral and institutional reform within some religious orders. And while these efforts received strong support from several secular rulers, the papacy showed little interest in them. In Spain, for example, reforming activities directed by Cardinal Francisco Ximenes de Cisneros (1436–1517) led to the imposition of strict rules of behavior and the elimination of abuses prevalent among the clergy. Ximenes (he-MEN-ez) also helped to regenerate the spiritual life of the Spanish Church. In Italy, meanwhile, earnest clerics labored to make the Italian Church more worthy of its prominent position. Reforming existing monastic orders was a difficult task, not least because the papal court set such a poor example; but Italian reformers did manage to establish several new orders dedicated to high ideals of piety and social service. In northern Europe, Christian humanists such as Erasmus and Thomas More also played a role in this Catholic reform movement, not only by criticizing abuses and editing sacred texts but also by encouraging the laity to lead lives of sincere religious piety (see Chapter 12).

As a response to the challenges posed by Protestantism, however, these internal reforms proved entirely inadequate. Starting in the 1530s, therefore, a more aggressive phase of reform began to gather momentum under a new style of vigorous papal leadership. The leading Counter-Reformation popes—Paul III (r. 1534–49), Paul IV (r. 1555–59), Pius V (r. 1566–72), and Sixtus V (r. 1585–90)—were the most zealous reformers of the Church since the eleventh century. All led upright lives; some, indeed, were so grimly ascetic that contemporaries longed for the bad old days. As a Spanish councilor wrote of Pius V in 1567, "We should like

THE COUNCIL OF TRENT. This fresco depicts the General Council of the Catholic Church, which met at intervals for nearly twenty years between 1545 and 1563 in the city of Trent (in modern-day Italy) in order to enact significant internal reforms.

THE INSPIRATION OF SAINT JEROME **BY GUIDO RENI (1635).** The Council of Trent declared Saint Jerome's Latin translation of the Bible, the Vulgate, to be the official version of the Catholic Church. Since biblical scholars had known since the early sixteenth century that Saint Jerome's translation contained numerous mistakes, Catholic defenders of the Vulgate insisted that even his mistakes had been divinely inspired. ▪ *How does Guido Reni's painting attempt to make this point?*

it even better if the present Holy Father were no longer with us, however great, inexpressible, unparalleled, and extraordinary His Holiness may be." In confronting Protestantism, however, an excessively holy pope was vastly preferable to a self-indulgent one. And these Counter-Reformation popes were not merely holy men. They were also accomplished administrators who reorganized papal finances and filled ecclesiastical offices with bishops and abbots no less renowned for austerity and holiness than were the popes themselves.

Papal reform efforts intensified at the Council of Trent, a general council of the entire Church convoked by Paul III in 1545, which met at intervals thereafter until 1563. The decisions taken at Trent (a provincial capital of the Holy Roman Empire, located in modern-day Italy) provided the foundations on which a new Catholic Church would be erected. Although the council began by debating some form of compromise with Protestantism, it ended by reaffirming all of the Catholic tenets challenged by Protestant critics. "Good works" were affirmed as necessary for salvation, and all seven sacraments were declared indispensable means of grace, without which salvation was impossible. Transubstantiation, purgatory, the invocation of saints, and the rule of celibacy

for the clergy were all confirmed as dogmas—essential elements—of the Catholic faith. The Bible, in its imperfect Vulgate form, and the traditions of apostolic teaching were held to be of equal authority as sources of Christian truth. Papal supremacy over every bishop and priest was expressly maintained, and the supremacy of the pope over any Church council was taken for granted outright, signaling a final defeat of the still-active conciliar movement. The Council of Trent even reaffirmed the doctrine of indulgences that had touched off the Lutheran revolt, although it condemned the worst abuses connected with their sale.

The legislation of Trent was not confined to matters of doctrine. To improve pastoral care of the laity, bishops and priests were forbidden to hold more than one spiritual office. To address the problem of an ignorant priesthood,

Analyzing Primary Sources

The Demands of Obedience

The necessity of obedience in the spiritual formation of monks and nuns can be traced back to the Rule of Saint Benedict *in the early sixth century, and beyond. In keeping with the mission of its founder, Ignatius of Loyola (1491–1556), the Society of Jesus brought a new militancy to this old ideal.*

Rules for Thinking with the Church

1. Always to be ready to obey with mind and heart, setting aside all judgment of one's own, the true spouse of Jesus Christ, our holy mother, our infallible and orthodox mistress, the Catholic Church, whose authority is exercised over us by the hierarchy.

2. To commend the confession of sins to a priest as it is practised in the Church; the reception of the Holy Eucharist once a year, or better still every week, or at least every month, with the necessary preparation. . . .

4. To have a great esteem for the religious orders, and to give the preference to celibacy or virginity over the married state. . . .

6. To praise relics, the veneration and invocation of Saints: also the stations, and pious pilgrimages, indulgences, jubilees, the custom of lighting candles in the churches, and other such aids to piety and devotion. . . .

9. To uphold especially all the precepts of the Church, and not censure them in any manner; but, on the contrary, to defend them promptly, with reasons drawn from all sources, against those who criticize them.

10. To be eager to commend the decrees, mandates, traditions, rites, and customs of the Fathers in the Faith or our superiors. . . .

11. That we may be altogether of the same mind and in conformity with the Church herself, if she shall have defined anything to be black which to our eyes appears to be white, we ought in like manner to pronounce it to be black. For we must undoubtingly believe, that the Spirit of our Lord Jesus Christ, and the Spirit of the Orthodox Church His Spouse, by which Spirit we are governed and directed to salvation, is the same. . . .

From the Constitutions of the Jesuit Order

Let us with the utmost pains strain every nerve of our strength to exhibit this virtue of obedience, firstly to the Highest Pontiff, then to the Superiors of the Society; so that in all things . . . we may be most ready to obey his voice, just as if it issued from Christ our Lord . . . leaving any work, even a letter, that we have begun and have not yet finished; by directing to this goal all our strength and intention in the Lord, that holy obedience may be made perfect in us in every respect, in performance, in will, in intellect; by submitting to whatever may be enjoined on us with great readiness, with spiritual joy and perseverance; by persuading ourselves that all things [commanded] are just; by rejecting with a kind of blind obedience all opposing opinion or judgment of our own. . . .

Source: Henry Bettenson, ed., *Documents of the Christian Church,* 2nd ed. (Oxford: 1967), pp. 259–61.

Questions for Analysis

1. How might Loyola's career as a soldier have inspired the language used in his "Rules for Thinking with the Church"?

2. In what ways do these Jesuit principles respond directly to the challenges of Protestant reformers?

---

a theological seminary was to be established in every diocese. The council also suppressed a variety of local religious practices and saints' cults, replacing them with new cults authorized and approved by Rome. To prevent heretical ideas from corrupting the faithful, the council further decided to censor or suppress dangerous books. In 1564, a specially appointed commission published the first *Index of Prohibited Books*, an official list of writings forbidden to faithful Catholics. Ironically, all of Erasmus's works were immediately placed on the *Index*, even though he had been a chosen champion of the Church against Martin Luther only forty years before. A permanent agency known as the

Congregation of the Index was later set up to revise the list, which was maintained until 1966, when it was abolished after the Second Vatican Council (1962–1965). For centuries, it was to become symbolic of the doctrinal intolerance that characterized sixteenth-century Christianity, both in its Catholic and Protestant varieties.

Ignatius Loyola and the Society of Jesus

In addition to the concerted activities of popes and the legislation of the Council of Trent, a third main force propelling the Counter-Reformation was the foundation of the Society of Jesus (commonly known as the Jesuits) by Ignatius Loyola (1491–1556). In the midst of a career as a mercenary, this young Spanish nobleman was wounded in battle in 1521, the same year in which Luther defied authority at the Diet of Worms. While recuperating, he turned from the reading of chivalric romances to a romantic vernacular retelling of the life of Jesus—and the impact of this experience convinced him to become a spiritual soldier of Christ.

For ten months, Ignatius lived as a hermit in a cave near the town of Manresa, where he experienced ecstatic visions and worked out the principles of his subsequent guidebook, the *Spiritual Exercises*. This manual, completed in 1535 and first published in 1541, offered practical advice on how to master one's will and serve God through a systematic program of meditations on sin and the life of Christ. It eventually became the basic handbook for all Jesuits and has been widely studied by Catholic laypeople as well. Indeed, Loyola's *Spiritual Exercises* ranks alongside Calvin's *Institutes* as the most influential religious text of the sixteenth century.

The Jesuit order originated as a small group of six disciples who gathered around Loyola during his belated career as a student in Paris. They vowed to serve God in poverty, chastity, and missionary work and were formally constituted by Pope Paul III in 1540. By the time of Loyola's death, the Society of Jesus already numbered some 1,500 members. It was by far the most militant of the religious orders fostered by the Catholic reform movements of the sixteenth century—not merely a monastic society but a company of soldiers sworn to defend the faith. Their weapons were not bullets and swords but eloquence, persuasion, and instruction in correct doctrines; yet the Society also became accomplished in more worldly methods of exerting influence. Its organization was patterned after that of a military unit, whose commander-in-chief enforced the iron discipline of all members. Individuality was suppressed, and a stoical obedience was required from the rank and file. Indeed, the Jesuit general, sometimes known as the "black pope" (from the color of the order's habit), was elected for life and answered only to the pope in Rome, to whom all senior Jesuits took a special vow of strict obedience. As a result of this vow, all Jesuits were held to be at the pope's disposal at all times.

The activities of the Jesuits consisted primarily of proselytizing and establishing schools. This meant they were ideal missionaries. Accordingly, Jesuits were soon dispatched to preach to non-Christians in India, China, and Spanish America. One of Loyola's closest associates, Francis Xavier (ZAY-vyer, 1506–1552), baptized thousands of people and traveled thousands of miles in South and East Asia. Although Loyola had not at first conceived of his society as a batallion of "shock troops" in the fight against Protestantism, that is what it primarily became. Through preaching and diplomacy—sometimes at the risk of their lives—Jesuits in the second half of the sixteenth century helped to colonize the world. In many places, they were instrumental in keeping rulers and their subjects loyal to Catholicism; in others, they met martyrdom; and in some others, notably Poland and parts of Germany and France, they succeeded in regaining territory previously lost to followers of Luther and Calvin. Wherever they were allowed to settle, they set up schools and colleges, on the grounds that only a vigorous Catholicism nurtured by widespread literacy and education could combat Protestantism.

A New Catholic Christianity

The greatest achievement of these reform movements was the revitalization of the Church. Had it not been for such determined efforts, Catholicism would not have swept over the globe during the seventeenth and eighteenth centuries—or reemerged in Europe as a vigorous spiritual force. There were some other consequences as well. One was the rapid advancement of lay literacy in Catholic countries. Another was the growth of intense concern for acts of charity; because Catholicism continued to emphasize good works as well as faith, charitable activities took on an extremely important role.

There was also a renewed emphasis on the role of religious women. Reformed Catholicism did not exalt marriage as a route to holiness to the same degree as did Protestantism, but it did encourage the piety of a female religious elite. For example, it embraced the mysticism of Saint Teresa of Avila (1515–1582) and established new orders of nuns, such as the Ursulines and the Sisters of Charity. Both Protestants

TERESA OF AVILA. Teresa of Avila (1515–1582) was one of many female religious figures who played an important role in the reformed Catholic Church. She was canonized in 1622. This image is dated 1576. The Latin wording on the scroll unfurled above Teresa's head reads: "I will sing forever of the mercy of the Holy Lord."

and Catholics continued to exclude women from the priesthood or ministry, but Catholic women could pursue religious lives with at least some degree of independence, and the convent continued to be a route toward spiritual and even political advancement in Catholic countries.

The reformed Catholic Church did not, however, perpetuate the tolerant Christianity of Erasmus. Instead, Christian humanists lost favor with the papacy, and even scientists such as Galileo were regarded with suspicion (see Chapter 16). Yet contemporary Protestantism was just as intolerant, and even more hostile to the cause of rational thought. Indeed, because Catholic theologians turned for guidance to the scholasticism of Thomas Aquinas, they tended to be much more committed to the dignity of human reason than were their Protestant counterparts, who emphasized the literal interpretation of the Bible and the importance of unquestioning faith. It is no coincidence that René Descartes, one of the pioneers of rational philosophy ("I think, therefore I am"), was educated by Jesuits.

It would be wrong, therefore, to claim that the Protestantism of this era was more forward-looking or progressive than Catholicism. Both were, in fact, products of the same troubled time. Each variety of Protestantism responded to specific historical conditions and the needs of specific peoples in specific places, while carrying forward certain aspects of the Christian tradition considered valuable by those communities. The Catholic Church also responded to new spiritual, political, and social realities—to such an extent that it must be regarded as distinct from either the early Church of the later Roman Empire or even the oft-reformed Church of the Middle Ages. That is why the phrase "Roman Catholic Church" has not been used in this book prior to this chapter, because the Roman Catholic Church as we know it emerged for the first time in the sixteenth century. Like Protestantism, it is a more modern phenomenon.

CONCLUSION

The Reformation grew out of complex historical processes that we have been tracing in the last few chapters. Foremost among these was the increasing power of Europe's sovereign states. As we have seen, those German princes who embraced Protestantism were moved to do so by the desire for sovereignty. The kings of Denmark, Sweden, and England followed suit for many of the same reasons. Since Protestant leaders preached absolute obedience to godly rulers, and since the state in Protestant countries assumed direct control of its churches, Protestantism bolstered state power. Yet the power of the state had been growing for a long time prior to this, especially in such countries as France and Spain, where Catholic kings already exercised most of the same rights that were seized by Lutheran authorities and by Henry VIII of England in the course of their own reformations. Those rulers who aligned themselves with Catholicism, then, had the same need to bolster their sovereignty and power.

Ideas of national identity, too, were already influential and thus available for manipulation by Protestants and Catholics alike. These religions, in turn, became new sources of both identity and disunity. Prior to the Reformation, peoples in the different regions of Germany spoke such different dialects that they had difficulty understanding each other. But Luther's Bible gained such currency that it eventually became the linguistic standard for all these disparate regions, which eventually began to conceive of themselves as part of a single nation. Yet religion alone could not achieve the political unification of Germany, which did not occur for another 300 years (see Chapter 21); indeed, it contributed to existing divisions by cementing the opposition of Catholic princes and peoples. Elsewhere in Europe—as in the Netherlands, where Protestants fought successfully against a foreign, Catholic overlord—religion created a shared identity where politics could not. In England, where it is arguable that a sense of nationalism had already been fostered before the Reformation, membership in the Church of England became a new, but not uncontested, attribute of "Englishness."

Ideals characteristic of the Renaissance also contributed something to the Reformation and the Catholic responses to it. The criticisms of Christian humanists helped to prepare Europe for the challenges of Lutheranism, and close textual study of the Bible led to the publication of the newer, more accurate editions used by Protestant reformers. For example, Erasmus's improved edition of the Latin New Testament enabled Luther to reach some crucial conclusions concerning the meaning of penance and became the foundation for Luther's own translation of the Bible. However, Erasmus was no supporter of Lutheran principles and most other Christian humanists followed suit, shunning Protestantism

After You Read
This Chapter

Ⓢ Visit StudySpace for quizzes, additional review materials, and multimedia documents. **wwnorton.com/web/westernciv18**

REVIEWING THE OBJECTIVES

- The main premises of Luther's theology had religious, political, and social implications. What were they?
- Switzerland fostered a number of different Protestant movements. Why was this the case?
- The Reformation had a profound effect on the basic structures of family life and on attitudes toward marriage and morality. Describe these changes.
- The Church of England was established in response to a specific political situation. What was this?
- How did the Catholic Church respond to the challenge of Protestantism?

as soon as it became clear to them what Luther was actually teaching. Indeed, in certain basic respects, Protestant doctrine was completely at odds with the principles, politics, and beliefs of most humanists, who became staunch supporters of the Catholic Church.

In the New World and Asia, both Protestantism and Catholicism became forces of imperialism and new catalysts for competition. The race to secure colonies and resources now became a race for converts, too, as missionaries of both faiths fanned out over the globe. In the process, the confessional divisions of Europe were mapped onto these regions, often with violent results. Over the course of the ensuing century, newly sovereign nation-states would struggle for hegemony at home and abroad, setting off a series of religious wars that would cause as much destruction as any plague. Meanwhile, western civilizations' extension into the Atlantic would create new kinds of ecosystems, forms of wealth, and types of bondage.

PEOPLE, IDEAS, AND EVENTS IN CONTEXT

- How did **MARTIN LUTHER**'s attack on **INDULGENCES** tap into more widespread criticism of the papacy? What role did the printing press and the German vernacular play in the dissemination of his ideas?
- Why did many German principalities and cities rally to Luther's cause? Why did his condemnation at the **DIET OF WORMS** not lead to his execution on charges of heresy?
- How did the Protestant teachings of **ULRICH ZWINGLI**, **JOHN CALVIN**, and the **ANABAPTISTS** differ from one another and from those of Luther?
- What factors made some of Europe's territories more receptive to **PROTESTANTISM** than others? What was the meaning of the principle *CUIUS REGIO, EIUS REGIO*, established by the Peace of Augsburg?
- How did the **REFORMATION** alter the status and lives of women in Europe? Why did it strengthen male authority in the family?
- Why did **HENRY VIII** break with Rome? How did the **CHURCH OF ENGLAND** differ from other Protestant churches in Europe?
- What decisions were made at the **COUNCIL OF TRENT**? What were the founding principles of **IGNATIUS LOYOLA**'s **SOCIETY OF JESUS**, and what was its role in the **COUNTER-REFORMATION** of the **CATHOLIC CHURCH**?

THINKING ABOUT CONNECTIONS

- Our study of Western civilizations has shown that reforming movements are nothing new: Christianity has been continuously reformed throughout its long history. What made this Reformation so different?
- Was a Protestant break with the Catholic Church inevitable? Why or why not?
- The political, social, and religious structures put in place during this era continue to shape our lives in such profound ways that we scarcely notice them—or we assume them to be inevitable and natural. In your view, what is the most far-reaching consequence of this age of dissent and division, and why? In what ways has it formed your own values and assumptions?

STORY LINES

- By the middle of the sixteenth century, the Atlantic Ocean became a central space for colonization, commerce, migration, and settlement, as the peoples of this Atlantic world confronted one another.

- In the wake of the Reformation, Europe itself remained politically unstable. Devastating religious wars were waged on the Continent. In England, mounting pressures caused a crisis that resulted in civil war and the execution of the reigning king.

- At the same time, competition in the wider Atlantic world exported these political and religious conflicts to the new European colonies.

- This widening world and its pervasive violence caused many Europeans to question the beliefs of earlier generations. Intellectuals and artists sought new sources of authority and new ways of explaining the complex circumstances of their time.

CHRONOLOGY

1555	Peace of Augsburg
1562–1598	French wars of religion
1588	Destruction of the Spanish Armada
1566–1609	Dutch wars with Spain
1598	Henry IV issues the Edict of Nantes
1607	English colony of Jamestown founded
1608	French colony in Québec founded
1611	William Shakespeare's play, *The Tempest*, is performed in London
1618	Thirty Years' War begins
1621	Dutch West India Company founded
1642–1649	English Civil War
1648	Beginning of the Fronde rebellions; the Thirty Years' War ends
1660	Restoration of the English monarchy

Before
You
Read
This
Chapter

Europe in the Atlantic World, 1550–1660

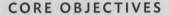

CORE OBJECTIVES

- **TRACE** the new linkages between Western civilizations and the Atlantic world, and describe their consequences.

- **DESCRIBE** the different forms of unfree labor that developed in European colonies during this period.

- **IDENTIFY** the monarchies that dominated Europe and the Atlantic world and the newer powers whose influence was expanding.

- **EXPLAIN** the reasons for Europe's religious and political instability and its consequences for Europe's monarchies and the Atlantic world.

- **UNDERSTAND** how artists and intellectuals responded to the crises and uncertainties of this era.

he Atlantic Ocean thrashes the western shores of Europe and Africa with wind-driven waves that have traveled thousands of miles from the American coasts. Its immense area links continents shaped by a wide variety of climates, including the arid desert of the Sahara, the more temperate zones of Europe and North America, the tropical islands of the Gulf of Mexico and the Caribbean, and the rain forests of the Amazon basin in South America. This ecological diversity, and the hitherto infrequent and limited movement of peoples on opposite sides of the ocean, meant that each of these regions nurtured its own forms of plant and animal life, its own unique microbes and pathogens.

In the sixteenth century, the emergence of the Atlantic world as an arena of cultural and economic exchange broke down the isolation of these ecosystems. Transatlantic commerce and migration now eclipsed the importance of trade and movement in the Mediterranean, which had been the crucial connector of Western civilizations since the Bronze Age (see Chapter 2). Populations—humans, animals, and plants—on once-remote shores came into frequent and intense contact. On the one hand, Europeans brought diseases that devastated the peoples of the Americas, along with

453

gunpowder and a hotly divided Christianity. On the other, the huge influx of silver from South America transformed (and eventually exploded) the cash-starved European economy while the arrival of American stimulants such as tobacco, sugar, and chocolate fostered new consumer appetites that could only be satisfied by new regimes of unfree labor.

Eventually, the need for slaves to power the plantations that supplied these consumer products fostered a vast industry of human trafficking, which led to the forcible removal of nearly 11 million people from Africa over the course of three centuries. Colonial settlement in North and South America also created new social hierarchies and new forms of inequality, which unsettled even long-established structures in Europe. The peoples of the Americas were forced to deal with the presence of newly

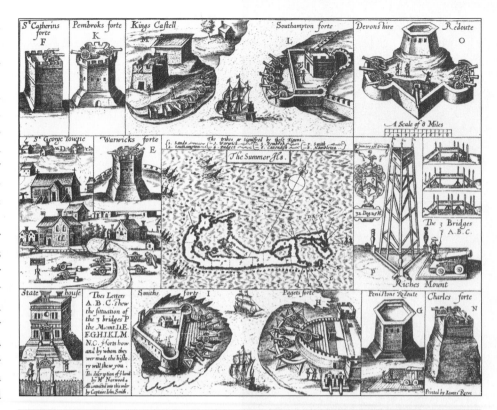

THE ISLAND OF BERMUDA. This map of "The Summer Isle" and the accompanying images of its major fortifications and sites, was drawn by Captain John Smith and published in *The Generall Historie of Virginia, New-England, and the Summer Isles* (1624). ▪ *Why would such features be of interest to readers of this pamphlet?*

arrived settlers, and settlers in turn confronted both indigenous peoples and the meddling interference of distant imperial bureaucracies.

Meanwhile, these European states were riven by internal dissent and engaged in deadly competitions among themselves—and these, too, were exported to the Atlantic world. Galvanized by the crisis of the Reformation (see Chapter 13), the Roman Catholic Church sought to redress the loss of religious dominance in Europe by spreading its influence to the Americas and Asia through the work of new missionary orders. The Spanish crown, which controlled the most developed colonial empire of the time, was also the most zealous defender of the Catholic faith—which meant that wars within Spain's Protestant Dutch provinces and with Protestant England affected colonial politics, too. Similar attempts by the Catholic Habsburg monarchy to enforce religious uniformity among the varied territories of central Europe led to the Thirty Years' War, one of the longest and bloodiest conflicts in history. In both direct and indirect ways, these deadly disputes stimulated the migration of persecuted minorities (Catholic and Protestant) across the Atlantic, replanting and propagating these rivalries.

But religion was not the only cause of conflict within Europe. Another was the growing tension between powerful monarchs and landowning elites, who disputed the right of the crown and its administrators to raise revenues through increased taxation. Supporting colonial expansion in the Atlantic world and fighting wars within Europe were expensive projects, and they placed strain on traditional alliances and ideas of kingship. Political and moral philosophers accordingly struggled to redefine the role of government in a world of religious pluralism and to articulate new political ideologies that did not necessitate violence among people of different faiths. Intellectuals and artists also strove to reassess Europeans' place in this expanding Atlantic world, to process the flood of new information and commodities, and to make sense of the profound changes in daily life.

THE EMERGENCE OF THE ATLANTIC WORLD

With the few exceptions that we have noted in previous chapters, even the most skilled of Europe's sailors were limited to coastal cruising along the Atlantic's eastern shores until the fifteenth century. But after the Portuguese and Spanish established settlements on the Canary Islands, this archipelago off the northwestern coast of Africa became a permanent base of operations for successive exploratory ventures. From here, generations of Portuguese sailors learned to navigate the West African coast, after which they successfully rounded the Cape of Good Hope and began to establish trading colonies in the Indian Ocean (see Chapter 12). During these years, Portuguese sailors also launched the first kidnapping raids for slaves along the Atlantic coast of Senegal. When they found that some African chieftains were willing to facilitate the capture of people from rival tribes, the Portuguese began to set up coastal outposts where they could trade livestock, foodstuffs, cotton, copper, and iron for ivory, gold, finished textiles, and human beings.

Competing Colonial Ventures

At the same time, Spanish successes in Mexico soon encouraged other European kingdoms to attempt imperial ventures of their own. Finding that Spanish and Portuguese holds on the Caribbean and South America were firm in practice as well as in theory—Protestant rulers were obviously not bound by the Treaty of Tordesillas (1494) and all subsequent papal pronouncements that favored Catholic colonial ventures—northern European explorers targeted the North American coast. Although the Englishman John Cabot had explored the mouth of the St. Lawrence River in 1497–98, it was nearly a century before Walter Raleigh's attempt to start an English colony just north of Spanish Florida in 1585. The settlement at Roanoke Island (present-day North Carolina) was intended to solidify English claims to the territory of Virginia, named for England's "Virgin Queen" Elizabeth and originally encompassing the North American seaboard from South Carolina to Maine, including Bermuda.

This ill-conceived experiment ended with the disappearance of the first colonists, but it was followed by Christopher Newport's expedition to the Chesapeake Bay in 1606, a voyage funded by a private London firm called the Virginia Company. Newport and his followers did not conceive of themselves as empire builders. They were not being sponsored by the English king, and they probably did not intend to settle permanently in the New World. They were "gentleman planters" whose goal was to provide agricultural goods for the European market and so to make their fortunes before returning home. Nevertheless, with the Spanish model much in mind, Newport's band reserved the right to "conquer" any peoples who proved uncooperative. So when Native Americans of the Powhatan tribe killed one-third of the settlers during a raid in 1622, the colonists responded by crushing the Powhatans and seizing their lands.

For decades thereafter, the native populations of North America remained capable of both threatening and fostering the survival of fragile settlements that had gained a toehold on the continent. Bitter conflicts and occasional cooperation between newcomers and indigenous peoples are part of a larger history of intermittent struggle and coexistence that began the moment Columbus first landed on Hispaniola. Especially in the early years of colonization, when the number of European immigrants was small, some Native American peoples sought to take advantage of these new contacts, to trade for goods otherwise unavailable to them. European settlers, for their part, often exhibited a combination of paternalism and contempt for the peoples they encountered. Some hoped to convert Americans to Christianity, others sought to use them as labor for their economic enterprises. Ultimately, however, the balance was tipped by larger environmental, biological, and demographic factors that lay outside the control of individuals.

The Columbian Exchange

The accelerating rate of global connections in the sixteenth century precipitated an extraordinary movement of peoples, plants, animals, goods, cultures, and diseases. This is known as the "Columbian exchange," a term coined by the historian Alfred Crosby in 1972, with reference to Columbus's voyage. Yet this exchange soon came to encompass lands that still lay far beyond the purview of Columbus and his contemporaries: not just the African and Eurasian landmass and the vast terrain of the Americas but Australia and the Pacific Islands, too.

Because of its profound consequences for human populations and for the environment, the Columbian exchange is considered a fundamental turning point in both human history and the history of the earth's ecology. The exchange put new agricultural products into circulation, introduced new domesticated species of animals, and accidentally encouraged the spread of deadly diseases and the devastating takeovers of invasive plants and animals. Both natural ecosystems and human immune systems around the world were destroyed or transformed. For example, the introduction of pigs and dogs on islands in the Atlantic and Pacific resulted in the extinction of indigenous animals and birds. The landscapes of Central America and southwestern North America were denuded of vegetation after Spanish settlers turned to large-scale herding and ranching operations. Honeybees displaced native insect populations and encouraged the propagation of harmful plant species.

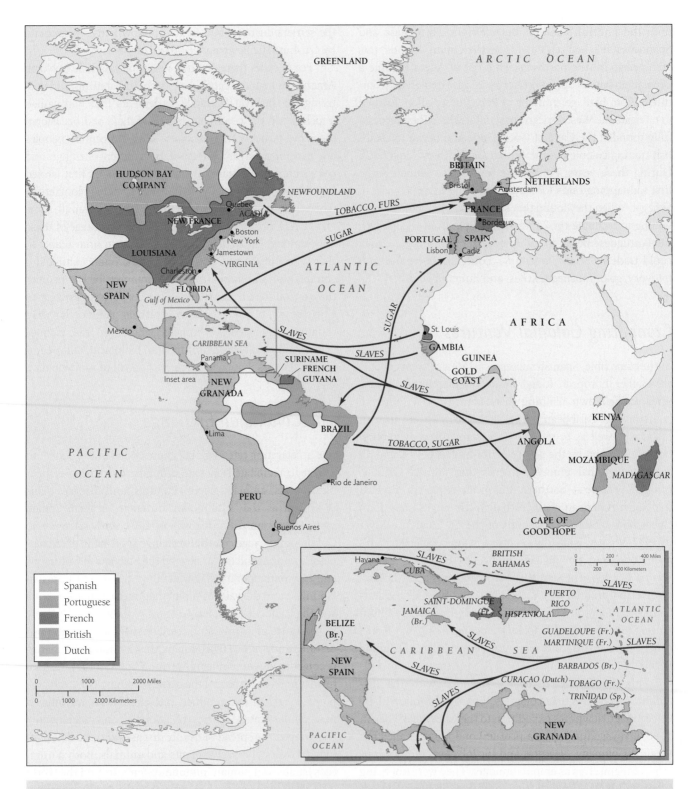

THE ATLANTIC WORLD. ▪ *Trace the routes of the triangular trade. What products did French and British colonies in North America provide to the European market?* ▪ *Which colonies were most dependent on slave labor?* ▪ *What products did they produce, and how did these enter into the triangle?*

Then there were the unintended exchanges: gray squirrels and raccoons from North America found their way to Britain and the European continent. Brown rats and even some species of earthworms were accidentally transported to the Americas. Insects from all over the world traveled to new environments and spread unfamiliar forms of bacteria and pollen.

Obviously, the transfer of human populations in the form of settlers, soldiers, merchants, sailors, indentured servants, and slaves accelerated the process of change. Some groups were wiped out through violence, forced resettlement, and bacteria. As much as 90 percent of the pre-Columbian population of the Americas died from communicable diseases such as smallpox, cholera, influenza, typhoid, measles, malaria, and bubonic plague—all brought from Europe. Syphilis, by contrast, appears to have been brought to Europe from the Americas; some scholars have even asserted that it was Columbus's own sailors who transmitted the disease across the Atlantic.

Meanwhile, the importation of foodstuffs from one part of the world to another, and their cultivation in new habitats, revolutionized the diets of local populations. The American potato (which could be grown in substandard soil and stored for long periods) eventually became the staple diet of the European poor. Tomatoes, although not widely consumed in Europe until the nineteenth century, are now an essential ingredient in many regional Italian dishes. Indeed, the foods and flavors that characterize today's iconic cuisines are, to an extraordinary degree, the result of the Columbian exchange—suggesting that many new, exotic foods quickly become fashionable and then habitual. Who can imagine an English meal without potatoes? Switzerland or Belgium without chocolate? Thai food without chili peppers? Or, on the other side of the Atlantic, Hawaii without pineapples? Florida without oranges? Colombia without coffee? Of the components that make up the quintessential American hamburger—ground-beef patties on a bun with lettuce, tomato, pickles, onion, and (if you like) cheese—only one of these ingredients is indigenous to America. Everything else is Old World: the beef, the wheat for the bun, the cucumber for the pickle, the onion, the lettuce. Even the name is European, a reference to the town of Hamburg in Germany.

Colonial Populations Compared

In contrast to the more than 7 million slaves who were taken from Africa to labor and die on plantations across the Atlantic, only about 1.5 million Europeans immigrated to the Americas in the two centuries after Columbus's first voyage. The total number who initially emigrated from Spain is estimated at 200,000 to 250,000; most of these were men. By 1570, given the high mortality of migrants and some returns to Europe, the population had been reduced to about 150,000. The Spanish crown did what it could to encourage a new wave of settlement, but even in a period of demographic growth the number of those who chose to seek their fortunes abroad remained relatively small. Transatlantic travel was expensive and uncertain, and the demand for a European labor force remained low as long as Native Americans could be conscripted and enslaved.

The population of the Spanish Americans thus remained largely urban during this period, with most colonists living in the military and administrative centers of the empire. Even the owners of large plantations lived in cities, corresponding from afar with the foremen who managed their estates. Only those who had been granted *encomiendas* tended to live on the lands entrusted to them by the Spanish crown (the Spanish verb *encomendar* means "to trust"). The *encomienda* system reminds us that Spanish conquests in the New World were an extension of the earlier Reconquista (see Chapter 12) of Spain itself. Originally set up to manage

---

THE COLUMBIAN EXCHANGE

The following list names just a few of the commodities and contagions that moved between the Old and New Worlds in this era.

Old World → New World	New World → Old World
• Wheat	• Corn
• Sugar	• Potatoes
• Bananas	• Beans
• Rice	• Squash
• Wine vines	• Pumpkins
• Horses	• Tomatoes
• Pigs	• Avocados
• Chickens	• Chili peppers
• Sheep	• Pineapples
• Cattle	• Cocoa
• *Smallpox*	• Tobacco
• *Measles*	• *Syphilis*
• *Typhus*	

Muslim populations in territories captured by Christian crusaders, this arrangement as carried forward in the new colonies of South America made *encomenderos* agents of the crown. Technically, the lands they oversaw were still owned by native peoples. But in practice, many *encomenderos* were able to exploit the land for their own profit, treating native workers like serfs. Some were descendants of the first conquistadors, others were drawn from Aztec and Inca elites. Many were women: the daughters of the Aztec emperor Montezuma had been given extensive lands to hold in trust after their father's capitulation to Cortés.

In North America, by contrast, English colonies in New England and the Chesapeake Bay were small and rural. But they also grew more quickly, with settlers numbering about 250,000 by 1700. Part of the reason for this was the greater impetus for emigration caused by overpopulation in the British Isles. The persecution of various Protestant groups also played an important role in driving immigration, especially to the New England colonies, where the relocation of entire families and even communities was common. The colonies in Virginia offered further incentives by granting 100 acres to each settler.

But these factors did not swell the numbers of migrants so much as the encouragement of indentured servitude, a practice that brought thousands of "free" European laborers across the Atlantic to work under terms that made them little different from slaves. Perhaps 75 to 80 percent of the people who arrived in the Chesapeake colony in the 1600s were indentured servants, and nearly a quarter of these were women. The successful use of indentured servants to grow tobacco in North America led some landowners to try the same system on plantations in the Caribbean islands. Ultimately, however, the plantation system rendered its greatest profits through the use of African slaves.

New Social Hierarchies in New Spain

After the conquests of the Aztec and Inca Empires (see Chapter 12), the Spanish established colonial governments in Peru and Mexico, controlled from a central bureaucracy in Madrid. This centralization was facilitated by the highly organized structure of Aztec society in Mexico and that of the Incas in Peru. Native peoples already lived, for the most part, in large, well-regulated villages and towns. The Spanish government could therefore work closely with local elites to maintain order. Indeed, the *encomienda* system was initially so effective because it was built on these existing structures and did not attempt to uproot or eliminate existing native cultures. Instead, it focused on controlling and exploiting native labor, especially in extracting mineral resources. Although farming

and ranching were encouraged in Central and South America, and later in Florida and California, the Spanish colonial economy was dominated by mining for a century and a half.

While the Spanish collected tribute from all the communities of their empire and worked assiduously to convert native peoples to Catholicism, they did not attempt to change basic patterns of life. The result was widespread cultural assimilation by the relatively small numbers of (usually male) settlers, which was also assisted by the normalcy of intermarriage between (male) colonizers and (female) colonial subjects. This pattern gave rise to a complex and distinctive caste system in New Spain, with a few "pure-blooded" Spanish immigrants at the top, a very large number of Creoles (peoples of mixed descent) in the middle, and Native Americans at the bottom.

In theory, these racial categories corresponded to class distinctions, but in practice race and class did not always coincide. Racial concepts and practices were extremely flexible, and prosperous individuals or families of mixed descent often found ways to establish their "pure" Spanish ancestry by adopting the social practices of the new Spanish colonial elites. The lingering effects of this complicated stratification are still evident in Latin America today.

Sugar, Slaves, and the Transatlantic Triangle

The Europeans who settled in the Americas faced a major problem: labor. Mining and plantation agriculture required many workers, and the indigenous labor supply of the Americas was limited; as we have seen, the introduction of new diseases resulted in the deaths of millions of Native Americans in the space of only a few decades. Meanwhile, the return of the bubonic plague to Europe in the seventeenth century, along with the slowing population growth that accompanied the wars of religion, meant that colonists could not look to Europe to satisfy their labor needs. Colonial agents thus began to import slaves from Africa to bolster the labor force and to produce the wealth they so avidly sought. And overwhelmingly, that wealth was derived not from gold or silver but from a new commodity for which there was an insatiable appetite in Europe: sugar.

Sugar was also at the center of the "Triangular Trade" that linked markets for goods in Africa, the Americas, and Europe—all of which were driven by slave labor. For example, slave ships that transported African slaves to the Caribbean might trade their human cargo for molasses made on the sugar plantations of the islands. These ships would then proceed to New England where the molasses

Enslaved Native Laborers at Potosí

Since the Spanish crown received one-fifth of all revenues from the mines of New Spain, as well as maintaining a monopoly over the mercury used to refine the silver ore into silver, it had an important stake in ensuring the mines' productivity. To this end, the crown granted colonial mine owners the right to conscript native peoples and gave them considerable freedom when it came to the treatment of the workers. This account, dated to about 1620, describes the conditions endured by these native laborers at Potosi (also discussed in Chapter 12).

According to His Majesty's warrant, the mine owners on this massive range [at Potosí] have a right to the conscripted labor of 13,300 Indians in the working and exploitation of the mines, both those [mines] which have been discovered, those now discovered, and those which shall be discovered. It is the duty of the *Corregidor* [municipal governor] of Potosí to have them rounded up and to see that they come in from all the provinces between Cuzco . . . and as far as the frontiers of Tarija and Tomina. . . .

The conscripted Indians go up every Monday morning to the . . . foot of the range; the *Corregidor* arrives with all the provincial captains or chiefs who have charge of the Indians assigned him for his miner or smelter; that keeps him busy till 1 P.M., by which time the Indians are already turned over to these mine and smelter owners.

After each has eaten his ration, they climb up the hill, each to his mine, and go in, staying there from that hour until Saturday evening without coming out of the mine; their wives bring them food, but they stay constantly underground, excavating and carrying out the ore from which they get the silver. They all have tallow candles, lighted day and night; that is the light they work with, for as they are underground, they have need for it all the time. . . .

These Indians have different functions in the handling of the silver ore; some break it up with bar or pick, and dig down in, following the vein in the mine; others bring it up; others up above keep separating the good and the poor in piles; others are occupied in taking it down from the range to the mills on herds of llamas; every day they bring up more than 8,000 of these native beasts of burden for this task. These teamsters who carry the metal are not conscripted, but are hired.

Source: Antonio Vázquez de Espinosa, *Compendium and Description of the West Indies*, trans. Charles Upson Clark (Washington, DC: 1968), p. 62.

Questions for Analysis

1. From the tone of this account, what do you think was the narrator's purpose in writing? Who is his intended audience?

2. Reconstruct the conditions in which these laborers worked. What would you estimate to be the human costs of this week's labor? Why, for example, would a fresh workforce be needed every Monday?

would be traded to distillers who used the sugary syrup to make rum. Loaded up with a consignment of rum, the slaver would return to the African coast to repeat the process. An alternative triangle might see cheap manufactured goods move from England to Africa, where they would be traded for slaves. Those slaves would then be shipped to Virginia and exchanged for tobacco, which would be shipped back to England to be processed and distributed.

Although the transatlantic slave trade was theoretically controlled by the governments of European colonial powers—Britain officially entered this trade in 1564, the year of William Shakespeare's birth—private entrepre-neurs and working-class laborers were active at every stage of the supply chain: in the ports of West Africa, where captured slaves cast their eyes on their homelands for the last time; on the ships where these captives were imprisoned; and in the slave markets of the Americas, as agents for the landowners and merchants who bid against one another to purchase the human chattel that had survived the terrible voyage.

Many other branches of the economy in Europe and the Americas were also linked to the slave trade: from the investors in Amsterdam, London, Lisbon, and Bordeaux who financed the slave trader's journey, to the insurance brokers who negotiated complex formulas for protecting these investments, to the financial agents who offered a range of credit instruments, to those seeking to enter into the expensive and risky business of transatlantic trade. And this is to say nothing of the myriad ways in which the everyday lives of average people were bound to slavery. All those who bought the commodities produced by slave labor, or who manufactured the implements and weapons that enabled enslavement, were also implicated. The slave trade was not, as is sometimes assumed, a venture carried forward by a few unscrupulous men. It created wealth and prestige for every sector of European society, not merely for those who had direct contact with it. It was the engine that created the modern globalized economy.

Counting the Human Cost of the Slave Trade

The Portuguese were the first to bring African slaves to their sugarcane plantations in Brazil, in the 1540s. By this time, slavery was already crucial to the domestic economies of West African kingdoms. In the following decades, however, the ever-increasing demand for slaves would cause the permanent disintegration of political order in this region, by creating an incentive for war and raiding among rival tribes. Moreover, the increased traffic in human beings called for more highly systematized methods for corralling, sorting, and shipping them. At the end of the sixteenth century, accordingly, the Portuguese government established a fortified trading outpost on an island known as Luanda on the central African coast (near what is now Angola). Additional trading posts were then established at multiple places along the coast, to assist in processing the increasing number of captives.

On board ship, enslaved humans were shackled below decks in spaces barely wider than their own bodies, without sanitary facilities of any kind. It might seem surprising that the mortality rate on these voyages was relatively low: probably 10 or 11 percent. But this was only because the slaves chosen for transport were healthy to begin with, and slave traders were anxious to maintain their goods so as to sell at a profit. Those Africans who were actually transported, then, were already the hardy survivors of unimagi-

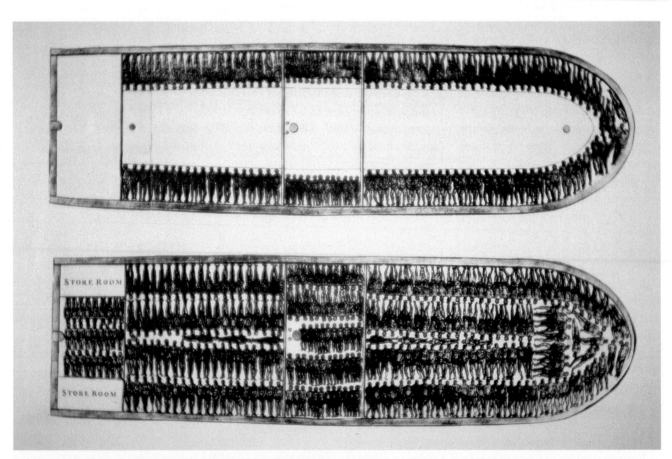

HOW SLAVES WERE STOWED ABOARD SHIP DURING THE MIDDLE PASSAGE. Men were "housed" on the right, women on the left, children in the middle. The human cargo was jammed onto platforms six feet wide without sufficient headroom to permit an adult to sit up. This diagram is from evidence gathered by English abolitionists and depicts conditions on the Liverpool slave ship *Brookes*.

nable hardships. For in order to place the above statistic in a larger context, we need to consider how many would have died before the ships were ready to transport them. One historian has estimated that 36 out of 100 people captured in the African interior would perish in the six-month-long forced march to the coast of Angola. Another dozen or so would die in the prisons there. Eventually, perhaps 57 of the original 100 captives would be taken on board a slave ship. Some 51 would survive the journey and be sold into slavery on arrival. If the destination was Brazil's sugar plantations, only 40 would still be alive after two years. In other words, the actual mortality rate of these new slaves was something more like 60 percent—and this doesn't begin to account for their life expectancy.

The people consigned to this fate struggled against it, and their initiatives helped to shape the emerging Atlantic world. When the opportunity presented itself, slaves banded together in revolt—a perpetual possibility that haunted slave owners and led to draconian regimes of violence and punishment (as in ancient Rome; see Chapter 5). When revolt was impossible, there were other forms of resistance, among them suicide and infanticide. Above all, slaves sought to escape. Almost as soon as the slave trade escalated, there were communities of escaped slaves throughout the Americas. Many of these independent settlements were large enough to assert and defend their autonomy. One such community, founded in 1603 in the hinterlands of Brazil's Pernambuco Province, persisted for over a century and had as many as 20,000 inhabitants. Most others were much smaller and more ephemeral, but their existence testifies to the limits of imperial authority at the fringes of the new American colonies.

CONFLICT AND COMPETITION IN EUROPE AND THE ATLANTIC WORLD

Most of Europe had enjoyed steady economic growth since the middle of the fifteenth century. The colonization of the Americas seemed to promise prosperity for the decades to come, while providing an outlet for European expansion and aggression. But in the second half of the sixteenth century, prolonged political, religious, and economic crises destabilized Europe. These crises were, in essential ways, the product of long-term developments within and between Europe's most powerful states, but they were exacerbated by these same states' imperial ambitions. Inevitably, then, European conflicts spread to European colonial holdings. Eventually,

the outcome of these conflicts would determine which European powers were best positioned to enlarge their presence in the Atlantic world—and beyond.

New World Silver and Old World Economies

In the latter half of the sixteenth century, an unprecedented inflation in prices profoundly destabilized the European economy. And because nothing on this scale had ever happened before, even during the Roman Empire's turbulent third century (see Chapter 6), it caused widespread panic. Although the twentieth century would see more dizzying inflations than this, skyrocketing prices were a terrifying novelty in this era, causing what some historians have termed a "price revolution."

Two developments in particular underlay this phenomenon. The first was demographic. After the plague-induced decline of the fourteenth century (see Chapter 11), Europe's population grew from roughly 50 million people

PEASANTS HARVESTING WHEAT, SIXTEENTH CENTURY.
The inflation that swept through Europe in the late sixteenth century affected poorer workers most acutely as the abundant labor supply dampened wages while at the same time the cost of food rose because of poor harvests.

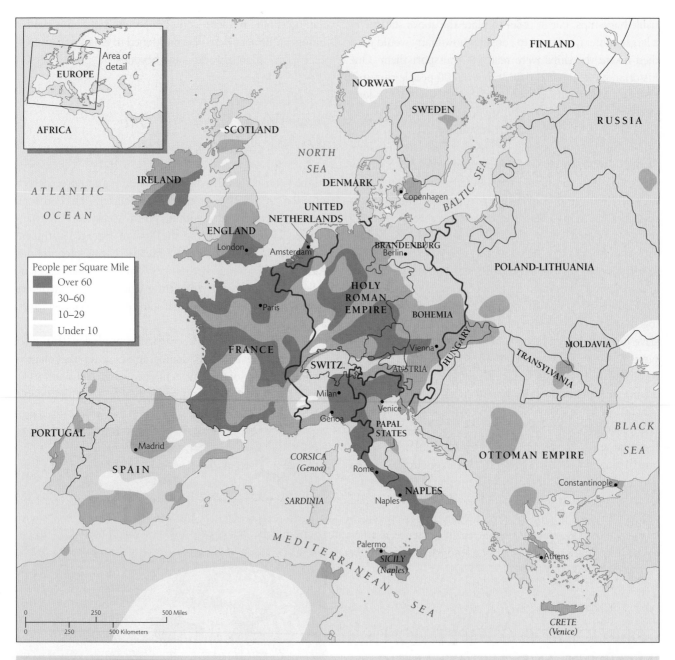

People per Square Mile
- Over 60
- 30–60
- 10–29
- Under 10

POPULATION GROWTH c. 1600. ▪ *In what regions did the population grow more rapidly?* ▪ *Why were the largest gains in population on the coasts?* ▪ *How would urbanization affect patterns of life and trade?*

in 1450 to 90 million in 1600: that is, it increased by nearly 80 percent in a relatively short span of time. Yet Europe's food supply remained nearly constant, meaning that food prices were driven sharply higher by the greater demand for basic commodities. Meanwhile, the enormous influx of silver and gold from Spanish America flooded Europe's previously cash-poor economy (see Chapter 12). This sudden availability of ready coin drove prices higher still.

How? In just four years, from 1556 to 1560, about 10 million ducats' worth of silver passed through the Spanish port of Seville: that is roughly equivalent to 10 billion U.S. dollars in today's currency. (A single gold ducat, the standard unit of monetary exchange for long-distance trade, would be worth nearly a thousand dollars.) Consequently, the market was flooded with coins whose worth quickly became debased because there were so many of them. And still silver poured in, cheapening the coinage even more: between 1576 and 1580, the amount of imported silver had doubled, becoming 20 million ducats; and between 1591 and 1595 it more than quadrupled. Because most of this money was used by the Spanish crown to pay its armies and the many creditors who had financed its imperial ventures, a huge volume of coinage was put quickly into circulation through European banks, making the problem of inflation even more widespread. Since some people suddenly had more money to pay for goods and services, those who supplied these commodities could charge higher and higher prices. "I learned a proverb here," said a French traveler in Spain in 1603: "Everything costs a lot, except silver."

The New European Poor

In this climate, aggressive entrepreneurs profited from financial speculation, landholders from the rising prices of agricultural produce, and merchants from increasing demand for luxury goods. But laborers were caught in a vice. Prices were rising steeply, but wages were not keeping pace owing to the population boom that kept labor relatively cheap. As the cost of food staples rose, poor people had to spend an ever-greater percentage of their paltry incomes on necessities. In Flanders, for example, the cost of wheat tripled between 1550 and 1600; grain prices in Paris quadrupled; and the overall cost of living in England more than doubled in Shakespeare's lifetime. When disasters such as wars or bad harvests drove grain prices out of their reach, as they frequently did, the poor starved to death.

The price revolution also placed new pressures on the sovereign states of Europe. Inflation depressed the real value of money, so fixed incomes derived from taxes and rents yielded less and less actual wealth. Governments were therefore forced to raise taxes merely to keep their revenues constant. Yet most states needed even more revenue than before, because they were engaging in more wars and warfare was becoming increasingly expensive. The only recourse, then, was to raise taxes precipitously. Hence, governments faced continuous threats of defiance and even armed resistance from their citizens, who could not afford to foot these bills.

Although prices rose less rapidly after 1600, as both population growth and the flood of silver began to slow, the ensuing decades were a time of economic stagnation. A few areas—notably the Netherlands (see below)—bucked the trend, and the rich were usually able to hold their own, but the laboring poor made no advances. Wages continued to rise far more slowly than prices. Indeed, the lot of the poor in many places deteriorated further, as helpless civilians were plundered by rapacious tax collectors, looting soldiers, or sometimes both. In England, peasants who had been dispossessed of property or driven off once-common lands were branded as vagrants, and vagrancy itself became a criminal offense. It was this population of newly impoverished Europeans who became the indentured servants or deported criminals of the American colonies.

The Legacy of the Reformation: The French Wars of Religion

Compounding these economic problems were the wars that erupted within many European states. As we began to observe in Chapter 9, most medieval kingdoms were created through the colonization of smaller, traditionally autonomous territories—either by conquest or through marriage alliances with ruling families. Now these enlarged monarchies began to make ever-greater financial claims on their citizens while at the same time demanding religious uniformity among them. The result was regional and civil conflict, as local populations and even elites rebelled against the centralizing demands of monarchs who often embraced a different religion than that of their subjects. Although the Peace of Augsburg (1555) had established that each territory would follow the religion of its ruler, in an effort to end civil strife (see Chapter 13), it was based on the premise that no state can tolerate religious diversity. This was a dangerous precedent, considering the rapid spread of new religious ideas throughout Europe and their export to the New World.

France was the first of these monarchies to be enflamed by religious warfare. Calvinist missionaries from Geneva had made significant headway there (Calvin himself was French), assisted by the conversion of many aristocratic Frenchwomen, who in turn converted their husbands. By the 1560s, French Calvinists—known as Huguenots (HEW-guh-nohz)—made up between 10 and 20 percent of the population. But there was no open warfare until dynastic politics led factions within the government to break down along religious lines, pitting the (mostly southern) Huguenots against the (mostly northern) Catholic aristocracy. In some places, mobs incited by members of the clergy on both sides used this opportunity to settle local scores.

While the Huguenots were not strong enough to win any major scuffle, there were too many to be ignored, and in 1572 the two sides almost brokered a truce: the presumptive heir to the throne, Prince Henry of Navarre—who had become a Protestant—was to marry the Catholic sister of the reigning king, Henry III. But the compromise was undone by the Queen Mother, Catherine de Medici, whose Catholic faction plotted to kill all the Huguenot leaders while they were assembled in Paris for her daughter's wedding. In the early morning of St. Bartholomew's Day (August 24), most of these Protestant aristocrats were

HENRY IV OF FRANCE. The rule of Henry of Navarre (r. 1589–1610) initiated the Bourbon dynasty that would rule France until 1792 and ended the bitter civil war between Catholic and Huguenot factions.

France had a regional component, the edict also reinforced a tradition of regional autonomy in southwestern France, in spite of the monarchy's centralized power. The success of this effort can be measured by the fact that peace was maintained in France even after Henry IV was assassinated by a Catholic in 1610.

The wars of religion may be one reason that France did not enter the competition for Atlantic wealth until the seventeenth century, despite their early involvement in North American explorations. It was not until 1608 that French colonial settlements received much royal support, after which Catholic (but not Huguenot) immigration to "New France" was encouraged. Meanwhile, there were three failed attempts to establish French outposts in Portuguese Brazil, the last of which (in 1612–15) resulted only in the export of six Amazonian villagers to France, where they aroused great curiosity in an organized tour of French towns. The Brazilians' Catholic hosts even arranged for them to be publicly baptized as part of an attempt to bolster support for the Catholic cause: an episode that further illustrates the strong connection between the expansion of European influence abroad and the politics of religion at home.

The Revolt of the Netherlands and the Dutch Trading Empire

Warfare between Catholics and Protestants also broke out in the Netherlands during this period. Controlled for almost a century by the same Habsburg family that ruled Spain and its overseas empire, the Netherlands had prospered through intense involvement with trade in the Atlantic world. Their inhabitants had the greatest per capita wealth in all Europe, and the metropolis of Antwerp was northern Europe's leading commercial and financial center. So when the Spanish king and emperor Philip II (r. 1556–98) attempted to tighten his hold there in the 1560s, the fiercely independent Dutch cities resented this imperial intrusion and were ready to fight it.

This conflict took on a religious dynamic because Calvinism had spread into the Netherlands from France. Philip, an ardent defender of the Catholic faith, could not tolerate this combination of political and religious disobedience. When crowds began ransacking and desecrating Catholic churches throughout the country, Philip dispatched an army of 10,000 Spanish soldiers to wipe out Protestantism in his Dutch territories. A reign of terror ensued: some 12,000 people were rounded up on charges of heresy or sedition, thousands of whom were convicted and executed for treason.

murdered in their beds, and thousands of humble Protestants were slaughtered in the streets or drowned in the Seine. When word of the Parisian massacre spread to the provinces, local massacres proliferated.

Henry of Navarre escaped, along with his bride, but the war continued for more than two decades. Finally, Catherine's death in 1589 was followed by that of her son, Henry III, who had produced no heir to supplant Henry of Navarre. He became Henry IV, renouncing his Protestant faith in order to placate France's Catholic majority. Then, in 1598, Henry made a landmark effort to end conflict by issuing the Edict of Nantes, which recognized Catholicism as the official religion of the realm but enabled Protestants to practice their religion in specified places. This was an important step toward a policy of religious tolerance: for the first time, French Protestants were allowed to hold public office and to enroll in universities and work in hospitals, and they were even allowed to fortify some towns for their own military defense. And because the religious divide in

PROTESTANTS RANSACKING A CATHOLIC CHURCH IN THE NETHERLANDS.
Protestant destruction of religious images provoked a stern response from Philip II.
■ *Why would Protestants have smashed statuary and other devotional artifacts?*

These events catalyzed the Protestant opposition. A Dutch aristocrat, William of Orange, emerged as the anti-Spanish leader and sought help from religious allies in France, Germany, and England. Organized bands of Protestant privateers (that is, privately owned ships) began harassing the Spanish navy in the waters of the North Atlantic. In 1572, William's Protestant army seized control of the Netherlands' northern provinces. Although William was assassinated in 1584, his efforts were instrumental in forcing the Spanish crown to recognize the independence of a northern Dutch Republic in 1609. Once united, these seven northern provinces became wholly Calvinist; the southern region, still largely Catholic, remained under Spanish rule.

After gaining its independence, the new Dutch Republic emerged as the most prosperous European commercial empire of the seventeenth century. Indeed, its reach extended well beyond the Atlantic world, targeting the Indian Ocean and East Asia as well. In general, the Dutch colonial project owed more to the strategic "fort and factory" model of expansion favored by the Portuguese than to the Spanish technique of territorial conquest and settlement. For example, the Dutch established a colony on the Cape of Good Hope at the southern tip of Africa, which facilitated the eastward spread of their influence. Many of its early initiatives were spurred by the establishment of the Dutch East India Company, a private mercantile corporation that came to control Sumatra, Borneo, and the Moluccas (the so-called Spice Islands). This meant that the Dutch had a lucrative monopoly on the European trade in pepper, cinnamon, nutmeg, mace, and cloves. The company also secured an exclusive right to trade with Japan and maintained military and trading outposts in China and India, too.

In the Atlantic world itself, the Dutch did not have much of a significant presence. However, they did establish an outpost in North America, the colony known as New Amsterdam—until it was surrendered to the English in 1667, when it was renamed New York. Their remaining territorial holdings in the Atlantic were Dutch Guyana (present-day Surinam) on the coast of South America, and the islands of Curaçao and Tobago in the Caribbean. But if the Dutch did not match the Spanish or the English in their accumulation of land, the establishment of a second merchant enterprise, the Dutch West India Company, allowed them to dominate the Atlantic slave trade with Africa after 1621.

In constructing this new transoceanic trading empire in slaves and spices, the Dutch pioneered a new financial mechanism for investing in colonial enterprises: the joint-stock company. The Dutch East and West India Companies were early examples, raising cash by selling shares to individual investors whose liability was limited to the sum of their investment. These investors were not part of the company's management, but they were entitled to a share in the profits. Originally, the Dutch East India Company intended to pay off its investors within ten years, but when the period was up, they convinced investors who wanted to realize their profits immediately to sell their shares on the open market. The creation of a market in shares—we now call it a stock market—was an innovation that spread quickly. Arguably, stock markets now control the world's economy.

The Struggle of England and Spain

Religious strife could spark civil war, as in France, or political rebellion, as in the Netherlands. But it could also provoke warfare between sovereign states, as in the struggle between England and Spain. In this case, religious conflict was entangled with both dynastic claims and economic competition in the Atlantic world.

The dynastic competition came from the English royal family's division along confessional lines. The Catholic queen Mary (r. 1553–58), eldest daughter of Henry VIII and granddaughter of Ferdinand and Isabella of Spain (see Chapter 13), had married her cousin Philip II of Spain in 1554 and ruled at a time of great strife between Catholics and Protestants

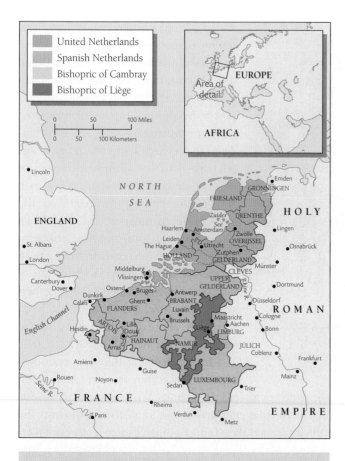

Map legend:
- United Netherlands
- Spanish Netherlands
- Bishopric of Cambray
- Bishopric of Liège

EUROPE
Area of detail
AFRICA

NORTH SEA

ENGLAND

HOLY

ROMAN

EMPIRE

FRANCE

THE NETHERLANDS AFTER 1609. ■ *What were the two main divisions of the Netherlands?* ■ *Which was Protestant, and which was Catholic?* ■ *How could William of Orange and his allies use the geography of the northern Netherlands against the Spanish?*

on the high seas. In a particularly dramatic exploit lasting from 1577 to 1580, prevailing winds and a lust for booty propelled Drake all the way around the world, to return with stolen Spanish treasure worth twice as much as Queen Elizabeth's annual revenue.

After suffering numerous such attacks over a period of two decades, King Philip finally resolved to fight back after Elizabeth's government openly supported the Dutch rebellion against Spain in 1585. In 1588, he dispatched an enormous fleet, confidently called the "Invincible Armada," whose mission was to invade England. But the invasion never occurred. After an indecisive initial encounter between the two fleets, a fierce storm—hailed as a "Protestant wind" by the lucky English—drove the Spanish galleons off course, many of them wrecking off the coast of Ireland. The shattered flotilla eventually limped home after a disastrous circumnavigation of the British isles, with almost half its ships lost. Meanwhile, Elizabeth took credit for her country's miraculous escape. In subsequent years, continued threats from Spain and sporadic skirmishes nurtured a renewed sense of English nationalism and also fueled anti-Catholic sentiment in that realm.

England's Colonial Ambitions

In the early decades of the seventeenth century, the English challenge to Spanish supremacy in the Atlantic began to bear fruit. Unlike New Spain, England's North American colonies had no significant mineral wealth; instead, as we noted above, English colonists sought to profit from the establishment of large-scale agricultural settlements in North America and the Caribbean. The first permanent colony was founded at Jamestown, Virginia, in 1607. Although this settlement was not particularly successful, more than twenty autonomous settlements were planted over the next forty years by a total of about 80,000 English immigrants.

Many of these were motivated by a desire for religious freedom—hence the name we still give to the Pilgrims who landed at Plymouth, Massachusetts, in 1620. These radical Protestants were known as Puritans, and because they were also political dissidents they were almost as unwelcome as Catholics in an England whose church was, after all, an extension of the monarchy. Strikingly, however, English colonists showed little interest in trying to convert Native American peoples to Christianity. Missionizing played a much larger role in Spanish efforts to colonize Central and South America and in French efforts to penetrate the North American hinterlands.

Another difference between Spanish and English colonialism is the fact that these English colonies did not

in England. After Mary's death, her Protestant half sister Elizabeth (r. 1558–1603) came to the throne, and relations with Spain rapidly declined. They declined further when Catholic Ireland—an English colony—rose in rebellion in 1565, with Spain quietly supporting the Irish. Although it took almost thirty bloody years, English forces eventually suppressed the rebellion. Elizabeth then cemented the Irish defeat by encouraging intense colonial settlement in Ireland. Somewhat ironically, she did so in conscious imitation of Spanish policy in the Americas, sending thousands of Protestant English settlers to occupy land in Ireland in the hopes of creating a colonial state with a largely English identity. Instead, these measures created the deep ethnic and religious conflicts that still trouble the island.

England's conflict with Spain, meanwhile, was worsened by the fact that English economic interests were directly opposed to those of Spain. English traders were making steady inroads into Spanish commercial networks in the Atlantic, as English sea captains such as Sir Francis Drake and Sir John Hawkins plundered Spanish vessels

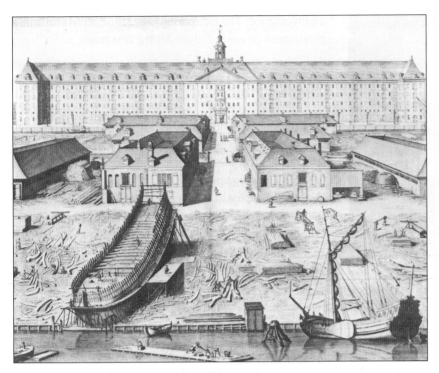

THE DUTCH EAST INDIA COMPANY WAREHOUSE AND TIMBER WHARF AT AMSTERDAM. The substantial warehouse, the stockpiles of lumber, and the company ship under construction in the foreground illustrate the degree to which overseas commerce could stimulate the economy of the mother country.

THE "ARMADA PORTRAIT" OF ELIZABETH. This is one of several portraits that commemorated the defeat of the Spanish Armada in 1588. Through the window on the left (the queen's right hand), an English flotilla sails serenely on sunny seas; on the right, Spanish ships are wrecked by a "Protestant wind." Elizabeth's right hand rests protectively—and commandingly—on the globe. ■ *How would you interpret this image?*

begin as royal enterprises. They were private ventures, farmed either by individual landholders (as in Maryland and Pennsylvania) or managed by joint-stock companies (as in Virginia and the Massachusetts Bay Colony). Building on their experience in Ireland, where colonies had been called "plantations," many English settlers established plantations—planned communities—that attempted to replicate as many features of English life as possible. Geography largely dictated the foundation locations of these English settlements, which were located along the northeast Atlantic coast and on rivers and bays that provided good harbors. Aside from the Hudson, however, there were no great rivers to lead colonists very far inland, so the English colonies clung to the coastline and to each other. The densely populated corridor along the Atlantic seaboard is a direct result of these early settlement patterns.

Since most land in the Old World was owned by royal and aristocratic families, the accumulation of wealth through the control of land was a new and exciting prospect for small-and medium-scale landholders in the new English colonies. This helps to explain their rural, agricultural character—in contrast to the great cities of New Spain. But this focus on agricultural holdings also resulted from the demographic catastrophe that had decimated native populations in this region, as in so many others: by the early seventeenth century, a great deal of rich land had been abandoned simply because there were so few native farmers to till it. As a result, indigenous peoples who had not already succumbed to European diseases were now under threat from colonists who wanted complete and exclusive control over their lands.

To this end, the English soon set out to eliminate, through expulsion and massacre, the former inhabitants of the region. There were a few exceptions; in the Quaker colony of Pennsylvania, colonists and Native Americans maintained friendly relations for more than half a

CHARLES I. King Charles of England was a connoisseur of the arts and a patron of artists. He was adept at using portraiture to convey the magnificence of his tastes and the grandeur of his conception of kingship. ▪ *How does this portrait by Anthony van Dyck compare to the engravings of the "martyred" king on page 480 in* **Interpreting Visual Evidence?**

seized control of the government. In order to ensure that the Puritan agenda would be carried out, he ejected all the moderates from Parliament by force. This "Rump" (remaining) Parliament then proceeded to put the king on trial and eventually to condemn him to death for treason against his own subjects. Charles Stuart was publicly beheaded on January 30, 1649: the first time in history that a reigning king had been legally deposed and executed. Europeans reacted to his death with horror, astonishment, or rejoicing, depending on their own political convictions (see *Interpreting Visual Evidence* on page 480).

After the king's execution, his son (the future King Charles II) joined with the remaining royalist forces in an attempt to restore the monarchy. But he was defeated by Cromwell's army and fled to France. With the heir to the English throne in exile, Cromwell and his supporters abolished Parliament's hereditary House of Lords and declared England a Commonwealth: an English translation of the Latin *res publica*. Technically, the Rump Parliament continued as the legislative body; but Cromwell, with the army at his command, possessed the real power and soon became exasperated by legislators' attempts to enrich themselves by confiscating their opponents' property. In 1653, he

and England as the state religion. But a radical minority of Puritans, commonly known as Independents, insisted on religious freedom for themselves and all other Protestants. Their leader was Oliver Cromwell (1599–1658), who had risen to command the Roundhead army, which he had reconstituted as "the New Model Army." Ultimately, he became the new leader of Parliament, too.

The Fall of Charles Stuart and Oliver Cromwell's Commonwealth

Taking advantage of the dissension within the ranks of his opponents, Charles renewed the war in 1648. But he was forced to surrender after a brief campaign, and Cromwell

OLIVER CROMWELL AS PROTECTOR OF THE COMMONWEALTH. This coin, minted in 1658, shows the lord protector wreathed with laurel garlands like a classical hero or a Roman consul, but it also proclaims him to be "by the Grace of God Protector of the Commonwealth." ▪ *What mixed messages does this coin convey?*

marched a detachment of troops into the Rump Parliament and disbanded it.

The short-lived Commonwealth was thus replaced by the "Protectorate," a thinly disguised autocracy established under a constitution drafted by officers of the army. Called the *Instrument of Government*, this text is the nearest approximation to a written constitution England has ever had. Extensive powers were given to Cromwell as Lord Protector for life, and his office was made hereditary.

The Restoration of the Monarchy

Many intellectuals noted the similarities between these events and those that had given rise to the Principate of Augustus after the death of Julius Caesar (Chapter 5). And among the people, Cromwell's Puritan military dictatorship was growing unpopular, not least because it prohibited public recreation on Sundays and closed London's theatres. Many became nostalgic for the milder and more tolerant Church of England and began to hope for a restoration of the old royalist regime. The opportunity came with Cromwell's death in 1658. His son Richard had no sooner succeeded to the office of Lord Protector when a faction within the army removed him from power. As groups of royalists plotted an uprising, a new Parliament was organized, and, in April of 1660, it declared that King Charles II had been the ruler of England since his father's execution in 1649. Almost overnight, England became a monarchy again.

Charles II (r. 1660–85) revived the Church of England and was careful not to return to the provocative religious policies of his father. Quipping that he did not wish to "resume his travels," he agreed to respect Parliament and to observe the Petition of Right that had so enraged Charles I. He also accepted all the legislation passed by Parliament immediately before the outbreak of civil war in 1642, including the requirement that Parliament be summoned at least once every three years. England thus emerged from its civil war as a limited monarchy, in which power was exercised by "the king in Parliament." It remains a constitutional monarchy to this day.

The English Civil War and the Atlantic World

These tumultuous events had a significant influence on the development of a new political sensibility within England's Atlantic colonies. The English landed aristocracy had sided with the king during this conflict, but many in the colonies had sympathized with Parliament in its claims to protect the liberties of small landowners, who also bore a dispro-portionate share of taxation. Even after the Restoration of the monarchy in 1660, many colonial leaders retained an antimonarchist and antiaristocratic bias.

The fact that the royal government had been almost entirely concerned with the business of putting down rebellion at home also meant that England's colonies became used, at an early stage, to a large degree of independence. As a result, once government was restored, all of Parliament's efforts to extend more control over the colonies would result in greater and greater friction (see Chapter 15). Slogans declaring the rights of "free-born Englishmen" would echo among farmers, while "free trade" became a rallying cry against royal interference in colonial commerce. The bitter religious conflicts that had divided the more radical Puritans from the Church of England also forced the colonies to come to grips with the problem of religious diversity. Some, like Massachusetts, took the opportunity to impose their own brand of Puritanism on settlers. Others experimented with forms of religious toleration that sometimes went beyond the forms of religious freedom that existed back in England.

Paradoxically, though, the spread of ideas about the protection of liberties and citizens' rights coincided with a rapid and considerable expansion of unfree labor in the colonies. Prior to the 1640s, the English colonies in North America and the Caribbean had been assured of a steady stream of immigrants, like the Puritan Pilgrims of Massachusetts in 1620. The outbreak of war in 1642 and the subsequent triumph of the Puritans under Cromwell caused a drop in this migration, since many who might have thought of emigrating decided to stay in England. In North America, the decline in the arrival of new settlers was so sudden that it caused a depression in local economies.

Meanwhile, the demand for labor was increasing rapidly owing to the expansion of tobacco plantations in Virginia and sugar plantations in Barbados and Jamaica, which the British captured from the Spanish in 1655. These plantations, with their punishing working conditions and high mortality rates from disease, were insatiable in their demand for workers. Plantation owners thus sought to meet this demand by investing ever more heavily in forms of unfree labor, including indentured servants and African slaves. The social and political crisis unleashed by the English Civil War also led to the forced migration of paupers and political prisoners, especially from Scotland, Wales, and Ireland; and this pattern continued during Cromwell's reign. These exiles, many without resources, swelled the ranks of the unfree and the very poor in England's Atlantic colonies, spurring the formation of new social hierarchies as earlier arrivals sought to distance themselves from newer immigrants they regarded

Competing Viewpoints

Debating the English Civil War

The English Civil War raised fundamental questions about political rights and responsibilities. Many of these are addressed in the two excerpts below. The first comes from a lengthy debate held within the General Council of Cromwell's army in October of 1647. The second is taken from the speech given by King Charles, moments before his execution in 1649.

The Army Debates, 1647

Colonel Rainsborough: Really, I think that the poorest man that is in England has a life to live as the greatest man, and therefore truly, sir, I think it's clear, that every man that is to live under a government ought first by his own consent to put himself under that government, and I do think that the poorest man in England is not at all bound in a strict sense to that government that he has not had a voice to put himself under . . . insomuch that I should doubt whether I was an Englishman or not, that should doubt of these things.

General Ireton: Give me leave to tell you, that if you make this the rule, I think you must fly for refuge to an absolute natural right, and you must deny all civil right, and I am sure it will come to that in the consequence. . . . For my part, I think it is no right at all. I think that no person has a right to an interest or share in the disposing of the affairs of the kingdom, and in determining or choosing those that shall determine what laws we shall be ruled by here, no person has a right to this that has not a permanent fixed interest in this kingdom, and those persons together are properly the represented of this kingdom who, taken together, and consequently are to make up the representers of this kingdom. . . .

We talk of birthright. Truly, birthright there is. . . . [M]en may justly have by birthright, by their very being born in England, that we should not seclude them out of England. That we should not refuse to give them air and place and ground, and the freedom of the highways and other things, to live amongst us, not any man that is born here, though he in birth or by his birth there come nothing at all that is part of the permanent interest of this kingdom to him. That I think is due to a man by birth. But that by a man's being born here he shall have a share in that power that shall dispose of the lands here, and of all things here, I do not think it is a sufficient ground.

Source: David Wootton, ed., *Divine Right and Democracy: An Anthology of Political Writing in Stuart England* (New York: 1986), pp. 286–87 (language modernized).

---

as inferiors. The crisis of kingship in England thus led to a substantial increase in the African slave trade and a sharpening of social and economic divisions in the English colonies. This is yet another indication of Europe's inseparable relationship with the Atlantic world.

THE PROBLEM OF DOUBT AND THE ART OF BEING HUMAN

On the first day of November in 1611, a new play by William Shakespeare premiered in London, at the royal court. *The Tempest* takes place on a remote island, where an exiled duke from the Italian city-state of Milan has used his magical arts to subjugate the island's inhabitants. This plot drew on widespread reports from the new European colonies of the Atlantic, especially the Caribbean, where slaves were called Caribans and where (it was rumored) cannibalism flourished—hence the name Shakespeare chose for the play's rebellious slave Caliban, who seeks to revenge himself on the magician Prospero, his oppressive master. When reminded that he owes his knowledge of the English language to the civilizing influence of Prospero's daughter, Miranda, Caliban retorts, "You taught me language, and my profit on't / Is, I know how to curse."

According to Caliban, the benefits of a European education could not outweigh the evils of colonization—and

Charles I on the Scaffold, 1649

think it is my duty, to God first, and to my country, for to clear myself both as an honest man, a good king, and a good Christian.

I shall begin first with my innocence. In truth I think it not very needful for me to insist long upon this, for all the world knows that I never did begin a war with the two Houses of Parliament, and I call God to witness, to whom I must shortly make an account, that I never did intend to incroach upon their privileges. . . .

As for the people—truly I desire their liberty and freedom as much as anybody whatsoever. But I must tell you that their liberty and freedom consists in having of government those laws by which their lives and goods may be most their own. It is not for having share in government. That is nothing pertaining to them. A subject and a sovereign are clean different things, and therefore, until they do

that—I mean that you do put the people in that liberty as I say—certainly they will never enjoy themselves.

Sirs, it was for this that now I am come here. If I would have given way to an arbitrary way, for to have all laws changed according to the power of the sword, I needed not to have come here. And therefore I tell you (and I pray God it be not laid to your charge) that I am the martyr of the people.

Source: Brian Tierney, Donald Kagan, and L. Pearce Williams, eds., *Great Issues in Western Civilization* (New York: 1967), pp. 46–47.

Questions for Analysis

1. What fundamental issues are at stake in both of these excerpts? How do the debaters within the parliamentary army (first excerpt) define "natural" and "civil" rights?

2. How does Charles defend his position? What is his theory of kingship, and how does it compare to that of Cardinal Richelieu's (page 475)? How does it conflict with the ideas expressed in the army's debate?

3. It is interesting that none of the participants in these debates seems to have recognized the implications their arguments might have for the political rights of women. Why would that have been the case?

could, in fact, be used to resist it. Shakespeare's audience was thus confronted with a spectacle of their own colonial ambitions gone awry, as well as with a number of other contemporary problems, including the perils of civil war, the struggle for political legitimacy, the fear of sorcery, and the availability of exotic commodities.

The doubt and uncertainty caused by Europe's extension into the Atlantic world were primary themes and motivators of this era's creative arts, which both documented and critiqued contemporary trends while emphasizing the redemptive qualities of human suffering and compassion. Another example of this artistic response is the novel *Don Quixote*, which its author, Miguel de Cervantes (*sehr-VAHN-tehs*, 1547–1616), composed largely in prison. It recounts the

adventures of an idealistic Spanish gentleman, Don Quixote of La Mancha, who becomes deranged by his constant reading of chivalric romances and sets out to have delusional adventures of his own. His sidekick, Sancho Panza, is his exact opposite: a plain, practical man content with modest bodily pleasures. Together, they represent different facets of human nature. On the one hand, *Don Quixote* is a devastating satire of Spain's decline. On the other, it is a sincere celebration of the human capacity for optimism and goodness.

Throughout the long century between 1550 and 1660, Europeans confronted a world in which all that they had once taken for granted was cast into confusion. Vast continents had been discovered, populated by millions of people whose very existence challenged Western civilizations'

Shakespeare's Popular Appeal

Although the plays of William Shakespeare are frequently described as elite entertainments, their enduring appeal can hardly be explained in those terms. In fact, Shakespeare wrote for a diverse audience—and a group of actors—who would have been more likely to see the inside of a prison than a royal court. His plays combine high politics, earthy comedy, and deeply human stories that still captivate and motivate audiences at the reconstructed Globe Theatre in London (left). They also lend themselves to inventive adaptations that comment on our own contemporary world, as in the recent film of *Coriolanus*.

 Watch related author interview on StudySpace
wwnorton.com/web/westernciv18

The Artists of Southern Europe

The ironies and tensions inherent in this age were also explored in the visual arts. In Italy and Spain, many painters cultivated a highly dramatic style sometimes known as "Mannerism." The most unusual of these artists was El Greco ("the Greek," c. 1541–1614), a pupil of the Venetian master Tintoretto (1518–1594). Born Domenikos Theotokopoulos on the Greek island of Crete, El Greco absorbed some of the stylized elongation characteristic of Byzantine icon painting (see Chapter 7) before traveling to Italy. He eventually settled in Spain. Many of his paintings were too strange to be greatly appreciated in his own day and even now appear so avant-garde as to be almost surreal. His *View of Toledo*, for example, is a transfigured landscape, mysteriously lit from within. Equally amazing are his swirling biblical scenes and the stunning portraits of gaunt, dignified saints who radiate austerity and spiritual insight.

In the seventeenth century, the dominant artistic style of southern Europe was that of the Baroque, a school whose name has become a synonym for elaborate, highly wrought sculpture and architectural details. This style originated in Rome during the Counter-Reformation and promoted a glorified Catholic worldview. Its most imaginative and influential figure was the architect and sculptor Gianlorenzo Bernini (1598–1680), a frequent employee of the papacy who created a magnificent celebration of papal grandeur in the sweeping colonnades leading up to St. Peter's Basilica. Breaking with the more serene classicism of Renaissance styles (see Chapter 12), Bernini's work drew inspiration from the restless motion and artistic bravado of Hellenistic statuary (see Chapter 4).

Characteristics of this Baroque style can also be found in paintings like those of the great Spanish master Diego Velázquez (*vay-LAH-skwez*, 1599–1660), who served the Spanish Habsburg court in Madrid. Although

VIEW OF TOLEDO BY EL GRECO. This is one of many landscape portraits representing the hilltop city that became the artist's home in later life. Its supple Mannerist style almost defies historical periodization.

DAVID BY BERNINI (1598–1680). Whereas the earlier conceptions of David by the Renaissance sculptors Donatello and Michelangelo were serene and dignified (see page 000), the Baroque sculptor Bernini chose to portray his young hero at the peak of physical exertion. ■ *Can you discern the influence of Hellenistic sculpture (see Chapter 4) in this work?* ■ *What are some shared characteristics?*

many of his canvases display a Baroque attention to motion and drama, those most characteristic of his own style are more conceptually thoughtful and daring. An example is *The Maids of Honor*, completed around 1656 and a masterpiece of self-referentiality. It shows the artist himself at work on a double portrait of the Spanish king and queen, but the scene is dominated by the children and servants of the royal family.

Dutch Painting in the Golden Age

Southern Europe's main rival in the visual arts was the Netherlands, where many exemplary but dissimilar painters explored the theme of man's greatness and wretchedness to the full. Pieter Bruegel the Elder (*BROY-ghul*, c. 1525–1569) exulted in portraying the busy, elemental life of the peasantry. Most famous in this respect are his rollicking *Peasant Wedding* and *Peasant Wedding Dance* and his spacious *Harvesters*, in which field hands are taking a well-deserved break under the noonday sun. Such vistas celebrate the uninterrupted rhythms of life; but late in his career, Bruegel became appalled by the intolerance and bloodshed he witnessed during the Calvinist riots and the Spanish repression of the Netherlands, expressing his criticism in works like *The Massacre of the Innocents*. From a distance, this looks like a snug scene of village

THE MAIDS OF HONOR (LAS MEÑINAS) BY DIEGO VELÁZQUEZ. The artist himself (at left) is shown working at his easel and gazing out at the viewer—or at the subjects of his double portrait, the Spanish king and queen, depicted in a distant mirror. But the real focus of the painting is the delicate, impish princess in the center, flanked by two young ladies-in-waiting, a dwarf, and another royal child. Courtiers in the background look on.

life. In fact, however, soldiers are methodically breaking into homes and slaughtering helpless infants, as Herod's soldiers once did and as warring armies were doing in Bruegel's own day.

Another Dutch painter, Peter Paul Rubens (1577–1640), was inspired by very different politics. A native of Antwerp, still part of the Spanish Netherlands, Rubens was a staunch Catholic who glorified the Roman Church and the local aristocrats who supported the Habsburg regime. Even when his intent was not propagandistic, Rubens reveled in the sumptuous extravagance of the Baroque style; he is most famous today for the pink and rounded flesh of his well-nourished nudes. But Rubens was not lacking in subtlety or depth. Although he celebrated martial valor for most of his career, his late painting of *The Horrors of War* movingly captures what

he called "the grief of unfortunate Europe, which, for so many years now, has suffered plunder, outrage, and misery."

In some ways a blend of Bruegel and Rubens, Rembrandt van Rijn (*vahn-REEN*, 1606–1669) defies all attempts at easy characterization. Living across the border from the Spanish Netherlands in the staunchly Calvinist Dutch Republic, Rembrandt managed to put both realistic and Baroque traits to new uses. In his early career, he gained fame and fortune as a painter of biblical scenes and was also active as a portrait painter who knew how to flatter his subjects—to the great advantage of his purse. But as personal tragedies mounted in his middle and declining years, the painter's art gained in dignity, subtlety, and mystery. His later portraits, including several self-portraits, are highly introspective and suggest

THE MASSACRE OF THE INNOCENTS BY BRUEGEL (c. 1525–1569). This painting shows how effectively art can be used as a means of political and social commentary. Here, Bruegel depicts the suffering of the Netherlands at the hands of the Spanish in his own day, with reference to the biblical story of Herod's slaughter of Jewish children after the birth of Jesus—thereby collapsing these two historical incidents.

***THE HORRORS OF WAR* BY RUBENS (1577–1640).** In his old age, Rubens took a far more critical view of war than he had done for most of his earlier career. Here, the war-god Mars casts aside his mistress Venus, goddess of love, and threatens humanity with death and destruction.

SELF-PORTRAITS. Self-portraits became common during the sixteenth and seventeenth centuries, reflecting the intense introspection of the period. Left: Rembrandt painted more than sixty self-portraits; this one, dating from around 1660, captures the artist's creativity, theatricality (note the costume), and honesty of self-examination. Right: Judith Leyster was a contemporary of Rembrandt who pursued a successful career during her early twenties, before she married. Respected in her own day, she was all but forgotten for centuries thereafter but is once again the object of much attention.

that only part of the story is being told. Equally fearless is the frank gaze of Rembrandt's slightly younger contemporary, Judith Leyster (1609–1660), who looks out of her own self-portrait with a refreshingly optimistic and good-humored expression.

CONCLUSION

It would take centuries for Europeans to adapt themselves to the changes brought about by their integration into the Atlantic world and to process its implications. Finding new

ability to project his authority into the remote corners of his realm and to do so in a way that diminished the power of other elites. During his long reign (1643–1715), Louis XIV systematically pursued such a policy on many fronts, asserting his power over the nobility, the clergy, and the provincial courts. Increasingly, these elites were forced to look to the crown to guarantee their interests, and their own power became more closely connected with the sacred aura of the monarchy itself. Louis XIV's model of kingship was so successful that it became known as absolute monarchy. In recognition of the success and influence of Louis XIV's political system, the period from around 1660 (when the English monarchy was restored and Louis XIV began his personal rule in France) to 1789 (when the French Revolution erupted) is traditionally known as the age of absolutism. This is a crucial period in the development of modern, centralized, bureaucratic states in Europe.

Absolutism was a political theory that encouraged rulers to claim complete sovereignty within their territories. An absolute monarch could make law, dispense justice, create and direct a bureaucracy, declare war, and levy taxation, without the approval of any other governing body. Assertions of absolute authority were buttressed by claims that rulers governed by divine right, just as fathers ruled over their households. After the chaos and religious wars of the previous century, many Europeans came to believe that it was only by exalting the sovereignty of absolute rulers that order could be restored to European life.

European monarchs also continued to project their power abroad during this period. By 1660, as we have seen, the French, Spanish, Portuguese, English, and Dutch had all established important colonies in the Americas and in Asia. These colonies created trading networks that brought profitable new consumer goods such as sugar, tobacco, and coffee to a wide public in Europe. They also encouraged the colonies' reliance on slavery to produce these goods. Rivalry among colonial powers to control the trade in slaves and consumer goods was intense and often led to wars that were fought both in Europe and in contested colonies. These wars, in turn, increased the motivation of absolutist rulers to extract as much revenue as they could from their subjects and encouraged the development of institutions that enhanced their power: armies, navies, tax systems, tariffs and customs controls.

Absolutism was not universally successful during this period. The English monarchy, restored in 1660 after the turbulent years of the Civil War, attempted to impose absolutist rule but met with resistance from parliamentary leaders who insisted on more inclusive institutions of government. After 1688, England, Scotland, the Dutch Republic, Switzerland, Venice, Sweden, and Poland-Lithuania were all either limited monarchies or republics. In Russia, on the other hand, an extreme autocracy emerged that gave the tsar a degree of control over his subjects' lives and property far beyond anything imagined by western European absolutists. Even in Russia, however, absolutism was never unlimited in practice. Even the most absolute monarchs could rule effectively only with the consent of their subjects (particularly the nobility). When serious opposition erupted, even powerful kings were forced to back down. King George III of Britain discovered this when his North American colonies declared their independence in 1776, creating the United States of America. In 1789, an even more sweeping revolution began in France, and the entire structure of absolutism came crashing to the ground (see Chapter 18).

THE DEFENSE OF CADÍZ AGAINST THE ENGLISH BY FRANCISCO ZURBARAN. The rivalry between European powers that played out over the new colonial possessions further proved the decline of Spain, which lost the island of Jamaica and ships in the harbor of Cadíz to the English in the 1650s.

THE APPEAL AND JUSTIFICATION OF ABSOLUTISM

Absolutism's promise of stability and order was an appealing alternative to the disorder of the "iron century" that preceded it. The early theorists of absolutism such as Jean Bodin and Thomas Hobbes looked to strong royal governments as an answer to the violence of religious wars and the crisis of the sixteenth and seventeenth centuries (see Chapter 14). Louis XIV himself was profoundly disturbed by an aristocratic revolt that occurred while he was still a child. When marauding Parisians entered his bedchamber one night in 1651, Louis saw the intrusion as an affront not only to his own person but to the majesty of the French state. Such experiences convinced him that he needed to rule assertively and without limits to his power.

Absolutist monarchs sought control of the state's armed forces and its legal system, and they demanded the right to collect and spend the state's financial resources at will. To achieve these goals, they also needed to create an efficient, centralized bureaucracy that owed its allegiance directly to the monarch. Creating and sustaining such a bureaucracy was expensive but necessary in order to weaken the special interests that hindered the free exercise of royal power. The nobility and the clergy, with their traditional legal privileges; the political authority of semiautonomous regions; and representative assemblies such as parliaments, diets, or estates-general were all obstacles—in the eyes of absolutists—to strong, centralized monarchical government. The history of absolutism is the history of kings who attempted to bring such institutions to heel.

In most Protestant countries, the power of the church had already been subordinated to the state when the age of absolutism began. Even where Roman Catholicism remained the state religion, such as in France, Spain, and Austria, absolutist monarchs now devoted considerable attention to bringing the Church and its clergy under royal control. Louis XIV took an active role in religious matters, appointing his own bishops and encouraging the repression of religious dissidents. Unlike his predecessors, however, he rarely appointed members of the clergy to offices within his administration.

The most important potential opponents of royal absolutism were not churchmen, however, but nobles. Louis XIV deprived the French nobility of political power in the provinces but increased their social prestige by making them live at his lavish court at Versailles. Peter the Great of Russia (1689–1725) forced his nobles into lifelong government service, and successive monarchs in Brandenburg-Prussia managed to co-opt the powerful aristocracy by granting them immunity to taxation and giving them the right to enserf their peasants. In exchange, they ceded administrative control to the increasingly bureaucratized Prussian state. In most European monarchies, including Spain, France, Prussia, and England, the nobility retained their preponderant role within the military.

Struggles between monarchs and nobles frequently affected relations between local and central government. In France, the requirement that nobles live at the king's court undermined the provincial institutions that the nobility used to exercise their political power. In Spain, the monarchy, based in Castile, battled the independent-minded nobles of Aragon and Catalonia. Prussian rulers asserted control over formerly "free" cities by claiming the right to police and tax their inhabitants. The Habsburg emperors tried, unsuccessfully, to suppress the largely autonomous nobility of Hungary. Rarely, however, was the path of confrontation between crown and nobility successful in the long run. The most effective absolutist monarchies of the eighteenth century continued to trade privileges for allegiance, so that nobles came to see their own interests as tied to those of the crown. For this reason, wary cooperation between kings and nobles was more common than open conflict during the eighteenth century.

THE ABSOLUTISM OF LOUIS XIV

In Louis XIV's state portrait, it is almost impossible to discern the human being behind the facade of the absolute monarch dressed in his coronation robes and surrounded by the symbols of his authority. That facade was artfully constructed by Louis, who recognized, more fully than any other early modern ruler, the importance of theater to effective kingship. Louis and his successors deliberately staged spectacular demonstrations of their sovereignty to enhance their position as rulers endowed with godlike powers.

Performing Royalty at Versailles

Louis's most elaborate staging of his authority took place at his palace at Versailles (vuhr-SY), outside of Paris. The main facade of the palace was a third of a mile in length. Inside, tapestries and paintings celebrated French military victories and royal triumphs; mirrors reflected shimmering light throughout the building. In the vast gardens outside, statues of the Greek god Apollo, god of the sun, recalled Louis's claim to be the "Sun King" of France. Noblemen vied to attend him when he arose from bed, ate his meals

The Performance and Display of Absolute Power at the Court of Louis XIV

istorians studying the history of absolutism and the court of Louis XIV in particular have emphasized the Sun King's brilliant use of symbols and display to demonstrate his personal embodiment of sovereignty. Royal portraits, such as that painted by Hyacinthe Rigaud in 1701, vividly illustrate the degree to which Louis's power was based on a studied performance. His pose, with his exposed and shapely calf, was an important indication of power and virility, necessary elements of legitimacy for a hereditary monarch. In the elaborate rituals of court life at Versailles, Louis often placed his own body at the center of attention, performing in one instance as the god Apollo in a ballet before his assembled courtiers. His movements through the countryside, accompanied by a retinue of soldiers, servants, and aristocrats, were another occasion for highly stylized ritual demonstrations of his quasi-divine status. Finally, of course, the construction of his palace at Versailles, with its symmetrical architecture and its sculpted gardens, was a demonstration that his power extended over the natural world as easily as it did over the lives of his subjects.

Questions for Analysis

1. Who was the intended audience for the king's performance of absolute sovereignty?

2. Who were Louis's primary competitors in this contest for eminence through the performance of power?

3. What possible political dangers might lie in wait for a regime that invested so heavily in the sumptuous display of semidivine authority?

A. Hyacinthe Rigaud's 1701 portrait of Louis XIV.

B. Louis XIV as the Sun King.

C. *The Royal Procession of Louis XIV*, 1664, by Adam Franz van der Meulen.

D. Louis XIV arrives at the Palace of Versailles.

Competing Viewpoints

Absolutism and Patriarchy

These selections show how two political theorists justified royal absolutism by deriving it from the absolute authority of a father over his household. Bishop Jacques-Bénigne Bossuet (1627–1704) was a famous French preacher who served as tutor to the son of King Louis XIV of France before becoming bishop of Meaux. Sir Robert Filmer (1588–1653) was an English political theorist. Filmer's works attracted particular attention in the 1680s, when John Locke directed the first of his Two Treatises of Government *to refuting Filmer's views on the patriarchal nature of royal authority.*

Bossuet on the Nature of Monarchical Authority

There are four characteristics or qualities essential to royal authority. First, royal authority is sacred; Secondly, it is paternal; Thirdly, it is absolute; Fourthly, it is subject to reason. . . . All power comes from God. . . . Thus princes act as ministers of God, and his lieutenants on earth. It is through them that he exercises his empire. . . . In this way . . . the royal throne is not the throne of a man, but the throne of God himself. . . .

We have seen that kings hold the place of God, who is the true Father of the human race. We have also seen that the first idea of power that there was among men, is that of paternal power; and that kings were fashioned on the model of fathers. Moreover, all the world agrees that obedience, which is due to public power, is only found . . . in the precept which obliges one to honor his parents. From all this it appears that the name "king" is a father's name, and that goodness is the most natural quality in kings. . . .

Royal authority is absolute. In order to make this term odious and insupportable, many pretend to confuse absolute government and arbitrary government. But nothing is more distinct, as we shall make clear when we speak of justice. . . . The prince need account to no one for what he ordains. . . . Without this absolute authority, he can neither do good nor suppress evil: his power must be such that no one can hope to escape him. . . . [T]he sole defense of individuals against the public power must be their innocence. . . .

One must, then, obey princes as if they were justice itself, without which there is neither order nor justice in affairs. They are gods, and share in some way in divine independence. . . . It follows from this that he who does not want to obey the prince . . . is condemned irremissibly to death as an enemy of public peace and of human society. . . . The prince can correct himself when he knows that he has done badly; but against his authority there can be no remedy. . . .

Source: Jacques-Bénigne Bossuet, *Politics Drawn from the Very Words of Holy Scripture*, trans. Patrick Riley (Cambridge: 1990), pp. 46–69 and 81–83.

(usually stone cold after having traveled the distance of several city blocks from kitchen to table), strolled in his gardens (even the way the king walked was choreographed by the royal dancing master), or rode to the hunt. France's leading nobles were required to reside with Louis at Versailles for a portion of the year; the splendor of Louis's court was deliberately calculated to blind them to the possibility of disobedience while raising their prestige by associating them with himself. At the same time, the almost impossibly detailed rules of etiquette at court left these privileged nobles in constant suspense, forever fearful of offending the king by committing some trivial violation of proper manners.

Of course, the nobility did not surrender social and political power entirely. The social order was still hierarchical, and noblemen retained enormous privileges and rights over local peasants within their jurisdiction. The absolutist system forced the nobility to depend on the crown, but it did not seek to undermine their superior place in society. In this sense, the relationship between

Filmer on the Patriarchal Origins of Royal Authority

The first government in the world was monarchical, in the father of all flesh, Adam being commanded to multiply, and people the earth, and to subdue it, and having dominion given him over all creatures, was thereby the monarch of the whole world; none of his posterity had any right to possess anything, but by his grant or permission, or by succession from him. . . . Adam was the father, king and lord over his family: a son, a subject, and a servant or a slave were one and the same thing at first. . . .

I cannot find any one place or text in the Bible where any power . . . is given to a people either to govern themselves, or to choose themselves governors, or to alter the manner of government at their pleasure. The power of government is settled and fixed by the commandment of "honour thy father"; if there were a higher power than the fatherly, then this commandment could not stand and be observed. . . .

All power on earth is either derived or usurped from the fatherly power, there being no other original to be found of any power whatsoever. For if there should be granted two sorts of power without any subordination of one to the other, they would be in perpetual strife which should be the supreme, for two supremes cannot agree. If the fatherly power be supreme, then the power of the people must be subordinate and depend on it. If the power of the people be supreme, then the fatherly power must submit to it, and cannot be exercised without the licence of the people, which must quite destroy the frame and course of nature. Even the power which God himself exercises over mankind is by right of fatherhood: he is both the king and father of us all. As God has exalted the dignity of earthly kings . . . by saying they are gods, so . . . he has been pleased . . . [t]o humble himself by assuming the title of a king to express his power, and not the title of any popular government.

Source: Robert Filmer, "Observations upon Aristotle's Politiques," in *Divine Right and Democracy: An Anthology of Political Writing in Stuart England*, ed. David Wootton (Harmondsworth, UK: 1986), pp. 110–118. First published 1652.

Questions for Analysis

1. Bossuet's definition of *absolutism* connected the sacred power of kings with the paternal authority of fathers within the household. What consequences does he draw from defining the relationship between king and subjects in this way?

2. What does Filmer mean when he says, "All power on earth is either derived or usurped from the fatherly power"? How many examples does he give of paternal or monarchical power?

3. Bossuet and Filmer make obedience the basis for order and justice in the world. What alternative political systems did they most fear?

Louis XIV and the nobility was more of a negotiated settlement than a complete victory of the king over other powerful elites. Louis XIV understood this, and in a memoir that he prepared for his son on the art of ruling he wrote, "The deference and the respect that we receive from our subjects are not a free gift from them but payment for the justice and the protection that they expect from us. Just as they must honor us, we must protect and defend them." In their own way, absolutists depended on the consent of those they ruled.

Administration and Centralization

Louis defined his responsibilities in absolutist terms: to concentrate royal power so as to produce domestic tranquillity. In addition to convincing the nobility to cede political authority, he also recruited the upper bourgeoisie as royal intendants, administrators responsible for running the thirty-six *generalités* into which France was divided. Intendants usually served outside the region where they were born and were thus unconnected with

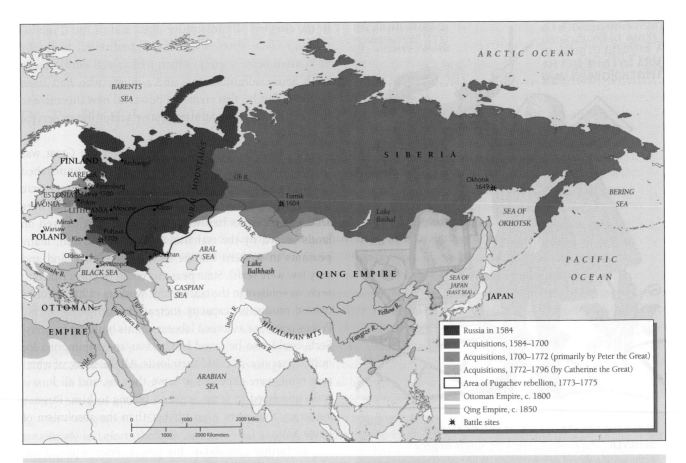

THE GROWTH OF THE RUSSIAN EMPIRE. ▪ *How did Peter the Great expand the territory controlled by Russia?* ▪ *What neighboring dynasties would have been the most affected by Russian expansion?* ▪ *How did the emergence of a bigger, more powerful Russia affect the European balance of power?*

Black Sea, his enemy was the Ottomans. Here, however, he had little success; although he captured the port of Azov in 1696, he was forced to return it in 1711. Russia would not secure its position in the Black Sea until the end of the eighteenth century. Nevertheless, Peter continued to push against the Ottoman Empire in the North Caucasus region throughout his reign. This mountainous area on Russia's southern flank became important sites for Russia's experiments in colonial expansion into central Asia, which began during the sixteenth century and would later mirror the process of colonial conquest undertaken by European powers and the United States in North and South America. Like France and Britain, the Russian state bureaucracy was built during a period of ambitious colonialism; and like Spain, the monarchy's identity was shaped by a long contest with Muslim power on its borders.

Since the late sixteenth century, successive Russian leaders had extended their control over bordering territories of central Asia to the south and east. Although merchants helped fund early expeditions into Siberia, this expansion

was primarily motivated by geopolitical concerns; the tsar sought to gain access to the populations of Russia's border areas and bring them into the service of the expanding Russian state. In this sense, Russian colonialism during this period differed from western European expansion into the Atlantic world, which had primarily been motivated by hopes of commercial gain. Nevertheless, tsarist Russia's colonization of central Asia was similar to the process of European colonial expansion elsewhere in some respects. Like European colonizers in the Americas, Russian expansion brought Russian troops into contact with a variety of peoples with different religious beliefs and their own political structures. Some, such as the Muslim Kumyks of northern Dagestan had a highly centralized government. Others, such as the Kabardinians or the Chechens, were more fragmented politically.

In its early stages, as successive Russian emperors moved Russian troops into the region, they relied on a process of indirect rule, often seeking to co-opt local elites. Later in the eighteenth century, they had more success settling

Russians in border regions who ruled over local populations directly. Religion also provided a cover for expansion, and Peter and his successors funded missionary work by Georgian Christians among Muslims in the Caucasus. Efforts to convert Muslim populations to Orthodox Christianity had little effect, and in fact the opposite occurred: the region's commitment to Islam was continuously renewed through contact with different strains of Islamic practice coming from neighboring Ottoman lands and Persia.

Peter could point to more concrete success to the north. In 1700, he began what would become a twenty-one-year war with Sweden, then the dominant power in the Baltic Sea. By 1703, Peter had secured a foothold on the Gulf of Finland and immediately began to build a new capital city there, which he named St. Petersburg. After 1709, when Russian armies, supported by Prussia, decisively defeated the Swedes at the battle of Poltava, work on Peter's new capital city accelerated. An army of serfs was now conscripted to build the new city, whose centerpiece was a royal palace designed to imitate and rival Louis XIV's Versailles.

The Great Northern War with Sweden ended in 1721 with the Peace of Nystad. This treaty marks a realignment of power in eastern Europe comparable to that effected by the Treaty of Utrecht in the West. Sweden lost its North Sea territories to Hanover and its Baltic German territories to Prussia. Its eastern territories, including the entire Gulf of Finland, Livonia, and Estonia, passed to Russia. Sweden was now a second-rank power in the northern European world. Poland-Lithuania survived but it too was a declining power; by the end of the eighteenth century, the kingdom would disappear altogether, its territories swallowed up by its more powerful neighbors (see Chapter 17). The victors at Nystad were the Prussians and the Russians. These two powers secured their position along the Baltic coast, positioning themselves to take advantage of the lucrative eastern European grain trade with western Europe. Peter's accomplishments came at enormous cost. Direct taxation in Russia increased 500 percent during his reign, and his army in the 1720s numbered more than 300,000 men. Peter made Russia a force to be reckoned with on the European scene; but in so doing, he also aroused great resentment, especially among his nobility. Peter's only son and heir, Alexis, became the focus for conspiracies against the tsar, until finally Peter had him arrested and executed in 1718. As a result, when Peter died in 1725, he left no son to succeed him. A series of ineffective tsars followed, mostly creatures of the palace guard, under whom the resentful nobles reversed many of Peter the Great's reforms. In 1762, however, the crown passed to Catherine the Great, a ruler whose ambitions and determination were equal to those of her great predecessor (see Chapter 17).

CONCLUSION

By the time of Peter the Great's death in Russia in 1725, the power of Europe's absolutist realms to reinvigorate European political institutions was visible to all. Government had become more bureaucratic, state service had been more professionalized, administrators loyal to the king had become more numerous, more efficient, and more demanding. Despite the increasing scope of government, however, the structure and principles of government changed relatively little. Apart from Great Britain and the Dutch Republic, the great powers of eighteenth-century Europe were still governed by rulers who styled themselves as absolutist monarchs in the mold of Louis XIV, who claimed an authority that came directly from God and who ruled over a society where social hierarchies based on birth were taken for granted.

These absolutist regimes could not hide the fact, however, that their rule depended on a kind of negotiated settlement with other powerful elites within European society, in particular with landed aristocrats and with religious leaders. Louis XIV used his power to curb the worst excesses of nobles who abused their position, and he defended Catholic orthodoxy against dissident Catholics and Protestants. He could not hide the fact, however, that his power depended on a delicate exchange of favors—French aristocrats would surrender their political authority to the state in exchange for social and legal privileges and immunity from many (but not all) forms of taxation. The Church made a similar bargain. Peter the Great's autocratic rule in Russia worked out a slightly different balance of powers between his state and the Russian aristocracy, one that tied aristocrats more closely to an ideal of state service, a model that also worked well for the rulers of Brandenburg-Prussia. Even in England, the establishment of a limited constitutional monarchy and a king who ruled alongside parliament was not really a radical departure from the European absolutist model. It was merely a different institutional answer to the same problem—what relationship should the monarchical state have with other elites within society?

The demands of state building during this period required that kings raise enormous revenues—for the sumptuous displays of their sovereignty in royal residences like Louis XIV's palace at Versailles, for the sponsorship of royal academies and the patronage of artists, but most of all, for war. Territorial expansion within Europe and holding on to colonial empires in the Atlantic world was costly. Distributing the burden of taxation to pay for these endeavors became an intensely fought political issue for European monarchs during this period, and the financing of royal debt became an increasingly sophisticated art. Colbert's mercantilist policy was an attempt to harness the full power of the economy for the benefit of royal government, and the competition among Spain, Holland, England, and France to control the revenue flows coming from the Atlantic world forced Europe's monarchs to recognize that the "balance of powers" was increasingly being played out on a global stage.

These themes—the expansion of state powers; conflicts between the monarchy and the aristocracy or with religious dissidents; the intensification of the tax burden on the population; and the opening up of Europe to ever more frequent interactions with other peoples in the Atlantic world, the Indian Ocean, and eventually, the Pacific—prompted many in eighteenth-century Europe to reflect on the consequences of these developments. What were the limits to state power, and by what criteria were the actions of rulers to be judged? What was the proper measure of economic prosperity, and who was it for? Could

After You Read This Chapter

Visit StudySpace for quizzes, additional review materials, and multimedia documents. **wwnorton.com/web/westernciv18**

REVIEWING THE OBJECTIVES

- Absolutist rulers claimed a monopoly of power and authority within their realms. Who were the most important absolutist rulers, how did they justify their innovations, and what did they do to achieve their goals?
- Mercantilism was an economic doctrine that guided the policies of absolutist rulers. What did mercantilists believe?
- Between 1660 and 1688, political leaders in England continued to debate the nature of the state, the role of Parliament, and religious divisions. What was the significance of these dates, and what was the outcome of these debates?
- What circumstances led to the decline of the Dutch Republic's power in this period?
- The wars begun by Louis XIV after 1680 drove his opponents to ally with one another to achieve a balance of power. What was the result of these conflicts in Europe and in the Atlantic world?

a well-ordered society tolerate religious diversity? Given Europe's growing awareness of cultures in other parts of the world with different religions, different political systems, and different ways of expressing their moral and ethical values, how might Europeans justify or take the measure of their own beliefs and customs? The intellectuals who looked for answers to these questions were similar to earlier generations of scientific researchers in their respect for reason and rational thought, but they turned their attention beyond problems of natural philosophy and science to the messy world of politics and culture. Their movement—known as the Enlightenment—reached its peak in the middle decades of the eighteenth century, and created the basis for a powerful critique of Europe's absolutist regimes. The Enlightenment itself emerged slowly from a revolution in scientific thinking that had begun earlier in the early modern period, and it is to this history that we now turn.

PEOPLE, IDEAS, AND EVENTS IN CONTEXT

- What did **LOUIS XIV** of France and **PETER THE GREAT** of Russia have in common? How did they deal with those who resisted their attempts to impose absolutist rule?

- Compare the religious policies of **LOUIS XIV** of France with the religious policies of the English Stuart kings **CHARLES II** and **JAMES II**. In what way did religious disagreements limit their ability to rule effectively?

- How did European monarchies use the economic theory known as **MERCANTILISM** to strengthen the power and wealth of their kingdoms, and how did this theory influence **FRENCH COLONIALISM**?

- What was the **CONTRACT THEORY OF GOVERNMENT** according to the English political thinker **JOHN LOCKE**?

- What limits to royal power were recognized in Great Britain as a result of the **GLORIOUS REVOLUTION**?

- What was significant about the new **BALANCE OF POWERS** that developed in Europe as a result of **LOUIS XIV**'s wars?

- What does the **TREATY OF UTRECHT** (1713) tell us about the diminished influence of Spain and the corresponding rise of Britain and France as European and colonial powers?

- What was different about the attempts by rulers in Habsburg Austria and Brandenburg-Prussia to impose **ABSOLUTISM** in central Europe?

- What innovations did **PETER THE GREAT** bring to Russia?

THINKING ABOUT CONNECTIONS

- What makes absolutism different from earlier models of kingship in earlier periods?

- Was the absolutist monarchs' emphasis on sumptuous displays of their authority something new? Is it different from the way that political power is represented today in democratic societies?

Before You Read This Chapter

The New Science of the Seventeenth Century

CORE OBJECTIVES

- **DEFINE** *scientific revolution* and explain what is meant by *science* in this historical context.

- **UNDERSTAND** the older philosophical traditions that were important for the development of new methods of scientific investigation in the seventeenth century.

- **IDENTIFY** the sciences that made important advances during this period and understand what technological innovations encouraged a new spirit of investigation.

- **EXPLAIN** the differences between the Ptolemaic view of the universe and the new vision of the universe proposed by Nicolas Copernicus.

- **UNDERSTAND** the different definitions of *scientific method* that emerged from the work of Francis Bacon and René Descartes.

Doubt thou the stars are fire,
Doubt that the sun doth move,
Doubt truth to be a liar,
But never doubt I love.

SHAKESPEARE, *HAMLET*, II.2

"Doubt thou the stars are fire" and "that the sun doth move." Was Shakespeare alluding to controversial ideas about the cosmos that contradicted the teachings of medieval scholars? *Hamlet* (c. 1600) was written more than fifty years after Copernicus had suggested, in his treatise *On the Revolutions of the Heavenly Spheres* (1543), that the sun did not move and that the earth did, revolving around the sun. Shakespeare probably knew of such theories, although they circulated only among small groups of learned Europeans. As Hamlet's love-torn speech to Ophelia makes clear, they were considered conjecture—or strange mathematical hypotheses. These theories were not exactly new—a heliocentric universe had been proposed as early as the second century B.C.E. by ancient Greek astronomers.

519

But they flatly contradicted the consensus that had set in after Ptolemy proposed an earth-centered universe in the second century C.E., and to Shakespeare's contemporaries, they defied common sense and observation. Learned philosophers, young lovers, shepherds, and sailors alike could watch the sun and the stars move from one horizon to the other each day and night, or so they thought.

Still, a small handful of thinkers did doubt. Shakespeare was born in 1564, the same year as Galileo. By the time the English playwright and the Italian natural philosopher were working, the long process of revising knowledge about the universe, and discovering a new set of rules that explained how the universe worked was under way. By the end of the seventeenth century a hundred years later, the building blocks of the new view had been put in place. This intellectual transformation brought sweeping changes to European philosophy and to Western views of the natural world and of humans' place in it.

Science entails at least three things: a body of knowledge, a method or system of inquiry, and a community of practitioners and the institutions that support them and their work. The *scientific revolution* of the seventeenth century (usually understood to have begun in the mid-sixteenth century and culminated in 1687 with Newton's *Principia*) involved each of these three realms. As far as the content of knowledge is concerned, the scientific revolution saw the emergence and confirmation of a heliocentric (sun-centered) view of the planetary system, which displaced the earth—and humans—from the center of the universe. Even more fundamental, it brought a new mathematical physics that described and confirmed such a view. Second, the scientific revolution established a method of inquiry for understanding the natural world: a method that emphasized the role of observation, experiment, and the testing of hypotheses. Third, *science* emerged as a distinctive branch of knowledge. During the period covered in this chapter, people referred to the study of matter, motion, optics, or the circulation of blood as natural philosophy (the more theoretical term), experimental philosophy, medicine, and—increasingly—science. The growth of societies and institutions dedicated to what we now commonly call scientific research was central to the changes at issue here. Science required not only brilliant thinkers but patrons, states, and communities of researchers; the scientific revolution was thus embedded in other social, religious, and cultural transformations.

The scientific revolution was not an organized effort. Brilliant theories sometimes led to dead ends, discoveries were often accidental, and artisans grinding lenses for telescopes played a role in the advance of knowledge just as surely as did great abstract thinkers. Educated women also claimed the right to participate in scientific debate, but their efforts were met with opposition or indifference. Old and new worldviews often overlapped as individual thinkers struggled to reconcile their discoveries with their faith or to make their theories (about the earth's movements, for instance) fit with received wisdom. Science was slow to work its way into popular understanding. It did not necessarily undermine religion, and it certainly did not intend to; figures like Isaac Newton thought their work confirmed and deepened their religious beliefs. In short, change came slowly and fitfully. But as the new scientific method began to produce radical new insights into the workings of nature, it eventually came to be accepted well beyond the small circles of experimenters, theologians, and philosophers with whom it began.

THE INTELLECTUAL ORIGINS OF THE SCIENTIFIC REVOLUTION

The scientific revolution marks one of the decisive breaks between the Middle Ages and the modern world. For all its novelty, however, it was rooted in earlier developments. Medieval artists and intellectuals had been observing and illustrating the natural world with great precision since at least the twelfth century. Medieval sculptors carved plants and vines with extraordinary accuracy, and fifteenth-century painters and sculptors devoted the same careful attention to the human face and form. Nor was the link among observation, experiment, and invention new to the sixteenth century. The magnetic compass had been known in Europe since the thirteenth century; gunpowder since the early fourteenth; printing, which permeated the intellectual life of the period and opened new possibilities—disseminating ideas quickly, collaborating more easily, buying books, and building libraries—since the middle of the fifteenth. "Printing, firearms, and the compass," wrote Francis Bacon, "no empire, sect or star appears to have exercised a greater power and influence on human affairs than these three mechanical discoveries." A fascination with light, which was a powerful symbol of divine illumination for medieval thinkers, encouraged the study of optics and, in turn, new techniques for grinding lenses. Lens grinders laid the groundwork for the seventeenth-century inventions of the telescope and microscope, creating reading glasses along the way. Astrologers were also active in the later Middle Ages, charting the heavens in the firm belief that the stars controlled the fates of human beings.

Behind these efforts to understand the natural world lay a nearly universal conviction that the natural world had been created by God. Religious belief spurred scientific study. One school of thinkers (the Neoplatonists) argued that nature was a book written by its creator to reveal the ways of God to humanity. Convinced that God's perfection must be reflected in nature, Neoplatonists searched for the ideal and perfect structures they believed must lie behind the "shadows" of the everyday world. Mathematics, particularly geometry, were important tools in this quest. The mathematician and astronomer Johannes Kepler, for example, was deeply influenced by Neoplatonism.

Renaissance humanism also helped prepare the grounds for the scientific revolution. The humanists' educational program placed a low value on natural philosophy, directing attention instead toward the recovery and study of classical antiquity. Humanists revered the authority of the ancients. Yet the energies the humanists poured into recovering, translating, and understanding classical texts (the source of conceptions of the natural world) made many of those important works available for the first time, and to a wider audience. Previously, Arabic sources had provided Europeans with the main route to ancient Greek learning; Greek classics were translated into Arabic and then picked up by late medieval scholars in Spain and Sicily. The humanists' return to the texts themselves—and the fact that the new texts could be more easily printed and circulated—encouraged new study and debate. Islamic scholars knew Ptolemy better than did Europeans until the humanist scholar and printer Johannes Regiomontanus recovered and prepared a new summary of Ptolemy's work. The humanist rediscovery of works by Archimedes—the great Greek mathematician who had proposed that the natural world operated on the basis of mechanical forces, like a great machine, and that these forces could be described mathematically—profoundly impressed important late-sixteenth- and seventeenth-century thinkers, including the Italian scientist Galileo, and shaped mechanical philosophy in the 1600s.

The Renaissance also encouraged collaboration between artisans and intellectuals. Twelfth- and thirteenth-century thinkers had observed the natural world, but they rarely tinkered with machines and they had little contact with the artisans who developed expertise in constructing machines for practical use. During the fifteenth century, however, these two worlds began to come together. Renaissance artists such as Leonardo da Vinci were accomplished craftsmen; they investigated the laws of perspective and optics, they worked out geometric methods for supporting the weight of enormous architectural domes, they studied the human body, and they devised new and more effective weapons for war. The Renaissance brought a vogue for alchemy and astrology; wealthy amateurs built observatories and measured the courses of the stars. These social and intellectual developments laid the groundwork for the scientific revolution.

What of the voyages of discovery? Sixteenth-century observers often linked the exploration of the globe to new knowledge of the cosmos. An admirer wrote to Galileo that he had kept the spirit of exploration alive: "The memory of Columbus and Vespucci will be renewed through you, and with even greater nobility, as the sky is more worthy than the earth." The parallel does not work quite so neatly. Columbus had not been driven by an interest in science.

PTOLEMAIC ASTRONOMICAL INSTRUMENTS. Armillary sphere, 1560s, built to facilitate the observation of planetary positions relative to the earth, in support of Ptolemy's theory of an earth-centered universe. In the sphere, seven concentric rings rotated about different axes. When the outermost ring was set to align with a north–south meridian, and the next ring was set to align with the celestial pole (the North Star, or the point around which the stars seem to rotate), one could determine the latitude of the place where the instrument was placed. The inner rings were used to track the angular movements of the planets, key measurements in validating the Ptolemaic system. ■ *What forms of knowledge were necessary to construct such an instrument?* ■ *How do they relate to the breakthrough that is known as the scientific revolution?*

Past and Present

Has Science Replaced Religion?

Galileo recanted his claims about the movement of heavenly bodies when challenged by the Church (left); but physicists persisted in their research, leading eventually to the development of modern particle accelerators like the one located in this lab in Grenoble, France (right). Few would say, however, that science has replaced religion in the modern world.

 Watch related author interview on StudySpace
wwnorton.com/web/westernciv18

Moreover, it took centuries for European thinkers to process the New World's implications for different fields of study, and the links between the voyages of discovery and breakthroughs in science were largely indirect. The discoveries made the most immediate impact in the field of natural history, which was vastly enriched by travelers' detailed accounts of the flora and fauna of the Americas. Finding new lands and cultures in Africa and Asia and the revelation of the Americas, a world unknown to the ancients and unmentioned in the Bible, also laid bare gaps in Europeans' inherited body of knowledge. In this sense, the exploration of the New World dealt a blow to the authority of the ancients.

In sum, the late medieval recovery of ancient texts long thought to have been lost, the expansion of print culture and reading, the turmoil in the church and the fierce wars and political maneuvering that followed the Reformation,

and the discovery of a new world across the oceans to explore and exploit all shook the authority of older ways of thinking. What we call the scientific revolution was part of the intellectual excitement that surrounded these challenges, and, in retrospect, the scientific revolution enhanced and confirmed the importance of these other developments.

THE COPERNICAN REVOLUTION

Medieval cosmologists, like their ancient counterparts and their successors during the scientific revolution, wrestled with the contradictions between ancient texts and the evidence of their own observations. Their view of an earth-centered universe was particularly influenced by the teachings of Aristotle (384–322 B.C.E.), especially as they were systematized by Ptolemy of Alexandria (100–178 C.E.). In fact, Ptolemy's vision of an earth-centered universe contradicted an earlier proposal by Aristarchus of Samos (310–230 B.C.E.), who had deduced that the earth and other planets revolve around the sun. Like the ancient Greeks, Ptolemy's medieval followers used astronomical observations to support their theory, but the persuasiveness of the model for medieval scholars also derived from the ways that it fit with their Christian beliefs (see Chapter 4). According to Ptolemy, the heavens orbited the earth in a carefully organized hierarchy of spheres. Earth and the heavens were fundamentally different, made of different matter and subject to different laws of motion. The sun, moon, stars, and planets were formed of an unchanging (and perfect) quintessence or ether. The earth, by contrast, was composed of four elements (earth, water, fire, and air), and each of these elements had its natural place: the heavy elements (earth and water) toward the center and the lighter ones farther out. The heavens—first the planets, then the stars—traced perfect circular paths around the stationary earth. The motion of these celestial bodies was produced by a prime mover, whom Christians identified as God. The view fit Aristotelian physics, according to which objects could move only if acted on by an external force, and it fit with a belief that each fundamental element of the universe had a natural place. Moreover, the view both followed from and confirmed belief in the purposefulness of God's universe.

By the late Middle Ages astronomers knew that this cosmology, called the "Ptolemaic system," did not correspond exactly to what many had observed. Orbits did not conform to the Aristotelian ideal of perfect circles. Planets, Mars in particular, sometimes appeared to loop backward before continuing on their paths. Ptolemy had managed to account for these orbital irregularities, but with complicated mathematics. By the early fifteenth century, the efforts to make the observed motions of the planets fit into the model of perfect circles in a geocentric (earth-centered) cosmos had produced astronomical charts that were mazes of complexity. Finally, the Ptolemaic system proved unable to solve serious difficulties with the calendar. That practical crisis precipitated Nicolaus Copernicus's intellectual leap forward.

By the early sixteenth century, the old Roman calendar was significantly out of alignment with the movement of the heavenly bodies. The major saints' days, Easter, and the other holy days were sometimes weeks off where they should have been according to the stars. Catholic authorities tried to correct this problem, consulting mathematicians and astronomers all over Europe. One of these was a Polish church official and astronomer, Nicolaus Copernicus (1473–1543). Educated in Poland and northern Italy, he was a man of diverse talents. He was trained in astron-

omy, canon law, and medicine. He read Greek. He was well versed in ancient philosophy. He was also a careful mathematician and a devout Catholic, who did not believe that God's universe could be as messy as the one in Ptolemy's model. His proposed solution, based on mathematical calculations, was simple and radical: Ptolemy was mistaken; the earth was neither stationary nor at the center of the planetary system; the earth rotated on its axis and orbited with the other planets around the sun. Reordering the Ptolemaic system simplified the geometry of astronomy and made the orbits of the planets comprehensible.

Copernicus was in many ways a conservative thinker. He did not consider his work to be a break with either the Church or with the authority of ancient texts. He believed, rather, that he had restored a pure understanding

NICOLAUS COPERNICUS. This anonymous portrait of Copernicus characteristically blends his devotion and his scientific achievements. His scholarly work (behind him in the form of an early planetarium) is driven by his faith (as he turns toward the image of Christ triumphant over death). ▪ *What relationship between science and religion is evoked by this image?*

of God's design, one that had been lost over the centuries. Still, the implications of his theory troubled him. His ideas contradicted centuries of astronomical thought, and they were hard to reconcile with the observed behavior of objects on earth. If the earth moved, why was that movement imperceptible? Copernicus calculated the distance from the Earth to the Sun to be at least 6 million miles. Even by Copernicus's very low estimate, the earth was hurtling around the sun at the dizzying rate of many thousands of miles an hour. How did people and objects remain standing? (The earth is actually about 93 million miles from the sun, moving through space at 67,000 miles an hour and spinning on its axis at about 1,000 miles an hour!)

Copernicus was not a physicist. He tried to refine, rather than overturn, traditional Aristotelian physics, but his effort to reconcile that physics with his new model of a sun-centered universe created new problems and inconsistencies that he could not resolve. These frustrations and complications dogged Copernicus's later years, and he hesitated to publish his findings. Just before his death, he consented to the release of his major treatise, *On the Revolutions of the Heavenly Spheres* (*De Revolutionibus*), in 1543. To fend off scandal, the Lutheran scholar who saw his manuscript through the press added an introduction to the book declaring that Copernicus's system should be understood as an abstraction, a set of mathematical tools for doing astronomy and not a dangerous claim about the nature of heaven and earth. For decades after 1543, Copernicus's ideas were taken in just that sense—as useful but not realistic mathematical hypotheses. In the long run, however, as one historian puts it, Copernicanism represented the first "serious and systematic" challenge to the Ptolemaic conception of the universe.

TYCHO'S OBSERVATIONS AND KEPLER'S LAWS

Within fifty years, Copernicus's cosmology was revived and modified by two astronomers also critical of the Ptolemaic model of the universe: Tycho Brahe (*TI-koh BRAH-hee*, 1546–1601) and Johannes Kepler (1571–1630). Each was considered the greatest astronomer of his day. Tycho was born into the Danish nobility, but he abandoned his family's military and political legacy to pursue his passion for astronomy. He was hotheaded as well as talented; at twenty, he lost part of his nose in a duel. Like Copernicus, he sought to correct the contradictions in traditional astronomy.

Unlike Copernicus, who was a theoretician, Tycho championed observation and believed careful study of the heavens would unlock the secrets of the universe. He first made a name for himself by observing a completely new star, a "nova," that flared into sight in 1572. The Danish king Friedrich II, impressed by Tycho's work, granted him the use of a small island, where he built a castle specially designed to house an observatory. For over twenty years, Tycho meticulously charted the movements of each significant object in the night sky, compiling the finest set of astronomical data in Europe.

Tycho was not a Copernican. He suggested that the planets orbited the sun and the whole system then orbited a stationary earth. This picture of cosmic order, though clumsy, seemed to fit the observed evidence better than the Ptolemaic system, and it avoided the upsetting physical and theological implications of the Copernican model. In the late 1590s, Tycho moved his work and his huge collection of data to Prague, where he became court astronomer to the Holy Roman emperor Rudolph II. In Prague, he was assisted by a young mathematician from a troubled family, Johannes Kepler. Kepler was more impressed with the Copernican model than was Tycho, and Kepler combined study of Copernicus's work with his own interest in mysticism, astrology, and the religious power of mathematics.

Kepler believed that everything in creation, from human souls to the orbits of the planets, had been created according to mathematical laws. Understanding those laws would thus allow humans to share God's wisdom and penetrate the inner secrets of the universe. Mathematics was God's language. Kepler's search for the pattern of mathematical perfection took him through musical harmonies, nested geometric shapes inside the planets' orbits, and numerical formulas. After Tycho's death, Kepler inherited Tycho's position in Prague, as well as his trove of observations and calculations. That data demonstrated to Kepler that two of Copernicus's assumptions about planetary motion simply did not match observations. Copernicus, in keeping with Aristotelian notions of perfection, had believed that planetary orbits were circular. Kepler calculated that the planets traveled in elliptical orbits around the sun; this finding became his First Law. Copernicus held that planetary motion was uniform; Kepler's Second Law stated that the speed of the planets varied with their distance from the sun. Kepler also argued that magnetic forces between the sun and the planets kept the planets in orbital motion, an insight that paved the way for Newton's law of universal gravitation formulated nearly eighty years later, at the end of the seventeenth century.

Each of Kepler's works, beginning with *Cosmographic Mystery* in 1596 and continuing with *Astronomia Nova* in 1609 and *The Harmonies of the World* in 1619, revised and augmented Copernicus's theory. His version of Copernicanism fit with remarkable accuracy the best observations of the time (which were Tycho's). Kepler's search for rules of motion that could account for the earth's movements in its new position was also significant. More than Copernicus, Kepler broke down the distinction between the heavens and the earth that had been at the heart of Aristotelian physics.

TYCHO BRAHE, 1662. This seventeenth-century tribute shows the master astronomer in his observatory. ▪ *How much scientific knowledge does one need to understand this image?* ▪ *Is this image, which celebrates science and its accomplishments, itself a scientific statement?* ▪ *What can one learn about seventeenth-century science from such imagery?*

NEW HEAVENS, NEW EARTH, AND WORLDLY POLITICS: GALILEO

Kepler had a friend deliver a copy of *Cosmographic Mystery* to the "mathematician named Galileus Galileus," then teaching mathematics and astronomy at Padua, near Venice. Galileo (1564–1642) thanked Kepler in a letter that nicely illustrates the Italian's views at the time (1597).

> So far I have only perused the preface of your work, but from this I gained some notion of its intent, and I indeed congratulate myself of having an associate in the study of Truth who is a friend of Truth. . . . I adopted the teaching of Copernicus many years ago, and his point of view enables me to explain many phenomena of nature which certainly remain inexplicable according to the more current hypotheses. I have written many arguments in support of him and in refutation of the opposite view—which, however, so far I have not dared to bring into the public light. . . . I would certainly dare to publish my reflections at once if more people like you existed; as they don't, I shall refrain from doing so.

Kepler replied, urging Galileo to "come forward!" Galileo did not answer.

At Padua, Galileo couldn't teach what he believed; Ptolemaic astronomy and Aristotelian cosmology were the established curriculum. By the end of his career, however, Galileo had provided powerful evidence in support of the Copernican model and laid the foundation for a new physics. What was more, he wrote in the vernacular (Italian) as well as in Latin. Kepler may have been a "friend of Truth," but his work was abstruse and bafflingly mathematical. (So was Copernicus's.) By contrast, Galileo's writings were widely translated and widely read, raising awareness of changes in natural philosophy across Europe.

Ultimately, Galileo made the case for a new relationship between religion and science, challenging in the process some of the most powerful churchmen of his day. His discoveries made him the most famous scientific figure of his time, but his work put him on a collision course with Aristotelian philosophy and the authority of the Catholic Church.

Galileo became famous by way of discoveries with the telescope. In 1609, he heard reports from Holland of a lens grinder who had made a spyglass that could magnify very distant objects. Excited, Galileo quickly devised his own telescope; trained it first on earthly objects to demonstrate that it worked; and then, momentously, pointed

Interpreting Visual Evidence

Astronomical Observations and the Mapping of the Heavens

One (often-repeated) narrative about the scientific revolution is that it marked a crucial break separating modern science from an earlier period permeated by an atmosphere of superstition and theological speculation. In fact, medieval scholars tried hard to come up with empirical evidence for beliefs that their faith told them must be true, and

without these traditions of observation, scientists like Copernicus would never have been led to propose alternative cosmologies (see "Ptolemaic Astronomical Instruments" on page 521).

The assumption, therefore, that the "new" sciences of the seventeenth century marked an extraordinary rupture with a more ignorant or superstitious past is thus not entirely correct. It would be closer to the truth to suggest

that works such as that of Copernicus or Galileo provided a new context for assessing the relationship between observations and knowledge that came from other sources. Printed materials provided opportunities for early modern scientists to learn as much from each other as from more ancient sources.

The illustrations here are from scientific works on astronomy both before and after the appearance of Coperni-

A. The Ptolemaic universe, as depicted in Peter Apian, *Cosmographia* (1540).

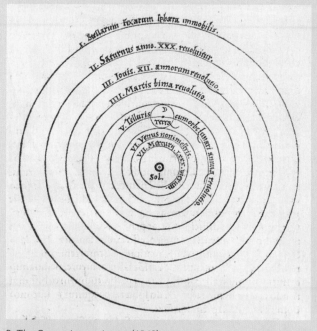

B. The Copernican universe (1543).

it at the night sky. Galileo studied the moon, finding on it mountains, plains, and other features of an earthlike landscape. His observations suggested that celestial bodies resembled the earth, a view at odds with the conception of the heavens as an unchanging sphere of heavenly perfection, inherently and necessarily different from the earth. He saw moons orbiting Jupiter, evidence that earth was not

at the center of all orbits. He saw spots on the sun. Galileo published these results, first in *The Starry Messenger* (1610) and then in *Letters on Sunspots* in 1613. *The Starry Messenger*, with its amazing reports of Jupiter's moons, was short, aimed to be read by many, and bold. It only hinted at Galileo's Copernicanism, however. The *Letters on Sunspots* declared it openly.

cus's work. All of them were based on some form of observation and claimed to be descriptive of the existing universe. Compare the abstract illustrations of the Ptolemaic (image A) and Copernican (image B) universes with Tycho Brahe's (image C) attempt to reconcile heliocentric observations with geocentric assumptions or with Galileo's illustration of sunspots (image D) observed through a telescope.

Questions for Analysis

1. What do these illustrations tell us about the relationship between knowledge and observation in sixteenth- and seventeenth-century science? What kinds of knowledge were necessary to produce these images?

2. Are the illustrations A and B intended to be visually accurate, in the sense that they represent what the eye sees?

Can one say the same of D? What makes Galileo's illustration of the sunspots different from the others?

3. Are the assumptions about observation contained in Galileo's drawing of sunspots (D) applicable to other sciences such as biology or chemistry? How so?

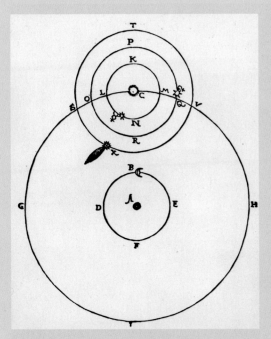

C. Brahe's universe (c. 1572, A, earth; B, moon; C, sun).

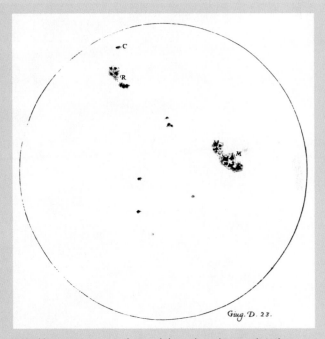

D. Galileo's sunspots, as observed through a telescope (1612).

A seventeenth-century scientist needed powerful and wealthy patrons. As a professor of mathematics, Galileo chafed at the power of university authorities who were subject to church control. Princely courts offered an inviting alternative. The Medici family of Tuscany, like others, burnished its reputation and bolstered its power by surrounding itself with intellectuals as well as artists. Per-

suaded he would be freer at its court than in Padua, Galileo took a position as tutor to the Medicis and flattered and successfully cultivated the family. He addressed *The Starry Messenger* to them. He named the newly discovered moons of Jupiter "the Medicean stars." He was rewarded with the title of chief mathematician and philosopher to Cosimo de' Medici, the grand duke of Tuscany. Now well positioned in Italy's networks of power and patronage, Galileo was able to pursue his goal of demonstrating that Copernicus's heliocentric (sun-centered) model of the planetary system was correct.

This pursuit, however, was a high-wire act, for he could not afford to antagonize the Catholic Church. In 1614, however, an ambitious and outspoken Dominican monk denounced Galileo's ideas as dangerous deviations from biblical teachings. Other philosophers and churchmen began to ask Galileo's patrons, the Medicis, whether their court mathematician was teaching heresy.

Disturbed by the murmurings against Copernicanism, Galileo penned a series of letters to defend himself, by addressing the relationship between natural philosophy and religion, and he argued that one could be a sincere Copernican and a sincere Catholic (see *Analyzing Primary Sources* on page 529). The Church, Galileo said, did the sacred work of teaching scripture and saving souls. Accounting for the workings of the physical world was a task better left to natural philosophy, grounded in observation and mathematics. For the Church to take a side in controversies over natural science might compromise the Church's spiritual authority and credibility. Galileo envisioned natural philosophers and theologians as partners in a search for truth, but with very different roles. In a brilliant rhetorical moment, he quoted Cardinal Baronius in support of his own argument: the purpose of the Bible was to "teach us how to go to heaven, not how heaven goes."

Nevertheless, in 1616, the Church moved against Galileo. The Inquisition ruled that Copernicanism was "foolish and absurd in philosophy and formally heretical." Copernicus's *De Revolutionibus* was placed on the Index of Prohibited Books, and Galileo was warned not to teach Copernicanism.

GALILEO GALILEI BEFORE THE INQUISITION **BY FRANÇOIS FLEURY-RICHARD.** This nineteenth-century painting of Galileo before the Holy Office dramatizes the conflict between science and religion and depicts the Italian natural philosopher as defiant. In fact, Galileo submitted but continued his work under house arrest and published, secretly, in the Netherlands. ▪ *Would Galileo himself have subscribed to the message of this much later painting, that religion and science were opposed to one another?*

Analyzing Primary Sources

Galileo on Nature, Scripture, and Truth

One of the clearest statements of Galileo's convictions about religion and science comes from his 1615 letter to the grand duchess Christina, mother of Galileo's patron, Cosimo de' Medici, and a powerful figure in her own right. Galileo knew that others objected to his work. The church had warned him that Copernicanism was inaccurate and impious; it could be disproved scientifically, and it contradicted the authority of those who interpreted the Bible. Thoroughly dependent on the Medicis for support, he wrote to the grand duchess to explain his position. In this section of the letter, Galileo sets out his understanding of the parallel but distinct roles of the Church and natural philosophers. He walks a fine line between acknowledging the authority of the Church and standing firm in his convictions.

Possibly because they are disturbed by the known truth of other propositions of mine which differ from those commonly held, and therefore mistrusting their defense so long as they confine themselves to the field of philosophy, these men have resolved to fabricate a shield for their fallacies out of the mantle of pretended religion and the authority of the Bible. . . .

Copernicus never discusses matters of religion or faith, nor does he use arguments that depend in any way upon the authority of sacred writings which he might have interpreted erroneously. He stands always upon physical conclusions pertaining to the celestial motions, and deals with them by astronomical and geometrical demonstrations, founded primarily upon sense experiences and very exact observations. He did not ignore the Bible, but he knew very well that if his doctrine were proved, then it could not contradict the Scriptures when they were rightly understood. . . .

I think that in discussions of physical problems we ought to begin not from the authority of scriptural passages, but from sense-experiences and necessary demonstrations; for the holy Bible and the phenomena of nature proceed alike from the divine Word, the former as the dictate of the Holy Ghost and the latter as the observant executrix of God's commands. It is necessary for the Bible, in order to be accommodated to the understanding of every man, to speak many things which appear to differ from the absolute truth so far as the bare meaning of the words is concerned. But Nature, on the other hand, is inexorable and immutable; she never transgresses the laws imposed upon her, or cares a whit whether her abstruse reasons and methods of operation are understandable to men. For that reason it appears that nothing physical which sense-experience sets before our eyes, or which necessary demonstrations prove to us, ought to be called in question (much less condemned) upon the testimony of biblical passages which may have some different meaning beneath their words. For the Bible is not chained in every expression to conditions as strict as those which govern all physical effects; nor is God any less excellently revealed in Nature's actions than in the sacred statements of the Bible. . . .

Source: Galileo, "Letter to the Grand Duchess Christina," in *The Discoveries and Opinions of Galileo Galilei*, ed. Stillman Drake (Garden City, NY: 1957), pp. 177–83.

Questions for Analysis

1. How does Galileo deal with the contradictions between the evidence of his senses and biblical teachings?

2. For Galileo, what is the relationship between God, man, and nature?

3. Why did Galileo need to defend his views in a letter to Christina de' Medici?

For a while, he did as he was asked. But when his Florentine friend and admirer Maffeo Barberini was elected pope as Urban VIII in 1623, Galileo believed the door to Copernicanism was (at least half) open. He drafted one of his most famous works, *A Dialogue Concerning the Two Chief World Systems* published in 1632. The *Dialogue* was a hypothetical debate between supporters of the old Ptolemaic system, represented by a character he named Simplicio (simpleton), on the one hand, and proponents of the new astronomy, on the other. Throughout, Galileo gave the best lines to the Copernicans. At the very end, however, to satisfy the letter of the Inquisition's decree, he had them capitulate to Simplicio.

The Inquisition banned the *Dialogue* and ordered Galileo to stand trial in 1633. Pope Urban, provoked by Galileo's scorn and needing support from Church conservatives during a difficult stretch of the Thirty Years' War, refused to protect his former friend. The verdict of the secret trial shocked Europe. The Inquisition forced Galileo to repent his Copernican position, banned him from working on or even discussing Copernican ideas, and placed him under house arrest for life. According to a story that began to circulate shortly afterward, as he left the court for house arrest he stamped his foot and muttered defiantly, looking down at the earth: "Still, it moves."

The Inquisition could not put Galileo off his life's work. He refined the theories of motion he had begun to develop early in his career. He proposed an early version of the theory of inertia, which held that an object's motion stays the same until an outside force changed it. He calculated that objects of different weights fall at almost the same speed and with a uniform acceleration. He argued that the motion of objects follows regular mathematical laws. The same laws that govern the motions of objects on earth (which could be observed in experiments) could also be observed in the heavens—again a direct contradiction of Aristotelian principles and an important step toward a coherent physics based on a sun-centered model of the universe. Compiled under the title *Two New Sciences* (1638), this work was smuggled out of Italy and published in Protestant Holland.

Among Galileo's legacies, however, was exactly the rift between religion and science that he had hoped to avoid. Galileo believed that Copernicanism and natural philosophy in general need not subvert theological truths, religious belief, or the authority of the Church. But his trial seemed to show the contrary, that natural philosophy and Church authority could not coexist. Galileo's trial silenced Copernican voices in southern Europe, and the Church's leadership retreated into conservative reaction. It was therefore in northwest Europe that the new philosophy Galileo had championed would flourish.

METHODS FOR A NEW PHILOSOPHY: BACON AND DESCARTES

As the practice of the new sciences became concentrated in Protestant northwest Europe, new thinkers began to spell out standards of practice and evidence. Sir Francis Bacon and René Descartes (*deh-KAHRT*) loomed especially large

in this development, setting out methods or the rules that should govern modern science. Bacon (1561–1626) lived at roughly the same time as Kepler and Galileo—and Shakespeare; Descartes (1596–1650) was slightly younger. Both Bacon and Descartes came to believe that theirs was an age of profound change, open to the possibility of astonishing discovery. Both were persuaded that knowledge could take the European moderns beyond the ancient authorities. Both set out to formulate a philosophy to encompass the learning of their age.

FRONTISPIECE TO BACON'S *NOVUM ORGANUM* (1620). The illustration suggests that scientific work is like a voyage of discovery, similar to a ship setting out through uncharted waters. Is it a voyage of conquest? Compare this image with the fanciful image of Tycho Brahe at work in his observatory (page 525).

■ *What metaphors and allegorical imagery did scientists use during this period to characterize the significance of their work?*

"Knowledge is power." The phrase is Bacon's and captures the changing perspective of the seventeenth century and its new confidence in the potential of human thinking. Bacon trained as a lawyer, served in Parliament and, briefly, as lord chancellor to James I of England. His abiding concern was with the assumptions, methods, and practices that he believed should guide natural philosophers and the progress of knowledge. The authority of the ancients should not constrain the ambition of modern thinkers. Deferring to accepted doctrines could block innovation or obstruct understanding. "There is but one course left . . . to try the whole thing anew upon a better plan, and to commence a total reconstruction of sciences, arts, and all human knowledge, raised upon the proper foundations." To pursue knowledge did not mean to think abstractly and leap to conclusions; it meant observing, experimenting, confirming ideas, or demonstrating points. If thinkers will be "content to begin with doubts," Bacon wrote, "they shall end with certainties." We thus associate Bacon with the gradual separation of scientific investigation from philosophical argument.

Bacon advocated an *inductive* approach to knowledge: amassing evidence from specific observations to draw general conclusions. In Bacon's view, many philosophical errors arose from beginning with assumed first principles. The traditional view of the cosmos, for instance, rested on the principles of a prime mover and the perfection of circular motion for planets and stars. The inductive method required accumulating data (as Tycho had done, for example) and then, after careful review and experiment, drawing appropriate conclusions about the motions of heavenly bodies. Bacon argued that scientific knowledge was best tested through the cooperative efforts of researchers performing experiments that could be repeated and verified. The knowledge thus gained would be predictable and useful to philosophers and artisans alike, contributing to a wide range of endeavors from astronomy to shipbuilding.

Bacon's vision of science and progress is vividly illustrated by two images. The first, more familiar, is the title page of Bacon's *Novum Organum* (1620) with its bold ships sailing out beyond the Straits of Gibraltar, formerly the limits of the West, into the open sea, in pursuit of unknown but

FROM RENÉ DESCARTES, *L'HOMME* (1729; ORIGINALLY PUBLISHED AS *DE HOMINI*, 1662). Descartes's interest in the body as a mechanism led him to suppose that physics and mathematics could be used to understand all aspects of human physiology, and his work had an important influence on subsequent generations of medical researchers. In this illustration, Descartes depicts the optical properties of the human eye. ■ *How might such a mechanistic approach to human perception have been received by proponents of Baconian science, who depended so much on the reliability of human observations?*

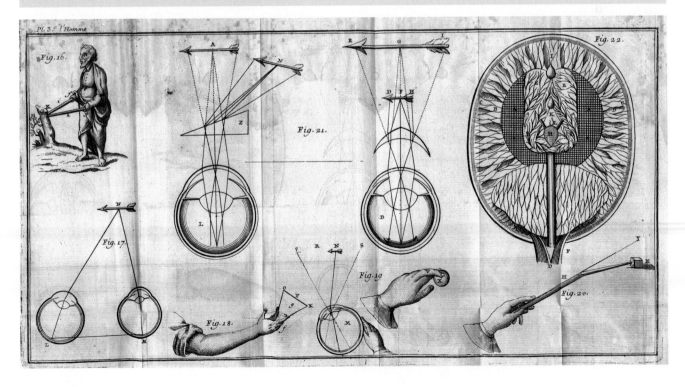

Competing Viewpoints

The New Science and The Foundations of Certainty

Francis Bacon (1561–1626) and René Descartes (1596–1650) were both enthusiastic supporters of science in the seventeenth century, but they differed in their opinions regarding the basis for certainty in scientific argumentation. Bacon's inductive method emphasized the gathering of particular observations about natural phenomena, which he believed could be used as evidence to support more general conclusions about causes, regularity, and order in the natural world. Descartes, on the other hand, defended a deductive method: he believed that certainty could be built only by reasoning from first principles that one knew to be true and was less certain of the value of evidence that came from the senses alone.

Aphorisms from *Novum Organum*

XXXI

It is idle to expect any advancement in science from the super-inducing and engrafting of new things upon old. We must begin anew from the very foundations, unless we would revolve forever in a circle with mean and contemptible progress. . . .

XXXVI

One method of delivery alone remains to us which is simply this: we must lead men to the particulars themselves, and their series and order; while men on their side must force themselves for a while to lay their notions by and begin to familiarize themselves with facts. . . .

XLV

The human understanding of its own nature is prone to suppose the existence of more order and regularity in the world than it finds. And though there be many things in nature which are singular and unmatched, yet it devises for them parallels and conjugates and relatives which do not exist. Hence the fiction that all celestial bodies move in perfect circles. . . . Hence too the element of fire with its orb is brought in, to make up the square with the other three which the sense perceives. . . . And so on of other dreams. And these fancies affect not dogmas only, but simple notions also. . . .

XCV

Those who have handled sciences have been either men of experiment or men of dogmas. The men of experiment are like the ant, they only collect and use; the reasoners resemble spiders, who make cobwebs out of their own substance. But the bee takes a middle course: it gathers its material from the flowers of the garden and of the field, but transforms and digests it by a power of its own. Not unlike this is the true business of philosophy; for it neither relies solely or chiefly on the powers of the mind, nor does it take the matter which it gathers from natural history and mechanical experiments and lay it up in the memory whole . . . but lays it up in the understanding altered and digested. Therefore, from a closer and purer league between these two faculties, the experimental and the rational (such as has never yet been made), much may be hoped. . . .

Source: Michael R. Matthews, ed., *The Scientific Background to Modern Philosophy: Selected Readings* (Indianapolis, IN: 1989), pp. 47–48, 50–52.

From *A Discourse on Method*

Just as a great number of laws is often a pretext for wrong-doing, with the result that a state is much better governed when, having only a few, they are strictly observed; so also I came to believe that in the place of the great number of precepts that go to make up logic, the following four would be sufficient for my purposes, provided that I took a firm but unshakeable decision never once to depart from them.

The first was never to accept anything as true that I did not *incontrovertibly* know to be so; that is to say, carefully to avoid both *prejudice* and premature conclusions; and to include nothing in my judgments other than that which presented itself to my mind so *clearly* and *distinctly*, that I would have no occasion to doubt it.

The second was to divide all the difficulties under examination into as many parts as possible, and as many as were required to solve them in the best way.

The third was to conduct my thoughts in a given order, beginning with the *simplest* and most easily understood objects, and gradually ascending, as it were step by step, to the knowledge of the most *complex;* and *positing* an order even on those which do not have a natural order of precedence.

The last was to undertake such complete enumerations and such general surveys that I would be sure to have left nothing out.

The long chain of reasonings, every one simple and easy, which geometers habitually employ to reach their most difficult proofs had given me cause to suppose that all those things which fall within the domain of human understanding follow on from each other in the same way, and that as long as one stops oneself taking anything to be true that is not true and sticks to the right order so as to deduce one thing from another, there can be nothing so remote that one cannot eventually reach it, nor so hidden that one cannot discover it. . . .

[B]ecause I wished . . . to concentrate on the pursuit of truth, I came to think that I should . . . reject as completely false everything in which I could detect the least doubt, in order to see if anything thereafter remained in my belief that was completely indubitable. And so, because our senses sometimes deceive us, I decided to suppose that nothing was such as they lead us to imagine it to be. And because there are men who make mistakes in reasoning, even about the simplest elements of geometry, and commit logical fallacies, I judged that I was as prone to error as anyone else, and I rejected as false all the reasoning I had hitherto accepted as valid proof. Finally, considering that all the same thoughts which we have while awake can come to us while asleep without any one of them then being true, I resolved to pretend that everything that had ever entered my head was no more true than the illusions of my dreams. But immediately afterwards I noted that, while I was trying to think of all things being false in this way, it was necessarily the case that I, who was thinking them, had to be something; and observing this truth: *I am thinking therefore I exist,* was so secure and certain that it could not be shaken by any of the most extravagant suppositions of the sceptics, I judged that I could accept it without scruple, as the first principle of the philosophy I was seeking.

Source: René Descartes, *A Discourse on the Method,* trans. Ian Maclean (New York: 2006), pp. 17–18, 28.

Questions for Analysis

1. Descartes's idea of certainty depended on a "long chain of reasonings" that departed from certain axioms that could not be doubted and rejected evidence from the senses. What science provided him with the model for this idea of certainty? What was the first thing that he felt he could be certain about? Did he trust his senses?

2. Bacon's idea of certainty pragmatically sought to combine the benefits of sensory knowledge and experience (gathered by "ants") with the understandings arrived at through reason (cobwebs constructed by "spiders"). How would Descartes have responded to Bacon's claims? According to Bacon, was Descartes an ant or a spider?

3. What do these two thinkers have in common?

great things to come. The second is Bacon's description of an imagined factory of discovery, "Solomon's house," at end of his utopian *New Atlantis* (1626). Inside the factory, "sifters" would examine and conduct experiments, passing on findings to senior researchers who would draw conclusions and develop practical applications. The work of these scholars would be supplemented by accounts sent in by their emissaries abroad, traveling ambassadors of science who would gather data and information about the natural world and human societies in other places. Bacon's utopian image of patient researchers and experimenters anticipated the modern university.

René Descartes was French, though he lived all over Europe. He was intellectually restless as well; he worked in geometry, cosmology, optics, and physiology—for a while dissecting cow carcasses daily. He was writing a (Copernican) book on physics when he heard of Galileo's condemnation in 1633, a judgment that impressed on him the dangers of "expressing judgements on this world." Descartes's *Discourse on Method* (1637), for which he is best known, began simply as a preface to three essays on optics, geometry, and meteorology. It is personal, recounting Descartes's dismay at the "strange and unbelievable" theories he encountered in his traditional education. His first response, as he described it, was to systematically doubt everything he had ever known or been taught. Better to clear the slate, he believed, than to build an edifice of knowledge on received assumptions. His first rule was "never to receive anything as a truth which [he] did not clearly know to be such." He took the human ability to think as his point of departure, summed up in his famous and enigmatic *Je pense, donc je suis,* later translated into Latin as *cogito ergo sum* and into English as "I think, therefore I am." As the phrase suggests, Descartes's doubting led (quickly, by our standards) to self-assurance and truth: the thinking individual existed, reason existed, God existed. For Descartes, then, doubt was a ploy, or a piece that he used in an intellectual chess game to defeat skepticism. Certainty, not doubt, was the centerpiece of the philosophy he bequeathed to his followers.

Descartes, like Bacon, sought a "fresh start for knowledge" or the rules for understanding of the world as it was. Unlike Bacon, Descartes emphasized *deductive* reasoning, proceeding logically from one certainty to another. "So long as we avoid accepting as true what is not so," he wrote in *Discourse on Method*, "and always preserve the right order of deduction of one thing from another, there can be nothing too remote to be reached in the end, or too well hidden to be discovered." For Descartes, mathematical thought expressed the highest standards of reason, and his work contributed greatly to the authority of mathematics as a model for scientific reasoning.

Descartes made a particularly forceful statement for *mechanism,* a view of the world shared by Bacon and Galileo and one that came to dominate seventeenth-century scientific thought. As the name suggested, mechanical philosophy proposed to consider nature as a machine. It rejected the traditional Aristotelian distinction between the works of humans and those of nature and the view that nature, as God's creation, necessarily belonged to a different—and higher—order. In the new picture of the universe that was emerging from the discoveries and writings of the early seventeenth century, it seemed that all matter was composed of the same material and all motion obeyed the same laws. Descartes sought to explain everything, including the human body, mechanically. As he put it firmly, "There is no difference between the machines built by artisans and the diverse bodies that nature alone composes." Nature operated according to regular and predictable laws and was thus accessible to human reason. The belief guided, indeed inspired, much of the scientific experiment and argument of the seventeenth century.

The Power of Method and the Force of Curiosity: Seventeenth-Century Experimenters

For nearly a century after Bacon and Descartes, most of England's natural philosophers were Baconian, and most of their colleagues in France, Holland, and elsewhere in northern Europe were Cartesians (followers of Descartes). The English Baconians concentrated on performing experiments in many different fields, producing results that could then be debated and discussed. The Cartesians turned instead toward mathematics and logic. Descartes himself pioneered analytical geometry. Blaise Pascal (1623–1662) worked on probability theory and invented a calculating machine before applying his intellectual skills to theology. The Cartesian thinker Christian Huygens (1629–1695) from Holland combined mathematics with experiments to understand problems of impact and orbital motion. The Dutch Cartesian Baruch Spinoza (1632–1677) applied geometry to ethics and believed he had gone beyond Descartes by proving that the universe was composed of a single substance that was both God and nature.

English experimenters pursued a different course. They began with practical research, putting the alchemist's tool, the laboratory, to new uses. They also sought a different kind of conclusion: empirical laws or provisional generalizations based on evidence rather than absolute statements of deductive truth. Among the many English laboratory scientists of the era were the physician William Harvey (1578–1657), the chemist Robert Boyle (1627–1691), and the inventor and experimenter Robert Hooke (1635–1703).

Harvey's contribution was enormous: he observed and explained that blood circulated through the arteries, heart, and veins. To do this, he was willing to dissect living animals (vivisection) and experiment on himself. Boyle performed experiments and established a law (known as Boyle's law) showing that at a constant temperature the volume of a gas decreases in proportion to the pressure placed on it. Hooke introduced the microscope to the experimenter's tool kit. The compound microscope had been invented in Holland early in the seventeenth century. But it was not until the 1660s that Hooke and others demonstrated its potential by using it to study the cellular structure of plants. Like the telescope before it, the microscope revealed an unexpected dimension of material phenomena. Examining even the most ordinary objects revealed detailed structures of perfectly connected smaller parts and persuaded many that

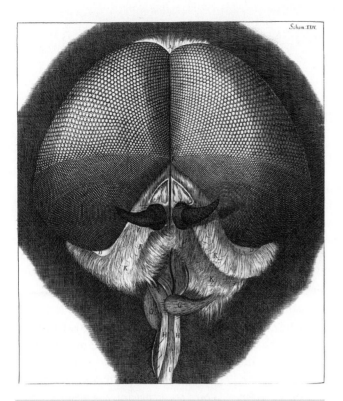

ROBERT HOOKE'S *MICROGRAPHIA*. Hooke's diagram of a fly's eye as seen through a microscope seemed to reveal just the sort of intricate universe the mechanists predicted. ▪ *Compare this image with that of Galileo's sunspots (page 527). What do these two images have in common?*

newly crowned King Charles II granted a group of natural philosophers and mathematicians a royal charter (1662) to establish the Royal Society of London, for the "improvement of natural knowledge" and committed to experimentation and collaborative work among natural philosophers. The founders of the Royal Society, in particular Boyle, believed it could serve a political as well as an intellectual purpose. The Royal Society would pursue Bacon's goal of collective research in which members would conduct formal experiments, record the results, and share them with other members. These members would in turn study the methods, reproduce the experiment, and assess the outcome. The enterprise would give England's natural philosophers a common sense of purpose and a system to reach reasoned, gentlemanly agreement on "matters of fact." By separating systematic scientific research from the dangerous language of politics and religion that had marked the civil war, the Royal Society could also help restore a sense of order and consensus to English intellectual life.

with improved instruments they would uncover even more of the world's intricacies.

The microscope also provided what many regarded as new evidence of God's existence. The way each minute structure of a living organism, when viewed under a microscope, corresponded to its purpose testified not only to God's existence but to God's wisdom as well. The mechanical philosophy did not exclude God but in fact could be used to confirm his presence. If the universe was a clock, after all, there must be a clock maker. Hooke himself declared that only imbeciles would believe that what they saw under the microscope was "the production of chance" rather than of God's creation.

The State, Scientific Academies, and Women Scientists

Seventeenth-century state building (see Chapter 14) helped secure the rise of science. In 1660, England's monarchy was restored after two decades of revolution and civil war. The

***OBSERVING THE TRANSIT OF VENUS* (1673).** Elisabetha (1647–1693) and Johannes Hevelius (1611–1687) believed that precise observations about the timing of Venus's passage across the face of the sun when observed from different parts of the earth could be used to calculate the distance from the earth to the sun. This German-speaking husband and wife astronomy team from Gdansk in present-day Poland worked together on many of their projects. After Johannes's death, Elisabetha published their jointly written star catalog.

Gassendi on the Science of Observation and the Human Soul

Pierre Gassendi (1592–1655) was a seventeenth-century French Catholic priest and philosopher. A contemporary of Descartes's, Gassendi was part of a group of intellectuals in France who sought a new philosophy of nature that could replace the traditional teachings of Aristotle that had been so severely criticized by Copernicus and his followers. Gassendi had no doubt that his faith as a Christian was compatible with his enthusiasm for the new sciences of observation, but in order to demonstrate this to his contemporaries he had to show that the mechanical explanations of the universe and the natural world did not necessarily lead to a heretical materialism or atheism. In the following passage, taken from his posthumously published work Syntagma Philosophicum *(1658), Gassendi attempted to demonstrate that one might infer the existence of the human soul, even if it was not accessible to the senses.*

There are many such things for which with the passage of time helpful appliances are being found that will make them visible to the senses. For example, take the little animal the mite, which is born under the skin; the senses perceived it as a certain unitary little point without parts; but since, however, the senses saw that it moved by itself, reason had deduced from this motion as from a perceptible sign that this little body was an animal and because its forward motion was somewhat like a turtle's, reason added that it must get about by the use of certain tiny legs and feet. And although this truth would have been hidden to the senses, which never perceived these limbs, the microscope was recently invented by which sight could perceive that matters were actually as predicted. Likewise, the question had been raised what the galaxy in the sky with the name of the Milky Way was. Democritus, concerning whom it was said that even when he did not know something he was knowing, had deduced from the perceptible sign of its filmy whiteness that it was nothing more than an innumerable multitude of closely packed little stars which could not be seen separately, but produced that effect of spilt milk when many of them were joined together. This truth had become known to him, and yet had remained undisclosed to the senses until our day and age, until the moment that the telescope, recently discovered, made it clear that things were in fact what he had said. But there are many such things which, though they were hidden from the ancients, have now been made manifest for our eyes. And who knows but a great many of those which are concealed in our time, which we perceive only through the intelligence, will one day also be clearly perceived by the senses through the agency of some helpful appliance thought up by our descendants? . . .

Secondly, if someone wonders whether a certain body is endowed with a soul or not, the senses are not at all capable of determining that by taking a look as it were at the soul itself; yet there are operations which when they come to the senses' notice, lead the intellect to deduce as from a sign that there is some soul beneath them. You will say that this sign belongs to the empirical type, but it is not at all of that type, for it is not even one of the indicative signs since it does not inform us of something that the senses have ever perceived in conjunction with the sign, as they have seen fire with smoke, but informs us instead of something that has always been impenetrable to the senses themselves, like our skin's pores or the mite's feet before the microscope.

You will persist with the objection that we should not ask so much whether there is a soul in a body as what its nature is, if it is the cause of such operations, just as there is no question that there is a force attracting iron in a magnet or that there is a tide in the sea, but there are questions over what their nature is or what they are caused by. But let me omit these matters which are to be fully treated elsewhere, and let it be enough if we say that not every truth can be known by the mind, but at least some can concerning something otherwise hidden, or not obvious to the senses themselves. And we bring up the example of the soul both because vital action is proposed by Sextus Empiricus as an example of an indicative sign and because even though it pertains not so much to the nature of the soul as to its existence, still a truth of existence of such magnitude as this, which it is most valuable for us to know, is made indisputable. For when among other questions we hear it asked if God is or exists in the universe, that is a truth of existence which it would be a great service to establish firmly even if it is not proven at the same time what he is or what his nature is. Although God is such that he can no more come under the perusal of the senses than the soul can, still we infer that the soul exists in the body from the actions that occur before the senses and are so peculiarly appropriate to a soul that if one were not present, they would not be either. In the same way we deduce that God exists in the universe from his effects perceived by the senses, which could not be produced by anything but God and which therefore would not be observed unless God were present in the world, such as the great order of the universe, its great beauty, its grandeur, its harmony, which are so great that they can only result from a sovereignly wise, good, powerful, and inexhaustible cause. But these things will be treated elsewhere at greater length.

Source: Craig B. Brush, ed., *The Selected Works of Pierre Gassendi* (New York: 1972), pp. 334–36.

Questions for Analysis

1. What is the relationship between new knowledge and new scientific tools (the microscope and the telescope) in Gassendi's examples of the mite and the Milky Way? Is he a Baconian or a Cartesian?

2. What are the limitations of the senses when it comes to questions of the human soul, according to Gassendi?

3. Given these limitations, does Gassendi conclude that science will never be able to say anything about his religious faith?

The society's journal, *Philosophical Transactions*, reached out to professional scholars and experimenters throughout Europe. Similar societies began to appear elsewhere. The French Academy of Sciences was founded in 1666 and was also tied to seventeenth-century state building, in this case Bourbon absolutism (see Chapter 15). Royal societies, devoted to natural philosophy as a collective enterprise, provided a state (or princely) sponsored framework for science and an alternative to the important but uncertain patronage of smaller nobles or to the religious (and largely conservative, Aristotelian) universities. Scientific societies reached rough agreement about what constituted legitimate research. They established the modern scientific custom of crediting discoveries to those who were first to publish results. They enabled information and theories to be exchanged more easily across national boundaries, although philosophical differences among Cartesians, Baconians, and traditional Aristotelians remained very difficult to bridge. Science began to take shape as a discipline.

The early scientific academies did not have explicit rules barring women, but with few exceptions they contained only male members. This did not mean that women did not practice science, though their participation in scientific research and debate remained controversial. In some cases, the new science could itself become a justification for women's inclusion, as when the Cartesian philosopher François Poullain de la Barre used anatomy to declare in 1673 that "the mind has no sex." Since women possessed the same physical senses as men and the same nervous systems and brains, Poullain asked, why should they not equally occupy the same roles in society? In fact, historians have discovered more than a few women who taught at European universities in the sixteenth and seventeenth centuries, above all in Italy. Elena Cornaro Piscopia received her doctorate of philosophy in Padua in 1678, the first woman to do so. Laura Bassi became a professor of physics at the University of Bologna after receiving her doctorate there in 1733, and based on her exceptional contributions to mathematics she became a member of the Academy of Science in Bologna. Her papers—including titles such as "On the Compression of Air" (1746), "On the Bubbles Observed in Freely Flowing Fluid" (1747), "On Bubbles of Air That Escape from Fluids" (1748)—gained her a stipend from the academy.

Italy appears to have been an exception in allowing women to get formal recognition for their education and research in established institutions. Elsewhere, elite women could educate themselves by associating with learned men. The aristocratic Margaret Cavendish (1623–1673), a natural philosopher in England, gleaned the information necessary to start her career from her family and their friends, a network that included Thomas Hobbes and, while in exile in France in the 1640s, René Descartes. These connections were not enough to overcome the isolation she felt working in a world of letters that was still largely the preserve of men, but this did not prevent her from developing her own speculative natural philosophy and using it to critique those who would exclude her from scientific debate. The "tyrannical government" of men over women, she wrote, "hath so dejected our spirits, that we are become so stupid, that

FROM MARIA SYBILLA MERIAN, *METAMORPHOSIS OF THE INSECTS OF SURINAM* (1705). Merian, the daughter of a Frankfurt engraver, learned in her father's workshop the skills necessary to become an important early entymologist and scientific illustrator and conducted her research on two continents.

kept on in such capacity, mouths would gape even wider." In spite of this rejection, Winkelmann continued to work as an astronomer, training both her son and two daughters in the discipline.

Like Winkelmann, the entymologist Maria Sibylla Merian (1647–1717) also made a career based on observation. And like Winkelmann, Merian was able to carve out a space for her scientific work by exploiting the precedent of guild women who learned their trade in family workshops. Merian was the daughter of an engraver and illustrator in Frankfurt, and she served as an informal apprentice to her father before beginning her own career as a scientific illustrator, specializing in detailed engravings of insects and plants. Traveling to the Dutch colony of Surinam, Merian supported herself and her two daughters by selling exotic insects and animals she collected and brought back to Europe. She fought the colony's sweltering climate and malaria to publish her most important scientific work, *Metamorphosis of the Insects of Surinam*, which detailed the life cycles of Surinam's insects in sixty ornate illustrations. Merian's *Metamorphosis* was well received in her time; in fact, Peter I of Russia proudly displayed Merian's portrait and books in his study.

"AND ALL WAS LIGHT": ISAAC NEWTON

Sir Isaac Newton's work marks the culmination of the scientific revolution. Galileo, peering through his telescope in the early 1600s, had come to believe that the earth and the heavens were made of the same material. Galileo's experiments with pendulums aimed to discover the laws of motion, and he proposed theories of inertia. It was Newton who articulated those laws and presented a coherent, unified vision of how the universe worked. All bodies in the universe, Newton said, whether on earth or in the heavens, obeyed the same basic laws. One set of forces and one pattern, which could be expressed mathematically, explained why planets orbited in ellipses and why (and at what speed) apples fell from trees. An Italian mathematician later commented that Newton was the "greatest and most fortunate of mortals"—because there was only one universe, and he had discovered its laws.

Isaac Newton (1642–1727) was born on Christmas Day to a family of small landowners. His father died before his birth, and it fell to a succession of relatives, family friends, and schoolmasters to spot, then encourage, his genius. In

beasts being but a degree below us, men use us but a degree above beasts. Whereas in nature we have as clear an understanding as men, if we are bred in schools to mature our brains."

The construction of observatories in private residences enabled some women living in such homes to work their way into the growing field of astronomy. Between 1650 and 1710, 14 percent of German astronomers were women, the most famous of whom was Maria Winkelmann (1670–1720). Winkelmann had worked with her husband, Gottfried Kirch, in his observatory, and when he died she had already done significant work, discovering a comet and preparing calendars for the Berlin Academy of Sciences. When Kirch died, she petitioned the academy to take her husband's place in the prestigious body but was rejected. Gottfried Leibniz, the academy's president, explained, "Already during her husband's lifetime the society was burdened with ridicule because its calendar was prepared by a woman. If she were now to be

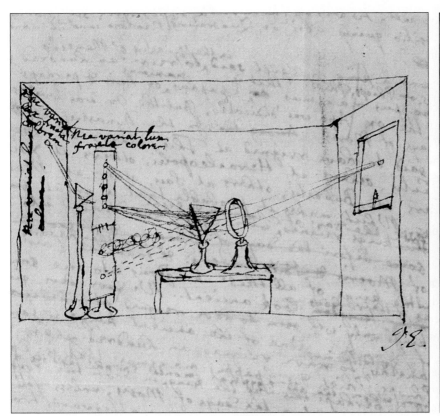

NEWTON'S EXPERIMENTS WITH LIGHT (1672). Newton's own sketch (left) elegantly displays the way he proved that white light was made up of differently colored light rays. Earlier scientists had explained the color spectrum produced by shining sunlight through a prism by insisting that the colors were a by-product of contaminating elements within the prism's glass. Newton disproved this theory by shining the sunlight through two consecutive prisms. The first produced the characteristic division of light into a color spectrum. When one of these colored beams passed through a second prism, however, it emerged on the other side unchanged, demonstrating that the glass itself was not the cause of the dispersal. He was not yet thirty when he published the results of this experiment.

1661, he entered Trinity College in Cambridge University, where he would remain for the next thirty-five years, first as a student, then as the Lucasian Professor of Mathematics. The man who came to represent the personification of modern science was reclusive, secretive about his findings, and obsessive. During his early work with optics, he experimented with his own eyes, pressing them to see how different shapes would change the effects of light and then, intrigued by what he found, inserting a very thick needle "betwixt my eye and the bone as neare to the backside of my eye as I could" to actually curve his eyeball. (Please do not try this at home.)

Newton's first great burst of creativity came at Cambridge in the years from 1664 to 1666, "the prime of my age for invention." During these years, Newton broke new ground in three areas. The first was optics. Descartes believed that color was a secondary quality produced by the speed of particulate rotation but that light itself was white. Newton, using prisms he had purchased at a local fair, showed that white light was composed of different-colored rays (see image on this page). The second area in which Newton produced innovative work during these years was in mathematics. In a series of brilliant insights, he invented both integral calculus and differential calculus, providing mathematical tools to model motion in space. The third area of his creative genius involved his early works on gravity. Newton later told different versions of the same story: the idea about gravity had come to him when he was in a "contemplative mood" and was "occasioned by the fall of an apple." Why did the apple "not go sideways or upwards, but constantly to the earth's center? . . . Assuredly the reason is, that the earth draws it. There must be a drawing power in matter." Voltaire, the eighteenth-century French essayist, retold the story to dramatize Newton's simple brilliance. But the theory of gravity rested on mathematical formulations, it was far from simple, and it would not be fully worked out until *Principia,* more than twenty years later.

Newton's work on the composite nature of white light led him to make a reflecting telescope, which used a curved mirror rather than lenses. The telescope earned him election to the Royal Society (in 1672) and drew him out of his sheltered obscurity at Cambridge. Encouraged by the Royal Society's support, he wrote a paper describing his theory of optics and allowed it to be published in *Philosophical Transactions.* Astronomers and scientists across Europe applauded the work. Robert Hooke, the Royal Society's curator of experiments, did not. Hooke was not persuaded by Newton's mode of argument; he found Newton's claims that science had to be mathematical both dogmatic and high-handed; and he objected—in a series of sharp exchanges with the reclusive genius—that Newton had not provided any physical explanation for his results. Stung by the conflict with Hooke and persuaded that few natural philosophers could understand his theories, Newton withdrew to Cambridge and long refused to share his work. Only the patient effort of friends and fellow scientists like the astronomer Edmond Halley (1656–1742), already well known for his astronomical observations in the Southern Hemisphere and the person for whom Halley's Comet is named, convinced Newton to publish again.

Newton's *Principia Mathematica* (Mathematical Principles of Natural Philosophy) was published in 1687. It was prompted by a visit from Halley, in which the astronomer asked Newton for his ideas on a question being discussed at the Royal Society: was there a mathematical basis for the elliptical orbits of the planets? Halley's question inspired Newton to expand calculations he had made earlier into an all-encompassing theory of celestial—and terrestrial—dynamics. Halley not only encouraged Newton's work but supervised and financed its publication (though he had less money than Newton); and on several occasions he had to persuade Newton, enraged again by reports of criticism from Hooke and others, to continue with the project and to commit his findings to print.

Principia was long and difficult—purposefully so, for Newton said he did not want to be "baited by little smatterers in mathematics." Its central proposition was that gravitation was a universal force and one that could be expressed mathematically. Newton built on Galileo's work on inertia, Kepler's findings concerning the elliptical orbits of planets, the work of Boyle and Descartes, and even his rival Hooke's work on gravity. He once said, "If

I have seen further, it is by standing on the shoulders of giants." But Newton's universal theory of gravity, although it drew on work of others before him, formulated something entirely new. His synthesis offered a single, descriptive account of mass and motion. "All bodies whatsoever are endowed with a principle of mutual gravitation." The law of gravitation was stated in a mathematical formula and supported by observation and experience; it was, literally, universal.

The scientific elite of Newton's time was not uniformly persuaded. Many mechanical philosophers, particularly Cartesians, objected to the prominence in Newton's theory of forces acting across empty space. Such attractions smacked of mysticism (or the occult); they seemed to lack any driving mechanism. Newton responded to these criticisms in a note added to the next edition of the *Principia* (*General Scholium,* 1713). He did not know what *caused* gravity, he said, and he did not "feign hypotheses." "For whatever is not deduced from the phenomena must be called hypothesis," he wrote, and has "no place in the experimental philosophy." For Newton, certainty

NEWTON AND SATIRE. The English artist and satirist William Hogarth mocking both philosophy and "Newton worship" in 1763. The philosophers' heads are being weighed on a scale that runs from "absolute gravity" to "absolute levity" or "stark fool."

Newton on the Purposes of Experimental Philosophy

When Newton added his General Scholium to the second edition of Principia *in 1713, he was seventy-one, president of the Royal Society, and widely revered. Responding to continental critics, he set out his general views on science and its methods, arguing against purely deductive reasoning and reliance on hypotheses about ultimate causes.*

itherto we have explained the phenomena of the heavens and of our sea by the power of gravity, but have not yet assigned the cause of this power. This is certain, that it must proceed from a cause that penetrates to the very centres of the sun and planets, without suffering the least diminution of its force; that operates not according to the quantity of the surfaces of the particles on which it acts (as mechanical causes used to do), but according to the quantity of the solid matter which they contain, and propagates its virtue on all sides to immense distances, decreasing always as the inverse square of the distances. . . . [H]itherto I have not been able to discover the cause of those properties of gravity from phenomena, and I frame no hypothesis; for whatever is not deduced from the phenomena is to be called an hypothesis and hypotheses, whether metaphysical or physical, whether of occult qualities or mechanical, have no place in experimental philosophy. In this philosophy particular propositions are inferred from the phenomena, and afterwards rendered general by induction. . . . And to us it is enough that gravity does really exist, and acts according to the laws which we have explained, and abundantly serves to account for all the motions of the celestial bodies, and of our sea.

Source: Michael R. Matthews, ed., *The Scientific Background to Modern Philosophy: Selected Readings* (Indianapolis, IN: 1989), p. 152.

Questions for Analysis

1. Why did Isaac Newton declare that "hypotheses, whether metaphysical or physical, whether of occult qualities or mechanical, have no place in experimental philosophy"?

2. Is Newton's thinking similar to Bacon's, or does he argue in ways similar to Descartes's?

and objectivity lay in the precise mathematical characterization of phenomena—"the mathematization of the universe," as one historian puts it. Science could not, and need not, always uncover causes. It did describe natural phenomena and accurately predict the behavior of objects as confirmed by experimentation.

Other natural philosophers immediately acclaimed Newton's work for solving long-standing puzzles. Thinkers persuaded that the Copernican version of the universe was right had been unable to piece together the physics of a revolving earth. Newton made it possible to do so. Halley provided a poem to accompany the first edition of *Principia*. "No closer to the gods can any mortal rise," he wrote, of the man with whom he had worked so patiently. Halley did have a financial as well as an intellectual interest in the book, and he also arranged for it to be publicized and reviewed in influential journals. John Locke (whose own *Essay Concerning Human Understanding* was written at virtually the same time, in 1690) read *Principia* twice and summarized it in French for readers across the Channel. By 1713, pirated editions of *Principia* were being published in Amsterdam for distribution throughout Europe. By the time Newton died, in 1727, he had become an English national hero and was given a funeral at Westminster Abbey. The poet Alexander Pope expressed the awe that Newton inspired in some of his contemporaries in a famous couplet:

Nature and nature's law lay hid in night;
God said, "Let Newton be!" and all was light.

Voltaire, the French champion of the Enlightenment (discussed in the next chapter), was largely responsible for Newton's reputation in France. In this, he was helped by a woman who was a brilliant mathematician in her own right, Emilie du Châtelet. Du Châtelet coauthored a book with

Voltaire introducing Newton to a French audience; and she translated *Principia*, a daunting scientific and mathematical task and one well beyond Voltaire's mathematical abilities. Newton's French admirers and publicists disseminated Newton's findings. In their eyes, Newton also represented a cultural transformation, a turning point in the history of knowledge.

Science and Cultural Change

From the seventeenth century on, science stood at the heart of what it meant to be "modern." It grew increasingly central to the self-understanding of Western culture, and scientific and technological power became one of the justifications for the expansion of Western empires and the subjugation of other peoples. For all these reasons, the scientific revolution was and often still is presented as a thorough-going break with the past, a moment when Western culture was recast. But, as one historian has written, "no house is ever built of entirely virgin materials, according to a plan bearing no resemblance to old patterns, and no body of culture is able to wholly reject its past. Historical change is not like that, and most 'revolutions' effect less sweeping changes than they advertise or than are advertised for them."

To begin with, the transformation we have canvassed in this chapter involved elite knowledge. Ordinary people inhabited a very different cultural world. Second, natural philosophers' discoveries—Tycho's mathematics and Galileo's observations, for instance—did not undo the authority of the ancients in one blow. They did not seek to do so. Third, science did not subvert religion. Even when traditional concepts collapsed in the face of new discoveries, natural philosophers seldom gave up on the project of restoring a picture of a divinely ordered universe. Mechanists argued that the intricate universe revealed by the discoveries of Copernicus, Kepler, Galileo, Newton, and others was evidence of God's guiding presence. Robert Boyle's will provided the funds for a lecture series on the "confutation of atheism" by scientific means. Isaac Newton was happy to have his work contribute to that project. "Nothing," he wrote to one of the lecturers in 1692, "can rejoice me more than to find [*Principia*] usefull for that purpose." The creation of "the Sun and Fixt stars," "the motion which the Planets now have could not spring from any naturall cause alone but were imprest with a divine Agent." Science was thoroughly compatible with belief in God's providential design, at least through the seventeenth century.

The greatest scientific minds were deeply committed to beliefs that do not fit present-day notions of science. Newton, again, is the most striking case in point. The great twentieth-century economist John Maynard Keynes was one of the first to read through Newton's private manuscripts. On the three hundredth anniversary of Newton's birth (the celebration of which was delayed because of the Second World War), Keynes offered the following reappraisal of the great scientist:

I believe that Newton was different from the conventional picture of him. . . .

In the eighteenth century and since, Newton came to be thought of as the first and greatest of the modern age of scientists, a rationalist, one who taught us to think on the lines of cold and untinctured reason.

I do not see him in this light. I do not think that any one who has pored over the contents of that box which he packed up when he finally left Cambridge in 1696 and which, though partly dispersed, have come down to us, can see him like that. Newton was not the first of the age of reason. He was the last of the magicians, the last of the Babylonians and Sumerians, the last great mind which looked out on the visible and intellectual world with the same eyes as those who began to build our intellectual inheritance rather less than 10,000 years ago.

Like his predecessors, Newton saw the world as God's message to humanity, a text to be deciphered. Close reading and study would unlock its mysteries. This same impulse led Newton to read accounts of magic, investigate alchemist's claims that base metals could be turned into gold, and to immerse himself in the writings of the Church fathers and in the Bible, which he knew in intimate detail. If these activities sound unscientific from the perspective of the present, it is because the strict distinction between rational inquiry and belief in the occult or religious traditions simply did not exist in his time. Such a distinction is a product of the long history of scientific developments after the eighteenth century. Newton, then, was the last representative of an older tradition, and also, quite unintentionally, the first of a new one.

What, then, did the scientific revolution change? Seventeenth-century natural philosophers had produced new answers to fundamental questions about the physical world. Age-old questions about astronomy and physics had been recast and, to some extent (although it was not

ESTABLISHMENT OF THE ACADEMY OF SCIENCES AND FOUNDATION OF THE OBSERVATORY, 1667. The 1666 founding of the Academy of Sciences was a measure of the new prestige of science and the potential value of research. Louis XIV sits at the center, surrounded by the religious and scholarly figures who offer the fruits of their knowledge to the French state. ▪ *What was the value of science for absolutist rulers like Louis?*

yet clear to what extent), answered. In the process, there had developed a new approach to amassing and integrating information in a systematic way, an approach that helped yield more insights into the workings of nature as time went on. In this period, too, the most innovative scientific work moved out of the restrictive environment of the Church and the universities. Natural philosophers began talking to and working with each other in lay organizations that developed standards of research. England's Royal Society spawned imitators in Florence and Berlin and later in Russia. The French Royal Academy of Sciences had a particularly direct relationship with the monarchy and the French state. France's statesmen exerted control over the academy and sought to share in the rewards of any discoveries its members made.

New, too, were beliefs about the purpose and methods of science. The practice of breaking a complex problem down into parts made it possible to tackle more and different questions in the physical sciences. Mathematics assumed a more central role in the new science. Finally,

rather than simply confirming established truths, the new methods were designed to explore the unknown and provide means to discover new truths. As Kepler wrote to Galileo, "How great a difference there is between theoretical speculation and visual experience, between Ptolemy's discussion of the Antipodes and Columbus's discovery of the New World." Knowledge itself was reconceived. In the older model, to learn was to read: to reason logically, to argue, to compare classical texts, and to absorb a finite body of knowledge. In the newer one, to learn was to discover, and what could be discovered was boundless.

CONCLUSION

The pioneering natural philosophers remained circumspect about their abilities. Some sought to lay bare the workings of the universe; others believed humans could

to plays and operas. The intellectual movement that lay behind the Enlightenment thus had broad consequences for the creation of a new kind of elite based not on birth but on the acquisition of knowledge and the encouragement of open expression and debate. A new sphere of public opinion had come into existence, one which was difficult for the state to monitor and to control, and one which would have profound consequences in the nineteenth and twentieth centuries.

The prosperity that had made the Enlightenment possible remained very unevenly distributed in late eighteenth-century Europe. In the cities, rich and poor lived separate lives in separate neighborhoods. In the countryside, regions bypassed by the developing commercial economy of the period continued to suffer from hunger and famine, just as they had done in the sixteenth and seventeenth centuries. In eastern Europe, the contrasts between rich and poor were even more extreme, as many peasants fell into a new style of serfdom that would last until the end of the nineteenth century. War, too, remained a fact of European life, bringing death and destruction to hundreds of thousands of people across the Continent and around the world—yet

After You Read This Chapter

 Visit StudySpace for quizzes, additional review materials, and multimedia documents. **wwnorton.com/web/westernciv18**

REVIEWING THE OBJECTIVES

- Many eighteenth-century thinkers used the term *Enlightenment* to describe what their work offered to European society. Who were they, and what did they mean by the term?
- Enlightenment ideas spread rapidly throughout Europe and in European colonies. How did this expanded arena for public discussion shape the development of Enlightenment thought?
- Enlightenment debates were shaped by the availability of new information about peoples and cultures in different parts of the globe. How did Enlightenment thinkers incorporate this new information into their thought?
- Enlightenment thinkers were often critical of widely held cultural and political beliefs. What was radical about the Enlightenment?

another consequence of the worldwide reach of these European colonial empires.

Finally, the Atlantic revolutions (the American Revolution of 1776, the French Revolution of 1789, and the Latin American upheavals of the 1830s) were steeped in the language of the Enlightenment. The constitutions of the new nations formed by these revolutions made reference to the fundamental assumptions of Enlightenment liberalism: on the liberty of the individual conscience and the freedom from the constraints imposed by religious or government institutions. Government authority could not be arbitrary; equality and freedom were natural; and humans sought happiness, prosperity, and the expansion of their potential. These arguments had been made earlier, though tentatively, and even after the Atlantic revolutions, their aspirations were only partially realized. But when the North American colonists declared their independence from Britain in 1776, they called such ideas "self-evident truths." That bold declaration marked both the distance traveled since the late seventeenth century and the self-confidence that was the Enlightenment's hallmark.

PEOPLE, IDEAS, AND EVENTS IN CONTEXT

- How did the **COMMERCIAL REVOLUTION** change social life in Europe?
- Who were the **PHILOSOPHES**? What gave them such confidence in **REASON**?
- What did **DAVID HUME** owe to **ISAAC NEWTON**? What made his work different from that of the famous physicist?
- What did **VOLTAIRE** admire about the work of **FRANCIS BACON AND JOHN LOCKE**? What irritated Voltaire about French society?
- What was **MONTESQUIEU**'s contribution to theories of government?
- What made **DENIS DIDEROT'S** *ENCYCLOPEDIA* such a definitive statement of the Enlightenment's goals?
- What influence did **CESARE BECCARIA** have over legal practices in Europe?
- What contributions did **ADAM SMITH** make to economic theory?
- What was radical about **JEAN-JACQUES ROUSSEAU**'s views on education and politics?
- What does the expansion of the **PUBLIC SPHERE** in the eighteenth century tell us about the effects of the Enlightenment?

THINKING ABOUT CONNECTIONS

- Compare the Enlightenment as an intellectual movement to the Reformation of the sixteenth century. What is similar about the two movements? What is distinctive?
- Did increases in literacy; the rise of print culture; and the emergence of new forms of intellectual sociability such as salons, reading societies, and coffeehouses really make public opinion more rational? How has our understanding of public opinion changed since the eighteenth century?

STORY LINES

- The French Revolution of 1798–1799 overthrew Louis XVI and created a government committed in principle to the rule of law, the liberty of the individual, and an idea of the nation as a sovereign body of citizens. These political changes also opened the way for the expression of a wide variety of social grievances by peasants, laborers, women, and other social groups in Europe.

- The French Revolution encouraged the spread of democratic ideas, but it also led to an increase in the power of centralized nation-states in Europe. The pressures of the revolutionary wars led governments to develop larger national bureaucracies, modern professional armies, new legal codes, and new tax structures.

- The French Revolution was part of a broader set of changes that rocked the Atlantic world at the end of the eighteenth century. Along with the Haitian Revolution and the American Revolution, this wave of cataclysmic change reshaped the political order of Europe and the Americas.

CHRONOLOGY

May 1789	The Estates General meets
June 1789	The Tennis Court Oath
July 1789	The Fall of the Bastille
September 1792	First French Republic
January 1793	Execution of King Louis XIV
September 1793– July 1794	The Terror
1798–1799	Napoleon's invasion of Egypt
January 1804	Haitian independence
1804	Napoleon crowned emperor
1804	Civil code
1808	Invasion of Spain
1812	Invasion of Russia
1814–1815	Napoleon's abdication and defeat

The French Revolution

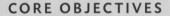

CORE OBJECTIVES

- **UNDERSTAND** the origins of the French Revolution in 1789.

- **EXPLAIN** the goals of French revolutionaries and the reactions of people elsewhere in Europe and the Atlantic world.

- **DESCRIBE** the events that made the Revolution more radical in 1792–1794.

- **IDENTIFY** the connections between the Revolution and Napoleon's regime after 1799, and the effects of Napoleon's conquests on Europe.

- **CONSIDER** the links between the French Revolution and the Atlantic world, which also saw revolutions in the Americas and in the Caribbean during these decades.

When a crowd of Parisians attacked the antiquated and nearly empty royal prison known as the Bastille on July 14, 1789, they were doing several things all at once. On the one hand, the revolt was a popular expression of support for the newly created National Assembly. This representative body had only weeks earlier declared an intention to put an end to absolutism in France by writing a constitution that made the nation, rather than the king, the sovereign authority in the land. But the Parisians in the street on July 14 did not express themselves like members of the National Assembly, who spoke the language of the Enlightenment. The actions of the revolutionary crowd were an expression of violent anger at the king's soldiers, who they feared might turn their guns on the city in a royal attempt to restore order by force. When the governor of the Bastille prison opened fire on the attackers, killing as many as a hundred, they responded with redoubled fury. By the end of the day, the prison had fallen, and the governor's battered body was dragged to the square before the city hall, where he was beheaded. Among the first to meet such an end as a consequence of revolution in France, he would not be the last.

This tension between noble political aspirations and cruel violence lies at the heart of the French Revolution. The significance of this contradiction was not lost on the millions of people throughout Europe who watched in astonishment as France was engulfed in turmoil in the 1790s. In 1789, one European out of every five lived in France, a kingdom that many considered to be the center of European culture. Other kingdoms were not immune to the same social and political tensions that divided the French. Aristocrats across Europe and the colonies resented monarchical inroads on their ancient freedoms. Members of the middle classes chafed under a system of official privilege that they increasingly saw as unjust and outmoded. Peasants fiercely resented the endless demands of central government on their limited resources. Nor were resentments focused exclusively on absolutist monarchs. Bitter resentments and tensions existed between country and city dwellers, between rich and poor, overprivileged and underprivileged, slave and free. The French Revolution was the most dramatic and tumultuous expression of all of these conflicts.

This age of revolution opened on the other side of the Atlantic Ocean. The American Revolution of 1776 was a crisis of the British Empire, linked to a long series of conflicts between England and France over colonial control of North America. It led to a major crisis of the old regime in France. Among "enlightened" Europeans, the success with which citizens of the United States had thrown off British rule and formed a republic based on Enlightenment principles was a source of tremendous optimism. Change would come, many believed. Reform was possible. The costs would be modest.

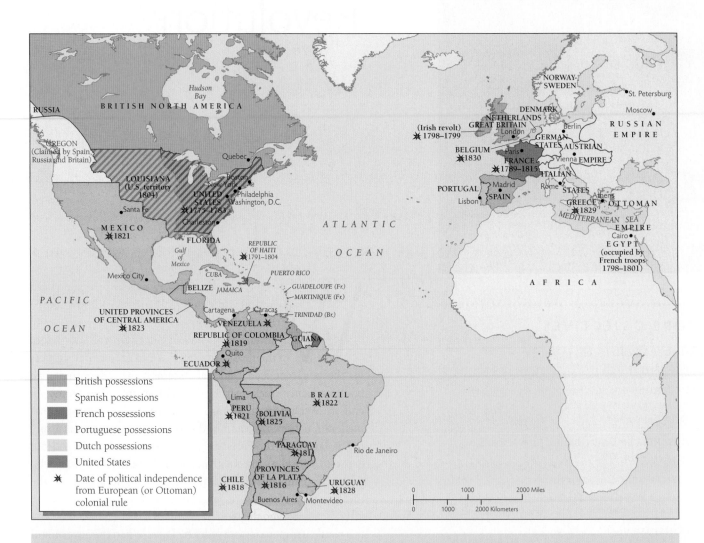

THE ATLANTIC REVOLUTIONS. The Atlantic revolutions shook nations and empires on both sides of the ocean, challenging the legitimacy of Europe's dynastic realms, lending further support to notions of popular sovereignty and forcing contemporaries to rethink the meanings of citizenship in a context of intense political and economic struggle. ▪ *How many of these struggles took place within Europe?* ▪ *How many appear to have taken place on the periphery of the Atlantic world?* ▪ *What circumstances may have made it more difficult for such revolutionary movements to develop within Europe itself?*

The French Revolution did not live up to these expectations, though change certainly did come. By any measure, the accomplishments of the revolutionary decade were extraordinary: it successfully proved that the residents of an old monarchy in the heart of Europe could come together to constitute themselves as citizens of a new political idea, the nation. Freed from the shackles of tradition, revolutionaries in France posed new questions about the role of women in public life, about the separation of church and state, about the rights of Jews and other minorities. A slave revolt in the French colonies convinced the revolutionaries that the new liberties they defended so ardently also belonged to African slaves, though few had suggested such a thing at the outset. Meanwhile, the European wars precipitated by the revolution marked the first time that entire populations were mobilized as part of a new kind of devastating international conflict, the first "total wars." In other words, in spite of the optimism of those who began the revolution in 1789, it quickly became something much more costly, complex, and violent. Its effects were to resonate throughout Europe for the next half century.

THE FRENCH REVOLUTION: AN OVERVIEW

The term *French Revolution* is a shorthand for a complex series of events between 1789 and 1799. (Napoleon ruled from 1799 to 1814–1815.) To simplify, those events can be divided into four stages. In the first stage, running from 1788 to 1792, the struggle was constitutional and relatively peaceful. An increasingly bold elite articulated its grievances against the king. Like the American revolutionaries, French elites refused taxation without representation; attacked despotism, or arbitrary authority; and offered an Enlightenment-inspired program to rejuvenate the nation. Reforms, many of them breathtakingly wide ranging, were instituted—some accepted or even offered by the king, and others passed over his objections. The peaceful, constitutional phase did not last. Unlike the American Revolution, the French Revolution did not stabilize around one constitution or one set of political leaders, for many reasons.

Reforms met with resistance, dividing the country. The threat of dramatic change within one of the most powerful countries in Europe created international tensions. In 1792, these tensions exploded into war, and the crises of war, in turn, spelled the end of the Bourbon monarchy and the beginning of the republic. This second stage of the revolution, which lasted from 1792 to 1794, was one of acute crisis, consolidation, and repression. A ruthlessly central-ized government mobilized all the country's resources to fight the foreign enemy as well as counterrevolutionaries at home, to destroy traitors and the vestiges of the Old Regime.

The Terror, as this policy was called, did save the republic, but it exhausted itself in factions and recriminations and collapsed in 1794. In the third phase, from 1794 to 1799, the government drifted. France remained a republic. It continued to fight with Europe. Undermined by corruption and division, the state fell prey to the ambitions of a military leader, Napoleon Bonaparte. Napoleon's rule, punctuated by astonishing victories and catastrophes, stretched from 1799 to 1815. It began as a republic, became an empire, and ended—after a last hurrah—in the muddy fields outside the Belgian village of Waterloo. After Napoleon's final defeat, the other European monarchs restored the Bourbons to the throne. That restoration, however, would be short lived, and the cycle of revolution and reaction continued into the nineteenth century.

THE COMING OF THE REVOLUTION

What were the long-term causes of the revolution in France? Historians long ago argued that the causes and outcomes should be understood in terms of class conflict. According to this interpretation, a rising bourgeoisie, or middle class, inspired by Enlightenment ideas and by its own self-interest, overthrew what was left of the aristocratic order. This interpretation drew on the writings of the nineteenth-century philosopher Karl Marx and on much twentieth-century sociology.

Historians have substantially modified this bold thesis. To be sure, the origins of the revolution lie in eighteenth-century French society. Yet that society was not simply divided between a bourgeois class and the aristocracy. Instead, it was increasingly dominated by a new elite or social group that brought together aristocrats, officeholders, professionals, and—to a lesser degree—merchants and businessmen. To understand the revolution, we need to understand this new social group and its conflicts with the government of Louis XVI.

French society was legally divided into Three Estates. (An individual's *estate* marked his standing, or status, and it determined legal rights, taxes, and so on.) The First Estate comprised all the clergy; the Second Estate, the nobility. The Third Estate, by far the largest, included everyone else, from wealthy lawyers and businessmen to urban laborers and poor peasants. Within the political and social elite of the country, a small but powerful group, these legal distinctions often seemed artificial. To begin with, in the upper reaches of society, the social boundaries between nobles and wealthy commoners were ill defined. Noble title was accessible to those who could afford to buy an ennobling office. For example, close to 50,000 new nobles were created between 1700 and 1789. The nobility depended on a constant infusion of talent and economic power from the wealthy social groups of the Third Estate.

To preserve their elite status, aristocrats spoke of a distinction between the nobility of the sword and of the robe, the former supposedly of a more ancient and distinguished lineage derived from military service, the latter aristocrats because they had purchased administrative or judicial office (hence the robe).

Nevertheless, wealth did not take predictable forms. Most noble wealth was proprietary—that is, tied to land, urban properties, purchased offices, and the like. Yet noble families did not disdain trade or commerce, as historians long thought. In fact, noblemen financed most industry, and they also invested heavily in banking and such enterprises as ship owning, the slave trade, mining, and metallurgy. Moreover, the very wealthy members of the Third Estate also preferred to invest in secure, proprietary holdings. Thus, throughout the century, much middle-class wealth was transformed into noble wealth, and a significant num-

ber of rich bourgeois became noblemen. Wealthy members of the bourgeoisie did not see themselves as a separate class. They thought of themselves as different from—and often opposed to—the common people, who worked with their hands, and they identified with the values of a nobility to which they frequently aspired.

There were, nonetheless, important social tensions. Less prosperous lawyers—and there were an increasing number of them—were jealous of the privileged position of a favored few in their profession. Over the course of the century, the price of offices rose, making it more difficult to buy one's way into the nobility, and creating tensions between middling members of the Third Estate and the very rich in trade and commerce who, by and large, were the only group able to afford to climb the social ladder. Less wealthy nobles resented the success of rich, upstart commoners whose income allowed them to live in luxury. In sum, several fault lines ran through the elite and the middle classes. All these social groups could nonetheless join in attacking a government and an economy that were not serving their interests.

The Enlightenment had changed public debate (see Chapter 17). Although ideas did not cause the revolution, they played a critical role in articulating grievances. The political theories of Locke, Voltaire, and Montesquieu could appeal to both discontented nobles and members of the

PREREVOLUTIONARY PROPAGANDA. Political cartoons in late-eighteenth-century France commonly portrayed the Third Estate as bearing the burden of taxation while performing the bulk of the nation's productive work. On the left, a peasant bears the burden of his tools and his harvest, as a cleric and a nobleman look on; on the right, the commoner is literally carrying his social superiors. ▪ *What visual cues indicate the status of individuals in these images?* ▪ *Would one expect the nobility or the clergy to defend their status on the basis of their usefulness to society?* ▪ *Can one detect the power of certain Enlightenment ideas behind these forms of social critique?* ▪ *Which ones?* ▪ *How might an opponent of Enlightenment thought have confronted such arguments?*

middle class. Voltaire was popular because of his attacks on noble privileges; Locke and Montesquieu gained widespread followings because of their defense of private property and limited sovereignty. Montesquieu's ideas appealed to the noble lawyers and officeholders who dominated France's powerful law courts, the *parlements*. They read his doctrine of checks and balances as support for their argument that parlements could provide a check to the despotism of the king's government. When conflicts arose, noble leaders presented themselves as defenders of the nation threatened by the king and his ministers.

The campaign for change was also fueled by economic reformers. The "physiocrats" urged the government to simplify the tax system and free the economy from mercantilist regulations. They advocated an end to price controls in the grain trade, which had been imposed to keep the cost of bread low. Such interventions, they argued, interfered with the market's ability to find an equilibrium between supply and demand.

In the countryside, peasants did not think in terms of markets. They were caught in a web of obligations to landlords, church, and state: a tithe, or levy, on farm produce owed to the church; fees for the use of a landlord's mill or wine press; fees to the landlord; and fees when land changed hands. In addition, peasants paid a disproportionate share of both direct and indirect taxes—the most onerous of which was the salt tax—levied by the government. (For some time, the production of salt had been a state monopoly; every individual was required to buy at least seven pounds a year from the government works. The result was a commodity whose cost was often as much as fifty or sixty times its actual value.) Further grievances stemmed from the requirement to maintain public roads (the corvée) and from the hunting privileges that nobles for centuries had regarded as the distinctive badge of their order.

Social and economic conditions deteriorated on the eve of the revolution. A general price increase during much of the eighteenth century, which permitted the French economy to expand by providing capital for investment, created hardship for the peasantry and for urban tradesmen and laborers. Their plight deteriorated further at the end of the 1780s, when poor harvests sent bread prices sharply higher. In 1788, families found themselves spending more than 50 percent of their income on bread, which made up the bulk of their diet. The following year the figure rose to as much as 80 percent. Poor harvests reduced demand for manufactured goods, and contracting markets in turn created unemployment. Many peasants left the countryside for the cities, hoping to find work there—only to discover that urban unemployment was far worse than that in rural areas. Evidence indicates that between 1787 and 1789 the unemployment rate in many parts of urban France was as high as 50 percent.

Failure and Reform

An inefficient tax system further weakened the country's financial position. Taxation differed according to social standings and varied from region to region—some areas were subject to a much higher rate than others. Special exemptions made the task of collectors more difficult. The financial system, already burdened by debts incurred under Louis XIV, all but broke down completely under the increased expenses brought on by French participation in the American Revolution. The cost of servicing the national debt in the 1780s consumed 50 percent of the nation's budget.

Problems with the economy reflected weaknesses in France's administrative structure, ultimately the responsibility of the country's absolutist monarch, Louis XVI (1774–1792).

LOUIS XVI. The last prerevolutionary French king, who was to lose his life in the Terror, combined in his person a strong attachment to the monarchy's absolutist doctrine with an inability to find workable solutions to the financial crisis facing his government. His royal portrait mimicked the forms of spectacular display that proved so useful to Louis XIV in shoring up the power of the monarchy. ■ *What made this display so much less potent in the late eighteenth century?* ■ *What caused the monarchy to lose its aura?*

What is the Third Estate? (1789)

The Abbé Emmanuel-Joseph Sieyès (1748–1836) was, by virtue of his office in the Church, a member of the First Estate of the Estates General. Nevertheless, his political savvy led him to be elected as a representative of the Third Estate from the district of Chartres. Sieyès was a formidable politician as well as a writer. His career during the revolution, which he ended by assisting Napoleon's seizure of power, began with one of the most important radical pamphlets of 1789. In What Is the Third Estate?, *Sieyès posed fundamental questions about the rights of the estate, which represented the great majority of the population and helped provoke its secession from the Estates General.*

 he plan of this book is fairly simple. We must ask ourselves three questions.

1. What is the Third Estate? *Everything.*

2. What has it been until now in the political order? *Nothing.*

3. What does it want to be? *Something.*

It suffices to have made the point that the so-called usefulness of a privileged order to the public service is a fallacy; that without help from this order, all the arduous tasks in the service are performed by the Third Estate; that without this order the higher posts could be infinitely better filled; that they ought to be the natural prize and reward of recognized ability and service; and that if the privileged have succeeded in usurping all well-paid and honorific posts, this is both a hateful iniquity towards the generality of citizens and an act of treason to the commonwealth.

Who is bold enough to maintain that the Third Estate does not contain within itself everything needful to constitute a complete nation? It is like a strong and robust man with one arm still in chains. If the privileged order were removed, the nation would not be something less but something more. What then is the Third Estate? All; but an "all" that is fettered and oppressed. What would it be without the privileged order? It would be all; but free and flourishing. Nothing will go well without the Third Estate; everything would go considerably better without the two others.

Source: Emmanuel-Joseph Sieyès, *What Is the Third Estate?*, ed. S. E. Finer, trans. M. Blondel, (London: 1964), pp. 53–63.

Questions for Analysis

1. How might contemporaries have viewed Sieyès's argument that the Three Estates should be evaluated according to their usefulness to the "commonwealth"?

2. Was Sieyès's language—accusing the privileged orders of "treason" and arguing for their "removal"—an incitement to violence?

3. What did Sieyès mean by the term *nation*? Could one speak of France as a nation in these terms before 1789?

Louis wished to improve the lot of the poor, abolish torture, and shift the burden of taxation onto the richer classes, but he lacked the ability to accomplish these tasks. He appointed reformers like Anne-Robert-Jacques Turgot, a physiocrat, and Jacques Necker, a Swiss Protestant banker, as finance ministers, only to arouse the opposition of traditionalists at court. When he pressed for new taxes to be paid by the nobility, he was defeated by the provincial parlements, who defended the aristocracy's immunity from taxation. He allowed his wife, the young but strong-willed Marie Antoinette—daughter of Austria's Maria Theresa—a free hand to dispense patronage among her friends. The result was constant intrigue and frequently reshuffled alliances at Versailles. By 1788, a weak monarch, together with a chaotic financial situation and severe social tensions, brought absolutist France to the edge of political disaster.

THE DESTRUCTION OF THE OLD REGIME

The fiscal crisis precipitated the revolution. In 1787 and 1788, the king's principal ministers, Charles de Calonne and Loménie de Brienne, proposed new taxes to meet the growing deficit, notably a stamp duty and a direct tax on the annual produce of the land.

Hoping to persuade the nobility to agree to these reforms, the king summoned an Assembly of Notables from among the aristocracy. This group insisted that any new tax scheme must be approved by the Estates General, the representative body of the Three Estates of the realm, and that the king had no legal authority to arrest and imprison arbitrarily. These proposed constitutional changes echoed the English aristocrats of 1688 and the American revolutionaries of 1776.

Faced with economic crisis and financial chaos, Louis XVI summoned the Estates General (which had not met since 1614) to meet in 1789. His action appeared to many as the only solution to France's deepening problems. Long-term grievances and short-term hardships produced bread riots across the country in the spring of 1789. Fear that the forces of law and order were collapsing and that the common people might take matters into their own hands

spurred the Estates General. Each of the three orders elected its own deputies—the Third Estate indirectly through local assemblies. These assemblies were charged as well with the responsibility of drawing up lists of grievances (*cahiers des doléances*), further heightening expectations for fundamental reform.

The delegates of the Third Estate, though elected by assemblies chosen in turn by artisans and peasants, represented the outlook of an elite. Only 13 percent were men of business. About 25 percent were lawyers; 43 percent were government officeholders of some sort.

By tradition, each estate met and voted as a body. In the past, this had generally meant that the First Estate (the clergy) had combined with the Second (the nobility) to defeat the Third. Now the Third Estate made it clear it would not tolerate such an arrangement. The Third's interests were articulated most memorably by the Abbé Emmanuel Sieyès, a radical member of the clergy. "What is the Third Estate?" asked Sieyès, in his famous pamphlet

THE TENNIS COURT OATH BY JACQUES LOUIS DAVID (1748–1825). In June 1789, the members of the Third Estate, now calling themselves the National Assembly, swear an oath not to disband until France has a constitution. In the center stands Jean Bailly, president of the new assembly. The Abbé Sieyès is seated at the table. In the foreground, a clergyman, an aristocrat, and a member of the Third Estate embrace in a symbol of national unity. The single deputy who refused to take the oath sits at far right, his hands clasped against his chest. ▪ *What is the significance of this near unanimity expressed in defiance of the king?* ▪ *What options were available to those who did not support this move?*

of January 1789. Everything, he answered, and pointed to eighteenth-century social changes to bolster his point. In early 1789, Sieyès's views were still unusually radical. But the leaders of the Third Estate agreed that the three orders should sit together and vote as individuals. More important, they insisted that the Third Estate should have twice as many members as the First and Second.

The king first opposed "doubling the Third" and then changed his position. His unwillingness to take a strong stand on voting procedures cost him support he might otherwise have obtained from the Third Estate. Shortly after the Estates General opened at Versailles in May 1789, the Third Estate, angered by the king's attitude, took the revolutionary step of leaving the body and declaring itself the National Assembly. Locked out of the Estates General meeting hall on June 20, the Third Estate and a handful of sympathetic nobles and clergymen moved to a nearby indoor tennis court.

Here, under the leadership of the volatile, maverick aristocrat Mirabeau and the radical clergyman Sieyès, they bound themselves by a solemn oath not to separate until they had drafted a constitution for France. This Tennis Court Oath, sworn on June 20, 1789, can be seen as the beginning of the French Revolution. By claiming the authority to remake the government in the name of the people, the National Assembly was asserting its right to act as the highest sovereign power in the nation. On June 27, the king virtually conceded this right by ordering all the delegates to join the National Assembly.

First Stages of the French Revolution

The first stage of the French Revolution extended from June 1789 to August 1792. In the main, this stage was moderate, its actions dominated by the leadership of liberal nobles and men of the Third Estate. Yet three events in the summer and fall of 1789 furnished evidence that their leadership would be challenged.

POPULAR REVOLTS

From the beginning of the political crisis, public attention was high. It was roused not merely by interest in political reform but also by the economic crisis that, as we have seen, brought the price of bread to astronomical heights. Many believed that the aristocracy and the king were conspiring to punish the Third Estate by encouraging scarcity and high prices. Rumors circulated in Paris during the latter days of June 1789 that the king's troops were mobilizing to march on the city. The electors of Paris (those who had voted for the Third Estate—workshop masters, artisans, and shop-keepers) feared not only the king but also the Parisian poor, who had been parading through the streets and threatening violence. The common people would soon be referred to as *sans-culottes* (*sahn koo-LAWTS*). The term, which translates to "without breeches," was an antiaristocratic badge of pride: a man of the people wore full-length trousers rather than aristocratic breeches with stockings and gold-buckled shoes. Led by the electors, the people formed a provisional municipal government and organized a militia of volunteers to maintain order. Determined to obtain arms, they made their way on July 14 to the Bastille, an ancient fortress where guns and ammunition were stored. Built in the Middle Ages, the Bastille had served as a prison for many years but was no longer much used. Nevertheless, it symbolized hated royal authority. When crowds demanded arms from its governor, he procrastinated and then, fearing a frontal assault, opened fire, killing ninety-eight of the attackers. The crowd took revenge, capturing the fortress (which held only seven prisoners—five common criminals and two people confined for mental incapacity) and decapitating the governor. Similar groups took control in other cities across France. The fall of the Bastille was the first instance of the people's role in revolutionary change.

The second popular revolt occurred in the countryside. Peasants, too, expected and feared a monarchical and aristocratic counterrevolution. Rumors flew that the king's armies were on their way, that Austrians, Prussians, or "brigands" were invading. Frightened and uncertain, peasants and villagers organized militias; others attacked and burned manor houses, sometimes to look for grain but usually to find and destroy records of manorial dues. This "Great Fear," as historians have labeled it, compounded the confusion in rural areas. The news, when it reached Paris, convinced deputies at Versailles that the administration of rural France had simply collapsed.

The third instance of popular uprising, the "October Days of 1789," was brought on by economic crisis. This time, Parisian women from the market district, angered by the soaring price of bread and fired by rumors of the king's continuing unwillingness to cooperate with the assembly, marched to Versailles on October 5 and demanded to be heard. Not satisfied with its reception by the assembly, the crowd broke through the gates to the palace, calling for the king to return to Paris from Versailles. On the afternoon of the following day the king yielded and returned to Paris, accompanied by the crowd and the National Guard.

Each of these popular uprisings shaped the political events unfolding at Versailles. The storming of the Bastille persuaded the king and nobles to agree to the creation of the National Assembly. The Great Fear compelled the most

WOMEN OF PARIS LEAVING FOR VERSAILLES, OCTOBER 1789. A crowd of women, accompanied by Lafayette and the National Guard, marched to Versailles to confront the king about shortages and rising prices in Paris. ■ *Did the existence of the National Assembly change the meaning of such popular protests?*

sweeping changes of the entire revolutionary period. In an effort to quell rural disorder, on the night of August 4 the assembly took a giant step toward abolishing all forms of privilege. It eliminated the Church tithe (tax on the harvest), the labor requirement known as the corvée, the nobility's hunting privileges, and a wide variety of tax exemptions and monopolies. In effect, these reforms obliterated the remnants of feudalism. One week later, the assembly abolished the sale of offices, thereby sweeping away one of the fundamental institutions of the Old Regime. The king's return to Paris during the October Days of 1789 undercut his ability to resist further changes.

THE NATIONAL ASSEMBLY AND THE RIGHTS OF MAN

The assembly issued its charter of liberties, the Declaration of the Rights of Man and of the Citizen, in September 1789. It declared property to be a natural right, along with liberty, security, and "resistance to oppression." It declared freedom of speech, religious toleration, and liberty of the press inviolable. All citizens were to be treated equally before the law. No one was to be imprisoned or punished without due process of law. Sovereignty resided in the people,

who could depose officers of the government if they abused their powers. These were not new ideas; they represented the outcome of Enlightenment discussions and revolutionary debates and deliberations. The Declaration became the preamble to the new constitution, which the assembly finished in 1791.

Whom did the Declaration mean by "man and the citizen"? The constitution distinguished between "passive" citizens, guaranteed rights under law, and "active" citizens, who paid a certain amount in taxes and could thus vote and hold office. About half the adult males in France qualified as active citizens. Even their power was curtailed, because they could vote only for "electors," men whose property ownership qualified them to hold office. Later in the revolution, the more radical republic abolished the distinction between active and passive, and the conservative regimes reinstated it. Which men could be trusted to participate in politics and on what terms was a hotly contested issue.

Also controversial were the rights of religious minorities. The revolution gave full civil rights to Protestants, though in areas long divided by religious conflict those rights were challenged by Catholics. The revolution did, hesitantly, give civil rights to Jews, a measure that sparked protest in areas of eastern France. Religious toleration, a central theme of the Enlightenment, meant ending persecution; it did not mean that the regime was prepared to accommodate religious difference. The assembly abolished serfdom and banned slavery in continental France. It remained silent on colonial slavery, and although delegations pressed the assembly on political rights for free people of color, the assembly exempted the colonies from the constitution's provisions. Events in the Caribbean, as we will see, later forced the issue.

The rights and roles of women became the focus of sharp debate, as revolutionaries confronted demands that working women participate in guilds or trade organizations, and laws on marriage, divorce, poor relief, and education were reconsidered. The Englishwoman Mary Wollstonecraft's milestone book *A Vindication of the Rights of Woman* (see Chapter 17) was penned during the revolutionary debate over national education. Should girls be educated? To what end? Wollstonecraft, as we have seen, argued strongly that reforming education required forging a new concept of independent and equal womanhood. Even Wollstonecraft, however, only hinted at political representation, aware that such an idea would "excite laughter."

Only a handful of thinkers broached the subject of women in politics: the aristocratic Enlightenment thinker the Marquis de Condorcet and, from another shore, Marie Gouze, the self-educated daughter of a butcher. Gouze became an intellectual and playwright and renamed herself Olympe de Gouges. Like many "ordinary" people, she found in the explosion of revolutionary activity the opportunity to address the public by writing speeches, pamphlets, or newspapers. She composed her own manifesto, the *Declaration of the Rights of Woman and the Citizen* (1791). Beginning with the proposition that "social distinctions can only be based on the common utility," she declared that women had the same rights as men, including resistance to authority, participation in government, and naming the fathers of illegitimate children. This last demand offers a glimpse of the shame, isolation, and hardship faced by an unmarried woman.

De Gouges's demand for equal rights was unusual, but many women nevertheless participated in the everyday activities of the revolution, joining clubs, demonstrations, and debates and making their presence known, sometimes forcefully. Women artisans' organizations had a well-established role in municipal life, and they used the revolution as an opportunity to assert their rights to produce and sell goods. Market women were familiar public figures, often central to the circulation of news and spontaneous popular demonstrations (the October Days are a good example). Initially, the regime celebrated the support of women "citizens," and female figures were favorite symbols for liberty, prudence, and the bounty of nature in

DECLARATION OF THE RIGHTS OF MAN (1789). Presented as principles of natural law inscribed on stone, this print gives a good indication of how the authors of the Declaration wished it to be perceived by the French people. Over the tablets is a beneficent and all-seeing deity accompanied by two female allegorical figures representing strength and virtue on one side and the French nation on the other. Two armed soldiers wear the uniform of the newly created National Guard. The image's symbols refer to Masonic lore (the triangle or pyramid with an eye at the center, the snake grasping its tail), and a set of historical references from the Roman Republic: a Phrygian cap, used by Romans as a symbol of liberty, is mounted on a spear emerging from a bundle of sticks. This bundle was known as a *faisceau* and was carried in ancient Rome by magistrates as symbols of their authority. ▪ *Given the absence of any monarchical symbolism or references to the Catholic Church, why was it important for the authors to come up with an alternative set of historical references?*

revolutionary iconography. When the revolution became more radical, however, some revolutionaries saw autonomous political activity by women's organizations as a threat to public order, and in 1793 the revolutionaries shut down the women's political clubs. Even so, many ordinary women were able to make use of the revolution's new legislation on marriage (divorce was legalized in 1792) and inheritance to support claims for relief from abusive husbands or absent

Declaration of the Rights of Man and of the Citizen

One of the first important pronouncements of the National Assembly after the Tennis Court Oath was the Declaration of the Rights of Man and of the Citizen. *The authors drew inspiration from the American Declaration of Independence, but the language is even more heavily influenced by the ideals of French Enlightenment philosophers, particularly Rousseau. Following are the* Declaration's *preamble and some of its most important principles.*

The representatives of the French people, constituted as the National Assembly, considering that ignorance, disregard, or contempt for the rights of man are the sole causes of public misfortunes and the corruption of governments, have resolved to set forth, in a solemn declaration, the natural, inalienable, and sacred rights of man, so that the constant presence of this declaration may ceaselessly remind all members of the social body of their rights and duties; so that the acts of legislative power and those of the executive power may be more respected . . . and so that the demands of the citizens, grounded henceforth on simple and incontestable principles, may always be directed to the maintenance of the constitution and to the welfare of all. . . .

Article 1. Men are born and remain free and equal in rights. Social distinctions can be based only on public utility.

Article 2. The aim of every political association is the preservation of the natural and imprescriptible rights of man. These rights are liberty, property, security, and resistance to oppression.

Article 3. The source of all sovereignty resides essentially in the nation. No body, no individual can exercise authority that does not explicitly proceed from it.

Article 4. Liberty consists in being able to do anything that does not injure another; thus the only limits upon each man's exercise of his natural laws are those that guarantee enjoyment of these same rights to the other members of society.

Article 5. The law has the right to forbid only actions harmful to society. No action may be prevented that is not forbidden by law, and no one may be constrained to do what the law does not order.

Article 6. The law is the expression of the general will. All citizens have the right to participate personally, or through representatives, in its formation. It must be the same for all, whether it protects or punishes. All citizens, being equal in its eyes, are equally admissable to all public dignities, positions, and employments, according to their ability, and on the basis of no other distinction than that of their virtues and talents. . . .

Article 16. A society in which the guarantee of rights is not secured, or the separation of powers is not clearly established, has no constitution.

Source: Declaration of the Rights of Man and of the Citizen, as cited in K. M. Baker, ed., *The Old Regime and the French Revolution* (Chicago: 1987), pp. 238–239.

Questions for Analysis

1. Who is the Declaration addressed to? Is it just about the rights of the French, or do these ideas apply to all people?

2. What gave a group of deputies elected to advise Louis XVI on constitutional reforms the right to proclaim themselves a National Assembly? What was revolutionary about this claim to represent the French nation?

3. Article 6, which states that "law is the expression of general will," is adapted from Rousseau's *Social Contract*. Does the Declaration give any indication of how the "general will" can be known?

---

fathers, claims that would have been impossible under the prerevolutionary legislation.

THE NATIONAL ASSEMBLY AND THE CHURCH

In November 1789 the National Assembly decided to confiscate all Church lands to use them as collateral for issuing interest-bearing notes known as *assignats*. The assembly hoped that this action would resolve the economy's infla-

tionary crisis, and eventually these notes circulated widely as paper money. In July 1789, the assembly enacted the Civil Constitution of the Clergy, bringing the Church under state authority. The new law forced all bishops and priests to swear allegiance to the state, which henceforth paid their salaries. The aim was to make the Catholic Church of France a national institution, free from interference from Rome.

These reforms were bitterly divisive. Many people resented the privileged status of the Church, and its vast monastic land holdings. On the other hand, for centuries the parish church had been a central institution in small towns and villages, providing poor relief and other services, in addition to baptisms and marriages. The Civil Constitution of the Clergy sparked fierce resistance in some parts of rural France. When the pope threatened to excommunicate priests who signed the Civil Constitution, he raised the stakes: allegiance to the new French state meant damnation. Many people, especially peasants in the deeply Catholic areas of western France, were driven into open revolt.

The National Assembly made a series of economic and governmental changes with lasting effects. To raise money, it sold off Church lands, although few of the genuinely needy could afford to buy them. To encourage the growth of economic enterprise, it abolished guilds. To rid the country of local aristocratic power, it reorganized local governments, dividing France into eighty-three equal departments. These measures aimed to defend individual liberty and freedom from customary privilege. Their principal beneficiaries were, for the most part, members of the elite, people on their way up under the previous regime who were able to take advantage of the opportunities, such as buying land or being elected to office, that the new one offered. In this realm as elsewhere, the social changes of the revolution endorsed changes already under way in the eighteenth century.

A NEW STAGE: POPULAR REVOLUTION

In the summer of 1792, the revolution's moderate leaders were toppled and replaced by republicans, who repudiated the monarchy and claimed to rule on behalf of a sovereign people. Why this abrupt and drastic change? Was the revolution blown off course? These are among the most difficult questions about the French Revolution. Historians have focused on three factors to explain the revolution's radical turn: changes in popular politics, a crisis of leadership, and international polarization.

First, the revolution politicized the common people, especially in cities. Newspapers filled with political and social commentary multiplied, freed from censorship. From 1789 forward, a wide variety of political clubs became part of daily political life. Some were formal, almost like political parties, gathering members of the elite to debate issues facing the country and influence decisions in the assembly. Other clubs opened their doors to those excluded from formal politics, and they read aloud from newspapers and discussed the options facing the country, from the provisions of the constitution to the trustworthiness of the king and his ministers.

This political awareness was heightened by nearly constant shortages and fluctuating prices. Prices particularly exasperated the working people of Paris who had eagerly awaited change since their street demonstrations of 1789. Urban demonstrations, often led by women, demanded cheaper bread; political leaders in clubs and newspapers called for the government to control rising inflation. Club leaders spoke for men and women who felt cheated by the constitution.

A second major reason for the change of course was a lack of effective national leadership. Louis XVI remained a weak monarch. He was forced to support measures personally distasteful to him, in particular the Civil Constitution of the Clergy. He was sympathetic to the plottings of the queen, who was in contact with her brother Leopold II of Austria. Urged on by Marie Antoinette, Louis agreed to attempt an escape from France in June 1791, hoping to rally foreign support for counterrevolution. The members of the royal family managed to slip past their palace guards in Paris, but they were apprehended near the border at Varennes and brought back to the capital. The constitution of 1791 declared France a monarchy, but after the escape to Varennes, Louis was little more than a prisoner of the assembly.

The Counterrevolution

The third major reason for the dramatic turn of affairs was war. From the outset of the revolution, men and women across Europe had been compelled, by the very intensity of events in France, to take sides in the conflict. In the years immediately after 1789, the revolution in France won the enthusiastic support of a wide range of thinkers. The British poet William Wordsworth, who later became disillusioned, recalled his initial mood: "Bliss was it in that dawn to be alive." His sentiments were echoed across the Continent by poets and philosophers, including the German Johann Gottfried von Herder, who declared the revolution the most important historical moment since the Reformation. In Britain, the Low Countries, western Germany, and Italy, "patriots" proclaimed their allegiance to the new revolution.

Others opposed the revolution from the start. Exiled nobles, who fled France for sympathetic royal courts in Germany and elsewhere, did all they could to stir up counterrevolutionary sentiment. In Britain, the conservative cause was strengthened by the publication in 1790 of Edmund Burke's *Reflections on the Revolution in France*. A Whig politician who had sympathized with the American revolutionaries, Burke deemed the revolution in France a monstrous crime against the social order (see **Competing Viewpoints** on pages 594–95).

Analyzing Primary Sources

Social Grievances on the Eve of the Revolution (1789)

During the elections to the Estates General, communities drew up "notebooks of grievances" to be presented to the government. The following comes from a rural community, Lignère la Doucelle.

For a long time now, the inhabitants have been crushed beneath the excessive burden of the multiplicity of taxes that they have been obliged to pay. Their parish is large and spread out, but it is a hard land with many uncultivated areas, almost all of it divided into small parcels. There is not one single farm of appreciable size, and these small properties are occupied either by the poor or by people who are doing so poorly that they go without bread every other day. They buy bread or grain nine months of the year. No industries operate in this parish, and from the time they began complaining, no one has ever listened. The cry of anguish echoed all to the way to the ministry after having fruitlessly worn out their intendants. They have always seen their legitimate claims being continuously denied, so may the fortunate moment of equality revive them.

* * *

That all lords, country gentlemen, and others of the privileged class who, either directly or through their proxies, desire to make a profit on their wealth, regardless of the nature of that wealth, pay the same taxes as the common people.

* * *

That the seigneur's mills not be obligatory, allowing everyone to choose where he would like to mill his grain.

* * *

That the children of common people living on a par with nobles be admitted for military service, as the nobility is.

That the king not bestow noble titles upon someone and their family line, but that titles be bestowed only upon those deserving it.

That nobility not be available for purchase or by any fashion other than by the bearing of arms or other service rendered to the State.

* * *

That church members be only able to take advantage of one position. That those who are enjoying more than one be made to choose within a fixed time period.

That future abbeys all be placed into the hands of the king, that His Majesty benefit from their revenue as the head abbots have been able to.

That in towns where there are several convents belonging to the same order, there be only one, and the goods and revenue of those that are to be abolished go to the profit of the crown.

That the convents where there are not normally twelve residents be abolished.

That no tenth of black wheat be paid to parish priests, priors or other beneficiaries, since this grain is only used to prepare the soil for the sowing of rye.

That they also not be paid any tenths of hemp, wool, or lamb. That in the countryside they be required to conduct burials and funerals free of charge. That the ten sous for audit books, insinuations, and the 100 [sous] collected for the parish be abolished.

* * *

That grain be taxed in the realm at a fixed price, or rather that its exportation abroad be forbidden except in the case where it would be sold at a low price.

Source: Armand Bellée, ed., *Cahiers de plaintes & doléances des paroisses de la province du Maine pour les Etats-généraux de 1789*, vol. 2 (Le Mans: 1881–1892), pp. 578–582.

Questions for Analysis

1. Do these grievances reflect the interests of only one social group, or can one hear demands being made from different groups within this rural community?

2. What do you think were the main problems faced by this community?

3. How did the revolutionaries receive these grievances?

Debating the French Revolution: Edmund Burke and Thomas Paine

The best-known debate on the French Revolution set the Irish-born conservative Edmund Burke against the British radical Thomas Paine. Burke opposed the French Revolution from the beginning. His Reflections on the Revolution in France *was published early, in 1790, when the French king was still securely on the throne. Burke disagreed with the premises of the revolution. Rights, he argued, were not abstract and "natural" but the results of specific historical traditions. Remodeling the French government without reference to the past and failing to pay proper respect to tradition and custom had, in his eyes, destroyed the fabric of French civilization.*

Thomas Paine was one of many to respond to Burke. The Rights of Man *(1791–1792) defended the revolution and, more generally, conceptions of human rights. In the polarized atmosphere of the revolutionary wars, simply possessing Paine's pamphlet was cause for imprisonment in Britain.*

Edmund Burke

You will observe, that from the Magna Carta to the Declaration of Rights, it has been the uniform policy of our constitution to claim and assert our liberties, as an entailed inheritance derived to us from our forefathers.... We have an inheritable crown; an inheritable peerage; and a house of commons and a people inheriting privileges, franchises, and liberties, from a long line of ancestors....

You had all these advantages in your ancient states, but you chose to act as if you had never been moulded into civil society, and had every thing to begin anew. You began ill, because you began by despising every thing that belonged to you.... If the last generations of your country appeared without much luster in your eyes, you might have passed them by, and derived your claims from a more early race of ancestors.... Respecting your forefathers, you would have been taught to respect yourselves. You would not have chosen to consider the French as a people of yesterday, as a nation of low-born servile wretches until the emancipating year of 1789.... [Y]ou would not have been content to be represented as a gang of Maroon slaves, suddenly broke loose from the house of bondage, and therefore to be pardoned for your abuse of liberty to which you were not accustomed and ill fitted....

... The fresh ruins of France, which shock our feelings wherever we can turn our eyes, are not the devastation of civil war; they are the sad but instructive monuments of rash and ignorant councel in time of profound peace. They are the display of inconsiderate and presumptuous, because unresisted and irresistible authority....

Nothing is more certain, than that of our manners, our civilization, and all the good things which are connected with manners, and with civilization, have, in this European world of ours, depended upon two principles; and were indeed the result of both combined; I mean the spirit of a gentleman, and the spirit of religion. The nobility and the clergy, the one by profession, the other by patronage, kept learning in existance, even

Burke's famous book aroused some sympathy for the counterrevolutionary cause, but active opposition came slowly. The first European states to express public concern about events in revolutionary France were Austria and Prussia, declaring in 1791 that order and the rights of the monarch of France were matters of "common interest to all sovereigns of Europe." The leaders of the French assembly pronounced the declaration an affront to national sovereignty. Nobles who had fled France played into their hands with plots and pronouncements against the government. Oddly, perhaps, both supporters and opponents of the revolution in France believed war would serve their cause. The National Assembly's leaders expected an aggressive policy to shore up the people's loyalty and bring freedom to the rest

in the midst of arms and confusions.... Learning paid back what it received to nobility and priesthood.... Happy if they had all continued to know their indissoluble union, and their proper place. Happy if learning, not debauched by ambition, had been satisfied to continue the instructor, and not aspired to be the master! Along with its natural protectors and guardians, learning will be cast into the mire, and trodden down under the hoofs of a swinish multitude.

Source: Edmund Burke, *Reflections on the Revolution in France (1790)* (New York: 1973), pp. 45, 48, 49, 52, 92.

Thomas Paine

Mr. Burke, with his usual outrage, abuses the *Declaration of the Rights of Man*.... Does Mr. Burke mean to deny that man has any rights? If he does, then he must mean that there are no such things as rights any where, and that he has none himself; for who is there in the world but man? But if Mr. Burke means to admit that man has rights, the question will then be, what are those rights, and how came man by them originally?

The error of those who reason by precedents drawn from antiquity, respecting the rights of man, is that they do not go far enough into antiquity. They stop in some of the intermediate stages of an hundred or a thousand years, and produce what was then a rule for the present day. This is no authority at all....

To possess ourselves of a clear idea of what government is, or ought to be, we must trace its origin. In doing this, we shall easily discover that governments must have arisen either *out* of the people, or *over* the people. Mr. Burke has made no distinction....

What were formerly called revolutions, were little more than a change of persons, or an alteration of local circumstances. They rose and fell like things of course, and had nothing in their existance or their fate that could influence beyond the spot that produced them. But what we now see in the world, from the revolutions of America and France, is a renovation of the natural order of things, a system of principles as universal as truth and the existance of man, and combining moral with political happiness and national prosperity.

Source: Thomas Paine, *The Rights of Man (1791)* (New York: 1973), pp. 302, 308, 383.

Questions for Analysis

1. How does Burke define *liberty*? Why does he criticize the revolutionaries for representing themselves as slaves freed from bondage?

2. What does Paine criticize about Burke's emphasis on history? According to Paine, what makes the French Revolution different from previous changes of regime in Europe?

3. How do these two authors' attitudes about the origins of human freedoms shape their understandings of the revolution?

of Europe. Counterrevolutionaries hoped the intervention of Austria and Prussia would undo all that had happened since 1789. Radicals, suspicious of aristocratic leaders and the king, believed that war would expose traitors with misgivings about the revolution and flush out those who sympathized with the king and European tyrants. On April 20, 1792, the assembly declared war against Austria and Prussia. Thus began the war that would keep the Continent in arms for a generation.

As the radicals expected, the French forces met serious reverses. By August 1792, the allied armies of Austria and Prussia had crossed the frontier and were threatening to capture Paris. Many, including soldiers, believed that the military disasters were evidence of the king's treason.

On August 10, Parisian crowds, organized by their radical leaders, attacked the royal palace. The king was imprisoned and a second and far more radical revolution began.

The French Republic

From this point, the country's leadership passed into the hands of the more egalitarian leaders of the Third Estate. These new leaders were known as Jacobins, the name of a political club to which many of them belonged. Although their headquarters were in Paris, their membership extended throughout France. Their members included large numbers of professionals, government officeholders, and lawyers; but they proclaimed themselves spokesmen for the people and the nation. An increasing number of artisans joined Jacobin clubs as the movement grew, and other, more democratic clubs expanded as well.

The National Convention, elected by free white men, became the effective governing body of the country for the next three years. It was elected in September 1792, at a time when enemy troops were advancing, spreading panic. Rumors flew that prisoners in Paris were plotting to aid the enemy. They were hauled from their cells, dragged before hastily convened tribunals, and killed. The "September Massacres" killed more than a thousand "enemies of the Revolution" in less than a week. Similar riots engulfed Lyons, Orléans, and other French cities.

The newly elected convention was far more radical than its predecessor, and its leadership was determined to end the monarchy. On September 21, the convention declared France a republic. In December, it placed the king on trial, and in January 1793 he was condemned to death by a narrow margin. The heir to the grand tradition of French absolutism met his end bravely as "citizen Louis Capet," beheaded by the guillotine. Introduced as a swifter

THE EXECUTION OF LOUIS XVI. The execution of Louis XVI shocked Europe. Even committed revolutionaries in France debated the necessity of such a dramatic act. The entire National Convention (over 700 members) acted as jury, and although the assembly was nearly unanimous in finding the king guilty of treason, a majority of only one approved the final death sentence. Those who voted for Louis XVI's execution were known forever after as "regicides." ▪ *What made this act necessary from the point of view of the most radical of revolutionaries?* ▪ *What made it repugnant from the point of view of the revolution's most heated enemies?*

and more humane form of execution, the frightful mechanical headsman came to symbolize revolutionary fervor.

The convention took other radical measures. It confiscated the property of enemies of the revolution, breaking up some large estates and selling them on easier terms to less-wealthy citizens. It abruptly canceled the policy of compensating nobles for their lost privileges. It repealed primogeniture, so that property would not be inherited exclusively by the oldest son but would be divided in substantially equal portions among all immediate heirs. It abolished slavery in French colonies (see below). It set maximum prices for grain and other necessities. In an astonishing effort to root out Christianity from everyday life, the convention adopted a new calendar. The calendar year began with the birth of the republic (September 22, 1792) and divided months in such a way as to eliminate the Catholic Sunday.

Most of this program was a hastily improvised response to crisis and political pressure from the common people in the cities and their leaders. In the three years after 1790, prices had risen staggeringly: wheat by 27 percent, beef by 136 percent, potatoes by 700 percent. While the government imposed its maximums in Paris, small vigilante militias, representing the sans-culottes, attacked those they considered hoarders and profiteers.

The convention also reorganized its armies, with astonishing success. By February 1793, Britain, Holland, Spain, and Austria were in the field against the French. Britain came into the war for strategic and economic reasons: it feared a French threat to Britain's growing global power. The allied coalition, though united only in its desire to contain France, was nevertheless a formidable force. To counter it, the revolutionary government mustered all men capable of bearing arms. The revolution flung fourteen hastily drafted armies into battle under the leadership of newly promoted, young, and inexperienced officers. What they lacked in training and discipline they made up for in organization, mobility, flexibility, courage, and morale. In 1793–1794, the French armies preserved their homeland. In 1794–1795, they occupied the Low Countries; the Rhineland; and parts of Spain, Switzerland, and Savoy. In 1796, they invaded and occupied key parts of Italy and broke the coalition that had arrayed itself against them.

The Reign of Terror

In 1793, however, those victories lay in a hard-to-imagine future. France was in crisis. In 1793, the convention drafted a new democratic constitution based on male suffrage. That constitution never took effect—suspended indefinitely by wartime emergency. Instead, the convention prolonged its own life year after year and increasingly delegated its responsibilities to a group of twelve leaders, the Committee of Public Safety. The committee's ruthlessness had two purposes: to seize control of the revolution and to prosecute all the revolution's enemies—"to make terror the order of the day." The Terror lasted less than two years but left a bloody and authoritarian legacy.

Perhaps the three best-known leaders of the radical revolution were Jean Paul Marat, Georges Jacques Danton, and Maximilien Robespierre, the latter two members of the Committee of Public Safety. Marat was educated as a physician and by 1789 had already earned enough distinction in that profession to be awarded an honorary degree by St. Andrews University in Scotland. Marat opposed nearly all of his moderate colleagues' assumptions, including their admiration for Great Britain, which Marat considered corrupt and despotic. Persecuted by powerful factions in the constituent assembly who feared his radicalism, he was forced to take refuge in unsanitary sewers and dungeons.

THE DEATH OF MARAT. This painting by the French artist Jacques-Louis David in 1793 immortalized Marat. The note in the slain leader's hand is from Charlotte Corday, his assassin. ■ *Why was it important to represent Marat as a martyr?*

He persevered as the editor of the popular news sheet *The Friend of the People*. Exposure to infection left him with a chronic and painful skin disease, from which baths provided the only relief. In the summer of 1793, at the height of the crisis of the revolution, he was stabbed in his bath by Charlotte Corday, a young royalist, and thus became a revolutionary martyr.

Danton, like Marat, was a popular political leader, well known in the more plebian clubs of Paris. Elected a member of the Committee of Public Safety in 1793, he had much to do with organizing the Terror. As time went on, however, he wearied of ruthlessness and displayed a tendency to compromise, which gave his opponents in the convention their opportunity. In April 1794, Danton was sent to the guillotine. On mounting the scaffold, he is reported to have said, "Show my head to the people; they do not see the like every day."

The most famous of the radical leaders was Maximilien Robespierre. Born of a family reputed to be of Irish descent, Robespierre trained in law and quickly became a modestly successful lawyer. His eloquence and his consistent, or ruthless, insistence that leaders respect the "will of the people" eventually won him a following in the Jacobin club. Later, he became president of the National Convention and a member of the Committee of Public Safety. Though he had little to do with starting the Terror, he was nevertheless responsible for enlarging its scope. Known as "the Incorruptible," he came to represent ruthlessness justified as virtue and necessary to revolutionary progress.

The two years of the radical republic (August 1792–July 1794) brought dictatorship, centralization, suspension of any liberties, and war. The committee faced foreign enemies and opposition from both the political right and left at home. In June 1793, responding to an escalating crisis, leaders of the "Mountain," a party of radicals allied with Parisian artisans, purged moderates from the convention. Rebellions broke out in the provincial cities of Lyons, Bordeaux, and Marseilles, mercilessly repressed by the committee and its local representatives. The government also faced counterrevolution in the western region known as the Vendée, where movements enlisted peasants and artisans, who believed their local areas were being invaded and who fought for their local priest or against the summons from the revolutionaries' conscription boards. By the summer, the forces in the Vendée posed a serious threat to the convention. Determined to stabilize France, whatever the cost, the committee redeployed its forces, defeated the counterrevolutionaries, and launched murderous campaigns of pacification—torching villages, farms, and fields and killing all who dared oppose them and many who did not.

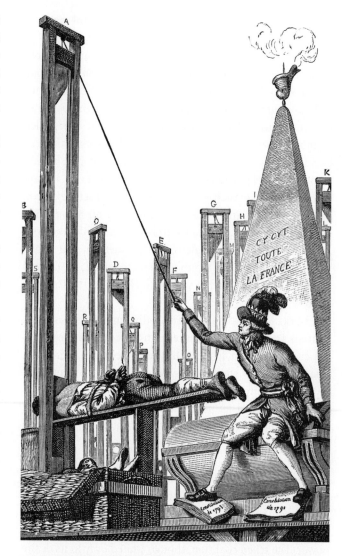

ROBESPIERRE GUILLOTINING THE EXECUTIONER. The original caption for this 1793 engraving read "Robespierre guillotines the executioner after having had all the French guillotined." In fact, Robespierre himself was guillotined after his fall from power in July 1794. ■ *What made the struggle for power and authority among revolutionaries so merciless and uncompromising?*

During the period of the Terror, from September 1793 to July 1794, the most reliable estimates place the number of deaths at close to 40,000 to about 16,500 from actual death sentences, with the rest resulting from extra-judicial killings and deaths in prison. Approximately 300,000 were incarcerated between March 1793 and August 1794. These numbers, however, do not include the pacification of the Vendée and rebellious cities in the Rhone Valley, which took more than 100,000 lives. Few victims of the Terror were aristocrats. Many more were peasants or laborers accused of hoarding, treason, or counterrevolutionary activity. Anyone who appeared to threaten the republic, no matter what his or her social or economic position, was at risk. When some time later the Abbé Sieyès was asked what he had done to distinguish himself during the Terror, he responded dryly, "I lived."

The Legacy of the Second French Revolution

The "second" French Revolution affected the everyday life of French men, women, and children in a remarkably direct way. Workers' trousers replaced the breeches that had been a sartorial badge of the middle classes and the nobility. A red cap, said to symbolize freedom from slavery, became popular headgear, and wigs vanished. Men and women addressed each other as "citizen" or "citizeness." Public life was marked by ceremonies designed to dramatize the break with the Old Regime and celebrate new forms of fraternity. In the early stages of the revolution, these festivals seem to have captured genuine popular enthusiasm for new ways of living and thinking. Under the Committee of Public Safety, they became didactic and hollow.

The radical revolution of 1792–1793 also dramatically reversed the trend toward decentralization and democracy. The assembly replaced local officials, some of them still royalist in sympathy, with "deputies on mission," whose task was to conscript troops and generate patriotic fervor. When these deputies appeared too eager to act independently, they were replaced by "national agents," with instructions to report directly to the committee. In another effort to stabilize authority, the assembly closed down all the women's political clubs, decreeing them a political and social danger. Ironically, those who claimed to govern in the name of the people found the popular movement threatening.

Finally, the revolution eroded the strength of those traditional institutions—church, guild, parish—that had for centuries given people a common bond. In their place now stood patriotic organizations and a culture that insisted on loyalty to one national cause. Those organizations had first emerged with the election campaigns, meetings, and pamphlet wars of 1788 and the interest they heightened. They included the political clubs and local assemblies, which at the height of the revolution (1792–1793) met every day of the week and offered an apprenticeship in politics. The army of the republic became the premier national institution.

On the one hand, the revolution divided France, mobilizing counterrevolutionaries as well as revolutionaries. At the same time, the revolution, war, and culture of sacrifice forged new bonds. The sense that the rest of Europe, carrying what the verses of the "Marseillaise," the most famous anthem of the revolution, called the "blood-stained flag of tyranny," sought to crush the new nation and its citizens unquestionably strengthened French national identity.

FROM THE TERROR TO BONAPARTE: THE DIRECTORY

The Committee of Public Safety might have saved France from enemy armies, but it could not save itself. Inflation became catastrophic. The long string of military victories convinced growing numbers that the committee's demands for continuing self-sacrifice and Terror were no longer justified. By July 1794, the committee was virtually without allies. On July 27 (9 Thermidor, according to the new calendar), Robespierre was shouted down while attempting to speak on the floor of the convention. The following day, along with twenty-one other conspirators, he met his death by guillotine.

Ending the Terror did not immediately bring moderation. Vigilante groups of royalists hunted down Jacobins. The repeal of price controls, combined with the worst winter in a century, caused widespread misery. Other measures that had constituted the Terror were gradually repealed. In 1795, the National Convention adopted a new and more conservative constitution. It granted suffrage to all adult male citizens who could read and write. Yet it set up indirect elections: citizens voted for electors, who in turn chose the legislative body. Wealthy citizens thus held authority. Eager

PATRIOTIC WOMEN'S CLUB. The members of this patriotic club wear constitutional bonnets to show their support for the revolution and the reforms of the convention. ▪ *What can one conclude about the atmosphere in Paris during the revolution from the existence of such associations?*

to avoid personal dictatorship, it vested executive authority in a board of five men known as the Directory, chosen by the legislative body. The new constitution included not only a bill of rights but also a declaration of the duties of the citizen.

The Directory lasted longer than its revolutionary predecessors. It still faced discontent on both the radical left and the conservative right. On the left, the Directory repressed radical movements to abolish private property and parliamentary-style government, including one led by the radical "Gracchus Babeuf." Dispatching threats from the right proved more challenging. In 1797, the first free elections held in France as a republic returned a large number of monarchists to the councils of government, alarming politicians who had voted to execute Louis XVI. Backed by the army, the Directory annulled most of the election results. After two years of more uprisings and purges, and with the country still plagued by severe inflation, the Directors grew desperate. This time they called for help from a brilliant young general named Napoleon Bonaparte.

Bonaparte's first military victory had come in 1793, with the recapture of Toulon from royalist and British forces, and had earned him promotion from captain to brigadier general at the age of twenty-four. After the Terror, he was briefly arrested for his Jacobin associations. But he proved his usefulness to the Directory in October 1795 when he put down an uprising with "a whiff of grapeshot," saving the new regime from its opponents. Promoted, he won a string of victories in Italy, forcing Austria to withdraw (temporarily) from the war. He attempted to defeat Britain by attacking British forces in Egypt and the Near East, a campaign that went well on land but ran into trouble at sea, where the French fleet was defeated by Admiral Horatio Nelson (Abukir Bay, 1798). Bonaparte found himself trapped in Egypt by the British and unable to win a decisive victory.

It was at this point that the call came from the Directory. Bonaparte slipped away from Egypt and appeared in Paris, already having agreed to participate in a coup d'état with the leading Director, that former revolutionary champion of the Third Estate, the Abbé Sieyès. On November 9, 1799 (18 Brumaire), Bonaparte was declared a "temporary consul." He was the answer to the Directory's prayers: a strong, popular leader who was not a king. Sieyès declared that Bonaparte would provide "[c]onfidence from below, authority from above." With those words Sieyès pronounced the end of the revolutionary period.

FRANCE AND ITS SISTER REPUBLICS. • The French revolutionaries, fighting against the conservative monarchs of Europe, conquered and annexed large sections of what three countries? • Who were potential supporters of the French Revolution in areas outside France during the Napoleonic era? • Who was most likely to oppose it in these areas?

NAPOLEON AND IMPERIAL FRANCE

Few figures in Western history have compelled the attention of the world as Napoleon Bonaparte did during the fifteen years of his rule in France. Few men lived on with such persistence as myth, not just in their own countries, but across the West. Why? For the great majority of ordinary Europeans, memories of the French Revolution were dominated by those of the Napoleonic Wars, which devastated Europe, convulsed its politics, and traumatized its peoples for a generation.

Yet Bonaparte's relationship to the revolution was not simple. His regime consolidated some of the revolution's political and social changes but sharply repudiated others. He presented himself as the son of the revolution, but he also borrowed freely from very different regimes, fashioning himself as the heir to Charlemagne or to the Roman Empire. His regime remade revolutionary politics and the French state; offered stunning examples of the new kinds of warfare; and left a legacy of conflict and legends of French glory that lingered in the dreams, or nightmares, of Europe's statesmen and citizens for more than a century.

Consolidating Authority: 1799–1804

Bonaparte's early career reinforced the claim that the revolution rewarded the efforts of able men. The son of a provincial Corsican nobleman, he attended the École Militaire in Paris. In prerevolutionary France he would have been unable to rise beyond the rank of major, which required buying a regimental command. The revolution, however, abolished the purchase of military office, and Bonaparte quickly became a general. Here, then, was a man who had risen from obscurity because of his own gifts, which he lent happily to the service of France's revolution.

Once in power, however, Bonaparte showed less respect for revolutionary principles. After the coup of 1799, he assumed the title of "first consul." A new constitution established universal white male suffrage and set up two legislative bodies. Elections, however, were indirect, and the power of the legislative bodies sharply curbed. "The government?" said one observer. "There is Bonaparte." Bonaparte instituted what has since become a common authoritarian device, the plebiscite, which put a question directly to popular vote. This allows the head of state to bypass politicians or legislative bodies who might disagree with him—as well as permitting local officials to tamper with ballot boxes. In 1802, flush with victory abroad, he asked the legislature to proclaim him consul for life. When the Senate refused to do so, Bonaparte's Council of State stepped in, offered him the title, and had it ratified by plebiscite. Throughout, his regime retained the appearance of consulting with the people, but its most important feature was the centralization of authority.

That authority came from reorganizing the state, and on this score Bonaparte's accomplishments were extraordinary and lasting. Bonaparte's regime confirmed the abolition of privilege, thereby promising "careers open to talent." Centralizing administrative departments, he accomplished what no recent French regime had yet achieved: an orderly and generally fair system of taxation. More efficient tax collection and fiscal management also helped halt the inflationary spiral that had crippled the revolutionary governments,

although Bonaparte's regime relied heavily on resources from areas he had conquered to fund his military ventures. As we have seen, earlier revolutionary regimes began to reorganize France's administration—abolishing the ancient fiefdoms with their separate governments, legal codes, privileges, and customs—setting up a uniform system of departments. Bonaparte continued that work, pressing it further and putting an accent on centralization. He replaced elected officials and local self-government with centrally appointed prefects and subprefects, who answered directly to the Council of State in Paris. The prefects wielded considerable power, much more than any elected representative: they were in charge of everything from collecting statistics and reporting on the economy and the population to education, roads, and public works. With more integrated administration, in which the different branches were coordinated (and supervised from above), a more professional bureaucracy, and more rational and efficient taxation (though the demands of war strained the system), Napoleon's state marked the transition from Bourbon absolutism to the modern state.

Law, Education, and a New Elite

Napoleon's most significant contribution to modern state building was the promulgation of a new legal code in 1804. Each revolutionary regime had taken up the daunting task of modernizing the laws; each had run out of time. Napoleon tolerated no delays, and threw himself into the project, pressing his own ideas and supervising half the meetings. The Napoleonic Code, as the civil code came to be called, pivoted on two principles that had remained significant through all the constitutional changes since 1789: uniformity and individualism. It cleared through the thicket of contradictory legal traditions that governed the ancient provinces of France, creating one uniform law. It confirmed the abolition of feudal privileges of all kinds: not only noble and clerical privileges but the special rights of craft guilds, municipalities, and so on. It set the conditions for exercising property rights: the drafting of contracts, leases, and stock companies. The code's provisions on the family, which Napoleon developed personally, insisted on the importance of paternal authority and the subordination of women and children. In 1793, during the most radical period of the revolution, men and women had been declared "equal in marriage"; now Napoleon's code affirmed the "natural supremacy" of the husband. Married women could not sell property, run a business, or have a profession without their husbands' permission. Fathers had the sole right to control their children's financial affairs, consent to their marriages, and (under the ancient right to correction) to imprison

reaction. Some countries and social groups collaborated enthusiastically, some negotiated, some resisted. Napoleon's image as a military hero genuinely inspired young men from the elite, raised in a culture that prized military honor. By contrast, Catholic peasants in Spain fought him from the beginning. In many small principalities previously ruled by princes—the patchwork states of Germany, for example, and the repressive kingdom of Naples—reforms that provided for more efficient, less corrupt administration, a workable tax structure, and an end to customary privilege were welcomed by most of the local population. Yet the Napoleonic presence proved a mixed

blessing. Vassal states contributed heavily to the maintenance of the emperor's military power. The French levied taxes, drafted men, and required states to support occupying armies. In Italy, the policy was called "liberty and requisitions"; and the Italians, Germans, and Dutch paid an especially high price for reforms—in terms of economic cost and numbers of men recruited. From the point of view of the common people, the local lord and priest had been replaced by the French tax collector and army recruiting board.

It is telling that even Napoleon's enemies came to believe that the upstart emperor represented the wave of the future,

NAPOLEON'S EUROPEAN EMPIRE AT ITS HEIGHT. At the height of his power in 1812, Napoleon controlled most of Europe, ruling either directly or through dependent states and allies. ▪ *Compared to the map on page 600, by what means had Napoleon expanded French control on continental Europe?* ▪ *Which major countries remained outside of French control?* ▪ *Which areas felt the most long-lasting impact of Napoleon's reign?*

NAPOLEON ON HORSEBACK AT THE ST. BERNARD PASS BY JACQUES-LOUIS DAVID, 1801, AND *LITTLE BONEY GONE TO POT* BY GEORGE CRUIKSHANK, 1814. The depth of Napoleon's celebrity in Europe can be measured in the equal shares of adulation and hatred that he stirred up within Europe among his supporters and his enemies. David's portrait, painted before he became emperor of France, captures the ardent hopes that many attached to his person. The painting explicitly compared Napoleon to two previous European conquerors, Charlemagne and the ancient Roman emperor Hannibal, by evoking their names in the stones at the base of the painting. In George Cruikshanks's bitter caricature, published after Napoleon's exile to Elba, the devil offers him a pistol to commit suicide, and the former emperor, seated on a chamber pot, says he might, but only if the firing mechanism is disabled. Both images use assumptions about virility and masculine authority to make their point. ▪ *Who are the intended audiences for these images, and how do they convey their respective arguments?*

particularly in regard to the reorganization of the state. Though they fought Napoleon, Prussian and Austrian administrators set about instituting reforms that resembled his: changing rules of promotion and recruitment, remodeling bureaucracies, redrawing districts, eliminating some privileges, and so on. Many who came of age under Napoleon's empire believed that, for better or worse, his empire was modern.

THE RETURN TO WAR AND NAPOLEON'S DEFEAT: 1806–1815

Napoleon's boldest attempt at consolidation, a policy banning British goods from the Continent, was a dangerous failure. Britain had bitterly opposed each of France's revolutionary regimes since the death of Louis XVI; now it tried to rally Europe against Napoleon with promises of generous financial loans and trade. Napoleon's Continental System, established in 1806, sought to starve Britain's trade and force its surrender. The system failed for several reasons. Throughout the war, Britain retained control of the seas. The British naval blockade of the Continent, begun in 1807, effectively countered Napoleon's system. While the French Empire strained to transport goods and raw materials overland to avoid the British blockade, the British successfully developed a lively trade with South America. A second reason for the failure of the system was its internal tariffs. Europe divided into economic camps, at odds with each other as they tried to subsist on what the Continent alone could produce and manufacture. Finally, the system hurt the Continent more than Britain. Stagnant trade in Europe's ports and unemployment in its manufacturing centers eroded public faith in Napoleon's dream of a working European empire.

The Continental System was Napoleon's first serious mistake. His ambition to create a European empire, modeled on Rome and ruled from Paris, was to become a second cause of his decline. The symbols of his empire—reflected in painting, architecture, and the design of furniture and clothing—were deliberately Roman in origin. Where early revolutionaries referred to the Roman Republic for their imagery, Napoleon looked to the more ostentatious style of the Roman emperors. In 1809, he divorced the empress Josephine and ensured himself a successor of royal blood by marrying a Habsburg princess, Marie Louise—the great-niece of Marie Antoinette. Such actions lost Napoleon the support of revolutionaries, former Enlightenment thinkers, and liberals across the Continent.

Over time, the bitter tonic of defeat began to have an effect on Napoleon's enemies, who changed their own approach to waging war. After the Prussian army was humiliated at Jena in 1806 and forced out of the war, a whole generation of younger Prussian officers reformed their military and their state by demanding rigorous practical training for commanders and a genuinely national army made up of patriotic Prussian citizens rather than well-drilled mercenaries.

The myth of Napoleon's invincibility worked against him as well, as he took ever greater risks with France's military and national fortunes. Russian numbers and Austrian artillery inflicted horrendous losses on the French at Wagram in 1809, although these difficulties were forgotten in the glow of victory. Napoleon's allies and supporters shrugged off the British admiral Horatio Nelson's victory at Trafalgar in 1805 as no more than a temporary check to the emperor's ambitions. But Trafalgar broke French naval power in the Mediterranean and led to a rift with Spain, which had been France's equal partner in the battle and suffered equally in the defeat. In the Caribbean, too, Napoleon was forced to cut growing losses (see below).

A crucial moment in Napoleon's undoing came with his invasion of Spain in 1808. Napoleon overthrew the Spanish king, installed his own brother on the throne, and then imposed a series of reforms similar to those he had instituted elsewhere in Europe. Napoleon's blow against the Spanish monarchy weakened its hold on its colonies across the Atlantic, and the Spanish crown never fully regained its grip (see Chapter 20). But in Spain itself,

NAPOLEON ON THE BATTLEFIELD OF EYLAU. Amid bitter cold and snow, Napoleon engaged with the Russian army in February 1807. Although technically a victory for the French, it was only barely that, with the French losing at least 10,000 men and the Russians twice as many. This painting, characteristic of Bonaparte propaganda, emphasizes not the losses but the emperor's saintlike clemency—even enemy soldiers reach up toward him.

Napoleon reckoned without two factors that led to the ultimate failure of his mission: the presence of British forces and the determined resistance of the Spanish people, who detested Napoleon's interference in the affairs of the church. The Peninsular Wars, as the Spanish conflicts were called, were long and bitter. The smaller British force learned how to concentrate a devastating volume of gunfire on the French pinpoint attacks on the open battlefield and laid siege to French garrison towns. The Spanish quickly began to wear down the French invaders through guerrilla warfare. Terrible atrocities were committed by both sides; the French military's torture and execution of Spanish guerrillas and civilians was immortalized by the Spanish artist Francisco Goya (1746–1828) with sickening accuracy in his prints and paintings. Though at one point Napoleon himself took charge of his army, he could not achieve anything more than temporary victory. The Spanish campaign was the first indication that Napoleon could be beaten, and it encouraged resistance elsewhere.

The second, and most dramatic, stage in Napoleon's downfall began with the disruption of his alliance with Russia. As an agricultural country, Russia had suffered a severe economic crisis when it was no longer able to trade its surplus grain for British manufactures. The consequence was that Tsar Alexander I began to wink at trade with Britain and to ignore or evade the protests from Paris. By 1811, Napoleon decided that he could no longer endure this flouting of their agreement. He collected an army of 600,000 and set out for Russia in the spring of 1812. Only a third of the soldiers in this "Grande Armée" were French; nearly as many were Polish or German, joined by soldiers and adventurers from the rest of France's client states. It was the grandest of Napoleon's imperial expeditions, an army raised from across Europe and sent to punish the autocratic tsar. The invasion ended in disaster. The Russians refused to make a stand, drawing the French farther and farther into the heart of their country. Just before Napoleon reached the ancient Russian capital of Moscow, the Russian army drew the French forces into a bloody, seemingly pointless battle in the narrow streets of a town called Borodino, where both sides suffered terrible losses of men and supplies, harder on the French who were now so far from home. After the battle, the Russians permitted Napoleon to occupy Moscow. But on the night of his entry, Russian partisans put the city to the torch, leaving little but the blackened walls of the Kremlin palaces to shelter the French troops.

THE DISASTERS OF WAR BY FRANCISCO GOYA (1746–1828). Goya was a Spanish painter and political liberal who had initially supported the French revolution. After Napoleon invaded Spain in 1807, Spaniards rose up in revolt, leading to the Peninsular War of 1808–1814. Between 1810 and 1820, Goya documented the war's violence in a series of black-and-white prints containing stark images of atrocity, rape, and the aftermath of famine. Note the absence of political imagery and the pointed and bitter irony of Goya's caption: "A great heroic feat! With dead people!" ▪ *Who or what is the target of Goya's sarcasm here?*

Hoping that the tsar would eventually surrender, Napoleon lingered amid the ruins for more than a month. On October 19, he finally ordered the homeward march. The delay was a fatal blunder. Long before he had reached the border, the terrible Russian winter was on his troops. Frozen streams, mountainous drifts of snow, and bottomless mud slowed the retreat almost to a halt. To add to the miseries of frostbite, disease, and starvation, mounted Cossacks rode out of the blizzard to harry the exhausted army. Each morning the miserable remnant that pushed on left behind circles of corpses around the campfires of the night before. Temperatures dropped to −27°F. On December 13, a few thousand broken soldiers crossed the frontier into Germany—a fragment of the once proud Grande Armée. Nearly 300,000 of its soldiers and untold thousands of Russians lost their lives in Napoleon's Russian adventure.

After the retreat from Russia, the anti-Napoleonic forces took renewed hope. United by a belief that they might finally succeed in defeating the emperor, Prussia, Russia, Austria, Sweden, and Britain renewed their attack. Citizens of many German states in particular saw this as a war of liberation, and indeed most of the fighting took place in Germany. The climax of the campaign occurred in October 1813 when, at what was thereafter known as the Battle of the Nations, fought near Leipzig, the allies dealt the French a resounding defeat. Meanwhile, allied armies won significant victories in the Low Countries and Spain. By the beginning of 1814, they had crossed the Rhine into France. Left with an army of inexperienced youths, Napoleon retreated to Paris, urging the French people to resist despite constant setbacks at the hands of the larger invading armies. On March 31, Tsar Alexander I of Russia and King Frederick William III of Prussia made their triumphant entry into Paris. Napoleon was forced to abdicate unconditionally and was sent into exile on the island of Elba, off the Italian coast.

Napoleon was back on French soil in less than a year. In the interim, the allies had restored the Bourbon dynasty to the throne, in the person of Louis XVIII, brother of Louis XVI. Despite his administrative abilities, Louis could not fill the void left by Napoleon's abdication. It was no surprise that when the former emperor staged his escape from Elba, his fellow countrymen once more rallied to his

Napoleon the "Liberator"?

Did Napoleon continue the work of the French Revolution? These two documents, from early and late moments in Napoleon's career, allow one to judge the extent to which Napoleon's regime shared the goals of revolutionaries who preceded him.

The first document concerns Napoleon's decision to reestablish slavery in French colonies. The slaves of Saint-Domingue had freed themselves by insurrection in 1791, and the French revolutionary government made this freedom official by abolishing slavery on French territory in 1794. In 1802, Napoleon launched an expeditionary force to reimpose French control over the colony, and in the course of this conflict it became clear that his goal was reenslavement. The former slaves of Saint-Domingue defeated Napoleon's troops and established Haiti as an independent nation, but in the nearby French colonies of Tobago, Martinique, and Guadeloupe, as well as in French holdings in the Indian Ocean, Napoleon reinstituted slavery. The first excerpt below is from a preliminary draft for the law on reenslavement that Napoleon drew up himself.

The second selection is excerpted from a proclamation that Napoleon addressed to the sovereigns of Europe on his return to France in March 1815, after escaping from his exile on the island of Elba. It is an excellent illustration of Napoleon's self-image at the end of his career, his rhetoric, and his belief that he represented the force of history itself.

Letter to Consul Cambacères, April 27, 1802

he consuls of the Republic and informed council of State decree:

Article One: According to the reports made to the captain-general of the colony of _____ by those individuals who will commit to this result, a list will be composed comprising first the names of black people who enjoyed freedom before 26 Pluviôse, Year II, and second, the names of blacks who have united to defend the territory of the Republic from its enemies, or who, in any other matter, have served the state.

Article Two: All the individuals named on this list will be declared free.

Article Three: Those among them who do not own property, and who have not trade or skill which can assure their subsistence, will be subjected to the regulations of the police who will assign them to property owners who will support them in agricultural work, determine their pay, and will stipulate above all arrangements for preventing vagabondage and insubordination.

Article Four: Insubordinates and outspoken vagabonds will be, in cases determined by the regulations, struck from the list and deprived of the advantages which result from it. One can substitute for this arrangement deportation to colonies where the emancipation laws have not been enacted.

Article Five: All blacks not included on the aforementioned list in article one will be subjected to the laws which in 1789 comprised the Black Code in the colonies [the Black Code was the law regulating the practice of slavery].

Article Six: It will be permitted to import blacks in the colony of _____ in accordance with the laws and regulations of the trade which were in place in 1789. The minister of the marine is charged with the execution of the present order.

Source: Laura Mason and Tracey Rizzo, *The French Revolution: A Document Collection* (Boston: 1999), pp. 349–50.

side. By the time Napoleon reached Paris, he had generated enough support to cause Louis to flee the country. The allies, meeting in Vienna to conclude peace treaties with the French, were stunned by the news of Napoleon's return. They dispatched a hastily organized army to meet the emperor's typically bold offensive push into the Low Countries. At the battle of Waterloo, fought over three bloody days from June 15 to 18, 1815, Napoleon was stopped by the forces of his two most persistent enemies, Britain and Prussia, and suffered his final defeat. This time, the allies took no chances and shipped their prisoner off to the bleak island of St. Helena in the South Atlantic. The once-mighty emperor, now the exile Bonaparte, lived out a dreary existence writing self-serving memoirs until his death in 1821.

Circular Letter to the Sovereigns of Europe, April 4, 1815

onsieur, My Brother,

You will have learnt, during the course of last month, of my landing again in France, of my entry into Paris, and of the departure of the Bourbon family. Your Majesty must by now be aware of the real nature of these events. They are the work of an irresistible power, of the unanimous will of a great nation conscious of its duties and of its rights. A dynasty forcibly reimposed upon the French people was no longer suitable for it: the Bourbons refused to associate themselves with the natural feelings or the national customs; and France was forced to abandon them. The popular voice called for a liberator. The expectation which had decided me to make the supreme sacrifice was in vain. I returned; and from the place where my foot first touched the shore I was carried by the affection of my subjects into the bosom of my capital.

My first and heartfelt anxiety is to repay so much affection by the maintenance of an honourable peace. The re-establishment of the Imperial throne was necessary for the happiness of Frenchmen: my dearest hope is that it may also secure repose for the whole of Europe. Each national flag in turn has had its gleam of glory: often enough, by some turn of fortune, great victories have been followed by great defeats. . . . I have provided the world in the past with a programme of great contests; it will please me better in future to acknowledge no rivalry but that of the advocates of peace, and no combat but a crusade for the felicity of mankind. It is France's pleasure to make a frank avowal of this noble ideal. Jealous of her independence, she will always base her policy upon an unqualified respect for the independence of other peoples. . . .

Monsieur my Brother,

Your good Brother,

Napoleon

Source: K. M. Baker, ed., *The Old Regime and the French Revolution* (Chicago: 1987), pp. 419–420, 426–427.

Questions for Analysis

1. Who in the Caribbean colonies did Napoleon intend to send back into slavery in 1802? Who was to remain free? What did Napoleon hope to accomplish by returning to the prerevolutionary legislation that authorized slavery?

2. In his 1815 address to the monarchs of Europe, can one still detect certain aspects of revolutionary rhetoric in Napoleon's words, even as he harnessed this rhetoric to his project of reestablishing the empire after his 1814 defeat?

3. Looking back on his career of ambitious conquests, what can Napoleon have hoped to accomplish in 1815 by boasting that France's "jealous" protection of her own independence gave her an "unqualified respect for the independence of other peoples"? Do his statements reveal a contradiction between the French revolution's commitment to the "universal" rights of man and the pursuit of national self-interests?

Liberty, Politics, and Slavery: The Haitian Revolution

In the French colonies across the Atlantic, the revolution took a different course, with wide-ranging ramifications. The Caribbean islands of Guadeloupe, Martinique, and Saint-Domingue occupied a central role in the eighteenth-century French economy because of the sugar trade. Their planter elites had powerful influence in Paris. The French National Assembly (like its American counterpart) declined to discuss the matter of slavery in the colonies, unwilling to encroach on the property rights of slave owners and fearful of losing the lucrative sugar islands to their British or Spanish rivals should discontented slave owners talk of independence from France. (Competition between the European powers for the islands of the Caribbean was intense; that islands would change hands was a real possibility.) French men in the National Assembly also had to consider the question of

Past and Present

The Atlantic Revolutions and Human Rights

The eighteenth-century revolutions in the Atlantic world, such as the slave revolt in Saint Domingue (left), were based on the idea that individual rights were universal—they applied to everybody. Since the world is divided into autonomous nation-states, however, it has been challenging for defenders of universal human rights, like the organization Amnesty International (right), to ensure their enforcement globally.

 Watch related author interview on StudySpace
wwnorton.com/web/westernciv18

rights for free men of color, a group that included a significant number of wealthy owners of property (and slaves).

Saint-Domingue had about 40,000 whites of different social classes, 30,000 free people of color, and 500,000 slaves, most of them recently enslaved in West Africa. In 1790, free people of color from Saint-Domingue sent a delegation to Paris, asking to be seated by the assembly, underscoring that they were men of property and, in many cases, of European ancestry. The assembly refused. Their refusal sparked a rebellion among free people of color in Saint-Domingue. The French colonial authorities repressed the movement quickly—and brutally. They captured Vincent Ogé, a member of the delegation to Paris and one of the leaders of the rebellion, and publicly executed him and his allies by breaking on the wheel and decapitation. Radical deputies in Paris, including Robespierre, expressed outrage but could do little to change the assembly's policy.

In August 1791, the largest slave rebellion in history broke out in Saint-Domingue. How much that rebellion owed to revolutionary propaganda is unclear; like many rebellions during the period, it had its own roots. The British and the Spanish invaded, confident they could crush the rebellion and take the island. In the spring of 1792, the French government, on the verge of collapse and war with Europe, scrambled to win allies in Saint-Domingue by making free men of color citizens. A few months later (after the revolution of August 1792), the new French Republic dispatched commissioners to Saint-Domingue with troops and instructions to hold the island. There they faced a combination of different forces: Spanish and British troops, defiant Saint-Domingue planters, and slaves in rebellion. In this context, the local French commissioners reconsidered their commitment to slavery; in 1793, they promised freedom to slaves who would join the French. A year later, the assembly in Paris extended to slaves in all the colonies a liberty that had already been accomplished in Saint-Domingue, by the slave rebellion.

Emancipation and war brought new leaders to the fore, chief among them a former slave, Toussaint Bréda, later Toussaint L'Ouverture (*too-SAN LOO-vehr-tur*), meaning "the one who opened the way." Over the course of the next five years, Toussaint and his soldiers, now allied with the French army, emerged victorious over the French planters, the British (in 1798), and the Spanish (in 1801). Toussaint also broke the power of his rival generals in both the mulatto and former slave armies, becoming the statesman of the revolution. In 1801, Toussaint set up a constitution, swearing allegiance to France but denying France any right to interfere in Saint-Domingue affairs. The constitution abolished slavery, reorganized the military, established Christianity as the state religion (this entailed a rejection of vodoun, a blend of Christian and various West and Central African traditions), and made Toussaint governor for life. It was an extraordinary moment in the revolutionary period: the formation of an authoritarian society but also an utterly unexpected symbol of the universal potential of revolutionary ideas.

TOUSSAINT L'OUVERTURE. A portrait of L'Ouverture, leader of what would become the Haitian Revolution, as a general.

Toussaint's accomplishments, however, put him on a collision course with the other French general he admired and whose career was remarkably like his own: Napoleon Bonaparte. Saint-Domingue stood at the center of Bonaparte's vision of an expanded empire in the New World, an empire that would recoup North American territories France had lost under the Old Regime and pivot around the lucrative combination of the Mississippi, French Louisiana, and the sugar and slave colonies of the Caribbean. In January 1802, Bonaparte dispatched 20,000 troops to bring the island under control. Toussaint, captured when he arrived for discussions with the French, was shipped under heavy guard to a prison in the mountains of eastern France, where he died in 1803. Fighting continued in Saint-Domingue, however, with fires now fueled by Bonaparte's decree reestablishing slavery where the convention had abolished it. The war turned into a nightmare for the French. Yellow fever killed thousands of French troops, including one of Napoleon's best generals and brother-in-law. Armies on both sides committed atrocities. By December 1803, the French army had collapsed. Napoleon scaled back his vision of an American empire and sold the Louisiana territories to Thomas Jefferson. "I know the value of what I abandon . . . I renounce it with the greatest regret," he told an aide. In Saint-Domingue, a general in the army of former slaves, Jean-Jacques Dessalines, declared the independent state of Haiti in 1804.

The Haitian Revolution remained, in significant ways, an anomaly. It was the only successful slave revolution in history and by far the most radical of the revolutions that occurred in this age. It suggested that the emancipatory ideas of the revolution and Enlightenment might apply to non-Europeans and enslaved peoples—a suggestion that residents of Europe attempted to ignore but one that struck home with planter elites in North and South America. Combined with later rebellions in the British colonies, it contributed to the British decision to end slavery in 1838. And it cast a long shadow over nineteenth-century slave societies from the southern United States to Brazil. The Napoleonic episode, then, had wide-ranging effects across the Atlantic: in North America, the Louisiana purchase; in the Caribbean, the Haitian Revolution; in Latin America, the weakening of Spain and Portugal's colonial empires.

CONCLUSION

The tumultuous events in France formed part of a broad pattern of late-eighteenth-century democratic upheaval. The French Revolution was the most violent, protracted, and contentious of the revolutions of the era; but the dynamics of revolution were much the same everywhere. One of the most important developments of the French Revolution was the emergence of a popular movement, which included political clubs representing people previously excluded from politics, newspapers read by and to the common people, and political leaders who spoke for the sans-culottes. In the French Revolution, as in other revolutions, the popular movement challenged the early and moderate revolutionary leadership, pressing for more radical and democratic measures. And, as in other revolutions, the popular movement in France was defeated, and authority was reestablished by a quasi-military figure. Likewise, the revolutionary ideas of liberty, equality, and fraternity were not specifically French; their roots lay in the social structures of the eighteenth century and in the ideas and culture of the Enlightenment. Yet French armies brought them, literally, to the doorsteps of many Europeans.

What was the larger impact of the revolution and the Napoleonic era? Its legacy is partly summed up in three key concepts: liberty, equality, and nation. Liberty meant individual rights and responsibilities and, more

After You Read This Chapter

(S) Visit StudySpace for quizzes, additional review materials, and multi-media documents. **wwnorton.com/web/westernciv18**

REVIEWING THE OBJECTIVES

- The French Revolution resulted both from an immediate political crisis and long-term social tensions. What was this crisis, and how did it lead to popular revolt against the monarchy?
- The revolutionaries in the National Assembly in 1789 set out to produce a constitution for France. What were their political goals, and what was the reaction of monarchs and peoples elsewhere in Europe?
- After 1792, a more radical group of revolutionaries seized control of the French state. How did they come to power, and how were their political goals different from their predecessors?
- Napoleon's career began during the revolution. What did he owe to the revolution, and what was different about his regime?
- Three major revolutions took place in the Atlantic world at the end of the eighteenth century: the American Revolution, the French Revolution, and the Haitian Revolution. What was similar about these revolutions? What was different?

specifically, freedom from arbitrary authority. By equality, as we have seen, the revolutionaries meant the abolition of legal distinctions of rank among European men. Though their concept of equality was limited, it became a powerful mobilizing force in the nineteenth century. The most important legacy of the revolution may have been the new term *nation*. Nationhood was a political concept. A nation was formed of citizens, not a king's subjects; it was ruled by law and treated citizens as equal before the law; sovereignty did not lie in dynasties or historic fiefdoms but in the nation of citizens. This new form of nation gained legitimacy when citizen armies repelled attacks against their newly won freedoms; the victories of "citizens in arms" lived on in myth and history and provided the most powerful images of the period. As the war continued, military nationhood began to overshadow its political cousin. By the Napoleonic period, this shift became decisive; a new political body of freely associated citizens was most powerfully embodied in a centralized state, its army and a kind of citizenship defined by individual commitment to the needs of the nation at war. This understanding of national identity spread throughout Europe in the coming decades.

PEOPLE, IDEAS, AND EVENTS IN CONTEXT

- Why was **LOUIS XVI** forced to convene the **ESTATES GENERAL** in 1789?
- What argument did **ABBÉ SIEYÈS** make about the role of the **THIRD ESTATE**?
- What made the **TENNIS COURT OATH** a revolutionary act?
- What was the role of popular revolt (the attack on the **BASTILLE**, the **GREAT FEAR**, the **OCTOBER DAYS**) in the revolutionary movements of 1789?
- What was the connection between the French Revolution with the **SLAVE REVOLT IN SAINT-DOMINGUE** that began in 1791?
- What was the **DECLARATION OF THE RIGHTS OF MAN AND OF THE CITIZEN**?
- What was the **CIVIL CONSTITUTION OF THE CLERGY**?
- What circumstances led to the abolition of the monarchy in 1792?
- Why did the **JACOBINS** in the **NATIONAL CONVENTION** support a policy of the **TERROR**?
- What were **NAPOLEON**'s most significant domestic accomplishments in France? What significance did Napoleon's military campaigns have for other parts of Europe and for the French Empire?
- What was the significance of the **HAITIAN REVOLUTION** of 1804?

THINKING ABOUT CONNECTIONS

- Popular movements in favor of democracy, social justice, or national self-determination in the more than two centuries since 1789 have often used the French Revolution as a point of reference or comparison. Obvious comparisons are those movements that saw themselves as "revolutionary," such as the Russian Revolution of 1917 or the Chinese Revolution of 1949. More recent comparisons might be the popular movements for democratic change in eastern Europe that resulted in the end of the Cold War in 1989 or the Arab Spring of 2011.
- Make a list of factors or circumstances that one might want to compare in considering the outcome of such movements. You might consider the degree to which elites support the current regime, the degree of consensus, and the goals of those who are protesting the status quo, economic circumstances, or international support for either the regime or for revolutionaries. What other factors might determine the outcome of revolutionary situations?

STORY LINES

- Industrialization put Europe on the path to a new form of economic development, based on the concentration of labor and production in areas with easy access to new sources of energy. This led to rapid growth of new industrial cities and to the development of new transportation to connect industrial centers to growing markets.

- Industrialization created new social groups in society, defined less by their status at birth than by their place in the new economy. Workers faced new kinds of discipline in the workplace, and women and children entered the new industrial workforce in large numbers. A new elite, made up of businessmen, entrepreneurs, bankers, engineers, and merchants, emerged as the primary beneficiaries of industrialization.

- Population growth in rural areas spurred migration to cities where laborers and the middle classes did not mix socially. They adopted different dress, speech, and leisure activities and had significantly different opportunities when it came to marriage, sex, and children.

CHRONOLOGY

1780s	Industrialization begins in Britain
1825	First railroad in Britain
1830s	Industrialization begins in France and Belgium
1845–1849	Irish potato famine
1850s	Industrialization begins in Prussia and German states of central Europe
1861	Russian tsar emancipates the serfs

Before
You
Read
This
Chapter

The Industrial Revolution and Nineteenth-Century Society

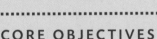

CORE OBJECTIVES

- **UNDERSTAND** the circumstances that allowed for industrialization to begin in Great Britain.

- **IDENTIFY** the industries that were the first to adopt new systems for mechanical production and the regions in Europe in which they thrived.

- **DESCRIBE** the changes in the nature of work, production, and employment that occurred as a result of the mechanization of industry.

- **EXPLAIN** the effects of industrialization on social life in Europe, especially in the new urban centers associated with industrial development.

- **IDENTIFY** the essential characteristics of the new "middle classes" in nineteenth-century Europe and their differences from property-owning groups prior to the Industrial Revolution.

James Watt, a Scottish mechanic and instrument maker, changed the course of human history when he took the primitive steam engine designed by Thomas Newcomen around 1712 and added a separate condenser, which allowed it to generate more power using less coal as fuel. Newcomen's engine used repeated heating and cooling of a steam container to generate a vacuum that could be used to pump water. Watt's engine, which he marketed after 1775 in a partnership with Matthew Boulton, was soon adapted to produce a rotary motion that could be used industrially in a multitude of ways, including grinding, milling, sawing, and weaving. The spread of Watt's steam technology throughout the north of England at the end of the eighteenth century transformed the manufacturing world, reshaped the landscape of the English countryside, and began a revolution in the way that people lived and worked.

The condensing steam engine also made Watt a very wealthy man—and he was well aware that wealth like his was different from that possessed by Britain's traditional elites. He distinguished this wealth from that of the landed aristocrat by linking it to his own efforts as an inventor and

617

entrepreneur: "The Squire's land has not been so much of his own making as the condensing engine has been of mine. He has only passively inherited his property, while this invention has been the product of my own labour and of God knows how much anguish of mind and body."

Watt was correct in his claim that his wealth and status were different from the status claimed by the landed aristocracy, but this wealth was not the product of his labor alone. In addition to his engineering predecessors, like Newcomen, Watt's engine could only be profitable in a world in which foresters, cotton merchants, and landowners could see profits in the purchase of expensive industrial sawmills, mechanical looms, and steam-driven threshers. Watt's invention also depended on the labor of men and women who dug coal from the ground and who smelted the iron and copper that he used to produce his machines. The profits of industrial entrepreneurs, meanwhile, depended on their ability to find sawyers, weavers, and fieldworkers who were willing to accept a new way of working, where they no longer owned their own tools but rather worked as wage laborers for men of business seeking returns on their investment. Business owners also required customers for the larger amounts of finished timber, woven cloth, and grain that they were now bringing to market. Technology such as Watt's was an important part of the changes that historians call the "Industrial Revolution," but technology alone cannot explain the complicated social and economic transformation contained in the phrase.

The Industrial Revolution led to the proliferation of more capital-intensive enterprises, new ways of organizing human labor, and the rapid growth of cities. It was made possible by new sources of energy and power, which led to faster forms of mechanized transportation, higher productivity, and the emergence of large consumer markets for manufactured goods. In turn, these interrelated developments triggered social and cultural changes with revolutionary consequences for Europeans and their relationship to the rest of the world.

Of all the changes, perhaps the most revolutionary came at the very root of human endeavor: new forms of energy. Over the space of two or three generations, a society and an economy that had drawn on water, wind, and wood for most of its energy needs came to depend on machines driven by steam engines and coal. In 1800, the world produced 10 million tons of coal. In 1900, it produced 1 billion—a hundred times more. The Industrial Revolution brought the beginning of the fossil-fuel age, altering as it did so the balance of humanity and the environment.

Mechanization made possible enormous gains in productivity in some sectors of the economy, but the new machines were limited to a few sectors of the economy, especially at the outset, and did not always lead to a dramatic break with older techniques. Above all, technology did not dispense with human toil. Historians emphasize that the Industrial Revolution intensified human labor—carrying water on iron rails, digging trenches, harvesting cotton, sewing by hand, or pounding hides—much more often than it eased it. One historian has suggested that we would do better to speak of the "industrious revolution." This revolution did not lie solely in machines but in a new economic system based on mobilizing capital and labor on a much larger scale. The industrious economy redistributed wealth and power, creating new social classes and producing new social tensions.

It also prompted deep-seated cultural shifts. The English critic Raymond Williams has pointed out that in the eighteenth century, *industry* referred to a human quality: a hardworking woman was "industrious," an ambitious clerk showed "industry." By the middle of the nineteenth century, industry had come to mean an economic system, one that followed its own logic and worked on its own—seemingly independent of humans. This is our modern understanding of the term, and it was born in the early nineteenth century. As the Industrial Revolution altered the foundations of the economy, it also changed the very assumptions with which people approached economics and the ways in which they regarded the role of human beings in the economy. These new assumptions could foster a sense of power but also anxieties about powerlessness.

The dramatic changes of the late eighteenth and early nineteenth centuries emerged out of earlier developments. Overseas commercial exploration opened new territories to European trade. India, Africa, and the Americas had already been brought into the web of the European economy. Expanding trade networks created new markets for goods and sources for raw materials, and the need to organize commerce over long distances fostered financial innovations and sophisticated credit schemes for managing risk. These developments paved the way for industrialization. Within Europe, the commercialization of agriculture and the spread of handicraft manufacturing in rural areas also changed the economy in ways that anticipated later industrial developments. A final factor seems to have been population growth, which began to accelerate in the eighteenth century. Because these earlier developments did not affect all areas in Europe the same way, industrialization did not always follow the same pattern across the Continent. It happened first in Great Britain, and that is where we will begin.

THE INDUSTRIAL REVOLUTION IN BRITAIN, 1760–1850

Great Britain in the eighteenth century had a fortunate combination of natural, economic, and cultural resources. It was a small and secure island nation with a robust empire and control over crucial lanes across the oceans. It had ample supplies of coal, rivers, and a well-developed network of canals.

In addition, agriculture in Britain was already more thoroughly commercialized than elsewhere. British agriculture had been transformed by a combination of new techniques, new crops, and by the "enclosure" of fields and pastures, which turned small holdings, and in many cases commonly held lands, into large fenced tracts that were privately owned and individually managed by commercial landlords. The British Parliament encouraged enclosure with a series of bills in the second half of the eighteenth century. Commercialized agriculture was more productive and yielded more food for a growing and increasingly urban population. The concentration of property in fewer hands drove small farmers off the land, sending them to look for work in other sectors of the economy. Last, commercialized agriculture produced higher profits, wealth that would be invested in industry.

A key precondition for industrialization, therefore, was Britain's growing supply of available capital, in the forms of private wealth and well-developed banking and credit institutions. London had become the leading center for international trade, and the city was a headquarters for the transfer of raw material, capital, and manufactured products throughout the world. This capital was readily available to underwrite new economic enterprises and eased the transfer of money and goods—importing, for instance, silks from the East or Egyptian and North American cottons.

Social and cultural conditions also encouraged investment in enterprises. In Britain far more than on the Continent, the pursuit of wealth was perceived to be a worthy goal. European nobility cultivated the notion of gentlemanly conduct, in part to hold the line against those moving up from below. British aristocrats respected commoners with a talent for making money and did not hesitate to invest themselves. Their scramble to enclose their

ENCLOSED FIELDS IN CENTRAL BRITAIN. The large, uniform square fields in the background of this photograph are fields that were enclosed from smaller holdings and common lands in the 1830s. They contrast with the smaller and older strip fields in the foreground. The larger enclosed fields were more profitable for their owners, who benefited from legislation that encouraged enclosure, but the process created hardship for the village communities that depended on the use of these lands for their survival. ▪ *What circumstances made enclosure possible?* ▪ *What connection have historians made between enclosure and early industrialization?*

lands reflected a keen interest in commercialization and investment. Outside the aristocracy, an even lower barrier separated merchants from the rural gentry. Many of the entrepreneurs of the early Industrial Revolution came from the small gentry or independent farmer class. Eighteenth-century Britain was not by any means free of social snobbery: lords looked down on bankers and bankers looked down on craft workers. But a lord's disdain might well be tempered by the fact that his own grandfather had worked in the counting house.

Growing domestic and international markets made eighteenth-century Britain prosperous. The British were voracious consumers. The court elite followed and bought up yearly fashions, and so did most of Britain's landed and professional society. "Nature may be satisfied with little," one London entrepreneur declared. "But it is the wants of fashion and the desire of novelties that causes trade." The country's small size and the fact that it was an island encouraged the development of a well-integrated domestic market. Unlike continental Europe, Britain did not have a system of internal tolls and tariffs, so goods could be moved freely to wherever they might fetch the best price. A constantly improving transportation system boosted that freedom of movement. So did a favorable political climate. Some members of Parliament were businessmen themselves; others were investors. And both groups were eager to encourage by legislation the construction of canals, the establishment of banks, and the enclosure of common lands.

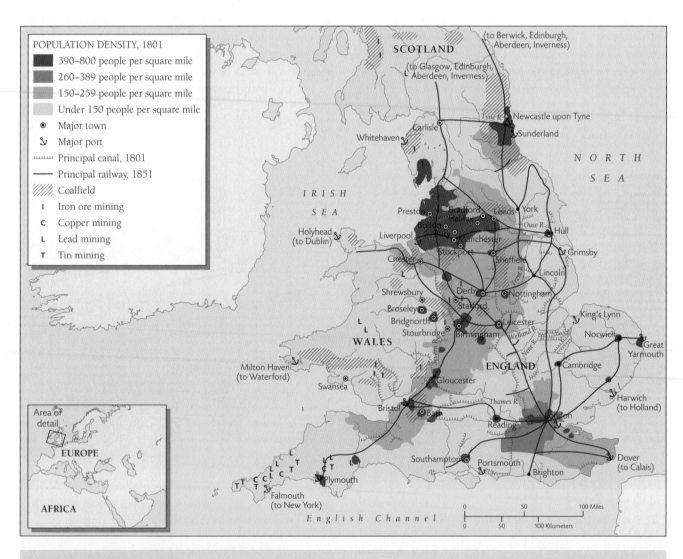

THE FIRST INDUSTRIAL NATION. Large-scale mechanization of industry developed first in Britain. ▪ *The accumulation of large deposits of what two natural resources caused urban growth outside of London?* ▪ *What new forms of transportation were critical for moving natural resources to market?* ▪ *What else was necessary for industrialization to develop as it did?*

Foreign markets promised even greater returns than domestic ones, though with greater risks. British foreign policy responded to its commercial needs. At the end of every major eighteenth-century war, Britain wrested overseas territories from its enemies. At the same time, Britain penetrated hitherto unexploited territories, such as India and South America. In 1759, over one-third of all British exports went to the colonies; by 1784, if we include the former colonies in North America, that figure had increased to one-half. Production for export rose by 80 percent between 1750 and 1770; production for domestic consumption gained just 7 percent over the same period. The British possessed a merchant marine capable of transporting goods around the world and a navy practiced in the art of protecting its commercial fleets. By the 1780s, Britain's markets, together with its fleet and its established position at the center of world commerce, gave its entrepreneurs unrivaled opportunities for trade and profit.

Innovation in the Textile Industries

The Industrial Revolution began with dramatic technological leaps in a few industries, the first of which was cotton textiles. The industry was already long established. Tariffs prohibiting imports of East Indian cottons, which Parliament had imposed to protect British woolen goods, had spurred the manufacture of British cotton. British textile manufacturers imported raw materials from India and the American South and borrowed patterns from Indian spinners and weavers. What, then, were the revolutionary breakthroughs?

In 1733, John Kay's invention of the flying shuttle speeded the process of weaving. The task of spinning thread, however, had not kept up. A series of comparatively simple mechanical devices eliminated this spinning-to-weaving bottleneck. The most important device was the spinning jenny, invented by James Hargreaves, a hand-loom weaver, in 1764. The spinning jenny was a compound spinning wheel capable of producing sixteen threads at once—though the threads were not strong enough to be used for the longitudinal fibers, or warp, of cotton cloth. The invention of the water frame by Richard Arkwright, a barber, in 1769, made it possible to produce both warp and woof (latitudinal fibers) in great quantity. In 1799, Samuel Compton invented the spinning mule, which combined the features of both the jenny and the frame. All of these important technological changes were accomplished by the end of the eighteenth century.

COTTON SPINNING, 1861. An illustration from a series showing spinning at Walter Evans and Company, cotton manufacturers in Derby, England. ▪ *Why did textile factories prefer female employees?*

A jenny could spin from six to twenty-four times more yarn than a hand spinner. By the end of the eighteenth century, a mule could produce 200 to 300 times more. Just as important, the new machines made better-quality—stronger and finer—thread. These machines revolutionized production across the textile industry. Last, the cotton gin, invented by the American Eli Whitney in 1793, mechanized the process of separating cotton seeds from the fiber, thereby speeding up the production of cotton and reducing its price. The supply of cotton fibers could now expand to keep pace with rising demand from cotton cloth manufacturers. This cotton gin had many effects, including, paradoxically, making slavery more profitable in the United States. The cotton-producing slave plantations in the American South became enmeshed in the lucrative trade with manufacturers who produced cotton textiles in the northern United States and England.

The first textile machines were inexpensive enough to be used by spinners in their own cottages. But as machines

JAMES HARGREAVES'S SPINNING JENNY, 1764. Earlier innovations in textile looms allowed weavers to produce cloth more quickly, but the industry was stymied by the slowness of traditional spinning methods. Thread production simply could not keep up with the demand created by new weaving methods. Hargreaves found a solution in a spinning jenny, which allowed spinners to spin thread and yarns on multiple spindles simultaneously—this image from Germany shows a jenny with sixteen spindles. The spinning jenny was capable of producing thread so quickly that it flooded the market, driving down the price of cotton thread. Local spinners were so outraged at this affront to their livelihood that they broke into Hargreaves's workshop and destroyed his machines, forcing him to flee and set up a new manufacture elsewhere in secret. (See also "Ned Ludd and the Luddites" on page 623.)

grew in size and complexity, they were housed instead in workshops or mills located near water that could be used to power the machines. Eventually, the further development of steam-driven equipment allowed manufacturers to build mills wherever they could be used. Frequently, those mills went up in towns and cities in the north of England, away from the older commercial and seafaring centers but nearer to the coal fields that provided fuel for new machines. From 1780 on, British cotton textiles flooded the world market. In 1760, Britain imported 2.5 million pounds of raw cotton; in 1787, 22 million pounds; in 1837, 366 million pounds. By 1815, the export of cotton textiles amounted to 40 percent of the value of all domestic goods exported from Great Britain. Although the price of manufactured cotton goods fell dramatically, the market expanded so rapidly that profits continued to increase.

Behind these statistics lay a revolution in clothing and consumption. Cotton in the form of muslins and calicos was fine enough to appeal to wealthy consumers. Cotton was also light and washable. For the first time, ordinary people could have sheets, table linens, curtains, and underwear. (Wool was too scratchy.) As one writer commented in 1846, the revolution in textiles had ushered in a "brilliant trans-

formation" in dress. "Every woman used to wear a blue or black dress that she kept ten years without washing it for fear that it would fall to pieces. Today her husband can cover her in flower-printed cotton for the price of a day's wages."

The explosive growth of textiles also prompted a debate about the benefits and tyranny of the new industries. The British Romantic poet William Blake famously wrote in biblical terms of the textile mills' blight on the English countryside:

> And did the Countenance Divine
> Shine forth upon our clouded hills?
> And was Jerusalem builded here
> Among these dark Satanic mills?

By the 1830s, the British House of Commons was holding hearings on employment and working conditions in factories, recording testimony about working days that stretched from 3:00 A.M. to 10:00 P.M., the employment of very young children, and workers who lost hair and fingers in the mills' machinery. Women and children counted for roughly two-thirds of the labor force in textiles. The principle of regulating any labor (and emphatically that of adult men), however, was controversial. Only gradually did a series of factory acts prohibit hiring children under age nine and limit the labor of workers under age eighteen to ten hours a day.

Coal and Iron

Meanwhile, decisive changes were transforming the production of iron. As in the textile industry, many important technological changes came during the eighteenth century. A series of innovations (coke smelting, rolling, and puddling) enabled the British to substitute coal (which they had in abundance) for wood (which was scarce and inefficient) to heat molten metal and make iron. The new "pig iron" was higher quality and could be used in building an enormous variety of iron products: machines, engines, railway tracks, agricultural implements, and hardware. Those iron products became, literally, the infrastructure of industrialization. Britain found itself able to export both coal and iron to rapidly expanding markets around the industrializing regions of the world. Between 1814 and 1852, exports of British iron doubled, rising to over 1 million tons of iron, more than half of the world's total production.

Rising demand for coal required mining deeper veins. In 1711, Thomas Newcomen's cumbersome but remarkably effective steam engine was immensely useful to the

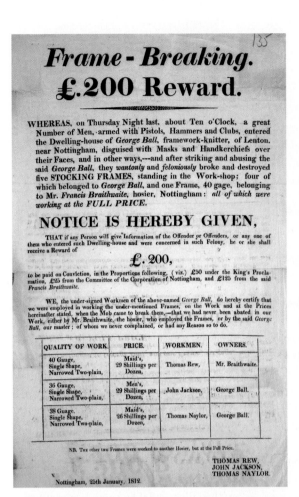

NED LUDD AND THE LUDDITES. In 1811 and 1812, in northern England, bands of working men who resented the adoption of new mechanical devices in the weaving industries attacked several establishments and destroyed the frames used to weave cloth. The movement took the name Luddites from Ned Ludd, a man who had broken the frames belonging to his employer in 1779. His mythological presence in the movement is depicted in the illustration at the right. Although their anger was directed at the machines, the real target of their resentment may have been a new pricing scheme imposed on them by the merchants who bought finished work. The debate about prices is a central part of the poster on the left, which offers a reward for information leading to the conviction of frame breakers. The poster is signed by several workers of the establishment, who published the price they received for each piece of clothing and their lack of complaints about their employer. ▪ *How might the need to adjust to the price fluctuations of a market economy have been perceived by weavers accustomed to getting fixed prices for their goods?*

coal industry for pumping water from mines. After 1763, as we have seen, James Watt improved on Newcomen's machine, and by 1800 Watt and his partner, Matthew Boulton, had sold 289 engines for use in factories and mines. Watt and Boulton made their fortune from their invention's efficiency; they earned a regular percentage of the increased profits from each mine that operated an engine.

Steam power was still energy consuming and expensive and so only slowly replaced traditional water power. Even in its early form, however, the steam engine decisively transformed the nineteenth-century world with one application: the steam-driven locomotive. Railroads revolution-

ized industry, markets, public and private financing, and ordinary people's conceptions of space and time.

THE COMING OF RAILWAYS

Transportation had improved during the years before 1830, but moving heavy materials, particularly coal, remained a problem. It is significant that the first modern railway, built in England in 1825, ran from the Durham coal field of Stockton to Darlington, near the coast. Coal had traditionally been hauled short distances via tramways, or tracks along which horses pulled coal carts. The locomotives on the Stockton-Darlington line traveled at fifteen miles per hour, the fastest rate at which machines had yet moved goods overland. Soon they would move people as well, transforming transportation in the process.

Building railways became a massive enterprise and a risky but potentially profitable opportunity for investment. No sooner did the first combined passenger and goods service open in 1830, operating between Liverpool and Manchester, England, than plans were formulated and money pledged to extend rail systems throughout Europe, the Americas, and beyond. In 1830, there were no more than a few dozen miles of railway in the world. By 1840, there were over 4,500 miles; by 1850, over 23,000. British engineers, industrialists, and investors were quick to realize the global opportunities available in constructing railways overseas; a large part of Britain's industrial success in the later nineteenth century came through building other nations' infrastructures. The English contractor Thomas Brassey, for instance, built railways in Italy, Canada, Argentina, India, and Australia.

Throughout the world, a veritable army of construction workers built the railways. In Britain, they were called "navvies," derived from *navigator,* a term first used for the construction workers on Britain's eighteenth-century canals. Navvies were a rough lot, living with a few women in temporary encampments as they migrated across the countryside. Often they were immigrant workers and faced local hostility. A sign posted by local residents outside a mine in Scotland in 1845 warned the Irish navvies to get "off the ground and out of the country" in a week or else be driven out "by the strength of our armes and a good pick shaft." Later in the century railway building projects in Africa and the Americas were lined with camps of immigrant Indian and Chinese laborers, who also became targets of nativist (a term that means "opposed to foreigners") anger.

The magnitude of the navvies' accomplishment was extraordinary. In Britain and in much of the rest of the world, mid-nineteenth-century railways were constructed almost entirely without the aid of machinery. An assistant engineer on the London-to-Birmingham line calculated that the labor involved was the equivalent of lifting 25 billion cubic feet of earth and stone 1 foot high. He compared this feat with building the Great Pyramid, a task he estimated had involved the hoisting of some 16 billion tons. The building of the pyramid, however, had required over 200,000 men and had taken twenty years. The construction

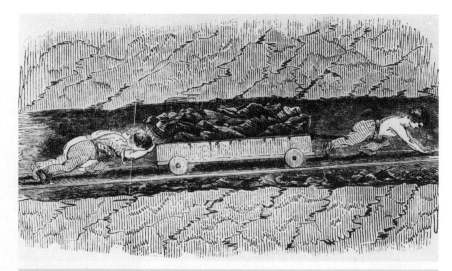

CHILD LABOR IN THE MINES. This engraving of a young worker pulling a coal cart up through the narrow shaft of a mine accompanied a British Parliamentary report on child labor. ▪ *What attitudes about government and the economy made it difficult for legislatures to regulate working conditions in the new industries?*

of the London-to-Birmingham railway was accomplished by 20,000 men in less than five years. If we translated this into individual terms, a navvy was expected to move an average of 20 tons of earth per day. Railways were produced by toil as much as by technology, by human labor as much as by engineering; they illustrate why some historians prefer to use the term *industrious revolution.*

Steam engines, textile machines, new ways of making iron, and railways—all these were interconnected. Changes in one area endorsed changes in another. Pumps run by steam engines made it possible to mine deeper veins of coal; steam-powered railways made it possible to trans-

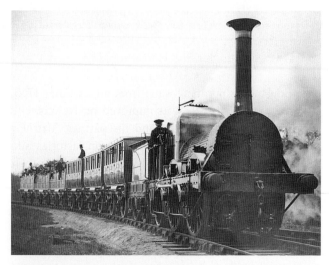

MANCHESTER TO LIVERPOOL, LATE NINETEENTH CENTURY. Lower-class passengers, physically separated from their social superiors, are packed into the rear of the train.

BARRY DOCK AND ISLAND, WALES, 1895. The convergence of coal, steam power, railways, and maritime shipping were at the center of industrialization in Britain. ▪ *In what way did the circular relationship between coal and iron production and the larger transportation revolution associated with the construction of railroads and, later, steamships help sustain the initial growth associated with industrial development?*

port coal. Mechanization fueled the production of iron for machines and the mining of coal to run steam engines. The railway boom multiplied the demand for iron products: rails, locomotives, carriages, signals, switches, and the iron to make all of these. Building railroads called for engineering expertise: scaling mountains, designing bridges and tunnels. Railway construction, which required capital investment beyond the capacity of any single individual, forged new kinds of public and private financing. The scale of production expanded and the tempo of economic activity quickened, spurring the search for more coal, the production of more iron, the mobilization of more capital, and the recruitment of more labor. Steam and speed were becoming the foundation of the economy and of a new way of life.

THE INDUSTRIAL REVOLUTION ON THE CONTINENT

Continental Europe followed a different path. Eighteenth-century France, Belgium, and Germany did have manufacturing districts in regions with raw materials, access to markets, and long-standing traditions of craft and skill.

Yet for a variety of reasons, changes along the lines seen in Britain did not occur until the 1830s. Britain's transportation system was highly developed; those of France and Germany were not. France was far larger than England: its rivers more difficult to navigate; its seaports, cities, and coal deposits farther apart. Much of central Europe was divided into small principalities, each with its own tolls and tariffs, which complicated the transportation of goods over any considerable distance. The Continent had fewer raw materials, coal in particular, than Britain. The abundance and cheapness of wood discouraged exploration that might have resulted in new discoveries of coal. It also meant that coal-run steam engines were less economical on the Continent. Capital, too, was less readily available. Early British industrialization was underwritten by private wealth; this was less feasible elsewhere. Different patterns of landholding formed obstacles to the commercialization of agriculture. In the East, serfdom was a powerful disincentive to labor-saving innovations. In the West, especially in France, the large number of small peasants, or farmers, stayed put on the land.

The wars of the French Revolution and Napoleon disrupted economies. During the eighteenth century, the population had grown and mechanization had begun in a few key industries. The ensuing political upheaval and the

The Factory System, Science, and Morality: Two Views

Reactions to the Industrial Revolution and the factory system it produced ranged from celebration to horror. Dr. Andrew Ure, a Scottish professor of chemistry, was fascinated with these nineteenth-century applications of Enlightenment science. He believed that the new machinery and its products would create a new society of wealth, abundance, and, ultimately, stability through the useful regimentation of production.

Friedrich Engels (1820–1895) was one of the many socialists to criticize Dr. Ure as shortsighted and complacent in his outlook. Engels was himself part of a factory-owning family and so was able to examine the new industrial cities at close range. He provides a classic nineteenth-century analysis of industrialization. The Condition of the Working Class in England *is compellingly written, angry, and revealing about middle-class concerns of the time, including female labor.*

Dr. Andrew Ure (1835)

This island [Britain] is preeminent among civilized nations for the prodigious development of its factory wealth, and has been therefore long viewed with a jealous admiration by foreign powers. This very pre-eminence, however, has been contemplated in a very different light by many influential members of our own community, and has even been denounced by them as the certain origin of innumerable evils to the people, and of revolutionary convulsions to the state. . . .

The blessings which physico-mechanical science has bestowed on society, and the means it has still in store for ameliorating the lot of mankind, has been too little dwelt upon; while, on the other hand, it has been accused of lending itself to the rich capitalists as an instrument for harassing the poor, and of exacting from the operative an accelerated rate of work. It has been said, for example, that the steam-engine now drives the power-looms with such velocity as to urge on their attendant weavers at the same rapid pace; but that the hand-weaver, not being subjected to this restless agent, can throw his shuttle and move his treddles at his convenience. There is, however, this difference in the two cases, that in the factory, every member of the loom is so adjusted, that the driving force leaves the attendant nearly nothing at all to do, certainly no muscular fatigue to sustain, while it produces for him good, unfailing wages, besides a healthy workshop *gratis:* whereas the non-factory weaver, having everything to execute by muscular exertion, finds the labour irksome, makes in consequence innumerable short pauses, separately of little account, but great when added together; earns therefore proportionally low wages, while he loses his health by poor diet and the dampness of his hovel.

Source: Andrew Ure, *The Philosophy of Manufacturers: Or, An Exposition of the Scientific, Moral, and Commercial Economy of the Factory System of Great Britain, 1835,* as cited in J. T. Ward, *The Factory System,* vol. 1 (New York: 1970), pp. 140–41.

financial strains of warfare did virtually nothing to help economic development. Napoleon's Continental System and British destruction of French merchant shipping hurt commerce badly. The ban on British-shipped cotton stalled the growth of cotton textiles for decades, though the armies' greater demand for woolen cloth kept that sector of textiles humming. Iron processing increased to satisfy the military's rising needs, but techniques for making iron remained largely unchanged. Probably the revolutionary change most beneficial to industrial advance in Europe was the removal of previous restraints on the movement of capital and labor—for example, the abolition of craft guilds and the reduction of tariff barriers across the Continent.

After 1815, a number of factors combined to change the economic climate. In those regions with a well-established commercial and industrial base—the northeast of France, Belgium, and swaths of territory across the Rhineland, Saxony, Silesia, and northern Bohemia (see map on page 000)—population growth further boosted economic development. Rising population did not by itself produce industrialization, however: in Ireland, where other necessary factors were absent, more people meant less food.

Friedrich Engels (1844)

Histories of the modern development of the cotton industry, such as those of Ure, Baines, and others, tell on every page of technical innovations. . . . In a well-ordered society such improvements would indeed be welcome, but social war rages unchecked and the benefits derived from these improvements are ruthlessly monopolized by a few persons. . . . Every improvement in machinery leads to unemployment, and the greater the technical improvement the greater the unemployment. Every improvement in machinery affects a number of workers in the same way as a commercial crisis and leads to want, distress, and crime. . . .

Let us examine a little more closely the process whereby machine-labour continually supersedes hand-labour. When spinning or weaving machinery is installed practically all that is left to be done by the hand is the piecing together of broken threads, and the machine does the rest. This task calls for nimble fingers rather than muscular strength. The labour of grown men is not merely unnecessary but actually unsuitable. . . . The greater the degree to which physical labour is displaced by the introduction of machines worked by water- or steam-power, the fewer grown men need be employed. In any case women and children will work for lower wages than men and, as has already been observed, they are more skillful at piecing than grown men. Consequently it is women and children who are employed to do this work. . . . When women work in factories, the most important result is the dissolution of family ties. If a woman works for twelve or thirteen hours a day in a factory and her husband is employed either in the same establishment or in some other works, what is the fate of the children? They lack parental care and control. . . . It is not difficult to imagine that they are left to run wild.

Source: Friedrich Engels, *The Condition of the Working Class in England in 1844*, ed. and trans. W. O. Henderson and W. H. Chaloner (New York: 1958), pp. 150–151, 158, 160.

Questions for Analysis

1. According to Andrew Ure, why was industrialization good for Britain? How can the blessings of "physico-mechanical science" lead to the improvement of humanity?

2. What criticism did Engels level at Ure and other optimists on industrialization? Why did Engels think conditions for workers were getting worse instead of better?

3. What consequences do these two writers see for society in the wake of technological change? What assumptions do they make about the relationship between economic development and the social order?

Transportation improved. The Austrian Empire added over 30,000 miles of roads between 1830 and 1847; Belgium almost doubled its road network in the same period; France built not only new roads but also 2,000 miles of canals. These improvements, combined with the construction of railroads in the 1830s and 1840s, opened up new markets and encouraged new methods of manufacturing. In many of the Continent's manufacturing regions, however, industrialists continued to tap large pools of skilled but inexpensive labor. Thus, older methods of putting out industry and handwork persisted alongside new-model factories longer than in Britain.

In what other ways was the continental model of industrialization different? Governments played a considerably more direct role in industrialization. France and Prussia granted subsidies to private companies that built railroads. After 1849, the Prussian state took on the task itself, as did Belgium and, later, Russia. In Prussia, the state also operated a large proportion of that country's mines. Governments on the Continent provided incentives for industrialization. Limited-liability laws, to take the most important example, allowed investors to own shares in a corporation or company without becoming liable for the company's debts—and they enabled enterprises to recruit investors to put together the capital for railroads, other forms of industry, and commerce.

Mobilizing capital for industry was one of the challenges of the century. In Great Britain, overseas trade had created well-organized financial markets; on the Continent, capital was dispersed and in short supply. New joint-stock investment banks, unlike private banks, could sell bonds to and take deposits from individuals and smaller companies. They could offer start-up capital in the form of long-term, low-interest commercial loans to aspiring entrepreneurs. The French Crédit Mobilier, for instance, founded in 1852 by the wealthy and well-connected Périere brothers, assembled enough capital to finance insurance companies; the Parisian bus system; six municipal gas companies; transatlantic shipping; enterprises in other European countries; and, with the patronage of the state, the massive railroad-building spree of the 1850s. The Crédit Mobilier collapsed in scandal, but the revolution in banking was well under way.

Finally, continental Europeans actively promoted invention and technological development. They were willing for the state to establish educational systems whose aim, among others, was to produce a well-trained elite capable of assisting in the development of industrial technology. In sum, what Britain had produced almost by chance, the Europeans began to reproduce by design.

Industrialization after 1850

Until 1850, Britain remained the preeminent industrial power. Between 1850 and 1870, however, France, Germany, Belgium, and the United States emerged as challengers to the power and place of British manufacturers. The British iron industry remained the largest in the world (in 1870 Britain still produced half the world's pig iron), but it grew more slowly than did its counterparts in France or Germany. Most of continental Europe's gains came as a result of continuing changes in those areas we recognize as important for sustained industrial growth: transport, commerce, and government policy.

The spread of railways encouraged the free movement of goods. International monetary unions were established and restrictions removed on international waterways such as the Danube. Free trade went hand in hand with removing guild barriers to entering trades and ending restrictions on practicing business. Guild control over artisanal production was abolished in Austria in 1859 and in most of Germany by the mid-1860s. Laws against usury, most of which had ceased to be enforced, were officially abandoned in Britain, Holland, Belgium, and in many parts of Germany. Governmental regulation of mining was surrendered by the Prussian state in the 1850s, freeing entrepreneurs to develop resources as they saw fit. Investment banks continued to form, encouraged by an increase in the money supply and an easing of credit after the California gold fields opened in 1849.

The first phase of the Industrial Revolution, one economic historian reminds us, was confined to a narrow set of industries and can be summed up rather simply: "cheaper and better clothes (mainly made of cotton), cheaper and better metals (pig iron, wrought iron, and steel) and faster travel (mainly by rail)." The second half of the century brought changes farther afield and in areas where Great Britain's early advantages were no longer decisive. Transatlantic cable

INTERIOR OF A CANUT HOUSEHOLD IN LYON C. 1830. The growth of the silk industry in Lyon in eighteenth-century France attracted many weavers and their families to the city's central neighborhoods: by the mid-1800s, there were 80,000 master artisans with their own shops in the trade and a further 40,000 *compagnons*, trained weavers who had not yet set up their own establishment and who worked as employees in the shops of others. The Canuts, as these weavers were called, worked as many as eighteen hours a day, and they were known for their militancy and their activism. They rose up in revolt in 1831, 1834, and 1848, and they were among the first examples of workers' insurrections in the nineteenth century. In the above image of a Canut household, the labor of nearly all the members of the family—weaving, spinning, and preparing the thread—can be identified.

(starting in 1865) and the telephone (invented in 1876) laid the ground for a revolution in communications. New chemical processes, dyestuffs, and pharmaceuticals emerged. So did new sources of energy: electricity, in which the United States and Germany led both invention and commercial development; and oil, which was being refined in the 1850s and widely used by 1900. Among the early exploiters of Russian oil discoveries were the Swedish Nobel brothers and the French Rothschilds. The developments that eventually converged to make the automobile came primarily from Germany and France. The internal combustion engine, important because it was small, efficient, and could be used in a very wide variety of situations, was developed by Carl Benz and Gottlieb Daimler in the 1880s. The removable pneumatic tire was patented in 1891 by Edouard Michelin, a painter who had joined with his engineer brother in running the family's small agricultural-equipment business. These developments are discussed fully in Chapter 23, but their pioneers' familiar names illustrate how industry and invention had diversified over the course of the century.

In eastern Europe, the nineteenth century brought different patterns of economic development. Spurred by the ever-growing demand for food and grain, large sections of eastern Europe developed into concentrated, commercialized agriculture regions that played the specific role of exporting food to the West. Many of those large agricultural enterprises were based on serfdom and remained so, in the face of increasing pressure for reform, until 1850. Peasant protest and liberal demands for reform only gradually chipped away at the nobility's determination to hold on to its privilege and system of labor. Serfdom was abolished in most parts of eastern and southern Europe by 1850 and in Poland and Russia in the 1860s.

Although industry continued to take a backseat to agriculture, eastern Europe had several important manufacturing regions. In the Czech region of Bohemia, textile industries, developed in the eighteenth century, continued to thrive. By the 1830s, there were machine-powered Czech cotton mills and iron works. In Russia, a factory industry producing coarse textiles—mostly linens—had grown up around Moscow. At mid-century, Russia was purchasing 24 percent of the total British machinery exports to mechanize its own mills. Many who labored in Russian industry actually remained serfs until the 1860s—about 40 percent of them employed in mines. Of the over 800,000 Russians engaged in manufacturing by 1860, however, most were employed in small workshops of about 40 persons.

By 1870, then, the core industrial nations of Europe included Great Britain, France, Germany, Italy, the Netherlands, and Switzerland. Austria stood at the margins. Russia, Spain, Bulgaria, Greece, Hungary, Romania, and Serbia formed the industrial periphery—and some regions of these nations seemed virtually untouched by the advance of industry. What was more, even in Great Britain, the most fully industrialized nation, agricultural laborers still constituted the single largest occupational category in 1860 (although they formed only 9 percent of the overall population). In Belgium, the Netherlands, Switzerland, Germany, France, Scandinavia, and Ireland, 25 to 50 percent of the population still worked on the land. In Russia, the number was 80 percent. *Industrial*, moreover, did not mean automation or machine production, which long remained confined to a few sectors of the economy. As machines were introduced in some sectors to do specific tasks, they usually intensified the tempo of handwork in other sectors. Thus even in the industrialized regions, much work was still accomplished in tiny workshops—or at home.

Industry and Empire

From an international perspective, nineteenth-century Europe was the most industrial region of the world. Europeans, particularly the British, jealously guarded their international advantages. They preferred to do so through financial leverage. Britain, France, and other European nations gained control of the national debts of China, the Ottoman Empire, Egypt, Brazil, Argentina, and other non-European powers. They also supplied large loans to other states, which bound those nations to their European investors. If the debtor nations expressed discontent, as Egypt did in the 1830s when it attempted to establish its own cotton textile industry, they confronted financial pressure and shows of force. Coercion, however, was not always necessary or even one-sided. Social change in other empires—China, Persia, and the Mughal Empire of India, for example—made those empires newly vulnerable and created new opportunities for the European powers and their local partners. Ambitious local elites often reached agreements with Western governments or groups such as the British East India Company. These trade agreements transformed regional economies on terms that sent the greatest profits to Europe after a substantial gratuity to the Europeans' local partners. Where agreements could not be made, force prevailed, and Europe took territory and trade by conquest (see Chapter 22).

Industrialization tightened global links between Europe and the rest of the world, creating new networks of trade and interdependence. To a certain extent, the world economy divided between the producers of manufactured goods—Europe itself—and suppliers of the necessary

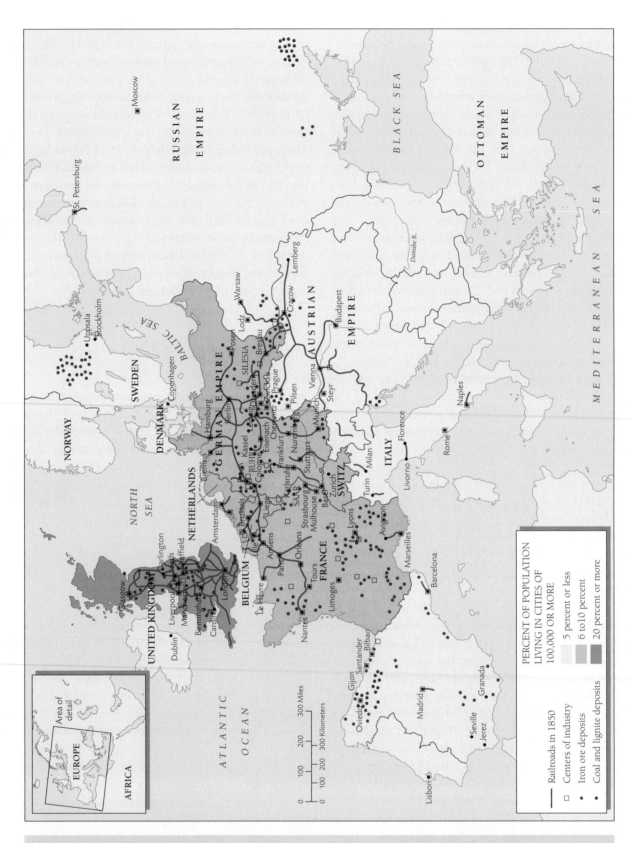

THE INDUSTRIAL REVOLUTION. Rapid industrial growth depended on a circular network of relationships. ▪ *According to the map key, what elements made up the circular networks of relationships?* ▪ *How were these elements connected, and how might they have reinforced one another, contributing to rapid growth?* ▪ *Why do you think the percentage of populations living in cities was so much greater in the United Kingdom?*

raw materials and buyers of finished goods—everyone else. Cotton growers in the southern United States, sugar growers in the Caribbean, and wheat growers in Ukraine accepted their arrangements with the industrialized West and typically profited by them. If there were disputes, however, those suppliers often found that Europe could look elsewhere for the same goods or dictate the terms of trade down the business end of a bank ledger or a cannon barrel.

In 1811, Britain imported 3 percent of the wheat it consumed. By 1891, that portion had risen to 79 percent. Why? In an increasingly urban society, fewer people lived off the land. The commercialization of agriculture, which began early in Britain, had taken even firmer hold elsewhere, turning new regions—Australia, Argentina, and North America (Canada and the United States)—into centers of grain and wheat production. New forms of transportation, finance, and communication made it easier to shuttle commodities and capital through international networks. Those simple percentages, in other words, dramatize the new interdependence of the nineteenth century; they illustrate as well as any statistics can how ordinary Britons' lives—like their counterparts' in other nations—were embedded in an increasingly global economy.

BRITISH CLIPPER SHIPS IN CALCUTTA HARBOR, 1860. Calcutta, a long-established city on the eastern coast of India, was one of the hubs of the British Empire—a center for trade in cotton, jute, opium, and tea. The dazzling new clipper ships, first built in the 1830s and 1840s, were very fast and central to the global economy of the nineteenth century. ▪ *What was the significance of this trade for the Indian economy?* ▪ *Could Indian merchants compete on equal terms with U.S. cotton producers in 1860?*

THE SOCIAL CONSEQUENCES OF INDUSTRIALIZATION

We have mentioned population growth as one factor in industrial development, but it deserves treatment on its own terms. By any measure, the nineteenth century constituted a turning point in European demographic history. In 1800, the population of Europe as a whole was estimated roughly at 205 million. By 1850, it had risen to 274 million; by 1900, 414 million; on the eve of the First World War, it was 480 million. (Over the same span of time, the world population went from about 900 million to 1.6 billion.) Britain, with its comparatively high standard of living, saw its population rise from 16 to 27 million. Increases, however, came in the largely rural regions as well. In Russia, the population rose from 39 million to 60 million during the same period.

Population

This population explosion did not occur because people were living longer—declines in mortality were not observable on a large scale until late in the nineteenth century, when improvements in hygiene and medicine had significant impact on the number of people who survived childhood to reach adulthood. Even in 1880, the average male life expectancy at birth in Berlin was no more than thirty years (in rural districts nearby, it was forty-three). Population growth in the nineteenth century resulted from increasing fertility—there were simply more babies being born. Men and women married earlier, which raised the average number of children born to each woman and increased the size of families. Peasants tended to set up households at a younger age. The spread of rural manufacturing allowed couples in the countryside to marry and set up households—even before they inherited any land. Not only did the age of marriage fall, but more people married. And because population growth increased the proportion of young and fertile people, the process reinforced itself in the next generation, setting the stage for a period of prolonged growth.

Interpreting Visual Evidence

Learning to Live in a Global Economy

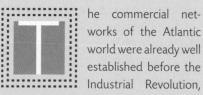The commercial networks of the Atlantic world were already well established before the Industrial Revolution, and Europeans were also trading widely with South and East Asia before the end of the eighteenth century. Nevertheless, the advent of an industrial economy in Europe at the beginning of the nineteenth century created such a demand for raw materials and such a need for new markets abroad that it became profitable for manufacturers and merchants to ship much larger amounts of goods over long distances than ever before. As different industrialized regions in Europe became more and more dependent on overseas markets, people in Europe came to be aware of the extent to which their own activities were linked to other parts of the world. Awareness of these linkages did not always mean that they possessed complete or accurate information about the people who produced the cotton that they wore, or who purchased the manufactured goods that they made, but the linkages stimulated their imagination and changed their consciousness of their place in the world.

This awareness is well illustrated in the cartoons shown here, which come from the British illustrated news in the 1850s and 1860s. The first (image A) depicts John Bull (representing British textile manufacturers) looking on as U.S. cotton suppliers fight one another during the Civil War in the United States. He states, "Oh! If you two like fighting better than business, I shall deal at the other shop." In the background, an Indian cotton merchant is happy to have him as a customer.

The second cartoon (image B) depicts the ways that the increasingly interconnected global economy might

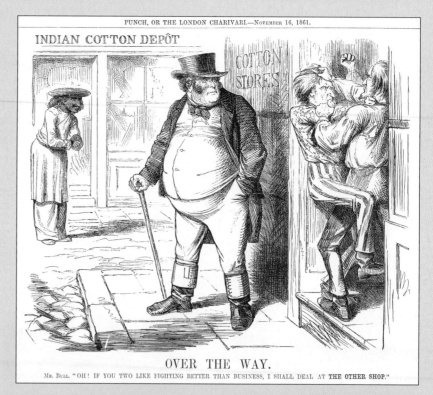

A. John Bull and cotton merchants.

Life on the Land: The Peasantry

Even as the West grew more industrial, the majority of people continued to live on the land. Conditions in the countryside were harsh. Peasants—as farmers of humble origin were called in Europe—still did most of their sowing and harvesting by hand. Millions of tiny farms produced, at most, a bare subsistence living, and families wove, spun, made knives, and sold butter to make ends meet. The average daily diet for an entire family in a good year might amount to no more than two or three pounds of bread—a total of about 3,000 calories daily. By many measures,

stimulate a new kind of political awareness. Emperor Napoleon III has placed a French worker in irons for participating in a revolutionary movement. The worker compares his situation to that of an African slave seated next to him, saying, "Courage, my friend! Am I not a man and a brother?" On the wall behind the two men a poster refers to the Portuguese slave trade—Napoleon III himself came to power by overthrowing the Second Republic in France, a government that had abolished the slave trade in French territories.

Questions for Analysis

1. What constellation of private and national interests were at play in the relationships portrayed in image A? What significance might contemporaries have attached to the possibility that the British may have chosen to buy their cotton from an Asian source "over the way" rather than from North America?

2. In image B, what is the message of the cartoon's suggestion that the slave and the worker might discover their equality only in the fact that they are both in chains? What was at stake in comparing a worker to a slave in mid-nineteenth-century Europe? Why does the caption read "Poor Consolation?"

3. How does the racial imagery of these images relate to their intended message?

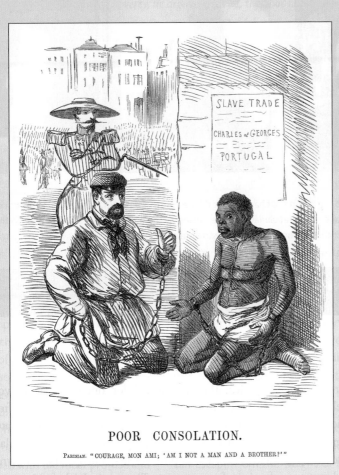

POOR CONSOLATION.

PARISIAN. "COURAGE, MON AMI; 'AM I NOT A MAN AND A BROTHER?'"

B. Increasing global awareness in France.

living conditions for rural inhabitants of many areas in Europe grew worse in the first half of the nineteenth century, a fact of considerable political importance in the 1840s. Rising population put more pressure on the land. Small holdings and indebtedness were chronic problems in regions where peasants scraped by on their own lands.

Over the course of the century, some 37 million people—most of them peasants—left Europe, eloquent testimony to the bleakness of rural life. They settled in the United States, South America, northern Africa, New Zealand, Australia, and Siberia. In many cases, governments encouraged emigration to ease overcrowding.

IRISH POTATO FAMINE, 1845–1849. The Irish potato famine was widely held by many in Ireland to have human as well as natural causes. Historians have noted that food exports from Ireland continued and may have even increased for some products during the famine, as merchants sought higher prices abroad. The cartoon at left depicts armed soldiers keeping starving Irish Catholic families at bay as sacks of potatoes are loaded onto a ship owned by a prosperous Irish Protestant trader. At right, an 1848 engraving from the *Illustrated London News* depicts an impoverished tenant family being evicted from their cottage by their landlord for nonpayment of rent. Thousands of such evictions took place, adding to the misery of the tenant farmers, who were thus unable to plant new crops after losing the potato harvest to blight.

the political regime: in 1820, the liberal regime passed legislation encouraging the free transfer of land; when absolutism was restored in 1823, the law was repealed. In Russia some of the largest landowners possessed over half a million acres. Until the emancipation of the serfs in the 1860s, landowners claimed the labor of dependent peasant populations for as much as several days per week. But the system of serfdom gave neither landowners nor serfs much incentive to improve farming techniques.

European serfdom, which bound hundreds of thousands of men, women, and children to particular estates for generations, made it difficult to buy and sell land freely and created an obstacle to the commercialization of agriculture. Yet the opposite was also the case. In France, peasant landholders who had benefited from the French Revolution's sale of lands and laws on inheritance stayed in the countryside, continuing to work their small farms. Although French peasants were poor, they could sustain themselves on the land. This had important consequences. France suffered less agricultural distress, even in the 1840s, than did other European countries; migration from country to city was slower than in the other nations; far fewer peasants left France for other countries.

Industrialization came to the countryside in other forms. Improved communication networks not only afforded rural populations a keener sense of events and opportunities elsewhere but also made it possible for governments to intrude into the lives of these men and women to a degree previously impossible. Central bureaucracies now found it easier to collect taxes from the peasantry and

to conscript sons of peasant families into armies. Some rural cottage industries faced direct competition from factory-produced goods, which meant less work or lower piece rates and falling incomes for families, especially during winter months. In other sectors of the economy, industry spread out into the countryside, making whole regions producers of shoes, shirts, ribbons, cutlery, and so on in small shops and workers' homes. Changes in the market could usher in prosperity, or they could bring entire regions to the verge of starvation.

Vulnerability often led to political violence. Rural rebellions were common in the early nineteenth century. In southern England in the late 1820s, small farmers and day laborers joined forces to burn barns and haystacks, protesting the introduction of threshing machines, a symbol of the new agricultural capitalism. They masked and otherwise disguised themselves, riding out at night under the banner of their mythical leader, "Captain Swing." Their raids were preceded by anonymous threats, such as the one received by a large-scale farmer in the county of Kent: "Pull down your threshing machine or else [expect] fire without delay. We are five thousand men [a highly inflated figure] and will not be stopped." In the southwest of France, peasants, at night and in disguise, attacked local authorities who had barred them from collecting wood in the forests. Since forest wood was in demand for new furnaces, the peasants' traditional gleaning rights had come to an end. Similar rural disturbances broke out across Europe in the 1830s and 1840s: insurrections against landlords; against tithes, or taxes to the church; against laws curtailing customary rights; against unresponsive governments. In Russia, serf uprisings were a reaction to continued bad harvests and exploitation.

Many onlookers considered the nineteenth-century cities dangerous seedbeds of sedition. Yet conditions in the countryside and frequent flare-ups of rural protest remained the greatest source of trouble for governments, and rural politics exploded, as we will see, in the 1840s. Peasants were land poor, deep in debt, and precariously dependent on markets. More important, however, a government's inability to contend with rural misery made it look autocratic, indifferent, or inept—all political failings.

The Urban Landscape

The growth of cities was one of the most important facts of nineteenth-century social history, and one with significant cultural reverberations. Over the course of the nineteenth century, as we have seen, the overall population of Europe doubled. The percentage of that population living in cities tripled—that is, urban populations rose sixfold. In mining and manufacturing areas or along newly built railway lines, it sometimes seemed that cities (like Manchester, Birmingham, and Essen) sprang up from nowhere. Sometimes the rates of growth were dizzying. Between 1750 and 1850, London (Europe's largest city) grew from 676,000 to 2.3 million. The population of Paris went from 560,000 to 1.3 million, adding 120,000 new residents between 1841 and 1846 alone! Berlin, which like Paris became the hub of a rapidly expanding railway system, nearly tripled in size during the first half of the century. Such rapid expansion was almost necessarily unplanned and brought in its wake new social problems.

Almost all nineteenth-century cities were overcrowded and unhealthy, their largely medieval infrastructures strained by the burden of new population and the demands of industry. Construction lagged far behind population growth, and working men and women who had left families behind in the country often lived in temporary lodging houses. The poorest workers dwelled in wretched basement or attic rooms, often without any light or drainage. A local committee appointed to investigate conditions in the British manufacturing town of Huddersfield—by no means the worst of that country's urban centers—reported that there were large areas without paving, sewers, or drains, "where garbage and filth of every description are left on the surface to ferment

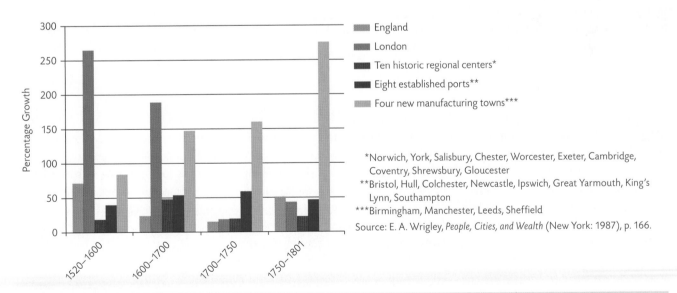

*Norwich, York, Salisbury, Chester, Worcester, Exeter, Cambridge, Coventry, Shrewsbury, Gloucester
**Bristol, Hull, Colchester, Newcastle, Ipswich, Great Yarmouth, King's Lynn, Southampton
***Birmingham, Manchester, Leeds, Sheffield
Source: E. A. Wrigley, *People, Cities, and Wealth* (New York: 1987), p. 166.

URBAN GROWTH IN EARLY MODERN ENGLAND. This figure shows the percentage increases in population in England as a whole, as well as in several distinct groups of population centers. London showed its greatest percentage increases in the periods 1520–1600 and 1600–1700, *before* the period of industrial expansion. The historic regional centers—cathedral and market towns—showed steady but unspectacular growth across these years, as did English port cities. The most remarkable growth, however, was observed in the new industrial areas of the north in the last half of the eighteenth century. *What can one conclude about the nature of population growth in England from this figure? What other sorts of information would allow you to draw more certain conclusions about the nature of these demographic shifts?*

Competing Viewpoints

The Irish Famine: Interpretations and Responses

When the potato blight appeared for the second year in a row in 1846, famine came to Ireland. The first letter excerpted here is from Father Theobald Mathew, a local priest, to Charles Edward Trevelyan, the English official in charge of Irish relief. While Father Mathew attributes the potato blight to "divine providence," he also worries that businessmen opposed to government intervention in a free market will let the Irish starve.

The second and third excerpts are from letters that Trevelyan wrote to other British officials concerned with the crisis. Trevelyan makes clear that although he does not want the government to bear responsibility for starving its people, he believes that the famine will work to correct "social evils" in Ireland, by which he means everything from families having too many children to farmers failing to plant the right crops. In the nineteenth century, reactions to food crises were reshaped by the rise of new economic doctrines, changing social assumptions, and the shifting relationship between religion and government. These letters provide good examples of those changes and how they affected government officials.

The Reverend Theobald Mathew to Trevelyan

Cork, 7 August 1846.

Divine providence, in its inscrutable ways, has again poured out upon us the viol [*sic*] of its wrath. A blot more destructive than the simoom of the desert has passed over the land, and the hopes of the poor potato-cultivators are totally blighted, and the food of a whole nation has perished. On the 27th of last month I passed from Cork to Dublin, and this doomed plant bloomed in all the luxuriance of an abundant harvest. Returning on the 3rd instant, I beheld, with sorrow, one wide waste of putrefying vegetation. In many places the wretched people were seated on the fences of their decaying gardens, wringing their hands and wailing bitterly the destruction that had left them foodless.

It is not to harrow your benevolent feelings, dear Mr. Trevelyan, I tell this tale of woe. No, but to excite your sympathy in behalf of our miserable peasantry. It is rumoured that the capitalists in the corn and flour trade are endeavoring to induce government not to protect the people from famine, but to leave them at their mercy. I consider this a cruel and unjustifiable interference.

Trevelyan to Routh

Treasury, 3 February 1846.

That indirect permanent advantages will accrue to Ireland from the scarcity and the measures taken for its relief, I entertain no doubt; but if we were to pursue these incidental objects to the neglect of any of the precautions immediately required to save the people from actual starvation, our responsibility would be fearful indeed. Besides, the greatest improvement of all which could take place in Ireland would be to teach the people to depend upon themselves for developing the resources of their country, instead of having recourse to the assistance of the government on every occasion. Much has been done of late years to put this important matter on its proper footing; but if a firm stand is not made against the prevailing disposition to take advantage of this crisis to break down all barriers, the true permanent interest of the country will, I am convinced, suffer in a manner which will be irreparable in our time.

Trevelyan to Lord Monteagle

To the Right Hon. Lord Monteagle.

My Dear Lord,

I need not remind your lordship that the ability even of the most powerful government is extremely limited in dealing with a social evil of this description. It forms no part of the functions of government to provide supplies of food or to increase the productive powers of the land. In the great institution of the business of society, it falls to the share of government to protect the merchant and the agriculturist in the free exercise of their respective employments; but

not itself to carry on those employments; and the condition of a community depends upon the result of the efforts which each member of it makes in his private and individual capacity. . . .

I must give expression to my feelings by saying that I think I see a bright light shining in the distance through the dark cloud which at present hangs over Ireland. A remedy has been already applied to that portion of the maladies of Ireland which was traceable to political causes, and the morbid habits which still to a certain extent survive are gradually giving way to a more healthy action. The deep and inveterate root of social evil remains, and I hope I am not guilty of irreverence in thinking that, this being altogether beyond the power of man, the cure has been applied by the direct stroke of an all-wise providence in a manner as unexpected and unthought of as it is likely to be effectual. God grant that we may rightly perform our part and not turn into a curse what was intended for a blessing. The ministers of religion and especially the pastors of the Roman Catholic Church, who possess the largest share of influence over the people of Ireland, have well performed their part; and although few indications appear from any proceedings which have yet come before the public that the landed proprietors have even taken the first step of preparing for the conversion of the land now laid down to potatoes to grain cultivation, I do not despair of seeing this class in society still taking the lead which their position requires of them, and preventing the social revolution from being so extensive as it otherwise must become.

Believe me, my dear lord,
yours very sincerely,
C. E. Trevelyan.
Treasury, 9 October 1846.

Source: Noel Kissane, *The Irish Famine: A Documentary History* (Dublin: 1995), pp. 17, 47, 50–51.

Questions for Analysis

1. Reverend Mathew's letter suggests that although the potato blight seems to be an act of God, the response to the crisis by those in government and in commerce plays a role in determining who has enough to eat. What relationship between hunger and the market does Mathew fear most?

2. What are the stakes in the crisis for Trevelyan, as the English official responsible for relief of the food shortage? What interests does he appear to serve and in what order of preference? What exactly is the responsibility of the government in the face of such an emergency, according to his view?

3. Do Mathew and Trevelyan agree on the relationship that should exist between the government and the economy? What accounts for their difference of opinion? Are the religious values of the reverend and the economic calculations of the official compatible with one another?

---

and rot; where pools of stagnant water are almost constant; where dwellings adjoining are thus necessarily caused to be of an inferior and even filthy description; thus where disease is engendered, and the health of the whole town perilled."

Governments gradually adopted measures in an attempt to cure the worst of these ills, if only to prevent the spread of catastrophic epidemics. Legislation was designed to rid cities of their worst slums by tearing them down and to improve sanitary conditions by supplying both water and drainage. Yet by 1850, these projects had only just begun. Paris, perhaps better supplied with water than any other European city, had enough for no more than two baths per person per year; in London, human waste remained uncollected in 250,000 domestic cesspools; in Manchester, fewer than one-third of the dwellings were equipped with toilets of any sort.

Industry and Environment in the Nineteenth Century

The Industrial Revolution began many of the environmental changes of the modern period. Nowhere were those changes more visible than in the burgeoning cities. Dickens's description of the choking air and polluted water of "Coketown," the fictional city in *Hard Times* (1854) is deservedly well known:

It was a town of red brick, or of brick that would have been red if the smoke and ashes had allowed it. . . . It was a town of machines and tall chimneys, out of which interminable serpents of smoke trailed themselves forever and ever, and never got uncoiled. It had a black canal in it, and a river that ran purple with ill-smelling dye, and vast piles of building full of windows where there was a rattling and a trembling all day long.

Wood-fired manufacturing and heating for homes had long spewed smoke across the skies, but the new concentration of industrial activity and the transition to coal made the air measurably worse. In London especially, where even homes switched to coal early, smoke from factories, railroads, and domestic chimneys hung heavily over the city; and the last third of the century brought the most intense pollution in its history. Over all of England, air pollution took an enormous toll on health, contributing to the bronchitis and tuberculosis that accounted for 25 percent of British deaths. The coal-rich and industrial regions of North America (especially Pittsburgh) and central Europe were other concentrations of pollution; the Ruhr, in particular, by the end of the century had the most polluted air in Europe.

Toxic water—produced by industrial pollution and human waste—posed the second critical environmental hazard in urban areas. London and Paris led the way in building municipal sewage systems, though those emptied into the Thames and the Seine. Cholera, typhus, and tuberculosis were natural predators in areas without adequate sewage facilities or fresh water. The Rhine River, which flowed through central Europe's industrial heartland and intersected with the Ruhr, was thick with detritus from coal mining, iron processing, and the chemical industry. Spurred by several epidemics of cholera, in the late nineteenth century the major cities began to purify their water supplies; but conditions in the air, rivers, and land continued to worsen until at least the mid-twentieth century.

The Social Question

Against the backdrop of the French Revolution of 1789 and subsequent revolutions in the nineteenth century (as we will see in the following chapters), the new "shock" cities of the nineteenth century and their swelling multitudes posed urgent questions. Political leaders, social scientists,

VIEW OF LONDON WITH SAINT PAUL'S CATHEDRAL IN THE DISTANCE BY WILLIAM HENRY CROME. Despite the smog-filled skies and intense pollution, many entrepreneurs and politicians celebrated the new prosperity of the Industrial Revolution. As W. P. Rend, a Chicago businessman, wrote in 1892, "Smoke is the incense burning on the altars of industry. It is beautiful to me. It shows that men are changing the merely potential forces of nature into articles of comfort for humanity."

and public health officials across all of Europe issued thousands of reports—many of them several volumes long—on criminality, water supply, sewers, prostitution, tuberculosis and cholera, alcoholism, wet nursing, wages, and unemployment. Radicals and reformers grouped all these issues under a broad heading known as "the social question." Governments, pressed by reformers and by the omnipresent rumblings of unrest, felt they had to address these issues before complaints swelled into revolution. They did so, in the first social engineering: police forces, public health, sewers and new water supplies, inoculations, elementary schools, Factory Acts (regulating work hours), poor laws (outlining the conditions of receiving relief), and new urban regulation and city planning. Central Paris, for instance, would be almost entirely redesigned in the nineteenth century—the crowded, medieval, and revolutionary poor neighborhoods gutted; markets rebuilt; streets widened and lit (see Chapter 21). From the 1820s on, the social question hung over Europe like a cloud, and it formed part of the backdrop to the revolutions of 1848 (discussed in Chapter 21). Surveys and studies, early social science, provided direct inspiration for novelists such as Honoré de Balzac, Charles Dickens, and Victor Hugo. In his novel *Les Misérables* (1862), Hugo even used the sewers of Paris as a central metaphor for the general condition of urban existence. Both Hugo and Dickens wrote sympathetically of the poor, of juvenile delinquency, and of child labor; revolution was never far from their minds. The French writer

Balzac had little sympathy for the poor, but he shared his fellow writers' views on the corruption of modern life. His *Human Comedy* (1829–55) was a series of ninety-five novels and stories, including *Eugenie Grandet, Old Goriot, Lost Illusions,* and *A Harlot High and Low.* Balzac was biting in his observations about ruthless and self-promoting young men and about the cold calculations behind romantic liaisons. And he was but one of many writers to use prostitution as a metaphor for what he considered the deplorable materialism and desperation of his time.

Sex in the City

Prostitution flourished in nineteenth-century cities; in fact, it offers a microcosm of the nineteenth-century urban economy. At mid-century, the number of prostitutes in

PROSTITUTION IN NINETEENTH-CENTURY EUROPEAN CITIES. This sketch by Constantin Guys (1802–1892) captures the moment when two *grisettes* (slang for flirtatious working-class women) entertain a proposition from two soldiers in the street. Guys's portrayal of the men's indistinct facial features and the saucy posture of the women captured the impersonal nature of the exchange as well as the mercenary intentions of all parties. ■ *How did the construction of new cities, with expanded streets designed to facilitate the efficient mixing and movement of peoples, change the way that individuals interacted with one another in modern cities?*

Vienna was estimated to be 15,600; in Paris, where prostitution was a licensed trade, 50,000; in London, 80,000. London newspaper reports of the 1850s cataloged the elaborate hierarchies of the vast underworld of prostitutes and their customers. Those included entrepreneurs with names like Swindling Sal who ran lodging houses; the pimps and "fancy men" who managed the trade of prostitutes on the street; and the relatively few "prima donnas" or courtesans who enjoyed the protection of rich, upper-middle-class lovers, who entertained lavishly and whose wealth allowed them to move on the fringes of more respectable high society. The heroines of Alexandre Dumas's novel *La Dame aux Camélias* ("The Lady of the Camellias") and of Giuseppe Verdi's opera *La Traviata* ("The Fallen Woman") were modeled on these women. Yet the vast majority of prostitutes were not courtesans but rather women (and some men) who worked long and dangerous hours in port districts of cities or at lodging houses in the overwhelmingly male working-class neighborhoods. Most prostitutes were young women who had just arrived in the city or working women trying to manage during a period of unemployment. Single women in the cities were very vulnerable to sexual exploitation. Many were abandoned by their partners if they became pregnant; others faced the danger of rape by their employers. Such experiences—abandonment and rape—could lead to prostitution since women in these circumstances were unlikely to secure "respectable" employment.

THE MIDDLE CLASSES

Nineteenth-century novelists such as Charles Dickens and William Thackeray in Britain, Victor Hugo and Honoré Balzac in France, and Theodor Fontane in Germany painted a sweeping portrait of middle-class society in the nineteenth century. Their novels are peopled with characters from all walks of life—journalists, courtesans, small-town mayors, mill owners, shopkeepers, aristocrats, farmers, laborers, and students. The plots of these stories explore the ways that older hierarchies of rank, status, and privilege were gradually giving way to a new set of gradations based on wealth and social class. In this new world, money trumped birth, and social mobility was an accepted fact rather than something to be hidden. One of Thackeray's characters observes caustically that "[o]urs is a ready-money society. We live among bankers and city big-wigs . . . and every man, as he talks to you, is jingling his guineas in his pocket." Works of literature need to be approached cautiously, for their characters express their authors' points of view. Still, literature and art offer an extraordinary source of social historical detail and insight. And we can safely say that the rising visibility of the middle classes and their new political and social power—lamented by some writers but hailed by others—were central facts of nineteenth-century society.

Who were the middle classes? (Another common term for this social group, the *bourgeoisie,* originally meant "city [*bourg*] dweller.") Its ranks included shopkeepers and their households, the families of lawyers, doctors, and other professionals, as well as well-off factory owners who might aspire to marry their daughters to titled aristocrats. At the lower end of the social scale the middle classes included the families of salaried clerks and office workers for whom white-collar employment offered hope of a rise in status.

Movement within middle-class ranks was often possible in the course of one or two generations. Very few, however, moved from the working class into the middle class. Most middle-class success stories began in the middle class itself, with the children of relatively well-off farmers, skilled artisans, or professionals. Upward mobility was almost impossible without education, and education was a rare, though not unattainable, luxury for working-class children. Careers open to talents, that goal achieved by the French Revolution, frequently meant opening jobs to middle-class young men who could pass exams. The examination system was an important path upward within government bureaucracies.

The journey from middle class to aristocratic, landed society was equally difficult. In Britain, mobility of this sort was easier to achieve than on the Continent. Sons from wealthy upper-middle-class families, if they were sent to elite schools and universities and if they left the commercial or industrial world for a career in politics, might actually move up. William Gladstone, son of a Liverpool merchant, attended the exclusive educational preserves of Eton (a private boarding school) and Oxford University, married into the aristocratic Grenville family, and became prime minister of England. Yet Gladstone was an exception to the rule, even in Britain, and most upward mobility was much less spectacular.

Nevertheless, the European middle class helped sustain itself with the belief that it was possible to get ahead by means of intelligence, pluck, and serious devotion to work. The Englishman Samuel Smiles, in his extraordinarily successful how-to-succeed book *Self-Help* (1859), preached a gospel dear to the middle class: "The spirit of self-help is the root of all genuine growth in the individual." As Smiles also suggested, those who succeeded were obliged to follow middle-class notions of respectability. The middle-class's

THE LEGISLATIVE BELLY BY HONORE DAUMIER, 1834. Daumier's caricatures of bourgeois politicians mock the close link between politics and a prosperous elite made up of men of property.

claim to political power and cultural influence rested on arguments that they constituted a new and deserving social elite, superior to the common people yet sharply different from the older aristocracy, and the rightful custodians of the nation's future. Thus, middle-class respectability, like a code, stood for many values. It meant financial independence, providing responsibly for one's family, avoiding gambling and debt. It suggested merit and character as opposed to aristocratic privilege and hard work as opposed to living off noble estates. Respectable middle-class gentlemen might be wealthy, but they should live modestly and soberly, avoiding conspicuous consumption, lavish dress, womanizing, and other forms of dandyish behavior associated with the aristocracy. Of course, these were aspirations and codes, not social realities. They nonetheless remained key to the middle-class sense of self and understanding of the world.

Private Life and Middle-Class Identity

Family and home played a central role in forming middle-class identity. Few themes were more common in nineteenth-century fiction than men and women pursuing mobility and status by or through marriage. Families served intensely practical purposes: sons, nephews, and cousins were expected to assume responsibility in family firms when it came their turn; wives managed accounts; and parents-in-law provided business connections, credit, inheritance, and so on. The family's role in middle-class thought, however, did not arise only from these practical considerations; family was part of a larger worldview.

A well-governed household offered a counterpoint to the business and confusion of the world, and families offered continuity and tradition in a time of rapid change.

Gender and the Cult of Domesticity

There was no single type of middle-class family or home. Yet many people held powerful convictions about how a respectable home should be run. According to advice manuals, poetry, and middle-class journals, wives and mothers were supposed to occupy a "separate sphere" of life, in which they lived in subordination to their spouses. "Man for the field and woman for the hearth; man for the sword and for the needle she. . . . All else confusion," wrote the British poet Alfred, Lord Tennyson in 1847. These prescriptions were directly applied to young people. Boys were educated in secondary schools; girls at home. This nineteenth-century conception of separate spheres needs to be understood in relation to much longer-standing traditions of paternal authority, which were codified in law. Throughout Europe, laws subjected women to their husbands' authority. The Napoleonic Code, a model for other countries after 1815, classified women, children, and the mentally ill together as legally incompetent. In Britain, a woman transferred all her property rights to her husband on marriage. Although unmarried women did enjoy a degree of legal independence in France and Austria, laws generally assigned them to the "protection" of their fathers. Gender relations in the nineteenth century rested on this foundation of legal inequality. Yet the idea or doctrine of separate spheres was meant to underscore that men's and women's spheres complemented each other. Thus, for instance, middle-class writings were full of references to spiritual equality between men and women; and middle-class people wrote, proudly, of marriages in which the wife was a "companion" and "helpmate."

It is helpful to recall that members of the middle class articulated their values in opposition to aristocratic customs, on the one hand, and the lives of the common people, on the other. They argued, for instance, that middle-class marriages did not aim to found aristocratic dynasties and were not arranged to accumulate power and privilege; instead they were to be based on mutual respect and division of responsibilities. A respectable middle-class woman should be free from the unrelenting toil that was the lot of a woman of the people. Called in Victorian Britain the "angel in the house," the middle-class woman was responsible for the moral education of her children. It was understood that being a good wife and mother was a demanding task, requiring an elevated character. This belief, sometimes called the "cult of domesticity," was central to middle-class Victorian thinking about women. Home life and, by extension, the woman's role in that life were infused with new meaning. As one young woman put it after reading a popular book on female education, "What an important sphere a woman fills! How thoroughly she ought to be qualified for it—I think hers the more honourable employment than a man's." In sum, the early nineteenth century brought a general reassessment of femininity. The roots of this reassessment lay in early-nineteenth-century religion and efforts to moralize society, largely to guard against the disorders of the French and Industrial Revolutions.

As a housewife, a middle-class woman had the task of keeping the household functioning smoothly and harmoniously. She maintained the accounts and directed the activities of the servants. Having at least one servant was a mark of middle-class status; and in wealthier families governesses and nannies cared for children, idealized views of motherhood notwithstanding. The middle classes, however, included many gradations of wealth, from a well-housed banker with a governess and five servants to a village preacher with one. Moreover, the work of running and maintaining a home was enormous. Linens and clothes had to be made and mended. Only the wealthy had the luxury of running water, and others had to carry and heat water for cooking, laundry, and cleaning. Heating with coal and lighting with kerosene involved hours of cleaning. If the "angel in the house" was a cultural ideal, it was partly because she had real economic value.

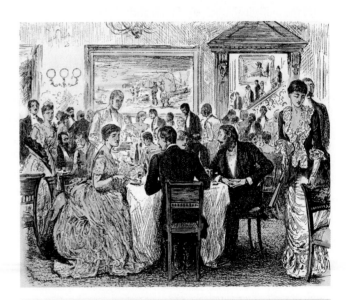

ILLUSTRATION FROM A VICTORIAN BOOK ON MANNERS.
Advice books such as this were very popular in the nineteenth century—a mark, perhaps, of preoccupation with status and the emergence of new social groups. ▪ *Why would people be concerned about "respectability" in an age of greater social mobility?*

Marriage, Sexuality, and the Facts of Life

In the nineteenth century, sexuality became the subject of much anxious debate, largely because it raised other issues: the roles of men and women, morality, and social respectability. Doctors threw themselves into the discussion, offering their expert opinions on the health (including the sexual lives) of the population. Yet doctors did not dictate people's private lives. Nineteenth-century men and women responded to what they experienced as the facts of life more than to expert advice. The first document provides an example of medical knowledge and opinion in 1870. The second offers a glimpse of the daily realities of family life in 1830.

A French Doctor Denounces Contraception (1870)

One of the most powerful instincts nature has placed in the heart of man is that which has for its object the perpetuation of the human race. But this instinct, this inclination, so active, which attracts one sex towards the other, is liable to be perverted, to deviate from the path nature has laid out. From this arises a number of fatal aberrations which exercise a deplorable influence upon the individual, upon the family and upon society. . . .

We hear constantly that marriages are less fruitful, that the increase of population does not follow its former ratio. I believe that this is mainly attributable to genesiac frauds. It might naturally be supposed that these odious calculations of egotism, these shameful refinements of debauchery, are met with almost entirely in large cities, and among the luxurious classes, and that small towns and country places yet preserve that simplicity of manners attributed to primitive society, when the *pater familias* was proud of exhibiting his numerous offspring. Such, however, is not the case, and I shall show that those who have an unlimited confidence in the patriarchal habits of our country people are deeply in error. At the present time frauds are practiced by all classes. . . .

The laboring classes are generally satisfied with the practice of Onan [withdrawal]. . . . They are seldom familiar with the sheath invented by Dr. Condom, and bearing his name.

Among the wealthy, on the other hand, the use of this preservative is generally known. It favors frauds by rendering them easier; but it does not afford complete security. . . .

Case X.—This couple belongs to two respectable families of vintners. They are both pale, emaciated, downcast, sickly. . . .

They have been married for ten years; they first had two children, one immediately after the other, but in order to avoid an increase of family, they have had recourse to conjugal frauds. Being both very amorous, they have found this practice very convenient to satisfy their inclinations. They have employed it to such an extent, that up to a few months ago, when their health began to fail, the husband had intercourse with his wife habitually two and three times in twenty-four hours.

The following is the condition of the woman: She complains of continual pains in the lower part of the abdomen and kidneys. These pains disturb the functions of the stomach and render her nervous. . . . By the touch we find a very intense heat, great sensibility to pressure, and all the signs of a chronic metritis. The patient attributes positively her present state to the too frequent approaches of her husband.

Outside the home, women had very few respectable options for earning a living. Unmarried women might act as companions or governesses—the British novelist Charlotte Brontë's heroine Jane Eyre did so and led a generally miserable life until "rescued" by marriage to her difficult employer. But nineteenth-century convictions about women's moral nature, combined as they were with middle-class aspirations to political leadership, encouraged middle-class wives to undertake voluntary charitable work or to campaign for social reform. In Britain and the United States, women played an important role in the struggle to abolish the slave trade and slavery in the British Empire. Many of these movements also drew on the energies of religious, especially Protestant, organizations, committed to the eradication of social evils

The husband does not attempt to exculpate himself, as he also is in a state of extreme suffering. It is not in the genital organs, however, that we find his disorder, but in the whole general nervous system; his history will find its place in the part of this work relative to general disturbances. . . .

Source: Louis-François-Etienne Bergeret, *The Preventive Obstacle, or Conjugal Onanism*, trans. P. de Marmon (New York: 1870), pp. 3–4, 12, 20–22, 25, 56–57, 100–101, 111–113. Originally published in Paris in 1868.

Death in Childbirth (1830)

rs. Ann B. Pettigrew was taken in Labour after returning from a walk in the garden, at 7 o'clock in the evening of June 30, 1830. At 40 minutes after 11 o'clock, she was delivered of a daughter. A short time after, I was informed that the Placenta was not removed, and, at 10 minutes after 12 was asked into the room. I advanced to my dear wife, and kissing her, asked her how she was, to which she replied, I feel very badly. I went out of the room, and sent for Dr. Warren.

I then returned, and inquired if there was much hemorrhage, and was answered that there was. I then asked the midwife (Mrs. Brickhouse) if she ever used manual exertion to remove the placenta. She said she had more than fifty times. I then, fearing the consequences of hemorrhage, observed, Do, my dear sweet wife, permit Mrs. Brickhouse to remove it: To which she assented. . . .

After the second unsuccessful attempt, I desired the midwife to desist. In these two efforts, my dear Nancy suffered exceedingly and frequently exclaimed: "O Mrs. Brickhouse you will kill me," and to me, "O I shall die, send for the Doctor." To which I replied, "I have sent."

After this, my feelings were so agonizing that I had to retire from the room and lay down, or fall. Shortly after which, the midwife came to me and, falling upon her knees, prayed most fervently to God and to me to forgive her for saying that she could do what she could not. . . .

The placenta did not come away, and the hemorrhage continued with unabated violence until five o'clock in the morning, when the dear woman breathed her last 20 minutes before the Doctor arrived.

So agonizing a scene as that from one o'clock, I have no words to describe. O My God, My God! have mercy on me. I am undone forever. . . .

Source: Cited in Erna Olafson Hellerstein, Leslie Parker Hume, and Karen M. Offen, eds., *Victorian Women: A Documentary Account of Women's Lives in Nineteenth-Century England, France, and the United States.* (Stanford, CA: 1981) pp. 193–94, 219–20.

Questions for Analysis

1. The French doctor states that the impulse to have sexual relations is "one of the most powerful instincts" given to humans by nature, while simultaneously claiming that this natural instinct is "liable to be perverted." What does this reveal about his attitude toward "nature"?

2. What does he mean by "genesiac frauds"? Who is being deceived by this fraud? What consequences for individuals and for society as a whole does the doctor fear from this deception?

3. What does the story of Mrs. Pettigrew's death reveal about the dangers of childbirth and the state of obstetric medicine in the nineteenth century?

and moral improvement. Throughout Europe, a wide range of movements to improve conditions for the poor in schools and hospitals, for temperance, against prostitution, or for legislation on factory hours were often run by women. Florence Nightingale, who went to the Crimean Peninsula in Russia to nurse British soldiers fighting there in the 1850s, remains the most famous of those women, whose determination to right

social wrongs compelled them to defy conventional notions of woman's "proper" sphere. Equally famous—or infamous, at the time—was the French female novelist George Sand (1804–1876), whose real name was Amandine Aurore Dupin Dudevant. Sand dressed like a man and smoked cigars, and her novels often told the tales of independent women thwarted by convention and unhappy marriage.

Queen Victoria, who came to the British throne in 1837, labored to make her solemn public image reflect contemporary feminine virtues of moral probity and dutiful domesticity. Her court was eminently proper, a marked contrast to that of her uncle George IV, whose cavalier ways had set the style for high life a generation before. Though possessing a bad temper, Victoria trained herself to curb it in deference to her ministers and her public-spirited, ultrarespectable husband, Prince Albert of Saxe-Coburg. She was a successful queen because she embodied the traits important to the middle class, whose triumph she seemed to epitomize and whose habits of mind we have come to call Victorian. Nineteenth-century ideas about gender had an impact on masculinity as well as femininity. Soon after the revolutionary and Napoleonic period, men began to dress in sober, practical clothing—and to see as effeminate or dandyish the wigs, ruffled collars, and tight breeches that had earlier been the pride of aristocratic masculinity.

"Passionlessness": Gender and Sexuality

Victorian ideas about sexuality are among the most remarked-on features of nineteenth-century culture. They have become virtually synonymous with anxiety, prudishness, and ignorance. An English mother counseling her daughter about her wedding night is said to have told her to "lie back and think of the empire." Etiquette apparently required that piano legs be covered. Many of these anxieties and prohibitions, however, have been caricatured. More recently, historians have tried to disentangle the teachings or prescriptions of etiquette books and marriage manuals from the actual beliefs of men and women. Equally important, they have sought to understand each on its own terms. Beliefs about sexuality followed from convictions, described earlier, concerning separate spheres. Indeed, one of the defining aspects of nineteenth-century ideas about men and women is the extent to which they rested on scientific arguments about nature. Codes of morality and methods of science combined to reinforce the certainty that specific characteristics were inherent to each sex. Men and women had different social roles, and those differences were rooted in their bodies. The French social thinker Auguste Comte provides a good example: "Biological philosophy teaches us that, through the whole animal scale, and while the specific type is preserved, radical differences, physical and moral, distinguish the sexes." Comte also spelled out the implications of biological difference: "[T]he equality of the sexes, of which so much is said, is incompatible with all social existence. . . . The economy of the human family could never be inverted without an entire

change in our cerebral organism." Women were unsuited for higher education because their brains were smaller or because their bodies were fragile. "Fifteen or 20 days of 28 (we may say nearly always) a woman is not only an invalid, but a wounded one. She ceaselessly suffers from love's eternal wound," wrote the well-known French author Jules Michelet about menstruation.

Finally, scientists and doctors considered women's alleged moral superiority to be literally embodied in an absence of sexual feeling, or "passionlessness." Scientists and doctors considered male sexual desire natural, if not admirable—an unruly force that had to be channeled. Many governments legalized and regulated prostitution—which included the compulsory examination of women for venereal disease—precisely because it provided an outlet for male sexual desire. Doctors disagreed about female sexuality, but the British doctor William Acton stood among those who asserted that women functioned differently:

I have taken pains to obtain and compare abundant evidence on this subject, and the result of my inquiries I may briefly epitomize as follows:— I should say that the majority of women (happily for society) are not very much troubled with sexual feeling of any kind. What men are habitually, women are only exceptionally.

Like other nineteenth-century men and women, Acton also believed that more open expressions of sexuality were disreputable and, also, that working-class women were less "feminine."

Convictions like these reveal a great deal about Victorian science and medicine, but they did not necessarily dictate people's intimate lives. As far as sexuality was concerned, the absence of any reliable contraception mattered more in people's experiences and feelings than sociologists' or doctors' opinions. Abstinence and withdrawal were the only common techniques for preventing pregnancy. Their effectiveness was limited, since until the 1880s doctors continued to believe that a woman was most fertile during and around her menstrual period. Midwives and prostitutes knew of other forms of contraception and abortifacients (all of them dangerous and most ineffective), and surely some middle-class women did as well, but such information was not respectable middle-class fare. Concretely, then, sexual intercourse was directly related to the very real dangers of frequent pregnancies. In England, 1 in 100 childbirths ended in the death of the mother; at a time when a woman might become pregnant eight or nine times in her life, this was a sobering prospect. Those dangers varied with social class, but even among wealthy and better-cared-for women, they took a real toll. It is not surprising that middle-class women's diaries and letters are full of their anticipations of childbirth, both joyful and anxious. Queen Victoria, who bore nine children, declared that childbirth was the "shadow side" of marriage—and she was a pioneer in using anesthesia!

Middle-Class Life in Public

The public life of middle-class families literally reshaped the nineteenth-century landscape. Houses and their furnishings were powerful symbols of material security. Solidly built, heavily decorated, they proclaimed the financial worth and social respectability of those who dwelt within. In provincial cities they were often freestanding villas. In London, Paris, Berlin, and Vienna, they might be in rows of five- or six-story townhouses or large apartments. Whatever particular shape they took, they were built to last a long time. The rooms were certain to be crowded with furniture, art objects, carpets, and wall hangings. The size of the rooms, the elegance of the furniture, the number of servants—all depended, of course, on the extent of one's income. A bank clerk did not live as elegantly as a bank director. Yet they shared many standards and aspirations, and those common values helped bind them to the same class, despite the differences in their material way of life.

As cities grew, they became increasingly segregated. Middle-class people lived far from the unpleasant sights and smells of industrialization. Their residential areas, usually built to the west of the cities, out of the path of the prevailing breeze and therefore of industrial pollution, were havens from congestion. The public buildings in the center, many constructed during the nineteenth century, were celebrated as signs of development and prosperity. The middle classes increasingly managed their cities' affairs, although members of the aristocracy retained considerable power, especially in central Europe. And it was these new middle-class civic leaders who provided new industrial cities with many of their architectural landmarks: city halls, stock exchanges, museums, opera houses, outdoor concert halls, and department stores. One historian has called these buildings the new cathedrals of the industrial age; projects intended to express the community's values and represent public culture, they were monuments to social change.

The suburbs changed as well. The advent of the railways made outings to concerts, parks, and bathing spots popular. They made it possible for families of relatively moderate means to take one- or two-week-long trips to the mountains or to the seashore. New resorts opened, offering racetracks, mineral springs baths, and cabanas on the beach. Mass

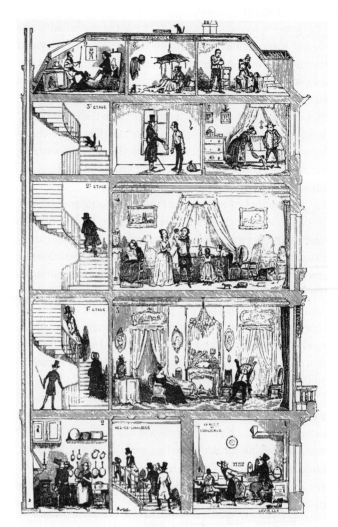

APARTMENT LIVING IN PARIS. This print shows that on the Continent, rich and poor often lived in the same buildings—the rich on the lower floors, the poor at the top. This sort of residential mixing was less common in Britain.

tourism would not come until the twentieth century. But the now-familiar impressionist paintings of the 1870s and 1880s testify to something that was dramatically new in the nineteenth century: a new range of middle-class leisures.

Working-Class Life

Like the middle class, the working class was divided into various subgroups and categories, determined in this case by skill, wages, gender, and workplace. Workers' experiences varied, depending on where they worked, where they lived, and, above all, how much they earned. A skilled textile worker lived a life far different from that of a ditch digger, the former able to afford the food, shelter, and clothing necessary for a decent existence, the latter barely able to scrape by.

Some movement from the ranks of the unskilled to the skilled was possible, if children were provided, or provided themselves, with at least a rudimentary education. Yet education was considered by many parents a luxury, especially since children could be put to work at an early age to supplement a family's meager earnings. Downward mobility from skilled to unskilled was also possible, as technological change—the introduction of the power loom, for example—drove highly paid workers into the ranks of the unskilled and destitute.

Working-class housing was unhealthy and unregulated. In older cities single-family dwellings were broken up into apartments, often of no more than one room per family. In new manufacturing centers, rows of tiny houses, located close by smoking factories, were built back to back, thereby eliminating any cross-ventilation or space for gardens. Crowding was commonplace. A newspaper account from the 1840s noted that in Leeds, a textile center in northern Britain, an ordinary worker's house contained no more than 150 square feet, and that in most cases those houses were "crammed almost to suffocation with human beings both day and night."

Household routines, demanding in the middle classes, were grinding for the poor. The family remained a survival network, in which everyone played a crucial role. In addition to working for wages, wives were expected to house, feed, and clothe the family on the very little money different members of the family earned. A good wife was able to make ends meet even in bad times. Working women's daily lives involved constant rounds of carrying and boiling water, cleaning, cooking, and doing laundry—in one- and two-room crowded, unventilated, poorly lit apartments. Families could not rely on their own gardens to help supply them with food. City markets catered to their needs for cheap goods, but these were regularly stale, nearly rotten, or dangerously adulterated. Formaldehyde was added to milk to prevent spoilage. Pounded rice was mixed into sugar. Fine brown earth was introduced into cocoa.

WORKING WOMEN IN THE INDUSTRIAL LANDSCAPE

Few figures raised more public anxiety and outcry in the nineteenth century than the working woman. Contemporaries worried out loud about the "promiscuous mixing of the sexes" in crowded and humid workshops. Nineteenth-century writers, starting in England and France, chronicled what they considered to be the economic and moral horrors of female labor: unattended children running in the streets, small children caught in accidents at the mills or the mines, pregnant women hauling coal, or women laboring alongside men in shops.

Women's work was not new, but industrialization made it more visible. Both before and after the Industrial Revolution labor was divided by gender, but as employers implemented new manufacturing processes, ideas about which jobs were appropriate for women shifted. In traditional textile production, for example, women spun and men operated the looms. In industrial textile factories, on the other hand, employers preferred women and children, both because they were considered more docile and less likely to make trouble and because it was believed that their smaller hands were better suited to the intricate job of tying threads on the power looms. Manufacturers sought to recruit women mill hands from neighboring villages, paying good wages by comparison with other jobs open to women. Most began to work at the age of ten or eleven, and when they had children they either put their children out to a wet nurse, brought them to the mills, or continued to work doing piecework at home. This transformation of the gendered structure of work caused intense anxiety in the first half of the nineteenth century and is one of the reasons that the emerging labor movement began to include calls for excluding women from the workplace in their programs.

Most women did not work in factories, however, and continued to labor at home or in small workshops—"sweatshops," as they came to be called—for notoriously low wages paid not by the hour but by the piece for each shirt stitched or each matchbox glued. The greatest number of unmarried working-class women worked less visibly in domestic service, a job that brought low wages and, to judge by the testimony of many women, coercive sexual relationships with male employers or their sons. Domestic service, however, provided room and board. In a time when a single woman simply could not survive on her own wages, a young woman who had just arrived in the city had few choices: marriage, which was unlikely to happen right away; renting a room in a boardinghouse, many of which were often centers of prostitution; domestic service; or living with someone. How women balanced the demands for money and the time for household work varied with the number and age of their children. Mothers were actually more likely to work when their children were very small, for there were more mouths to feed and the children were not yet old enough to earn wages.

Poverty, the absence of privacy, and the particular vulnerabilities of working-class women made working-class sexuality very different from its middle-class counterpart. Illegitimacy rose dramatically between 1750 and 1850. In Frankfurt, Germany, for example, where the illegitimacy rate had been a mere 2 percent in the early 1700s, it reached 25 percent in 1850. In Bordeaux, France, in 1840, one-third of the recorded births were illegitimate. Reasons for

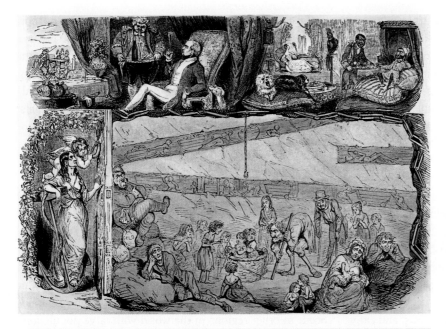

CAPITAL AND LABOUR. In its earliest years, the British magazine *Punch*, though primarily a humorous weekly, manifested a strong social conscience. This 1843 cartoon shows the capitalists enjoying the rewards of their investments while the hungry workers shiver in cold. ▪ *How would a defender of the new industrial order respond to this cartoon?*

ality was a fact of life, midwives could help desperate pregnant girls, marriage was an avenue to respectability, and so on. The gulf that separated these expectations and codes from those of middle-class women was one of the most important factors in the development of nineteenth-century class identity.

A Life Apart: "Class Consciousness"

The new demands of life in an industrial economy created common experiences and difficulties. The factory system denied skilled workers the pride in craft they had previously enjoyed. Stripped of the protections of guilds and apprenticeships and prevented from organizing by legislation in France, Germany, and Britain in the first half of the nineteenth century, workers felt vulnerable in the face of their socially and politically powerful employers. Factory hours were long—usually twelve to fourteen hours. Textile mills were unventilated, and minute particles of lint lodged in workers' lungs. Machines were unfenced and posed dangers to child workers. British physicians cataloged the toll that long hours tending machines took on children, including spinal curvature and bone malformations. Children were also employed in large numbers in mines—over 50,000 worked in British mines in 1841.

Factories also imposed new routines and disciplines. Artisans in earlier times worked long hours for little pay, but they set their own schedules and controlled the pace of work, moving from their home workshops to their small garden plots as they wished. In a factory, all hands learned the discipline of the clock. To increase production, the factory system encouraged the breaking down of the manufacturing process into specialized steps, each with its own time. Workers began to see machinery itself as the tyrant that changed their lives and bound them to industrial slavery. A radical working-class song written in Britain in the 1840s expressed the feeling:

> There is a king and a ruthless king;
> Not a king of the poet's dream;
> But a tyrant fell, white slaves know well,
> And that ruthless king is steam.

this increase are difficult to establish. Greater mobility and urbanization meant weaker family ties, more opportunities for young men and women, and more vulnerabilities. Premarital sex was an accepted practice in preindustrial villages, but because of the social controls that dominated village life, it was almost always followed by marriage. These controls were weaker in the far more anonymous setting of a factory town or commercial city. The economic uncertainties of the early industrial age meant that a young working-man's promise of marriage based on his expectation of a job might frequently be difficult to fulfill. Economic vulnerability drove many single women into temporary relationships that produced children and a continuing cycle of poverty and abandonment. Historians have shown, however, that in the city as in the countryside, many of these temporary relationships became enduring ones: the parents of illegitimate children would marry later. Again, nineteenth-century writers dramatized what they considered the disreputable sexuality of the "dangerous classes" in the cities. Some of them attributed illegitimacy, prostitution, and so on to the moral weakness of working-class people, others to the systematic changes wrought by industrialization. Both sides, however, overstated the collapse of the family and the destruction of traditional morality. Working-class families transmitted expectations about gender roles and sexual behavior: girls should expect to work, daughters were responsible for caring for their younger siblings as well as for earning wages, sexu-

Yet the defining feature of working-class life was vulnerability—to unemployment, sickness, accidents in dangerous jobs, family problems, and spikes in the prices of food. Seasonal unemployment, high in almost all trades, made it impossible to collect regular wages. Markets for manufactured goods were small and unstable, producing cyclical economic depressions; when those came, thousands of workers found themselves laid off with no system of unemployment insurance to sustain them. The early decades of industrialization were also marked by several severe agricultural depressions and economic crises. During the crisis years of the 1840s, half the working population of Britain's industrial cities was unemployed. In Paris, 85,000 went on relief in 1840. Families survived by working several small jobs, pawning their possessions, and getting credit from local wineshops and grocery stores. The chronic insecurity of working-class life helped fuel the creation of workers' self-help societies, fraternal associations, and early socialist organizations. It also meant that economic crises could have explosive consequences (see Chapter 21).

By mid-century, various experiences were beginning to make working people conscious of themselves as different from and in opposition to the middle classes. Changes in the workplace—whether the introduction of machines and factory labor, speedups, subcontracting to cheap labor, or the loss of guild protections—were part of the picture. The social segregation of the rapidly expanding nineteenth-century cities also contributed to the sense that working people lived a life apart. Class differences seemed embedded in a very wide array of everyday experiences and beliefs: work, private life, expectations for children, the roles of men and women, and definitions of respectability. Over the course of the nineteenth century all of these different experiences gave concrete, specific meaning to the word *class*.

CONCLUSION

Why did the Industrial Revolution occur at this moment in human history? Why did it begin in Europe? Why did it not occur in other regions in the world with large populations and advanced technologies, such as China or India? These fundamental questions remain subject to serious debate among historians. One school of explanations focuses on the fact that the mechanization of industry occurred first in northern Europe and seeks to explain the Industrial Revolution's origins in terms of this region's vibrant towns,

After You Read This Chapter

Visit StudySpace for quizzes, additional review materials, and multimedia documents. **wwnorton.com/web/westernciv18**

REVIEWING THE OBJECTIVES

- The Industrial Revolution in Europe began in northern Great Britain. What circumstances made this process of economic development begin there?
- Certain industries were particularly suitable for the kinds of technological developments that encouraged industrialization. What were these industries, and where did they exist in Europe?
- Industrial development changed the nature of work and production in significant ways. What were these changes, and how did they change the relations between laborers and their employers, or local producers and wider markets?
- Industrialization had social effects far beyond the factories. What larger changes in European society were associated with the Industrial Revolution?
- A large and diverse group of middle-class people emerged in Europe as a result of the social changes brought on by industrialization. What kinds of people qualified as middle class during the nineteenth century, and how were they different from other social groups?

its well-developed commercial markets, and the presence of a prosperous land-owning elite that had few prejudices against entrepreneurial activity. These historians have suggested that industrialization is best understood as a process rooted in European culture and history.

More recently, however, historians with a more global approach have argued that it may be incorrect to assert that industrialization developed as it did because of the advantages enjoyed by a central, European, core. Instead, they have explored the possibility that the world's economies constituted a larger interlocking system that had no definitive center until *after* the takeoff of European industrialization. Before that period, when it came to agricultural practices, ecological constraints, population densities, urbanization, and technological development, *many* global regions were not so different from the western European model. In the end, suggest these historians, Europe was able to move more quickly to industrial production because its economies were better positioned to mobilize the resources available to them on the periphery of their trading sphere. The access enjoyed by European traders to agricultural products from slave-owning societies in the Americas helped them escape the ecological constraints imposed by their own intensely farmed lands and made the move to an industrial economy possible. Contingent factors—such as patterns of disease and epidemic or the location of coal fields—may have also played a role.

There is less debate about the consequences of the Industrial Revolution within Europe. New forms of industrial production created a new economy and changed the nature of work for both men and women. Industrialization changed the landscape of Europe and changed the structures of families and the private lives of people in both the cities and the countryside. Industrialization created new forms of wealth along with new kinds of poverty. It also fostered an acute awareness of the disparity between social groups. In the eighteenth century, that disparity would have been described in terms of birth, rank, or privilege. In the nineteenth century, it was increasingly seen in terms of class. Both champions and critics of the new industrial order spoke of a "class society." The identities associated with class were formed in the crowded working-class districts of the new cities, in experiences of work, and in the new conditions of respectability that determined life in middle-class homes. These new identities would be sharpened in the political events to which we now turn.

PEOPLE, IDEAS, AND EVENTS IN CONTEXT

- Why was **ENCLOSURE** an important factor in the Industrial Revolution?
- What was the **SPINNING JENNY**? What was the **COTTON GIN**? What effect did these machines have on industrial development?
- What was the significance of **EUROPEAN EMPIRE** and overseas expansion for industrialization?
- How did industrialization affect **POPULATION GROWTH** in Europe? What effects did it have on the **PEASANTRY**? On **URBAN POPULATIONS**?
- What environmental changes were associated with the use of new sources of fuel such as coal or the construction of large and concentrated centers of industrial manufacture?
- What was the **IRISH POTATO FAMINE**, and how was it related to the economic developments of nineteenth-century Europe? What might **THOMAS MALTHUS** have thought about the potato famine?

THINKING ABOUT CONNECTIONS

- What might the changes associated with the Industrial Revolution have done to people's conceptions of time and space? How might they have perceived their lives against what they knew of the experience of their parents' generation or what they anticipated for their children?
- Awareness that these changes made the present radically different from the recent past gave many people the sensation that time was hurtling ever faster into a future whose outlines could only dimly be perceived.
- In the early twenty-first century, innovations in information technology have created a similar sensation of accelerated change and diminishing distances in a more interconnected globe. What are the similarities between our own period and the period between the 1780s and 1830s, when large numbers of people first began to think of the power of technology to change the way that society was organized and to conceive of history as a headlong rush into the future? What are the differences?

public, begun in the Enlightenment, continued. The word *citizen* (and the liberal political ideas contained within it) was controversial in the aftermath of the French Revolution, but it was difficult to banish the term from political debates. Liberalism's fundamental principles—equality before the law, freedom of expression, and the consent of the governed—were still a potent threat to Europe's dynastic rulers, especially when coupled with the emotions stirred up by popular nationalism. Liberal nationalists believed that legitimate sovereignty could only be exercised by citizens acting collectively as a nation. Such a conception of sovereignty was diametrically opposed to conservative monarchs who believed their authority came not from the people but from God.

At the same time, the political opposition to the conservative order in Europe began to be infused with new and more radical political ideologies. Some liberals were comfortable living under a constitutional monarch—one who agreed to rule in accordance with the law. Others accepted the idea of representation but believed that voting was a privilege that should be extended only to wealthy property owners. Much more radical were republicans who called for universal (male) suffrage and an end to monarchy altogether. Socialists, disturbed by the inequalities produced in the new market economy of industrial society, went even further and argued that political reform was not enough to free the people from want and exploitation. To socialists, justice was possible only with a radical reordering of society that redistributed property equitably. Between 1815 and 1848, none of these more radical oppositional movements succeeded in carrying the day, but their ideas circulated widely and occupied the attention of conservative monarchs (and their police spies) throughout Europe.

In culture as well as in politics, imagination and a sense of possibility were among the defining characteristics of the first half of the century. Romanticism broke with what many artists considered the cold Classicism and formality of eighteenth-century art. The Enlightenment had championed reason; the Romantics prized subjectivity, feeling, and spontaneity. Their revolt against eighteenth-century conventions had ramifications far beyond literature and painting. The Romantics had no single political creed: some were fervent revolutionaries and others fervent traditionalists who looked to the past, to religion or history, for inspiration. Their sensibility, however, infused politics and culture. And to look ahead, their collective search for new means of expression sent nineteenth-century art off in a new direction.

THE SEARCH FOR ORDER IN EUROPE, 1815–1830

In 1814, the European powers—including the France of the restored king, Louis XVIII—met at the Congress of Vienna to settle pressing questions about the post-Napoleonic political order and to determine the territorial spoils of their victory over the French emperor. An observer of the lavish balls and celebrations that accompanied the Congress's diplomatic negotiations might well have assumed that the calendar had been turned back several decades, to a time when the European nobility had not yet been humiliated and terrorized by violent revolutionaries. But the celebrations of Louis XVIII's return to the throne and the glittering display of aristocratic men in wigs and fine clothes, accompanied by their bejeweled wives (and mistresses), could not hide the fact that twenty years of war, revolution, and political experimentation had changed Europe in fundamental ways. The task of the Congress of Vienna was to reinforce Europe's monarchical regimes against the powerful social and political forces that had been unleashed in the years since 1789.

The Congress of Vienna and the Restoration

The Russian tsar Alexander I (r. 1801–25) and the Austrian diplomat Klemens von Metternich (1773–1859) dominated the Congress of Vienna. After Napoleon's fall, Russia became the most powerful continental state. Alexander I presented himself during the Napoleonic Wars as the "liberator" of Europe, and many feared that he would substitute an all-powerful Russia for an all-powerful France. The French prince Charles Maurice de Talleyrand (1754–1838) had a surprisingly strong supporting role. Talleyrand had been a bishop and a revolutionary and survived the Terror in exile in the United States before becoming first Napoleon's foreign minister and then occupying the same post under Louis XVIII. That he was present at Vienna testified to his diplomatic skill—or opportunism.

Metternich, the architect of the peace, had witnessed the popular violence connected with the French Revolution while a student at the University of Strasbourg in 1789. It left him with a lifelong hatred of revolutionary movements. At the Congress of Vienna, his central concerns were checking Russian expansionism and preventing political

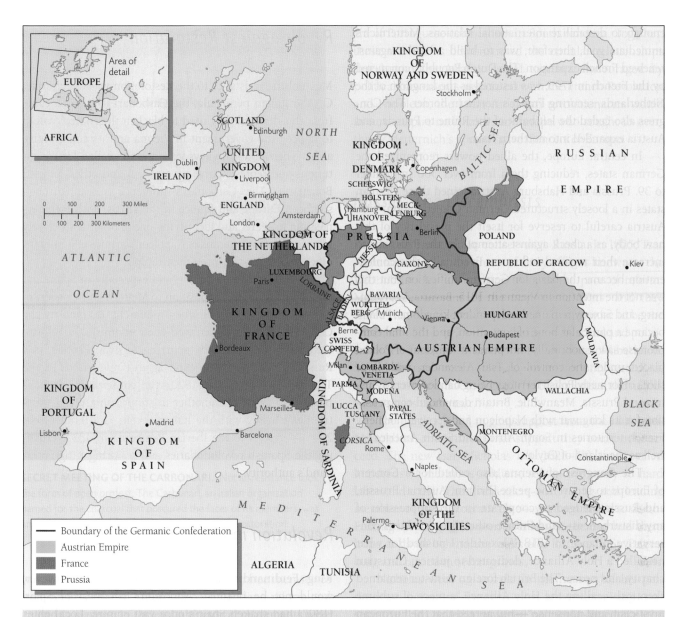

THE CONGRESS OF VIENNA. Note how the borders of European nations were established after the final defeat of Napoleon in 1815, and compare these boundaries to Europe in 1713 after the Peace of Utrecht (page 508). ▪ *What major changes had occurred in the intervening years in central Europe?* ▪ *Which territorial powers played an active role in determining the balance of power at the Congress of Vienna?* ▪ *What social or political developments might disrupt this balance?*

and social change. He favored treating the defeated French with moderation. Nevertheless, he remained an archconservative who readily resorted to harsh repressive tactics, including secret police and spying. But the peace he crafted was enormously significant and helped prevent a major European war until 1914.

The Congress sought to restore order by insisting that Europe's dynastic rulers were the only legitimate political authority. It recognized Louis XVIII as the legitimate sovereign of France and confirmed the restoration of Bourbon rulers in Spain and the Two Sicilies. Other European monarchs had no interest in undermining the French restoration: Louis XVIII was a bulwark against revolution. But after Napoleon's Hundred Days, the allies imposed an indemnity of 700 million francs and an occupying army for five years. France's borders remained the same as in 1789—less than the revolution's "greater France" but not as punitive as they might have been.

The guiding principle of the peace was the balance of power, according to which no country should be powerful on newspapers, allowing house searches, and restricting rights of assembly.

British political leaders reversed their opposition to reform in response to pressure from below. The reforms actually began under the conservative Tory Party, when Catholics and non-Anglican Protestants were allowed to participate in public life. The Tories nevertheless refused to reform representation in the House of Commons. About two-thirds of the members of the House of Commons owed their seats to the patronage of the richest titled landowners in the country. In districts known as "rotten" or "pocket" boroughs, landowners used their power to return members of Parliament who would serve their interests. Defenders of this system argued that the interests of landed property coincided with the nation at large.

Liberals in the Whig Party, the new industrial middle class, and radical artisans argued passionately for reform. They were not necessarily democrats—liberals in particular wanted only to enfranchise responsible citizens—but they made common cause with organized middle-class and working-class radicals to push for reform. A Birmingham banker named Thomas Atwood, for example, organized the Political Union of the Lower and Middle Classes of the People. By July 1830, similar organizations arose in several cities, and some clashed with the army and police. Middle-class shopkeepers announced they would withhold taxes and form a national guard. The country appeared to be on the verge of serious general disorder, if not outright revolution. Lord Grey, head of the Whig Party, seized the opportunity to push through reform.

The Reform Bill of 1832 eliminated the rotten boroughs and reallocated 143 parliamentary seats, mostly from the rural south, to the industrial north. The bill expanded the franchise, but only one in six men could vote. Landed aristocrats had their influence reduced but not destroyed. This modest reform nevertheless brought British liberals and members of the middle class into a junior partnership with a landed elite that had ruled Britain for centuries.

What changes did this more liberal parliament produce? It abolished slavery in the British colonies in 1838 (see Chapter 21). The most significant example of middle-class power came in the repeal of the Corn Laws in 1846. The Corn Laws (the British term for grain is *corn*) protected British landowners and farmers from foreign com-petition by establishing tariffs for imports, and they kept bread prices high. The middle class increasingly saw this as an unfair protection of the aristocracy and pushed for their repeal in the name of free trade. The Anti-Corn Law League held meetings throughout the north of England and lobbied Parliament, eventually resulting in a repeal of the law and a free-trade policy that lasted until the 1920s.

British Radicalism and the Chartist Movement

Reformers disappointed with the narrow gains of 1832 pushed for expanded political reforms. Their attention focused on a petition known as the "People's Charter," which contained six demands: universal white male suffrage, a secret ballot, an end to property qualifications as a condition of public office, annual parliamentary elections, salaries for members of the House of Commons, and equal electoral districts. The Chartists organized committees across the country, and the charter was eventually signed by millions.

Chartism spread in a climate of economic hardship during the 1840s. The movement tapped into local traditions of worker self-help, but the Chartists often disagreed about tactics and goals. Should Irish Catholics be included in the movement or excluded as dangerous competitors? Should women be included in the franchise?

THE GREAT CHARTIST RALLY OF APRIL 10, 1848. The year 1848 brought revolution to continental Europe and militant protest to England. This photo shows the April rally in support of the Chartists' six points, which included expanding the franchise, abolishing property qualifications for representatives, and instituting a secret ballot.

Women in the Anti-Corn Law League, 1842

Members of the Anti-Corn Law League sought to repeal the protectionist laws that prohibited foreign grain from entering the British market. The laws were seen as an interference with trade that kept bread prices artificially high, benefiting British landowners and grain producers at the expense of the working population. The campaign to repeal the Corn Laws enlisted many middle-class women in its ranks, and some later campaigned for woman suffrage. This article, hostile to the reform, deplored women's participation in the reform movement.

e find that the council of the Manchester Anti-Corn Law Association had invited the inhabitants to "an *anti-Corn-law tea-party*, to be held on the 20th of May, 1841—gentlemen's tickets, 2s.; ladies 1s. 6d." ... [L]adies were advertised as *stewardesses* of this assembly. So now the names of about 300 Ladies were pompously advertised as the *Patroness* and *Committee* of the *National Bazaar*. We exceedingly wonder and regret that the members of the Association ... and still more that anybody else, should have chosen to exhibit their wives and daughters in the character of political agitators; and we most regret that so many ladies—modest, excellent, and amiable persons we have no doubt in their domestic circles—should have been persuaded to allow

their names to be *placarded* on such occasions—for be it remembered, this Bazaar and these *Tea-parties* did not even pretend to be for any *charitable* object, but entirely for the purposes of *political agitation*. ...

We have before us a letter from Mrs. Secretary Woolley to one body of workmen. ... She "appeals to them to stand forth and denounce as *unholy*, unjust, and cruel all restrictions on the food of the people." She acquaints them that "the ladies are resolved to perform *their* arduous part in the attempt to *destroy a monopoly* which, for *selfishness* and its *deadly* effects, has no parallel in the history of the world." "We therefore," she adds, "ask you for contributions. ..." Now surely ... not only should the *poorer classes* have been exempt from such unreasonable solicitations, but whatever subscriptions might be obtain-

able from the wealthier orders should have been applied, not to *political agitation* throughout England, but to charitable relief at home.

Source: J. Croker, "Anti-Corn Law Legislation," *Quarterly Review* (December 1842), as cited in Patricia Hollis, ed., *Women in Public: The Women's Movement 1850–1900* (London: 1979), p. 287.

Questions for Analysis

1. Why does the article highlight the participation of women in the Anti-Corn Law Association? What does this argument tell us about attitudes toward women's political activity?

2. Does the article actually mention any of the arguments in favor of repealing the Corn Laws? What alternative to repeal does the article appear to support?

The Chartist William Lovett, a cabinetmaker, was a fervent believer in self-improvement and advocated a union of educated workers that could claim its fair share of the nation's increasing industrial wealth. The Chartist Fergus O'Connor appealed to the more impoverished and desperate class of workers by attacking industrialization and the resettlement of the poor on agricultural allotments. Chartist James Bronterre O'Brien shocked the crowds by openly expressing his admiration for Robespierre and attacking "the big-bellied, little-brained, numbskull aristocracy." Chartism had many faces, but

the movement's common goal was social justice through political democracy.

In spite of the Chartists' efforts to present massive petitions to the Parliament in 1839 and 1842, the Parliament rejected them both times. Members of the movement resorted to strikes, trade union demonstrations, and attacks on factories and manufacturers who imposed low wages and long hours or who harassed unionists. The movement peaked in April 1848. Inspired by revolutions in continental Europe (see Chapter 21), the Chartists' leaders planned a major demonstration in London. Twenty-five thousand workers carried to Parliament a petition with 6 million signatures. Confronted with the specter of class conflict, special constables and regular army units were marshaled by the aged Duke of Wellington to resist any threat to public order. In the end, only a small delegation presented the petition, and rain and an unwillingness to do battle with the constabulary put an end to the Chartist movement. A relieved liberal observer, Harriet Martineau, observed, "From that day it was a settled matter that England was safe from revolution."

THE POLITICS OF SLAVERY AFTER 1815

These political conflicts within nations about citizenship, sovereignty, and equality were also linked to a transnational debate about slavery and its legitimacy, which was taking place at the same time. When the age of revolution opened in the 1770s, slavery was legal everywhere in the Atlantic world. By 1848, slavery remained legal only in the southern United States, Brazil, and Cuba. (It endured, too, in most of Africa and parts of India and the Islamic world.) Given the importance of slavery to the Atlantic economy, this was a remarkable shift. The debate about slavery was fundamental, because it challenged the defenders of citizenship rights to live up to the claims of universality that had been a central part of Enlightenment political thought. If "all men" were "created equal," how could some be enslaved?

Slavery, Enlightenment, and Revolution

In fact, the revolutions of the eighteenth century by no means brought emancipation in their wake. Eighteenth-century Enlightenment thinkers had persuaded many Europeans that slavery contradicted natural law and natural freedom (see Chapter 17). As one historian trenchantly puts it, however, "Slavery became a metaphor for everything that was bad—except the institution of slavery itself." Thus, Virginia planters who helped lead the American Revolution angrily refused to be "slaves" to the English king while at the same time defending plantation slavery. The planters' success in throwing off the British king expanded their power and strengthened slavery.

Likewise, the French revolutionaries denounced the tyranny of a king who would "enslave" them but refused to admit free people of color to the revolutionary assembly for fear of alienating the planters in the lucrative colonies of Martinique, Guadeloupe, and Saint-Domingue. Only a slave rebellion in Saint-Domingue in 1791 forced the French revolutionaries, eventually, to contend with the contradictions of revolutionary policy. Napoleon's failure to repress that rebellion allowed for the emergence of Haiti in 1804 (see Chapter 18). The Haitian Revolution sent shock waves through the Americas, alarming slave owners and offering hope to slaves and former slaves. In the words of a free black sailmaker in Philadelphia, the Haitian nation signaled that black people "could not always be detained in their present bondage."

Yet the revolution in Haiti had other, contradictory consequences. The "loss" of slave-based sugar production in the former Saint-Domingue created an opportunity for its expansion elsewhere, in Brazil, where slavery expanded in the production of sugar, gold, and coffee, and in the American South. Slavery remained intact in the French, British, and Spanish colonial islands in the Caribbean, backed by the Congress of Vienna in 1815.

The Slow Path to Abolition

An abolitionist movement did emerge, in England. The country that ruled the seas was "the world's leading purchaser and transporter of African slaves," and the movement aimed to abolish that trade. From the 1780s on, pamphlets and books (the best known is *The Interesting Narrative of the Life of Olaudah Equiano*, 1789) detailed the horrors of the slave ships to an increasingly sympathetic audience. Abolitionist leaders like William Wilberforce believed that the slave trade was immoral and hoped that banning it would improve conditions for the enslaved, though like most abolitionists Wilberforce did not want to foment revolt. In 1807, the reform movement compelled Parliament to pass a bill declaring the "African Slave Trade to be contrary to the principles of justice, humanity and sound policy" and prohibiting British ships from participating in it, effective 1808. The United States joined in the agreement; ten years later the Portuguese agreed to a limited ban on traffic north of the equator. More treaties followed, which slowed but did not stop the trade.

What roots did abolitionism tap? Some historians argue that slavery was becoming less profitable and that its decline made humanitarian concern easier to accept. Others argue that slavery was expanding: among other things, ships carried 2.5 million slaves to markets in the Americas in the four decades *after* the abolition of the slave trade.

Some historians believe economic factors undermined slavery. Adam Smith and his followers argued that free labor, like free trade, was more efficient. This was not necessarily the case, but such arguments still had an effect. Critics claimed slavery was wasteful as well as cruel. Economic calculations, however, did less to activate abolitionism than did a belief that the slave trade and slavery itself represented the arrogance and callousness of wealthy British traders, their planter allies, and the British elite in general. In a culture with high literacy and political traditions of activism, calls for "British liberty" mobilized many.

In England, and especially in the United States, religious revivals supplied much of the energy for the abolitionist movement. The hymn "Amazing Grace" was written by a former slave trader turned minister, John Newton, to describe his conversion experience and salvation. The moral and religious dimensions of the struggle made it acceptable for women, who would move from antislavery to the Anti-Corn Law League and, later, to woman suffrage. Finally, the issue spoke to laborers whose sometimes brutal working conditions and sharply limited political rights we have discussed in the previous chapters. To oppose slavery and to insist that labor should be dignified, honorable, and minimally free resonated broadly in the social classes accustomed to being treated as "servile." The issue, then, cut across material interests and class politics, and antislavery petitions were signed by millions in the 1820s and 1830s.

Slave rebellions and conspiracies to rebel also shook opinion, especially after the success of the Haitian Revolution (see Chapter 19). In 1800, slaves rebelled in Virginia; in 1811, there was an uprising in Louisiana; and in 1822, an alleged conspiracy took hold in South Carolina. The British colonies saw significant rebellions in the Barbados (1816); Demerara, just east of Venezuela (1823); and, most important, the monthlong insurrection in Jamaica (1831). All of these were ferociously repressed. Slave rebellions had virtually no chance of succeeding and usually erupted only when some crack in the system opened up: divisions within the white elite or the (perceived) presence of a sympathetic outsider. Still, these rebellions had important

consequences. They increased slaveholders' sense of vulnerability and isolation. They polarized debate. Outsiders (in England or New England) often recoiled at the brutality of repression. Slave owners responded to antislavery sentiment much as Russian serf owners had responded to their critics, by insisting that slavery was vital to their survival, that emancipation of inferior peoples would sow chaos, and that abolitionists were dangerously playing with fire.

In Great Britain, the force of abolitionism wore down the defense of slavery. In the aftermath of the Great Reform Bill of 1832, Great Britain emancipated 800,000 slaves in its colonies—effective in 1838, after four years of "apprenticeship." In France, republicans took the strongest antislavery stance, and emancipation came to the French colonies when the revolution of 1848 brought republicans, however briefly, to power (see Chapter 21).

In Latin America, slavery's fate was determined by demographics, economics, and the politics of breaking away from the Spanish and Portuguese empires. In most of mainland Spanish America (in other words, not Cuba or Brazil), slavery had been of secondary importance, owing to the relative ease of escape and the presence of other sources of labor. As the struggles for independence escalated, nationalist leaders recruited slaves and free people of

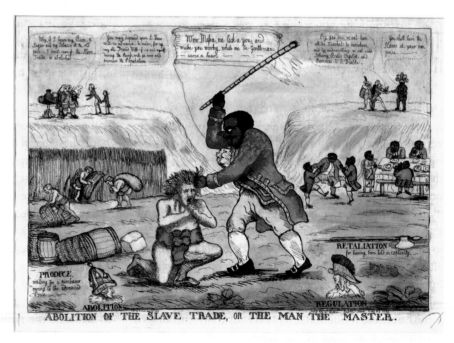

FEAR OF SLAVE VIOLENCE. This cartoon, published in Britain in 1789 in opposition to the movement to end slavery, played on public fears of the consequences of abolition. The former slaves, dressed in the fashionable attire of the landed gentry, dine at their former master's table, and beat the master in retaliation for what they have suffered. In the background, other former slave owners are stooped in labor in the cane fields. By the logic of this cartoon, such a reversal was intolerable, and given the choice between "Abolition" and "Regulation" (the two heads at the bottom) the cartoonist chose "Regulation" as the wiser course.

Competing Viewpoints

Karl Marx and Pierre-Joseph Proudhon, *Correspondence*

Karl Marx was both a prolific political and economic theorist and a political militant who corresponded with socialists and other political radicals throughout Europe. Along with Friedrich Engels, Marx was the author of The Communist Manifesto *(1848), a widely circulated polemical critique of the capitalist economic system, which predicted the emergence of a revolutionary movement led by Europe's industrial working classes. This exchange of letters with a prominent French socialist thinker, Pierre-Joseph Proudhon, reveals disagreements among socialists in Europe about the desirability of revolution, as well as Marx's ideas about how intellectuals such as himself might participate in the revolutionary movement.*

Brussels, 5 May 1846

My dear Proudhon,

...I have made arrangements with the German communists and socialists for a constant interchange of letters which will be devoted to discussing scientific questions, and to keeping an eye on popular writings, and the socialist propaganda that can be carried on in Germany by this means. The chief aim of our correspondence, however, will be to put the German socialists in touch with the French and English socialists; to keep foreigners constantly informed of the socialist movements that occur in Germany and to inform the Germans in Germany of the progress of socialism in France and England. In this way differences of opinion can be brought to light and an exchange of ideas and impartial criticism can take place. It will be a step made by the social movement in its *literary* manifestation to rid itself of the barriers of *nationality*. And when the moment for action comes, it will clearly be much to everyone's advantage to be acquainted with the state of affairs abroad as well as at home.

Our correspondence will embrace not only the communists in Germany, but also the German socialists in Paris and London. Our relations with England have already been established. So far as France is concerned, we all of us believe that we could find no better correspondent than yourself. As you know, the English and Germans have hitherto estimated you more highly than have your own compatriots.

So it is, you see, simply a question of establishing a regular correspondence and ensuring that it has the means to keep abreast of the social movement in the different countries, and to acquire a rich and varied interest, such as could never be achieved by the work of one single person. . . .

Yours most sincerely

Karl Marx

the nation designated the aristocracy, or those who shared noble birthright. The French nobility also referred to itself as a nation. Those earlier and unfamiliar usages are important. They highlight the most significant development of the late eighteenth and early nineteenth centuries: the French Revolution redefined *nation* to mean "the sovereign people." The revolutionaries of 1789 boldly claimed that the nation, and no longer the king, was the sovereign power. *Vive la nation*, or "long live the nation"— a phrase found everywhere, from government decrees to revolutionary festivals, engravings, and memorabilia— celebrated a new political community, not a territory or

Lyon, 17 May 1846

My dear Monsieur Marx,

I am happy to become a recipient of your correspondence, whose goal and organization seem to me to be very useful. I cannot promise to write you at length or often, however, as my many occupations and my natural laziness will not permit such epistolary efforts. I would also like to take the liberty of expressing several reservations about a few of the passages in your letter.

First, [. . .] I believe that it is my duty, and the duty of all socialists, to maintain for the time being a skeptical or critical perspective, in a word, I claim [in matters of economics] an almost absolute anti-dogmatism.

Let us search together, if you wish, the laws of society, and the ways that these laws make themselves felt, and the process of development that allows us to discover them; but by God, after having demolished all the *a priori* dogmatisms, let us not dream of then indoctrinating the people ourselves, do not fall into the same contradiction faced by your compatriot Martin Luther, who after having overthrown Catholic theology, set about at once excommunicating others, in order to found a Protestant theology. [. . .] I applaud with all my heart your idea of bringing forth all possible opinions; let us therefore pursue a good and loyal argument; let us offer the world an example of a wise and perceptive toleration, but we should not, simply because we are the leaders of a movement, seek to pose as the apostles of a new religion, even if this religion is that of logic, of reason. Under these terms, I am happy to join your association, but if not—then No!

I would also like to comment on these words in your letter: *At the moment of action.* You may still think that no reform is possible at present without a bold stroke, without what was formerly called a revolution [. . .] Having myself held this opinion for a long time, I confess now that my more recent works have made me revisit this idea completely. I believe that we do not need [a revolution] to succeed, because this alleged solution would simply be an appeal to force, to something arbitrary, in short, a contradiction. I see the problem like this: *to find a form of economic combination that would restore to society the wealth that has been taken from it by another form of economic combination.* In other words, [. . .] to turn Property against Property, in such a way as to establish what you German socialists call *community*, and which I limit myself to calling *liberty, equality.* [. . .] I prefer to burn Property with a slow fuse, rather than to give it new energy by massacring the property owners.

Your very devoted
Pierre-Joseph Proudhon

Source: Karl Marx, Frederick Engels, *Collected Works*, vol. 38 (New York: International Publishers, 1982), pp. 38–40. P.-J. Proudhon, Amédée Jérôme, *Correspondance de P.-J. Proudhon* (Paris: A. Lacroix, 1875), pp. 198–200.

Questions for Analysis

1. What is the purpose of the network of correspondents that Marx was inviting Proudhon to join, and why did he believe it necessary to overcome "the barriers of nationality"?

2. Why does Proudhon compare Marx's analysis of "scientific questions" or "the laws of society" to religious dogmas?

3. Why does Proudhon reject Marx's assumption that a revolution is necessary, and what alternative does he propose?

---

an ethnicity. Philosophically, the French revolutionaries and the others who developed their views took from Jean-Jacques Rousseau the argument that a regenerated nation, based on the equality of its members (or on the limits of that equality; see Chapter 18), was not only more just but also more powerful. On a more concrete level, the revolutionaries built a national state, a national army, and a national legal system whose jurisdiction trumped the older regional powers of the nobility and local courts. In the aftermath of the French Revolution of 1789, the nation became what one historian calls "the collective image of modern citizenry."

Legend:
- Slavic
- Hellenic
- Germanic
- Celtic
- Baltic
- Latin
- Other
- 1848 boundaries

0   250   500 Miles
0   250   500 Kilometers

MAJOR EUROPEAN LANGUAGE GROUPS, c. 1850. Compare the distribution of language groups in Europe with the political boundaries of European nations in 1848. ▪ *Do they line up?* ▪ *Which political units were forced to deal with a multitude of languages within their borders?* ▪ *How might this distribution of language groups be related to the history of European nationalisms?*

In the early nineteenth century, then, *nation* symbolized legal equality, constitutional government, and unity, or an end to feudal privileges and divisions. Conservatives disliked the term. National unity and the creation of national political institutions threatened to erode the local power of aristocratic elites. New nations rested on constitutions, which, as we have seen, conservatives considered dangerous abstractions. Nationalism became an important rallying cry for liberals across Europe in the early nineteenth century precisely because it was associated with political transformation. It celebrated the achievements and political awakening of the common people.

Nationalism also went hand in hand with liberal demands for economic modernity. Economists, such as the influential German Friedrich List (1789–1846), sought to develop national economies and national infrastructures:

larger, stronger, better integrated, and more effective systems of banking, trade, transportation, production, and distribution. List linked ending the territorial fragmentation of the German states and the development of manufacturing to "culture, prosperity, and liberty."

Nationalism, however, could easily undermine other liberal values. When liberals insisted on the value and importance of individual liberties, those committed to building nations replied that their vital task might require the sacrifice of some measure of each citizen's freedom. The Napoleonic army, a particularly powerful symbol of nationhood, appealed to conservative proponents of military strength and authority as well as to liberals who wanted an army of citizens.

Nineteenth-century nationalists wrote as if national feeling were natural, inscribed in the movement of history. They waxed poetic about the sudden awakening of feelings slumbering within the collective consciousness of a "German," an "Italian," a "French," or a "British" people. This is misleading. National identity (like religious, gender, or ethnic identities) developed and changed historically. It rested on specific nineteenth-century political and economic developments; on rising literacy; on the creation of national institutions such as schools or the military; and on the new importance of national rituals, from voting to holidays, village festivals, and the singing of anthems. Nineteenth-century governments sought to develop national feeling, to link their peoples more closely to their states. State-supported educational systems taught a "national" language, fighting the centrifugal forces of traditional dialects. Italian became the official language of the Italian nation, despite the fact that only 2.5 percent of the population spoke it. In other words, even a minority could define a national culture. Textbooks and self-consciously nationalist theater, poetry, and painting helped elaborate and sometimes "invent" a national heritage.

Political leaders associated the nation with specific causes. But ordinary activities, such as reading a daily newspaper in the morning, helped people imagine and identify with their fellow citizens. As one influential historian puts it, "All communities larger than primordial villages of face-to-face contact (and perhaps even these) are imagined." The nation is imagined as "limited," "sovereign," and "finally, it is imagined as a community, because regardless of the actual inequality and exploitation that may prevail . . . , the nation is always conceived as a deep, horizontal comradeship." The different meanings of *nationhood*, the various political beliefs it evoked, and the powerful emotions it tapped made nationalism exceptionally unpredictable.

Eventually, conservatives, liberals, and republicans all implicitly recognized the power of nationalism by attempting to describe a vision of the nation that was compatible with their core principles. Conservatives linked dynastic ruling families and aristocratic elites to "national" traditions embodied in the history of territorially rooted peasant cultures and their traditional rulers. Liberals and republicans praised the nation as a body of free citizens. Marxist socialists, on the other hand, rejected the claims of nationalists, saying that the interest of social classes trumped national identity. The resolutely internationalist message of *The Communist Manifesto* was embodied in its concluding motto: "Workers of the world unite!"

Conservatism, liberalism, republicanism, socialism, and nationalism were the principal political ideologies of the early nineteenth century. They were rooted in the eighteenth century but brought to the forefront by the political turmoil of the early nineteenth century. Some nineteenth-century ideologies were continuations of the French revolutionary trio: liberty (from arbitrary authority), equality (or the end of legal privilege), and fraternity (the creation of new communities of citizens). Others, like conservatism, were reactions against the French Revolution. All could be reinterpreted. All became increasingly common points of reference as the century unfolded.

CULTURAL REVOLT: ROMANTICISM

Romanticism, the most significant cultural movement in the early nineteenth century, touched all the arts and permeated politics as well. It marked a reaction against the Classicism of the eighteenth century and the Enlightenment. Whereas Classicism aspired to reason, discipline, and harmony, Romanticism stressed emotion, freedom, and imagination. Romantic artists prized intense individual experiences and considered intuition and emotion to be better guides to truth and human happiness than reason and logic.

British Romantic Poetry

Romanticism developed first in England and Germany as a reaction against the Enlightenment. Early Romantics developed ideas originating from some of the Enlightenment's dissenters, such as Jean-Jacques Rousseau (see Chapter 17). The poet William Wordsworth (1770–1834) took up Rousseau's central themes—nature, simplicity, and feeling—in his *Lyrical Ballads* (1798). For Wordsworth, poetry was "the spontaneous overflow of powerful feelings," and like Rousseau, he also emphasized the ties of compassion that bind all humankind, regardless of social class. "We have all of us one human heart," he wrote, "men who do not wear fine cloths can feel deeply." Wordsworth considered nature to be humanity's most trustworthy teacher and the source of true feeling. His poems were inspired by the wild hills and tumbledown cottages of England's Lake District. In "The Ruined Cottage," he quoted from the Scottish Romantic poet Robert Burns:

> Give me a spark of Nature's fire,
> 'Tis the best learning I desire . . .
> My muse, though homely in attire,
> May touch the heart.

Wordsworth's poetry, along with that of his colleague Samuel Taylor Coleridge (1772–1834), offered a key theme of nineteenth-century Romanticism: a view of nature that rejected the abstract mechanism of eighteenth-century Enlightenment thought. Nature was not a system to be dissected by science but the source of a sublime power that nourished the human soul.

The poet William Blake (1757–1827) sounded similar themes in his fierce critique of industrial society and the factories (which he called "dark satanic mills") that blighted the English landscape. Blake championed the individual imagination and poetic vision, seeing both as transcending the limits of the material world. Imagination could awaken human sensibilities and sustain belief in different values, breaking humanity's "mind-forged manacles." Blake's poetry paralleled early socialist efforts to imagine a better world. And like many Romantics, Blake looked back to a past in which he thought society had been more organic and humane.

English Romanticism peaked with the next generation of poets—Lord Byron (1788–1824); Percy Bysshe Shelley (1792–1822); and John Keats (1795–1821). Their lives and loves often appealed to readers as much as their writings. Byron was an aristocrat, rich, handsome, and defiant of convention. Poetry, he wrote, was the "lava of the imagination, whose eruption prevents an earthquake." His love affairs helped give Romantics their reputation as rebels against conformity, but they were hardly carefree. Byron treated his wife cruelly and drove her away after a year. Byron also rebelled against Britain's political leaders, labeling them corrupt and repressive. A Romantic hero, he defended working-class movements and fought in the war for Greek independence, during which he died of tuberculosis. Byron's friend Percy Shelley emphasized similar themes of individual audacity in his poem, *Prometheus*

***NEWTON* BY WILLIAM BLAKE, 1795.** Blake was also a brilliant graphic artist. Here, he depicts Sir Isaac Newton shrouded in darkness, distracted by his scientific calculations from the higher sphere of the imagination. Blake's image is a Romantic critique of Enlightenment science, for which Newton had become a hero.

Unbound (1820). Prometheus defied an all-powerful god, Zeus, by stealing fire for humanity and was punished by being chained to a rock while an eagle tore out his heart. The poem celebrated the title character as a selfless mythic hero, comparable to Christ in his willingness to sacrifice himself for others. Shelley himself in his correspondence described the play as a parable about revolutionary change, and the need to overthrow tyranny in the name of a new political ideal of struggle and hope, a sentiment captured in the play's closing lines:

> To suffer woes which Hope thinks infinite;
> To forgive wrongs darker than Death or Night;
> To defy Power, which seems omnipotent;
> To love, and bear; to hope till Hope creates
> From its own wreck the thing it contemplates;
> Neither to change nor falter nor repent
> This, like thy glory, Titan! is to be
> Good, great, and joyous, beautiful and free;
> This is alone Life, Joy, Empire, and Victory.

Women Writers, Gender, and Romanticism

No romantic work was more popular than Mary Shelley's *Frankenstein* (1818). Shelley was the daughter of radical celebrities—the philosopher William Godwin and the feminist Mary Wollstonecraft (see Chapter 17), who died as her daughter was born. Mary Godwin met Percy Shelley when she was sixteen, had three children by him before they were married, and published *Frankenstein* at twenty. The novel captured the Romantic critique of science and Enlightenment reason and tells the story of an eccentric doctor determined to find the secret of human life. Conducting his research on corpses and body parts retrieved from charnel houses, Dr. Frankenstein produced life in the form of a monster. The monster had human feelings but was overwhelmed by loneliness and self-hatred when his creator cast him out. Shelley told the story as a twisted creation myth, a study of individual genius gone wrong. The novel remains one of the most memorable characterizations in literature of the limits of reason and the impossibility of controlling nature.

The Romantic's belief in individuality and creativity led in several directions. It became a cult of artistic genius—of the "inexplicably and uniquely creative individual" who could see things others could not. It also led people to seek out experiences that would elicit intense emotions and spark their imagination and creativity, ranging from foreign travel to using opium. The Romantic style encouraged the daring to defy convention as did Lord Byron, the Shelleys, and the French writer George Sand (1804–1876). Sand, like Byron, cultivated a persona—in her case, by living as a woman writer, taking lovers at her pleasure, and wearing men's clothing.

Women played an important role in Romantic writing, and Romanticism stimulated new thinking about gender and creativity. It was common at the time to assert that men were rational and women emotional or intuitive. Many Romantics, like their contemporaries, accepted such gender differences as natural, and some exalted the superior moral virtues of women. Since Romanticism placed such value on the emotions as an essential part of artistic creation, however, some female writers or painters were able to use these ideas to claim a place for themselves in the world of letters

MARY SHELLEY'S *FRANKENSTEIN*. Perhaps the best-known work of Romantic fiction, *Frankenstein* joined the Romantic critique of Enlightenment reason with early-nineteenth-century ambivalence about science to create a striking horror story. Shelley (pictured at left, around the time she published *Frankenstein*) was the daughter of the philosopher William Godwin and the feminist Mary Wollstonecraft; she married the poet Percy Shelley. On the right is an engraving from the first illustrated edition (1831) by Theodore von Holst.

MARY SHELLEY AT NINETEEN

and the arts. Germaine de Staël (1766–1817), for example, emigrated from revolutionary France to Germany and played a key part in popularizing German Romanticism in France. The language of Romanticism allowed Madame de Staël to describe herself as a genius, by way of explaining her own subversion of social norms. Romantics such as Madame de Staël suggested that men too could be emotional and that feelings were a part of a common human nature shared by both sexes. For many literate middle-class people, the language of Romanticism gave them a way to express their own search for individual expression and feeling in writing—and in thinking—about love. In this way, Romanticism reached well beyond small circles of artists and writers into the everyday writing and thoughts of European men and women.

Romantic Painting

Painters carried the Romantic themes of nature and imagination onto their canvases (see **Interpreting Visual Evidence** on pages 682–83). In Great Britain, John Constable (1776–1837) and J. M. W. Turner (1775–1851) developed more emotional and poetic approaches to depicting nature. "It is the soul that sees," wrote Constable, echoing Wordsworth. Constable studied Isaac Newton and the properties of light but aimed to capture the "poetry" of a rainbow. Turner's intensely subjective paintings were even more unconventional. His experiments with brushstroke and color produced remarkable images. Critics assailed the paintings, calling them incomprehensible, but Turner merely responded, "I did not paint it to be understood." In France, Théodore Géricault (1791–1824) and Eugène Delacroix (1799–1863) produced very different paintings from Turner's, but like the English painter they too were preoccupied by subjectivity and the creative process. The poet Charles Baudelaire credited Delacroix with showing him new ways to see: "The whole visible universe is but a storehouse of images and signs. . . . All the faculties of the human soul must be subordinated to the imagination." These Romantic experiments prepared the way for the later development of modernism in the arts.

Romantic Politics:
Liberty, History, and Nation

Victor Hugo (1802–1885) wrote that "Romanticism is only . . . liberalism in literature." Hugo's plays, poetry, and historical novels focused sympathetically on the experience of common people, especially *Notre Dame de Paris* (1831)

and *Les Misérables* (1862). Delacroix's painting *Liberty Leading the People* gave a revolutionary face to Romanticism, as did Shelley's and Byron's poetry. In works such as these, political life was no longer the preserve of social elites, and the commoners in the street could embrace new freedoms with a violent passion that would have surprised the *philosophes,* with their emphasis on reasoned debate.

Yet Romantics could also be ardently conservative. French conservative François Chateaubriand's *Genius of Christianity* (1802) emphasized the primacy of religious emotions and feeling in his claim that religion was woven into the national past and could not be ignored without threatening the culture as a whole. The period, in fact, witnessed a broad and popular religious revival and a renewed interest in medieval literature, art, and architecture, all of which drew heavily on religious themes.

Early nineteenth-century nationalism took the Romantic emphasis on individuality and turned it into a faith in the uniqueness of individual cultures. Johann von Herder, among the most influential of nationalist thinkers, argued that civilization sprang from the culture of the common people, not from a learned or cultivated elite, as the *philosophes* had argued in the Enlightenment. Herder extolled the special creative genius of the German people, the *Volk,* and insisted that each nation must be true to its own particular heritage and history.

The Romantic's keen interest in history and the lives of ordinary people led to new kinds of literary and historical works. The brothers Grimm, editors of the famous collection of fairy tales (1812–1815), traveled across Germany to study native dialects and folktales. The poet Friedrich Schiller retold the story of William Tell (1804) to promote German national consciousness, but the Italian composer Gioacchino Rossini turned Schiller's poem into an opera that promoted Italian nationalism. In Britain, Sir Walter Scott retold the popular history of Scotland and the Pole Adam Mickiewicz wrote a national epic *Pan Tadeusz* ("Lord Thaddeus") as a vision of a Polish past that had been lost. After 1848, these nationalist enthusiasms would overwhelm the political debates that divided conservatives from liberals and socialists in the first half of the nineteenth century (see Chapter 21).

Orientalism

This passion for theories and histories of distinctive cultures also created broad interest in what contemporary Europeans called the "Orient"—a catch-all term used rather indiscriminately and confusedly to refer to the non-European cultures of North Africa, the eastern Mediterranean, the

Arabian Peninsula, and eventually to the vast and densely populated lands of southern and eastern Asia. Napoleon wrote, "This Europe of ours is a molehill. Only in the East, where 600 million human beings live, is it possible to found great empires and realize great revolutions." The dozens of scholars who accompanied Napoleon on his invasion of Egypt in 1798 collected information on Egyptian history and culture. Among the artifacts the French took from Egypt was the Rosetta Stone, with versions of the same text in three different languages: hieroglyphic writing (pictorial script), demotic (an early alphabetic writing), and Greek, which scholars used to decode and translate the first two. The twenty-three volume, lavishly illustrated *Description of Egypt*, published in French between 1809 and 1828, was a major event, heightening the soaring interest in Eastern languages and history. "We are now all orientalists," wrote Victor Hugo in 1829. The political echoes to this cultural fascination with the East could be seen in great power rivalries that surfaced in the British incursion into India, in the Greek war for independence, and in the French invasion of Algeria in 1830.

Nineteenth-century Europeans cast the "Orient" as a contrasting mirror for their own civilization, a process that did more to create a sense of their own identity as Europeans than it did to promote an accurate understanding of the diversity of cultures that lay beyond Europe's uncertain eastern and southern frontiers. During the Greek war for independence, Europeans identified with Greek heritage against Oriental despotism. Romantic painters such as Delacroix depicted the landscapes of the East in bold and sensuous colors and emphasized the sensuality, mystery, and irrationality of Eastern peoples. The fascination with medieval history and religion shared by many Romantic writers also bred interest in the medieval crusades in the Holy Lands of the Middle East—important subjects for Romantics such as Scott and Chateaubriand. These habits of mind, encouraged by Romantic literature and art, helped to crystallize a sense of what were felt to be essential differences between the East and the West.

Goethe and Beethoven

Two important artists of the period are especially difficult to classify. Johann Wolfgang von Goethe (1749–1832) had an enormous influence on the Romantic movement with his early novel *The Passions of Young Werther* (1774), which told the story of a young man's failure in love and eventual suicide. The novel brought international fame to its young author, though many who sympathized with the main character perhaps missed the point about the self-destructiveness of

WOMEN OF ALGIERS BY EUGÈNE DELACROIX. This is one of many paintings done during Delacroix's trips through North Africa and a good example of the Romantics' Orientalism.

the "cult of feeling." Rumors spread that some in his audience identified so strongly with Werther's alienation that they killed themselves in imitation. Though scholars now doubt that such suicides occurred, the rumor itself indicates the fascination that Goethe's emotionally complex character exerted over the reading public. The significance of the novel lay in Goethe's ability to capture in prose the longing that many middle-class readers felt for something more meaningful than a life lived in strict conformity with social expectations. It also revealed that a new sense of self and aspirations for self-fulfillment might be emerging in Europe alongside the narrower definitions of individualism that one might find in liberal political or economic theory. In his masterpiece, *Faust*, published in part in 1790 and finished just before his death in 1832, Goethe retold the German story of a man who sold his soul to the devil for eternal youth and universal knowledge. *Faust*, written in dramatic verse, was more Classical in its tone, though it still expressed a Romantic concern with spiritual freedom and humanity's daring in probing life's divine mysteries.

The composer Ludwig van Beethoven (1770–1827) was steeped in the principles of Classical music composition, but his insistence that instrumental music without vocal

Romantic Painting

Romantic painters shared with Romantic poets a fascination with the power of nature. To convey this vision of nature as both an overwhelming power and source of creative energy, Romantic painters created new and poetic visions of the natural world, where human beings and their activities were reduced in significance, sometimes nearly disappearing altogether. At times, these visions also were linked to a backward-looking perspective, as if the dramatic changes associated with industrialization provoked a longing for a premodern past, where Europeans sought and found their sense of place in the world from an awareness of a quasi-divine natural setting invested with powerful mysteries. John Martin's *The Bard* (image A) shows a highly romanticized vision of a medieval subject: a single Welsh bard strides across rocky peaks above a mountain river, after escaping a massacre ordered by the English king Edward I. Across the river, Edward's troops can barely be seen leaving the scene of the crime, which still glows with destructive fires. The emotional qualities of this early expression of Romantic nationalism are reinforced by the forbidding and dynamic sky above, where the clouds merge into the Welsh mountaintops as if they were stirred by the hand of God himself.

Other Romantic painters minimized the significance of human activity in their landscapes, though without reference to history. John Constable's *Weymouth Bay* (image B) contains a tiny, almost imperceptible human figure in the middle ground, a man walking on the beach, near a thin stone wall that snakes up a hill in the background. These passing references to human lives are completely dominated, however, by Constable's sky and the movement of the clouds in particular, which seem to be the real subject of the painting.

Of all the Romantic painters, J. M. W. Turner (image C) may have tackled the tricky subject of the new industrialized landscape in the most novel way. His painting *Rain, Steam, Speed–The Great Western Railway* (1844) boldly places the most modern technology of the period,

A. John Martin, *The Bard*, 1817.

B. John Constable, *Weymouth Bay*, 1816.

C. J. M. W. Turner, *Rain, Steam, Speed—The Great Western Railway*, 1844.

the steam train on an arched bridge, into a glowing and radiant painting where both nature's forces and the tremendous new power unleashed by human activity seem to merge into one continuous burst of energy. To the left of the train, on the river's edge, a fire of indeterminate but evidently industrial origin burns, illuminating several small but ecstatic figures with its light. Most enigmatic of all, a tiny rabbit sprints ahead of the train between the rails (unfortunately invisible in this reproduction), highlighting the painting's complex message about nature and human creation. Are they heading in the same direction? Will one overtake the other and destroy it in the process?

Questions for Analysis

1. In Martin's *Bard*, what vision of the individual emerges from this painting, and how is it different from the rational, rights-bearing individual that political liberalism sought to protect?

2. Is Constable's painting concerned with nature as a source of nourishment for humans, or is it presented as a value in itself?

3. How is one to interpret Turner's explicit connection between the power of nature and the new force of industrial societies? Is he suggesting that contemplating the industrial landscape can be just as moving to a human observer as is the sight of nature's magnificence?

accompaniment could be more expressive of emotion made him a key figure for later Romantic composers. The glorification of nature and Romantic individuality rang clearly throughout his work. Like many of his contemporaries, Beethoven was enthusiastic about the French Revolution in 1789, but he became disillusioned with Napoleon. At the age of thirty-two he began to lose his hearing, and by 1819 he was completely deaf—the intensely personal crisis that this catastrophe produced in the young musician drove him to retreat into the interior of his own musical imagination, and the compositions of his later life expressed both his powerfully felt alienation as well as his extraordinary and heroic creativity in the face of enormous hardship.

Beethoven and Goethe marked the transition between eighteenth-century artistic movements that prized order and harmony to the turbulent and disruptive emotions of the nineteenth-century artists and writers. Their work embraced the cult of individual heroism, sympathized with the Romantic's quasi-mystical view of nature, and represented different aspects of a shared search for new ways of seeing and hearing. The many shapes of Romanticism make a simple definition of the movement elusive, but at the core, the Romantics sought to find a new way of expressing emotion, and in doing so, they sent nineteenth-century art in a new direction.

CONCLUSION

With the fizzling of the Chartist movement, the British monarchy avoided an outbreak of revolution in 1848. Monarchs on the Continent were not so lucky. As we will see in the next chapter, a wave of revolutionary activity unprecedented since the 1790s spread to nearly every capital in Europe in 1848. This resurgence of rebellion and revolt pointed to the powerful ways that the French Revolution of 1789 polarized Europe in the first half of the nineteenth century. In its aftermath, the Congress of Vienna aimed to establish a new conservative, international system and to prevent further revolutions. It succeeded in the first aim but only partially in the second. A combination of new political movements and economic hardship undermined the conservative order. Social grievances and political disappointments created powerful movements for change, first in Latin America and the Balkans and then in western Europe and Great Britain.

All of the contesting ideologies of these postrevolutionary decades could point to a longer history: conservatives could point to traditional religious justifications for royal authority and the absolutist's conception of indivisible monarchical power; liberals could point to the debates

After You Read
This Chapter

Ⓢ Visit StudySpace for quizzes, additional review materials, and multimedia documents. **wwnorton.com/web/westernciv18**

REVIEWING THE OBJECTIVES

- The European leaders who met at the Congress of Vienna possessed a conservative vision for post–Napoleonic Europe. What were their goals and what challenges did their political system face between 1815 and 1848?

- Slavery persisted long after the French Revolution. What accounts for the development of an abolition movement, and why did it persist in the United States, Latin America, and Cuba?

- Conservatives, liberals, and republicans differed from one another about the lessons to be learned from the French Revolution, while socialists sought to address the inequalities produced by the Industrial Revolution. What were the core principles of conservatism, liberalism, republicanism, and socialism?

- Nationalism reshaped the political landscape in Europe between 1815 and 1848. How did conservatives, liberals, republicans, and socialists view the claims of nationalists?

- Romanticism was a cultural movement defined in opposition to the Enlightenment. Who were the Romantics and what did they believe?

about the rule of law in the English revolution of the seventeenth century; even socialists could point to age-old collective traditions among rural communities as precedents for their defense of communal property and egalitarianism. Nevertheless, all of these ideologies were shaped and brought into clearer focus during these decades by the combined effects of the French Revolution and industrialization. Conservatives may have differed among themselves as to why they preferred a government of monarchs and landed aristocrats, but they were united by their horror of revolutionary violence and dismayed by the social disruptions that attended industrialization. Liberals may have disagreed with each other about who qualified for citizenship, but they defended the revolutionary's insistence that the only legitimate government was one whose institutions and laws reflected the consent of at least some, if not all, of the governed. Many socialists, Marx included, celebrated the insurrectionary tradition of the French revolutionaries, even as they demanded a reordering of society that went far beyond the granting of new political rights to include a redistribution of society's wealth. Meanwhile, nationalists throughout Europe remained inspired by the collective achievements of the French nation that was forged in revolution in the 1790s.

The reemergence of social and political conflict in 1848 pit the defenders of these ideologies against one another under the most dramatic of circumstances, making the revolutions of 1848 the opening act of a much larger drama. In France, as in 1792 and 1830, revolutionaries rallied around an expanded notion of representative government and the question of suffrage, though they were divided on how much responsibility their new government had for remedying social problems. In southern and central Europe, as we will see in the next chapter, the issues were framed differently, around new struggles for national identity. The eventual failure of these revolutions set a pattern that was also observed elsewhere: exhilarating revolutionary successes were followed by a breakdown of revolutionary unity and the emergence of new forms of conservative government. The crisis of 1848 became a turning point for all of Europe. The broad revolutionary alliances that had pushed for revolutionary change since 1789 were broken apart by class politics, and earlier forms of utopian socialism gave way to Marxism. In culture as in politics, Romanticism lost its appeal, its expansive sense of possibility replaced by the more biting viewpoint of realism. No nationalist, conservative, liberal, or socialist was exempt from this bitter truth after the violent conflicts of 1848.

PEOPLE, IDEAS, AND EVENTS IN CONTEXT

- Who was **KLEMENS VON METTERNICH** and what was the **CONCERT OF EUROPE**?

- How did the **CARBONARI** in Italy, the **DECEMBRISTS** in Russia, and **GREEK NATIONALISTS** in the Balkans in the 1820s disturb the conservative order in Europe after Napoleon's defeat?

- Where did revolutions occur in 1830–1832, and what was their outcome?

- What political changes did movements such as the **CHARTISTS** or the **ANTI-CORN LAW LEAGUE** accomplish in Britain? Why was there no revolution in Britain?

- What beliefs made **EDMUND BURKE** a conservative?

- What beliefs made **ADAM SMITH** and **JEREMY BENTHAM** liberals? What was **UTILITARIANISM**?

- What beliefs did **UTOPIAN SOCIALISTS** such as **ROBERT OWEN** and **CHARLES FOURIER** share? What made **KARL MARX**'s brand of socialism different from his predecessors'?

- How did the values of **ROMANTICISM** challenge Europeans to reconsider their assumptions about the differences between men and women?

- What beliefs led romantic writers such as **WILLIAM WORDSWORTH, WILLIAM BLAKE**, and **LORD BYRON** to reject the rationalism of the Enlightenment and embrace emotion and imagination as the most essential and vital aspects of human experience?

THINKING ABOUT CONNECTIONS

- What new ideas about historical change made it possible to think in terms of a political conflict between "conservatives" and "revolutionaries" during the decades immediately before and after 1800? Would such an opposition have been conceivable in earlier periods of history?

- Terms such as *conservative, liberal*, and *socialist* are still used today in contemporary political debates. Do they still mean the same thing as they did between 1815 and 1848?

that Karl Marx and Friedrich Engels published *The Communist Manifesto*, which announced as its goal an even more sweeping remaking of society than that imagined by the French revolutionaries of 1789. If 1848 was the last wave of the revolutionary movements that began in Europe and the Atlantic world at the end of the eighteenth century, it was also the first chapter in a new revolutionary movement that would have enormous consequences in the twentieth century.

Revolutionary regime change, territorial expansion, economic development, and debates about who deserved citizenship: all of these were issues in 1848, and all were related to the spread of nationalism and nation building in Europe and the Americas. As we saw in the last chapter, the term *nation* had taken on a new meaning at the end of the eighteenth century and had come to mean "a sovereign people." *Nationalism* was a related political ideal, based on the assumption that governments could be legitimate only if they reflected the character, history, and customs of the nation—that is, the common people. This idea undermined the assumptions of Europe's dynastic rulers, as hereditary monarchs had emphasized the differences between themselves and the people they ruled. Kings and aristocrats often did not even speak the same language as their subjects. Nobody would have thought this odd before 1789, since peasants often spoke regional dialects that were different from the language spoken in cities. But once the notion of national sovereignty emanating from the people became widespread, such discrepancies between the language and culture of elites and of the common people loomed larger as political questions that needed to be solved. Intellectuals, revolutionaries, and governments all propagated the radical new idea that nations of like peoples and the states that ruled over them should be congruent with one another. This simple idea lay at the heart of all forms of nationalism, but there was often bitter debate about who best represented the nation and what the goals of a unified nationalist government should be.

Between 1789 and 1848, Europeans commonly associated nationalism with liberalism. Liberals saw constitutions, the rule of law, and elected assemblies as necessary expressions of the people's will, and they sought to use popular enthusiasm for liberal forms of nationalism against the conservative monarchs of Europe. The upheavals of 1848 marked the high point of this period of liberal revolution, and their failure marked the end of that age. By the end of the nineteenth century, conservative governments also found ways to mobilize popular support by invoking nationalist themes. The only political movement to swim against the tide of nationalism was that of the socialists, who stressed the importance of class unity across national boundaries: Marx and his followers believed that German, French, and British workers had more in common with each other than with their middle-class employers. Even so, however, socialist movements in Europe developed in distinctly different nationalist political contexts, making traditions of French socialism different from German socialism, or from Italian socialism, for example.

The years following the 1848 revolutions witnessed a shift in the connections between liberalism, nationalism, and nation building. In the United States, territorial changes such as the treaty of Guadalupe Hidalgo transformed the boundaries of nations; equally significant was the American Civil War, which resulted in wrenching political change. The unification of Germany and Italy in the years after 1848 also involved the conquest of territory, but the process could not have been completed without political reforms and new state structures that changed how governments worked and how they related to their citizens. The governments of France, Britain, Russia, and Austria undertook vast projects of administrative reform during this period: they overhauled their bureaucracies, expanded their electorates, and reorganized relations among ethnic groups. The Russian tsar abolished serfdom, and Abraham Lincoln, an American president, abolished slavery, decades after the French and British had prohibited slavery in their territories.

As the process of nation building continued, the balance of power in Europe shifted toward the states that were the earliest to industrialize and most successful in building strong, centralized states. Older imperial powers such as the Habsburg Empire in Austria-Hungary or the Ottoman Empire found their influence waning, in spite of their long history of successful rule over vast territories with diverse populations. At the heart of this nineteenth-century period of nation building lay changing relations between states and those they governed, and these changes were hastened by reactions to the revolutionary upheavals of 1848.

THE REVOLUTIONS OF 1848

Throughout Europe, the spring of 1848 brought a dizzying sequence of revolution and repression. The roots of revolution lay in economic crisis, social antagonisms, and political grievances. But these revolutions were also shaped decisively by nationalism, especially in southern, central, and eastern Europe. To be sure, reformers and revolutionaries had liberal goals: representative government, an end to privilege, economic development, and so on. They also sought some form of national unity. Indeed, reformers in Germany, Italy, Poland, and the Austrian Empire believed that their liberal goals might be realized only in a vigorous, "modern" nation-state. The fate of the 1848 revolutions in these regions demonstrated nationalism's power to mobilize opponents of the regime and also its potential to splinter revolutionary alliances and to override other allegiances and values entirely.

The Hungry Forties

A deteriorating economic climate in Europe was an important contributing factor to the outbreak of revolution in 1848, one that helps to explain why revolutions occurred in so many places nearly simultaneously. Poor harvests in the early 1840s were followed by two years in 1845–46 when the grain harvest failed completely. A potato blight brought starvation in Ireland and hunger in Germany (see **Competing Viewpoints** on pages 690–91). Food prices doubled in 1846–47, and bread riots broke out across Europe. Villagers attacked carts carrying grain, refusing to let merchants take it to other markets. At times, hungry people seized the grain and forced the merchants to sell it at what they thought was a "just" price. Compounding the problem was a cyclical industrial slowdown that spread across Europe, throwing thousands into unemployment. Starving peasants and unemployed laborers swamped public-relief organizations in many European cities. The years 1846 and 1847 were "probably the worst of the entire century in terms of want and human suffering," and the decade has earned the name the "Hungry Forties."

GERMAN CONFEDERATION, 1815. Compare this map with the one on page 714. ▪ *What major areas were left out of the German Confederation?* ▪ *Why do you think they were left out?* ▪ *What obstacles made it difficult to establish a unified German nation during this period?*

Two Views of the June Days, France, 1848

> These two passages make for an interesting comparison. The socialist Karl Marx reported on the events of 1848 in France as a journalist for a German newspaper. For Marx, the bloodshed of the June Days shattered the "fraternal illusions" of February 1848, when the king had been overthrown and the provisional government established. That bloodshed also symbolized a new stage in history: one of acute class conflict.
>
> The French liberal politician Alexis de Tocqueville also wrote about his impressions of the revolution. (Tocqueville's account, however, is retrospective, for he wrote his memoirs well after 1848.) For Marx, a socialist observer, the June Days represented a turning point: "The working class was knocking on the gates of history." For Tocqueville, a member of the government, the actions of the crowd sparked fear and conservative reaction.

Karl Marx's Journalism

The last official remnant of the February Revolution, the Executive Commission, has melted away, like an apparition, before the seriousness of events. The fireworks of Lamartine [French Romantic poet and member of the provisional government] have turned into the war rockets of Cavaignac [French general, in charge of putting down the workers' insurrection]. *Fraternité,* the fraternity of antagonistic classes of which one exploits the other, this *fraternité,* proclaimed in February, on every prison, on every barracks—its true, unadulterated, its prosaic expression is civil war, civil war in its most fearful form, the war of labor and capital. This fraternity flamed in front of all the windows of Paris on the evening of June 25, when the Paris of the bourgeoisie was illuminated, whilst the Paris of the proletariat [Marxist term for the working people] burnt, bled, moaned.... The February Revolution was the beautiful revolution, the revolution of universal sympathy, because the antagonisms, which had flared up in it against the monarchy, slumbered peacefully side by side, still undeveloped, because the social struggle which formed its background had won only a joyous existence, an existence of phrases, of words. The June revolution is the ugly revolution, the repulsive revolution, because things have taken the place of phrases, because the republic uncovered the head of the monster itself, by striking off the crown that shielded and concealed it.—Order! was the battle cry of Guizot... Order! shouts Cavaignac, the brutal echo of the French National Assembly and of the republican bourgeoisie. Order! thundered his grape-shot, as it ripped up the body of the proletariat. None of the numerous revolutions of the French bourgeoisie since 1789 was an attack on order; for they allowed the rule of

Hunger itself cannot cause revolution. It does, however, test governments' abilities to manage a crisis, and failure can make a ruler seem illegitimate. When public relief foundered in France and troops repressed potato riots in Berlin, when regimes armed middle-class citizens to protect themselves against the poor, governments looked both authoritarian and inept. In the 1840s, European states already faced a host of political challenges: from liberals who sought constitutional government and limits on royal power, from republicans who campaigned for universal manhood suffrage, from nationalists who challenged the legitimacy of their hereditary rulers, and from socialists whose appeal lay in their claim to speak for the most economically vulnerable among the population. These political challenges were reinforced by the economic crisis of the 1840s, and the result was a wave of revolution that swept across Europe as one government after another lost the confidence of its people. The first of these revolutions came in France, and as elsewhere in 1848, it did not have the outcome that revolutionaries had hoped for.

the class, they allowed the slavery of the workers, they allowed the bourgeois order to endure, however often the political form of this rule and of this slavery changed. June has attacked this order. Woe to June!"

Source: *Neue Rheinische Zeitung* (New Rhineland Gazette), June 29, 1848, as cited in Karl Marx, *The Class Struggles in France* (New York: 1964), pp. 57–58.

Alexis de Tocqueville Remembers the June Days (1893)

Now at last I have come to that insurrection in June which was the greatest and the strangest that had ever taken place in our history, or perhaps in that of any other nation: the greatest because for four days more than a hundred thousand men took part in it, and there were five generals killed; the strangest, because the insurgents were fighting without a battle cry, leaders, or flag, and yet they showed wonderful powers of coordination and a military expertise that astonished the most experienced officers.

Another point that distinguished it from all other events of the same type during the last sixty years was that its object was not to change the form of government, but to alter the organiza-tion of society. In truth it was not a polit-ical struggle (in the sense in which we have used the word "political" up to now), but a class struggle, a sort of "Ser-vile War." . . . One should not see it only as a brutal and a blind, but as a powerful effort of the workers to escape from the necessities of their condition, which had been depicted to them as an illegitimate depression, and by the sword to open up a road towards that imaginary well-being that had been shown to them in the distance as a right. It was this mix-ture of greedy desires and false theories that engendered the insurrection and made it so formidable. These poor peo-ple had been assured that the goods of the wealthy were in some way the result of a theft committed against them-selves. They had been assured that

inequalities of fortune were as much opposed to morality and the interests of society as to nature. This obscure and mistaken conception of right, combined with brute force, imparted to it an energy, tenacity and strength it would never have had on its own.

Source: From Alexis de Tocqueville, *Recollec-tions: The French Revolution of 1848*, ed. J. P. Mayer and A. P. Kerr, trans. George Lawrence (New Brunswick, NJ: 1987), pp. 436–37.

Questions for Analysis

1. Was Tocqueville sympathetic to the revolutionaries of June?

2. Did Tocqueville think the events were historically significant?

3. Where did Tocqueville agree and dis-agree with Marx?

The French Revolution of 1848: A Republican Experiment

The French monarchy after the revolution of 1830 (see Chapter 20) seemed little different from its predecessor. King Louis Philippe gathered around him members of the banking and industrial elite. Confronted with demands to enlarge the franchise, the prime minister quipped that everyone was free to acquire enough property to qualify for the vote: "Enrich yourselves!" Building projects, especially the railway, presented ample opportunities for graft, and the reputation of the government suffered. Protest movements, in the form of republican societies, proliferated in French cities. In 1834, the government declared these organizations illegal. Rebellions broke out in Paris and Lyon, bringing a harsh repression that resulted in deaths and arrests. The gov-ernment's refusal to compromise drove even moderates into opposition. In 1847, the opposition organized a campaign for electoral reform around repeated political "banquets"—an attempt to get around the laws against assembly. When they called for a giant banquet on February 22, 1848, the king responded by banning the meeting. A sudden and surprising popular revolution in the streets caused Louis Philippe to abdicate his throne only days later. A hastily assembled group of French political figures declared France a republic, for the first time since 1792.

The provisional government of the new republic consisted of liberals, republicans, and—for the first time— socialists. They produced a new constitution, with elections based on universal male suffrage. Among their first acts was the abolition of slavery in France and French colonies (slavery had been abolished in 1794 during the revolution but reestablished by Napoleon in 1802). In spite of these accomplishments, tensions between propertied republicans and socialists shattered the unity of the coalition that toppled Louis Philippe. Suffering because of the economic crisis, working men and women demanded the "right to work," the right to earn a living wage. The provisional government responded by creating the National Workshops, a program of public works, to give jobs to the unemployed, headed by the socialist Louis Blanc. Initial plans were made to employ 10,000–12,000 workers, but unemployment was so high that 120,000 job-seekers had gathered in the city by June 1848. Meanwhile, voters in rural areas resented the increase in taxation that was required to pay for the public works program.

Popular politics flourished in Paris in 1848. The provisional government lifted restrictions on speech and assembly. One hundred seventy new journals and more than 200 clubs formed within weeks. Delegations claiming to represent the oppressed of Europe—Chartists, Hungarians, Poles—moved freely about the city. Women's clubs and newspapers appeared, demanding universal suffrage and living wages. Many middle-class Parisians were alarmed, and more conservative rural populations also looked for stern measures to restore order. When elections for parliament were held—the first elections ever in France under a regime of universal male suffrage—the conservative voices won out, and a majority of moderate republicans and monarchists were elected.

A majority in the new assembly believed the National Workshops were a financial drain and a threat to order. In May, they closed the workshops to new enrollment, excluded

THE BURNING OF THE THRONE (1848). A contemporary print shows revolutionaries burning the king's throne. Note the man with a top hat standing next to a man in a worker's smock. Delacroix used similar images to depict cooperation between workers and middle-class revolutionaries (see page 661).

recent arrivals to Paris, and sent members between the ages of eighteen and twenty-five into the army. On June 21, they abolished the workshops altogether. In defense of this social program, the workers of Paris—laborers, journeymen, the unemployed—rose in revolt, building barricades across Paris. For four days, June 23–26, they fought a hopeless battle against armed forces recruited from the provinces. The repression of the June Days shocked many observers. About 3,000 were killed and 12,000 arrested. Many of the prisoners were deported to Algerian labor camps. After this repression, support for the republic among the workers in Paris declined rapidly.

In the aftermath, the government moved quickly to restore order. The parliament hoped for a strong leader in the presidential election. Four candidates ran: Alphonse de Lamartine, the moderate republican and poet; General Louis Eugène de Cavaignac, who had perfected the art of urban warfare in the conquest of Algeria and who used these skills in repressing the workers' revolt in Paris; Alexandre Ledru-Rollin, a socialist; and Louis Napoleon Bonaparte, the nephew of the former emperor, who had spent his life in exile. Buoyed by enthusiastic support from rural voters, the upstart Louis Napoleon polled more than twice as many votes as the other three candidates combined.

"All facts and personages of great importance in world history occur twice . . . the first time as tragedy, the second as farce." Karl Marx's judgment on Louis Napoleon's relationship to his famous uncle was shared by many, but his name gave him wide appeal. Conservatives believed

BARRICADE IN THE RUE DE LA MORTELLERIE, JUNE, 1848 BY ERNEST MEISSONIER (1815–1891). A very different view of 1848, a depiction of the June Days.

he would protect property and order. Some on the left had read his book *The Extinction of Pauperism* and noted his correspondence with important socialists. One old peasant put it succinctly, "How could I help voting for this gentleman—I whose nose was frozen at Moscow?"

Louis Napoleon used his position to consolidate his power. He rallied the Catholics by restoring the Church to its former role in education and by sending an expedition to Rome to rescue the pope from revolutionaries (see Chapter 4). He banned radical activities, workers' associations, and suspended press freedoms. In 1851, he called for a plebiscite to give him the authority to change the constitution, and one year later another plebiscite allowed him to establish the Second Empire, ending the Republican experiment. He assumed the title of Napoleon III (r. 1852–70), emperor of the French.

The dynamics of the French Revolution of 1848—initial success, followed by divisions among the supporters of revolution, followed by a reassertion of authoritarian control—would be repeated elsewhere, especially evidenced in the pivotal role of the propertied middle classes. Louis Philippe's reign had been proudly bourgeois but alienated many of its supporters. Key groups in the middle class joined the opposition, allying with radicals who could not topple the regime alone. Yet demands for reform soon led to fears of disorder and the desire for a strong state. This dynamic led to the collapse of the republic and to the rule of Napoleon III. The abandonment of the revolution's social goals—most visibly evident in the National Workshops—led to a stark polarization along class lines, with middle-class and working-class people demanding different things from the state. This political conflict would grow even more intense as socialism came into its own as an independent political force.

Nationalism, Revolution, and the German Question in 1848

The revolutions of 1848 in the German-speaking lands of Europe shared some similarities with the revolutions in France. Like liberals in France, liberal Germans wanted a ruler who would abide by a constitution, allow for greater press freedoms, and accept some form of representative government, though not necessarily universal suffrage. As in France, artisans and urban laborers in German cities gravitated toward more radical ideologies of republicanism and socialism, and protested against new methods of industrial production. More so than in France, German peasants still faced the burden of feudal obligations owed to an entrenched and powerful aristocracy. The great difference between France and Germany in 1848, however, was that France already had a centralized state and a unified territory. In central Europe, a unified Germany did not exist in 1848. In 1815, the Congress of Vienna had created the German Confederation, a loose organization of thirty-nine states, including Habsburg Austria with its Catholic monarchy, and Prussia, ruled by a Protestant king. The German Confederation did not include Prussian and Austrian territories in Poland and Hungary with large non-German populations. This confederation was intended to provide only common defense. It had no real executive power. As a practical matter, Prussia and Austria competed with one another to occupy the dominant position in German politics, and as a result revolutionaries in the German states were forced to reckon with these two powers as they struggled to achieve the national unity that they hoped would allow them to achieve their political goals.

In 1806, Prussia had been defeated by the French under Napoleon. Many Prussians considered the defeat an indictment of the country's inertia since the reign of Frederick the Great (r. 1740–86). Aiming to revive "patriotism and a national honor and independence," they passed a series of aggressive reforms, imposed from above. Prussian

Frederick William IV Refuses the Throne

In March 1849, after months of deliberation and constitution making, the Frankfurt Assembly offered the throne of its proposed German state to the Prussian monarch Frederick William IV, who quickly turned it down. He had already reflected on the matter. In an earlier (December 1848) letter to one of his advisers, the diplomat Christian von Bunsen, he had set out his reasoning as follows.

I want the princes' approval of neither *this* election nor *this* crown. Do you understand the words emphasized here? For you I want to shed light on this as briefly and brightly as possible. First, *this* crown is no crown. The crown which a Hohenzoller [the Prussian royal house] could accept, *if* circumstances *permitted*, is not one *made* by an assembly sprung from a revolutionary seed in the genre of the crown of cobble stones of Louis Philippe—even if this assembly was established with the sanction of princes . . . but one which bears the stamp of God, one which makes [the individual] on whom it [the crown] is placed, after his anointment, a "divine right" monarch—just as it has elevated more than 34 princes to Kings of the Germans by divine right and just as it bonds the last of these to his predecessors. The crown worn by Ottonians, Staufens [earlier German royal houses], Habsburgs can of course also be worn by a Hohenzoller; it honors him overwhelmingly with the luster of a thousand years. But *this* one, to which you regrettably refer, overwhelmingly dishonors [its bearer] with its smell of the gunpowder of the 1848 revolution—the silliest, dumbest, worst, though—thank God!—not the most evil of this century. Such an imaginary headband, baked out of dirt and the letters of the alphabet, is supposed to be welcome to a legitimate divine right king: to put it more precisely, to the King of Prussia who is blessed with a crown which may not be the oldest but, of all those which have never been stolen, is the most noble? . . . I will tell you outright: if the thousand-year-old crown of the German nation . . . should be bestowed again, it will be *I* and my equals who will bestow it. And woe to those who assume [powers] to which they have no title.

Source: Ralph Menning, *The Art of the Possible: Documents on Great Power Diplomacy, 1814–1914* (New York: 1996), p. 82.

Questions for Analysis

1. For Frederick William IV, what was the only legitimate source of a monarch's authority?

2. Why did he call the crown offered to him by the Frankfurt Assembly a "crown of cobble stones . . . with its smell of gunpowder of the 1848 revolution"?

3. Frederick William referred to himself by his family name, Hohenzollern, and to his title, king of Prussia, but he also used the expression "German nation" once in his letter. What relationship did he see among his family, the kingdom of Prussia, and the possibility of a unified German nation?

---

spectacle of disintegration in the Habsburg Empire. This was the "Great German" position. It was countered by a minority who called for a "Small Germany," one that left out all lands of the Habsburg Empire, including German Austria. Great Germans had a majority but were stymied by other nationalities unwilling to be included in their fold. Many Czechs in Bohemia, for instance, wanted no part of Great Germany, believing that they needed the protection of the Habsburg monarchy to avoid being swallowed up by a new German state on one side and the Russian monarchy on the other. After a long and difficult debate, the Austrian emperor withdrew his support, and the assembly retreated to the Small German solution. In April 1849, the Frankfurt Assembly offered the crown of a new German nation to the Prussian king, Frederick William IV.

By this time, however, Frederick William was negotiating from a position of greater strength. Already in the fall of 1848, he had used the military to repress the radical revolutionaries in Berlin while the delegates debated the constitutional question in Frankfurt. He was also encouraged by a backlash against revolutionary movements in Europe after the bloody repression during the June Days

THE FRANKFURT PREPARLIAMENT MEETS AT ST. PAUL'S CHURCH, 1848. This assembly brought together 500 delegates from the various German states to establish a constitution for a new German nation. An armed militia lined the square, and lines of student gymnasts (dressed in white with wide-brimmed hats) escorted the delegates. Their presence was a sign that the organizers of the preparliament feared violence. The black, red, and gold banners were also associated with republicanism. ▪ *What image did the organizers mean to convey with this pageantry, the disciplined lines of students and delegates, their forms of dress, and their use of republican symbols?*

als began to have second thoughts about the pace of change. Peasants ransacked tax offices and burned castles; workers smashed machines in protests against industrialization. In towns and cities, citizen militias formed, threatening the power of established elites. New daily newspapers multiplied. So did political clubs. For the first time, many of these clubs admitted women (although they denied them the right to speak), and newly founded women's clubs demanded political rights. This torrent of popular unrest made moderate reformers uneasy; they considered universal manhood suffrage too radical. While peasant and worker protests had forced the king to make concessions in the early spring of 1848, moderate reformers now found those protests threatening. Throughout the German states, rulers took advantage of this shift in middle-class opinion to undo the concessions that they had granted in 1848 and to push through counterrevolutionary measures in the name of order.

For German liberals, national unification was now seen as necessary to maintain political stability. "In order to realize our ideas of freedom and equality, we want above all a strong and powerful government," claimed one candidate during the election campaigns for the Frankfurt Assembly. Popular sovereignty, he continued, "strengthened by the authority of a hereditary monarchy, will be able to repress with an iron hand any disorder and any violation of the law." In this context, nationhood stood for a new constitution and political community but also for a sternly enforced rule of law. After the failure of the Frankfurt Assembly, therefore, German liberals increasingly looked to a strong Prussian state as the only possible route toward national unification.

in Paris. He therefore refused to become a constitutional monarch on the terms offered by the Frankfurt Assembly. The proposed constitution, he said, was too liberal and receiving his crown from a parliament would be demeaning. The Prussian monarch wanted both the crown and a larger German state, but on his own terms, and he therefore dissolved the assembly before they could approve it with an official vote. After brief protests, summarily suppressed by the military, the Frankfurt delegates went home, disillusioned by their experience and convinced that their liberal and nationalist goals were incompatible. Some fled repression by immigrating to the United States. Others convinced themselves to sacrifice their liberal views for the seemingly realistic goal of nationhood. In Prussia itself, the army dispatched what remained of the revolutionary forces.

Elsewhere in the German-speaking states as popular revolution was taking its own course, many moderate liber-

Peoples against Empire: The Habsburg Lands

In the sprawling Habsburg (Austrian) Empire, nationalism played a different role. On the one hand, the Habsburg emperors could point to a remarkable record of political success: as

"NO PIECE OF PAPER WILL COME BETWEEN MYSELF AND MY PEOPLE" (1848). In this cartoon, Frederick William IV and a military officer refuse to accept the constitution for a new Germany offered to him by the Frankfurt Assembly. Note that the caption refers to a conservative definition of the relationship between a monarch and "his people." Compare this autocratic vision of the nation-state with the liberal nationalist's demand for a government that reflects the people's will. ▪ *What contrasting visions of the nation and its relation to the state are contained in this cartoon?*

HUNGARIAN REVOLUTIONARY LAJOS KOSSUTH, 1851. A leader of the Hungarian nationalist movement who combined aristocratic style with rabble-rousing politics, Kossuth almost succeeded in an attempt to separate Hungary from Austria in 1849.

heir to the medieval Holy Roman Empire, Habsburg kings had ruled for centuries over a diverse array of ethnicities and language groups in central Europe that included Germans, Czechs, Magyars, Poles, Slovaks, Serbs, and Italians, to name only the most prominent. In the sixteenth century, under Charles V, the empire had included Spain, parts of Burgundy, and the Netherlands. In the nineteenth century, however, the Habsburgs found it increasingly difficult to hold their empire together as the national demands of the different peoples in the realm escalated after 1815. Whereas the greater ethnic and linguistic homogeneity of the German-speaking lands allowed for a convergence between liberal ideas of popular sovereignty and national unification, no such program was possible in the Habsburg Empire. Popular sovereignty for peoples defined in terms of their ethnic identity implied a breakup of the Habsburg lands.

At the same time, however, the existence of nationalist movements did not imply unity, even within territories that spoke the same language. In the Polish territories of the empire, nationalist sentiment was strongest among aristocrats, who were especially conscious of their historic role as leaders of the Polish nation. Here, the Habsburg Empire successfully set Polish serfs against Polish lords, ensuring

that social grievances dampened ethnic nationalism. In the Hungarian region, national claims were likewise advanced by the relatively small Magyar aristocracy. (*Hungarian* is a political term; *Magyar,* which was often used, refers to the Hungarians' non-Slavic language.) Yet they gained an audience under the gifted and influential leadership of Lajos (Louis) Kossuth (*KAW-shut*). A member of the lower nobility, Kossuth was by turns a lawyer, publicist, newspaper editor, and political leader. To protest the closed-door policy of the empire's barely representative Diet (parliament), Kossuth published transcripts of parliamentary debates and distributed them to a broader public. He campaigned for independence and a separate Hungarian parliament, but he also (and more influentially) brought politics to the people. Kossuth staged political "banquets" like those in France, at which local and national personalities made speeches in the form of toasts and interested citizens could eat, drink, and participate in politics. The Hungarian political leader combined aristocratic style with rabble-rousing politics: a delicate balancing act but one that, when it worked, catapulted him to the center of Habsburg politics. He was as well known in the Habsburg capital of Vienna as he was in Pressburg and Budapest.

The other major nationalist movement that troubled the Habsburg Empire was pan-Slavism. Slavs included Russians, Poles, Ukrainians, Czechs, Slovaks, Slovenes, Croats, Serbs, Macedonians, and Bulgarians. Before 1848, pan-Slavism was primarily a cultural movement united by a general pro-Slavic sentiment. It was internally divided, however, by the competing claims of different Slavic languages and traditions. Pan-Slavism inspired the works of the Czech historian and political leader, František Palacký, author of the *History of the Bohemian People*, and the Slovak Jan Kollár, whose book *Salvy Dcera* ("Slava's Daughter") mourned the loss of identity among Slavs in the Germanic world. The movement also influenced the Polish Romantic poet Adam Mickiewicz (*mihtz-KYAY-vihch*), who sought to rekindle Polish nationhood against foreign oppression.

The fact that Russia and Austria were rivals in eastern Europe made pan-Slavism a volatile and unpredictable political force in the regions of eastern Europe where the two nations vied for power and influence. Tsar Nicholas of Russia sought to use pan-Slavism to his advantage, making arguments about "Slavic" uniqueness part of his "autocracy, orthodoxy, nationality" ideology after 1825. Yet the tsar's Russian-sponsored pan-Slavism alienated Western-oriented Slavs who resented Russia's ambitions. Here, as elsewhere, nationalism created a tangled web of alliances and antagonisms.

Austria and Hungary in 1848: Springtime of Peoples and the Autumn of Empire

The empire's combination of political, social, and ethnic tensions came to the point of explosion in 1848. The opening salvo came from the Hungarians. Emboldened by uprisings in France and Germany, Kossuth stepped up his reform campaigns, pillorying the "Metternich system" of Habsburg autocracy and control, demanding representative institutions throughout the empire and autonomy for the Hungarian Magyar nation. The Hungarian Diet prepared to draft its own constitution. In Vienna, the seat of Habsburg power, a popular movement of students and artisans demanding political and social reforms built barricades and attacked the imperial palace. A Central Committee of Citizens took shape, as did a middle-class militia, or national guard, determined at once to maintain order and to press demands for reform. The Habsburg regime tried to shut the movement down by closing the university, but that only unleashed more popular anger. The regime found itself forced to retreat almost entirely. Met-

ternich, whose political system had weathered so many storms, fled to Britain in disguise—a good indication of the political turmoil—leaving the emperor Ferdinand I in Vienna. The government conceded to radical demands for male suffrage and a single house of representatives. It agreed to withdraw troops from Vienna and to put forced labor and serfdom on a path to abolition. The government also yielded to Czech demands in Bohemia, granting that kingdom its own constitution. To the south, Italian liberals and nationalists attacked the empire's territories in Naples and Venice. In Milan, the forces of King Charles Albert of Piedmont routed the Austrians, raising hopes of victory. As what would be called "the springtime of peoples" unfolded, Habsburg control of its various provinces seemed to be coming apart.

Yet the explosion of national sentiment that shook the empire later allowed it to recoup its fortunes. The paradox of nationalism in central Europe was that no cultural or ethnic majority could declare independence in a given region without prompting rebellion from other minority groups that inhabited the same area. In Bohemia, for instance, Czechs and Germans who lived side by side had worked together to pass reforms scuttling feudalism. Within a month, however, nationalism began to fracture their alliance. German Bohemians set off to attend the all-important Frankfurt Assembly, but the Czech majority refused to send representatives and countered by convening a confederation of Slavs in Prague. What did the delegates at the Slav confederation want? Some were hostile to what the Russian anarchist Mikhail Bakunin called the "monstrous Austrian Empire." But the majority of delegates preferred to be ruled by the Habsburgs (though with some autonomy) than to be dominated by either the Germans or the Russians.

This bundle of animosities allowed the Austrians to divide and conquer. In May 1848, during the Slav Congress, a student- and worker-led insurrection broke out in Prague. On the orders of the newly installed liberal government, Austrian troops entered the city to restore order, sent the Slav Congress packing, and reasserted control in Bohemia. For economic as well as political reasons, the new government was determined to keep the empire intact. The regime also sent troops to regain control in the Italian provinces of Lombardy and Venetia, and quarrels among the Italians helped the Austrians succeed.

Nationalism and counternationalism in Hungary set the stage for the final act of the drama. The Hungarian parliament had passed a series of laws including new provisions for the union of Hungary and Austria. In the heat of 1848, Ferdinand I had little choice but to accept them. The Hungarian parliament abolished serfdom and ended noble privilege to prevent a peasant insurrection. It also established freedom

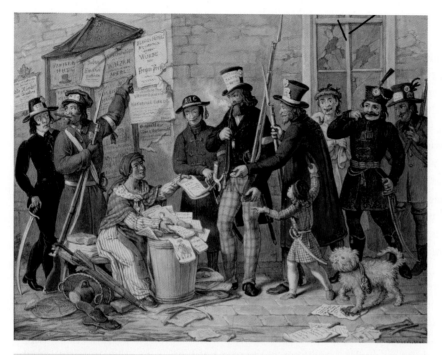

THE FIRST UNCENSORED NEWSPAPER AFTER THE REVOLUTION IN VIENNA, JANUARY 1848. This watercolor illustrates the power of public information during the 1848 revolution in the Austrian capital. An uncensored newspaper, wall posters, caps with political insignia and slogans, and an armed citizenry all are evidence of a vibrant and impassioned public discussion on the events of the day. Note, too, the modest dress of the woman selling the papers, the top hat and fashionable dress of the middle-class man smoking a pipe, and the presence of military uniforms, all of which illustrate support for the revolution among a broad portion of the population. ▪ *How does this vision of the public sphere in action compare with previous depictions of public debate in the Enlightenment (see page 571) or in the French Revolution (see page 599, or elsewhere in Europe in 1848 (see page 704)?*

dent organizations, and put twenty-five revolutionary leaders to death in front of a firing squad. Kossuth went into hiding and lived the rest of his life in exile.

Paradoxically, then, the Habsburg Empire of Austria was in part saved during the revolutions of 1848 by the very nationalist movements that threatened to tear it apart. Although nationalists in Habsburg lands, especially in Hungary, gained the support of significant numbers of people, the fact that different nationalist movements found it impossible to cooperate with one another allowed the new emperor, Franz Josef, to defeat the most significant challenges to his authority one by one and consolidate his rule (with Russian help), ultimately gaining popular support from many quarters, especially from middle-class populations that came to express a certain civic pride in the spirit of toleration that allowed so many peoples to live together within such a patchwork of peoples and tongues. Franz Josef would survive these crises, and many others, until his death in 1916 during World War I, a much larger conflict that would finally overwhelm and destroy the Habsburg Empire for good.

of the press and of religion and changed the suffrage requirements, enfranchising small property holders. Many of these measures (called the March laws) were hailed by Hungarian peasants, Jewish communities, and liberals. But other provisions—particularly the extension of Magyar control—provoked opposition from the Croats, Serbs, and Romanians within Hungary. On April 14, 1848, Kossuth upped the ante, severing all ties between Hungary and Austria. The new Austrian emperor, Franz Josef, now played his last card: he asked for military support from Nicholas I of Russia. The Habsburgs were unable to win their "holy struggle against anarchy," but the Russian army of over 300,000 found it an easier task. By mid-August 1849, the Hungarian revolt was crushed.

In the city of Vienna itself, the revolutionary movement had lost ground. When economic crisis and unemployment helped spark a second popular uprising, the emperor's forces, with Russian support, descended on the capital. On October 31, the liberal government capitulated. The regime reestablished censorship, disbanded the national guard and stu-

The Early Stages of Italian Unification in 1848

The Italian peninsula had not been united since the Roman Empire. At the beginning of the nineteenth century, like the German-speaking lands of central Europe, the area that is now Italy was a patchwork of small states (see map on page 655). Austria occupied the northernmost states of Lombardy and Venetia, which were also the most urban and industrial. Habsburg dependents also ruled Tuscany, Parma, and Modena, extending Austria's influence over the north of the peninsula. The independent Italian states included the southern kingdom of the Two Sicilies, governed by members of the Bourbon family; the Papal States, ruled by Pope Gregory XVI (1831–46); and most important, Piedmont-Sardinia, ruled by the reform-minded monarch Charles Albert (r. 1831–49) of the House of Savoy. Charles Albert had no particular commitment to creating an Italian

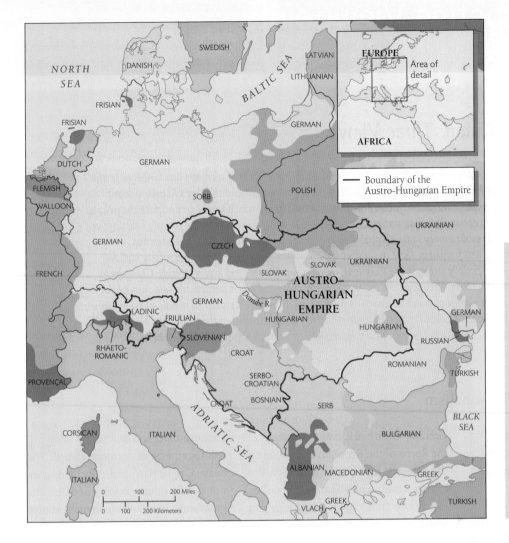

EUROPE

Area of detail

AFRICA

—— Boundary of the Austro-Hungarian Empire

LANGUAGES OF CENTRAL AND EASTERN EUROPE. In Habsburg Austria-Hungary, ethnic/linguistic boundaries did not conform to political boundaries between states. ■ *How many different language groups can you count in the Austrian Empire?* ■ *Why was it ultimately easier for the German states to unify when looking at this map?* ■ *How did the diversity of peoples in the Habsburg Empire make a convergence between liberal revolution and nationalism more difficult to achieve?*

national state, but by virtue of Piedmont-Sardinia's economic power, geographical location, and long tradition of opposition to the Habsburgs, Charles Albert's state played a central role in nationalist and anti-Austrian politics.

The leading Italian nationalist in this period—one whose republican politics Charles Albert disliked—was Giuseppe Mazzini (1805–1872) from the city of Genoa, in Piedmont. Mazzini began his political career as a member of the Carbonari (see Chapter 20), an underground society pledged to resisting Austrian control of the region and establishing constitutional rule. In 1831, Mazzini founded his own society, Young Italy, which was anti-Austrian and in favor of constitutional reforms but also dedicated to Italian unification. Charismatic and persuasive, Mazzini was one of the best-known nationalists of his time. He spoke in characteristically Romantic tones of the awakening of the Italian people and of the common people's mission to bring republicanism to the world. Under his leadership, Young Italy clubs multiplied. Yet the organization's favored tactics, plotting mutinies and armed rebellions, proved ineffective. In 1834, Mazzini launched an invasion of the kingdom of Sardinia. Without sufficient support, it fizzled, driving Mazzini into exile in England.

Mazzini's republican vision of a united Italy clashed with the goals of his potential allies. Many liberals shared his commitment to creating a single Italian state but not his enthusiasm for the people and popular movements. They hoped instead to merge existing governments into some form of constitutional monarchy or, in a few cases, for a government under the pope. Mazzini's insistence on a democratic republic committed to social and political transformation struck pragmatic liberals as utopian and well-to-do members of the middle classes as dangerous.

The turmoil that swept across Europe in 1848 raised hopes for political and social change and put Italian unification on the agenda. As in Germany, those who hoped for change were divided in their goals, but they shared a common hope that national unification might allow them to achieve the reforms they sought, whether it was a constitution, civil liberties, universal suffrage, or revolutionary social change that would benefit the working poor. In March

The New German Nation

In order to silence their critics at home and abroad, nationalists in Germany sought to create a vision of German history that made unification the natural outcome of a deep historical process that had begun hundreds of years before. In image A, the family of a cavalry officer prepares to hang a portrait of King William on the wall, next to portraits of Martin Luther, Frederick the Great, and Field Marshal von Blücher, who commanded the Prussian forces at Waterloo. In the lower left corner, two boys roll up a portrait of the defeated French emperor, Napoleon III. The implication, of course, was that the unification of Germany was the inevitable culmination of generations of German heroes who all worked toward the same goal.

This unity was itself controversial among German people. Image B, a pro-Bismarck cartoon, shows the German minister-president dragging the unwilling liberal members of the Prussian par-liament along with him as he pulls a triumphal chariot toward his military confrontation with Austria in 1866. The caption reads: "And in this sense, too, we are in agreement with Count Bismarck, and we have pulled the same rope as him." Image C, on the other hand, expresses reservations about Prussian dominance in the new empire. The title "Germany's Future" and the caption:

A. *Homage to Kaiser Wilhelm I* by Paul Bürde, 1871.

states that had not already been absorbed into the Prussian fold, except Austria, declared their allegiance to William I, henceforth emperor or kaiser. Four months later, at Frankfurt, a treaty between the French and the Germans ceded the border region of Alsace to the new German Empire and forced the French to pay an indemnity of 5 billion francs. Prussia accounted for 60 percent of the new state's territory and population. The Prussian kaiser, prime minister, army, and most of the bureaucracy remained intact, now reconfigured as the German nation-state. This was not the new nation for which Prussian liberals had hoped. It marked a "revolution from above" rather than from below. Still, the more optimistic believed that the German Empire would evolve in a different political direction and that they could eventually "extend freedom through unity."

The State and Nationality: Centrifugal Forces in the Austrian Empire

Germany emerged from the 1860s a stronger, unified nation. The Habsburg Empire faced a very different situation, with different resources, and emerged a weakened,

"Will it fit under one hat? I think it will only fit under a [Prussian] Pickelhaube." The *Pickelhaube*—the characteristic pointed helmet of the Prussian army—had already become a much-feared symbol of Prussian military force. Such an image may well have struck a chord with residents of the non-Prussian German states who now paid taxes to the Prussian monarchy and served in an army dominated by Prussian officers.

Questions for Analysis

1. What is the significance of the familial setting in image A? Why was it important for nationalists to emphasize a multigenerational family as the repository of German national spirit?

2. How do images B and C treat the question of Prussia's role within the new German nation? Was German national identity seen as something built from below or defined from above by a strong monarchy?

3. What is the place of the individual citizen in these representations of the German nation?

C. "Germany's Future" (1870).

B. Prussian liberals and Bismarck after Königgrätz (1866).

precariously balanced, multiethnic dual monarchy, also called Austria-Hungary.

As we have seen, ethnic nationalism was a powerful force in the Habsburg monarchy in 1848. Yet the Habsburg state, with a combination of military repression and tactics that divided its enemies, had proved more powerful. It abolished serfdom but made few other concessions to its opponents. The Hungarians, who had nearly won independence in the spring of 1848, were essentially reconquered. Administrative reforms created a new and more uniform legal system, rationalized taxation, and imposed a single-language policy that favored German. The issue of man-

aging ethnic relations, however, only grew more difficult. Through the 1850s and 1860s, the subject nationalities, as they were often called, bitterly protested the powerlessness of their local diets, military repression, and cultural disenfranchisement. The Czechs in Bohemia, for instance, grew increasingly alienated by policies that favored the German minority of the province. In response, they became more insistent on their Slavic identity—a movement welcomed by Russia, which became the sponsor of a broad pan-Slavism. The Hungarians, or Magyars, the most powerful of the subject nationalities, sought to reclaim the autonomy they had glimpsed in 1848.

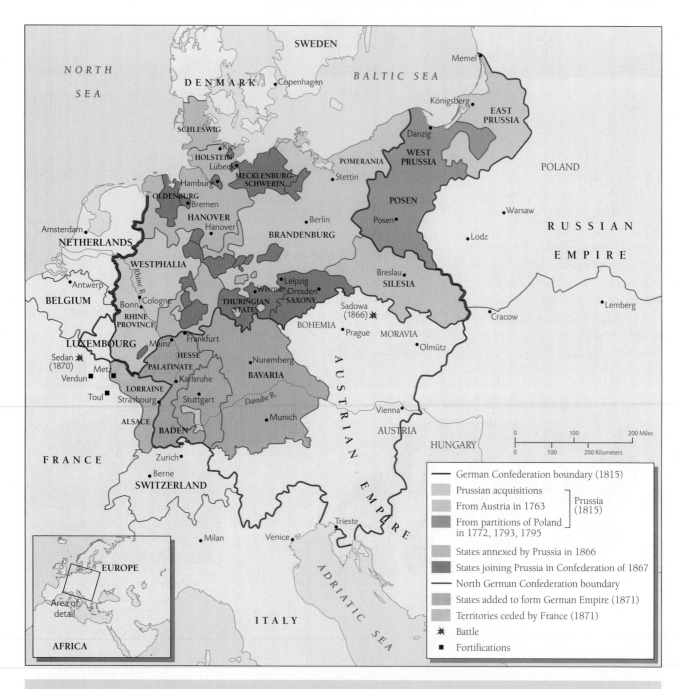

TOWARD THE UNIFICATION OF GERMANY. Note the many elements that made up a unified Germany and the stages that brought them together. ▪ *Did this new nation have any resemblance to the unified Germany envisioned by the liberal revolutionaries of the Frankfurt Preparliament in 1848? (See page 697.)* ▪ *How many stages were involved in the unification of Germany, and how many years did it take?* ▪ *What region filled with German-speaking peoples was not included in the new unified Germany and why?*

In this context, Austria's defeats at the hands of Piedmont-Sardinia in 1859 and Prussia in 1866 became especially significant. The 1866 war forced the emperor Franz Josef to renegotiate the very structure of the empire. To stave off a revolution by the Hungarians, Francis Joseph agreed to a new federal structure in the form of the Dual Monarchy. Austria-Hungary had a common system of taxa-tion, a common army, and made foreign and military policy together. Francis Joseph was emperor of Austria and king of Hungary. But internal and constitutional affairs were separated. The Ausgleich, or Settlement, allowed the Hungarians to establish their own constitution; their own legislature; and their own capital, combining the cities of Buda and Pest.

What of the other nationalities? The official policy of the Dual Monarchy stated that they were not to be discriminated against and that they could use their own languages. Official policy was only loosely enforced. More important, elevating the Hungarians and conferring on them alone the benefits of political nationhood could only worsen relations with other groups. On the Austrian side of the Dual Monarchy, minority nationalities such as the Poles, Czechs, and Slovenes resented their second-class status. On the Hungarian side, the regime embarked on a project of Magyarization, attempting to make the state, the civil service, and the schools more thoroughly Hungarian—an effort that did not sit well with Serbs and Croats.

In spite of these divisions, however, the Austro-Hungarian Empire succeeded for a time in creating a different kind of political and culture space within a Europe that was increasingly given over to nation-states who perceived their interests to be irrevocably opposed. The Austrian capital of Vienna developed a reputation for intellectual and cultural refinement that was in part a product of the many different peoples who made up the Habsburg lands, including Germans, Jews, Hungarians, Italians, Czechs, Poles, Serbs, Croats, and Balkan Muslims from lands that formerly belonged to the Ottoman Empire. This polyglot culture produced Béla Bartók (1881–1945), the great Hungarian composer and admirer of folk musical traditions; Gustav Mahler (1860–1911), a German-Austrian composer whose romantic symphonies and conducting prowess made him a global celebrity by the time of his death. From the same intellectual milieu came Sigmund Freud (1856–1939), a German-speaking Jewish doctor from Vienna whose writings helped shape modern psychology; and Gustav Klimt (1862–1918), a painter and founding member of the Viennese Secession movement, which rejected the reigning classicism of the Austrian art world and made the Austrian capital an important center for the birth of modern art.

The Austrian emperor's deep opposition to nationalism was not just geopolitical, therefore, but also a defense of a different relationship between the nation-state and culture. Unlike the governments of France, England, Italy, or Germany, the Habsburgs did not seek to build a nation-state based on a common cultural identity. It tried instead to build a state and administrative structure strong enough to keep the pieces from spinning off, at times playing different minorities off against each other, but also conceding greater autonomy to different groups when it seemed necessary. As the nineteenth century unfolded, however, discontented subject nationalities would appeal to other powers—Serbia, Russia, the Ottomans—and this balancing act would become more difficult.

NATION AND STATE BUILDING IN RUSSIA AND THE UNITED STATES

The challenges of nationalism and nation building also occupied Russia, the United States, and Canada. In all three countries, nation building entailed territorial and economic expansion, the incorporation of new peoples, and—in Russia and the United States—contending with the enormous problems of slavery and serfdom.

Territory, the State, and Serfdom: Russia

Serfdom in Russia, which had been legally formalized in 1649, had begun to draw significant protest from the intelligentsia under the reign of Catherine the Great (r. 1762–96). After 1789, and especially after 1848, the abolition of serfdom elsewhere in Europe made the issue more urgent. Abolishing serfdom became part of the larger project of building Russia as a modern nation. How that should happen was the subject of much debate. Two schools of thought emerged. The "Slavophiles," or Romantic nationalists, sought to preserve Russia's distinctive features. They idealized traditional Russian culture and the peasant commune, rejecting Western secularism, urban commercialism, and bourgeois culture. In contrast, the "westernizers" wished to see Russia adopt European developments in science, technology, and education, which they believed to be the foundation for Western liberalism and the protection of individual rights. Both groups agreed that serfdom must be abolished. The Russian nobility, however, tenaciously opposed emancipation. Tangled debates about how lords would be compensated for the loss of "their" serfs, and how emancipated serfs would survive without full-scale land redistribution, also checked progress on the issue. The Crimean War (see below) broke the impasse. In its aftermath, Alexander II (r. 1855–81) forced the issue. Worried that the persistence of serfdom had sapped Russian strength and contributed to its defeat in the war, and persuaded that serfdom would only continue to prompt violent conflict, he ended serfdom by decree in 1861.

The emancipation decree of 1861 was a reform of massive scope, but paradoxically it produced limited change. It granted legal rights to some 22 million serfs and authorized their title to a portion of the land they had worked. It also required the state to compensate landowners for the properties they relinquished. Large-scale landowners vastly inflated their compensation claims, however, and

Competing Viewpoints

The Abolition of Serfdom in Russia

The abolition of serfdom was central to Tsar Alexander II's program of modernization and reform after the Crimean War. Emancipated serfs were now allowed to own their land, ending centuries of bondage. The decree, however, emphasized the tsar's benevolence and the nobility's generosity—not peasant rights. The government did not want emancipation to bring revolution to the countryside; it sought to reinforce the state's authority, the landowners' power, and the peasants' obligations. After spelling out the detailed provisions for emancipation, the decree added the paragraphs reprinted here.

Emancipation did not solve problems in the Russian countryside. On the contrary, it unleashed a torrent of protest, including complaints from peasants that nobles were undermining attempts to reform. These petitions in the second section detail the struggles that came in the wake of emancipation in two villages.

Tsar Alexander II's Decree Emancipating the Serfs, 1861

And We place Our hope in the good sense of Our people.

When word of the Government's plan to abolish the law of bondage [serfdom] reached peasants unprepared for it, there arose a partial misunderstanding. Some [peasants] thought about freedom and forgot about obligations. But the general good sense [of the people] was not disturbed in the conviction that anyone freely enjoying the goods of society correspondingly owes it to the common good to fulfill certain obligations, [a conviction held] both by natural reason and by Christian law, according to which "every soul must be subject to the governing authorities." . . . Rights legally acquired by the landlords cannot be taken from them without a decent return or [their] voluntary concession; and that it would be contrary to all justice to make use of the lords' land without bearing the corresponding obligation.

And now We hopefully expect that the bonded people, as a new future opens before them, will understand and accept with gratitude the important sacrifice made by the Well-born Nobility for the improvement of their lives.

Source: James Cracraft, ed., *Major Problems in the History of Imperial Russia* (Lexington, MA: 1994), pp. 340–44.

Emancipation: The View from Below

Petition from Peasants in Podosinovka (Voronezh Province) to Alexander II, May 1863

The most merciful manifesto of Your Imperial Majesty from 19 February 1861, with the published rules, put a limit to the enslavement of the people in blessed Russia. But some former serfowners—who desire not to improve the peasants' life, but to oppress and ruin them—apportion land contrary to the laws, choose the best land from all the fields for themselves, and give the poor peasants . . . the worst and least usable lands.

To this group of squires must be counted our own, Anna Mikhailovna Raevskaia. . . . Of our fields and resources, she chose the best places from amidst our strips, and, like a cooking ring in a hearth, carved off 300 dessiatines [measures of land] for herself. . . .

But our community refused to accept so ruinous an allotment and requested that we be given an allotment in accordance with the local Statute. . . . The peace arbitrator . . . and the police chief . . . slandered us before the governor, alleging that we were rioting and that it is impossible for them to enter our village.

The provincial governor believed this lie and sent 1,200 soldiers of the penal

command to our village. . . . Without any cause, our village priest Father Peter—rather than give an uplifting pastoral exhortation to stop the spilling of innocent blood—joined these reptiles, with the unanimous incitement of the authorities. . . . They summoned nine township heads and their aides from other townships. . . . In their presence, the provincial governor—without making any investigation and without interrogating a single person—ordered that the birch rods be brought and that the punishment commence, which was carried out with cruelty and mercilessness. They punished up to 200 men and women; 80 people were at four levels (with 500, 400, 300 and 200 blows); some received lesser punishment . . . and when the inhuman punishment of these innocent people had ended, the provincial governor said: "If you find the land unsuitable, I do not forbid you to file petitions wherever you please," and then left. . . .

We dare to implore you, Orthodox emperor and our merciful father, not to reject the petition of a community with 600 souls, including wives and children. Order with your tsarist word that our community be allotted land . . . as the law dictates without selecting the best sections of fields and meadows, but in straight lines. . . . [Order that] the meadows and haylands along the river Elan be left to our community without any restriction; these will enable us to feed our cattle and smaller livestock, which are necessary for our existence.

Petition from Peasants in Balashov District to Grand Duke Constantin Nikolaevich, January 25, 1862

Your Imperial Excellency! Most gracious sire! Grand Duke Konstantin Nikolaevich! . . .

After being informed of the Imperial manifesto on the emancipation of peasants from serfdom on 1861 . . . we received this [news] with jubilation. . . . But from this moment, our squire ordered that the land be cut off from the entire township. But this is absolutely intolerable for us: it not only denies us profit, but threatens us with a catastrophic future. He began to hold repeated meetings and [tried to] force us to sign that we agreed to accept the above land allotment. But, upon seeing so unexpected a change, and bearing in mind the gracious manifesto, we refused. . . . After assembling the entire township, they tried to force us into making illegal signatures accepting the land cut-offs. But when they saw that this did not succeed, they had a company of soldiers sent in. . . . Then [Colonel] Globbe came from their midst, threatened us with exile to Siberia, and ordered the soldiers to strip the peasants and to punish seven people by flogging in the most inhuman manner. They still have not regained consciousness.

Source: Gregory L. Freeze, ed., *From Supplication to Revolution: A Documentary Social History of Imperial Russia* (New York: 1988), pp. 170–73.

Questions for Analysis

1. What did Tsar Alexander II fear most in liberating the serfs from bondage? What provisions did he make to ensure that the emancipation would not destabilize his regime?

2. What issues mattered most to the peasantry? What is their attitude toward the tsar?

3. Given the immediate danger to social peace, why did the tsar feel that emancipating the serfs was necessary?

managed to retain much of the most profitable acreage for themselves. As a result, the land granted to peasants was often of poor quality and insufficient to sustain themselves and their families. Moreover, the newly liberated serfs had to pay in installments for their land, which was not granted to them individually but rather to a village commune, which collected their payments. As a result, the pattern of rural life in Russia did not change drastically. The system of payment kept peasants in the villages—not as freestanding farmers but as agricultural laborers for their former masters.

While the Russian state undertook reforms, it also expanded its territory. After midcentury, the Russians pressed east and south. They invaded and conquered several independent Islamic kingdoms along the former Silk Road and expanded into Siberia in search of natural resources. Russian diplomacy wrung various commercial concessions from the Chinese that led to the founding of the Siberian city of Vladivostok in 1860. Racial, ethnic, and religious differences made governing a daunting task. In most cases, the Russian state did not try to assimilate the populations of the new territories: an acceptance of ethnic particularity was a pragmatic response to the difficulties of governing such a heterogeneous population. When the state did attempt to impose Russian culture, the results were disastrous. Whether power was wielded by the nineteenth-century tsars or, later, by the Soviet Union, powerful centrifugal forces pulled against genuine unification. Expansion helped Russia create a vast empire that was geographically of one piece but by no means one nation.

Territory and the Nation: The United States

The American Revolution had bequeathed to the United States a loose union of slave and free states, tied together in part by a commitment to territorial expansion. The so-called Jeffersonian Revolution combined democratic aspirations with a drive to expand the nation's boundaries. Leaders of the movement, under the Democratic-Republican president Thomas Jefferson (1801–1809), campaigned to add the Bill of Rights to the Constitution and were almost exclusively responsible for its success. Though they supported, in principle, the separation of powers, they believed in the supremacy of the people's representatives and viewed with alarm attempts of the executive and judicial branches to increase their power. They supported a political system based on an aristocracy of "virtue and talent," in which respect for personal liberty would be the guiding principle. They opposed the establishment of a national religion and special privilege, whether of birth or of wealth. Yet the Jeffersonian vision of the republic rested on the independence of yeoman farmers, and the independence and prosperity of those farmers depended on the availability of new lands. This made territorial expansion, as exemplified by the Louisiana Purchase in 1803, central to Jeffersonian America. Expansion brought complications. While it did provide land for many yeoman farmers in the north and south, it also added millions of acres of prime cotton land, thus extending the empire of slavery. The purchase of the port of New Orleans made lands in the south well worth developing but led the American republic forcibly to remove Native Americans from the Old South west of the Mississippi River. This process of expansion and expropriation stretched from Jefferson's administration through the age of Jackson, or the 1840s.

Under Andrew Jackson (1829–1837), the Democrats (as some of the Democratic-Republicans were now called) transformed the circumscribed liberalism of the Jeffersonians. They campaigned to extend the suffrage to all white males; they argued that all officeholders

THE EMANCIPATION OF THE SERFS. This engraving depicts officials delivering the formal decree liberating serfs. A massive reform granting legal rights to millions of people, emancipation was undermined by the payments serfs owed to their former owners.

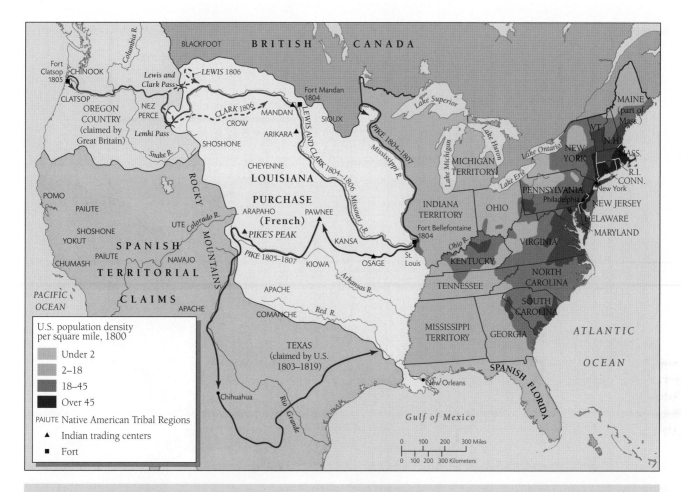

AMERICAN EXPANSION IN THE EARLY NINETEENTH CENTURY. ▪ *What three European powers had a substantial role to play in American expansion?* ▪ *What events enabled the United States to acquire all lands west of the Mississippi River?* ▪ *How did the loss of these lands affect European powers?*

should be elected rather than appointed; and they sought the frequent rotation of men in positions of political power—a doctrine that permitted politicians to use patronage to build national political parties. Moreover, the Jacksonian vision of democracy and nationhood carried over into a crusade to incorporate more territories into the republic. It was the United States' "Manifest Destiny," wrote a New York editor, "to overspread the continent allotted by Providence for the free development of our yearly multiplying millions." That "overspreading" brought Oregon and Washington into the Union through a compromise with the British and brought Arizona, Texas, New Mexico, Utah, Nevada, and California through war with Mexico—all of which led to the wholesale expropriation of Native American lands. Territorial expansion was key to nation building, but it was built on increasingly impossible conflict over slavery.

The American Civil War, 1861–1865

The politics of slavery had already led to its abolition in France and Britain (see Chapter 20), but in the United States the combination of a growing abolitionist movement, a slave-owning class that feared the economic power of the north, and territorial expansion created deadlock and crisis. As the country expanded west, the North and South engaged in a protracted tug of war about whether new states were to be "free" or "slave." In the North, territorial expansion heightened calls for free labor; in the South, it deepened whites' commitment to an economy and society based on plantation slavery. Ultimately, the changes pushed southern political leaders toward secession. The failure of a series of elaborate compromises led to the outbreak of the Civil War in 1861.

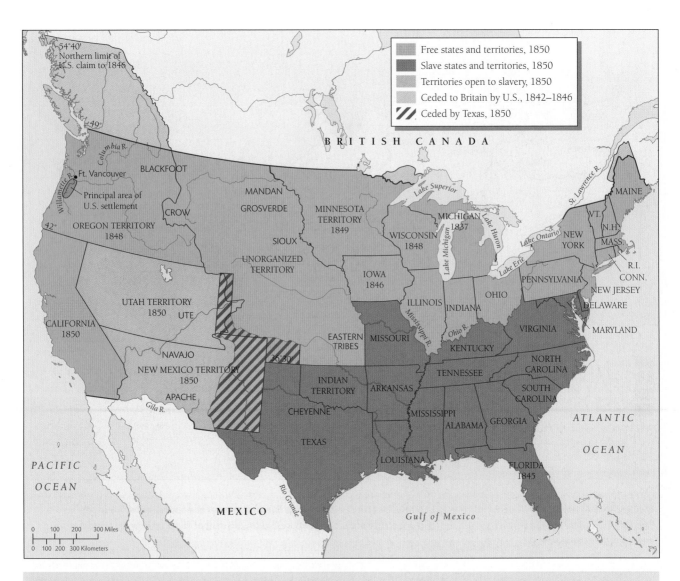

AMERICAN EXPANSION IN THE LATE NINETEENTH CENTURY. Note the stages of American settlement across the North American continent and the dates for the extension of slavery into new territories. ■ *How did the question of slavery shape the way that new territories were absorbed into the republic?* ■ *Compare American expansion with European colonialism?*

The protracted and costly struggle proved a first experience of the horrors of modern war and prefigured the First World War. It also decisively transformed the nation. First, it abolished slavery. Second, it established the preeminence of the national government over states' rights. The Fourteenth Amendment to the Constitution stated specifically that all Americans were citizens of the United States and not of an individual state or territory. In declaring that no citizen was to be deprived of life, liberty, or property without due process of law, it established that "due process" was to be defined by the national, not the state or territorial, government. Third, in the aftermath of the Civil War, the U.S. economy expanded with stunning rapidity. In 1865, there were 35,000 miles of railroad track in the United States; by 1900, there were almost 200,000. Industrial and agricultural production rose, putting the United States in a position to compete with Great Britain. As we will see later on, American industrialists, bankers, and retailers introduced innovations in assembly-line manufacturing, corporate organization, and advertising that startled their European counterparts and gave the United States new power in world politics. These developments were all part of the process of nation building. They did not overcome deep racial, regional, or class divides. Though the war brought the South back into the Union, the rise of northern capitalism magnified the backwardness of the South as an underdeveloped agricultural region whose wealth was extracted by northern industrialists. The railroad corporations, which pieced together the national infrastructure, became the classic foe of labor and agrarian reformers. In

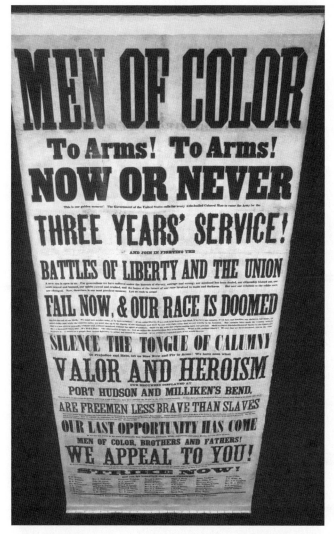

CIVIL WAR RECRUITING POSTER. This poster, created by northern African American abolitionists, exhorts fellow blacks to fight in the American Civil War.

these ways, the Civil War laid the foundations for the modern American nation-state.

"EASTERN QUESTIONS": INTERNATIONAL RELATIONS AND THE DECLINE OF OTTOMAN POWER

During the nineteenth century, questions of national identity and international power were inextricable from contests over territory. War and diplomacy drew and redrew boundaries as European nations groped toward a sustainable balance of power. The rise of new powers, principally the German Empire, posed one set of challenges to continental order. The waning power of older regimes posed another. The Crimean War, which lasted from 1853 to 1856, was a particularly gruesome attempt to cope with the most serious such collapse. As the Ottoman Empire lost its grip on its provinces in southeastern Europe, the "Eastern Question" of who would benefit from Ottoman weakness drew Europe into war. At stake were not only territorial gains but also strategic interests, alliances, and the balance of power in Europe. And though the war occurred before the unification of the German and Italian states, it structured the system of Great Power politics that guided Europe until (and indeed toward) the First World War.

The Crimean War, 1853–1856

The root causes of the war lay in the Eastern Question and the decline of the Ottoman Empire. The crisis that provoked it, however, involved religion—namely French and Russian claims to protect religious minorities and the holy places of Jerusalem within the Muslim Ottoman Empire. In 1853, a three-way quarrel among France (on behalf of Roman Catholics), Russia (representing Eastern Orthodox Christians), and Turkey devolved into a Russian confrontation with the Turkish sultan. Confident that Turkey would be unable to resist, concerned that other powers might take advantage of Turkish weakness, and persuaded (mistakenly) that they had British support, the Russians moved troops into the Ottoman-governed territories of Moldavia and Walachia (see the map on page 722). In October 1853, Turkey, also persuaded they would be supported by the British, declared war on Russia. The war became a disaster for the Turks, who lost their fleet at the battle of Sinope in November. But Russia's success alarmed the British and the French, who considered Russian expansion a threat to their interests in the Balkans, the eastern Mediterranean, and, for the British, the route to India. Determined to check that expansion, France and Britain each declared war on Russia in March 1854. In September, they landed on the Russian peninsula of Crimea and headed for the Russian naval base at Sevastopol, to which they laid siege. France, Britain, and the Ottomans were joined in 1855 by the small but ambitious Italian state of Piedmont-Sardinia, all fighting against the Russians. This was the closest Europe had come to a general war since 1815.

The war was relatively short, but its conduct was devastating. Conditions on the Crimean peninsula were dire, and the disastrous mismanagement of supplies and hygiene by the British and French led to epidemics among the troops.

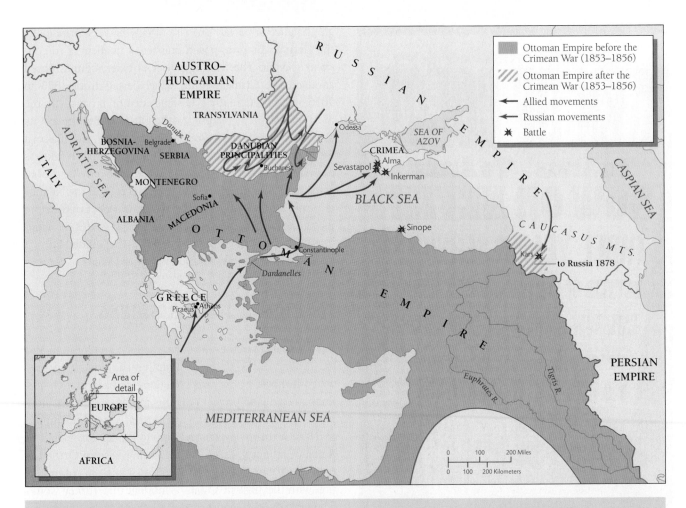

THE CRIMEAN WAR. Note the theater of operations and the major assaults of the Crimean War. ▪ *Which empires and nations were in a position to take advantage of Ottoman weakness?* ▪ *Who benefited from the outcome, and who was most harmed?* ▪ *In what ways was the Crimean War the first modern war?*

At least as many soldiers died from typhus or cholera as in combat. The fighting was bitter, marked by such notoriously inept strategies as the British "charge of the Light Brigade," in which a British cavalry unit was slaughtered by massed Russian artillery. Vast battles pitted tens of thousands of British and French troops against Russian formations, combat that was often settled with bayonets. Despite the disciplined toughness of the British and French troops, and despite their nations' dominance of the seas around Crimea, the Russians denied them a clear victory. Sevastopol, under siege for nearly a year, did not fall until September 1855. The bitter, unsatisfying conflict was ended by treaty in 1856.

For the French and Sardinians, the bravery of their soldiers bolstered positive national sentiments at home; for the British and Russians, however, the poorly managed war provoked waves of intense criticism. As far as international relations were concerned, the peace settlement dealt a blow to Russia, whose influence in the Balkans was drastically curbed. The provinces of Moldavia and Walachia were united as Romania and became an independent nation. Austria's refusal to come to the aid of Russia cost Russia the support of its powerful former ally. The Crimean War embarrassed France and left Russia and Austria considerably weaker, opening an advantage for Bismarck in the 1860s, as we saw earlier.

The Crimean War was important in other ways as well. Though fought largely with the same methods and mentalities employed in the Napoleonic Wars forty years earlier, the war brought innovations that forecast the direction of modern warfare. It saw the first significant use of rifled muskets, underwater mines, and trench warfare as well as the first tactical use of railroads and telegraphs.

In addition, the war was covered by the first modern war correspondents and photojournalists, making it the most public war to date. Reports from the theater of war were sent "live" by telegraph to Britain and France with

CAPTAIN DAMES OF THE ROYAL ARTILLERY, 1855. Roger Fenton studied painting in London and then Paris, where he learned about and started to experiment with photography. He developed a mobile darkroom and ventured into the English countryside. In 1855, he went to the Crimea, subsidized by the British government. Photographs of movement and troops in battle were still impossible, and political restraint kept him from photographing the horrors of the increasingly unpopular Crimean War. Still, his were the first war photographs.

objective and sobering detail; the (London) *Times* reporter William Howard Russell, for instance, heaped criticism on the government for the deplorable conditions British soldiers endured. The care and supply of the troops became national scandals in the popular press, prompting dramatic changes in the military's administrative and logistical systems and making heroes of individual doctors and nurses such as Florence Nightingale. The British government and commercial publishers both sent photographers to document the war's progress and perhaps also to counter charges that troops were undersupplied and malnourished. Roger Fenton, the most prominent and prolific of these war photographers, employed the new medium to capture the grim realities of camp life. Technological limitations and political considerations kept him from photographing the more gruesome carnage of the battlefield, but Fenton's photographs introduced a new level of realism and immediacy to the public's conception of war.

CONCLUSION

The decades between 1848 and 1870 brought intense nation building in the Western world. The unification of Germany and Italy changed the map of Europe, with important consequences for the balance of power. The emergence of the United States as a major power also had international ramifications. For old as well as new nation-states, economic development and political transformation—often on a very large scale—were important means of increasing and securing the state's power. Even though the liberal revolutionaries of 1848 had not achieved the goals

THE STONE BREAKERS BY GUSTAVE COURBET, 1849. Courbet was a French realist painter who depicted everyday men and women in an honest and unromantic manner. Considered one of his most important works, this painting of two ordinary peasants building a road was destroyed in Dresden during the Second World War.

AUTHOR LEO TOLSTOY. Although a wealthy landowner, Tolstoy often dressed as a peasant. He became increasingly ascetic, casting off the corruptions of the world, and pacifist. In this picture, he is leaving his home for a hermitage.

they sought, their demands for more representative government, the abolition of privilege, and land reform still had to be reckoned with, as did the systems of slavery and serfdom. Trailing the banner of nationhood was an explosive set of questions about how to balance the power and interests of minorities and majorities, of the wealthy and poor, of the powerful and the dispossessed. Nation building not only changed states, it transformed relations between states and their citizens.

These transformations were anything but predictable. Nationalism showed itself to be a volatile, erratic, and malleable force during the mid-nineteenth century. It provided

After You Read This Chapter

Visit StudySpace for quizzes, additional review materials, and multimedia documents. **wwnorton.com/web/westernciv18**

REVIEWING THE OBJECTIVES

- Revolutions broke out in 1848 in almost every capital of Europe except for London and St. Petersburg. What accounts for this wave of simultaneous revolutionary movements?

- Liberal revolutionaries in France in 1848 did not have the same goals as their socialist allies. What were their goals and why did they fail to achieve them?

- Liberal revolutionaries in the German-speaking lands of central Europe in 1848 were forced to reckon with Austrian and Prussian states in their bid for national unification. What did they want, and why did they fail?

- Nationalists in both Germany and Italy were divided between those who supported the creation of a new nation from below, through popular movements, and those who preferred nation building from above. How did these divisions work themselves out in the process of national unification?

- Creating a modern nation in Russia entailed the end of serfdom, whereas in the United States, political leaders from the North and South debated the place of slavery in the modern nation-state. In what ways were national debates about citizenship in these countries shaped by the widespread practices of bondage?

- The three major European wars of this period were of relatively short duration, but they had profound effects on the international balance of power in Europe. Which countries emerged stronger from these conflicts, and which found their interests most damaged?

much of the fuel for revolutionary movements in 1848, but it also helped tear their movements apart, undermining revolutionary gains. Those who had linked their democratic goals to the rise of new nation-states were sorely disappointed. In the aftermath of the defeated revolutions, most nation building took a conservative tack. Nationalism came to serve the needs of statesmen and bureaucrats who did not seek an "awakening of peoples" and who had serious reservations about popular sovereignty. For them, nations simply represented modern, organized, and stronger states.

The result of these many tensions was an age that seemed a contradictory mix of the old and the new, of monarchies beset with debates about nationality and citizenship, of land-owning aristocratic elites rubbing elbows with newly wealthy industrialists, and of artisan handworkers meeting up with factory laborers in worker's associations that debated the proper path toward realizing their socialist goals. Remarkably, the result of this period of intense nation building was a period of unusual stability on the Continent, which ushered in an era of unprecedented capitalist and imperial expansion. The antagonisms unleashed by German unification and the crumbling of the Ottoman Empire would reemerge, however, in the Great Power politics that precipitated the First World War.

PEOPLE, IDEAS, AND EVENTS IN CONTEXT

- What circumstances led to the downfall of **LOUIS PHILIPPE**'s government in France? What divisions between supporters of the revolution led to the **JUNE DAYS** in Paris in 1848?

- What role did the **ZOLLVEREIN** and the **FRANKFURT PARLIAMENT** play in the creation of a unified Germany?

- How and why did **OTTO VON BISMARCK** aim for a policy of German national unification during his time in office?

- How did **GIUSEPPE GARIBALDI** and **CAMILLO BENSO DI CAVOUR** initially see the process of Italian unification? Whose vision came closest to reality?

- Who was **NAPOLEON III**, and how did his policies contribute to nation building in France?

- What was the contribution of **JOHN STUART MILL** to debates about citizenship in Britain?

- Why were nationalist movements such as **PAN-SLAVISM** or **MAGYAR NATIONALISM** such a danger to the Austro-Hungarian Empire?

- Why did **TSAR ALEXANDER II** decide to **EMANCIPATE THE SERFS**?

- What made the **CRIMEAN WAR** different from previous conflicts and more like the wars of the twentieth century?

THINKING ABOUT CONNECTIONS

- Revolutionaries in 1848, whether they were in Paris, Rome, Berlin, or Vienna, must have been aware of connections between their own struggles and the historical example of the French Revolution of 1789–99. Did revolutionaries in 1848 have goals that were similar to the goals of French revolutionaries at the end of the eighteenth century?

- How might the failure of the 1848 revolutions have shaped the beliefs of European conservatives and liberals or the beliefs of supporters of more radical ideologies such as republicanism and socialism?

of government officials, schoolteachers, and engineers. Nineteenth-century imperialism produced new forms of government and management in the colonies, and as it did so, it forged new interactions between Europeans and indigenous peoples.

The New Imperialism and Its Causes

As early as 1902, British author J. A. Hobson charged that the interests of a small group of wealthy financiers had driven the "scramble for Africa." British taxpayers subsidized armies of conquest and occupation, and journalists whipped up the public's enthusiasm for imperialism. Hobson, a reformer and a social critic, argued that international finance and business had distorted conceptions of England's real national interests. He hoped that a genuine democracy would curb the country's imperial policies.

Hobson's analysis inspired an influential Marxist critique of imperialism made by Vladimir Ilyich Lenin. Like Hobson, Lenin believed that imperialism was best understood on economic grounds. Unlike Hobson, however, Lenin believed that imperialism was an integral part of late-nineteenth-century capitalism. With domestic markets saturated and growth limited by competition at home, capitalists were forced to invest and search for new markets overseas, producing an ever more intensive pressure for the expansion of European imperialism. Lenin published *Imperialism: The Highest Stage of Capitalism* (1917) at the height of the First World War, and he used this argument to assert that hopes for a democratic reform of capitalism were misplaced and that the only solution was the replacement of capitalism with a revolutionary new economic order.

Historians now agree that economic pressures were only one of the causes of imperialism. Only half of Britain's £4 billion in foreign investments was at work within its empire, and in France the proportion was even smaller: one fifth of French capital was invested overseas. The French had more capital invested in their ally Russia than in all their colonial possessions. Nevertheless, Europeans expected the colonies to produce profits. French newspapers, for instance, reported that the Congo was "rich, vigorous, and fertile virgin territory" with "fabulous quantities" of gold, copper, ivory, and rubber. Such hopes contributed to expansionism, even if the profits did not meet expectations.

A second interpretation of imperialism emphasized strategic and nationalist motives. International rivalries made European powers more determined to control less-developed nations and territories. French politicians hoped that imperialism would restore the honor France had lost in their defeat by the Prussians in 1870. The British looked with alarm at Germany's industrialization and feared losing their share of world markets. The Germans, recently unified into a modern nation-state, saw overseas empire as the only way to become a great power.

This interpretation suggests a link between imperialism and nineteenth-century state and nation building. Colonies demonstrated military power; they showed the vigor of a nation's economy; the strength of its citizens, the force of its law, the power of its culture. A strong national community could assimilate others, bringing progress to new lands and new peoples. One German proponent of expansion called colonialism the "national continuation of the German desire for unity." Lobby groups such as the German Colonial Society, the French Colonial Party, and the Royal Colonial Institute in Britain argued for empire in similar terms, as did newspapers, which recognized the profits to be made in selling sensational stories of overseas conquest.

Finally, imperialism had important cultural dimensions. A French diplomat once described the British imperial adventurer Cecil Rhodes as a "force cast in an idea"; the same might be said of imperialism itself. Scottish missionary David Livingston believed that the British conquest of Africa would end the East African slave trade and "introduce the Negro family into the body of corporate nations." Taking arms against the slave trade, famine, disorder, and illiteracy seemed to many Europeans not only a reason to invade Africa but also a duty and proof of a somehow superior civilization. These convictions did not cause imperialism, but they illustrate how central empire building became to the West's self-image.

In short, it is difficult to disentangle the economic, political, and strategic causes of imperialism. It is more important to understand how the motives overlapped. Economic interests often helped convince policy makers that strategic interests were at stake. Different constituencies—the military, international financiers, missionaries, colonial lobby groups at home—held different and often clashing visions of the purpose and benefits of imperialism. Imperial policy, therefore, was less a matter of long-range planning than a series of quick responses, often improvised, to particular situations. And of course, Europeans were not the only players on the stage. Their goals and intentions were shaped by social changes in the countries in which they became involved; by the independent interests of local peoples; and by resistance, which, as often as not, Europeans found themselves unable to understand and powerless to stop.

EUROPEAN EMPIRES IN 1900. ■ *Where were Britain's major imperial interests, and what trade routes did they have most incentive to protect?* ■ *Where were France's most important imperial holdings and who was their major competitor?* ■ *How substantial were German, Dutch, Portuguese, or U.S. colonies in comparison to British and French holdings?*

Britain
France
Germany
Portugal
Spain
Netherlands
Belgium
Denmark
Italy
United States
Ottoman
Russia
Japan
Independent

Past and Present

The Legacy of Colonialism

Decolonization in the 1950s and 1960s brought an end to the era of European imperialism (left), but the colonial past continues to shape the relations among European nations and former colonies elsewhere in the world. These links are reinforced by the large number of people from former colonies that now live in Europe, including the diverse neighborhood of Southall, London (right).

 Watch related author interview on StudySpace
wwnorton.com/web/westernciv18

Civil-service reform opened new positions to members of the Indian upper classes. The British had to reconsider their relationship to Indian cultures. Missionary activity was no longer encouraged, and the British channeled their reforming impulses into the more secular projects of economic development, railways, roads, irrigation, and so on. Still, consensus on effective colonial strategies was lacking. Some administrators counseled more reform; others sought to support the princes. The British tried both policies, in fits and starts, until the end of British rule in 1947.

In India, the most prominent representative of the new imperialism was Lord Curzon, the viceroy of India from 1898 to 1905. Curzon deepened British commitments to the region. Concerned about the British position in the world, he warned of the need to fortify India's borders against Russia. He urged continued economic investment. Curzon worried that the British would be worn down by resistance to the raj and that, confronted with their apparent inability to

transform Indian culture, they would become cynical, get "lethargic and think only of home." In the same way that Rudyard Kipling urged the British and the Americans to "take up the white man's burden" (see **Competing Viewpoints** on pages 756–57), Curzon pleaded with his countrymen to see how central India was to the greatness of Britain.

What did India do for Great Britain? By the eve of the First World War, India was Britain's largest export market. One tenth of all the British Empire's trade passed through India's port cities of Madras, Bombay, and Calcutta. India mattered enormously to Britain's balance of payments; surpluses earned there compensated for deficits with Europe and the United States. Equally important to Great Britain were the human resources of India. Indian laborers worked on tea plantations in Assam, near Burma, and they built railways and dams in southern Africa and Egypt. Over a million indentured Indian servants left their country in the second half of the century to work elsewhere in the empire.

India also provided the British Empire with highly trained engineers, land surveyors, clerks, bureaucrats, schoolteachers, and merchants. The nationalist leader Mohandas Gandhi, for instance, first came into the public eye as a young lawyer in Pretoria, South Africa, where he worked for an Indian law firm. The British deployed Indian troops across the empire. (They would later call up roughly 1.2 million troops in the First World War.) For all these reasons, men such as Curzon found it impossible to imagine their empire, or even their nation, without India.

How did the British raj shape Indian society? The British practice of indirect rule sought to create an Indian elite that would serve British interests, a group "who may be the interpreters between us and the millions whom we govern—a class of persons Indian in colour and blood, but English in tastes, in opinion, in morals, and in intellect," as one British writer put it. Eventually, this practice created a class of British-educated Indian civil servants and businessmen, well trained for government and skeptical about British claims that they brought progress to the subcontinent. This group provided the leadership for the nationalist movement that challenged British rule in India. At the same time, this group became increasingly distant from the rest of the nation. The overwhelming majority of Indians remained desperately poor peasants struggling to subsist on diminishing plots of land and, in many cases, in debt to British landlords. Meanwhile, villagers working in the textile trade were beaten down by imports of cheap manufactured goods from England.

IMPERIALISM IN CHINA

In China, too, European imperialism began early, well before the period of the new imperialism. Yet there it took a different form. Europeans did not conquer and annex whole regions. Instead, they forced favorable trade agreements at gunpoint, set up treaty ports where Europeans lived and worked under their own jurisdiction, and established outposts of European missionary activity. The Chinese spoke of their country as being "carved up like a melon."

Since the seventeenth century, European trade with China focused on coveted luxuries such as silk, porcelain, art objects, and tea. The Chinese government, however, was determined to keep foreign traders, and foreign influence in general, at bay. By the early nineteenth century, Britain's global ambitions and rising power were setting the stage for a confrontation. Freed from the task of fighting Napoleon, the British set their sights on improving the terms of the China trade, demanding the rights to come into open harbors and to have special trading privileges. The other source of constant friction involved the harsh treatment of British subjects by Chinese law courts—including the summary execution of several Britons convicted of crimes. By the 1830s, these diplomatic conflicts had been intensified by the opium trade.

The Opium Trade

Opium provided a direct link among Britain, British India, and China. Since the sixteenth century, the drug had been produced in India and carried by Dutch and, later, British traders. In fact, opium (derived from the poppy plant) was one of the very few commodities that Europeans could sell in China. For this reason, it became crucial to the balance of East–West trade. When the British conquered northeast India, they also annexed one of the world's richest opium-growing areas and became deeply involved in the trade—so much so that historians have called the East India Company's rule a "narco-military empire." British agencies designated specific poppy-growing regions and gave cash advances to Indian peasants who cultivated the crop. Producing opium was a labor-intensive process: peasant cultivators collected sap from the poppy seeds, and others cleaned the sap and formed it into opium balls that were dried before being weighed and shipped out. In the opium-producing areas northwest of Calcutta, "factories" employed as many as a thousand Indian workers, who formed and cured the opium, as well as young boys, whose job it was to turn the opium balls every four days.

From India, the East India Company sold the opium to "country traders"—small fleets of British, Dutch, and Chinese shippers who carried the drug to Southeast Asia and China. The East India Company used the silver it earned from the sale of opium to buy Chinese goods for the European market. The trade, therefore, was not only profitable, but it was also key to a triangular European-Indian-Chinese economic relationship. Production and export rose dramatically in the early nineteenth century, in spite of the Chinese emperor's attempts to discourage the trade. By the 1830s, when the British-Chinese confrontation was taking shape, opium provided British India with more revenues than any other source except taxes on land.

People all over the world consumed opium, for medicinal reasons as well as for pleasure. The Chinese market was especially lucrative. Eighteenth-century China witnessed a craze for tobacco smoking that taught users how to smoke opium. A large, wealthy Chinese elite of merchants and government officials provided much of the market, but opium smoking also became popular among

AN OPIUM FACTORY IN PATNA, INDIA, c. 1851. Balls of opium dry in a huge warehouse before being shipped to Calcutta for export to China and elsewhere.

sovereignty and to proselytize and open schools. The Chinese government could not accept these challenges to its authority, and war flared up several times over the course of the century. After the first war of 1839–42, in which British steam vessels and guns overpowered the Chinese fleet, the Treaty of Nanking (1842) compelled the Chinese to give the British trading privileges, the right to reside in five cities, and the port of Hong Kong "in perpetuity." After a second war, the British secured yet more treaty ports and privileges, including the right to send in missionaries. In the aftermath of those agreements between the Chinese and the British, other countries demanded similar rights and economic opportunities. By the end of the nineteenth century, the French, Germans, and Russians had claimed mining rights and permission to build railroads, to begin manufacturing with cheap Chinese labor, and to arm and police European communities in Chinese cities. In Shanghai, for instance, 17,000 foreigners lived with their own courts, schools, churches, and utilities. The United States, not wanting to be shouldered aside, demanded its own Open Door Policy. Japan was an equally active imperialist power in the Pacific, and the Sino-Japanese War of 1894–95 was a decisive moment in the history of the region. The Japanese victory forced China to concede trading privileges, the independence of Korea, and the Liaotung Peninsula in Manchuria. It opened a scramble for spheres of influence and for mining and railway concessions. The demand for reparations forced the Chinese government to levy greater taxes. All these measures heightened resentment and destabilized the regime.

Surrendering privileges to Europeans and the Japanese seriously undermined the authority of the Chinese Qing (Ching) emperor at home and heightened popular hostility to foreign intruders. Authority at the imperial center had been eroding for more than a century by 1900, hastened by the Opium Wars and by the vast Taiping Rebellion (1852–64), an enormous, bitter, and deadly conflict in which radical Christian rebels in south-central China challenged the authority of the emperors. On the defensive against the rebels, the dynasty hired foreign generals, including the British commander Charles Gordon, to lead its forces. The war devastated China's agricultural heartland; and the death toll, never confirmed, may have reached 20 million.

soldiers, students, and Chinese laborers. In the nineteenth century, opium imports followed Chinese labor all over the world—to Southeast Asia and San Francisco. In 1799, in an effort to control the problem, the Chinese government banned opium imports, prohibited domestic production, criminalized smoking, and in the 1830s began a full-scale campaign to purge the drug from China. That campaign set the Chinese emperor on a collision course with British opium traders. In one confrontation, the Chinese drug commissioner Lin confiscated 3 million pounds of raw opium from the British and washed it out to sea. In another, the Chinese authorities blockaded British ships in port, and local citizens demonstrated angrily in front of British residences.

THE OPIUM WARS

In 1839, these simmering conflicts broke into what was called the first Opium War. Drugs were not the core of the matter. The dispute over the drug trade highlighted larger issues of sovereignty and economic status. The Europeans claimed the right to trade with whomever they pleased, bypassing Chinese monopolies. They wished to set up zones of European residence in defiance of Chinese

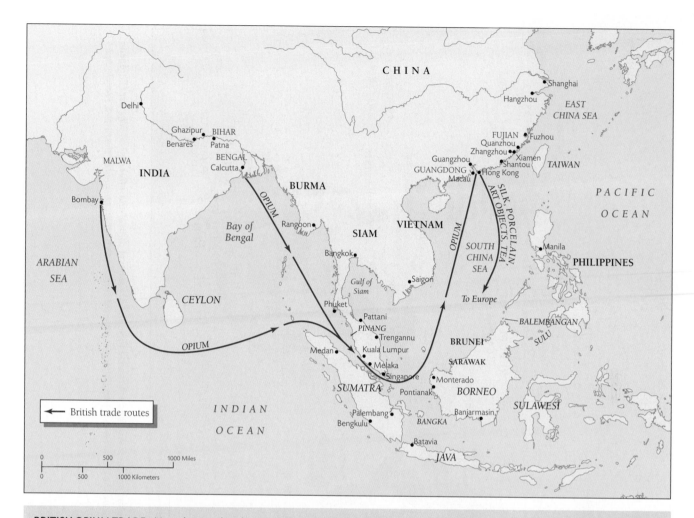

BRITISH OPIUM TRADE. Note the way that the British trade in opium linked the economies of India, China, and Europe. ▪ *What were the major products involved in trade between East Asia, South Asia, and Europe during this period?* ▪ *In what ways did the opium trade destabilize East Asia?* ▪ *What efforts did the Chinese government make to restrict the sale of opium?* ▪ *What was the response of European nations involved in this trade?*

This ruinous disorder and the increasing inability of the emperor to keep order and collect the taxes necessary to repay foreign loans, led European countries to take more and more direct control of the China trade.

The Boxer Rebellion

From a Western perspective, the most important of the nineteenth-century rebellions against the corruptions of foreign rule was the Boxer Rebellion of 1900. The Boxers were a secret society of young men trained in Chinese martial arts and believed to have spiritual powers. Antiforeign and antimissionary, they provided the spark for a loosely organized but widespread uprising in northern China. Bands of Boxers attacked foreign engineers, tore up

railway lines, and in the spring of 1900 marched on Beijing. They laid siege to the foreign legations in the city, home to several thousand Western diplomats and merchants and their families. The legations' small garrison defended their walled compound with little more than rifles, bayonets, and improvised artillery; but they withstood the siege for fifty-five days until a large relief column arrived. The rebellion, particularly the siege at Beijing, mobilized a global response. Europe's Great Powers, rivals everywhere else in the world, drew together in response to this crisis to tear China apart. An expedition numbering 20,000 troops—combining the forces of Britain, France, the United States, Germany, Italy, Japan, and Russia—ferociously repressed the Boxer movement. The outside powers then demanded indemnities, new trading concessions, and reassurances from the Chinese government.

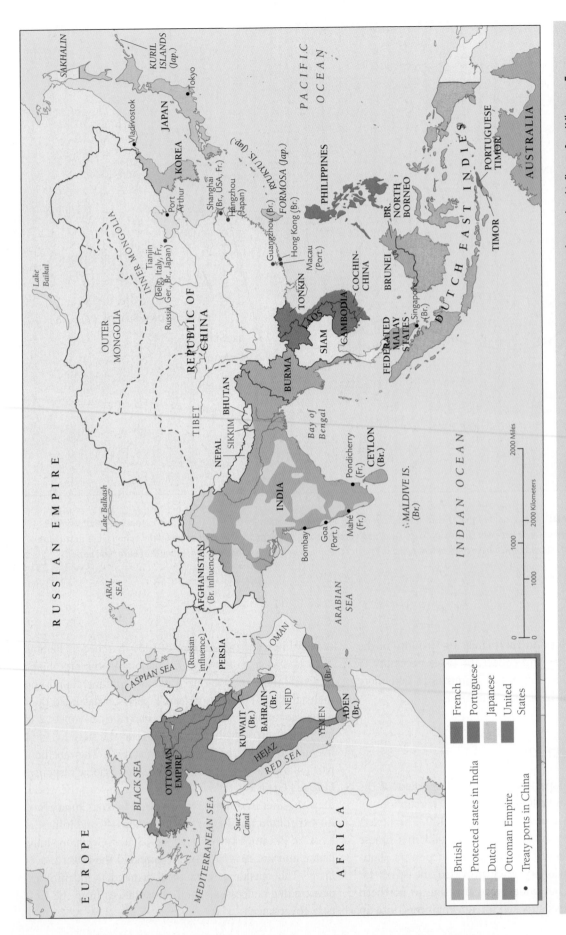

IMPERIALISM IN SOUTH AND EAST ASIA, c. 1914. ▪ *Which imperial powers were most present in Asia and where were their primary zones of control and influence?* ▪ *Why were European nations and the United States interested in establishing treaty ports in China?* ▪ *How were the Chinese treaty ports different from the territorial conquest pursued by the British, French, and Dutch in their respective Asian colonies?*

THE OPIUM TRADE, 1880s. A European merchant examines opium. At first, European traders were forced to carry silver to China to pay for the luxury goods they wanted. The discovery that they could sell this highly addictive narcotic in China allowed them to correct this trade imbalance and increase their profits.

The Boxer Rebellion was one of several anti-imperialist movements at the end of the nineteenth century. The rebellion testified to the vulnerability of Europeans' imperial power. It dramatized the resources Europeans would have to devote to maintaining their far-flung influence. In the process of repression, the Europeans became committed to propping up corrupt and fragile governments to protect their agreements and interests, and they were drawn into putting down popular uprisings against local inequalities and foreign rule.

In China, the age of the new imperialism capped a century of conflict and expansion. By 1900, virtually all of Asia had been divided up among the European powers. Japan, an active imperial power in its own right, maintained its independence. British rule extended from India across Burma, Malaya, Australia, and New Zealand. The Dutch, Britain's longstanding trade rivals, secured Indonesia. Thailand remained independent. During the 1880s, the French moved into Indochina. Imperial rivalries (among Britain, France, and Russia, China and Japan, Russia and Japan) drove European powers to press for influence and economic advantage in Asia; that struggle, in turn, encouraged the development of nationalist feeling among local populations. Imperial expansion was showing its destabilizing effects.

AN AMERICAN CARICATURE OF THE BOXER REBELLION.
Uncle Sam (to the obstreperous Boxer), "I occasionally do a little boxing myself."

Russian Imperialism

Russia championed a policy of annexation—by conquest, treaty, or both—of lands bordering on the existing Russian state throughout the nineteenth century. Beginning in 1801, with the acquisition of Georgia after a war with Persia, the tsars continued to pursue their expansionist dream. Bessarabia and Turkestan (taken from the Turks) and Armenia (from the Persians) vastly increased the empire's size. This southward colonization brought large Muslim populations in central Asia into the Russian Empire. It also brought the Russians close to war with the British twice: first in 1881, when Russian troops occupied territories in the trans-Caspian region, and again in 1884–87, when the tsar's forces advanced to the frontier of Afghanistan. In both cases, the British feared incursions into areas they deemed within their sphere of influence in the Middle East. They were concerned, as well, about a possible threat to India. The maneuvering, spying, and support of friendly puppet governments by Russia and Britain became known

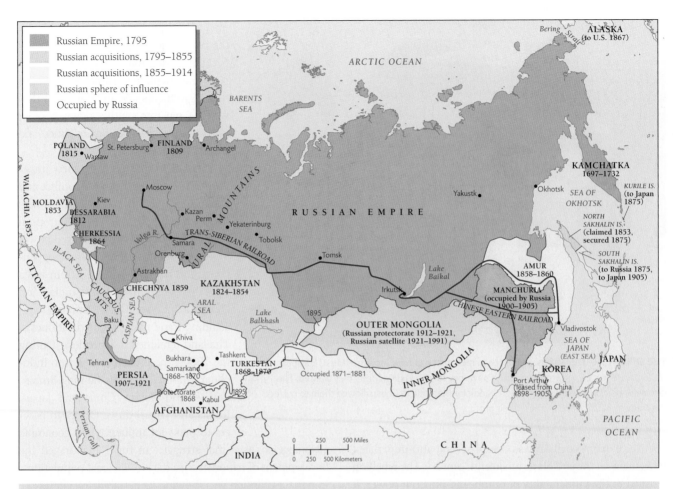

BUILDING THE RUSSIAN EMPIRE. ■ *In what directions did the Russian Empire primarily expand after 1795?* ■ *What drove Russian expansion?* ■ *Which areas were most contentious and why?*

as the "Great Game" and foreshadowed Western countries' jockeying for the region's oil resources in the twentieth century.

Russian expansion also moved east. In 1875, the Japanese traded the southern half of Sakhalin Island for the previously Russian Kurile Islands. The tsars' eastward advance was finally halted in 1904, when Russian expansion in Mongolia and Manchuria came up against Japanese expansion. In the Russo-Japanese War of 1904, Russia's huge imperial army more than met its match. Russia's navy was sent halfway around the world to reinforce the beleaguered Russian troops but was ambushed and sunk by the better-trained and -equipped Japanese fleet. This national humiliation helped provoke a revolt in Russia and led to an American-brokered peace treaty in 1905 (see Chapter 23). The defeat shook the already unsteady regime of the tsar and proved that European nations were not the only ones who could play the imperial game successfully.

THE FRENCH EMPIRE AND THE CIVILIZING MISSION

Like British expansion into India, French colonialism in northern Africa began before the new imperialism of the late nineteenth century. By the 1830s, the French had created a general government of their possessions in Algeria, the most important of which were cities along the Mediterranean coast. From the outset, the Algerian conquest was different from most other colonial ventures: Algeria became a settler state, one of the few apart from South Africa. Some of the early settlers were utopian socialists, out to create ideal communities; some were workers the French government deported after the revolution of 1848 to be "resettled" safely as farmers; some were winegrowers whose vines at home had been destroyed by an insect infestation. The settlers were by no means all French; they included Italian, Spanish, and Maltese merchants and shopkeepers of modest means, laborers, and

THE ENTRY OF THE CRUSADERS INTO CONSTANTINOPLE BY EUGÉNE DELACROIX, 1840. The invasion of Algeria in 1830 became an occasion for thinking about Europe's long historical relationship with Muslim civilizations in Africa and the Middle East. Delacroix's work, painted while the conquest of Algeria was going on, portrays these civilizations as exotic and subservient, even as it glorifies the figures of conquering Christian armies. ▪ *How might this long historical view have shaped European attitudes toward conquest in the nineteenth century?*

peasants. By the 1870s, in several of the coastal cities, this new creole community outnumbered indigenous Algerians, and within it, other Europeans outnumbered the French. With the French military's help, the settlers appropriated land, and French business concerns took cork forests and established mining in copper, lead, and iron. Economic activity was for European benefit. The first railroads, for instance, did not even carry passengers; they took iron ore to the coast for export to France, where it would be smelted and sold.

The settlers and the French government did not necessarily pursue common goals. In the 1870s, the new and still-fragile Third Republic (founded after Napoleon III was defeated in 1870; see Chapter 21), in an effort to ensure the settlers' loyalty, made the colony a department of France. This gave the French settlers the full rights of republican citizenship. It also gave them the power to pass laws in Algeria that consolidated their privileges and community (naturalizing all

Europeans, for instance) and further disenfranchised indigenous Muslim populations, who had no voting rights at all. French politicians in Paris occasionally objected to the settlers' contemptuous treatment of indigenous peoples, arguing that it subverted the project of "lifting up" the natives. The French settlers in Algeria had little interest in such a project; although they paid lip service to republican ideals, they wanted the advantages of Frenchness for themselves. Colonial administrators and social scientists differentiated the "good" mountain-dwelling Berbers, who they believed could be brought into French society, from the "bad" Arabs, whose religion made them supposedly unassimilable. France's divide and rule strategy, which treated European settlers, Arabs, Berbers, and Jews very differently, illustrates the contradictions of "the civilizing mission" in action.

Before the 1870s, colonial activities aroused relatively little interest among the French at home. But after the

SLAVES IN CHAINS, 1896. In Africa, native labor was exploited by Europeans and by other Africans.

humiliating defeat in the Franco-Prussian War (1870–71) and the establishment of the Third Republic, colonial lobby groups and politicians became increasingly adamant about the benefits of colonialism. These benefits were not simply economic. Taking on the "civilizing mission" would reinforce the international influence of the French republic and the prestige of the French people. It was France's duty "to contribute to this work of civilization." Jules Ferry, a republican leader, successfully argued for expanding the French presence in Indochina, saying, "We must believe that if Providence deigned to confer upon us a mission by making us masters of the earth, this mission consists not of attempting an impossible fusion of the races but of simply spreading or awakening among the other races the superior notions of which we are the guardians." Those "superior notions" included a commitment to economic and technological progress and to liberation from slavery, political oppression, poverty, and disease. Ferry argued that "the superior races have a right vis-à-vis the inferior races . . . they have a right to civilize them."

Under Ferry, the French acquired Tunisia (1881), northern and central Vietnam (Tonkin and Annam; 1883), and Laos and Cambodia (1893). They also carried this civilizing mission into their colonies in West Africa. European and Atlantic trade with the west coast of Africa—in slaves, gold, and ivory—had been well established for centuries. In the late nineteenth century, trade gave way to formal administration. The year 1895 saw the establishment of a Federation of French West Africa, a loosely organized administration to govern an area nine times the size of France, including Guinea, Senegal, and the Ivory

Coast. Even with reforms and centralization in 1902, French control remained uneven. Despite military campaigns of pacification, resistance remained. The French dealt gingerly with tribal leaders, at times deferring to their authority and at others trying to break their power. They established French courts and law only in cities, leaving Islamic or tribal courts to run other areas. The federation aimed to rationalize the economic exploitation of the area and to replace "booty capitalism" with a more careful management and development of resources. The French called this "enhancing the value" of the region, which was part of the civilizing mission of the modern republic. The federation embarked on an ambitious program of public works. Engineers rebuilt the huge harbor at Dakar, the most important on the coast, to accommodate rising exports. With utopian zeal they redesigned older cities, tried to improve sanitation and health, improved water systems, and built roads and railways. The French republic was justifiably proud of the Pasteur Institute for bacteriological research, which opened in France in 1888; overseas institutes became part of the colonial enterprise. One plan called for a large-scale West African railroad network to lace through the region. A public-school program built free schools in villages not controlled by missionaries. Education, though, was not compulsory and was usually for boys.

Such programs plainly served French interests. "Officially this process is called civilizing, and after all, the term is apt, since the undertaking serves to increase the degree of prosperity of our civilization," remarked one Frenchman who opposed the colonial enterprise. None of these measures aimed to give indigenous peoples political rights. As one historian puts it, "the French Government General was in the business not of making citizens, but of civilizing its subjects." More telling, however, the French project was not often successful. The French government did not have the resources to carry out its plans, which proved much more expensive and complicated than anyone imagined. Transportation costs ran very high. Labor posed the largest problems. Here as elsewhere, Europeans faced massive resistance from the African peasants, whom they wanted to do everything from building railroads to working mines and carrying rubber. The Europeans resorted to forced labor, signing agreements with local tribal leaders to deliver workers, and they turned a blind eye to the continuing use of slave labor in the interior. For all of these reasons, the colonial project did not produce the profits some expected. In important respects, however, the French investment in colonialism was cultural.

Railroads, schools, and projects such as the Dakar harbor were, like the Eiffel Tower (1889), symbols of the French nation's modernity, power, and world leadership.

THE "SCRAMBLE FOR AFRICA" AND THE CONGO

French expansion into West Africa was only one instance of Europe's voracity on the African continent. The scope and speed with which the major European powers conquered and asserted formal control was astonishing. The effects were profound. In 1875, 11 percent of the continent was in European hands. By 1902, the figure was 90 percent. European powers mastered logistical problems of transport and communication; they learned how to keep diseases at bay. They also had new weapons. The Maxim gun, adopted by the British army in 1889 and first used by British colonial troops, pelted out as many as 500 rounds a minute; it turned encounters with indigenous forces into bloodbaths and made armed resistance virtually impossible.

The Congo Free State

In the 1870s, the British had formed new imperial relationships in the north and west of Africa and along the southern and eastern coasts. A new phase of European involvement struck right at the heart of the continent. Until the latter part of the nineteenth century, this territory had been out of bounds for Europeans. The rapids downstream on such strategic rivers as the Congo and the Zambezi made it difficult to move inland, and tropical diseases were lethal to most European explorers. But during the 1870s, a new drive into central Africa produced results. The target was the fertile valleys around the river Congo, and the European colonizers were a privately financed group of Belgians paid by their king, Leopold II (1865–1909). They followed in the footsteps of Henry Morton Stanley, an American newspaperman and explorer who later became a British subject and a knight of the realm. Stanley hacked his way through thick canopy jungle into territory where no European had previously set foot. His "scientific" journeys inspired the creation of a society of researchers and students of African culture in Brussels, in reality a front organization for the commercial company set up by Leopold. The ambitiously named International Association for the Exploration and Civilization of the Congo was set up in 1876 and soon set about signing treaties with local elites, which opened the whole Congo River basin to commercial exploitation. The vast resources

of palm oil and natural rubber and the promise of minerals (including diamonds) were now within Europeans' reach.

The strongest resistance that Leopold's company faced came from other colonial powers, particularly Portugal, which objected to this new drive for occupation. In 1884, a conference was called in Berlin to settle the matter of control over the Congo River basin. It was chaired by the master of European power politics, Otto von Bismarck, and attended by all the leading colonial nations as well as by the United States. The conference established ground rules for a new phase of European economic and political expansion. Europe's two great overseas empires, Britain and France, and the strongest emerging power inside Europe, Germany, joined forces in a settlement that seemed to be perfectly in line with nineteenth-century liberalism. The Congo valleys would be open to free trade and commerce; a slave trade still run by some of the Islamic kingdoms in the region would be suppressed in favor of free labor; and a Congo Free State would be set up, denying the region to the formal control of any single European country.

In reality, the Congo Free State was run by Leopold's private company, and the region was opened up to unrestricted exploitation by a series of large European corporations. The older slave trade was suppressed, but the European companies took the "free" African labor guaranteed in Berlin and placed workers in equally bad conditions. Huge tracts of land, larger than whole European countries, became diamond mines or plantations for the extraction of palm oil, rubber, or cocoa. African workers labored in appalling conditions, with no real medicine or sanitation, too little food, and according to production schedules that made European factory labor look mild by comparison. Hundreds of thousands of African workers died from disease and overwork. Because European managers did not respect the different cycle of seasons in central Africa, whole crop years were lost, leading to famines. Laborers working in the heat of the dry season often carried individual loads on their backs that would have been handled by heavy machinery in a European factory. Thousands of Africans were pressed into work harvesting goods Europe wanted. They did so for little or no pay, under the threat of beatings and mutilation for dozens of petty offenses against the plantation companies, who made the laws of the Free State. Eventually the scandal of the Congo became too great to go on unquestioned. A whole generation of authors and journalists, most famously Joseph Conrad in his *Heart of Darkness,* publicized the arbitrary brutality and the vast scale of suffering. In 1908, Belgium was forced to take direct control of the Congo, turning it into a Belgian colony. A few restrictions at least were imposed on the activities of the great plantation companies that had brought a vast new store of raw materials to European industry by using slavery in all but name.

The Partition of Africa

The occupation of Congo, and its promise of great material wealth, pressured other colonial powers into expanding their holdings. By the 1880s, the "scramble for Africa" was well under way, hastened by stories of rubber forests or diamond mines in other parts of central and southern Africa. The guarantees made at the 1884 Berlin conference allowed the Europeans to take further steps. The French and Portuguese increased their holdings. Italy moved into territories along the Red Sea, beside British-held land and the independent kingdom of Ethiopia.

Germany came relatively late to empire overseas. Bismarck was reluctant to engage in an enterprise that he believed would yield few economic or political advantages. Yet he did not want either Britain or France to dominate Africa, and Germany seized colonies in strategic locations. The German colonies in Cameroon and most of modern Tanzania separated the territories of older, more established powers. Though the Germans were not the most enthusiastic colonialists, they were fascinated by the imperial adventure and jealous of their territories. When the Herero people of German Southwest Africa (now Namibia) rebelled in the early 1900s, the Germans responded with a vicious campaign of village burning and ethnic killing that nearly annihilated the Herero.

Great Britain and France had their own ambitions. The French aimed to move west to east across the continent, an important reason for the French expedition to Fashoda (in the Sudan) in 1898 (discussed later). Britain's part in the scramble took place largely in southern and eastern Africa and was encapsulated in the dreams and career of one man: the diamond tycoon, colonial politician, and imperial visionary Cecil Rhodes. Rhodes, who made a fortune from the South African diamond mines in the 1870s and 1880s and founded the diamond-mining company DeBeers, became prime minister of Britain's Cape Colony in 1890. (He left part of this fortune for the creation of the Rhodes scholarships to educate future leaders of the empire at Oxford.) In an uneasy alliance with the Boer settlers in their independent republics and with varying levels of support from London, Rhodes pursued two great personal and imperial goals. The personal goal was to build a southern African empire that was founded on diamonds. "Rhodesia" would fly the Union Jack out of pride but send its profits into Rhodes's own companies. Through bribery, double dealing, careful coalition politics with the British and Boer settlers, warfare, and outright theft, Rhodes helped carve out territories occupying the modern nations of Zambia, Zimbabwe, Malawi, and Botswana—most of the savannah of southern Africa. Rhodes had a broader imperial vision, one that he shared with the new British colonial secretary in the late 1890s, Joseph Chamberlain. The first part of that vision was a British presence along the whole of eastern Africa, symbolized by the goal of a Cape-to-Cairo railway. The second was that the empire should make Britain self-sufficient, with British

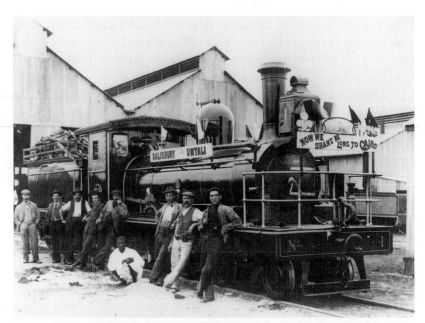

"THE RHODES COLOSSUS" (left). This cartoon, which appeared in *Punch* magazine, satirized the ambitions of Cecil Rhodes, the driving force behind British imperialism in South Africa. **"NOW WE SHANT BE LONG TO CAIRO" (right).** So read the banner across Engine No. 1, taking the first train from Umtali to Salisbury, Rhodesia. In Cecil Rhodes's vision, the Capetown-to-Cairo railway symbolized British domination of the African continent.

industry able to run on the goods and raw materials shipped in from its colonies, then exporting many finished products back to those lands. Once the territories of Zambeziland and Rhodesia were taken, Rhodes found himself turning against the European settlers in the region, a conflict that led to the Boer war in 1899 (discussed later in this chapter).

This battle over strategic advantage, diamonds, and European pride was typical of the scramble. As each European power sought its "place in the sun," in the famous phrase of the German kaiser William II, they brought more and more of Africa under direct colonial control. It created a whole new scale of plunder as companies were designed and managed to strip the continent of its resources. African peoples thus faced a combination of direct European control and indirect rule, which allowed local elites friendly to European interests to lord over those who resisted. The partition of Africa was the most striking instance of the new imperialism, with broad consequences for the subject peoples of European colonies and for the international order as a whole.

IMPERIAL CULTURE

Imperialism was thoroughly anchored in the culture of late-nineteenth-century Europe and the United States. Images of empire were everywhere, not just in the propagandist literature of colonialism's supporters but on tins of tea and boxes of cocoa and as background themes in posters advertising everything from dance halls to sewing machines. Museums and world's fairs displayed the products of empire and introduced spectators to "exotic peoples." Music halls rang to the sound of imperialist songs. Empire was present in novels of the period, sometimes appearing as a faraway setting for fantasy, adventure, or stories of self-discovery. Even the tales of Sherlock Holmes, set in London and not overtly imperialist, often used references to empire—tiger carpets, hookahs and opium dens, Malaysian servants—to add mystery and fascination to their plots. The popular literature of empire showed a particular fascination with sexual practices in faraway places—photos and postcards of North African harems and unveiled Arab women were common in European pornography, as were colonial memoirs that chronicled the sexual adventures of their authors.

Empire thus played an important part in establishing European identity during these years. In France, the "civilizing mission" demonstrated to French citizens the grandeur of their nation. Building railroads and "bringing progress to other lands" illustrated the vigor of the French republic. Many British writers spoke in similar tones. One author wrote, "The British race may safely be called a missionary race. The command to go and teach all nations is

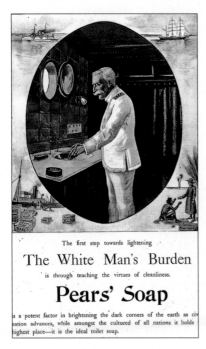

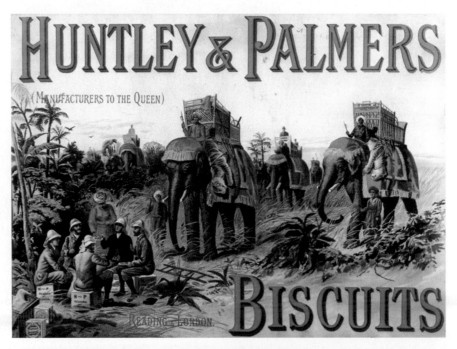

THINKING ABOUT EMPIRE AT HOME. By the end of the nineteenth century, advertisers had begun to use images of empire to sell their products to consumers. The advertisement for Pears' Soap appeared in the American magazine *McClure's* in 1899. The image of the white-uniformed officer washing his hands connects the theme of cleanliness and personal hygiene to notions of racial superiority and the necessity of bringing civilization to "the dark corners of the earth." The packaging of Huntley & Palmers Biscuits, on the other hand, transported the familiar domestic scene of teatime to an exotic imperial location with a supporting cast of elephants. The image, which adorned biscuit boxes in many English parlors during the late Victorian period, seemed to reinforce the idea that essential aspects of British culture could be maintained even as they traveled to distant parts of the globe.

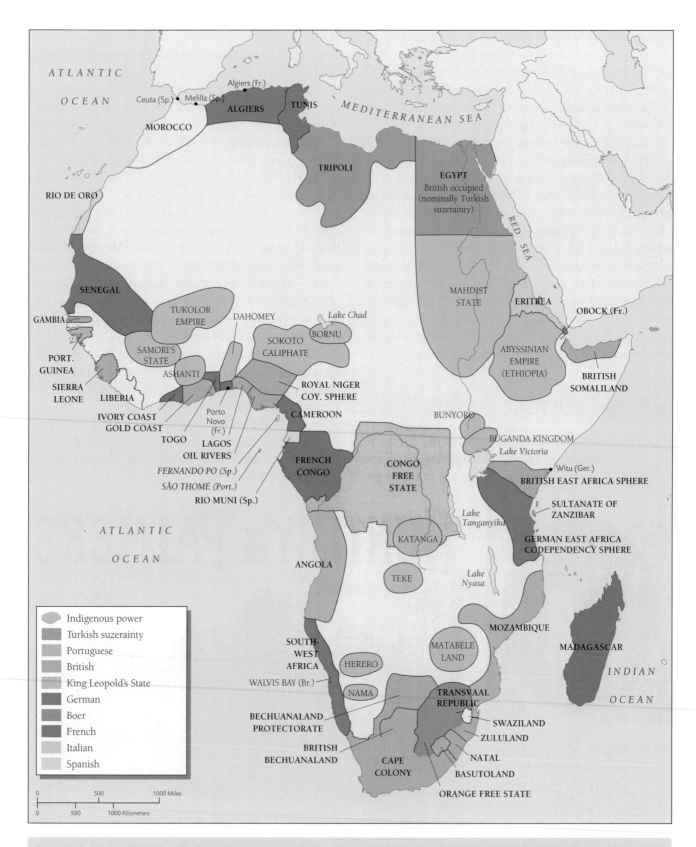

ATLANTIC OCEAN

MEDITERRANEAN SEA

Algiers (Fr.)
Ceuta (Sp.) Melilla (Sp.)
ALGIERS TUNIS
MOROCCO

TRIPOLI

EGYPT
British occupied
(nominally Turkish
suzerainty)

RIO DE ORO

RED SEA

SENEGAL

MAHDIST
STATE

ERITREA

OBOCK (Fr.)

GAMBIA

TUKOLOR
EMPIRE

DAHOMEY

Lake Chad

BORNU

ABYSSINIAN
EMPIRE
(ETHIOPIA)

PORT.
GUINEA

SAMORI'S
STATE

SOKOTO
CALIPHATE

BRITISH
SOMALILAND

SIERRA
LEONE

ASHANTI

LIBERIA

IVORY COAST
GOLD COAST

Porto
Novo
(Fr.)

ROYAL NIGER
COY. SPHERE

CAMEROON

BUNYORO

TOGO LAGOS
OIL RIVERS

FERNANDO PO (Sp.)

SÃO THOMÉ (Port.)

RIO MUNI (Sp.)

FRENCH
CONGO

CONGO
FREE
STATE

BUGANDA KINGDOM
Lake Victoria

Witu (Ger.)

BRITISH EAST AFRICA SPHERE

SULTANATE OF
ZANZIBAR

Lake
Tanganyika

GERMAN EAST AFRICA
CODEPENDENCY SPHERE

ATLANTIC

OCEAN

KATANGA

ANGOLA

TEKE

Lake
Nyasa

MOZAMBIQUE

MADAGASCAR

INDIAN

OCEAN

Indigenous power
Turkish suzerainty
Portuguese
British
King Leopold's State
German
Boer
French
Italian
Spanish

SOUTH-
WEST
AFRICA

HERERO

MATABELE
LAND

WALVIS BAY (Br.)

NAMA

TRANSVAAL
REPUBLIC

SWAZILAND

ZULULAND

BECHUANALAND
PROTECTORATE

NATAL

BRITISH
BECHUANALAND

CAPE
COLONY

BASUTOLAND

ORANGE FREE STATE

0 500 1000 Miles
0 500 1000 Kilometers

AFRICA, c. 1886. ▪ *What is the single biggest difference in terms of rulership between the two maps?* ▪ *Who were the winners and losers in the scramble for Africa before the First World War?* ▪ *What does the result of the scramble for Africa suggest about how European powers regarded each other?*

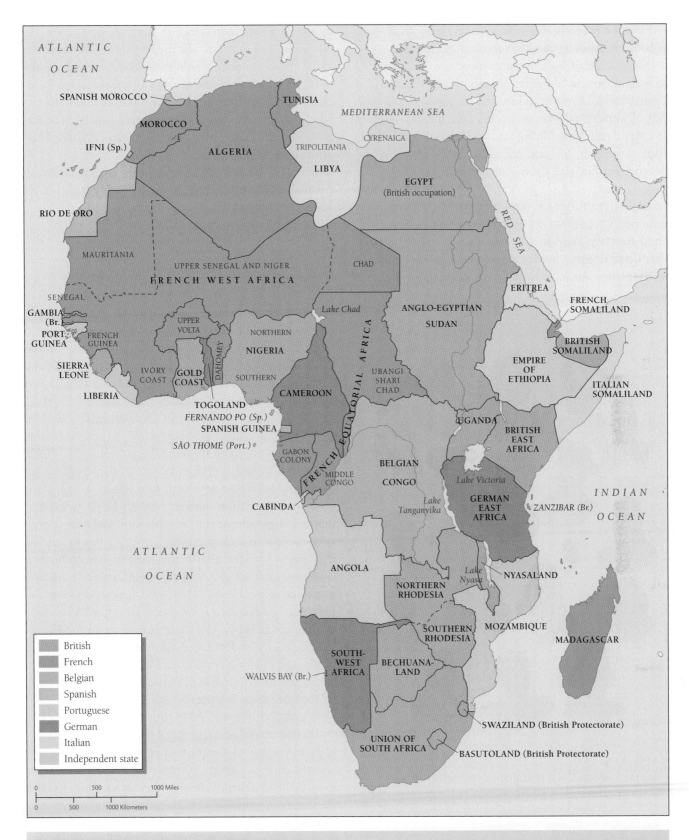

Legend:
- British
- French
- Belgian
- Spanish
- Portuguese
- German
- Italian
- Independent state

0   500   1000 Miles
0   500   1000 Kilometers

AFRICA, c. 1914.

ATLANTIC OCEAN

SPANISH MOROCCO

TUNISIA

MEDITERRANEAN SEA

MOROCCO

IFNI (Sp.)

ALGERIA

TRIPOLITANIA

CYRENAICA

LIBYA

EGYPT
(British occupation)

RIO DE ORO

RED SEA

MAURITANIA

UPPER SENEGAL AND NIGER

CHAD

ERITREA

FRENCH WEST AFRICA

FRENCH SOMALILAND

SENEGAL

Lake Chad

ANGLO-EGYPTIAN SUDAN

BRITISH SOMALILAND

GAMBIA (Br.)

UPPER VOLTA

NORTHERN

PORT. GUINEA

FRENCH GUINEA

NIGERIA

EMPIRE OF ETHIOPIA

SIERRA LEONE

IVORY COAST

GOLD COAST

DAHOMEY

SOUTHERN

CAMEROON

UBANGI SHARI CHAD

ITALIAN SOMALILAND

LIBERIA

TOGOLAND

FERNANDO PO (Sp.)

SPANISH GUINEA

UGANDA

BRITISH EAST AFRICA

SÃO THOMÉ (Port.)

GABON COLONY

FRENCH EQUATORIAL AFRICA

BELGIAN CONGO

Lake Victoria

INDIAN OCEAN

CABINDA

MIDDLE CONGO

Lake Tanganyika

GERMAN EAST AFRICA

ZANZIBAR (Br.)

ATLANTIC OCEAN

ANGOLA

Lake Nyasa

NYASALAND

NORTHERN RHODESIA

MOZAMBIQUE

MADAGASCAR

SOUTHERN RHODESIA

SOUTH-WEST AFRICA

BECHUANA-LAND

WALVIS BAY (Br.)

SWAZILAND (British Protectorate)

UNION OF SOUTH AFRICA

BASUTOLAND (British Protectorate)

one that the British people have, whether rightly or wrongly, regarded as specially laid upon themselves."

This sense of high moral purpose was not restricted to male writers or to figures of authority. In England, the United States, Germany, and France, the speeches and projects of women's reform movements were full of references to empire and the civilizing mission. Britain's woman suffrage movement, for example, was fiercely critical of the government but was also nationalist and imperialist. For these militants, women's participation in politics also meant the right to participate in imperial projects. British women reformers wrote about the oppression of Indian women by child marriage and sati and saw themselves shouldering the "white women's burden" of reform. In France, suffragist Hubertine Auclert criticized the colonial government

in Algeria for its indifference to the condition of Muslim women in their domains. She used an image of women suffering in polygamous marriages abroad to dramatize the need for reform. Arguments such as these enabled European women in their home countries to see themselves as bearers of progress, as participants in a superior civilization. Similarly, John Stuart Mill often used Hindu or Muslim culture as a foil when he wanted to make a point of freedom of speech and religion. This contrast between colonial backwardness and European civility and cultural superiority shaped Western culture and political debate about liberal ideas in particular.

Imperialism and Racial Thought

Imperial culture gave new prominence to racial thinking. Count Arthur de Gobineau (GOH-bih-noh, 1816–1882) wrote a massive work, *The Inequality of the Races*, in the 1850s, but it sparked little interest until the period of the new imperialism, when it was translated into English and widely discussed. For Gobineau, race offered the "master key" for understanding human societies in the modern world. "The racial question overshadows all other problems of history . . . the inequality of the races from whose fusion a people is formed is enough to explain the whole course of its destiny." Gobineau's work followed from Enlightenment investigations of different cultures in the world, but unlike Enlightenment authors who attributed these differences largely to environmental factors, Gobineau argued that "blood" was the determining factor in human history. Gobineau claimed that humans were originally divided into three races, "black," "white," and "yellow," and that the peoples of the present day were variously mixed from these original components. The white race, he argued, had preserved purer bloodlines and was therefore superior. The others suffered "adulteration" and were therefore degenerate and no longer capable of civilization. Gobineau's readers included some defenders of the confederacy during the American Civil War and Adolf Hitler.

Followers of Gobineau's racial thinking looked increasingly to science to legitimate their theories. The natural scientist Charles Darwin, no racist himself, attracted wide attention with a theory of evolution that sought to explain the variety of species observable in the natural world. Darwin suggested that only the most "fit" individuals in a species survived to bear viable offspring, and that this process of "natural selection" explained how species diverged from one another: variations that made individuals better able to find food and mates were likely to be passed on to future generations. Social scientists such as Herbert Spencer

RACIAL THINKING IN THE AGE OF EMPIRE. This plate was published in 1906 in England and the United States in a geography book that was aimed at a mass audience. It is a good example of the ways that racial categories were given scientific legitimacy and disseminated in a way that lent them credibility in the popular imagination of the reading public. ▪ *How does this print convey the notion of racial hierarchy, the idea that some "races" were superior to others? Is the idea of "race" contained in this print purely biological? Does it also contain implications about human history?*

sought to use a similar logic of competition among individuals for scarce resources to explain the evolution of social groups, suggesting that inequalities of wealth or ability could also be explained as the result of a process of "natural selection." Racial theorists and followers of Gobineau such as Houston Stewart Chamberlain (1855–1927) wasted little time in harnessing such scientific arguments to the claim that human "races" evolved over time. Chamberlain's books sold tens of thousands of copies in England and Germany.

Francis Galton (1822–1911), a half cousin of Charles Darwin and a scientist who studied evolution, went so far as to advocate improving the population's racial characteristics by selective breeding of "superior types." Galton and others feared that improvements in health care and hygiene might allow individuals with inferior traits to survive to reproductive age, and his system of racial management, which he called *eugenics*, would save European populations from a decline in their vitality and biological fitness. Theories such as Galton's or Gobineau's did not cause imperialism, and they were closely linked with other developments in European culture, in particular renewed anxieties about social class and a fresh wave of European anti-Semitism. Yet the increasingly scientific racism of late-nineteenth-century Europe made it easier for many to reconcile the rhetoric of progress, individual freedom, and the civilizing mission with contempt for other peoples.

Opposition to Imperialism

Support for imperialism was not unanimous. Hobson and Lenin condemned the entire enterprise as an act of greed and arrogance. Polish-born Joseph Conrad, a British novelist, shared much of the racism of his contemporaries, but he nevertheless believed that imperialism was an expression of deeply rooted pathologies in European culture. Other anti-imperialists were men and women from the colonies themselves who brought their case to the metropole. The British Committee of the Indian National Congress gathered together many members of London's Indian community to educate British public opinion about the exploitation of Indian peoples and resources.

Perhaps the most defiant anti-imperialist action was the London Pan-African Conference of 1900, staged at the height of the scramble for Africa and during the Boer War (discussed on page 000). The conference grew out of an international tradition of African American, British, and American antislavery movements and brought the rhetoric used earlier to abolish slavery to bear on the tactics of European imperialism. They protested forced labor in the mining compounds of South Africa as akin to slavery and asked in very moderate tones for some autonomy and representation

for African peoples. The Pan-African Conference of 1900 was small, but it drew delegates from the Caribbean, West Africa, and North America, including the thirty-two-year-old Harvard Ph.D. and leading African American intellectual, W. E. B. Du Bois (1868–1963). The conference issued a proclamation "To the Nations of the World," with a famous introduction written by Du Bois. "In the metropolis of the modern world, in this closing year of the nineteenth century," the proclamation read, "there has been assembled a congress of men and women of African blood, to deliberate solemnly upon the present situation and outlook of the darker races of mankind. The problem of the twentieth century is the problem of the colour-line." The British government ignored the conference, but pan-Africanism, like Indian nationalism, grew rapidly after the First World War.

Colonial Cultures

Imperialism also created new colonial cultures in other parts of the world. Cities such as Bombay, Calcutta, and Shanghai boomed, more than tripling in size. Treaty ports like Hong Kong were transformed as Europeans built banks, shipping enterprises, schools, and religious missions. As Europeans and indigenous peoples encountered and transformed one another, new hybrid cultures emerged. Elsewhere, new social instabilities were produced as European demands for labor brought men out of their villages, away from their families, and crowded them into shantytowns bordering sprawling new cities. Hopes that European rule would create a well-disciplined labor force were quickly dashed.

People on both sides of the colonial divide worried about preserving national traditions and identity in the face of these hybrid and changing colonial cultures. In Africa and the Middle East, Islamic scholars debated the proper response to European control. In China and India, suggestions that local populations adopt European models of education set off fierce controversies. Chinese elites, already divided over such customs as foot-binding and concubinage (the legal practice of maintaining formal sexual partners for men outside their marriage), found their dilemmas heightened as imperialism became a more powerful force. Should they defend such practices as integral to their culture? Should they argue for a Chinese path to reform? Proponents of change in China or India thus had to sort through their stance toward Western culture and traditional popular culture.

For their part, British, French, and Dutch authorities fretted that too much familiarity between colonized and colonizer would weaken European prestige and authority. In Phnom Penh, Cambodia (part of French Indochina),

Address to the Nations of the World by the Pan-African Conference in London, 1900

The Pan-African Conference that met in 1900 in London brought together a group of people of African heritage from many parts of the world who were determined to add their voices to those who were discussing and debating the consequences of European imperialism in the last decades of the nineteenth century. The declaration that they produced gives a clear picture of their vision of history, their sense of the injustices associated with colonial conquest, and their hopes for the future. The chair of the committee who wrote the address was W. E. B. Du Bois (1868–1963), an African American professor of history, sociology, and economics who had studied at Harvard and the University of Berlin and who in 1909 became a founding member of the National Association for the Advancement of Colored People.

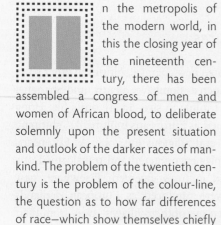

n the metropolis of the modern world, in this the closing year of the nineteenth century, there has been assembled a congress of men and women of African blood, to deliberate solemnly upon the present situation and outlook of the darker races of mankind. The problem of the twentieth century is the problem of the colour-line, the question as to how far differences of race—which show themselves chiefly in the colour of the skin and the texture of the hair—will hereafter be made the basis of denying to over half the world the right of sharing to their utmost ability the opportunities and privileges of modern civilization.

To be sure, the darker races are today the least advanced in culture according to European standards. This has not, however, always been the case in the past, and certainly the world's history, both ancient and modern, has given many instances of no despicable ability and capacity among the blackest races of men.

In any case, the modern world must remember that in this age when the ends of the world are being brought so near together the millions of black men in Africa, America, and the Islands of the Sea, not to speak of the brown and yellow myriads elsewhere, are bound to have a great influence upon the world in the future, by reason of sheer numbers and physical contact. If now the world of culture bends itself towards giving Negroes and other dark men the largest and broadest opportunity for education and self-development, then this contact and influence is bound to have a beneficial effect upon the world and hasten human progress. But if, by reason of carelessness, prejudice, greed and injustice, the black world is to be exploited and ravished and degraded, the results must be deplorable, if not fatal—not simply to them, but to the high ideals of justice, freedom and culture which a thousand years of Christian civilization have held before Europe.

And now, therefore, to these ideals of civilization, to the broader humanity of the followers of the Prince of Peace, we, the men and women of Africa in world congress assembled, do now solemnly appeal:

Let the world take no backward step in that slow but sure progress which has successively refused to let the spirit of class, of caste, of privilege, or of birth, debar from life, liberty and the pursuit of happiness a striving human soul.

Let not color or race be a feature of distinction between white and black men, regardless of worth or ability.

Let not the natives of Africa be sacrificed to the greed of gold, their liberties

French citizens lived separated from the rest of the city by a moat, and authorities required "dressing appropriately and keeping a distance from the natives." Sexual relations provoked the most anxiety and the most contradictory responses. "In this hot climate, passions run higher," wrote a French administrator in Algeria. "French soldiers seek out Arab women due to their strangeness and newness." "It was common practice for unmarried Englishmen resident in China to keep a Chinese girl, and I did as the others did," reported a British man stationed in Shanghai. He married an Englishwoman, however, and sent his Chinese mistress and their three children to England to avoid awkwardness. European administrators fitfully tried to prohibit liaisons between European men and local women, labeling such affairs as "corrupting." Such prohibitions only drove these relations underground, increasing the gap between the public facade of colonial rule and the private reality of colonial lives.

taken away, their family life debauched, their just aspirations repressed, and avenues of advancement and culture taken from them.

Let not the cloak of Christian missionary enterprise be allowed in the future, as so often in the past, to hide the ruthless economic exploitation and political downfall of less developed nations, whose chief fault has been reliance on the plighted faith of the Christian Church.

Let the British nation, the first modern champion of Negro Freedom, hasten to crown the work of Wilberforce, and Clarkson, and Buxton, and Sharpe, Bishop Colenso, and Livingstone, and give, as soon as practicable, the rights of responsible government to the black colonies of Africa and the West Indies.

Let not the spirit of Garrison, Phillips, and Douglass wholly die out in America; may the conscience of a great nation rise and rebuke all dishonesty and unrighteous oppression toward the American Negro, and grant to him the right of franchise, security of person and property, and generous recognition of the great work he has accomplished in a generation toward raising nine millions of human beings from slavery to manhood.

Let the German Empire, and the French Republic, true to their great past, remember that the true worth of colonies lies in their prosperity and progress, and that justice, impartial alike to black and white, is the first element of prosperity.

Let the Congo Free State become a great central Negro State of the world, and let its prosperity be counted not simply in cash and commerce, but in the happiness and true advancement of its black people.

Let the nations of the World respect the integrity and independence of the first Negro States of Abyssinia, Liberia, Haiti, and the rest, and let the inhabitants of these States, the independent tribes of Africa, the Negroes of the West Indies and America, and the black subjects of all nations take courage, strive ceaselessly, and fight bravely, that they may prove to the world their incontestible right to be counted among the great brotherhood of mankind.

Thus we appeal with boldness and confidence to the Great Powers of the civilized world, trusting in the wide spirit of humanity, and the deep sense of justice of our age, for a generous recognition of the righteousness of our cause.

ALEXANDER WALTERS (Bishop)
President Pan-African Association
HENRY B. BROWN
Vice-President
H. SYLVESTER-WILLIAMS
General Secretary
W. E. BURGHARDT DU BOIS
Chairman Committee on Address

Source: Ayodele Langley, *Ideologies of Liberation in Black Africa* (London: 1979), pp. 738–39.

Questions for Analysis

1. What value do the authors ascribe to "race" as a description of human difference?

2. According to the authors, what choices do European powers have to make as they exercise their power in Africa? What are their hopes for Africans in a world shaped by European expansion?

3. What are the specific "ideals of civilization" that the authors of this declaration invoke? Do they share these ideals with people from elsewhere?

4. Are there echoes of European liberalism or nationalism in the address's pan-Africanism?

CRISES OF EMPIRE AT THE TURN OF THE TWENTIETH CENTURY

The turn of the twentieth century brought a series of crises to the Western empires. Those crises did not end European rule. They did, however, create sharp tensions among Western nations. The crises also drove imperial nations to expand their economic and military commitments in territories overseas. They shook Western confidence. In all of these ways, they became central to Western culture in the years before the First World War.

Fashoda

In the fall of 1898, British and French armies nearly went to war at Fashoda, in the Egyptian Sudan. The crisis had

Interpreting Visual Evidence

Displays of Imperial Culture: The Paris Exposition of 1889

he French colonies were very visible during the celebration of the centenary of the French Revolution in 1889. In that year, the French government organized a "Universal Exposition" in the capital that attracted over 6 million visitors to a broad esplanade covered with exhibitions of French industry and culture, including the newly constructed Eiffel Tower, a symbol of modern French engineering.

At the base of the Eiffel Tower (image A), a colonial pavilion placed objects from France's overseas empire on display, and a collection of temporary architectural exhibits placed reproductions of buildings from French colonies in Asia and Africa as well as samples of architecture from other parts of the world. The photographs here show a reproduction of a Cairo Street (image B); the Pagoda of Angkor, modeled after

A. The Eiffel Tower in 1889.

the Khmer temples of Angkor Wat in Cambodia, a French protectorate (image C); and examples of West African dwellings (image D). The Cairo Street was the second most popular tourist destination at the fair, after the Eiffel Tower. It con-

tained twenty-five shops and restaurants, and employed dozens of Egyptian servers, shopkeepers, and artisans who had been brought to Paris to add authenticity to the exhibit. Other people on display in the colonial pavilion included Senegalese villagers and a Vietnamese theater troupe.

Questions for Analysis

1. What vision of history and social progress is celebrated in this linkage between France's colonial holdings and the industrial power on display in the Eiffel Tower?

2. What might account for the popularity of the Cairo Street exhibit among the public?

3. Why was it so important for the exposition to place people from European colonies on display for a French audience?

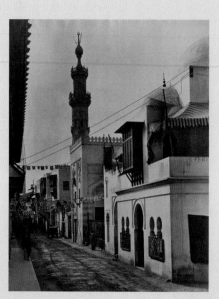

B. Reproduction of a Cairo Street at the Paris World's Fair, 1889.

C. Pagoda of Angkor at the Paris World's Fair, 1889.

D. West African houses at the Paris World's Fair, 1889.

complex causes: in the early 1880s, the British had used a local uprising in the Sudan as an excuse to move southward from Egypt in an attempt to control the headwaters of the Nile River. This project began with grandiose dreams of connecting Cairo to the Cape of Good Hope, but it ran into catastrophe when an army led by Britain's most flamboyant general, Charles Gordon, was massacred in Khartoum in 1885 by the forces of the Mahdi, a Sufi religious leader who claimed to be the successor to the prophet Muhammad. Avenging Gordon's death preoccupied the British for more than a decade, and in 1898 a second large-scale rebellion gave them the opportunity. An Anglo-Egyptian army commanded by General Horatio Kitchener attacked Khartoum and defeated the Mahdi's army using modern machine guns and artillery.

The victory brought complications, however. France, which held territories in central Africa adjacent to the Sudan, saw the British victory as a threat. A French expedition was sent to the Sudanese town of Fashoda (now Kodok) to challenge British claims in the area. The French faced off with troops from Kitchener's army, and for a few weeks in September 1898 the situation teetered on the brink of war. The matter was resolved diplomatically, however, and France ceded the southern Sudan to Britain in exchange for a stop to further expansion. The incident was a sobering reminder of the extent to which imperial competition could lead to international tensions between European powers.

EMPEROR MENELIK II. Ethiopia was the last major independent African kingdom, its prosperity a counter to the European opinion of African cultures. Menelik soundly defeated the Italian attempt to conquer his kingdom in 1896.

Ethiopia

During the 1880s and 1890s, Italy had been developing a small empire on the shores of the Red Sea. Italy annexed Eritrea and parts of Somalia, and shortly after the death of Gordon at Khartoum, the Italians defeated an invasion of their territories by the Mahdi's forces. Bolstered by this success, the Italians set out to conquer Ethiopia in 1896. Ethiopia was the last major independent African kingdom, ruled by a shrewd and capable emperor, Menelik II. His largely Christian subjects engaged in profitable trade on the East African coast, and revenues from this trade allowed Menelik to invest in the latest European artillery. When the Italian army—mostly Somali conscripts and a few thousand Italian troops—arrived, Menelik allowed them to penetrate into the mountain passes of Ethiopia. To keep to the roads, the Italians were forced to divide their forces into separate columns. Meanwhile, the Ethiopians moved over the mountains themselves, and at Adowa in March 1896 Menelik's army attacked, destroyed the Italian armies completely, and killed

6,000. Adowa was a national humiliation for Italy and an important symbol for African political radicals during the early twentieth century.

South Africa: The Boer War

In the late 1800s, competition between Dutch settlers in South Africa—known as Afrikaners or Boers—and the British led to a shooting war between Europeans. The Boers (an appropriation of the Dutch word for farmer) arrived in South Africa in the early nineteenth century and had long had a troubled relationship with their British neighbors in the colony. In the 1830s, the Boers trekked inland from the cape, setting up two republics away from British influence: the Transvaal and the Orange Free State. Gold reserves were found in the Transvaal in the 1880s, and Cecil Rhodes, the diamond magnate, tried to provoke war between Britain and the Boers to gain control of the Afrikaners' diamond mines. The war finally

Competing Viewpoints

Rudyard Kipling and His Critics

Rudyard Kipling (1865–1936) remains one of the most famous propagandists of empire. His novels, short stories, and poetry about the British imperial experience in India were defining texts for the cause in which he believed. Kipling's poem was—and continues to be—widely read, analyzed, attacked, and praised. His immediate goal was to influence American public opinion during the Spanish-American War, but he also wanted to celebrate the moral and religious values of European imperialism in general.

The White Man's Burden

Take up the White Man's burden—
　Send forth the best ye breed—
Go, bind your sons to exile
　To serve your captives' need;
To wait, in heavy harness,
　On fluttered folk and wild—
Your new-caught sullen peoples,
　Half devil and half child.

Take up the White Man's burden—
　In patience to abide,
To veil the threat of terror
　And check the show of pride;
By open speech and simple,
　An hundred times made plain,
To seek another's profit
　And work another's gain.

Take up the White Man's burden—
　The savage wars of peace—
Fill full the mouth of Famine,
　And bid the sickness cease;

And when your goal is nearest
　(The end for others sought)
Watch sloth and heathen folly
　Bring all your hope to nought.

Take up the White Man's burden—
　No iron rule of kings,
But toil of serf and sweeper—
　The tale of common things.
The ports ye shall not enter,
　The roads ye shall not tread,
Go, make them with your living
　And mark them with your dead.

Take up the White Man's burden,
　And reap his old reward—
The blame of those ye better
　The hate of those ye guard—
The cry of hosts ye humour
　(Ah, slowly!) toward the light:—
"Why brought ye us from bondage,
　Our loved Egyptian night?"

Take up the White Man's burden—
　Ye dare not stoop to less—
Nor call too loud on Freedom
　To cloak your weariness.
By all ye will or whisper,
　By all ye leave or do,
The silent sullen peoples
　Shall weigh your God and you.

Take up the White Man's burden!
　Have done with childish days—
The lightly-proffered laurel,
　The easy ungrudged praise:
Comes now, to search your manhood
　Through all the thankless years,
Cold, edged with dear-bought wisdom,
　The judgment of your peers.

Source: Rudyard Kipling, "The White Man's Burden," *McClure's Magazine* 12 (Feb. 1899).

To the Editor of *The Nation*

Sir: The cable informs us that "Kipling's stirring verses, the 'Call to America,' have created a . . . profound impression" on your side. What that impression may be, we can only conjecture. There is something almost sickening in this "imperial" talk of assuming and bearing burdens for the good of others. They are never assumed or held where they are not found to be of material advantage or ministering to honor or glory. Wherever empire (I speak of the United Kingdom) is extended, and the climate suits the white man, the aborigines are, for the benefit of the white man, cleared off or held in degradation for his benefit. . . .

Taking India as a test, no one moves a foot in her government that is not well paid and pensioned at her cost. No appointments are more eagerly

contended for than those in the Indian service. A young man is made for life when he secures one. The tone of that service is by no means one "bound to exile," "to serve . . . captives' need," "to wait in heavy harness," or in any degree as expressed in Mr. Kipling's highfalutin lines. It is entirely the contrary: "You are requested not to beat the servants" is a not uncommon notice in Indian hotels. . . . So anxious are we, where good pay is concerned, to save Indians the heavy burden of enjoying them, that, while our sons can study and pass at home for Indian appointments, her sons must study and pass in England; and even in India itself whites are afforded chances closed to natives. . . .

There never was a fostered trade and revenue in more disastrous consequences to humanity than the opium trade and revenue. There never was a more grinding and debilitating tax than that on salt. . . .

Source: Alfred Webb, "Mr. Kipling's Call to America," *The Nation* 68 (Feb. 23, 1899).

Questions for Analysis

1. What benefits did Kipling think imperialism brought, and to whom?

2. What, exactly, was the "burden"?

3. What were Webb's arguments against Kipling? Why did he think that imperial talk was "almost sickening"? Did Europeans really suffer in their colonial outposts? In British India, with its well-established civil service, Webb thought not. Why did he mention the opium trade and the salt tax?

broke out in 1899, but the British were unprepared for the ferocity of Boer resistance. British columns were shot to pieces by Afrikaner forces who knew the territory, and the British towns of Ladysmith and Mafeking were besieged. Angered by these early failures, the British replaced their commanders and began to fight in earnest, using the railroads built to service the diamond mines to bring in modern military hardware.

The Afrikaners responded by taking to the hills, fighting a costly guerilla war that lasted another three years. The British tactics became more brutal as the campaign went on, setting up concentration camps—the first use of the term—where Afrikaner civilians were rounded up and forced to live in appalling conditions so that they would not be able to help the guerillas. Nearly 20,000 civilians died in the camps owing to disease and poor sanitation over the course of two years. Black Africans, despised by both sides, also suffered the effects of famine and disease as the war destroyed valuable farmland.

Meanwhile, the concentration camps aroused opposition in Britain and internationally, and protesters campaigned against these violations of "European" rights, without saying anything about the fate of Africans in the conflict. In the end, the Afrikaners ceded control of their republics to a new British Union of South Africa that gave them a share of political power. In the aftermath of the

LA GUERRE AU TRANSVAAL
Les camps de reconcentration

AN ENGLISH CONCENTRATION CAMP DURING THE BOER WAR. In an attempt to block support to guerilla fighters, the English restricted Afrikaner civilians to camps where appalling conditions led to the death of nearly 20,000 people over two years. This illustration appeared in a French newspaper, *Le Petit Journal*, in 1901.

war, both British and Afrikaners preserved their high standards of living by relying on cheap African labor and, eventually, a system of racial segregation known as apartheid.

U.S. Imperialism: The Spanish-American War of 1898

Imperialism also brought Spain and the United States to war in 1898. American imperialism in the nineteenth century was closely bound up with nation building, the conquest of new territories, and the defeat of the North American Indians (see Chapter 21). In the 1840s, the United States provoked Mexico into war over Texas and California after unsuccessfully trying to purchase the territories. Mexico's defeat, and the treaty of Guadalupe Hidalgo that followed in 1848, gave the American Southwest to the United States, an enormous territorial gain that made the question of slavery more acute in the years before the American Civil War.

The conflict with Spain followed a similar pattern. In the 1880s and 1890s, Spain's imperial powers were considerably weakened, and they faced rebellion in their colonies in the Caribbean and the Pacific. American economic interests had considerable investments in Cuba, and when an American battleship accidentally exploded at port in Havana, advocates of empire and the press in general

IMPERIALISM IN THE BALANCE. This cartoon, titled "A Study—Imperialism" appeared in the United States in 1899 during the beginning of the Philippine-American War. The image shows the scales of justice weighing imperialism against the many victims of U.S. military action, and demonstrates that the populations of colonial powers were far from unanimous about the virtues of imperial expansion and the "civilizing mission."

After You Read This Chapter

Ⓢ Visit StudySpace for quizzes, additional review materials, and multimedia documents. **wwnorton.com/web/westernciv18**

REVIEWING THE OBJECTIVES

- European imperialism in the nineteenth century differed from earlier phases of colonial expansion. How was it different, and which parts of the globe were singled out for special attention by European imperial powers?
- European nations justified the cost and effort of their colonial policies in many ways. What were the major reasons for colonial expansion in the nineteenth century?
- The subjugated peoples of European colonies faced a choice between resistance and accommodation, though these choices were rarely exclusive of one another. What examples of resistance to colonialism can you identify? Of accommodation?
- Imperialism also shaped cultural developments within Europe in the nineteenth century. How did imperialism change the lives of Europeans and their sense of their place in the world?
- Imperialism unleashed destabilizing competitive forces that drove European colonial powers into conflict with one another by the end of the nineteenth century. Where were the flashpoints of these conflicts?

clamored for revenge. President William McKinley gave in to political necessity, in spite of his misgivings, and the United States declared war on Spain in 1898, determined to protect its economic interests in the Americas and the Pacific. The United States swiftly won.

In Spain, the Spanish-American War provoked an entire generation of writers, politicians, and intellectuals to national soul searching. The defeat undermined the Spanish monarchy, which fell in 1912. The ensuing political tensions resurfaced in the Spanish Civil War of the 1930s, an important episode in the origins of the Second World War.

In the United States, this "splendid little war" was followed by the annexation of Puerto Rico, the establishment of a protectorate over Cuba, and a short but brutal war against Philippine rebels who liked American colonialism no better than the Spanish variety. In the Americas, the United States intervened in a rebellion in Panama in 1903, quickly backing the rebels and helping establish a republic while building the Panama Canal on land leased from the new government. The Panama Canal opened in 1914, and like Britain's canal at Suez, it cemented U.S. dominance of the seas in the Western Hemisphere and the eastern Pacific. Later interventions in Hawaii and Santo Domingo gave further evidence of U.S. imperial power and committed the former colony to a broad role in its new and greater sphere of influence.

CONCLUSION

In the last quarter of the nineteenth century, the long-standing relationship between Western nations and the rest of the world entered a new stage. That stage was distinguished by the stunningly rapid extension of formal Western control, by new forms of economic exploitation, and by new patterns of social discipline and settlement. It was driven by the rising economic needs of the industrial West; by territorial conflict; and by nationalism, which by the late nineteenth century linked nationhood to empire. Among its immediate results was the creation of a self-consciously imperial culture in the West. At the same time, however, it plainly created unease and contributed powerfully to the sense of crisis that swept through the late-nineteenth-century West.

For all its force, this Western expansion was never unchallenged. Imperialism provoked resistance and required constantly changing strategies of rule. During the First World War, mobilizing the resources of empire would become crucial to victory. In the aftermath, reimposing the conditions of the late nineteenth century would become nearly impossible. And over the longer term, the political structures, economic developments, and racial ideologies established in this period would be contested throughout the twentieth century.

PEOPLE, IDEAS, AND EVENTS IN CONTEXT

- What was the **EAST INDIA COMPANY**? How did the British reorganize their rule in India after the **SEPOY MUTINY**?
- What did the French mean when they justified colonial expansion in the name of the **CIVILIZING MISSION**?
- How did the **OPIUM WARS** change the economic and political relationships between Europe and China?
- How did the **BERLIN CONFERENCE** of 1884 shape the subsequent colonization of Africa?
- What limits to the exercise of colonial power were revealed by the **BOXER REBELLION**, the failed **ITALIAN INVASION OF ETHIOPIA**, or the **RUSSO-JAPANESE WAR**?
- What expressions of anti-imperialism emerged from the London **PAN-AFRICAN CONFERENCE**?
- How did the **BOER WAR** and the **FASHODA INCIDENT** contribute to a sense of crisis among European colonial powers?
- What effects did the **SPANISH-AMERICAN WAR** have on attitudes toward imperialism in the United States, itself a former European colony?

THINKING ABOUT CONNECTIONS

- Compare the consequences of late-nineteenth-century European colonial conquest with earlier episodes of imperial expansion such as the Roman Empire or early modern colonization in the Atlantic world. What was similar? What was different?
- What challenges were faced by colonial regimes such as France and Britain, which expanded their institutions of representative and elected government at home even as they subjugated the conquered peoples in their new colonies during the nineteenth century?
- The histories of colonial conquest in the nineteenth century helped to establish a network of political and cultural connections that shaped the history of the world in the twentieth century. What was the legacy of these connections during the period of decolonization?
- How was the history of industrialization connected to the history of colonialism?

STORY LINES

- The second industrial revolution intensified the scope and effects of technological innovations, as new techniques for producing steel and chemicals became widespread and new sources of power—electricity and oil—provided alternatives to coal-burning machinery.

- The expansion of the electorate in many European nation-states created a different kind of politics, as workers and peasants were given voting rights for the first time while women continued to be excluded from voting. New political parties on the right and the left engaged in partisan struggles to win the support of new voters.

- Although the advances in technology and industry encouraged a sense of self-confidence about European society and progress, other scientific and cultural movements expressed doubt or anxiety about the effects of rapid modernization on European culture.

CHRONOLOGY

1850s–1870s	Production of steel alloys revolutionized
1859	Publication of Charles Darwin's *On the Origin of Species*
1861	Emancipation of the serfs in Russia
1871	Paris Commune
1871–1878	Bismarck's *Kulturkampf*
1880–1890s	Russia launches industrialization program
1890s	Electricity becomes available in many European cities
1894–1906	Dreyfus Affair
1899	Publication of Sigmund Freud's *The Interpretation of Dreams*
1901	Labour party founded in Britain
1903	Russian Marxists split into Bolsheviks and Mensheviks
1905	The First Russian Revolution

Modern Industry and Mass Politics, 1870–1914

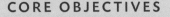

CORE OBJECTIVES

- **UNDERSTAND** the origins and consequences of the second industrial revolution.

- **DEFINE** *mass politics* and explain how the expansion of voting rights in European nations led to the development of organized political parties that sought the support of the working classes.

- **UNDERSTAND** the arguments both for and against woman suffrage during this period.

- **IDENTIFY** the ways that European liberalism and conservatism evolved as new social and political tensions emerged with the advent of mass politics and intensified industrial development.

- **EXPLAIN** the contributions of scientists and other cultural figures who came to prominence in the final decades of the nineteenth century and their contributions to debates about human nature, modern society, and the natural world.

"We are on the extreme promontory of ages!" decreed the Italian poet and literary editor F. T. Marinetti in 1909. In a bombastic manifesto—a self-described "inflammatory declaration" printed on the front page of a Paris newspaper—Marinetti introduced Europe to an aggressive art movement called futurism. Revolting against what he considered the tired and impotent conservatism of Italian culture, Marinetti called for a radical renewal of civilization through "courage, audacity, and revolt." Enamored with the raw power of modern machinery, with the dynamic bustle of urban life, he trumpeted "a new form of beauty, the beauty of speed." Most notable, Marinetti celebrated the heroic violence of warfare and disparaged the moral and cultural traditions that formed the bedrock of nineteenth-century liberalism.

Few Europeans embraced the modern era with the unflinching abandon of the futurists, but many would have agreed with Marinetti in his claim that modern life was above all characterized by flux, movement, and an accelerating rate of change. In the last decades of the nineteenth century, a second

761

industrial revolution produced new techniques for manufacturing and new sources of power, including electricity and petroleum-based fuels. These developments transformed the infrastructure of European towns and cities, and people felt the immediate effects of these changes in their daily lives.

At the same time, European nation-states faced new political realities as their electorates expanded and new blocs of voters began participating directly in shaping parliamentary bodies and their legislative agendas. New mass-based political parties brought new demands to the political arena, and national governments struggled to maintain order and legitimacy in the face of these challenges. Socialists mobilized growing numbers of industrial workers, while suffragists demanded the franchise for women. The ability of traditional elites to control the political life of nations was sorely tested, even in nations that continued to be governed by hereditary monarchs.

In the arts and sciences new theories challenged older notions of nature, society, truth, and beauty. Since the eighteenth century at least, science had been a frequent ally of political liberalism, as both liberals and scientists shared a common faith in human reason and an openness to rational inquiry into the laws of society and nature. In the late nineteenth century, however, this common agenda was strained by scientific investigations in new fields such as biology and psychology that challenged liberal assumptions about human nature. Meanwhile, in the arts, a new generation of artists and writers embraced innovation and rejected the established conventions in painting, sculpture, poetry, and literature. A period of intense experimentation in the arts followed, leading artists and writers to develop radically new forms of expression.

The nineteenth century, then, ended in a burst of energy as many Europeans embraced a vision of their society racing headlong into what they hoped was a more promising and better future. Behind this self-confidence, however, lay significant uncertainty about the eventual destination. What aspects of the European past would continue to be relevant in the modern age? In politics and social life and in the culture as a whole, such questions produced more conflict than consensus.

NEW TECHNOLOGIES AND GLOBAL TRANSFORMATIONS

In the last third of the nineteenth century, new technologies transformed the face of manufacturing in Europe, leading to new levels of economic growth and complex realignments among industry, labor, and national governments. Like Europe's first industrial revolution, which began in the late eighteenth century and centered on coal, steam, and iron, this second industrial revolution relied on innovation in three key areas: steel, electricity, and chemicals.

Harder, stronger, and more malleable than iron, steel had long been prized as a construction material. But until the mid-nineteenth century, producing steel cheaply and in large quantities was impossible. That changed between the 1850s and 1870s, as different processes for refining and mass-producing alloy steel revolutionized the metallurgical industry. Britain's shipbuilders made a quick and profitable switch to steel construction and thus kept their lead in the industry. Germany and America dominated the

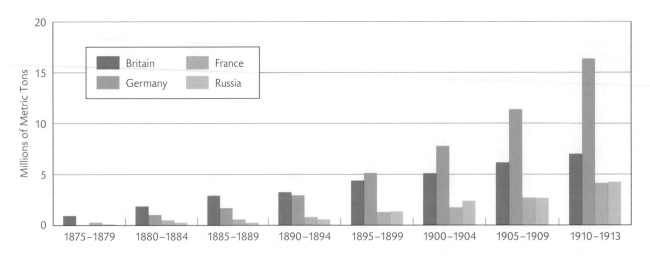

ANNUAL OUTPUT OF STEEL (IN MILLIONS OF METRIC TONS).
Source: Carlo Cipolla, *The Fontana Economic History of Europe*, vol. 3, pt. 2 (London: 1976), p. 775.

rest of the steel industry. By 1901, Germany was producing almost half again as much steel as Britain, allowing Germany to build a massive national and industrial infrastructure.

Like steel, electricity had been discovered earlier, and its advantages were similarly well known. Easily transmitted over long distances to be converted into heat, light, and other types of energy, electricity was made available for commercial and domestic use in the 1880s, after the development of alternators and transformers capable of producing high-voltage alternating current. By century's end, large power stations, which often used cheap water power, could send electric current over vast distances. In 1879, Thomas Edison and his associates invented the incandescent-filament lamp and changed electricity into light. The demand for electricity skyrocketed, and soon entire metropolitan areas were electrified. As a leading sector in the new economy, electrification powered subways, tramways, and, eventually, long-distance railroads; it made possible new techniques in the chemical and metallurgical industries, and gradually, it dramatically altered living habits in ordinary households.

The chemical industry was a third sector of important new technologies. The efficient production of alkali and sulfuric acid transformed the manufacture of such consumer goods as paper, soaps, textiles, and fertilizer. Britain and particularly Germany became leaders in the field. Heightened concerns for household hygiene and new techniques in mass marketing enabled the British entrepreneur Harold Lever to market his soaps and cleansers around the world. German production, on the other hand, focused on industrial use, such as developing synthetic dyes and methods for refining petroleum, and came to control roughly 90 percent of the world's chemical market.

Other innovations contributed to the second industrial revolution. The growing demand for efficient power spurred the invention of the liquid-fuel internal combustion engine. By 1914, most navies had converted from coal to oil, as had domestic steamship companies. The new engines' dependence on crude petroleum and distilled gasoline at first threatened their general application, but the discovery of oil fields in Russia, Borneo, Persia, and Texas around 1900 allayed fears. Protecting these oil reserves thus became a vital state prerogative. The adoption of oil-powered machinery had another important consequence:

THE SECOND INDUSTRIAL REVOLUTION. A German electrical engineering factory illustrates the scale of production during the second industrial revolution. ▪ *What changes in business practices and labor management made factories of this size possible?*

industrialists who had previously depended on nearby rivers or coal mines for power were free to take their enterprises to regions bereft of natural resources. The potential for worldwide industrialization was in place. Of course, the internal combustible engine would bring even more radical changes to twentieth-century transportation in the future, but the automobile and the airplane were both still in their infancies before 1914.

Changes in Scope and Scale

These technological changes were part of a much larger process—impressive increases in the scope and scale of industry. Technologies were both causes and consequences of the race toward a bigger, faster, cheaper, and more efficient world. At the end of the nineteenth century, size mattered. The rise of heavy industry and mass marketing had factories and cities growing hand in hand, while advances in media and mobility spurred the creation of national mass cultures. For the first time, ordinary people followed the news on national and global levels. They watched as European powers divided the globe, enlarging their empires with prodigious feats of engineering mastery; railroads, dams, canals, and harbors grew to monumental proportions. Such projects embodied the ideals of modern European industry. They also generated enormous income for builders, investors, bankers, entrepreneurs, and,

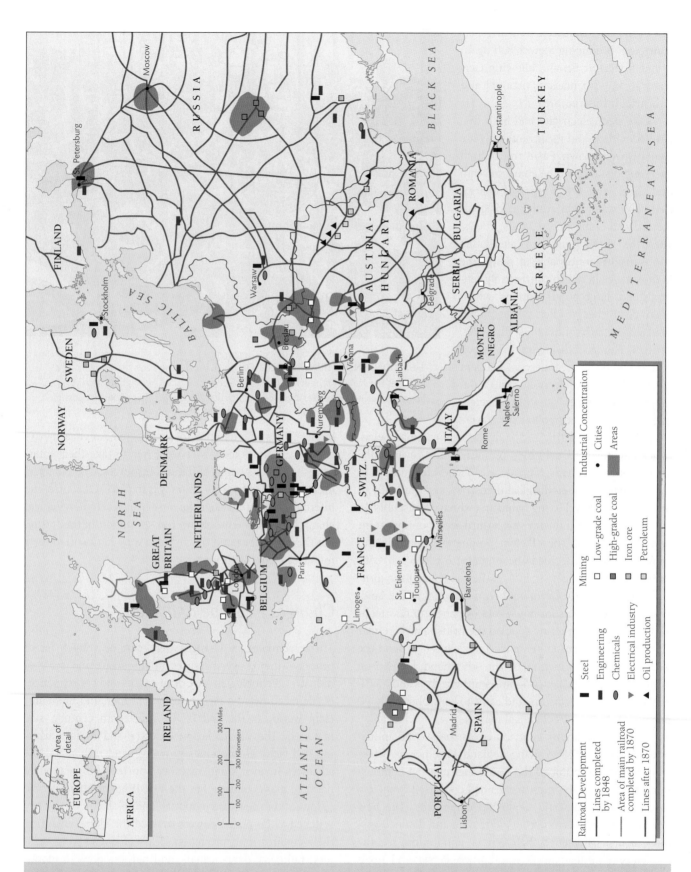

THE INDUSTRIAL REGIONS OF EUROPE. This map shows the distribution of mineral resources, rail lines, and industrial activity. ▪ *What nations enjoyed advantages in the development of industry and why?* ▪ *What resources were most important for industrial growth in the second half of the nineteenth century?* ▪ *What resources in England became dominant as a result of industrialization?*

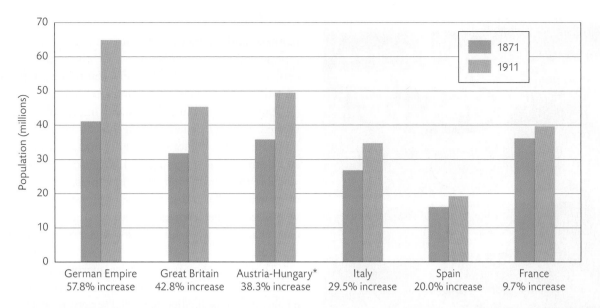

POPULATION GROWTH IN MAJOR STATES BETWEEN 1871 AND 1911 (POPULATION IN MILLIONS).
*Not including Bosnia-Herzegovina.
Source: Colin Dyer, *Population and Society in Twentieth-Century France* (New York: 1978), p. 5.

of course, makers of steel and concrete. Canals in central Europe, railroads in the Andes, and telegraph cables spanning the ocean floors: these "tentacles of empire," as one historian dubs them, stretched across the globe.

Yet industrialization also brought profound, if less spectacular, changes in Europe. The population grew constantly, particularly in central and eastern Europe. Russia's population increased by nearly a quarter and Germany's by half in the space of a generation. Britain's population, too, grew by nearly one-third between 1881 and 1911. Thanks to improvements in both crop yields and shipping, food shortages declined, which rendered entire populations less susceptible to illness and high infant mortality. Advances in medicine, nutrition, and personal hygiene diminished the prevalence of dangerous diseases such as cholera and typhus, and improved conditions in housing and public sanitation transformed the urban environment.

Credit and Consumerism

Changes in scope and scale not only transformed production but also altered consumption. Indeed it was during this period that consumption began to shift, slowly, to the center of economic activity and theory. The era in which economists would worry about consumer confidence and experts could systematically track the public's buying habits did not begin until the middle of the twentieth century, but developments pointed toward that horizon. Department stores offering both practical and luxury goods to the

middle class were one mark of the times—of urbanization, economic expansion, and the new importance attached to merchandising. Advertising took off as well. The lavishly illustrated posters of the late nineteenth century that advertised concert halls, soaps, bicycles, and sewing machines were only one sign of underlying economic changes. Even more significant, by the 1880s new stores sought to attract working-class people by introducing the all-important innovation of credit payment. In earlier times, working-class families pawned watches, mattresses, or furniture to borrow money; now they began to buy on credit, a change that would eventually have seismic effects on both households and national economies.

These new late-nineteenth-century patterns of consumption, however, were largely urban. In the countryside, peasants continued to save money under mattresses; pass down a few pieces of furniture for generations; make, launder, and mend their own clothes and linens; and offer a kilo of sugar as a generous household gift. Only slowly did retailers whittle away at these traditional habits. Mass consumption remained difficult to imagine in what was still a deeply stratified society.

The Rise of the Corporation

Economic growth and the demands of mass consumption spurred reorganization, consolidation, and regulation of capitalist institutions. Although capitalist enterprises had been financed by individual investors through the joint-stock

POSTER FOR *MOTOCYCLES COMIOT*, 1899. The rise of consumer spending in the middle class created a new industry and a new art: advertising. This advertisement, like many from the period, contrasted new with old, leisure with toil, and speed, or freedom, with inertia.

principle at least since the sixteenth century, it was during the late nineteenth century that the modern corporation came into its own. To mobilize the enormous funds needed for large-scale enterprises, entrepreneurs needed to offer better guarantees on investors' money. To provide such protection, most European countries enacted or improved their limited-liability laws, which ensured that stockholders could lose only the value of their shares in the event of bankruptcy. Insured in this way, many thousands of middle-class men and women now considered corporate investment a promising venture. After 1870, stock markets ceased to be primarily a clearinghouse for state paper and railroad bonds and instead attracted new commercial and industrial ventures.

Limited liability was one part of a larger trend of incorporation. Whereas most firms had been small or middle size, companies now incorporated to attain the necessary size for survival. In doing so, they tended to shift control

from company founders and local directors to distant bankers and financiers. Because financial institutions represented the interests of investors whose primary concern was the bottom line, bankers' control over industrial growth encouraged an ethos of impersonal finance capital.

Equally important, the second industrial revolution created a strong demand for technical expertise, which undercut traditional forms of family management. University degrees in engineering and chemistry became more valuable than on-the-job apprenticeships. The emergence of a white-collar class (middle-level salaried managers who were neither owners nor laborers) marked a significant change in work life and for society's evolving class structure.

The drive toward larger business enterprises was spurred by a desire for increased profits. It was also encouraged by a belief that consolidation protected society against the hazards of boom-and-bust economic fluctuations and against the wasteful inefficiencies of unbridled, "ruinous" competition. Some industries combined vertically, attempting to control every step of production from the acquisition of raw materials to the distribution of finished products. Andrew Carnegie's steel company in Pittsburgh controlled costs by owning the iron and coal mines necessary for steel production as well as by acquiring its own fleet of steamships and railways to transport ore to the mills. A second form of corporate self-protection was horizontal alignment. Organizing into cartels, companies in the same industry would band together to fix prices and control competition, if not eliminate it outright. Coal, oil, and steel companies were especially suited to the organization of cartels, since only a few major players could afford the huge expense of building, equipping, and running mines, refineries, and foundries. In 1894, for example, the Rhenish-Westphalian Coal Syndicate captured 98 percent of Germany's coal market by using ruthless tactics against small competitors, who could join the syndicate or face ruin. Through similar tactics, both legal and illegal, John D. Rockefeller's Standard Oil Company came to control the refined petroleum market in the United States, producing over 90 percent of the country's oil by the 1880s. The monopoly was sustained through the Standard Oil Trust, a legal innovation that enabled Rockefeller to control and manage assets of allied companies through the government. Cartels were particularly strong in Germany and America but less so in Britain, where dedication to free-trade policies made price fixing difficult, and in France, where family firms and laborers both opposed cartels and where there was also less heavy industry.

Though governments sometimes tried to stem the burgeoning power of cartels, the dominant trend of this period was increased cooperation between governments

The Dangers of Consumer Culture

By 1880 the Bon Marché in Paris, the world's first department store, was turning over the astronomical sum of 80 million francs annually and came to embody the new rhythm and tempo of mass consumer culture. The vast scale of selling sparked debate about the decline of the family store, the recreation of browsing and window shopping, and, above all, the "moral disaster" of women's limitless desire for goods. In writing the novel The Ladies' Paradise (1883), *Émile Zola noted he wanted to "write the poem of modern activity." The passage here captures the fascination for Denise, a clerk in her uncle's fabric shop, of the fictitious department store the Ladies' Paradise.*

But what fascinated Denise was the Ladies' Paradise on the other side of the street, for she could see the shop-windows through the open door. The sky was still overcast, but the mildness brought by rain was warming the air in spite of the season; and in the clear light, dusted with sunshine, the great shop was coming to life, and business was in full swing.

Denise felt that she was watching a machine working at high pressure; its dynamism seemed to reach to the display windows themselves. They were no longer the cold windows she had seen in the morning; now they seemed to be warm and vibrating with the activity within. A crowd was looking at them, groups of women were crushing each other in front of them, a real mob, made brutal by covetousness. And these passions in the street were giving life to the materials: the laces shivered, then drooped again, concealing the depths of the shop with an exciting air of mystery; even the lengths of cloth, thick and square, were breathing, exuding a tempting odour, while the overcoats were throwing back their shoulders still more on the dummies, which were acquiring souls, and the huge velvet coat was billowing out, supple and warm, as if on shoulders of flesh and blood, with heaving breast and quivering hips. But the furnace-like heat with which the shop was ablaze came above all from the selling, from the bustle at the counters, which could be felt behind the walls. There was the continuous roar of the machine at work, of customers crowding into the departments, dazzled by the merchandise, then propelled towards the cash-desk. And it was all regulated and organized with the remorselessness of a machine: the vast horde of women were as if caught in the wheels of an inevitable force. . . .

Source: Émile Zola, *The Ladies' Paradise,* trans. Brian Nelson (New York: 1995), pp. 15–16.

Questions for Analysis

1. Why did Zola choose to represent the new department store as a giant machine?

2. The first industrial revolution faced the challenge of production. In what ways was consumption the challenge of the late nineteenth century? What obstacles did merchants confront when encouraging people to consume?

---

and industry. Contrary to the laissez-faire mentality of early capitalism, corporations developed close relationships with the states in the West—most noticeably in colonial industrial projects, such as the construction of railroads, harbors, and seafaring steamships. These efforts were so costly, or so unprofitable, that private enterprise would not have undertaken them alone. But because they served larger political and strategic interests, governments funded them willingly. Such interdependence was underscored by the appearance of businessmen and financiers as officers of state. The German banker Bernhard Dernburg was the German secretary of state for colonies. Joseph Chamberlain, the British manufacturer and mayoral boss of industrial Birmingham, also served as the colonial secretary. And in France, Charles Jonnart, president of the Suez Canal Company and the Saint-Étienne steelwork, was later governor general of Algeria. Tied to imperial interests, the rise of modern corporations had an impact around the globe.

Global Economics

From the 1870s on, the rapid spread of industrialization heightened competition among nations. The search for markets, goods, and influence fueled much of the imperial expansion and, consequently, often put countries at odds with each other. Trade barriers arose again to protect home markets. All nations except Britain raised tariffs, arguing that the needs of the nation-state trumped laissez-faire doctrine. Yet changes in international economics fueled the continuing growth of an interlocking, worldwide system of manufacturing, trade, and finance. For example, the near universal adoption of the gold standard in currency exchange greatly facilitated world trade. Pegging the value of currencies, particularly Britain's powerful pound sterling, against the value of gold meant that currencies could be readily exchanged. The common standard also allowed nations to use a third country to mediate trade and exchange to mitigate trade imbalances—a common problem for the industrializing West. Almost all European countries, dependent on vast supplies of raw materials to sustain their rate of industrial production, imported more than they exported. To avoid the mounting deficits that this practice would otherwise incur, European economies relied on "invisible" exports: shipping, insurance, and banking services. The extent of Britain's exports in these areas was far greater than that of any other country. London was the money market of the world, to which would-be borrowers looked for assistance before turning elsewhere. By 1914, Britain had $20 billion invested overseas, compared with $8.7 billion for France and $6 billion for Germany. Britain also used its invisible trade to secure relationships with food-producing nations, becoming the major overseas buyer for the wheat of the United States and Canada, the beef of Argentina, and the mutton (lamb) of Australia. These goods, shipped cheaply aboard refrigerated vessels, kept down food prices for working-class families and eased the demand for increased wages.

During this period, the relationship between European manufacturing nations and the overseas sources of their materials—whether colonies or not—was transformed, as detailed in the last chapter. Those changes, in turn, reshaped economies and cultures on both sides of the imperial divide. Europeans came to expect certain foods on their tables; whole regions of Africa, Latin America, and Asia geared toward producing for the European market. This international push toward mass manufacturing and commodity production necessarily involved changes in deep-seated patterns in consumption and in production. It altered the landscape and habits of India as well as those of Britain. It brought new rhythms of life to women working in clothing factories in Germany, to porters carrying supplies to build railways in Senegal, to workers dredging the harbor of Dakar.

LABOR POLITICS, MASS MOVEMENTS

The rapid expansion of late-nineteenth-century industry brought a parallel growth in the size, cohesion, and activism of Europe's working classes. The men and women who worked as wage laborers resented corporate power—resentment fostered not only by the exploitation and inequalities they experienced on the job but also by living "a life apart" in Europe's expanding cities (see Chapter 19). Corporations had devised new methods of protecting and promoting their interests, and workers did the same. Labor unions, which were traditionally limited to skilled male workers in small-scale enterprises, grew during the late nineteenth century into mass, centralized, nationwide organizations. This "new unionism" emphasized organization across entire industries and, for the first time, brought unskilled workers into the ranks, increasing power to negotiate wages and job conditions. More important, though, the creation of national unions provided a framework for a new type of political movement: the socialist mass party.

Why did socialism develop in Europe after 1870? Changing national political structures provide part of the answer. Parliamentary constitutional governments opened the political process to new participants, including socialists. Now part of the legislative process, socialists in Parliament led efforts to expand voting rights in the 1860s and 1870s. Their success created new constituencies of working-class men. At the same time, traditional struggles between labor and management moved up to the national level; governments aligned with business interests, and legislators countered working-class agitation with antilabor and antisocialist laws. To radical leaders, the organization of national mass political movements seemed the only effective way to counter industrialists' political strength. Thus, during this period, socialist movements abandoned their earlier revolutionary traditions (exemplified by the romantic image of barricaded streets) in favor of legal, public competition within Europe's parliamentary systems.

The Spread of Socialist Parties— and Alternatives

The emergence of labor movements in Europe owed as much to ideas as to social changes. The most influential radical thinker was Karl Marx, whose early career was discussed

INDEPENDENT LABOR PARTY DEMONSTRATION IN ENGLAND, c. 1893. Activism among workers swelled in the late nineteenth century. Increasingly powerful labor unions had a profound impact on politics because male workers without property could now vote in local and national elections.

in Chapter 20. Since the 1840s, Marx and his collaborator Friedrich Engels had been intellectuals and activists, participating in the organization of fledgling socialist movements. In 1867, Marx published the first of three volumes of *Capital*, a work he believed was his greatest contribution to human emancipation. *Capital* attacked capitalism using the tools of economic analysis, allowing Marx to claim a scientific validity for his work, and he was contemptuous of other socialists whose opposition to industrial economies were couched only in moral terms. Marx's work claimed to offer a systematic analysis of how capitalism forced workers to exchange their labor for subsistence wages while enabling their employers to amass both wealth and power. Followers of Marx called for workers everywhere to ally with one another to create an independent political force, and few other groups pushed so strongly to secure civil liberties, expand conceptions of citizenship, or build a welfare state. Marxists also made powerful claims for gender equality, though in practice woman suffrage took a backseat to class politics.

Not all working-class movements were Marxist, however. Differences among various left-wing groups remained strong, and the most divisive issues were the role of violence and whether socialists should cooperate with liberal governments—and if so, to what end. Some "gradualists" were willing to work with liberals for piecemeal reform, while anarchists and syndicalists rejected parliamentary politics altogether. When European labor leaders met in 1864 at the first meeting of the International Working Men's Association, Marx argued strongly in favor of political mass movements, which would prepare the working classes for revolution. He was strongly opposed by the anarchist Mikhail Bakunin, who rejected any form of state or party organization and called instead for terror and violence to destabilize society.

Between 1875 and 1905, Marxist socialists founded political parties in Germany, Belgium, France, Austria, and Russia. These parties were disciplined workers' organizations that aimed to seize control of the state to make revolutionary changes in the social order. The most successful was the German Social Democratic party (SPD). Initially intending to work for political change within the parliamentary political system, the SPD became more radical in the face of Bismarck's oppressive antisocialist laws. By the outbreak of the First World War, the German Social Democrats were the largest, best-organized workers' party in the world. Rapid and extensive industrialization, a large urban working class, and a national government hostile to organized labor, made German workers particularly receptive to the goals and ideals of social democracy.

In Britain—the world's first and most industrialized economy—the socialist presence was much smaller and more moderate. Why? The answer lies in the fact that much of the socialist agenda was advanced by radical Liberals in Britain, which forestalled the growth of an independent socialist party. Even when a separate Labour party was formed in 1901, it remained moderate, committed to reforming capitalism with measures such as support for public housing or welfare benefits, rather than a complete overhaul of the economy. For the Labour party, and for Britain's many trade unions, Parliament remained a legitimate vehicle for achieving social change, limiting the appeal of revolutionary Marxism.

Militant workers seeking to organize themselves for political action found alternatives to Marxism in the ideas

SOCIALIST PARTY PAMPHLET, c. 1895. Socialism emerged as a powerful political force throughout Europe in the late nineteenth century, although appearing in different forms depending on the region. This German pamphlet quotes from Marx's *Communist Manifesto* of 1848, calling for workers of Asia, Africa, America, and Australia to unite under the banners of equality and brotherhood. ▪ *What was the significance of this claim for equality, given the image's apparent references to racial difference?*

of anarchists and syndicalists. Anarchists shared many values with Marxist socialists, but they were opposed to centrally organized economies and to the very existence of the state. Rather than participating in parliamentary politics, therefore, the anarchists aimed to establish small-scale, localized, and self-sufficient democratic communities that could guarantee a maximum of individual sovereignty. Renouncing parties, unions, and any form of modern mass organization, the anarchists fell back on the tradition of conspiratorial violence, which Marx had denounced. Anarchists assassinated Tsar Alexander II in 1881 and five other heads of state in the following years, believing that such "exemplary terror" would spark a popular revolt. Syndicalists, on the other hand, did not call for terror but embraced a strategy of strikes and sabotage by workers. Their hope was that a general strike of all workers would bring down the capitalist state and replace it with workers' syndicates or trade associations. Anarchism's opposition to any form of organization kept it from making substantial gains as a movement. Likewise, the syndicalists' refusal to participate in politics limited their ability to command wide influence, but the tradition was kept alive, especially in France, through participation in trade unions.

By 1895, popular socialist movements had made impressive gains in Europe: seven socialist parties had captured between a quarter and third of the votes in their countries. But just as socialists gained a permanent foothold in national politics, they were also straining under limitations and internal conflicts. Working-class movements, in fact, had never gained full worker support. Some workers remained loyal to older liberal traditions or to religious parties, and many others were excluded from socialist politics by its narrow definition of who constituted the working class—male industrial workers.

Furthermore, some committed socialists began to question Marx's core assumptions about the inevitability of workers' impoverishment and the collapse of the capitalist order. A German group of so-called revisionists, led by Eduard Bernstein, challenged Marxist doctrine and called for a shift to moderate and gradual reform, accomplished through electoral politics. Radical supporters of direct action were incensed at Bernstein's betrayal of Marxist theory of revolution, because they feared that the official reforms that favored workers might make the working class more accepting of the status quo. The radicals within the labor movement were inspired by the unexpected (and unsuccessful) revolution in Russia in 1905. German Marxists such as Rosa Luxembourg called for mass strikes, hoping to ignite a widespread proletarian revolution.

Conflicts over strategy peaked just before the First World War, but these divisions did not diminish the strength and appeal of socialism among workers. On the eve of the

Le Petit Journal

SUPPLÉMENT ILLUSTRÉ

DIMANCHE 30 AVRIL 1905

SANGLANTES ÉMEUTES A LIMOGES

Les manifestants essayent d'enfoncer les portes de la prison

"BLOODY RIOTS IN LIMOGES." Labor unions used strikes to draw attention to low wages and dangerous working conditions and to extract concessions from their employers. Some militant groups, known as syndicalists, hoped that a general strike of all workers would lead to a revolutionary change. Fear of labor militancy was a common theme in the popular press, as in this newspaper illustration from Limoges in France, where soldiers are depicted defending the gates of a prison from laborers brandishing the revolutionary red flag of socialism. ■ *What connection might this newspaper's readers have made with earlier revolutionary movements in Europe?*

war, governments discreetly consulted with labor leaders about workers' willingness to enlist and fight. Having built impressive organizational and political strength since the 1870s, working-class parties now affected the ability of nation-states to wage war. In short, they had come of age. Much to the disappointment of socialist leaders, however, European laborers—many of whom had voted for socialist candidates in previous elections—nevertheless donned the uniforms of their respective nations and marched off to war in 1914, proving that national identities and class identities were not necessarily incompatible with one another.

DEMANDING EQUALITY: SUFFRAGE AND THE WOMEN'S MOVEMENT

Since the 1860s, the combination of working-class activism and liberal constitutionalism had expanded male suffrage rights across Europe: by 1884, Germany, France, and Britain had enfranchised most men. But nowhere did women have the right to vote. Nineteenth-century political ideology relegated women to the status of second-class citizens, and even egalitarian-minded socialists seldom challenged this entrenched hierarchy. Excluded from the workings of parliamentary and mass party politics, women pressed their interests through independent organizations and through forms of direct action. The new women's movement won some crucial legal reforms during this period; and after the turn of the century, its militant campaign for suffrage fed the growing sense of political crisis, most notably in Britain.

Women's organizations, such as the General German Women's Association, pressed first for educational and legal reforms. In Britain, women's colleges were established at the same time that women won the right to control their own property. (Previously, women surrendered their property, including wages, to their husbands.) Laws in 1884 and 1910 gave Frenchwomen the same right and the ability to divorce their husbands. German women, too, won more favorable divorce laws by 1870, and in 1900 they were granted full legal rights.

After these important changes in women's status, suffrage crystallized as the next logical goal. Indeed, votes became *the* symbol for women's ability to attain full personhood. As the suffragists saw it, enfranchisement meant not merely political progress but economic, spiritual, and moral advancement as well. By the last third of the century, middle-class women throughout western Europe had founded clubs, published journals, organized petitions, sponsored assemblies, and initiated other public activities to press for the vote. The number of middle-class women's societies rapidly multiplied; some, such as the German League of Women's Voting Rights, established in 1902, were founded solely to advocate votes. To the left of middle-class movements were organizations of feminist socialists, women such as Clara Zetkin and Lily Braun who believed that only a socialist revolution would free women from economic as well as political exploitation. Meanwhile, the French celebrity journalist and novelist Gyp (the pseudonym of Sibylle de Riguetti de Mirabeau) carved out a name for herself on the nationalist and anti-Semitic right, with her acerbic commentary on current events.

In Britain, woman suffrage campaigns exploded in violence. Millicent Fawcett, a distinguished middle-class woman with connections to the political establishment, brought together sixteen different organizations into the National Union of Women's Suffrage Societies (1897), committed to peaceful, constitutional reform. But the movement lacked the political or economic clout to sway a male legislature. They became increasingly exasperated by their inability to win over either the Liberal or Conservative party, each of which feared that female suffrage would benefit the other. For this reason Emmeline Pankhurst founded the Women's Social and Political Union (WSPU) in 1903, which adopted tactics of militancy and civil disobedience. WSPU women chained themselves to the visitors' gallery in the House of Commons, slashed paintings in museums, inscribed "Votes for Women" in acid on the greens of golf courses, disrupted political meetings, burned politicians' houses, and smashed department-store windows. The government countered violence with repression. When arrested women went on hunger strikes in prisons, wardens fed them by force—tying them down, holding their mouths open with wooden and metal clamps, and running tubes down their throats. In 1910, the suffragists' attempt to enter the House of Commons set off a six-hour riot with policemen and bystanders, shocking and outraging a nation unaccustomed to such kinds of violence from women. The intensity of suffragists' moral claims was dramatically embodied by the 1913 martyrdom of Emily Wilding Davison who, wearing a "Votes for Women" sash, threw herself in front of the king's horse on Derby Day and was trampled to death.

FEMINIST PROTEST IN THE AGE OF MASS POLITICS. These two images demonstrate the variety of ways that supporters of the vote for women in Britain sought to use the public realm to their political advantage. Emily Davison, shown in the top image being fatally struck by the king's horse at a racetrack, sought to draw attention to the injustice of women's exclusion from political citizenship by disrupting the Epsom Derby, the richest race in Britain and an annual society event. Her death, widely seen as a martyrdom in the cause of women's rights by her supporters, became the occasion for a public funeral procession through London. The image on the bottom shows a woman reading a feminist paper, *Suffragette*, on a British tram. By the end of the nineteenth century, the penny press and growing literacy rates vastly increased the ability of organized political groups to get their message out.

Redefining Womanhood

The campaign for woman suffrage was perhaps the most visible and inflammatory aspect of a larger cultural shift, in which traditional Victorian gender roles were redefined. In the last third of the nineteenth century, economic, political, and social changes were undermining the view that men and women should occupy distinctly different spheres. Women became increasingly visible in the workforce as growing numbers of them took up a greater variety of jobs. Some working-class women joined the new factories and workshops in an effort to stave off their families' poverty, in spite of some working-class men's insistence that stable families required women at home. In addition, the expansion of government and corporate bureaucracies, coupled with a scarcity of male labor owing to industrial growth, brought middle-class women to the workforce as social workers and clerks. The increase in hospital services and the advent of national compulsory education required more nurses and teachers. Again, a shortage of male workers and a need to fill so many new jobs as cheaply as possible made women a logical choice. Thus women, who had campaigned vigorously for access to education, began to see doors opening to them. Swiss universities and medical schools began to admit women in the 1860s. In the 1870s and 1880s, British women established their own colleges at Cambridge and Oxford. Parts of the professional world began to look dramatically different: in Prussia, for instance, 14,600 full-time women teachers were staffing schools by 1896. These changes in women's employment began to deflate the myth of female domesticity.

Women became more active in politics—an area previously termed off limits. This is not to say that female political activity was unprecedented; in important ways, the groundwork for women's new political participation had been laid earlier in the century. Reform movements of the early nineteenth century depended on women and raised women's standing in public. First with charity work in religious associations and later with hundreds of secular associations, women throughout Europe directed their energies toward poor relief, prison reform, Sunday school, temperance, ending slavery and prostitution, and expanding educational opportunities for women. Reform groups brought women together outside the home, encouraging them to speak their minds as freethinking equals and to pursue political goals—a right denied them as individual females. And while some women in reform groups supported political emancipation, many others were drawn into reform politics by appeals to the belief that they had a special moral mission: they saw their public activities as merely an extension of feminine domestic duties. Nonetheless, nineteenth-century reform movements had opened up the world beyond the home, particularly for the middle classes, and widened the scope of possibilities for later generations.

These changes in women's roles were paralleled by the emergence of a new social type, dubbed the "new woman." A new woman demanded education and a job; she refused to be escorted by chaperones when she went out; she rejected the restrictive corsets of mid-century fashion. In other words, she claimed the right to a physically and intellectually active life and refused to conform to the norms that defined nineteenth-century womanhood. The new woman was an image—in part the creation of artists

CHANGES IN WHITE-COLLAR WORK. Clerical work was primarily male until the end of the nineteenth century, when cadres of women workers and the emergence of new industries and bureaucracies transformed employment. ▪ *How might these changing patterns of employment have affected family life or attitudes toward marriage and child-rearing?*

and journalists, who filled newspapers, magazines, and advertising billboards with pictures of women riding bicycles in bloomers (voluminous trousers with a short skirt); smoking cigarettes; and enjoying the cafés, dance halls, tonic waters, soaps, and other emblems of consumption. Very few women actually fit this image: among other things, most were too poor. Still, middle- and working-class women demanded more social freedom and redefined gender norms in the process. For some onlookers, women's newfound independence amounted to shirking domestic responsibilities, and they attacked women who defied convention as ugly "half-men," unfit and unable to marry. For supporters, though, these new women symbolized a welcome era of social emancipation.

Opposition to these changes was intense, sometimes violent, and not exclusively male. Men scorned the women who threatened their elite preserves in universities, clubs, and public offices; but a wide array of female antisuffragists also denounced the movement. Conservatives such as Mrs. Humphrey Ward maintained that bringing women into the political arena would sap the virility of the British Empire. Octavia Hill, a noted social worker, stated that women should refrain from politics and, in so doing, "temper this wild struggle for place and power." Christian commentators criticized suffragists for bringing moral decay through selfish individualism. Still others believed feminism would dissolve the family, a theme that fed into a larger discussion on the decline of the West amid a growing sense of cultural crisis. Indeed, the struggle for women's rights provided a flashpoint for an array of European anxieties over labor, politics, gender, and biology—all of which suggested that an orderly political consensus, so ardently desired by middle-class society, was slipping from reach.

LIBERALISM AND ITS DISCONTENTS: NATIONAL POLITICS AT THE TURN OF THE CENTURY

Having championed doctrines of individual rights throughout the nineteenth century, middle-class liberals found themselves on the defensive after 1870. Previously, political power had rested on a balance between middle-class interests and traditional elites. The landed aristocracy shared power with industrial magnates; monarchical rule coexisted with constitutional freedoms. During the late nineteenth century, the rise of mass politics upset this balance. An expanding franchise and rising expectations brought newcomers to the political stage. As we have seen, trade unions, socialists, and feminists all challenged Europe's governing classes by demanding that political participation be open to all. Governments responded in turn, with a mix of conciliatory and repressive measures. As the twentieth century approached, political struggles became increasingly fierce, and by the First World War the foundation of traditional parliamentary politics was crumbling. For both the left and the right, for both insiders and outsiders, negotiating this unfamiliar terrain required the creation of new and distinctly modern forms of mass politics.

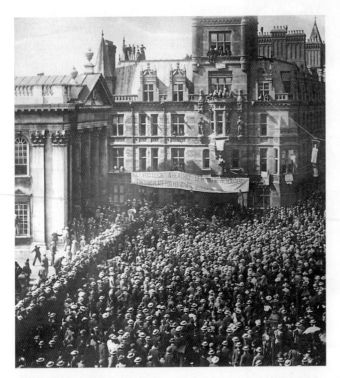

ORGANIZED ANTIFEMINISM. Male students demonstrate against admitting women to Cambridge University in England, 1881. A female figure is hung in effigy to the right of center, and the suspended banner reads (in part): "There's No Place for You Maids."

France: The Third Republic and the Paris Commune

The Franco-Prussian War of 1870, which completed the unification of the victorious Germany, was a bruising defeat for France. The government of the Second Empire folded. In its wake, the French proclaimed a republic whose legitimacy was contested from the start. Crafting a durable republican system proved difficult. The new constitution of the Third Republic, which was finally instituted in 1875, signaled a triumph of democratic and parliamentary principles. Establishing democracy, however, was a volatile process, and the Third Republic faced class conflicts, scandals and the rise of new forms of right-wing politics that would poison politics for decades to come.

No sooner had the government surrendered than it faced a crisis that pitted the nation's representatives against the radical city of Paris. During the war, the city had appointed its own municipal government, the Commune. Paris not only refused to surrender to the Germans but proclaimed itself the true government of France. The city had been besieged by the Germans for four months; most people who could afford to flee had done so; and the rest, hungry and radicalized, defied the French government sitting in Versailles and negotiating the terms of an armistice with the Germans. The armistice signed, the French government turned its attention to the city. After long and fruitless negotiations, in March 1871 the government sent troops to disarm the capital. Since the Commune's strongest support came from the workers of Paris, the conflict became a class war. For a week, the "communards" battled against the government's troops, building barricades to stop the invaders, taking and shooting hostages, and retreating very slowly into the northern working-class neighborhoods of the city. The French government's repression was brutal. At least 25,000 Parisians were executed, killed in fighting, or consumed in the fires that raged through the city; thousands more were deported to the penal colony of New Caledonia in the South Pacific. The Paris Commune was a brief episode, but it cast a long shadow and reopened old political wounds. For Marx, who wrote about the Commune, and for other socialists, it illustrated the futility of an older insurrectionary tradition on the left and the need for more mass-based democratic politics.

The Dreyfus Affair and Anti-Semitism as Politics

On the other side of the French political spectrum, new forms of radical right-wing politics emerged that would foreshadow developments elsewhere. As the age-old foundations of conservative politics, the Catholic Church and the landed nobility, slipped, more radical right-wing politics took shape. Stung by the defeat of 1870 and critical of the republic and its premises, the new right was nationalist, antiparliamentary, and antiliberal (in the sense of

commitment to individual liberties). Maurice Barrès, for instance, elected deputy in 1889, declared that parliamentary government had sown "impotence and corruption" and was too weak to defend the nation. During the first half of the nineteenth century, nationalism had been associated with the left (see Chapter 20). Now it was more often invoked by the right and linked to xenophobia (fear of foreigners) in general and anti-Semitism in particular.

The power of popular anti-Semitism in France was made clear by a public controversy that erupted in the 1890s known as the Dreyfus Affair. In 1894, a group of monarchist officers in the army accused Alfred Dreyfus, a Jewish captain on the general staff, of selling military secrets to Germany. Dreyfus was convicted and deported for life to Devil's Island, a ghastly South American prison colony in French Guiana. Two years later, an intelligence officer named Georges Picquart discovered that the documents used to convict Dreyfus were forgeries. The War Department refused to grant Dreyfus a new trial, and the case became an enormous public scandal, fanned on both sides by the involvement of prominent intellectual figures. Republicans, some socialists, liberals, and intellectuals such as the writer Émile Zola backed Dreyfus, claiming that the case was about individual rights and the legitimacy of the republic and its laws. Nationalists, prominent Catholics, and other socialists who believed that the case was a distraction from economic issues, opposed Dreyfus and refused to question the military's judgment. One Catholic newspaper insisted that the question was not whether Dreyfus was guilty or innocent but whether Jews and unbelievers were not the "secret masters of France."

The anti-Semitism of the anti-Dreyfus camp was a combination of three strands of anti-Jewish thinking in Europe: (1) long-standing currents of anti-Semitism within Christianity, which damned the Jewish people as Christ killers; (2) economic anti-Semitism, which insisted that the wealthy banking family of Rothschild was representative of all Jews; and (3) late-nineteenth-century racial thinking, which opposed a so-called Aryan (Indo-European) race to an inferior Semitic race. Anti-Dreyfus propagandists whipped these ideas into a potent form of propaganda in anti-Semitic newspapers such as Edouard Drumont's *La Libre Parole* ("*Free Speech*"), a French daily that claimed a circulation of 200,000 during the height of the Dreyfus Affair.

In 1899, Dreyfus was pardoned and freed by executive order. In 1906, the French Supreme Court declared him free of all guilt, and he was reinstated in the army as a major. A major consequence of the controversy was passage of laws between 1901 and 1905 that separated church and state in France. Convinced that the church and the army were

Competing Viewpoints

Liberalism and the State

In the second half of the nineteenth century, some British liberals responded to calls from an expanding electorate by moving away from a laissez-faire position that called for minimal state interference in society and the economy. This laissez-faire position still had its adherents among liberals, most notably the libertarian social philosopher Herbert Spencer. In the face of a more organized labor movement and what was perceived to be a very real threat of revolution, however, other liberals began to argue that some forms of government action to alleviate social distress were not only compatible with individual liberty in the economic realm but were in fact also necessary to preserve it. Compare Herbert Spencer's arguments against assistance to the poor from 1851 with L. T. Hobhouse's defense of state pension plans in 1911.

Herbert Spencer, *Social Statics* (1851)

In common with its other assumptions of secondary offices, the assumption by a government of the office of Reliever-general to the poor, is necessarily forbidden by the principle that a government cannot rightly do anything more than protect. In demanding from a citizen contributions for the mitigation of distress—contributions not needed for the due administration of men's rights—the state is, as we have seen, reversing its function, and diminishing that liberty to exercise the faculties which it was instituted to maintain. Possibly, unmindful of the explanations already given, some will assert that by satisfying the wants of the pauper, a government is in reality extending *his* liberty to exercise his faculties, inasmuch as it is giving him something without which the exercise of them is impossible; and that hence, though it decreases the rate-payer's sphere of action, it compensates by increasing that of the rate-receiver. But this statement of the case implies a confounding of two widely-different things. To enforce the fundamental law—to take care that every man has freedom to do all that he wills, provided he infringes not the equal freedom of any other man—this is the special purpose for which the civil power exists. Now insuring to each the right to pursue within the specified limits the objects of his desires without let or hindrance, is quite a separate thing from insuring him satisfaction. Of two individuals, one may use his liberty of action successfully—may achieve the gratifications he seeks after, or accumulate what is equivalent to many of them—property; whilst the other, having like privileges, may fail to do so. But with these results the state has no concern. All that lies within its commission is to see that each man is allowed to use such powers and opportunities as he possesses; and if it takes from him who has prospered to give to him who has not, it violates its duty

hostile to the republic, the Republican legislature passed new laws that prohibited any religious orders in France that were not authorized by the state and forbade clerics to teach in public schools.

The French Republic withstood the attacks of radical anti-Semites in the first decade of the twentieth century, but the same right-wing and nationalist forces made their voices known elsewhere in Europe. The mayor of Vienna in 1897 was elected on an anti-Semitic platform. The Russian secret police forged and published a book called *The Protocols of the Learned Elders of Zion* (1903 and 1905), which imagined a Jewish plot to dominate the world and held Jews responsible for the French Revolution and the dislocating effects of industrialization. Political anti-Semitism remained popular among a substantial number of Europeans who accepted its insistence that social and political problems could be understood in racial terms.

Zionism

Among the many people to watch with alarm as the Dreyfus Affair unfolded was Theodor Herzl (1860–1904), a Hungarian-born journalist working in Paris. The rise of

towards the one to do more than its duty towards the other. Or, repeating the idea elsewhere expressed, it breaks down the vital law of society, that it may effect what social vitality does not call for.

Source: Herbert Spencer, *Social Statics: or, The Conditions essential to Happiness specified, and the First of them Developed* (London: John Chapman, 1851), p. 311–12.

L. T. Hobhouse, *Liberalism* (1911)

For the mass of the people, therefore, to be assured of the means of a decent livelihood must mean to be assured of continuous employment at a living wage, or, as an alternative, of public assistance. Now, as has been remarked, experience goes to show that the wage of the average worker, as fixed by competition, is not and is not likely to become sufficient to cover all the fortunes and misfortunes of life, to provide for sickness, accident, unemployment and old age, in addition to the regular needs of an average family. In the case of accident the State has put the burden of making provision on the employer. In the case of old age it has, acting, as I think, upon a sounder principle, taken the burden upon itself. It is very important to realize precisely what the new departure involved in the Old Age Pensions Act amounted to in point of principle. The Poor Law already guaranteed the aged person and the poor in general against actual starvation. But the Poor Law came into operation only at the point of sheer destitution. It failed to help those who had helped themselves. Indeed, to many it held out little inducement to help themselves if they could not hope to lay by so much as would enable them to live more comfortably on their means than they would live in the workhouse. The pension system throws over the test of destitution. It provides a certain minimum, a basis to go upon, a foundation upon which independent thrift may hope to build up a sufficiency. It is not a narcotic but a stimulus to self help and to friendly aid or filial support, and it is, up to a limit, available for all alike. It is precisely one of the conditions of independence of which voluntary effort can make use, but requiring voluntary effort to make it fully available.

Source: L. T. Hobhouse, *Liberalism* (New York: Henry Holt & Co., 1911), pp. 177–78.

Questions for Analysis

1. According to Spencer, what is the primary function of government? Why does he deem assistance to the poor to be a violation of that duty?

2. According to Hobhouse, what circumstances make assistance to the poor, such as of state-sponsored pension plans, necessary?

3. What assumptions lie behind their disagreement about the state's responsibility to remedy social inequalities? What values do they share?

---

virulent anti-Semitism in the land of the French Revolution troubled Herzl deeply. He considered the Dreyfus Affair "only the dramatic expression of a much more fundamental malaise." Despite Jewish emancipation, or the granting of civil rights, Herzl came to believe Jewish people might never be assimilated into Western culture and that staking the Jewish community's hopes on acceptance and tolerance was dangerous folly. Herzl endorsed the different strategy of Zionism, the building of a separate Jewish homeland outside of Europe (though not necessarily in Palestine). A small movement of Jewish settlers, mainly refugees from Russia, had already begun to establish settlements outside of Europe. Herzl was not the first to voice these goals, but he was the most effective advocate of political Zionism. He argued that Zionism should be recognized as a modern nationalist movement, capable of negotiating with other states. In 1896, Herzl published *The State of the Jews*; a year later he convened the first Zionist Congress in Switzerland. Throughout, he was involved in high politics, meeting with British and Ottoman heads of state. Herzl's vision of a Jewish homeland had strong utopian elements, for he believed that building a new state had to be based on a new and transformed society, eliminating inequality and

JEWISH MIGRATION IN THE LATE NINETEENTH CENTURY. ▪ *Where did Jews primarily flee from in the late nineteenth century?* ▪ *What drove Jewish people to flee from eastern Europe in the late nineteenth century?* ▪ *To what areas did Jewish people migrate and why?*

establishing rights. Although Herzl's writings met with much skepticism, they received an enthusiastic reception among Jews who lived in areas of eastern Europe where anti-Semitism was especially violent. During the turmoil of the First World War, specific wartime needs prompted the British to become involved in the issue, embroiling Zionism in international diplomacy (see Chapter 24).

Germany's Search for Imperial Unity

Through deft foreign policy, three short wars, and a groundswell of national sentiment, Otto von Bismarck united Germany under the banner of Prussian conservatism during the years 1864 to 1871. In constructing a federal political system, Bismarck sought to create the centralizing institutions of a modern nation-state while safeguarding

Interpreting Visual Evidence

Anti-Semitism and the Popular Press in France

The Dreyfus Affair lasted twelve years, from 1894, when Captain Alfred Dreyfus was first arrested and convicted of treason by a military court, to 1906, when he was finally absolved of all guilt and reinstated in the army. During the affair, most people in France followed the events of the case through the popular press, which had undergone rapid expansion as public schooling became more general and literacy spread through the population. The newspapers milked every episode of the case for all of its sensational drama, and editors openly took sides in order to increase their circulation and profits. The illustrated press was particularly popular, and the images associated with expressions of anti-Semitism became ubiquitous in both the respectable and the more popular press. Image A shows Jakob Rothschild, a French Jewish banker, stretching his demonic hands around the globe. Edouard Drumont, the anti-Semitic editor of *La Libre Parole* used the scandal to launch his own political career. His celebrity status is evident in a caricature of himself that appeared in a competing paper, *Le Rire* (image B). Even illustrations that did not aim at caricature could carry a powerful message about the intensity of popular anti-Semitism in France during the affair, as in image C, which depicts young people burning Alfred Dreyfus's brother Mathieu in effigy during a demonstration. Mathieu Dreyfus played a key role in the effort to establish his brother's innocence.

Questions for Analysis

1. What fears about the economy are exploited in image A? (Compare this with the image on page 770 of socialists circling the globe, hand in hand.)

2. Is *Le Rire*'s portrait of Edouard Drumont (image B) an anti-Semitic image, or is it critical of Drumont's anti-Semitism?

3. Taken together, what do these images tell us about the connections among anti-Semitism, the popular press, and the definitions of national identity that were current in France during the affair?

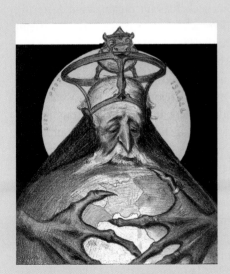

A. Anti-Semitic French cartoon with caricature of Jakob Rothschild, 1898.

B. "The Ogre's Meal," caricature of Edouard Drumont, editor of *La Libre Parole*, from *Le Rire*, 1896.

C. "Anti-Semitic Agitation in Paris: Mathieu Dreyfus burned in effigy in Montmartre (Paris)."

OTTO VON BISMARCK LEAVES OFFICE, 1890. This political cartoon shows Bismarck resigning as Kaiser Wilhelm II childishly plays with "Socialism," a doll made of dynamite. Germany anxiously watches the scene from the background.

trade and economic growth. To strengthen ties with these liberal coalitions, Bismarck unleashed an anti-Catholic campaign in Prussia. In what is known as the *Kulturkampf*, or "cultural struggle," Bismarck passed laws that imprisoned priests for political sermons, banned Jesuits from Prussia, and curbed the church's control over education and marriage. The campaign backfired, however, and public sympathy for the persecuted clergy helped the Catholic Center party win fully one-quarter of the seats in the Reichstag in 1874.

Bismarck responded by fashioning a new coalition that included agricultural and industrial interests as well as socially conservative Catholics. This new alliance passed protectionist legislation (grain tariffs, duties on iron and steel) that riled both laissez-faire liberals and the German working class, which was represented by the SPD. Just as Bismarck had used anti-Catholic sentiments to solidify his previous alliance, he now turned against a new enemy of the empire—Social Democrats—and couched his protectionist and antisocial legislation in terms of defending a "Christian moral order." In 1878, after two separate attempts on the life of the emperor, Bismarck declared a national crisis to push through a series of antisocialist laws that forbade Social Democrats to assemble or distribute their literature. Additional legislation further expelled socialists from major cities. In effect, these laws obliged the Social Democratic party to become a clandestine organization, fostering a subculture of workers who increasingly viewed socialism as the sole answer to their political needs.

Having made the stick to beat down organized-labor politics, Bismarck now offered a carrot to German workers with an array of social reforms. Workers were guaranteed sickness and accident insurance, rigorous factory inspection, limited working hours for women and children, a maximum workday for men, public employment agencies, and old-age pensions. By 1890, Germany had put together a raft of social legislation, with the exception of unemployment insurance, that became a prototype for the majority of Western nations in the decades to come. The laws nevertheless failed to achieve Bismarck's short-term political goal of winning workers' loyalty: votes for the SPD more than quadrupled between 1881 and 1890, the year that Bismarck resigned.

The embittered atmosphere created by Bismarck's domestic policies prompted the new kaiser, Wilhelm II, to

the privileges of Germany's traditional elites, including a dominant role for Prussia. Bismarck's constitution assigned administrative, educational, and juridical roles to local state governments and established a bicameral parliament to oversee Germany's national interests. The appointed delegates of the upper house (the Bundesrat) served as a conservative counterbalance to the more democratic lower house (the Reichstag), which was elected through universal male suffrage. In the executive branch, power rested solely with Wilhelm I, the Prussian king and German kaiser (emperor), who wielded full control of foreign and military affairs. Unlike in France or Britain, Germany's cabinet ministers had no responsibility to the Parliament but answered only to the kaiser.

Under a government that was neither genuinely federal nor democratic, building a nation with a sense of common purpose was no easy task. Three fault lines in Germany's political landscape especially threatened to crack the national framework: the divide between Catholics and Protestants; the growing Social Democratic party; and the potentially divisive economic interests of agriculture and industry.

Between 1871 and 1878, Bismarck governed principally with liberal factions interested in promoting free legalize the SPD. By 1912, the Social Democrats were the largest single bloc in the Reichstag, yet the kaiser refused to allow any meaningful political participation beyond a tight-knit circle of elites. Any conclusion to this volatile standoff was preempted by the outbreak of the First World War.

Britain: From Moderation to Militance

During the half century before 1914, the British prided themselves on what they believed to be an orderly and workable system of government. After the passage of the Second Reform Bill in 1867, which extended suffrage to more than a third of the nation's adult males, the two major political parties, Liberal and Conservative, vied with each other to win the support of this growing voting bloc. Parliament responded to new voters' concerns with laws that recognized the legality of trade unions, commissioned the rebuilding of large urban areas, provided elementary education for all children, and permitted male religious dissenters to attend the elite universities of Oxford and Cambridge. In 1884, suffrage expanded to include more than three-fourths of adult males.

Two central figures, the Conservative Benjamin Disraeli and the Liberal William Gladstone, dominated the new parliamentary politics. Disraeli, a converted Jew and bestselling novelist, was eminently pragmatic, whereas Gladstone, a devout Anglican, was committed to political and social reform out of a sense of moral obligation. Despite their opposing sensibilities and bitter parliamentary clashes, the two men led parties that, in retrospect, seem to share largely similar outlooks. Leaders of both parties were drawn from the upper middle class and the landed gentry, and both Liberals and Conservatives offered moderate programs that appealed to the widening electorate. Steered by men whose similar education and outlooks promised middling solutions, the British political system was stable and "reasonable."

Even Britain's working-class movements were notably moderate until the turn of the century, when at last new trade unions and middle-class socialist societies combined to create the independent Labour party in 1901. Pressed from the left, the Liberal ministry that took office in 1906 passed sickness, accident, old-age, and unemployment insurance acts, along with other concessions to trade unions. To pay for the new welfare programs—and for a larger navy to counter the German buildup—the chancellor of the exchequer (finance minister), David Lloyd George, proposed an explosively controversial budget in 1909, which included progressive income and inheritance taxes, designed to make the wealthy pay at higher rates. The bill provoked a rancorous showdown with the House of Lords, which was forced not only to pass the budget but also to surrender permanently its power to veto legislation passed by the Commons. The acrimony of this debate pointed to an increasingly militant tenor in British politics, which to many seemed headed for chaos.

Indeed, after 1900, Britain's liberal parliamentary framework, which had so successfully channeled the rising demands of mass society since the 1860s, began to buckle, as an array of groups rejected legislative activity in favor of radical action. Industrial militants launched enormous labor protests, including nationwide strikes of coal and rail workers and citywide transportation strikes in London and Dublin. Woman suffragists adopted violent forms of direct action (discussed earlier). Meanwhile, in Ireland, disagreements over Irish home rule, or self-government, threatened to produce armed confrontations between increasingly radical Irish nationalists and Protestants opposed to home rule.

Ireland had been put under the direct government of the British Parliament in 1800, and various political and military efforts to regain Irish sovereignty over the course of the nineteenth century had failed. By the 1880s, a modern nationalist party (the Irish Parliamentary party) had begun to make substantial political gains through the legislative process, but as with other reform-minded groups (such as woman suffrage), its agenda was increasingly eclipsed toward the turn of the century by more radical organizers. These proponents of "new nationalism" disdained the party's representatives as ineffectual and out of touch. New groups revived interest in Irish history and culture and provided organizational support to the radical movement, as did such militant political organizations as Sinn Féin and the Irish Republican Brotherhood. Firmly opposed to the nationalists was the Protestant Ulster Volunteer force, led by military officers who were determined to resist the imposition of home rule by force, if necessary. In 1913, as a Liberal plan to grant home rule was once again on the table, Britain now seemed on the verge of a civil war—a prospect delayed only by the outbreak of the First World War in Europe.

Russia: The Road to Revolution

The industrial and social changes that swept Europe proved especially unsettling in Russia. An autocratic political system was ill equipped to handle conflict and the pressures of modern society. Western industrialization challenged Russia's military might. Western political doctrines—liberalism, democracy, socialism—threatened its internal political stability. Like other nations, tsarist Russia negotiated these challenges with a combination of repression and reform.

In the 1880s and 1890s, Russia launched a program of industrialization that made it the world's fifth largest economy by the early twentieth century. The state largely directed this industrial development, for despite the creation of a mobile workforce after the emancipation of the serfs in 1861, no independent middle class capable of raising capital and stewarding industrial enterprises emerged. In fact, the Russian state financed more domestic industrial development than any other major European government during the nineteenth century.

Rapid industrialization heightened social tensions. The transition from country to city life was sudden and harsh. Men and women left agriculture for factory work, straining the fabric of village life and rural culture. In the industrial areas, workers lived in large barracks and were marched, military-style, to and from the factories, where working conditions were among the worst in Europe. They coped by leaving their villages only temporarily and returning to their farms for planting or the harvest. Social change strained Russia's legal system, which did not recognize trade unions or employers' associations. Laws still distinguished among nobles, peasants, clergy, and town dwellers, categories that did not correspond to an industrializing society. Outdated banking and financial laws failed to serve the needs of a modern economy.

Real legal reform, however, would threaten the regime's stability. When Alexander II (r. 1855–81), the liberator of the serfs, was killed by a radical assassin in 1881, his successor, Alexander III (r. 1881–94), steered the country sharply to the right. Russia had nothing in common with western Europe, Alexander III claimed; his people had been nurtured on mystical piety for centuries and would be utterly lost without a strong autocratic system. This principle guided stern repression. The regime curtailed all powers of local assemblies, increased the authority of the secret police, and subjected villages to the governmental authority of nobles appointed by the state. The press and schools remained under strict censorship.

Nicholas II (r. 1894–1917) continued these repressive policies. Like his father, he ardently advocated Russification, or government programs to extend the language, religion, and culture of greater Russia over the empire's non-Russian subjects. Russification amounted to coercion, expropriation, and physical oppression: Finns lost their constitution, Poles studied their own literature in Russian translation, and Jews perished in pogroms. (*Pogrom* is a Russian term for violent attacks on civilians, which in the late nineteenth century were usually aimed at Jewish communities.) The Russian government did not organize pogroms, but it was openly anti-Semitic and made a point of looking the other way when villagers massacred Jews and destroyed their homes, businesses, and synagogues. Other groups whose repression by the state led to long-lasting undercurrents of anti-Russian nationalism included the Georgians, Armenians, and Azerbaijanis of the Caucasus Mountains.

The most important radical political group in late-nineteenth-century Russia was a large, loosely knit group of men and women who called themselves populists. Populists believed that Russia needed to modernize on its own terms, not the West's. They envisioned an egalitarian Russia based on the ancient institution of the village commune (*mir*). Advocates of populism sprang primarily from the middle class; many of its adherents were young students, and women made up about 15 percent—a significantly large proportion for the period. They formed secret bands, plotting the overthrow of tsarism through anarchy and insurrection. They dedicated their lives to "the people," attempting wherever possible to live among common laborers so as to understand and express the popular will. Populism's emphasis on peasant socialism influenced the Social Revolutionary party, formed in 1901, which also concentrated on increasing the political power of the peasant and building a socialist society based on the agrarian communalism of the mir.

The emergence of industrial capitalism and a new, desperately poor working class created Russian Marxism. Organized as the Social Democratic party, Russian Marxists concentrated their efforts on behalf of urban workers and saw themselves as part of the international working-class movement. They made little headway in a peasant-dominated Russia before the First World War, but they provided disaffected urban factory workers and intellectuals alike with a powerful ideology that stressed the necessity of overthrowing the tsarist regime and the inevitability of a better future. Autocracy would give way to capitalism and capitalism to an egalitarian, classless society. Russian Marxism blended radical, activist opposition with a rational, scientific approach to history, furnishing revolutionaries with a set of concepts with which to understand the upheavals of the young twentieth century.

In 1903, the leadership of the Social Democratic party split over an important disagreement on revolutionary strategy. One group, temporarily in the majority and quick

The Age of Mass Politics

Granting the vote to all adult men ushered in an age of mass politics. Political groups competed with one another to gain the support of this new constituency, and to prevent opponents from gaining power (left, in this 1878 cartoon, Otto von Bismarck tries to put socialism back in the box). Then, as now, political groups sought simple messages that would give them an edge, leading to more sharply defined ideological competition, as well as populist demagoguery and scapegoating of minorities (right, Marine Le Pen at rally for the extreme-right party in France, the National Front).

 Watch related author interview on StudySpace
wwnorton.com/web/westernciv18

to name itself the Bolsheviks (majority group), believed that the Russian situation called for a strongly centralized party of active revolutionaries. The Bolsheviks also insisted that the rapid industrialization of Russia meant that they did not have to follow Marx's model for the West. Instead of working for liberal capitalist reforms, Russian revolutionaries could skip a stage and immediately begin to build a socialist state. The Mensheviks (which means minority) were more cautious or "gradualist," seeking slow changes and reluctant to depart from Marxist orthodoxy. When the Mensheviks regained control of the Social Democratic party, the Bolsheviks formed a splinter party under the leadership of the young, dedicated revolutionary Vladimir Ilyich Ulyanov, who lived in political exile in western Europe between 1900 and 1917. He wrote under the pseudonym of Lenin, from the Lena River in Siberia, where he had been exiled earlier.

Lenin's theoretical abilities and organizational energy commanded respect, enabling him to remain the leader of the Bolsheviks even while living abroad. From exile, Lenin preached unrelenting class struggle; the need for a coordinated revolutionary socialist movement throughout Europe; and, most important, the belief that Russia was passing into an economic stage that made it ripe for revolution. It was the Bolsheviks' responsibility to organize a revolutionary party on behalf of workers, for without the party's discipline, workers could not effect change. Lenin's treatise *What Is to Be Done?* (1902) set out his vision of Russia's special destiny, and it denounced gradualists who had urged collaboration with moderate parties. Lenin considered revolution the only answer to Russia's problems, and he argued that organizing for revolution needed to be done, soon, by vanguard agents of the party acting in the name of the working class.

AUTOCRACY AND REPRESENTATIVE GOVERNMENT. In response to the revolution of 1905 in Russia, Tsar Nicholas II allowed for the creation of a new legislative body for Russia in 1905, a form of parliament called the Duma. Although he later succeeded in limiting the powers of this body, its very existence indicated that even the autocratic and conservative Russian state was forced to pay lip service to the principle of representative government. In the image above, note the extent to which the opening ceremony evoked the traditional hierarchies of Russian society, exemplified in the presence of the tsar, the military, the aristocracy, and the clergy.

THE FIRST RUSSIAN REVOLUTION

The revolution that came in 1905, however, took all of these radical movements by surprise. Its unexpected occurrence resulted from Russia's resounding defeat in the Russo-Japanese War of 1904–5. But the revolution had deeper roots. Rapid industrialization had transformed Russia unevenly; certain regions were heavily industrial, whereas others were less integrated into the market economy. The economic boom of the 1880s and 1890s turned to bust in the early 1900s, as demand for goods tapered off, prices plummeted, and the nascent working class suffered high levels of unemployment. At the same time, low grain prices resulted in a series of peasant uprisings, which, combined with students' energetic radical organizing, became overtly political.

As dispatches reported the defeats of the tsar's army and navy, the Russian people grasped the full extent of the regime's inefficiency. Hitherto apolitical middle-class subjects clamored for change, and radical workers organized strikes and held demonstrations in every important city. Trust in the benevolence of the tsar was severely shaken on January 22, 1905—"Bloody Sunday"—when a group

of 200,000 workers and their families, led by a priest, Father Gapon, went to demonstrate their grievances at the tsar's winter palace in St. Petersburg. When guard troops killed 130 demonstrators and wounded several hundred, the government seemed not only ineffective but arbitrary and brutal.

Over the course of 1905, general protest grew. Merchants closed their stores, factory owners shut down their plants, lawyers refused to plead cases in court. The autocracy lost control of entire rural towns and regions as local authorities were ejected and often killed by enraged peasants. Forced to yield, Tsar Nicholas II issued the October Manifesto, pledging guarantees of individual liberties, a moderately liberal franchise for the election of a Duma, and genuine legislative veto powers for the Duma. Although the 1905 revolution brought the tsarist system perilously close to collapse, it failed to convince the tsar that fundamental political change was necessary. Between 1905 and 1907, Nicholas revoked most of the promises made in the October Manifesto. Above all, he deprived the Duma of its principal powers and decreed that it be elected indirectly on a class basis, which ensured a legislative body of obedient followers.

Nonetheless, the revolt of 1905 persuaded the tsar's more perceptive advisers that reform was urgent. The agrarian programs sponsored by the government's leading minister, Peter Stolypin, were especially significant. Between 1906 and 1911 the Stolypin reforms provided for the sale of 5 million acres of royal land to peasants, granted permission to peasants to withdraw from the mir and form independent farms, and canceled peasant property debts. Further decrees legalized labor unions, reduced the working day (to ten hours in most cases), and established sickness and accident insurance. Liberals could reasonably hope that Russia was on the way to becoming a progressive nation on the Western model, yet the tsar remained stubbornly autocratic. Russian agriculture remained suspended between an emerging capitalist system and the traditional peasant commune; Russian industry, though powerful enough to allow Russia to maintain its status as a world power, had hardly created a modern, industrial society capable of withstanding the enormous strains that Russia would face during the First World War.

Analyzing Primary Sources

Lenin's View of a Revolutionary Party

At the turn of the century, Russian revolutionaries debated political strategy. How could Russian autocracy be defeated? Should revolutionaries follow the programs of their counterparts in the West? Or did the Russian situation require different tactics? In What Is to Be Done? *(1902) Lenin (Vladimir Ilyich Ulyanov, 1870–1924) argued that Russian socialists needed to revise the traditional Marxist view, according to which a large and politically conscious working class would make revolution. In Russia, Lenin argued, revolution required a small but dedicated group of revolutionaries to lead the working class. Lenin's vision was important, for it shaped the tactics and strategies of the Bolsheviks in 1917 and beyond.*

he national tasks of Russian Social-Democracy are such as have never confronted any other socialist party in the world. We shall have occasion further on to deal with the political and organisational duties which the task of emancipating the whole people from the yoke of autocracy imposes upon us. At this point, we wish to state only that the *role of vanguard fighter can be fulfilled only by a party that is guided by the most advanced theory. . . .*

I assert: (1) that no revolutionary movement can endure without a stable organisation of leaders maintaining continuity; (2) that the broader the popular mass drawn spontaneously into the struggle, which forms the basis of the movement and participates in it, the more urgent the need for such an organisation, and the more solid this organisation must be (for it is much easier for all sorts of demagogues to side-track the more backward sections of the masses); (3) that such an organisation must consist chiefly of people professionally engaged in revolutionary activity; (4) that in an autocratic state, the more we *confine* the membership of such an organisation to people who are professionally engaged in revolutionary activity and who have been professionally trained in the art of combating the political police, the more difficult will it be to unearth the organisation; and (5) the *greater* will be the number of people from the working class and from the other social classes who will be able to join the movement and perform active work in it. . . .

Social-Democracy leads the struggle of the working class, not only for better terms for the sale of labour-power, but for the abolition of the social system that compels the propertyless to sell themselves to the rich. Social-Democracy represents the working class, not in its relation to a given group of employers alone, but in its relation to all classes of modern society and to the state as an organised political force. Hence, it follows that not only must Social-Democrats not confine themselves exclusively to the economic struggle. . . . We must take up actively the political education of the working class and the development of its political consciousness.

Source: Vladimir Lenin, *What Is to Be Done?* in *Collected Works of V. I. Lenin*, vol. 5 (Moscow: 1964), pp. 369–70, 373, 375.

Questions for Analysis

1. What were the key features of Lenin's thought?

2. Here Lenin more or less set down the rules for the revolutionary vanguard. What historical experiences and political theories shaped his thinking? In what ways was the Russian experience unique?

Nationalism and Imperial Politics: The Balkans

In southeastern Europe in the last decades of the nineteenth century, nationalism continued to divide the disintegrating Ottoman Empire. When the sultan's government repressed uprisings in Bosnia, Herzegovina, and Bulgaria in 1875–76, the Russians saw an opportunity to intercede following reports of atrocities committed against Christians in the region. In the ensuing Russo-Turkish War (1877–78), the tsar's armies won a smashing victory. The Treaty of San Stefano forced the sultan to surrender nearly all of his European territory, except for a remnant around Constantinople.

BLOODY SUNDAY. Demonstrating workers who sought to bring their grievances to the attention of the tsar were met and gunned down by government troops, January 1905.

under centralized Turkish control. That effort, intended to compensate for the loss of territories in Europe, undercut the popularity of the new reformist regime.

THE SCIENCE AND SOUL OF THE MODERN AGE

Nineteenth-century liberals believed in individualism, progress, and science. Not only did science deliver technological and material rewards but it also confirmed liberals' faith in the power of human reason to uncover and command the laws of nature. Toward the end of the century, however, scientific developments defied these expectations. Darwin's theory of evolution, psychology, and social science all introduced visions of humanity that were sharply at odds with conventional wisdom. At the same time, artists and intellectuals mounted their own revolt against nineteenth-century conventions. Morals, manners, institutions, traditions—all established values and assumptions were under question, as a generation of self-consciously avant-garde artists called for a radical break with the past. These upheavals in the world of ideas unsettled older conceptions of individuality, culture, and consciousness. The modern individual no longer seemed the free and rational agent of Enlightenment thought but rather the product of irrational inner drives and uncontrollable external circumstances. As Georg Simmel, one of the founders of modern sociology, wrote in 1902: "The deepest problems of modern life derive from the claim of the individual to preserve the autonomy and individuality of his existence in the face of overwhelming social forces, of historical heritage, of external culture, and of the technique of life."

Britain and Austria took action to ensure that Russia would not be the only beneficiary of the Ottoman withdrawal, and in 1878 a congress of great powers in Berlin divided the spoils: Bessarabia went to Russia, Thessaly to Greece, and Bosnia and Herzegovina fell under the control of the Austrian Empire. Montenegro, Serbia, and Romania became independent states, launching the modern era of Balkan nationalism. This trend continued in 1908, when the Bulgars succeeded in wresting independence for Bulgaria from the Ottomans—a move that drove the Austrians to annex Bosnia and Herzegovina outright. The power vacuum in the Orient significantly strained Europe's imperial balance of power.

A nationalist movement also emerged in the Ottoman Empire itself. Educated Turks had grown impatient with the sultan's weakness, and some began to call for national rejuvenation through the introduction of Western science and democratic reforms. These reformers called themselves "Young Turks," and in 1908 they successfully forced the sultan to establish a constitutional government. In the following year, they deposed Sultan Abdul Hamid II (1876–1909) and placed his brother, Mohammed V (1909–1918), on the throne. The powers of government were entrusted to a grand vizier and ministers responsible to an elected parliament. Non-Turkish inhabitants of the empire were not given the vote, however; and the Young Turks launched a vigorous effort to "Ottomanize" all their imperial subjects, trying to bring both Christian and Muslim communities

Darwin's Revolutionary Theory

If Marx changed conceptions of society, Charles Darwin did him one better, perhaps, for his theory of organic evolution by natural selection transformed conceptions of nature itself. As both a scientific explanation and an imaginative metaphor for political and social change, Darwin's theory of evolution introduced an unsettling new picture of human biology, behavior, and society. As with Marxism, its core concepts were embraced by some and abhorred by others,

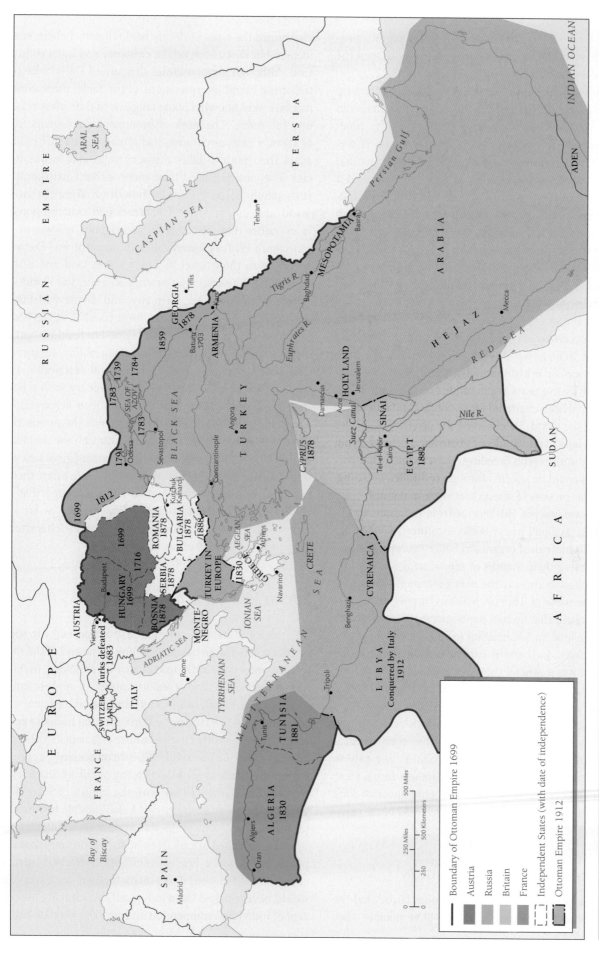

ARAL
SEA

RUSSIAN EMPIRE

CASPIAN SEA

PERSIA

Tehran

INDIAN OCEAN

ADEN

Persian Gulf

Basra

MESOPOTAMIA

GEORGIA
1878

Tiflis

Kars

ARMENIA

1859

1878

1783 1739

1784

SEA OF
AZOV

1783

1791

Odessa

Sevastopol

BLACK SEA

1812

1699

Constantinople

TURKEY

Angora

Batumi
1703

Tigris R.

Baghdad

Euphrates R.

Damascus

Acre

HOLY LAND
Jerusalem

Suez Canal

SINAI

Tel-el-Kebir

Cairo

Nile R.

ARABIA

HEJAZ

Mecca

RED SEA

SUDAN

EGYPT
1882

CYPRUS
1878

Kutchuk
Kainardji

ROMANIA
1878

1699

1716

HUNGARY
1699

BOSNIA
1878

SERBIA
1878

BULGARIA
1878

1888

TURKEY IN
EUROPE

1830

AEGEAN
SEA

GREECE

Athens

CRETE

CYRENAICA

Benghazi

AUSTRIA

Vienna
Turks defeated
1683

Budapest

MONTE-
NEGRO

Navarino

IONIAN
SEA

ADRIATIC SEA

Rome

ITALY

SWITZER-
LAND

FRANCE

TYRRHENIAN
SEA

MEDITERRANEAN SEA

Tripoli

LIBYA

Conquered by Italy
1912

TUNISIA
1881

Tunis

AFRICA

ALGERIA
1830

Algiers

Oran

SPAIN

Madrid

Bay of
Biscay

EUROPE

Boundary of Ottoman Empire 1699

Austria

Russia

Britain

France

Independent States (with date of independence)

Ottoman Empire 1912

500 Miles

500 Kilometers

250 Miles

250

0

0

THE DECLINE OF THE OTTOMAN EMPIRE, 1699–1912. ■ *What were the farthest points that that the Ottoman Empire reached into Europe and Africa?* ■ *How do you explain the slow decline of Ottoman power in relationship to Europe and the emerging global economy?* ■ *The decline of Ottoman power had enormous significance for relations among European nations themselves. Why?*

and were interpreted and deployed in a variety of unexpected, often conflicting, ways that profoundly shaped the late nineteenth and early twentieth centuries.

Theories of evolution did not originate with Darwin, but none of the earlier theories had gained widespread scientific or popular currency. Geologists in the nineteenth century had challenged the biblical account of creation with evidence that the world was formed by natural processes over millions of years, but no one had found a satisfactory explanation for the existence of different species. One important attempt at an answer was proposed in the early nineteenth century by the French biologist Jean Lamarck, who argued that behavioral changes could alter an animal's physical characteristics within a single generation and that these new traits would be passed on to offspring. Over time, Lamarck suggested, the inheritance of acquired characteristics produced new species of animals.

A more convincing hypothesis of organic evolution appeared in 1859, however, with the publication of *On the Origin of Species* by British naturalist Charles Darwin. Darwin traveled for five years as a naturalist on the HMS *Beagle,* a ship that had been chartered for scientific exploration on a trip around the world. He observed the diversity of species in different lands and wondered about their origins. From a familiarity with pigeon breeding, Darwin knew that particular traits could be selected through controlled breeding. Was a similar process of selection at work in nature?

His answer was yes. He theorized that variations within a population (such as longer beaks or protective coloring) made certain individual organisms better equipped for survival, increasing their chances of reproducing and passing their advantageous traits to the next generation. His theory drew on the work of Thomas Malthus, a political economist who argued that human populations grow faster than the available food supply, leading to a fatal competition for scarce resources. In Darwin's explanation, this Malthusian competition was a general rule of nature, where the strong survived and the weak perished. Competition with other individuals and struggle with the environment produced a "natural selection" of some traits over others, leading to a gradual evolution of different species over time. Eventually, Darwin applied this theory of evolution not only to plant and animal species but also to humans. In his view, the human race had evolved from an apelike ancestor, long since extinct but probably a common precursor of the existing anthropoid apes and humans.

DARWINIAN THEORY AND RELIGION

The implications of Darwin's writings went far beyond the domain of the evolutionary sciences. Most notably, they challenged the basis of deeply held religious beliefs, sparking a public discussion on the existence and knowability of God. Although popular critics denounced Darwin for contradicting literal interpretations of the Bible, those contradictions were not what made religious middle-class readers uncomfortable. The work of prominent theologians, such as David Friedrich Strauss, had already helped Christians adapt their faith to biblical inaccuracies and inconsistencies. They did not need to abandon either Christianity or faith simply because Darwin showed (or argued) that the world and its life forms had developed over millions of years rather than six days. What religious readers in the nineteenth century found difficult to accept was Darwin's challenge to their belief in a benevolent God and a morally guided universe. By Darwin's account, the world was governed not by order, harmony, and divine will but by random chance and constant, undirected struggle. Moreover, the Darwinian worldview seemed to redefine notions of good and bad only in terms of an ability to survive, thus robbing humanity of critical moral certainties. Darwin himself was able to reconcile his theory with a belief in God, but others latched on his work to fiercely attack Christian orthodoxy. One such figure was the philosopher Thomas Henry Huxley, who earned himself the nickname of "Darwin's bulldog" by inveighing against Christians who were appalled by the implications of Darwinian theory. Opposed to all forms of dogma, Huxley argued that the thinking person should simply follow reason "as far as it can take you" and recognize that the ultimate character of the universe lay beyond his or her grasp.

Social Darwinism

The theory of natural selection also influenced the social sciences, which were just developing at the end of the nineteenth century. New disciplines such as sociology, psychology, anthropology, and economics aimed to apply scientific methods to the analysis of society and introduced new ways of quantifying, measuring, and interpreting human experience. Under the authoritative banner of "science," these disciplines exerted a powerful influence on society, oftentimes to improve the health and well-being of European men and women. But, as we will see with the impact of Social Darwinism, the social sciences could also provide justification for forms of economic, imperial, and racial dominance.

The so-called Social Darwinists, whose most famous proponent was the English philosopher Herbert Spencer (1820–1903), adapted Darwinian thought in a way that would have shocked Darwin himself, by applying his concept of individual competition and survival to relationships among classes, races, and nations. Spencer, who coined the phrase *survival of the fittest*, used evolutionary theory to expound the virtues of free competition and attack state welfare programs. As a champion of individualism, Spencer condemned all forms of collectivism as primitive and counterproductive, relics of an earlier stage of social evolution. Government attempts to relieve economic and social hardships—or to place constraints on big business—were, in Spencer's view, hindrances to the vigorous advancement of civilization, which could occur only through individual adaptation and competition. Particularly in America, such claims earned Spencer high praise from some wealthy industrialists, who were no doubt glad to be counted among the fittest.

Unlike the science of biological evolution, a popularized Social Darwinism was easy to comprehend, and its concepts (centering on a struggle for survival) were soon integrated into the political vocabulary of the day. Proponents of laissez-faire capitalism and opponents of socialism used Darwinist rhetoric to justify marketplace competition and the "natural order" of rich and poor. Nationalists embraced Social Darwinism to rationalize imperialist expansion and warfare. Spencer's doctrine also became closely tied to theories of racial hierarchy and white superiority, which claimed that the white race had reached the height of evolutionary development and had thus earned the right to dominate and rule other races (see Chapter 25). Ironically, some progressive middle-class reformers relied on a similar set of racial assumptions: their campaigns to improve the health and welfare of society played to fears that Europe, though dominant, could move down the evolutionary ladder. Despite its unsettling potential, Darwinism was used to advance a range of political objectives and to shore up an array of ingrained prejudices.

Challenges to Rationality: Pavlov, Freud, and Nietzsche

Although the new social scientists self-consciously relied on the use of rational, scientific principles, their findings often stressed the opposite: the irrational, even animalistic nature of human experience. Darwin had already called into question the notion that humanity was fundamentally superior to the rest of the animal kingdom, and similarly discomfiting conclusions came from the new field of psychology. The Russian physician Ivan Pavlov (1849–1936) asserted that animal behavior could be understood as a series of trained responses to physical stimuli. Pavlov's famous experiment showed that if dogs were fed after they heard the ringing of a bell, the animals would eventually salivate at the sound of the bell alone, exactly as if they had smelled and saw food. Moreover, Pavlov insisted that such conditioning constituted a significant part of human behavior as well. Known as "behaviorism," this type of physiological psychology avoided vague concepts such as mind and consciousness, concentrating instead on the reaction of muscles, nerves, glands, and visceral organs. Rather than being governed by reason, human activity was recast by behaviorists as a bundle of physiological responses to stimuli in the environment.

Like behaviorism, a second major school of psychology also suggested that human behavior was largely motivated by unconscious and irrational forces. Founded by the Austrian physician Sigmund Freud (1856–1939), the discipline of psychoanalysis posited a new, dynamic, and unsettling theory of the mind, in which a variety of unconscious drives and desires conflict with a rational and moral conscience.

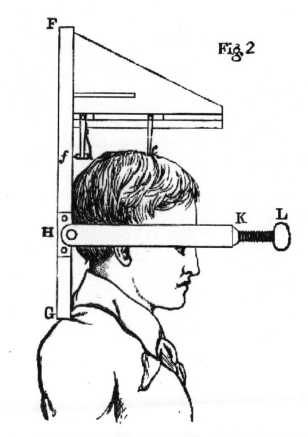

CEPHALOGRAPH. This illustration from Herbert Spencer's autobiography shows a device designed to measure skulls. He believed that the size of one's skull determined brain capacity and applied the idea of "survival of the fittest" to justify theories of white racial superiority.

Competing Viewpoints

Darwin and His Readers

> Charles Darwin's On the Origin of Species (1859) and his theory of natural selection transformed Western knowledge of natural history. The impact of Darwin's work, however, extended well beyond scientific circles. It assumed a cultural importance that exceeded even Darwin's scholarly contribution. How Darwinism was popularized is a complex question, for writers and readers could mold Darwin's ideas to fit a variety of political and cultural purposes. The first excerpt comes from the conclusion to On the Origin of Species itself, and it sets out the different laws that Darwin thought governed the natural world. The second excerpt comes from the autobiography of Nicholas Osterroth (1875–1933), a clay miner from western Germany. Osterroth was ambitious and self-educated. The passage recounts his reaction to hearing about Darwin and conveys his enthusiasm for late-nineteenth-century science.

On the Origin of Species

The natural system is a genealogical arrangement, in which we have to discover the lines of descent by the most permanent characters, however slight their vital importance may be.

The framework of bones being the same in the hand of a man, wing of a bat, fin of the porpoise, and leg of the horse,—the same number of vertebrae forming the neck of the giraffe and of the elephant,—and innumerable other such facts, at once explain themselves on the theory of descent with slow and slight successive modifications. The similarity of pattern in the wing and leg of a bat, though used for such different purposes,—in the jaws and legs of a crab,—in the petals, stamens, and pistils of a flower, is likewise intelligible on the view of the gradual modification of parts or organs, which were alike in the early progenitor of each class. . . .

It is interesting to contemplate an entangled bank, clothed with many plants of many kinds, with birds singing on the bushes, with various insects flitting about, and with worms crawling through the damp earth, and to reflect that these elaborately constructed forms, so different from each other, and dependent on each other in so complex a manner, have all been produced by laws acting around us. These laws, taken in the largest sense, being Growth with Reproduction; Inheritance which is almost implied by reproduction; Variability from the indirect and direct action of the external conditions of life, and from use and disuse; a Ratio of Increase so high as to lead to a Struggle for Life, and as a consequence to Natural Selection, entailing Divergence of Character and the Extinction of less-improved forms. Thus, from the war of nature, from famine and death, the most exalted object which we are capable of conceiving, namely, the production of the higher animals, directly follows. There is grandeur in this view of life, with its several powers, having been originally breathed into a few forms or into one; and that, whilst this planet has gone cycling on according to the fixed law of gravity, from so simple a beginning endless forms most beautiful and most wonderful have been, and are being, evolved.

Source: Charles Darwin, *On the Origin of Species* (Harmondsworth, UK: 1968), pp. 450–51, 458–60.

Developed over many years of treating patients with nervous ailments, Freud's model of the psyche contained three elements: (1) the id, or undisciplined desires for pleasure, sexual gratification, aggression, and so on; (2) the superego, or conscience, which registers the prohibitions of morality and culture; and (3) the ego, the arena in which the conflict between id and superego works itself out. Freud believed that most cases of mental disorder result from an irreconcilable tension between natural drives and the restraints placed on individuals. Freud believed that by studying

Nicholas Osterroth: A Miner's Reaction

The book was called *Moses or Darwin?*... Written in a very popular style, it compared the Mosaic story of creation with the natural evolutionary history, illuminated the contradictions of the biblical story, and gave a concise description of the evolution of organic and inorganic nature, interwoven with plenty of striking proofs.

What particularly impressed me was a fact that now became clear to me: that evolutionary natural history was monopolized by the institutions of higher learning; that Newton, Laplace, Kant, Darwin, and Haeckel brought enlightenment only to the students of the upper social classes; and that for the common people in the grammar school the old Moses with his six-day creation of the world still was the authoritative world view. For the upper classes there was evolution, for us creation; for them productive liberating knowledge, for us rigid faith; bread for those favored by fate, stones for those who hungered for truth!

Why do the people need science? Why do they need a so-called Weltanschauung [worldview]? The people must keep Moses, must keep religion; religion is the poor man's philosophy. Where would we end up if every miner and every farmhand had the opportunity to stick his nose into astronomy, geology, biology, and anatomy? Does it serve any purpose for the divine world order of the possessing and privileged classes to tell the worker that the Ptolemaic heavens have long since collapsed; that out there in the universe there is an eternal process of creation and destruction; that in the universe at large, as on our tiny earth, everything is in the grip of eternal evolution; that this evolution takes place according to inalterable natural laws that defy even the omnipotence of the old Mosaic Jehovah.... Why tell the dumb people that Copernicus and his followers have overturned the old Mosaic creator, and that Darwin and modern science have dug the very ground out from under his feet of clay?

That would be suicide! Yes, the old religion is so convenient for the divine world order of the ruling class! As long as the worker hopes faithfully for the beyond, he won't think of plucking the blooming roses in this world....

The possessing classes of all civilized nations need servants to make possible their godlike existence. So they cannot allow the servant to eat from the tree of knowledge.

Source: Alfred Kelly, ed., *The German Worker: Working-Class Autobiographies from the Age of Industrialization* (Berkeley, CA: 1987), pp. 185–86.

Questions for Analysis

1. Was the theory of evolution revolutionary? If so, how? Would it be fair to say that Darwin did for the nineteenth century what Newton did for the seventeenth and eighteenth centuries?

2. Why did people think the natural world was governed by laws? Was this a religious belief or a scientific fact?

3. What aspects of Darwin appealed to Osterroth and why?

such disorders, as well as dreams and slips of the tongue, scientists could glimpse the submerged areas of consciousness and thus understand seemingly irrational behavior. Freud's seach for an all-encompassing theory of the mind was deeply grounded in the tenets of nineteenth-century science. By stressing the irrational, however, Freud's theories fed a growing anxiety about the value and limits of human reason. Likewise, they brought to fore a powerful critique of the constraints imposed by the moral and social codes of Western civilization.

individual, or "superman," was one who abandoned the burdens of cultural conformity and created an independent set of values based on artistic vision and strength of character. Only through individual struggle against the chaotic universe did Nietzsche forecast salvation for Western civilization.

Religion and Its Critics

Faced with these various scientific and philosophical challenges, the institutions responsible for the maintenance of traditional faith found themselves on the defensive. The Roman Catholic Church responded to the encroachments of secular society by appealing to its dogma and venerated traditions. In 1864, Pope Pius IX issued a Syllabus of Errors, condemning what he regarded as the principal religious and philosophical errors of the time. Among them were materialism, free thought, and indifferentism (the idea that one religion is as good as another). The pope also convoked the first Church council since the Catholic Reformation, which in 1871 pronounced the dogma of papal infallibility. This meant that in his capacity "as pastor and doctor of all Christians," the pope was infallible in regard to all matters of faith and morals. Though generally accepted by pious Catholics, the claim of papal infallibility provoked a storm of protest and was denounced by the governments of several Catholic countries, including France, Spain, and Italy. The death of Pius IX in 1878 and the accession of Pope Leo XIII, however, brought a more accommodating climate to the Church. The new pope acknowledged that there was good as well as evil in modern civilization. He added a scientific staff to the Vatican and opened archives and observatories but made no further concessions to liberalism in the political sphere.

Protestants were also compelled to respond to a modernizing world. Since they were taught to understand God with the aid of little more than the Bible and a willing conscience, Protestants, unlike Catholics, had little in the way of doctrine to help them defend their faith. Some fundamentalists chose to ignore the implications of scientific and philosophical inquiry altogether and continued to believe in the literal truth of the Bible. Others were willing to agree with the school of American philosophers known as pragmatists (principally Charles S. Peirce and William James), who taught that "truth" was whatever produced useful, practical results; by their logic, if belief in God provided mental peace or spiritual satisfaction, then the belief was true. Other Protestants sought solace from religious doubt in founding missions, laboring among the poor,

SIGMUND FREUD. Freud's theory of the mind and the unconscious broke with many of the basic assumptions about human nature during his time. He remained, however, a committed nineteenth-century scientist and believed he had uncovered new laws that governed culture as well as individuals.

No one provided a more sweeping or more influential assault on Western values of rationality than the German philosopher Friedrich Nietzsche (*NEE-chuh*, 1844–1900). Like Freud, Nietzsche had observed a middle-class culture that he believed to be dominated by illusions and self-deceptions, and he sought to unmask them. In a series of works that rejected rational argumentation in favor of an elliptical, suggestive prose style, Nietzsche argued that bourgeois faith in such concepts as science, progress, democracy, and religion represented a futile, and reprehensible, search for security and truth. Nietzsche categorically denied the possibility of knowing truth or reality, since all knowledge comes filtered through linguistic, scientific, or artistic systems of representation. He famously ridiculed Judeo-Christian morality for instilling a repressive conformity that drained civilization of its vitality. Nietzsche's philosophy resounded with themes of personal liberation, especially freedom from the stranglehold of history and tradition. Indeed, Nietzsche's ideal

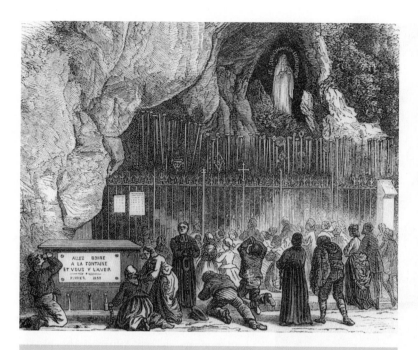

POPULAR RELIGION IN THE MODERN AGE. The political and social changes that accompanied the second industrial revolution and the advent of mass politics transformed European society in fundamental ways, but this did not lead to a waning of traditional religious faith. Instead, the practices of religious devotion changed with the society as a whole. A good example of this is the emergence of new popular destinations for Catholic pilgrimage, such as the Grotto of Lourdes, where a young girl had a series of visions of the Virgin Mary in 1858. After the vision was verified by a local bishop in 1860, the site became a pilgrimage site for the faithful. In 2012, it was estimated that 200 million people had visited the site since 1860. ▪ *What developments during the second industrial revolution helped to make this pilgrimage a global phenomenon?*

other places, from political speeches to novels and crime reports.

The diffusion of these new ideas was facilitated by rising literacy rates and by new forms of printed mass culture. Between 1750 and 1870, readership had expanded from the aristocracy to include middle-class circles and, thereafter, to an increasingly literate general population. In 1850, approximately half the population of Europe was literate. In subsequent decades, country after country introduced state-financed elementary and secondary education to provide opportunities for social advancement, to diffuse technical and scientific knowledge, and to inculcate civic and national pride. By 1900, approximately 85 percent of the population in Britain, France, Belgium, the Netherlands, Scandinavia, and Germany could read.

In those countries where literacy rates were highest, commercial publishers such as Alfred Harmsworth in Britain and William Randolph Hearst in the United States hastened to serve the new reading public. New newspapers appealed to the newly literate by means of sensational journalism and spicy, easy-to-read serials. Advertisements drastically lowered the costs of the mass-market newspapers, enabling even workers to purchase one or two newspapers a day. The yellow journalism of the penny presses merged entertainment and sensationalism with the news, aiming to increase circulation and thus secure more lucrative advertising sales. The era of mass readership had arrived, and artists, activists—and above all—governments would increasingly focus their message on this mass audience.

and other good works. Many adherents to this social gospel were also modernists who accepted the ethical teachings of Christianity but discarded beliefs in miracles and original sin.

New Readers and the Popular Press

The effect of various scientific and philosophical challenges on the men and women who lived at the end of the nineteenth century cannot be measured precisely. Millions undoubtedly went about the business of life untroubled by the implications of evolutionary theory, content to believe as they had believed before. Yet the changes we have been discussing eventually had a profound impact. Darwin's theory was not too complicated to be popularized. If educated men and women had neither the time nor inclination to read *On the Origin of Species,* they read magazines and newspapers that summarized (not always correctly) its implications. They encountered some of its central concepts in

The First Moderns: Innovations in Art

In the crucible of late-nineteenth-century Europe—bubbling with scientific, technological, and social transformations—artists across the Continent began critically and systematically to question the moral and cultural values of liberal, middle-class society. Some did so with grave hesitation, others with heedless abandon. In a dizzying array of experiments, innovations, ephemeral art movements, and bombastic manifestos, the pioneers of what would later be termed "modernism" developed the artistic forms and aesthetic values that came to dominate much of the twentieth century.

***BLACK LINES* BY WASSILY KANDINSKY, 1913.** Kandinsky broke from the traditional representational approach of nineteenth-century painting with his abstractions and was one of a generation of turn-of-the-century artists who reexamined and experimented with their art forms.

Modernism encompassed a diverse and often contradictory set of theories and practices that spanned the entire range of cultural production—from painting, sculpture, literature, and architecture to theater, dance, and musical composition. Despite such diversity, however, modernist movements did share certain key characteristics: first, a sense that the world had radically changed and that change should be embraced (hence the modernists' interest in science and technology); second, a belief that traditional values and assumptions were outdated; and third, a new conception of what art could do, one that stressed expression over representation and insisted on experiment and freedom.

Early modernism was also distinguished by a new understanding of the relationship between art and society. Some artists remained interested in purely aesthetic questions but many others embraced the notion that art could effect profound social and spiritual change. The abstract painter Wassily Kandinsky (1866–1944) believed that the materialism of the nineteenth century was a source of social and moral corruption, and he looked toward a future in which artists would nourish a human spirit that was threatened by the onset of industrial society. Other artists believed they had a duty to document unflinchingly what they saw as the pathological aspects of life in modern cities or the inward chaos of the human mind. In the political arena, modernist hostility toward conventional values sometimes translated into support for antiliberal or revolutionary movements of the extreme right or left.

THE REVOLT ON CANVAS

Like most artistic movements, modernism defined itself in opposition to a set of earlier principles. For painters in particular, this meant a rejection both of mainstream academic art, which affirmed the chaste and moral outlook of museumgoers, and of the socially conscious realist tradition, which strove for rigorous, even scientific exactitude in representing material reality. The rebellion of modern artists went even further, however, by discarding altogether the centuries-old tradition of realist representation. Since the Renaissance, Western art had sought to accurately depict three-dimensional visual reality; paintings were considered to be mirrors or windows on the world. But during the late nineteenth century, artists turned their backs to the visual world, focusing instead on subjective, psychologically oriented, intensely emotional forms of self-expression. As the Norwegian painter Edvard Munch claimed: "Art is the opposite of nature. A work of art can come only from the interior of man."

The first significant breaks with traditional representational art emerged with the French impressionists, who came to prominence as young artists in the 1870s. Strictly speaking, the impressionists were realists. Steeped in scientific theories about sensory perception, they attempted to record natural phenomena objectively. Instead of painting objects themselves, they captured the transitory play of light on surfaces, giving their works a sketchy, ephemeral quality that differed sharply from realist art. And though subsequent artists revolted against what they deemed the cold objectivity of this scientific approach, the impressionist painters, most famously Claude Monet (*moh-NAY*, 1840–1926) and Pierre-Auguste Renoir (1841–1919), left two important legacies to the European avant-garde. First, by developing new techniques without reference to past styles, the impressionists paved

SELF-PORTRAIT, BY EGON SCHIELE, 1912. The Viennese artist Schiele represents another side of early modernism that, instead of moving toward abstraction, sought to portray raw psychological expression.

PORTRAIT OF AMBROISE VOLLARD **BY PABLO PICASSO, 1909.** In the early twentieth century, Picasso and George Braque radically transformed painting with their cubist constructions, breaking the depiction of reality into fragmented planes. Vollard, an important art dealer of the period, loses recognizable form as his figure descends. ▪ *Compare this portrait with Schiele's self-portrait, at left. What do these paintings say about the task of the artist?* ▪ *What makes them "modern"?*

the way for younger artists to experiment more freely. Second, because the official salons rejected their work, the impressionists organized their own independent exhibitions from 1874 to 1886. These shows effectively undermined the French Academy's centuries-old monopoly on artistic display and aesthetic standards, and they established a tradition of autonomous outsider exhibits, which figures prominently in the history of modernism.

In the wake of impressionism, a handful of innovative artists working at the end of the nineteenth century laid the groundwork for an explosion of creative experimentation after 1900. Chief among them was the Frenchman Paul Cézanne (1839–1906). Perhaps more so than anyone, Cézanne shattered the window of representational art. Instead of a reflection of the world, painting became a vehicle for an artist's self-expression. The Dutchman Vincent van Gogh also explored art's expressive potential, with greater emotion and subjectivity. For Van Gogh, painting was a labor of faith, a way to channel his violent passions. For Paul Gauguin, who fled to the Pacific islands in 1891, art promised a utopian refuge from the corruption of Europe.

After the turn of the century, a diverse crop of avant-garde movements flowered across Europe. In Germany and Scandinavia, expressionists such as Emil Nolde (1867–1956), and Edvard Munch (1863–1944) turned to acid colors and violent figural distortions to express the interior consciousness of the human mind. The Austrian Egon Schiele (1890–1918) explored sexuality and the body with disturbingly raw, graphic imagery. In bohemian Paris, the Frenchman Henri Matisse (1869–1954) and Pablo Picasso (1881–1973), a Catalan Spaniard, pursued their groundbreaking aesthetic experiments in relative quiet. Clamoring for attention, on the other hand, were groups of artists who reveled in the energetic dynamism of modern life.

The cubists in Paris, vorticists in Britain, and futurists in Italy all embraced a hard, angular aesthetic of the machine age. While other modernists sought an antidote to end-of-the-century malaise by looking backward to so-called primitive cultures, these new movements embraced the future in all its uncertainty—often with the kind of aggressive, hyper-masculine language that later emerged as a hallmark of fascism. In the futurist *Manifesto,* for instance, F. T. Marinetti proclaimed: "We will glorify war—the only true hygiene of the world—militarism, patriotism, the destructive gesture of anarchist, the beautiful Ideas which kill." In Russia and Holland, meanwhile, a few intensely idealistic painters made perhaps the most revolutionary aesthetic leap of early modernism, into totally abstract, or "object-less" painting.

The breadth and diversity of modern art defy simple categories and explanations. Though they remained the province of a small group of artists and intellectuals before 1914, these radical revisions of artistic values entered the cultural mainstream soon after the First World War (see Chapter 25).

CONCLUSION

Many Europeans who had grown up in the period from 1870 to 1914, but lived through the hardships of the First World War, looked back on the prewar period as a golden age of

After You Read This Chapter

Visit StudySpace for quizzes, additional review materials, and multimedia documents. **wwnorton.com/web/westernciv18**

REVIEWING THE OBJECTIVES

- The second industrial revolution was made possible by technological innovations that stimulated the production of steel and new energy sources. What were the consequences of this era of rapid growth for the economy and for European society?

- Expanded electorates meant that more people were participating in politics, especially among the working classes. What parties and movements emerged to represent European workers, and what were their goals?

- At the end of the nineteenth century, militant agitation in favor of women's suffrage increased. What obstacles faced women who demanded the vote?

- Liberalism and nationalism were changed by the advent of mass politics. How did the expansion of the electorate change political life across Europe?

- Technological innovations and scientific ideas about human nature and modern society changed the way that people thought about their place in the world, stimulating artists and writers to new and revolutionary forms of creative expression. What were these scientific ideas and why were they so controversial at the end of the nineteenth century?

European civilization. In one sense, this retrospective view is apt. After all, the continental powers had successfully avoided major wars, enabling a second phase of industrialization to provide better living standards for the growing populations of mass society. An overall spirit of confidence and purpose fueled Europe's perceived mission to exercise political, economic, and cultural dominion in the far reaches of the world. Yet European politics and culture also registered the presence of powerful—and destabilizing—forces of change. Industrial expansion, relative abundance, and rising literacy produced a political climate of rising expectations. As the age of mass politics arrived, democrats, socialists, and feminists clamored for access to political life, threatening violence, strikes, and revolution. Marxist socialism especially changed radical politics, redefining the terms of debate for the next century. Western science, literature, and the arts explored new perspectives on the individual, undermining some of the cherished beliefs of nineteenth-century liberals. The competition and violence central to Darwin's theory of evolution, the subconscious urges that Freud found in human behavior, and the rebellion against representation in the arts all pointed in new and baffling directions. These experiments, hypotheses, and nagging questions accompanied Europe into the Great War of 1914. They would help shape Europeans' responses to the devastation of that war. After the war, the political changes and cultural unease of the period from 1870 to 1914 would reemerge in the form of mass movements and artistic developments that would define the twentieth century.

PEOPLE, IDEAS, AND EVENTS IN CONTEXT

- Why was the British **LABOUR PARTY** more moderate in its goals than the German **SOCIAL DEMOCRATIC PARTY**?

- What disagreements about political strategy divided **ANARCHISTS** and **SYNDICALISTS** from **MARXISTS** in European labor movements?

- What legal reforms were successfully achieved by **WOMEN'S ASSOCIATIONS** in late-nineteenth-century western European nations?

- What was the **DREYFUS AFFAIR**, and how was it related to the spread of popular **ANTI-SEMITISM** and the emergence of **ZIONISM** in European Jewish communities?

- What were the goals of the **BOLSHEVIKS** and the **MENSHEVIKS** in the **RUSSIAN REVOLUTION OF 1905**?

- Who were the **YOUNG TURKS**?

- What was **CHARLES DARWIN**'s **THEORY OF EVOLUTION**, and why did it stimulate so much debate between religious and secular thinkers?

- Why was the psychology of **SIGMUND FREUD** so troubling for liberals in Europe?

- What common ideas did the artists and writers who came to be known as **MODERNISTS** share?

THINKING ABOUT CONNECTIONS

- How did the expansion of the electorate and the spread of representative political institutions in Europe at the end of the nineteenth century change the nature of debates about the power of public opinion and the responsibility of government for the people?

- Compare the age of mass politics at the end of the nineteenth century in Europe with earlier periods of rapid change, such as the Reformation of the sixteenth century or the period of the French Revolution. What was similar? What was different?

- Compare the age of mass politics in Europe circa 1900 with the political life of Europe or the United States today. What has changed? What remains the same?

STORY LINES

- In 1914, the balance of power in Europe collapsed in a total war that mobilized the full resources of modern industrialized nations, their global empires, and their populations.

- The war transformed the relationship between state and society. Governments conscripted an entire generation of young men, encouraged women to work in industry, and took control of the economy to produce goods and material for the military.

- The war provoked the first successful socialist revolution in modern history when the Russian Empire collapsed and the Bolsheviks seized power in October 1917. The Russian Revolution set the stage for the major ideological confrontations of the twentieth century.

CHRONOLOGY

1879	The Dual Alliance (Germany and Austria-Hungary)
1904	The Triple Entente (France, Russia, and Britain)
June 1914	Assassination of Franz Ferdinand in Sarajevo
September 1914	Battle of the Marne
April 1915	Gallipoli campaign begins
May 1915	Italy enters the war against Austria-Hungary
February 1916	Battle of Verdun begins
July 1916	British offensive on the Somme begins
January 1917	Germany begins unrestricted submarine warfare
April 1917	United States enters the war
November 1917	Bolshevik Revolution
March 1918	Treaty of Brest-Litovsk
November 1918	Armistice
June 1919	Treaty of Versailles signed

Before
You
Read
This
Chapter

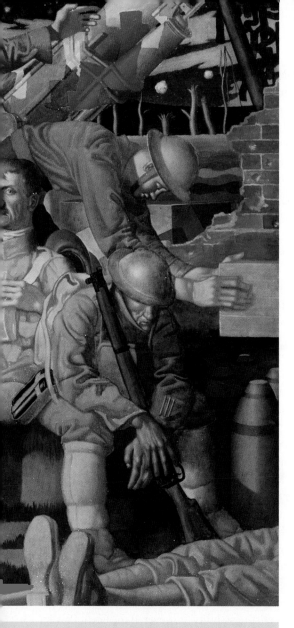

The First World War

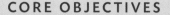

CORE OBJECTIVES

- **EXPLAIN** the origins of the First World War.

- **UNDERSTAND** the circumstances that led to trench warfare on the Western Front, and the consequences of the offensive strategy pursued by all sides.

- **IDENTIFY** the major effects of the war on civilian life.

- **EXPLAIN** the war's effects on territories beyond Europe's borders, in the Middle East, in Africa, and in Asia.

- **UNDERSTAND** the origins and goals of the Bolshevik movement in Russia and the circumstances that allowed them to seize power in 1917.

- **IDENTIFY** the people responsible for the final terms of the Versailles Peace Treaty and understand its goals.

The battle of the Somme began on June 24, 1916, with a fearsome British artillery barrage against German trenches along a twenty-five-mile front. Hour after hour, day and night, the British guns swept across the barbed wire and fortifications that faced their own lines, firing 1.5 million rounds over seven days. Mixing gas with explosive rounds, the gunners pulverized the landscape and poisoned the atmosphere. Deep in underground bunkers on the other side, the German defenders huddled in their masks. When the big guns went silent, tens of thousands of British soldiers rose up out of their trenches, each bearing sixty pounds of equipment, and made their way into the cratered No Man's Land that separated the two armies. They had been told that wire-cutting explosives would destroy the labyrinth of barbed wire between the trenches during the barrage, leaving them free to charge across and occupy the front trench before the stunned Germans could recover. To their horror, they found the barbed wire intact. Instead of taking the German trench, they found themselves caught in the open when the German machine-gunners manned the defensive parapets. The result proved all too eloquently the efficiency of the First World

War's mechanized methods of killing. Twenty-one thousand British soldiers were killed on the first day of the battle of the Somme. A further 30,000 were wounded. Because some British units allowed volunteers to serve with their friends—the "Pals Battalions"—there were neighborhoods and villages in Britain in which every married woman became a widow in the space of a few minutes. The British commanders pressed the offensive for nearly five more months, and the combined casualties climbed over a million. The German line never broke.

This contest between artillery and machine gun was a war that was possible only in an industrialized world. Before beginning the assault, the British had stockpiled 2.9 million artillery shells—Napoleon had only 20,000 at Waterloo. Although European armies marched off to war in 1914 with a confidence and ambition bred by their imperial conquests, they soon confronted the ugly face of industrial warfare and the grim capacities of the modern world. In a catastrophic combination of old mentalities and new technologies, the war left 9 million dead soldiers in its wake.

Soldiers were not the only casualties. Four years of fighting destroyed many of the institutions and assumptions of the previous century, from monarchies and empires to European economic dominance. It disillusioned many, even the citizens of the victorious nations. As the British writer Virginia Woolf put it, "It was a shock—to see the faces of our rulers in the light of shell-fire." The war led European states to take over their national economies, as they set quotas for production and consumption and took responsibility for sustaining the civilian population during the crisis. By toppling the Prussian and Austrian monarchies, the war banished older forms of authoritarianism, and by provoking the Russian Revolution of 1917, the war ushered in new ones that bore the distinctive mark of the twentieth century. Finally, the war proved nearly impossible to settle; antagonisms bred in battle only intensified in the war's aftermath and would eventually lead to the Second World War. Postwar Europe faced more problems than peace could manage.

THE JULY CRISIS

In the decades before 1914, Europe had built a seemingly stable peace. Through the complex negotiations of Great Power geopolitics, Europe had settled into two systems of alliance: the Triple Entente (later the Allied Powers) of Britain, France, and Russia rivaled the Triple Alliance (later the Central Powers) of Germany, Austria-Hungary, and Italy. Within this balance of power, the nations of Europe challenged one another for economic, military, and imperial advantage. The scramble for colonies abroad accompanied a fierce arms race at home, where military leaders assumed that superior technology and larger armies would result in a quick victory in a European war. Yet none of the diplomats, spies, military planners, or cabinet ministers of Europe—or any of their critics—predicted the war they eventually got. Nor did many expect that the Balkan crisis of July 1914 would touch off that conflict, engulfing all of Europe in just over a month's time.

The Balkan Peninsula had long been a satellite of the Ottoman Empire. During the nineteenth century, however, Ottoman power became severely weakened, and both the Austro-Hungarian Empire and the Russian monarchy competed with one another to replace the Ottomans as the dominant force in the region. The region was also home to ambitious national movements of Serbs and Bulgarians who took advantage of Ottoman decline to declare their independence in the decades before the First World War. Russia, as the most powerful Slavic monarchy, was the traditional sponsor of these Slavic nationalist movements and had a particularly close relationship with Serbia. Austria-Hungary, on the other hand, sought to minimize the influence of Slavic nationalisms because they constituted a threat to its own multi-ethnic empire. In 1912 and 1913, the region was destabilized by two wars involving the Ottoman Empire and the independent Balkan states of Serbia, Greece, Bulgaria, and Montenegro. The Great Powers steered clear of entanglement and these wars remained localized. The alliance system could only ensure stability, however, if the Great Powers could maintain this posture of nonintervention. Once one of them became embroiled in a local conflict, the system of alliances would lead directly to a wider war.

The spark came from the Balkan province of Bosnia, a multi-ethnic region of Serbs, Croats, and Bosnian Muslims that had been under Austrian rule since 1878. In Bosnia, members of the local Serb population longed to secede from Austrian rule altogether and join the independent state of Serbia. When Bosnian Serbs found their way blocked by the Austrians, some began to conspire with Serbia, and on June 28, 1914, a group of Bosnian Serbs assassinated the heir to the Austro-Hungarian throne, Franz Ferdinand (1889–1914) as he paraded through Sarajevo, the capital of Bosnia.

Shocked by Ferdinand's death, the Austrians treated the assassination as a direct attack by the Serbian government. Three weeks later, the Austrians announced an ultimatum to Serbia, demanding that they denounce the activities of Bosnian Serbs, abstain from propaganda that served their cause, and allow Austro-Hungarian officials to prosecute members of the Serbian government who they believed were involved in the assassination. The demands were deliberately unreasonable—the Austrians wanted war, to crush Serbia and restore order in Bosnia. The Serbs mobilized their army before agreeing to all but the most important demands, and Austria responded with its own mobilization order on July 28, 1914. Shaken from their summer distractions, Europeans began to realize that the treaty system they relied on for stability was actually leading to a much larger confrontation: Austria and its ally Germany were facing a war with Serbia, Serbia's ally Russia, and by extension, Russia's ally France.

Diplomats tried and failed to prevent the outbreak of wider war. When Russia announced a "partial mobilization" to defend Serbia against Austria, the German ministers telegraphed the French to find out if they intended to honor France's defensive treaty with Russia. The French responded that France would "act in accordance with her interests"—meaning that they would immediately mobilize against Germany. Facing the dual threat from both sides that they had long feared, Germany mobilized on August 1 and declared war on Russia—and two days later, on France. The next day, the German army invaded Belgium on its way to take Paris.

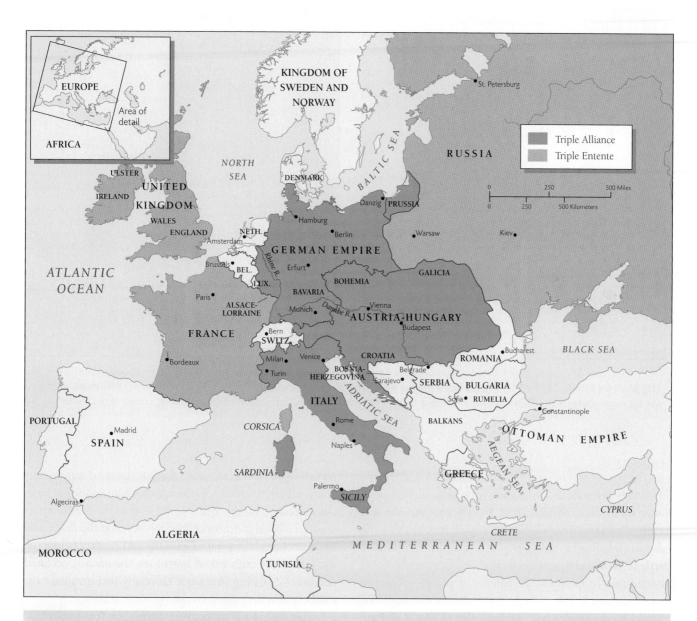

EUROPEAN ALLIANCES ON THE EVE OF THE FIRST WORLD WAR. ▪ *What major countries were part of the Triple Alliance?* ▪ *Of the Triple Entente?* ▪ *From the map, why would Germany have declared war on France so quickly once Russia began to mobilize?* ▪ *According to the map, why were the Balkan countries such a volatile region?*

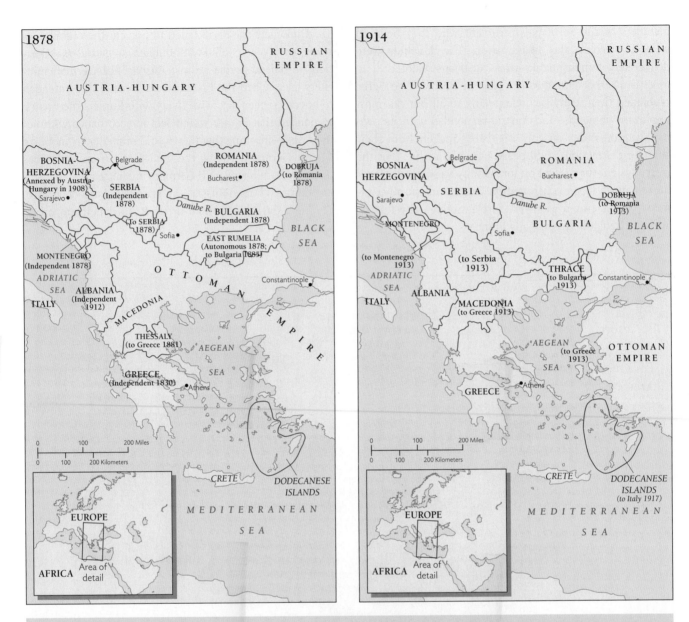

THE BALKAN CRISIS, 1878–1914. ▪ *What major empires were involved in the Balkans during this period?* ▪ *According to the maps, what was the major change in the Balkans between 1878 and 1914?* ▪ *What problems did nationalism, ethnicity, and race create in this region?*

The invasion of neutral Belgium provided a rallying cry for British generals and diplomats who wanted Britain to honor their secret obligations to France and join the war against Germany. This was not a foregone conclusion—the Liberal government was opposed to war and acquiesced partly to avoid being voted out of office. Proponents of war insisted that to maintain the balance of power—a central tenet of British foreign policy—no single nation should be allowed to dominate the continent. On August 4, Britain entered the war against Germany.

Other nations were quickly drawn into the struggle. On August 7, the Montenegrins joined the Serbs against Austria. Two weeks later, the Japanese declared war on Germany, mainly to attack German possessions in the Far East. On August 1, Turkey allied with Germany and in October began the bombardment of Russian ports on the Black Sea. Italy had been allied with Germany and Austria before the war, but at the outbreak of hostilities, the Italians declared neutrality, insisting that since Germany had invaded neutral Belgium, they owed Germany no protection.

The diplomatic maneuvers during the five weeks that followed the assassination at Sarajevo have been called a "tragedy of miscalculation." Austria's determination to punish Serbia, Germany's unwillingness to restrain their

FRANZ FERDINAND AND HIS WIFE, SOPHIE. The Austrian archduke and archduchess, in Sarajevo on June 28, 1914, approaching their car before they were assassinated.
- *What made their deaths the spark that unleashed a general war in Europe?*

Austrian allies, and Russia's desire to use Serbia as an excuse to extend their influence in the Balkans all played a part in making the war more likely. Diplomats were further constrained by the strategic thinking and rigid timetables set by military leaders, and all sides clearly felt that it was important to make a show of force during the period of negotiation that preceded the outbreak of war. It is clear, however, that powerful German officials were arguing that war was inevitable. They insisted that Germany should fight before Russia recovered from their 1905 loss to Japan and before the French army could benefit from its new three-year conscription law, which would put more men in uniform. This sense of urgency characterized the strategies of all combatant countries. The lure of a bold, successful strike against one's enemies, and the fear that too much was at stake to risk losing the advantage created a rolling tide of military mobilization that carried Europe into battle.

THE MARNE AND ITS CONSEQUENCES

Declarations of war were met with a mix of public fanfare and private concern. Though saber-rattling romantics envisioned a war of national glory and spiritual renewal, plenty of Europeans recognized that a continental war put decades of progress and prosperity at risk. Bankers and financiers, who might have hoped to profit from increased wartime production or from captured colonial markets, were among those most opposed to the war. They correctly predicted that a major war would create financial chaos. Many young men, however, enlisted with excitement. On the Continent, volunteer soldiers added to the strength of conscript armies, while in Britain (where conscription wasn't introduced until 1916) over 700,000 men joined the army in the first eight weeks alone. Like many a war enthusiast, these men expected the war to be over by Christmas.

If less idealistic, the expectations of the politicians and generals in charge were also soon to be disproved. Military planners foresaw a short, limited, and decisive war—a tool to be used where diplomacy failed. They thought that a modern economy simply could not function amid a sustained war effort and that modern weaponry made protracted war impossible. They placed their bets on size and speed: bigger armies, more powerful weapons, and faster offensives would win the war. But for all of their planning, they were unable to respond to the uncertainty and confusion of the battlefield.

The Germans based their offensive on what is often called the Schlieffen Plan, named for Count Alfred von Schlieffen (*SHLEE-fen*), chief of the German General Staff from 1890 to 1905. Schlieffen called for attacking France first to secure a quick victory that would neutralize the Western Front and free the German army to fight Russia in the east. With France expecting an attack through Alsace-Lorraine, the Germans would instead invade through Belgium and sweep down through northwestern France to fight a decisive battle near Paris. For over a month, the German army advanced swiftly, but the plan overestimated the army's physical and logistical capabilities. The speed of the operation—advancing twenty to twenty-five miles a day—was simply too much for soldiers and supply lines to keep up with. They were also slowed by the resistance of Belgian forces and by the intervention of Britain's small but highly professional field army. Fearing the Russians would move faster than expected, German commanders altered the offensive plan by dispatching some troops to the east instead of committing them all to the assault on France.

Toward the First World War: Diplomacy in the Summer of 1914

The assassination of Franz Ferdinand in Sarajevo on June 28, 1914, set off an increasingly desperate round of diplomatic negotiations. As the following exchanges show, diplomats and political leaders on both sides swung from trying to provoke war to attempting to avert or, at least, contain it. A week after his nephew, the heir to the throne, was shot, Franz Joseph set out his interpretation of the long-standing conflict with Serbia and its larger implications—reprinted here.

The second selection comes from an account of a meeting of the Council of Ministers of the Austro-Hungarian Empire on July 7, 1914. The ministers disagreed sharply about diplomatic strategies and about how crucial decisions should be made.

The British foreign secretary Sir Edward Grey, for one, was shocked by Austria's demands, especially its insistence that Austrian officials would participate in Serbian judicial proceedings. The Serbian government's response was more conciliatory than most diplomats expected, but diplomatic efforts to avert war still failed. The Austrians' ultimatum to Serbia included the following demands given in the final extract here.

Emperor Franz Joseph of Austria-Hungary to Kaiser Wilhelm II of Germany, July 5, 1914

The plot against my poor nephew was the direct result of an agitation carried on by the Russian and Serb Pan-Slavs, an agitation whose sole object is the weakening of the Triple Alliance and the destruction of my realm.

So far, all investigations have shown that the Sarajevo murder was not perpetrated by one individual, but grew out of a well-organized conspiracy, the threads of which can be traced to Belgrade. Even though it will probably be impossible to prove the complicity of the Serb government, there can be no doubt that its policy, aiming as it does at the unification of all Southern Slavs under the Serb banner, encourages such crimes, and that the continuation of such conditions constitutes a permanent threat to my dynasty and my lands. . . .

This will only be possible if Serbia, which is at present the pivot of Pan-Slav policies, is put out of action as a factor of political power in the Balkans.

You too are [surely] convinced after the recent frightful occurrence in Bosnia that it is no longer possible to contemplate a reconciliation of the antagonism between us and Serbia and that the [efforts] of all European monarchs to pursue policies that preserve the peace will be threatened if the nest of criminal activity in Belgrade remains unpunished.

Austro-Hungarian Disagreements over Strategy

C [Count Leopold Berchtold, foreign minister of Austria-Hungary] . . . both Emperor Wilhelm and [chancellor] Bethmann Hollweg had assured us emphatically of Germany's unconditional support in the event of military complications with Serbia. . . . It was clear to him that a military conflict with Serbia might bring about war with Russia. . . .

[Count Istvan Tisza, prime minister of Hungary] . . . We should decide what our demands on Serbia will be [but] should only present an ultimatum if Serbia rejected them. These demands must be hard but not so that they cannot be complied with. If Serbia accepted them, we could register a noteworthy diplomatic success and our prestige in the Balkans would be enhanced. If Serbia rejected our demands, then he too would favor military action. But he would already now go on record that we could aim at the down sizing but not the complete annihilation of Serbia because, first, this would provoke Russia to fight to the death and, second, he—as Hungarian premier—could never consent to the monarchy's annexation of a part of Serbia. Whether or not we ought to go to war with Serbia was not a matter for Germany to decide. . . .

[Count Berchtold] remarked that the history of the past years showed that diplomatic successes against Serbia might enhance the prestige of the monarchy temporarily, but that in reality the tension in our relations with Serbia had only increased.

[Count Karl Stürgkh, prime minister of Austria] ... agreed with the Royal Hungarian Prime Minister that we and not the German government had to determine whether a war was necessary or not ... [but] Count Tisza should take into account that in pursuing a hesitant and weak policy, we run the risk of not being so sure of Germany's unconditional support. ...

[Leo von Bilinsky, Austro-Hungarian finance minister] ... The Serb understands only force, a diplomatic success would make no impression at all in Bosnia and would be harmful rather than beneficial. ...

Austro-Hungary's Ultimatum to Serbia

The Royal Serb Government will publish the following declaration on the first page of its official *journal* of 26/13 July:

"The Royal Serb Government condemns the propaganda directed against Austria-Hungary, and regrets sincerely the horrible consequences of these criminal ambitions.

"The Royal Serb Government regrets that Serb officers and officials have taken part in the propaganda above-mentioned and thereby imperiled friendly and neighbourly relations.

"The Royal Government ... considers it a duty to warn officers, officials and indeed all the inhabitants of the kingdom [of Serbia], that it will in future use great severity against such persons who may be guilty of similar doings.

The Royal Serb Government will moreover pledge itself to the following.

1. to suppress every publication likely to inspire hatred and contempt against the Monarchy;

2. to begin immediately dissolving the society called *Narodna Odbrana*,* to seize all its means of propaganda and to act in the same way against all the societies and associations in Serbia, which are busy with the propaganda against Austria-Hungary;

3. to eliminate without delay from public instruction everything that serves or might serve the propaganda against Austria-Hungary, both where teachers or books are concerned;

4. to remove from military service and from the administration all officers and officials who are guilty of having taken part in the propaganda against Austria-Hungary, whose names and proof of whose guilt the I. and R. Government [Imperial and Royal, that is, the Austro-Hungarian empire] will communicate to the Royal Government;

5. to consent to the cooperation of I. and R. officials in Serbia in suppressing the subversive movement directed against the territorial integrity of the Monarchy;

6. to open a judicial inquest [*enquête judiciaire*] against all those who took part in the plot of 28 June, if they are to be found on Serbian territory; the I. and R. Government will delegate officials who will take an active part in these and associated inquiries;

The I. and R. Government expects the answer of the Royal government to reach it not later than Saturday, the 25th, at six in the afternoon. ...

*Narodna Odbrana, or National Defense, was pro-Serbian and anti-Austrian but nonviolent. The Society of the Black Hand, to which Franz Ferdinand's assassin belonged, considered Narodna Odbrana too moderate.

Source (for all three excerpts): Ralph Menning, *The Art of the Possible: Documents on Great Power Diplomacy, 1814–1914* (New York: 1996), pp. 400, 402–03, and 414–15.

Questions for Analysis

1. Emperor Franz Joseph's letter to Kaiser Wilhelm II tells of the Austrian investigation into the assassination of Archduke Franz Ferdinand. What did Franz seek from his German ally? What did the emperors understand by the phrase "if Serbia ... is put out of action as a factor of political power in the Balkans"? Why might the Germans support a war against Serb-sponsored terrorism?

2. Could the Serbians have accepted the Austrian ultimatum without total loss of face and sacrifice of their independence? British and Russian foreign ministers were shocked by the demands on Serbia. Others thought the Austrians were justified and that Britain would act similarly if threatened by terrorism. If, as Leo von Bilinsky said, "The Serb understands only force," why didn't Austria declare war without an ultimatum?

THE SCHLIEFFEN PLAN AND THE GERMAN OFFENSIVE. The map on the left details the offensive strategy developed (and modified several times) by Alfred von Schlieffen, chief of the German General Staff, and Helmuth von Moltke, his successor in the decade after 1890.
- *What strategy did they propose, and why?* - *The map on the right shows the German offensive. How was the plan modified, and why?*
- *With what consequences?* - *Why did the German offensive fail to achieve its ultimate goal?*

At first, French counterattacks into Alsace-Lorraine failed, and casualties mounted as the French lines retreated toward Paris. The French commander, Jules Joffre, nevertheless reorganized his armies and slowly drew the Germans into a trap. In September, with the Germans just thirty miles outside of the capital, Britain and France launched a successful counteroffensive at the battle of the Marne. The German line retreated to the Aisne River, and what remained of the Schlieffen Plan was dead.

After the Marne, unable to advance, the armies tried to outflank one another to the north, racing to the sea. After four months of swift charges across open ground, Germany set up a fortified, defensive position that the Allies could not break. Along an immovable front, stretching over 400 miles from the northern border of Switzerland to the English Channel, the Great Powers literally dug in for a protracted battle. By Christmas, trench warfare was born, and the war had just begun.

The Marne proved to be the most strategically important battle of the entire war. This single battle upended Europe's expectations of war and dashed hopes that it would quickly finish. The war of movement had stopped dead in its tracks, where it would remain for four years. Politicians and generals began a continual search for ways to break the stalemate and to bring the war out of trenches, seeking new allies, new theaters, and new weapons. But they also remained committed to offensive tactics on the Western Front. Whether through ignorance, stubbornness, callousness, or desperation, military leaders continued to order their men to go "over the top."

Allied success at the Marne resulted in part from an unexpectedly strong Russian assault in eastern Prussia, which pulled some German units away from the attack on the west. But Russia's initial gains were obliterated at the battle of Tannenberg, August 26–30. Plagued with an array of problems, the Russian army was tired and half-starved; the Germans devastated it, taking 92,000 prisoners and virtually destroying the Russian Second Army. The Russian general killed himself on the battlefield. Two weeks later, the Germans won another decisive victory at the battle of the Masurian Lakes, forcing the Russians to retreat from German territory. Despite this, Russian forces were able to defeat Austrian attacks to their south, inflicting terrible losses and thereby forcing the Germans to commit more troops to Russia. Through 1915 and 1916, the Eastern Front remained bloody and indecisive, with neither side able to capitalize on its gains.

RUSSIAN PRISONERS IN LATE AUGUST 1914, AFTER THE BATTLE OF TANNENBERG. The German army, under Paul von Hindenburg and Erich Ludendorff, crushed the Russians and took 92,000 prisoners. The Russians continued to fight, but the photograph highlights the weakness of even a massive army and the scale of the combat.

STALEMATE, 1915

In the search for new points of attack, both the Allies and the Central Powers added new partners. The Ottoman Empire (Turkey) joined Germany and Austria at the end of 1914. In May 1915, Italy joined the Allies, persuaded by the popular support of its citizens and lured by promises of financial reparations, parts of Austrian territory, and pieces of Germany's African colonies when (and if) the Allies won the war. Bulgaria also hoped to gain territory in the Balkans and joined the war on the side of the Central Powers a few months later. The entry of these new belligerents expanded the geography of the war and introduced the possibility of breaking the stalemate in the west by waging offensives on other fronts.

Gallipoli and Naval Warfare

Turkey's involvement, in particular, altered the dynamics of the war, for it threatened Russia's supply lines and endangered Britain's control of the Suez Canal. To defeat Turkey quickly—and in hopes of bypassing the Western Front—the British first lord of the admiralty, Winston Churchill (1911–15), argued for a naval offensive in the Dardanelles, the narrow strait separating Europe and Asia Minor. Under particularly incompetent leadership, however, the Royal

Navy lacked adequate planning, supply lines, and maps to mount a successful campaign, and quickly lost six ships. The Allies then attempted a land invasion of the Gallipoli Peninsula, in April 1915, with a combined force of French, British, Australian, and New Zealand troops. The Turks defended the narrow coast from positions high on fortified cliffs, and the shores were covered with nearly impenetrable barbed wire. During the disastrous landing, a British officer recalled, "the sea behind was absolutely crimson, and you could hear the groans through the rattle of musketry." The battle became entrenched on the beaches at Gallipoli, and the casualties mounted for seven months before the Allied commanders admitted defeat and ordered a withdrawal in December. The Gallipoli campaign—the first large-scale amphibious attack in history—brought death into London's neighborhoods and the cities of Britain's industrial north. Casualties were particularly devastating in the "white dominions"—practically every town and hamlet in Australia, New Zealand, and Canada lost young men, sometimes all the sons of a single family. The defeat cost the Allies 200,000 soldiers and did little to shift the war's focus away from the deadlocked Western Front.

By 1915, both sides realized that fighting this prolonged and costly "modern" war would require countries to mobilize all of their resources. As one captain put it in a letter home, "It is absolutely certainly a war of 'attrition,' as somebody said here the other day, and we have got to stick it out longer than the other side and go on producing men, money, and material until they cry quits, and that's about it, as far as I can see."

The Allies started to wage war on the economic front. Germany was vulnerable, dependent as it was on imports for at least one-third of its food supply. The Allies' naval blockade against all of central Europe aimed to slowly drain their opponents of food and raw materials. Germany responded with a submarine blockade, threatening to attack any vessel in the seas around Great Britain. On May 7, 1915, the German submarine *U-20*, without warning, torpedoed the passenger liner *Lusitania*, which was secretly carrying war supplies. The attack killed 1,198 people, including 128 Americans. The attack provoked the animosity of the United States, and Germany was forced to promise that it would no longer fire without warning. (This promise proved only temporary: in 1917, Germany

Interpreting Visual Evidence

War Propaganda

Poster art was a leading form of propaganda used by all belligerents in the First World War to enlist men, sell war bonds, and sustain morale on the home front. Posters also demonized the enemy and glorified the sacrifices of soldiers to better rationalize the unprecedented loss of life and national wealth. The posters shown here, from a wide range of combatant nations during the war, share a common desire to link the war effort to a set of assumptions about the different roles assigned to men and women in the national struggle.

A. British Poster: "Women of Britain say 'Go!'"

B. Russian Poster: "Women Workers! Take up the Rifle!"

Questions for Analysis

1. Why would nationalists resort to such gendered images in a time of crisis?

2. What do these images tell us about the way that feelings of national belonging are created and sustained in times of urgency?

3. How might the changes that the war brought about—an increase in the number of women working in industry or outside the home, increased autonomy for women in regard to their wages or management of their household affairs—have affected the way that individuals responded to such images?

C. German Poster: "Collect women's hair that has been combed out. Our industry needs it for drive belts."

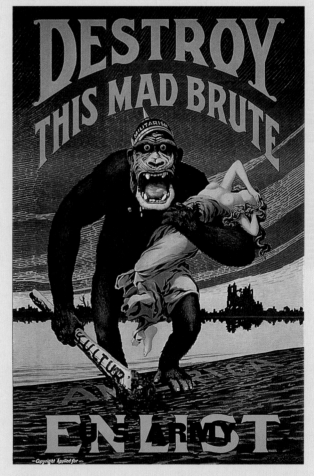

D. American Poster: "Destroy This Mad Brute. Enlist." The mad beast, meant to represent Germany, with *militarism* on his helmet, threatens American civilization with a club of *Kultur* (culture).

THE NEW TECHNOLOGIES OF WAR IN THE AIR AND AT SEA. The use of airplanes and submarines, both produced in large numbers during World War I, changed the nature of warfare. Air war helped dissolve the boundaries between the front line and the home front as civilian populations were brought within range of the enemy's destructive power. Germany's decision to use submarines against merchant ships trading with Britain and France led to the sinking of the *Lusitania* in 1915, which turned public opinion in the United States. The same issue led President Wilson to commit U.S. troops to the Allied side in 1917. The image on the left shows the German submarine base in Kiel, on the Baltic coast. On the right is a German plane attacking an English tank.

would again declare unrestricted submarine warfare, drawing America into the war.) Although the German blockade against Britain destroyed more tonnage, the blockade against Germany was more devastating in the long run, as the continued war effort placed increasing demands on the national economy.

Trench Warfare

While the war escalated economically and politically, life in the trenches—the "lousy scratch holes," as a soldier called them—remained largely the same: a cramped and miserable existence of daily routines and continual killing. Indeed, some 25,000 miles of trenches snaked along the Western Front, normally in three lines on each side of "No Man's Land." The front line was the attack trench, lying anywhere from fifty yards to a mile away from the enemy. Behind the front lay a maze of connecting trenches and lines, leading to a complex of ammunition dumps, telephone exchanges, water points, field hospitals, and command posts. These logistical centers were supposed to allow an army to project its power forward, but just as often, they acted as a tether, making it difficult to advance.

The common assertion that railroads, the central symbol of an industrial age, made war more mobile, is misleading. Trains might take men to the front, but mobility ended there. Machine guns and barbed wire gave well-supplied and entrenched defenders an enormous advantage

even against a larger attacking force, but logistics stymied generals' efforts to regain a war of movement.

The British and French trenches were wet, cold, and filthy. Rain turned the dusty corridors into squalid mud pits and flooded the floors up to waist level. "Hell is not fire," was the grim observation of a French soldiers' paper. "The real hell is the mud." Soldiers lived with lice and large black rats, which fed on the dead soldiers and horses that cast their stench over everything. Cadavers could go unburied for months and were often just embedded in the trench walls. It was little wonder that soldiers were rotated out of the front lines frequently—after only three to seven days—to be relieved from what one soldier called "this present, ever-present, eternally present misery, this stinking world of sticky, trickling earth ceilinged by a strip of threatening sky." Indeed, the threat of enemy fire was constant: 7,000 British men were killed or wounded daily. This "wastage," as it was called, was part of the routine, along with the inspections, rotations, and mundane duties of life on the Western Front. Despite this danger, the trenches were a relatively reliable means of protection, especially compared to the casualty rates of going on the offensive.

As the war progressed, new weapons added to the frightening dimensions of daily warfare. Besides artillery, machine guns, and barbed wire, the instruments of war now included exploding bullets, liquid fire, and poison gas. Gas, in particular, brought visible change to the battlefront. First used effectively by the Germans in April 1915 at the second battle of Ypres, poison gas was not only physically devastating—especially in its later forms—but also

POISON GAS. Poison gases (mustard gas, chlorine gas, and phosgene were the most commonly used) caused thousands of casualties in World War I and were greatly feared by the troops. Such weapons led to offensive breakthroughs when first used, but gas was difficult to control and did not change the balance of forces in the war. Both sides developed gas masks to protect their troops. The environmental damage was severe—concentrations of gas residue were intense enough to cause injury to farmers decades after the war ended, and unexploded gas shells are still occasionally found in former battlefields.

psychologically disturbing. The deadly cloud frequently hung over the trenches, although the quick appearance of gas masks limited its effectiveness. Like other new weapons, poison gas solidified the lines and took more lives but could not end the stalemate. The war dragged through its second year, bloody and stagnant. Soldiers grew accustomed to the stalemate, while their leaders plotted ways to end it.

SLAUGHTER IN THE TRENCHES: THE GREAT BATTLES, 1916–17

The bloodiest battles of all—those that epitomize the First World War—occurred in 1916–17, when first the Germans and later the British and French launched major offensives in attempts to end the stalemate. Massive campaigns in the war of attrition, these assaults produced hundreds of thousands of casualties and only minor territorial gains. These battles encapsulated the military tragedy of the war: a strategy of soldiers in cloth uniforms marching against machine guns. The result, of course, was carnage. The common response to these staggering losses was to replace the generals in charge. But though commanders changed, commands did not. Military planners continued to believe that their original strategies were the right ones and that their plans had simply been frustrated by bad luck and German determination. The "cult of the offensive" insisted that a breakthrough was possible with enough troops and enough weapons.

But the manpower needed could not be moved efficiently or protected adequately. Unprotected soldiers armed with rifles, grenades, and bayonets were simply no match for machine guns and deep trenches. Another major problem of military strategy—and another explanation for the continued slaughter—was the lack of effective communication between the front lines and general headquarters. If something went wrong at the front (which happened frequently) it was impossible for the leaders to know in time to make meaningful corrections. As the battles of the Great War illustrate, firepower had outpaced mobility, and the Allied generals simply did not know how to respond.

Verdun

The first of these major battles began with a German attack on the French stronghold of Verdun, near France's eastern border, in February 1916. Verdun had little strategic importance, but it quickly became a symbol of France's strength and was defended at all costs. Germany's goal was not necessarily to take the city but rather to break French morale—France's "remarkable devotion"—at a moment of critical weakness. As the German general Erich von Falkenhayn (1914–16) said, the offensive would "compel the French to throw in every man they have. If they do so the forces of France will bleed to death." One million shells were fired on the first day of battle, inaugurating a ten-month struggle of back-and-forth fighting offensives and counteroffensives of intense ferocity at enormous cost and zero gain. Led by General Henri Pétain (1914–18), the French pounded the Germans with artillery and received heavy bombardment in return. The Germans relied on large teams of horses, 7,000 of which were killed in a single day, to drag their guns through the muddy, cratered terrain. The French moved supplies and troops into Verdun continually. Approximately 12,000 delivery trucks were employed for service. So were 259 out of the 330 regiments of the French army. Neither side could gain a real advantage—one small village on the front changed hands thirteen times in one month alone—but both sides incurred devastating losses of life. By the end of June, over 400,000 French and German soldiers were dead. "Verdun," writes one historian, "had become a place of terror and death that could not yield victory." In the end, the advantage fell to the French, who survived and who bled the Germans as badly as they suffered themselves.

The Somme

Meanwhile, the British opened their own offensive against Germany farther west, beginning the battle of the Somme on June 24, 1916. The Allied attack began with a fierce bombardment, blasting the German lines with 1,400 guns. The blasts could be heard all the way across the English Channel. The British assumed that this preliminary attack would break the mesh of German wire, destroy Germany's trenches, and clear the way for Allied troops to advance forward. They were tragically wrong. The shells the British used were designed for surface combat, not to penetrate the deep, reinforced trenches dug by the Germans. The wire and trenches withstood the bombardment. When the British soldiers were ordered over the top toward enemy lines, they found themselves snared in wire and facing fully operational German machine guns. Each man carried sixty pounds of supplies that were to be used during the expected fighting in the German trenches. A few British commanders who had disobeyed orders and brought their men forward before the shelling ended were able to break through German lines. Elsewhere it was hardly a battle; whole British divisions were simply mowed down. Those who made it to the enemy trenches faced bitter hand-to-hand combat with pistols, grenades, knives, bayonets, and bare hands. On the first day of battle alone, a stunning 21,000 British soldiers died, and another 30,000 were wounded. The carnage continued from July until mid-November, resulting in massive casualties on both sides: 500,000 German, 400,000 British, and 200,000 French. The losses were unimaginable, and the outcome was equally hard to fathom: for all their

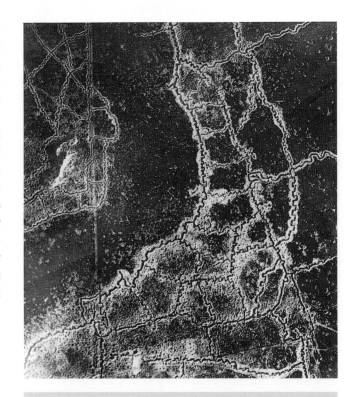

THE LINES OF BATTLE ON THE WESTERN FRONT. A British reconnaissance photo showing three lines of German trenches (right), No Man's Land (the black strip in the center), and the British trenches (partially visible to the left). The upper right-hand quadrant of the photo shows communications trenches linking the front to the safe area. ■ *What technologies gave these defenses such decisive advantages?*

sacrifices, neither side made any real gains. The first lesson of the Somme was offered later, by a war veteran: "Neither side had won, nor could win, the War. The War had won, and would go on winning." The futility of offensive war was not lost on the soldiers, yet morale remained surprisingly strong. Although mutinies and desertions occurred on both sides, they were rare before 1917; and surrenders became an important factor only in the final months of the war.

With willing armies and fresh recruits, military commanders maintained their strategy and pushed for victories on the Western Front again in 1917. The French general Robert Nivelle (1914–17) promised to break through the German lines with overwhelming manpower, but the "Nivelle Offensive" (April–May 1917) failed immediately, with first-day casualties like those at the Somme. The British also reprised the Somme at the third battle of Ypres (July–October 1917), in which a half-million casualties earned Great Britain only insignificant gains—and no breakthrough. The one weapon with the potential to break the stalemate, the tank, was finally introduced into

YPRES. Entrenched in craters, the Sixteenth Canadian Machine Gun Company endures the mud after the third battle of Ypres, usually called the Battle of Passchendaele (July–November 1917). ("Passiondale" in the British pronunciation.) Ypres, along the Yperlee River near the Belgian coast, was the object of three major battles during the war. The third, an Allied offensive, aimed to attack German submarine bases and to strengthen the Allied position if Russia withdrew from the war.

battle in 1916, but with such reluctance by tradition-bound commanders that its halfhearted employment made almost no difference. Other innovations were equally indecisive. Airplanes were used almost exclusively for reconnaissance, though occasional "dogfights" did occur between German and Allied pilots. And though the Germans sent zeppelins to raid London, they did little significant damage.

Off the Western Front, fighting produced further stalemate. The Austrians continued to fend off attacks in Italy and Macedonia, while the Russians mounted a successful offensive against them on the Eastern Front. The initial Russian success brought Romania into the war on Russia's side, but the Central Powers quickly retaliated and knocked the Romanians out of the war within a few months.

The war at sea was equally indecisive, with neither side willing to risk the loss of enormously expensive battleships. The British and German navies fought only one major naval battle early in 1916, which ended in stalemate. Afterward, they used their fleets primarily in the economic war of blockades.

As a year of great bloodshed and growing disillusionment, 1916 showed that not even the superbly organized Germans had the mobility or fast-paced communications to win the western ground war. Increasingly, warfare would be turned against entire nations, including civilian populations on the home front and in the far reaches of the European empires.

WAR OF EMPIRES

Coming as it did at the height of European imperialism, the Great War quickly became a war of empires, with far-reaching repercussions. As the demands of warfare rose, Europe's colonies provided soldiers and material support. Britain, in particular, benefited from its vast network of colonial dominions and dependencies, bringing in soldiers from Canada, Australia, New Zealand, India, and South Africa. Nearly 1.5 million Indian troops served as British forces, some on the Western Front and many more in the Middle East, fighting in Mesopotamia and Persia against the Turks. The French Empire, especially North and West Africa, sent 607,000 soldiers to fight with the Allies; 31,000 of them died in Europe. Colonial recruits were also employed in industry. In France, where even some French conscripts were put to work in factories, the international labor force numbered over 250,000, including workers from China, Vietnam, Egypt, India, the West Indies, and South Africa.

As the war stalled in Europe, colonial areas also became strategically important theaters for armed engagement. Although the campaign against Turkey began poorly for Britain with the debacle at Gallipoli, beginning in 1916 Allied forces won a series of battles, pushing the Turks out of Egypt and eventually capturing Baghdad, Jerusalem, Beirut, and other cities throughout the Middle East. The British commander in Egypt and Palestine was Edmund Allenby (1919–25), who led a multinational army against the Turks. In his campaigns, the support of different Arab peoples seeking independence from the Turks proved crucial. Allenby allied himself to the successful Bedouin (nomadic peoples speaking Arabic) revolts that split the Ottoman Empire; the British officer T. E. Lawrence (1914–18) popularized the Arabs' guerrilla actions. When one of the senior Bedouin aristocrats, the emir Abdullah, captured the strategic port of Aqaba in July 1917, Lawrence took credit and entered popular mythology as "Lawrence of Arabia."

Britain encouraged Arab nationalism for its own strategic purposes, offering a qualified acknowledgment of Arab political aspirations. At the same time, for similar but conflicting strategic reasons, the British declared their support of "the establishment in Palestine of a national home for the Jewish people." Britain's foreign secretary, Arthur Balfour,

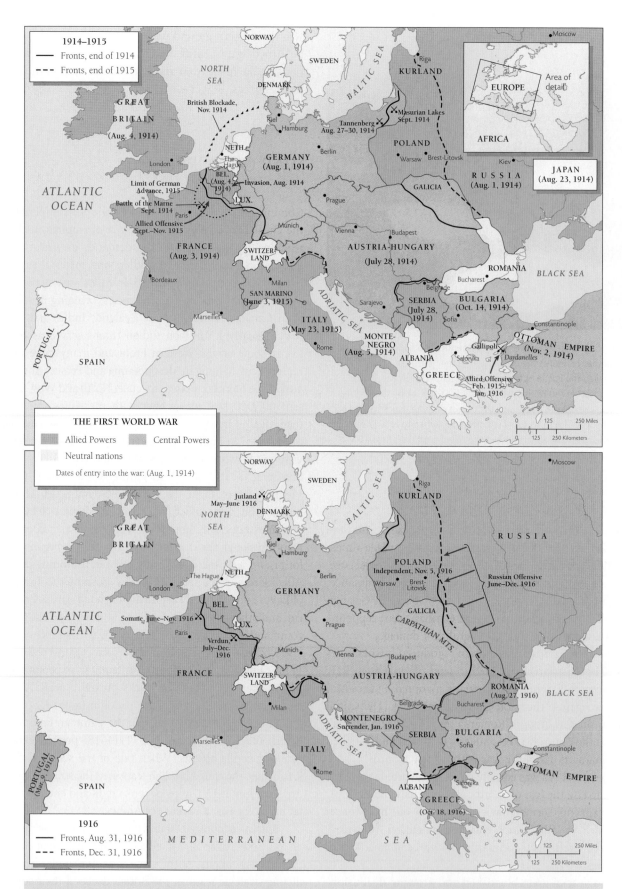

A. THE GREAT WAR, 1914–1916. ▪ *What were the farthest points of German expansion on both fronts?* ▪ *Why did the British blockade have a large impact on the war?* ▪ *Why did the war become stalemated?*

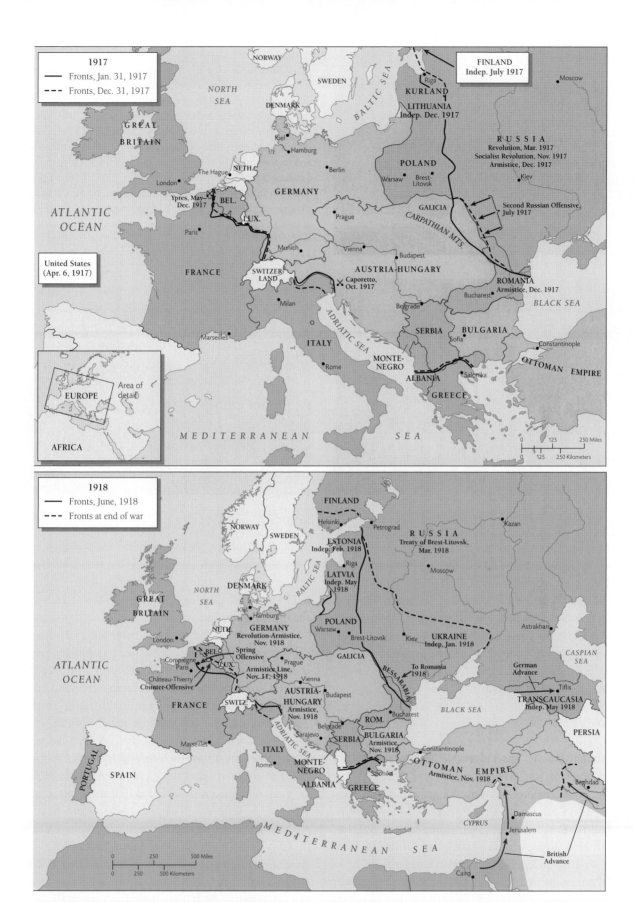

B. THE GREAT WAR, 1917–1918. ▪ *What were the key events of 1917, and how did they change the course of the war?*
▪ *Consider the map of 1918. Why might many German people have believed they nearly won the war?* ▪ *Why were developments in the Middle East significant in the war's aftermath?*

A GLOBAL WAR. The effects of World War 1 were immediately felt in other parts of the world. Japan entered the war in August 1914 on the side of France, Russia, and Britain in order to secure German territory in the Pacific and extend its influence over China. Turkey joined Germany and Austria-Hungary's alliance during the same month. Meanwhile, all the European colonial powers recruited laborers and soldiers from their imperial territories. In the image to the left, Japanese troops land in China at Tsingtao in 1915. In the image at bottom left, an Islamic cleric reads the proclamation of war before a mosque in the Turkish capital of Constantinople in 1914. In the image at bottom right, colonial troops in German East Africa march during World War 1.

made the pledge. European Zionists, who were seeking a Jewish homeland, took the Balfour Declaration very seriously. The conflicting pledges to Bedouin leaders and Zionists sowed the seeds of the future Arab-Israeli conflict. First the war and then the promise of oil drew Europe more deeply into the Middle East, where conflicting dependencies and commitments created numerous postwar problems.

Irish Revolt

The Ottoman Empire was vulnerable; so was the British. The demands of war strained precarious bonds to the breaking point. Before the war, long-standing tensions between Irish Catholics and the Protestant British government had reached fever pitch, and some feared civil war. The Sinn Féin (We Ourselves) party had formed in 1900 to fight for Irish independence, and a home rule bill had passed Parliament in 1912. But with the outbreak of war in 1914, national interests took precedence over domestic politics: the "Irish question" was tabled, and 200,000 Irishmen volunteered for the British army. The problem festered, however, and on Easter Sunday 1916 a group of nationalists

revolted in Dublin. The insurgents' plan to smuggle in arms from Germany failed, and they had few delusions of achieving victory. The British army arrived with artillery and machine guns; they shelled parts of Dublin and crushed the uprising within a week.

The revolt was a military disaster but a striking political success. Britain shocked the Irish public by executing the rebel leaders. Even the British prime minister David Lloyd George (1916–22) thought the military governor in Dublin exceeded his authority with these executions. The martyrdom of the "Easter Rebels" seriously damaged Britain's relationship with its Irish Catholic subjects. The deaths galvanized the cause of Irish nationalism and touched off guerrilla violence that kept Ireland in turmoil for years. Finally, a new home rule bill was enacted in 1920, establishing separate parliaments for the Catholic south of Ireland and for Ulster, the northeastern counties where the majority population was Protestant. The leaders of the so-called Dáil Éireann (Irish Assembly), which had proclaimed an Irish Republic in 1918 and therefore been outlawed by Britain, rejected the bill but accepted a treaty that granted dominion status to Catholic Ireland in 1921. Dominion was followed almost immediately by civil war between those who abided by the treaty and those who wanted to

BRITISH REPRESSION OF EASTER REBELLION, DUBLIN, 1916. British troops line up behind a moveable barricade made up of household furniture during their repression of the Irish revolt. The military action did not prevent further conflict.

absorb Ulster, but the conflict ended in an uneasy compromise. The Irish Free State was established, and British sovereignty was partially abolished in 1937. Full status as a republic came, with some American pressure and Britain's exhausted indifference, in 1945.

THE HOME FRONT

When the war of attrition began in 1915, the belligerent governments were unprepared for the strains of sustained warfare. The costs of war—in both money and manpower—were staggering. In 1914, the war cost Germany 36 million marks per day (five times the cost of the war of 1870), and by 1918 the cost had skyrocketed to 146 million marks per day. Great Britain had estimated it would need 100,000 soldiers but ended up mobilizing 3 million. The enormous task of feeding, clothing, and equipping the army became as much of a challenge as breaking through enemy lines; civilian populations were increasingly asked—or forced—to support these efforts. Bureaucrats and industrialists led

the effort to mobilize the home front, focusing all parts of society on the single goal of military victory. The term *total war* was introduced to describe this intense mobilization of society. Government propagandists insisted that civilians were as important to the war effort as soldiers, and in many ways they were. As workers, taxpayers, and consumers, civilians were vital parts of the war economy. They produced munitions; purchased war bonds; and shouldered the burden of tax hikes, inflation, and material privations.

The demands of industrial warfare led first to a transition from general industrial manufacturing to munitions production and then to increased state control of all aspects of production and distribution. The governments of Britain and France managed to direct the economy without serious detriment to the standard of living in their countries. Germany, meanwhile, put its economy in the hands of army and industry; under the Hindenburg Plan, named for Paul von Hindenburg (1916–19), the chief of the imperial staff of the German army, pricing and profit margins were set by individual industrialists.

Largely because of the immediate postwar collapse of the German economy, historians have characterized Germany's wartime economy as a chaotic, ultimately disastrous system governed by personal interest. New research, however, suggests that this was not the case: Germany's systems of war finance and commodity distribution, however flawed, were not decisively worse than those of Britain or France.

Women in the War

As Europe's adult men left farms and factories to become soldiers, the composition of the workforce changed: thousands of women were recruited into fields that had previously excluded them. Young people, foreigners, and unskilled workers were also pressed into newly important tasks; in the case of colonial workers, their experiences had equally critical repercussions. But because they were more visible, it was women who became symbolic of many of the changes brought by the Great War. In Germany, one-third of the labor force in heavy industry was female by the end of the war, and in France 684,000 women worked in the munitions industry alone. In England, the "munitionnettes," as they were dubbed, numbered nearly 1 million. Women also entered the clerical and service sectors. In the villages of France, England, and Germany, women became mayors, school principals, and mail carriers. Hundreds of thousands of women worked with the army as nurses and ambulance drivers, jobs that brought them very close to the front lines. With minimal supplies and under squalid conditions, they worked to save lives or patch bodies together.

In some cases, war offered new opportunities. Middle-class women often said that the war broke down the restrictions on their lives; those in nursing learned to drive and acquired rudimentary medical knowledge. At home, they could now ride the train, walk the street, or go out to dinner without an older woman present to chaperone them. In terms of gender roles, an enormous gulf sometimes seemed to separate the wartime world from nineteenth-century Victorian society. In one of the most famous autobiographies of the war, *Testament of Youth,* author Vera Brittain (1896–1970) recorded the dramatic new social norms that she and others forged during the rapid changes of wartime. "As a generation of women we were now sophisticated to an extent which was revolutionary when compared with the romantic ignorance of 1914. Where we had once spoken with polite evasion of 'a certain condition,' or 'a certain profession,' we now unblushingly used the words 'pregnancy' and 'prostitution.'" For every Vera Brittain who celebrated the changes, however, journalists, novelists, and other observers grumbled that women were now smoking, refusing to wear the corsets that gave Victorian dresses their hourglass shape, or cutting their hair into the new fashionable bobs. The "new woman" became a symbol of profound and disconcerting cultural transformation.

How long lasting were these changes? In the aftermath of the war, governments and employers scurried to send women workers home, in part to give jobs to veterans, in part to deal with male workers' complaints that women were undercutting their wages. Efforts to demobilize women faced real barriers. Many women wage earners—widowed, charged with caring for relatives, or faced with inflation and soaring costs—needed their earnings more than ever. It was also difficult to persuade women workers who had grown accustomed to the relatively higher wages in heavy industry to return to their poorly paid traditional sectors of employment: the textile and garment industries and domestic service. The demobilization of women after the war, in other words, created as many dilemmas as had their mobilization. Governments passed "natalist" policies to encourage women to go home, marry, and—most important—have children. These policies did make maternity benefits—time off, medical care, and some allowances for the poor—available to women for the first time. Nonetheless, birth rates had been falling across Europe by the early twentieth century, and they continued to do so after the war. One upshot of the war was the increased availability of birth control—Marie Stopes (1880–1958) opened a birth-control clinic in London in 1921—and a combination of economic hardship, increased knowledge, and the demand for freedom made men and women more likely to use it. Universal suffrage, and the vote for all adult men and women, and for women in particular, had been one of the most controversial issues in European politics before the war. At the end of the fighting it came in a legislative rush. Britain was first off the mark, granting the vote to all men and women over thirty with the Representation of the People Act in 1918; the United States gave women the vote with the Nineteenth Amendment the following year. Germany's new republic and the Soviet Union did likewise. France was much slower to offer woman suffrage (1945) but did provide rewards and incentives for the national effort.

Mobilizing Resources

Along with mobilizing the labor front, the wartime governments had to mobilize men and money. All the belligerent countries had conscription laws before the war, except for Great Britain. Military service was seen as a duty,

WOMEN AT WORK. The all-out war effort combined with a manpower shortage at home brought women into factories across Europe in unparalleled numbers. Men and women work side by side in a British shell factory (left); German women assemble military equipment (right). ▪ *How might the participation of women in the industrial workforce have changed attitudes toward women's labor?* ▪ *What tensions might this have created within families or between male and female workers?*

not an option. Bolstered by widespread public support for the war, this belief brought millions of young Europeans into recruitment offices in 1914. The French began the war with about 4.5 million trained soldiers, but by the end of 1914—just four months into the war—300,000 were dead and 600,000 injured. Conscripting citizens and mustering colonial troops became increasingly important. Eventually, France called up 8 million citizens: almost two-thirds of Frenchmen aged eighteen to forty. In 1916, the British finally introduced conscription, dealing a serious blow to civilian morale; by the summer of 1918, half its army was under the age of nineteen.

Government propaganda, while part of a larger effort to sustain both soldier and civilian morale, was also important to the recruitment effort. From the outset, the war had been sold to the people on both sides of the conflict as a moral and righteous crusade. In 1914, the French president Raymond Poincaré (1913–20) assured his fellow citizens that France had no other purpose than to stand "before the universe for Liberty, Justice and Reason." Germans were presented with the task of defending their superior *Kultur* (culture) against the wicked encirclement policy of the Allied nations: "May God punish England!" was practically a greeting in 1914. By the middle of the war, massive propaganda campaigns were under way. Film, posters, postcards, newspapers—all forms

of media proclaimed the strength of the cause, the evil of the enemy, and the absolute necessity of total victory. The success of these campaigns is difficult to determine, but it is clear that they had at least one painful effect—they made it more difficult for any country to accept a fair, nonpunitive peace settlement.

Financing the war was another heavy obstacle. Military spending accounted for 3 to 5 percent of government expenditure in the combatant countries before 1914 but soared to perhaps half of each nation's budget during the war. Governments had to borrow money or print more of it. The Allied nations borrowed heavily from the British, who borrowed even more from the United States. American capital flowed across the Atlantic long before the United States entered the war. And though economic aid from the United States was a decisive factor in the Allies' victory, it left Britain with a $4.2 billion debt and hobbled the United Kingdom as a financial power after the war. The situation was far worse for Germany, which faced a total blockade of money and goods. In an effort to get around this predicament, and lacking an outside source of cash, the German government funded its war effort largely by increasing the money supply. The amount of paper money in circulation increased by over 1,000 percent during the war, triggering a dramatic rise in inflation. During the war, prices in Germany rose about

Woman's Work in Wartime

Although women in Europe had worked in some industries—such as textiles—long before World War I, the mobilization of women during the war years brought an unprecedented number of them into the industrial workforce. Inevitably, such profound changes in conceptions of gender and work generated controversy. These two documents provide a window into this debate both from the point of view of the highest government authorities and from women who took advantage of the new opportunities available to them in war work. The first document is a letter from the German chief of the General Staff, General Paul von Hindenburg to Chancellor Bethmann Hollweg, written in October 1916. The second is the testimony taken in 1918 from Helen Ross, an African American woman who had worked in domestic service before taking a wartime job in Topeka, Kansas.

General Paul von Hindenburg to Chancellor Bethmann Hollweg, October 1916

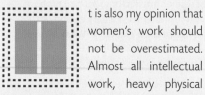 t is also my opinion that women's work should not be overestimated. Almost all intellectual work, heavy physical labour, as well as all real manufacturing work will still fall on men—in addition to the entire waging of the war. It would be good if clear, official expression were given to these facts and if a stop were put to women's agitation for parity in all professions, and thereby, of course, for political emancipation. I completely agree with your Excellency that compulsory labour for women would be an inappropriate measure. After the war, we will need the woman as spouse and mother....

If I *nevertheless* urge that the requirement to work be extended to all women who are either unemployed or working in trivial positions, now and for the duration of the war, I do so because, in my opinion, women can be employed in many areas to a still greater degree than previously and men can thereby be freed for other *work*. But first industry and agriculture must be urged even more to employ women. Further, the choice of occupation must not be left up to the women alone, but rather, it must [be] regulated according to ability, previous experience and social status. In particular, I want to stress again that I consider it especially wrong to keep secondary

schools and universities, which have been almost completely emptied of men by conscription, open only for women. It is valueless, because the scholarly gain is minimal; furthermore, because precisely that rivalry with the family that needs to be combated would be promoted; and *finally,* because it would represent the coarsest injustice if the young man, who is giving everything for his Fatherland, is forced behind the woman.

Source: Letter of Chief of the General Staff General Paul von Hindenburg to Chancellor Bethmann Hollweg, October 1916. Quoted in Ute Daniel, *The War from Within: German Working-Class Women in the First World War,* trans. Margaret Ries (Oxford: 1997), pp. 68–69, emphasis in the original.

---

400 percent, double the inflation in Britain and France. For middle-class people living on pensions or fixed incomes, these price hikes were a push into poverty.

The Strains of War, 1917

The demands of total war worsened as the conflict dragged into 1917. On the front lines, morale fell as war-weary soldiers began to see the futility of their commanders' strategies.

After the debacle of the Nivelle Offensive, the French army recorded acts of mutiny in two-thirds of its divisions; similar resistance arose in nearly all major armies in 1917. Military leaders portrayed the mutineers as part of a dangerous pacifist movement, but most were nonpolitical. As one soldier put it: "All we wanted was to call the government's attention to us, make it see that we are men, and not beasts for the slaughterhouse." Resistance within the German army was never organized or widespread but existed in subtler forms. Self-mutilation rescued some soldiers

Helen Ross, Employee of the Santa Fe Railroad, Topeka, Kansas, October 1918

All the colored women like this work and want to keep it. We are making more money at this than any work we can get, and we do not have to work as hard as at housework which requires us to be on duty from six o'clock in the morning until nine or ten at night, with might little time off and at very poor wages.... What the colored women need is an opportunity to make money. As it is, they have to take what employment they can get, live in old tumbled down houses or resort to street walking, and I think a woman ought to think more of her blood than to do that. What occupation is open to us where we can make really good wages? We are not employed as clerks, we cannot all be school teachers, and so we cannot see any use in working our parents to death to get educated. Of course we should like easier work than this if it were opened to us. With three dollars a day, we can buy bonds . . . , we can dress decently, and not be tempted to find our living on the streets.

Source: Helen Ross, Freight House, Santa Fe RR, Topeka, Kansas, 28 October 1918, File 55, Women's Service Section, Record Group 14 [Records of the United States Railroad Administration], National Archives, Washington, D.C. Also quoted in M. W. Greenwald, *Women, War and Work: The Impact of World War I on Women Workers in the United States* (Ithaca, NY: 1980, reprinted, 1990), p. 27.

Questions for Analysis

1. What reservations does Hindenburg express about demands made by women for political emancipation, and how does he connect this to the question of women's wartime employment? Why does he nevertheless support women's wartime labor in Germany?

2. How did Helen Ross perceive the opportunity to earn wages in her railroad job compared to her previous work as a domestic servant? How had her life changed?

3. What long-lasting effects might the experience of wartime labor have had for women who worked in such jobs?

from the horror of the trenches; many more were released because of various emotional disorders. Over 6,000 cases of "war neuroses" were reported among German troops—an indication, if not of intentional disobedience, then of the severe physical and psychological trauma that caused the mutinies.

The war's toll also mounted for civilians, who often suffered from the same shortages of basic supplies that afflicted the men at the front. In 1916–17, the lack of clothing, food, and fuel was aggravated in central Europe by abnormally cold, wet weather. These strains provoked rising discontent on the home front. Although governments attempted to solve the problem with tighter controls on the economy, their policies often provoked further hostilities from civilians. "The population has lost all confidence in promises from the authorities," a German official reported in 1917, "particularly in view of earlier experiences with promises made in the administration of food."

In urban areas, where undernourishment was worst, people stood in lines for hours to get food and fuel rations that scarcely met their most basic needs. The price of bread and potatoes—still the central staples of working-class meals—soared. Prices were even higher in the thriving black market that emerged in cities. Consumers worried aloud that speculators were hoarding supplies and creating artificial shortages, selling tainted goods, and profiting from others' miseries. They decried the government's "reckless inattention" to families. Governments, however, were concentrated on the war effort and faced difficult decisions about who needed supplies the most—soldiers at the front, workers in the munitions industry, or hungry and cold families.

Like other nations, Germany moved from encouraging citizens to restrain themselves—"those who stuff themselves full, those who push out their paunches in all directions, are traitors to the Fatherland"—to direct control, issuing ration cards in 1915. Britain was the last to institute control, rationing bread only in 1917 when Germany's submarines sank an average of 630,000 tons per month and brought British food reserves within two

Before You Read This Chapter

Turmoil between the Wars

CORE OBJECTIVES

- **UNDERSTAND** the direction taken by the Russian Revolution after 1917 and the consequences of Stalin's revolution from above in the 1930s.

- **DEFINE** fascism and explain Mussolini's rise to power in Italy in the 1920s.

- **DESCRIBE** the challenges faced by the Weimar Republic and other democracies in Britain, France, and the United States after the First World War.

- **EXPLAIN** Hitler's rise to power in Germany in 1933 and the reasons for the broad support the Nazis enjoyed among many Germans.

- **UNDERSTAND** the ways that the interwar atmosphere of social and political crisis was reflected in the world of the arts, literature, and popular culture.

Käthe Kollwitz, a Berlin painter and sculptor, understood as well as anybody in Europe the terrible costs and futility of the First World War. Her youngest son, Peter, was killed on October 22, 1914, in Germany's failed attack on France. Her diary recorded the last moments she spent with him, an evening walk from the barracks on October 12, the day before his departure for the front: "It was dark, and we went arm in arm through the wood. He pointed out constellations to me, as he had done so often before." Her entry for October 30 was more succinct, a quotation from the postcard she had received from his commanding officer: "Your son has fallen." Kollwitz's pain at this loss found expression in her later work, which explored in naked terms the grief and powerlessness that she and her family had felt during the war years. Her suffering found expression, too, in a commitment to socialism, a political ideology that provided her with an antidote to the nationalism that pervaded German society during the war years and after. Kollwitz's socialism drew her to the attention of the Gestapo after the Nazis came to power in 1933, and she was fired from her position at the Academy of Art. She put up with house searches and harassment but refused invitations from friends abroad to go into exile. She died in Germany in 1945, having survived long enough to see her cherished grandson, also named Peter, killed in a second war while fighting as a German soldier on the Eastern Front in Russia in 1942.

The story of Käthe Kollwitz and her family between 1914 and 1945 is only unusual for the fact that she was a well-known artist. The suffering was all too familiar to others, as was the search for new political ideologies that might save Europeans from their past. The Great War left 9 million dead in its wake and shattered the confidence that had been such a characteristic of nineteenth-century European culture. It led tragically to another world war, even more horrific than the first. Many in the interwar years shared Kollwitz's hope for a socialist or communist future, and many others turned to extremisms of the right. The result in the 1920s was a near collapse of democracy. By the late 1930s, few Western democracies remained. Even in those that did, most notably Britain, France, and the United States, regimes were frayed by the same pressures and strains that wrecked democratic governments elsewhere.

The foremost cause of democracy's decline in this period was a series of continuing disruptions in the world economy, caused first by the First World War and later, by the Great Depression of 1929–33. A second source of crisis lay in increased social conflict, exacerbated by the war. Although many hoped that these conflicts would be resolved by the peace and a renewed commitment to democratic institutions, the opposite occurred. Broad swathes of the electorate rallied to extremist political parties that promised radical transformations of nations and their cultures. Nationalism, sharpened by the war, proved a key source of discontent in its aftermath, and in Italy and Germany frustrated nationalist sentiment turned against their governments.

The most dramatic instance of democracy's decline came with the rise of new authoritarian dictatorships, especially in the Soviet Union, Italy, and Germany. The experiences of these three nations differed significantly as a result of varying historical circumstances and personalities. In each case, however, many citizens allowed themselves to be persuaded that only drastic measures could bring order

WIDOWS AND ORPHANS BY KÄTHE KOLLWITZ, 1919. Kollwitz (1867–1945), a German artist and socialist activist in Berlin, lost a son in the First World War and a grandson in the Second World War. Her work poignantly displayed the effects of poverty and war on the lives of ordinary people.

from chaos. Those measures, including the elimination of parliamentary government, strict restrictions on political freedom, and increasingly virulent repression of "enemies" of the state were implemented with a combination of violence, intimidation, and propaganda. That so many citizens seemed willing to sacrifice their freedoms—or those of others—was a measure of their alienation, impatience, or desperation.

THE SOVIET UNION UNDER LENIN AND STALIN

The Russian Civil War

The Bolsheviks seized power in October 1917. They signed a separate peace with Germany in March 1918 (the Treaty of Brest-Litovsk) and then turned to consolidating their own position. The October Revolution and withdrawing from the war, however, had divided Russian society, igniting a war that turned out to be far more costly than conflict with Germany. Fury at the terms of Brest-Litovsk mobilized the Bolsheviks' enemies. Known collectively as "Whites," the Bolsheviks' opponents were only loosely bound by their common goal of removing the "Reds" from power. Their military force came mainly from supporters of the old regime, including tsarist military officers, reactionary monarchists, the former nobility, and disaffected liberal supporters of the monarchy. The Whites were joined by groups as diverse as liberal supporters of the provisional government, Mensheviks, Social Revolutionaries, and anarchist peasant bands known as "Greens" who opposed all central state power. The Bolsheviks also faced insurrections from strong nationalist movements in some parts of the former Russian Empire: Ukraine, Georgia, and the north Caucasus regions. Finally, several foreign powers, including the United States, Great Britain, and Japan, launched small but threatening interventions on the periphery of the old empire. Outside support for the Whites proved to be an insignificant threat to the Bolsheviks, but it heightened Bolshevik mistrust of the capitalist world which, in the Marxists' view, would naturally oppose the existence of the world's first "socialist" state.

The Bolsheviks eventually won the civil war because they gained greater support—or at least tacit acceptance—from the majority of the population and because they were better organized for the war effort itself. Leon Trotsky, the revolutionary hero of 1905 and 1917, became the new commissar of war and created a hierarchical, disciplined military machine that grew to some 5 million men by 1920. Trotsky's Red Army triumphed over the White armies by the end of 1920, although fighting continued into 1922. The Bolsheviks also invaded Poland and nearly reached Warsaw before being thrown back.

When the civil war was over, the country had suffered some 1 million combat casualties, several million deaths from hunger and disease caused by the war, and 100,000–300,000 executions of noncombatants as part of Red and White terror. The barbarism of the war engendered lasting hatreds within the emerging Soviet nation, especially among ethnic minorities, and it brutalized the fledgling society that came into existence under the new Bolshevik regime.

The civil war also shaped the Bolsheviks' approach to the economy. On taking power in 1917, Lenin expected to create, for the short term at least, a state-capitalist system that resembled the successful European wartime economies. The new government took control of large-scale industry, banking, and all other major capitalist concerns while allowing small-scale private economic activity, including agriculture, to continue. The civil war pushed the new government toward a more radical economic stance known as "war communism." The Bolsheviks began to req-uisition grain from the peasantry, and they outlawed private trade in consumer goods as "speculation," militarized production facilities, and abolished money. Many believed that war communism would replace the capitalist system that had collapsed in 1917.

Such hopes were largely unfounded. War communism sustained the Bolshevik military effort but further disrupted the already war-ravaged economy. The civil war devastated Russian industry and emptied major cities. The population of Moscow fell by 50 percent between 1917 and 1920. The masses of urban workers, who had strongly supported the Bolshevik revolution, melted back into the countryside; and industrial output in 1920–21 fell to only 20 percent of prewar levels. Most devastating were the effects of war communism on agriculture. The peasants had initially benefited from the revolution when they spontaneously seized and redistributed noble lands. Nonetheless, the agricultural system was severely disrupted by the civil war, by the grain requisitioning of war communism, and by the outlawing of all private trade in grain. Large-scale famine resulted in 1921 and claimed some 5 million lives.

LENIN AND STALIN. Under Stalin, this picture was used to show his close relationship with Lenin. In fact, the photograph has been doctored. ▪ *What opportunities for propaganda and manipulation were offered by new technologies of photography and film?*

that granted independence to the papal residence in the Vatican City and established Roman Catholicism as the official religion of the state. The treaty also guaranteed religious education in the nation's schools and made religious marriage ceremonies mandatory.

In fact, Mussolini's regime did much to maintain the status quo. Party officers exercised some political supervision over bureaucrats yet did not infiltrate the bureaucracy in significant numbers. Moreover, Mussolini remained on friendly terms with the elites who had assisted his rise to power. Whatever he might proclaim about the distinctions between fascism and capitalism, the economy of Italy remained dependent on private enterprise.

The Italian dictator boasted that fascism had pulled the country back from economic chaos. Like other European economies, the Italian economy did improve in the late 1920s. The regime created the appearance of efficiency, and Mussolini's admirers famously claimed that he had at last "made the trains run on time." Fascism, however, did little to lessen Italy's plight during the worldwide depression of the 1930s.

GERMAN WOMEN SMOKING CIGARS DURING THE WEIMAR REPUBLIC, 1927. The Weimar years were marked by a new atmosphere of cultural experimentation, especially in German cities. The traumatic experience of World War 1, which destroyed so many families and overturned the social and political order, also made prewar social conventions about sex, marriage, and gender seem quaint and outdated. This scene, in which women are smoking and drinking in public, while wearing masculine hairstyles and casually demonstrating their affection for one another was almost unimaginable in 1910. In the 1920s, however, such scenes were common enough to provoke controversy and scandal, becoming fodder for the media, and providing material for best-selling novels. Similar debates over the "New Woman" of the 1920s took place in other European countries, and Hitler and the Nazi party used such images in their campaign to discredit Weimar society as "degenerate."

Like Nazism later, fascism had contradictory elements. It sought to restore traditional authority and, at the same time, mobilize all of Italian society for economic and nationalist purposes—a process that inevitably undercut older authorities. It created new authoritarian organizations and activities that comported with these goals: exercise programs to make the young fit and mobilized, youth camps, awards to mothers of large families, political rallies, and parades in small towns in the countryside. Activities like these offered people a feeling of political involvement though they no longer enjoyed political rights. This mobilized but essentially passive citizenship was a hallmark of fascism.

WEIMAR GERMANY

On November 9, 1918—two days before the armistice ending the First World War—a massive and largely unexpected uprising in Berlin resulted in the kaiser's abdication and the

birth of a new German republic. The leader of the new government was Friedrich Ebert, a member of the Social Democratic party (SPD) in the Reichstag. The revolution spread quickly. By the end of the month, councils of workers and soldiers controlled hundreds of German cities. The "November Revolution" was fast and far reaching, though not as revolutionary as many middle- and upper-class conservatives feared. The majority of socialists steered a cautious, democratic course: they wanted reforms but were willing to leave much of the existing imperial bureaucracy intact. Above all, they wanted a popularly elected national assembly to draft a constitution for the new republic.

Two months passed, however, before elections could be held—a period of crisis that verged on civil war. The revolutionary movement that had brought the SPD to power now threatened it. Independent socialists and a nascent Communist party wanted radical reforms, and in December 1918 and January 1919, they staged armed uprisings in the streets of Berlin. Fearful of a Bolshevik-style revolution, the Social Democratic government turned against its former allies and sent militant bands of workers and volunteers to crush the uprisings. During the conflict, the government's fighters murdered Rosa Luxemburg and Karl Liebknecht—two German communist leaders who became instant martyrs. Violence continued into 1920, creating a lasting bitterness among groups on the left.

More important, the revolutionary aftermath of the war gave rise to bands of militant counterrevolutionaries. Veterans and other young nationalists joined so-called *Freikorps* (free corps). Such groups developed throughout the country, drawing as many as several hundred thousand members. Former army officers who led these militias continued their war experience by fighting against Bolsheviks, Poles, and communists. The politics of the Freikorps were fiercely right wing. Anti-Marxist, anti-Semitic, and antiliberal, they openly opposed the new German republic and its parliamentary democracy. Many of the early Nazi leaders had fought in the First World War and participated in Freikorps units.

Germany's new government—known as the Weimar Republic (*VY-mahr*) for the city in which its constitution was drafted—rested on a coalition of socialists, Catholic centrists, and liberal democrats, a necessary compromise since no single party won a majority of the votes in the January 1919 election. The Weimar constitution was based on the values of parliamentary liberalism and set up an open, pluralistic framework for German democracy. Through a series of compromises, the constitution established universal suffrage (for both women and men) and a bill of rights that guaranteed not only civil liberties but also a range of social entitlements. On paper, at least, the revolutionary movement had succeeded.

Yet the Weimar government lasted just over a decade. By 1930, it was in crisis, and in 1933 it collapsed. What happened? Many of Weimar's problems were born from Germany's defeat in the First World War, which was not only devastating but also humiliating. Many Germans soon latched onto rumors that the army hadn't actually been defeated in battle but instead had been stabbed in the back by socialists and Jewish leaders in the German government. Army officers cultivated this story even before the war was over; and though untrue, it helped salve the wounded pride of German patriots. In the next decade, those in search of a scapegoat also blamed the republican regime, which had signed the Versailles treaty. What was needed, many critics argued, was authoritative leadership to guide the nation and regain the world's respect.

The Treaty of Versailles magnified Germany's sense of dishonor. Germany was forced to cede a tenth of its territory, accept responsibility for the war, and slash the size of its army to a mere hundred thousand men—a punishment

HYPERINFLATION. German children use stacks of money as toys. In July 1922, the American dollar was worth 670 German marks; in November 1923 it was worth 4,210,500,000,000.
■ *How might hyperinflation have affected attitudes in Germany toward the Weimar Republic's government?*

that riled the politically powerful corps of officers. Most important, the treaty saddled Germany with punitive reparations. Negotiating the $33 billion debt created problems for all the governments involved; it provoked anger from the German public and, in a global economy, had unintended effects on the recipients as well as the debtors. Some opponents of the reparations settlement urged the government not to pay, arguing that the enormous sum would doom Germany's economy. In 1924, Germany accepted a new schedule of reparations designed by an international committee headed by the American financier Charles G. Dawes. At the same time, the German chancellor Gustav Stresemann moved Germany toward a foreign policy of cooperation and rapprochement that lasted throughout the 1920s. Many German people, however, continued to resent reparations, Versailles, and the government that refused to repudiate the treaty.

Major economic crises also played a central role in Weimar's collapse. The first period of emergency occurred in the early 1920s. Still reeling from wartime inflation, the government was hard-pressed for revenues. Funding post-war demobilization programs, social welfare, and reparations forced the government to continue to print money. Inflation became nearly unstoppable. By 1923, as one historian writes, the economic situation had "acquired an almost surrealistic quality." A pound of potatoes cost about 9 marks in January, 40 million marks by October. Beef went for almost 2 trillion marks per pound. The government finally took drastic measures to stabilize the currency in 1924, but millions of Germans had already been ruined. For those on fixed incomes, such as pensioners and stockholders, savings and security had vanished. Middle-class employees, farmers, and workers were all hard hit by the economic crisis, and many of them abandoned the traditional political parties in protest. In their eyes, the parties that claimed to represent the middle classes had created the problems and proved incapable of fixing them.

Beginning in 1925, however, Germany's economy and government seemed to be recovering. By borrowing money, the country was able to make its scaled-down reparations payments and to earn money by selling cheap exports. In large cities, socialist municipal governments sponsored building projects that included schools, hospitals, and low-cost worker housing. But such economic and political stability was misleading. The economy remained dependent on large infusions of capital from the United States set up by the Dawes Plan as part of the effort to settle reparations. That dependence made the German economy especially vulnerable to American economic developments. When the U.S. stock market crashed in 1929, beginning the Great Depression (see below), capital flow to Germany virtually stopped.

The Great Depression pushed Weimar's political system to the breaking point. In 1929, there were 2 million unemployed; in 1932, 6 million. In those three years production dropped by 44 percent. Artisans and small shopkeepers lost both status and income. Farmers fared even worse, having never recovered from the crisis of the early 1920s. Peasants staged mass demonstrations against the government's agricultural policies even before the depression hit. For white-collar and civil service employees, the depression meant lower salaries, poor working conditions, and a constant threat of unemployment. Burdened with plummeting tax revenues and spiraling numbers of Germans in need of relief, the government repeatedly cut welfare benefits, which further demoralized the electorate. Finally, the crisis created an opportunity for Weimar's opponents. Many leading industrialists supported a return to authoritarian government, and they were allied with equally conservative landowners, united by a desire for protective economic policies to stimulate the sale of domestic goods and foodstuffs. Those conservative forces wielded considerable power in

Germany, beyond the control of the government. So too did the army and the civil service, which were staffed with opponents of the republic—men who rejected the principles of parliamentary democracy and international cooperation that Weimar represented.

HITLER AND THE NATIONAL SOCIALISTS

National Socialism in Germany emerged out of the bitterness of the defeat in the First World War, but Adolf Hitler's political party did not gain mass support until the economic crisis caused by the Depression in 1929 led many Germans to give up on the traditional political parties. At each stage in the movement's development, Hitler found a way to capitalize on the mistakes of his opponents and draw more support to his cause.

Adolf Hitler was born in 1889 in Austria, not Germany. The son of a petty customs official in the Austrian civil service, Hitler dropped out of school and went to Vienna in 1909 to become an artist. That failed. He was rejected by the academy and forced to eke out a dismal existence doing manual labor and painting cheap watercolors in Vienna. Meanwhile, he developed the violent political prejudices that would become the guiding principles of the Nazi regime. He ardently admired the Austrian politicians preaching anti-Semitism, anti-Marxism, and pan-Germanism. When war broke out in 1914, Hitler was among the jubilant crowds in the streets of Munich; and though he was an Austrian citizen, he enlisted in the German army, where he claimed to have finally found meaning in his life. After the war, he joined the newly formed German Workers' party, whose name changed in 1920 to the National Socialist Workers' party (abbreviated in popular usage to Nazi). The Nazis were but one among many small, militant groups of disaffected Germans devoted to racial nationalism and to the overthrow of the Weimar Republic. They grew out of the political milieu that refused to accept the defeat or the November Revolution and that blamed both on socialists and Jews.

Ambitious and outspoken, Hitler quickly moved up the rather short ladder of party leadership as a talented stump orator. By 1921, he was the *Führer*—the leader—to his followers in Bavaria. The wider public saw him as a "vulgar demagogue"—if they noticed him at all. In November 1923, during the worst days of the inflation crisis, the Nazis made a failed attempt (the Beer Hall Putsch in Munich) at overthrowing the state government of Bavaria. Hitler spent the next seven months in prison, where he wrote his autobiography and political manifesto *Mein Kampf* (*myn KAHMPF*;

Past and Present

The Great Depression and Today's Economy

What parallels can one see between the history of the Great Depression in the 1930s and the situation in the world's economy today, after the crisis of 2008? In both cases, the debate has focused on whether or not financial markets can operate without significant government oversight, and what responsibilities the government has to alleviate the pain of those whose jobs or wages are cut as a result of economic collapse. Left, in 1930s France, laborers battle police over wage cuts; right, in 2011, protesters demonstrate in Italy against the government's "austerity" policy, which saw reductions in pension benefits and job cuts.

 Watch related author interview on StudySpace
wwnorton.com/web/westernciv18

"*My Struggle*") in 1924. Combining anti-Semitism with anti-communism, the book set out at great length the popular theory that Germany had been betrayed by its enemies and that the country needed strong leadership to regain international prominence. The failed 1923 putsch proved an eye-opening experience for Hitler; he recognized that the Nazis would have to play politics if they wanted to gain power. Released from prison in 1924, Hitler resumed leadership of the party. In the next five years, he consolidated his power over a growing membership of ardent supporters. Actively cultivating the image of the Nazi movement as a crusade against Marxism, capitalism, and Jews, he portrayed himself as the heroic savior of the German people.

An equally important factor in Hitler's rise to power was the Nazis' ambitious and unprecedented campaign program. In the "inflation election" of 1924, the Nazis polled 6.6 percent of the vote as a protest party at the radical

fringe. With the economic stabilization of the mid-1920s, their meager share dropped to below 3 percent. But during this time of seeming decline, the Nazis were building an extensive organization of party activists that helped lay the foundation for the party's electoral gains later.

After 1928, political polarization between the right and left worked to Hitler's advantage and made it impossible for the Weimar government to put together a coalition that could support the continuation of democracy in Germany. Alienated voters, especially in rural areas, deserted the traditional political parties. The Nazis quickly learned how to benefit from this splintering of the electorate. Having failed to win over the German working class from the left, the Nazis stepped up their efforts to attract members of the rural and urban middle classes. Guided by their chief propagandist, Joseph Goebbels, the party hammered home its critique of Weimar society: its parliamentary system, the

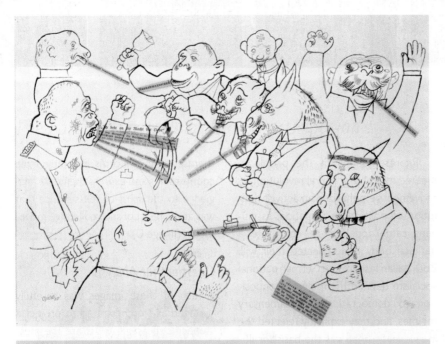

VOICE OF THE PEOPLE, VOICE OF GOD BY GEORGE GROSZ (1920). Industrialization, the First World War, and political change combined to make early-twentieth-century Berlin a center of mass culture and communication. In this drawing, the radical artist and social critic George Grosz deplores the newspapers' power over public opinion. That public opinion could be manipulated was a common theme for many who wrote about early-twentieth-century democracy. ▪ *How does this cynicism about the public sphere compare with earlier defenders of free speech, such as John Stuart Mill?*

FRITZ LANG'S M. In this film, Peter Lorre, a Jewish actor, played the role of a child murderer, who maintains that he should not be punished for his crimes. Lorre's speech at the end of the film was used in the Nazi propaganda film *The Eternal Jew* as proof that Jews were innate criminals who showed no remorse for their actions.

lower-class form of entertainment. In Europe, the cross-class appeal of American popular culture grated against long-standing social hierarchies. Conservative critics abhorred the fact that "the parson's wife sat nearby his maid at Sunday matinees, equally rapt in the gaze of Hollywood stars." American critics expressed many of the same concerns. Yet the United States enjoyed more social and political stability than Europe. War and revolution had shaken Europe's economies and cultures, and in that context "Americanization" seemed a handy shorthand for economic as well as cultural change. One critic expressed a common concern: "America is the source of that terrible wave of uniformity that gives everyone the same [*sic*]: the same overalls on the skin, the same book in the hand, the same pen between the fingers, the same conversation on the lips, and the same automobile instead of feet."

Authoritarian governments, in particular, decried these developments as decadent threats to national culture. Fascist, communist, and Nazi governments alike tried to control not only popular culture but also high culture and modernism, which were typically out of line with the designs of the dictators. Stalin much preferred socialist realism to the new Soviet avant-garde. Mussolini had a penchant for classical kitsch, though he was far more accepting of modern art than Hitler, who despised its decadence. Nazism had its own cultural aesthetic, promoting "Aryan" art and architecture and rejecting the modern, international style they associated with the "international Jewish conspiracy." Modernism, functionalism, and atonality were banned: the hallmarks of Weimar Germany's cultural preeminence were replaced by a state-sponsored revival of an alleged mystical and heroic past. Walter Gropius's acclaimed experiments in modernist architecture, for example, stood as monuments to everything the Nazis hated. The Bauhaus school was closed in 1933, and Hitler hired Albert Speer as his personal architect, commissioning him to design grandiose neoclassical buildings, including an extravagant plan to rebuild the entire city of Berlin.

The Nazis, like other authoritarian governments, used mass media as efficient means of indoctrination and control. Movies became part of the Nazis' pioneering use of "spectacular politics." Media campaigns, mass rallies, parades

Cinema: Fritz Lang on the Future of the Feature Film in Germany, 1926

Fritz Lang (1890–1976) came from Austria to Berlin after the First World War and became one of the German Weimar Republic's most brilliant movie directors, best known for Metropolis *(1926) and* M *(1931). In this essay, Lang reflects on the technological, artistic, and human potential of film. Like many European filmmakers he was fascinated by American movies. In 1932, Joseph Goebbels, dazzled by Lang's work, asked him to work on movies for the Nazis. Lang immediately left Germany for Paris and, from there, for the United States where he continued to make films in Hollywood.*

There has perhaps never before been a time so determined as ours in its search for new forms of expression. Fundamental revolutions in painting, sculpture, architecture, and music speak eloquently of the fact that people of today are seeking and finding their own means of lending artistic form to their sentiments. . . .

The speed with which film has developed in the last five years makes all predictions about it appear dangerous, for it will probably exceed each one by leaps and bounds. Film knows no rest. What was invented yesterday is already obsolete today. This uninterrupted drive for new modes of expression, this intellectual experimentation, along with the joy Germans characteristically take in overexertion, appear to me to fortify my contention that film as art will first find its form in Germany. . . .

Germany has never had, and never will have, the gigantic human and financial reserves of the American film industry at its disposal. To its good fortune. For that is exactly what forces us to compensate a purely material imbalance through an intellectual superiority. . . .

The first important gift for which we have film to thank was in a certain sense *the rediscovery of the human face.* Film has revealed to us the human face with unexampled clarity in its tragic as well as grotesque, threatening as well as blessed expression.

The second gift is that of visual empathy: in the purest sense the expressionistic representation of thought processes. No longer will we take part purely externally in the workings of the soul of the characters in film. We will no longer limit ourselves to seeing the effects of feelings, but will experience them in our own souls, from the instant of their inception on, from the first flash of a thought through to the logical last conclusion of the idea. . . .

The internationalism of filmic language will become the strongest instrument available for the mutual understanding of peoples, who otherwise have such difficulty understanding each other in all too many languages. To bestow upon film the double gift of ideas and soul is the task that lies before us. . . .

Source: Anton Kaes, Matin Jay, and Edward Dimendberg, *The Weimar Republic Sourcebook* (Los Angeles: 1994), pp. 622–23.

Questions for Analysis

1. Why does Lang suggest that his own time is in search of "new forms of expression"? Do artists always search for new forms, or might this be a specifically twentieth-century phenomenon?

2. What did Lang mean by calling "the rediscovery of the human face" and "visual empathy" gifts of film? Did television, video, and electronic media have comparable effects on how we see the world and other beings in it?

3. How does Lang see the technological, artistic, and human potential of film?

and ceremonies: all were designed to display the strength and glory of the Reich and to impress and intimidate spectators. In 1934, Hitler commissioned the filmmaker Leni Riefenstahl to record a political rally staged by herself and Albert Speer in Nuremberg. The film, titled *Triumph of the Will*, was a visual hymn to the Nordic race and the Nazi regime. Everything in the film was on a huge scale: masses of bodies stood in parade formation, and flags rose and fell in unison; the film invited viewers to surrender to the power of grand ritual and symbolism. The comedian Charlie Chaplin riposted in his celebrated lampoon *The Great Dictator* (1940), an enormously successful parody of Nazi pomposities.

The Nazis also tried to eliminate the influences of American popular culture, which even before 1933 had been decried as an example of biological and cultural degeneracy. For instance, critics associated American dances and jazz (which were increasingly popular in German cities) with what the Nazis deemed "racially inferior" blacks and Jews. With culture, however, the Nazis were forced to strike a balance between party propaganda and popular entertainment. The regime allowed many cultural imports, including Hollywood films, to continue while consciously cultivating German alternatives to American cinema, music, fashions, and even dances. Joseph Goebbels, the minister of propaganda who controlled most film production, placed a high value on economic viability. During the Third Reich, the German film industry turned out comedies, escapist fantasies, and sentimental romances. It developed its own star system and tried to keep audiences happy; meanwhile, it became a major competitor internationally. For domestic consumption, the industry also produced vicious anti-Semitic films, such as *The Eternal Jew* (1940) and *Jew Suss* (1940), a fictional tale of a Jewish moneylender who brings the city of Württemberg to ruin in the eighteenth century. In the final scene of the film, the town expels the entire Jewish community from its midst, asking that "posterity honor this law." Goebbels reported that the entire Reich cabinet had viewed the film and considered it "an incredible success."

After You Read This Chapter

Visit StudySpace for quizzes, additional review materials, and multimedia documents. **wwnorton.com/web/westernciv18**

REVIEWING THE OBJECTIVES

- After 1917, the Bolsheviks in Russia debated how fast they should move to reorganize society along the lines demanded by their revolutionary ideology. What circumstances determined the outcome of this debate and what were the consequences of Stalin's revolution from above in the 1930s?

- Mussolini's Fascist party offered an alternative to Italian voters disappointed with their government in the aftermath of the First World War. What was fascism, and how did Mussolini come to power?

- The Weimar Republic failed in its attempt to establish a stable democracy in Germany while other democracies in France, Britain, and the United States underwent severe strain. What challenges did democratic regimes face during the interwar period?

- Hitler came to power legally in 1933 through the German electoral system. What did he stand for, and why did so many Germans support his cause?

- Artists, writers, and other intellectuals in the interwar period could not help but reflect the atmosphere of social and political crisis in their work. How did artists and writers react to the crisis of the interwar period?

CONCLUSION

The strains of the First World War created a world that few recognized—transformed by revolution, mass mobilization, and loss. In retrospect, it is hard not to see the period that followed as a succession of failures. Capitalism foundered in the Great Depression, democracies collapsed in the face of authoritarianism, and the Treaty of Versailles proved hollow. Stalin's Soviet Union paid a terrible price for the creation of a modern industrial economy in the years of famine, political repression, and state terror. Hitler's Germany and Mussolini's Italy offered a vision of the future that held no comfort for those committed to basic human freedoms and equality under the law. Yet we better understand the experiences and outlooks of ordinary people if we do not treat the failures of the interwar period as inevitable. By the late 1920s, many were cautiously optimistic that the Great War's legacy could be overcome and that problems were being solved. The Great Depression wrecked these hopes, bringing economic chaos and political paralysis. Paralysis and chaos, in turn, created new audiences for political leaders offering authoritarian solutions and brought more voters to their political parties. Finally, economic troubles and political turmoil made contending with rising international tensions, to which we now turn, vastly more difficult. By the 1930s, even cautious optimism about international relations had given way to apprehension and dread.

PEOPLE, IDEAS, AND EVENTS IN CONTEXT

- What is the difference between the Bolshevik policies of **WAR COMMUNISM** and the **NEW ECONOMIC POLICY (NEP)**?
- What were **JOSEPH STALIN**'s goals in implementing his catastrophic plan for **COLLECTIVIZATION** of agriculture, and what did he hope to accomplish with his purging of an entire generation of Bolshevik leaders, along with millions of other Soviet citizens, in the **GREAT TERROR**?
- What was the basis of **BENITO MUSSOLINI**'s rejection of liberal democracy? What kinds of changes in Italian society followed from the adoption of **FASCISM** as the official state ideology?
- How important was **ANTI-SEMITISM** to **ADOLF HITLER**'s political career? What do events like **KRISTALLNACHT** tell us about the depth of German anti-Semitism?
- What effects did the **GREAT DEPRESSION** have on the European economy, and how did this economic crisis affect the political developments of the 1930s?
- How did the **NEW DEAL** attempt to deal with the economic crisis in the United States?

THINKING ABOUT CONNECTIONS

- What did Soviet communism, national socialism in Germany, and Italian fascism have in common during the years 1919–39? What made them different from one another?
- How much of the crisis of the interwar period can be attributed to the effects of World War I? To the economic upheaval of the Great Depression? Is it possible to see the ideological conflicts of these years as the result of a much longer history?

STORY LINES

- In the 1930s, Hitler's Germany and Mussolini's Italy allied with imperial Japan to form the Axis. The Axis eventually provoked a Second World War, against a group of Allied powers that included Britain, the United States, Canada, Australia, and the Soviet Union.

- The Nazi regime's military successes in 1939 brought almost all of Europe under German control. The Russian victory at Stalingrad in 1942 proved to be a turning point, and from 1942 to 1945 the Allies progressively rolled back the German and Japanese armies, leading to Allied victory in 1945.

- The Nazi state embarked on a genocidal project of mass murder to exterminate its racial and ideological enemies—Europe's Jews, homosexuals, and the Roma (Gypsies).

- Attacks on civilian populations and the plundering of resources by occupying armies made the Second World War a "total war" in which the distinction between military and home front meant little for many Europeans.

CHRONOLOGY

1931	Japanese invasion of Manchuria
1936–1939	Spanish Civil War
September 1938	Sudeten Crisis and Munich Conference
August 1939	Nazi-Soviet Pact
September 1939	German invasion of Poland
May 1940	German invasion of the Low Countries and France
June 1941	German invasion of the Soviet Union
December 1941	Japanese attack on Pearl Harbor
September 1942–January 1943	Battle of Stalingrad
June 1944	D-Day Invasion
May 1945	German surrender
August 1945	The United States drops atomic bombs on Hiroshima and Nagasaki
August 1945	Japanese surrender

Before You Read This Chapter

The Second World War

CORE OBJECTIVES

- **IDENTIFY** the broader political and economic causes of the Second World War.

- **EXPLAIN** the reasons for the British and French policy of "appeasement," when faced with Hitler's violations of international law.

- **UNDERSTAND** the consequences of German conquest and occupation for European nations and their populations and the challenges facing those who chose to resist.

- **DESCRIBE** how the Holocaust became possible after the conquest of territory in eastern Europe during the invasion of the Soviet Union.

- **UNDERSTAND** the military operations that led to the defeat of the Nazi regime and their allies in Europe.

- **EXPLAIN** the main areas of conflict in Asia and the Pacific and the circumstances that led to Japanese surrender in 1945.

I n 1939, Adolf Hitler wanted war. By the spring of that year, he had already revealed to the world the weakness of France and Britain, which had stood by while he dismantled Czechoslovakia, a democratic nation created at the end of World War I. He turned his eyes next to Poland, confident that Britain and France could do little to prevent him from fulfilling his pledge to unleash the full power of a rearmed Germany to conquer *Lebensraum*—"living space"—for the German people in the east. Before he could invade Poland, however, he needed to come to an understanding with another long-standing enemy—the Soviet Union of Josef Stalin. Since 1934, Stalin had participated in a broad-based anti-fascist coalition in Europe, the Popular Front, an alliance that had brought the Soviets to side with the "bourgeois democracies" that were their sworn enemies. The Popular Front had led to Soviet support for the Republican side in the Spanish Civil War, though the Republicans had lost to the Nationalists who were backed by Hitler's Germany and Mussolini's Italian fascists. Hitler's propaganda campaign against the Soviets was relentless. He portrayed the Soviet regime as a cabal run by Jewish communists and referred continuously to Stalin's commissar for foreign affairs, Maxim Litvinov, as "Finkelstein" (his brother was a rabbi). Given this history of conflict, what possible understanding could Hitler hope to achieve with Stalin?

In fact, by 1939, Stalin himself had been forced to recalculate his alliances in Europe. The loss in the Spanish Civil War, and the failure of France and Britain to uphold their obligations to preserve the international order guaranteed by the Versailles peace treaty led the Soviet leader to believe that his regime had no choice but to come to an agreement with Hitler, in an attempt to gain time and preserve the Soviet Union from an immediate war. The hope was that the other European powers—France, Britain, Italy, and Germany—would weaken themselves in a general war, thus benefiting the cause of the Soviet Union. To show his willingness to talk, he fired Litvinov on May 3 and replaced him with his closest adviser, Vyacheslav Molotov (1890–1986), an ethnic Russian. In August, Hitler responded by sending his own foreign minister, Joachim von Ribbentrop (1893–1946), to Moscow to meet with Stalin. When the German envoy arrived, the Moscow airport was decorated with swastikas. The two sides cynically agreed to carve Poland up between them, and when the agreement was announced on August 23, 1939, the world was shocked to discover that these two powers, sworn ideological enemies, had made common cause to destroy Poland. On September 1, 1939, Hitler invaded Poland. Stalin, looking to what was to become a global conflict, had already attacked Japanese forces along the Mongolian border in Central Asia on August 20. The Second World War had begun.

Like the First World War, the Second World War was triggered by threats to the European balance of power. Yet even more than the Great War, the Second World War was a conflict among nations, whole peoples, and fiercely opposing ideals. Adolf Hitler and his supporters in Germany and abroad cast the conflict as a racial war against the twin enemies of national socialism: the democracies in western Europe and the United States, on the one hand, and the communist order of the Soviet Union, on the other. Hitler's opponents in the West and the East believed just as fervently that they were defending a way of life and a vision of justice that was bigger than narrow definitions of national interest.

Belief that the world was now characterized by ideologies and worldviews that were necessarily in mortal combat with one another meant that the scale of the killing overtook even that of the First World War. In 1914, military firepower outmatched mobility, resulting in four years of static, mud-sodden slaughter. In 1939, mobility was joined to firepower on a massive scale, with terrifying results. On the battlefield, the tactics of high-speed armored warfare (*Blitzkrieg*), aircraft carriers sinking ships far below the horizon, and submarines used in vast numbers to dominate shipping lanes changed the scope and the pace of fighting. This was not a war of trenches and barbed wire but a war of motion, dramatic conquests, and terrible destructive power. The devastation of 1914–18 paled in comparison to this new, global conflict.

The other great change involved not tactics but targets. Much of the unprecedented killing power now available was aimed directly at civilians. Cities were laid waste by artillery and aerial bombing. Whole regions were put to the torch, and towns and villages were systematically cordoned off and leveled. Whole populations were targeted as well, in ways that continue to appall. The Nazi regime's systematic murder of gypsies, homosexuals, and other "deviants," along with the effort to exterminate the Jewish people completely, made the Second World War a horrifyingly unique event. So did the United States' use of a weapon whose existence would dominate politics and society for the next fifty years: the atomic bomb. The naive enthusiasm that had marked the outbreak of the Great War was absent from the start. Terrible memories of the first conflict lingered. Yet those who fought against the Axis Powers (and many of those who fought for them) found that their determination to fight and win grew as the war went on. Unlike the seemingly meaningless killing of the Great War, the Second World War was cast as a war of absolutes, of good and evil, of national and global survival. Nevertheless, the scale of destruction brought with it a profound weariness. It also provoked deep-seated questions about the value of Western "civilization" and the terms on which it, and the rest of the world, might live peaceably in the future.

THE CAUSES OF THE WAR: UNSETTLED QUARRELS, ECONOMIC FALLOUT, AND NATIONALISM

Historians have isolated four main causes for the Second World War: the punishing terms of the Versailles peace settlement, the failure to create international guarantees for peace and security after 1918, the successive economic crises of the interwar years, and the violent forms of nationalism that emerged in Europe in the 1930s.

The peace settlement of 1919–20 created as many problems as it solved. The senior Allied heads of state annexed German territory and created satellite states out of the eastern European empires. In doing so, the peacemakers created fresh bitterness and conflict. The Versailles treaty and its champions, such as President Woodrow Wilson, proclaimed the principle of self-determination for the peoples of eastern and southern Europe. Yet the new states created by the treaty crossed ethnic boundaries, created new minorities without protecting them, and frustrated many of the expectations they had raised. The unsteady new boundaries would be redrawn by force in the 1930s. The Allied powers also kept up the naval blockade against Germany after the end of the fighting. This forced the new German government to accept harsh terms that deprived Germany of its political power in Europe and saddled the German economy with the bill for the conflict in a "war guilt" clause. The blockade and its consequences created grievances that many angry, humiliated Germans considered legitimate.

Power politics persisted after the peace conference. Although Woodrow Wilson and other sponsors of the League of Nations acclaimed the League as a means to eliminate power struggles, it did nothing of the sort. The signatures on the peace treaties were hardly dry when the victors began carving out new alliances to maintain their supremacy, interfering in the new central European states and the mandate territories added to the British and French empires in the Middle East. Even the League itself was fundamentally an alliance of the victors against the vanquished. It is not surprising that politicians feared international relations would be undermined by this imbalance of power.

Another cause of the Second World War was the failure to create lasting, binding standards for peace and security. Diplomats spent the ten years after Versailles trying to restore such standards. Some put their faith in the legal and moral authority of the League. Others saw disarmament as the most promising means of guaranteeing peace. In 1925, an effort was made to secure the frontiers on the Rhine established at Versailles in order to reassure the French against any resurgence of German expansionism. In 1928, the Kellogg-Briand Pact attempted to make war an international crime. None of these pacts carried any real weight. Each nation tried to include special provisions and exceptions for "vital interests," and these efforts compromised the treaties from the start. Had the League of Nations been better organized, it might have relieved some of the tensions or at least prevented clashes between nations. But the League was never a league of all nations. Essential members were absent, since Germany and the Soviet Union were excluded for most of the interwar period and the United States never joined.

Economic conditions were a third important cause of renewed conflict. The huge reparations imposed on the Germans and France's occupation of much of Germany's industrial heartland helped slow Germany's recovery. German and French stubbornness about the pace of repayments combined disastrously to bring on the German inflation of the early 1920s. The spiraling inflation made German money nearly worthless, damaging the stability and credibility of Germany's young republic almost beyond repair.

The depression of the 1930s contributed to the coming of the war in several ways. It intensified economic nationalism. Baffled by problems of unemployment and business stagnation, governments imposed high tariffs in an effort to preserve the home market for their own producers. The collapse of investment and terrible domestic unemployment caused the United States to withdraw even further from world affairs. Although France suffered less than some other countries, the depression still inflamed tensions between management and labor. This conflict exacerbated political battles between left and right, making it difficult for either side to govern France. Britain turned to its empire, raising tariffs for the first time and guarding its financial investments jealously.

In Germany, the Great Depression was the last blow to the Weimar Republic. In 1933, power passed to the Nazis, who promised a total program of national renewal. In the fascist states (and, exceptionally, the United States), public works projects of one kind or another were prescribed as an answer to mass unemployment. This produced highways, bridges, and railroads; it also produced a new arms race.

Despite the misgivings of many inside the governments of Britain and France, Germany was allowed to ignore the terms of the peace treaties and rearm. Armaments expansion on a large scale first began in Germany in 1935, with the result that unemployment was reduced and the effects of the depression eased. Other nations followed the German example, not simply as a way to boost their economies but in response to growing Nazi military power. In the Pacific, the decline of Japanese exports meant that the nation did not have enough foreign currency to pay for vital raw materials from overseas. This played into the hands of Japan's military regime. Japanese national ambitions and Japanese leaders' perception of the political and cultural inferiority of the Chinese led Japan to fresh imperial adventures in the name of establishing economic stability in East Asia. They began in 1931 with the invasion of Manchuria and moved from there to create a "Greater Pacific Co-Prosperity Sphere," which involved seizing other territories as Japanese colonies. Raw materials could then be bought with Japanese money and more of Asia would serve the needs of Japan's empire.

Imperial success could serve as consolation when economic methods failed. As the depression dragged on in fascist Italy, Mussolini tried to distract his public with national conquests overseas, culminating in the invasion of Ethiopia in 1935.

In sum, the tremendous economic hardship of the depression, a contested peace treaty, and political weakness undermined international stability. But the decisive factor in the crises of the 1930s and the trigger for another world war lay in a blend of violent nationalism and modern ideologies that glorified the nation and national destiny. This blend, particularly in the forms of fascism and militarism, appeared around the world in many countries. By the middle of the 1930s, recognizing common interests, fascist Italy and Nazi Germany formed an Axis, an alliance binding their goals of national glory and international power. They were later joined by Japan's military regime. In Spain, the ultranationalist forces that tried to overthrow the Spanish Republic, setting off the Spanish Civil War (discussed below), believed they were reviving the stability, authority, and morality of the nation. Fascist, semifascist, or authoritarian regimes spread in eastern Europe, in Yugoslavia, Hungary, and Romania. One exception to this sobering trend toward authoritarianism was Czechoslovakia. Czechoslovakia boasted no ethnic majority. Although the Czechs practiced an enlightened policy of minority self-government, and though their government was remarkably stable, questions of nationality remained a potential source of friction. Those questions became a key factor as international tensions mounted in the late 1930s.

THE 1930s: CHALLENGES TO THE PEACE, APPEASEMENT, AND THE "DISHONEST DECADE"

The 1930s brought the tensions and failures caused by the treaties of 1919–20 to a head, creating a global crisis. Fascist and nationalist governments flouted the League of Nations by launching new conquests and efforts at national expansion. With the memories of 1914–18 still fresh, these new crises created an atmosphere of deepening fear and apprehension. Each new conflict seemed to warn that another, much wider war would follow unless it could somehow be averted. Ordinary people, particularly in Britain, France, and the United States, were divided. Some saw the actions of the aggressors as a direct challenge to civilization, one that had to be met with force if necessary. Others hoped to avoid premature

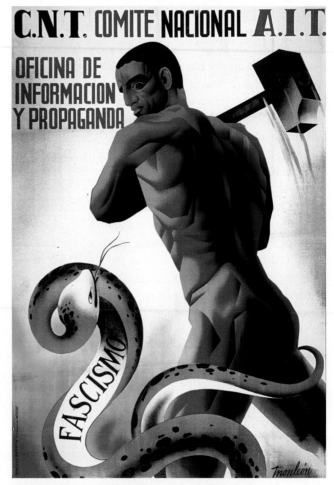

ANTIFASCIST PROPAGANDA, SPANISH CIVIL WAR. This poster, produced by a left-wing labor organization affiliated with the international anarchist movement, shows a worker delivering a killing blow to a fascist snake.

GIANT PORTRAIT OF MUSSOLINI IN ETHIOPIA, 1935. Central to Mussolini's popularity in Italy was his ability to connect a vision of his personal leadership with a militant and expansionist nationalism. This portrait stood over an Italian military camp in Ethiopia in November 1935 during the invasion of this East African nation.

or unnecessary conflict. Their governments tried instead at several points to negotiate with the fascists and keep a tenuous peace. Writers, intellectuals, and politicians on the left vilified these efforts. Many saw the period as a series of missed opportunities to prevent renewed warfare. In 1939, on the first day of the Second World War, the British poet and leftist W. H. Auden condemned the behavior of Western governments, calling the 1930s "a low, dishonest decade."

The object of Auden's venom was the policy of "appeasement" pursued by Western governments in the face of German, Italian, and Japanese aggression. Appeasement was neither simple power politics nor pure cowardice. It was grounded in three deeply held assumptions. The first assumption was that doing anything to provoke another war was unthinkable. The 1914–18 slaughter and its aftermath left many in the West embracing pacifism and not wanting to deal with the uncompromising aggression of the fascist governments, especially Nazi Germany. Second, many in Britain and the United States argued that Germany had been mistreated by the Versailles treaty and harbored legitimate grievances that should be acknowledged and resolved. Finally, many appeasers were staunch anticommunists. They believed that the fascist states in Germany and Italy were an essential bulwark against the advance of Soviet communism and that division among the major European states only played into the hands of the USSR. One group, however, believed that the Soviets posed the greater threat and that accommodating Hitler might create a common interest against a common enemy. The other faction believed that Nazi Germany presented the true threat to European stability. Nevertheless, they believed, Hitler would have to be placated until Britain and France finished rearming. At that point, they hoped, their greater military power would deter Hitler or Mussolini from risking a general European war. It took most of the 1930s for the debate among appeasers to come to a head. Meanwhile, the League of Nations faced more immediate and pressing challenges.

The 1930s brought three crucial tests for the League: crises in China, Ethiopia, and Spain. In China, the Japanese invasion of Manchuria in 1931 turned into an invasion of the whole country. Chinese forces were driven before the Japanese advance, and the Japanese deliberately targeted civilians to break the Chinese will to fight. In 1937, the Japanese laid siege to the strategic city of Nanjing. Their orders on taking the city were simple: "kill all, burn all, destroy all." More than 200,000 Chinese citizens were slaughtered in what came to be known as the "Rape of Nanjing." The League voiced shock and disapproval but did nothing. In

GUERNICA BY PABLO PICASSO (1937). One of Picasso's most influential paintings, *Guernica* was painted as a mural for the Spanish republican government as it fought for survival in the Spanish Civil War. The Basque town of Guernica had been bombed by German fighters just a few months earlier, in April 1937. Near the center a horse writhes in agony; to the left a distraught woman holds her dead child. Compare Picasso's image to the antifascist propaganda poster on page 876. ▪ *What is different about the way that the two images deliver their political messages?* ▪ *Does Picasso's rejection of realism diminish the power of his political message?* ▪ *Does the antifascist poster seek any outcome other than the annihilation of the enemy?*

1935, Mussolini began his efforts to make the Mediterranean an Italian empire by returning to Ethiopia to avenge the defeat of 1896. This time the Italians came with tanks, bombers, and poison gas. The Ethiopians fought bravely but hopelessly, and this imperial massacre aroused world opinion. The League attempted to impose sanctions on Italy and condemned Japan. But for two reasons, no enforcement followed. The first was British and French fear of communism and their hope that Italy and Japan would act as counterweights to the Soviets. The second reason was practical. Enforcing sanctions would involve challenging Japan's powerful fleet or Mussolini's newly built battleships. Britain and France were unwilling, and dangerously close to unable, to use their navies to those ends.

The Spanish Civil War

The third challenge came closer to home. In 1936, civil war broke out in Spain. A series of weak republican governments, committed to large-scale social reforms, could not overcome opposition to those measures and political polarization. War broke out as extreme right-wing military officers rebelled. Although Hitler and Mussolini had signed a pact of nonintervention with the other Western powers, both leaders sent troops and equipment to assist the rebel commander, Francisco Franco (1939–75). The Soviet Union countered with aid to communist troops serving under the banner of the Spanish Republic. Again Britain and France failed to act decisively. Thousands of volunteers from England, France, and the United States—including many working-class socialists and writers, such as George Orwell and Ernest Hemingway—took up arms as private soldiers for the Republican government. They saw the war as a test of the West's determination to resist fascism and military dictatorships. Their governments were much more hesitant. For the British, Franco was anticommunist at least, just like Mussolini and the Japanese. The French prime minister Léon Blum, a committed antifascist, stood at the head of a Popular Front government—an alliance of socialists, communists, and republicans. The Popular Front had been elected on a program of social reform and opposition to Hitler abroad and fascism in France. Yet Blum's margin of support was limited. He feared that intervening in Spain would further polarize his country, bring down his government, and make it impossible to follow through on any commitment to the conflict. In Spain, despite some heroic fighting, the Republican camp degenerated into a hornet's nest of competing factions: republican, socialist, communist, and anarchist.

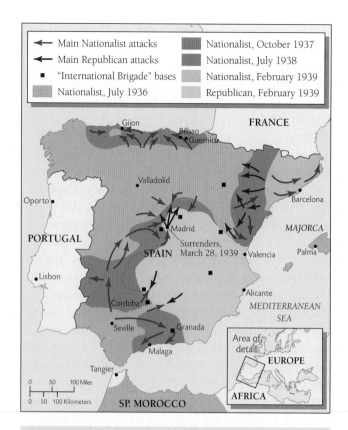

THE SPANISH CIVIL WAR. ■ *Why did thousands of foreign fighters join the war?* ■ *How did the strategies and weapons used in the war anticipate those used in the Second World War?* ■ *What were the consequences of Franco's victory?*

The Spanish Civil War was brutal. Both the German and the Soviet "advisers" saw Spain as a "dress rehearsal" for a later war between the two powers. They each brought in their newest weapons and practiced their skills in destroying civilian targets from the air. In April 1937, a raid by German dive bombers utterly destroyed the town of Guernica in northern Spain in an effort to cut off Republican supply lines and terrorize civilians. It shocked public opinion and was commemorated by Pablo Picasso in one of the most famous paintings of the twentieth century. Both sides committed atrocities. The Spanish Civil War lasted three years, ending with a complete victory for Franco in 1939. In the aftermath, Britain and France proved reluctant to admit Spanish Republicans as refugees, even though Republicans faced recriminations from Franco's regime. Franco sent 1 million of his Republican enemies to prison or concentration camps.

Hitler drew two lessons from Spain. The first was that if Britain, France, and the Soviet Union ever tried to contain fascism, they would have a hard time coordinating their efforts. The second was that Britain and France were deeply averse to fighting another European war. This meant that the Nazis could use every means short of war to achieve their goals.

German Rearmament and the Politics of Appeasement

Hitler took advantage of this combination of international tolerance and war weariness to advance his ambitions. As Germany rearmed, Hitler played on Germans' sense of shame and betrayal, proclaiming their right to regain their former power in the world. In 1933, he removed Germany from the League of Nations, to which it had finally been admitted in 1926. In 1935, he defied the disarmament provisions of the Treaty of Versailles and revived conscription and universal military training. Hitler's stated goals were the restoration of Germany's power and dignity inside Europe and the unification of all ethnic Germans inside his Third German Reich. As the first step in this process, Germany reoccupied the Rhineland in 1936. It was a risky move, chancing war with the much more powerful French army. But France and Britain did not mount a military response. In retrospect, this was an important turning point; the balance of power tipped in Germany's favor. While the Rhineland remained demilitarized and German industry in the Ruhr valley was unprotected, France held the upper hand. After 1936, it no longer did so.

In March 1938, Hitler annexed Austria, reaffirming his intention to bring all Germans into his Reich. Once more, no official reaction came from the West. The Nazis' next target was the Sudetenland in Czechoslovakia, a region with a large ethnic German population. With Austria now a part of Germany, Czechoslovakia was almost entirely surrounded by its hostile neighbor. Hitler declared that the Sudetenland was a natural part of the Reich and that he intended to occupy it. The Czechs did not want to give way. Hitler's generals were wary of this gamble. Czechoslovakia had a strong, well-equipped army and a line of fortifications along the border. Many in the French and Polish governments were willing to come to the Czechs' aid. According to plans already being laid for a wider European war, Germany would not be ready for another three to four years. But Hitler gambled, and the British prime minister, Neville Chamberlain, obliged him. Chamberlain decided to take charge of international talks about the Sudetenland and agreed to Hitler's terms. Chamberlain's logic was that this dispute was about the balance of power in Europe. If Hitler were allowed to unify all Germans in one state, he reasoned, then German ambitions would be satisfied. Chamberlain also believed that his country could not commit to a sustained war. Finally, defending eastern European boundaries against Germany ranked low on Great Britain's list of priorities, at least in comparison to ensuring free trade in western Europe and protecting the strategic centers of the British Empire.

On September 29, 1938, Hitler met with Chamberlain, Premier Édouard Daladier (1938–40) of France, and Mussolini in a four-power conference in Munich. The result was another capitulation by France and Britain. The four negotiators bargained away a major slice of Czechoslovakia while Czech representatives were left to await their fate outside the conference room. Chamberlain returned to London proclaiming "peace in our time." Hitler soon proved

GERMAN SOLDIERS ENTER RHINELAND IN COLOGNE, 1936. Hitler's reoccupation of the Rhineland—an area bordering France, Belgium, and the Netherlands—was a direct violation of the Treaty of Versailles, but it was difficult for the French and British governments to respond effectively, because voters in these nations were reluctant to go to war over Hitler's decision to move troops into what was, after all, German territory.

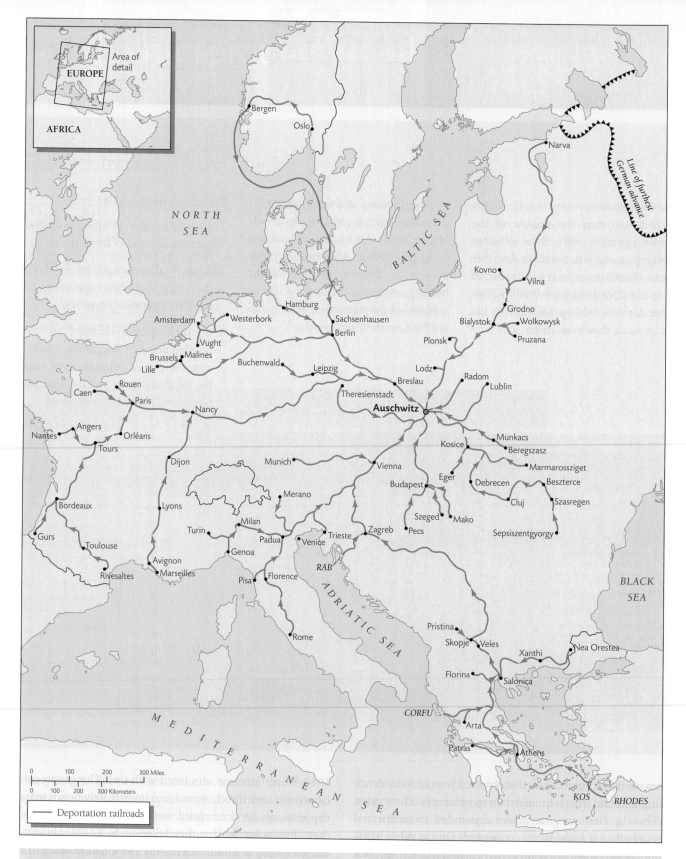

DEPORTATION RAILWAYS. Between March 1942 and November 1944, Jews are known to have been deported from every location on this map—as well as from numerous other locales. Note the effort made by the Nazis to transport Jews from the very frontiers of the empire at the height of a two-front war. ▪ *According to the map, to which site were most Jews deported?* ▪ *Looking back at Hitler's "Final Solution" map on page 895, why was Auschwitz in Poland chosen as the main deportation site?* ▪ *What does this say about the Nazi regime in particular and about other states willing to collaborate with the Nazis?*

Past and Present

European Integration Then and Now

Hitler's conquest of Europe was a plan for European integration, based on a theory of racial domination, whereby "pure" Aryan settlements (see photo from "model" Nazi village of Adolf Hitler-Koog) would take over territory from "racially inferior" people who would eventually be eliminated. The great success of European integration after the Second World War (see photo of German Chancellor Konrad Adenauer shaking hands with Jean Monnet, a key figure in European integration) was to create a structure for international cooperation based on democratic institutions and mutual economic interest.

 Watch related author interview on StudySpace
wwnorton.com/web/westernciv18

killed right away. In his famous account, the survivor Primo Levi writes: "Our language lacks words to express this offence, the demolition of a man. . . . It is not possible to sink lower than this; no human condition is more miserable than this, nor could it conceivably be so. Nothing belongs to us any more; they have taken away our clothes, our shoes, even our hair; if we speak, they will not listen to us, and if they listen, they will not understand." A few rebellions in Auschwitz and Treblinka were repressed with savage efficiency. In the villages of Poland, Ukraine, and elsewhere, people rounded up to be deported or shot had to make split-second decisions to escape. Saving oneself nearly always meant abandoning one's children or parents, which very few could—or would—do. The countryside offered no shelter; local populations were usually either hostile or too terrified to help. Reprisals horrified all. Families of Jews and gypsies were ordinary people whose lives could not have prepared them for the kind of violence that rolled over them.

The largest Jewish resistance came in the Warsaw ghetto, in the spring of 1943. The previous summer, the Nazis had deported 80 percent of the ghetto's residents to the camps, making it clear that those left behind had little hope of survival. Those in the ghetto had virtually no resources, yet when deportations started again, a small Jewish underground movement—a thousand fighters, perhaps, in a community of 70,000—took on the Nazis with a tiny arsenal of gasoline bombs, pistols, and ten rifles. The Nazis responded by burning the ghetto to the ground and executing and deporting to the camps nearly everyone who was left. Some 56,000 Jews died. "The Warsaw Ghetto is no more," reported the SS commander at the end. Word of the rising did spread, but the repression made it clear that the targets of Nazi extermination could choose only between death in the streets or death in the camps. Sustained resistance, as one person remarked, would have required "the prospect of victory."

The Holocaust claimed between 4.1 and 5.7 million Jewish lives. Even those numbers do not register the nearly total destruction of some cultures. In the Baltic states (Latvia and Lithuania), Germany, Czechoslovakia, Yugoslavia, and Poland, well over 80 percent of the long-established Jewish communities were annihilated. Elsewhere, the figures were closer to 50 percent. The Holocaust was part of a racial war and of an even longer period of ethnically motivated mass murder. Through both world wars and afterward ethnic and religious groups—Jews, Armenians, Poles, Serbian Orthodox, ethnic Germans—were hunted, massacred, and legally deported en masse. Hitler's government had planned to build a "new Europe," safe for ethnic Germans and their allies and secure against communism, on the graveyards of whole cultures.

TOTAL WAR: HOME FRONTS, THE WAR OF PRODUCTION, BOMBING, AND THE BOMB

The Second World War was a "total war." Even more than the First World War, it involved the combined efforts of whole populations, massive resources, and a mobilization of entire economies within combatant nations. Standards of living changed around the world. In the neutral nations of Latin America, which supplied vast amounts of raw materials to the Allies, wartime profits led to a wave of prosperity known as the "dance of the millions." In the lands occupied by Germany or Japan, economies of forced extraction robbed local areas of resources, workers, and even food. In East Asia, deprivations caused rising resentment of the Japanese, who had been seen initially as liberators ending the rule of the old colonial powers. In the United States, Detroit produced no new models of car or truck between 1940 and 1945. Work schedules were grueling. Women and the elderly, pressed back into wage work or working for the first time, put in long shifts (in Britain and Russia, these sometimes ran over twelve hours) before returning home to cook, clean, and care for families and neighbors also affected by enemy bombing and wartime shortages. Diets changed. Though Germany lived comfortably off the farmlands of Europe for several years and the United States could lean on its huge agricultural base, food, gasoline, and basic household goods were still rationed. In occupied Europe and the Soviet Union, rations were just above starvation level and sometimes fell below in areas near the fighting. Britain, dependent on its empire and other overseas sources for food and raw materials, ran a comprehensive

rationing system that kept up production and ensured a drab but consistent diet on the table.

Production—the industrial ability to churn out more tanks, tents, planes, bombs, and uniforms than the other side—was essential to winning the war. Britain, the Soviet Union, and America each launched comprehensive, well-designed propaganda campaigns that encouraged the production of war equipment on an unmatched scale. Appeals to patriotism, to communal interests, and to a common stake in winning the war struck a chord. The Allied societies proved willing to regulate themselves and commit to the effort. Despite strikes and disputes with government officials, the Allied powers devoted more of their economies to war production, more efficiently, than any nations in history. They built tanks, ships, and planes capable of competing with advanced German and Japanese designs by the tens of thousands, swamping the enemy with constant reinforcements and superior firepower. Japan nearly reached comparable levels of production but then slowly declined, as Allied advances on land and American subma-

"JUST A GOOD AFTERNOON'S WORK!" A British poster mobilizing women for part-time factory work.

rines cut off overseas sources of vital supplies. Germany, despite its reputation for efficiency and its access to vast supplies of slave labor, was less efficient in its use of workers and materials than the Allied nations. The Germans' ability to produce devastatingly successful weapons led to a damaging side effect—vast amounts of money and time spent developing the pet projects of high-ranking Nazi officials or trying to make unsuccessful designs work. Rather than losing time and resources pursuing perfection, the Allies developed working, standard designs and produced them in overwhelming numbers.

Because industry was essential to winning the war, centers of industry became vital military targets. The Allies began bombing German ports and factories almost as soon as the Germans started their own campaigns. Over time, American and British planners became equally ruthless on an even larger scale. Both of these Allied nations made a major commitment to strategic bombing, developing new planes and technology that allowed them to put thousands of bombers in the air both night and day over occupied Europe. As the war wore on and Germany kept fighting, the Allies expanded their campaign. They moved from pinpoint bombing of the military and industry in Germany to striking such targets across all of occupied Europe and bombing Germany's civilian population in earnest. For the British, despite a public debate about the morality of bombing, it was a war of retribution; for the Americans, it was an effort to grind the Germans down without sacrificing too many Allied lives. The Allies killed tens of thousands of German civilians as they struck Berlin, ports such as Hamburg, and the industrial cities of the Ruhr, but German war production persisted. At the same time, German fighter planes shot down hundreds of Allied bombers, causing heavy losses. After the Allied invasion of Europe, bombing expanded well beyond targets of military value. The German city of Dresden, a center of culture and education that lacked heavy industry, was firebombed with a horrifying death toll. This gave Allied generals and politicians pause, but strategic bombing continued. German industry was slowly degraded, but the German will to keep fighting, like Britain's or the Soviet Union's, remained intact.

The Race to Build the Bomb

Allied scientists in the United States also developed the world's first nuclear weapon during the war years, a bomb that worked by splitting the atom, creating a chain reaction that could release tremendous energy in an explosion. Physicists in Britain and Germany first suggested that such a weapon might be possible, but only the United States had the resources to build such a bomb before the end of the war. A group of physicists at the University of Chicago, under the leadership of Enrico Fermi and including many refugees from fascist regimes in Europe, built the world's first nuclear reactor. In December 1942, Fermi and his group staged the first controlled chain reaction at the site. Fearful that the Germans would develop a bomb of their own, the U.S. government built a laboratory at Los Alamos, New Mexico, and charged the physicists to build an atomic bomb. Physicist J. Robert Oppenheimer directed the top-secret plan, known to the researchers as the Manhattan Project. The idea was to perfect a bomb that could be dropped by plane and detonated above the target. The physicists successfully tested a device on July 16, 1945, in New Mexico, vaporizing the test tower in a wave of heat and fire that rose in a mushroom shape overhead. The United States now possessed the most destructive weapon ever devised.

THE ALLIED COUNTERATTACK AND THE DROPPING OF THE ATOMIC BOMB

Hitler had invaded the Soviet Union in June 1941. Within two years, the war in the East had become his undoing; within four years, it brought about his destruction.

The early successes of the German-led invasion were crippling. Nearly 90 percent of the Soviets' tanks, most of their aircraft, and huge stores of supplies were destroyed or captured. Nazi forces penetrated deep into European Russia. The Soviets fought regardless. By late 1941, German and Finnish forces had cut off and besieged Leningrad (St. Petersburg). Yet the city held out for 844 days—through three winters, massive destruction by artillery and aircraft, and periods of starvation—until a large relief force broke the siege. Russian partisans stepped up their campaigns of ambush and terrorism, and many of the Germans' former allies in Ukraine and elsewhere turned against them in reaction to Nazi pacification efforts.

The Eastern Front

In the East, the character of the war changed as Russians rallied to defend the *rodina*, the Russian motherland. Stalin's efforts were aided by the weather—successive winters took a heavy toll in German lives. At the same time, Soviet industry made an astonishing recovery during the war years. Whole industries were rebuilt behind the safety of the Ural mountains and entire urban populations were sent to work in them, turning out tanks, fighter planes, machine guns, and ammunition. Finally, the Germans were the victims of their own success with their *Blitzkrieg* tactics, as their lines extended deep into Russian territory, spreading their forces more thinly, and opening them up to attack from unexpected angles.

The turning point came in 1942–43, when the Germans attempted to take Stalingrad, in an effort to break the back of Soviet industry. The Russians drew the invading army into the city where they were bogged down in house-to-house fighting that neutralized the German tanks and gave the outnumbered Soviet forces greater chances of success, despite their lack of equipment. The Germans found their supplies running low as winter set in, and in November 1942 large Russian armies encircled the city and besieged the invaders in a battle that continued through a cruel winter. At the end of January 1943, the German commander defied his orders and surrendered. More than a half million German, Italian, and Romanian soldiers had been killed; Russian casualties were over a million, including a hundred thousand civilians.

After Stalingrad, a series of Soviet attacks drove the Germans back toward the frontier and beyond. In what may have been the largest battle ever fought, Soviet armies destroyed a German force at Kursk in the summer of 1943—the battle involved over 6,000 tanks and 2 million men. Following this victory, the Russians launched a major offensive into Ukraine, and by the spring of 1944 Ukraine was back in Soviet hands. Meanwhile, Leningrad was liberated and Romania forced to capitulate. Soviet armies

PRISONERS OF WAR. Over 90,000 captured German troops were forced to march through the streets of Stalingrad after a defeat by the Soviet forces. The combination of the battle and the Russian winter resulted in the German loss of over 300,000 men.

entered the Balkans where they met with Tito's partisans in Yugoslavia. In Poland, successive German armies collapsed, and the Soviets, joined by communist partisans from eastern Europe, retook large parts of Czechoslovakia. Hitler's ambitious goal of conquest in the East had brought the downfall of the Nazi regime and death to another generation of German soldiers.

The Western Front

When the Nazis invaded Russia, Stalin called on the Allies to open a second front in the West. In response, the Americans led an attack on Italy in 1943, beginning with an invasion of Sicily in July. Italy's government deposed Mussolini and surrendered in the summer of 1943 while the nation collapsed into civil war. Italian partisans, especially the communists, sided with the Americans, while dedicated fascists fought on. The Germans occupied Italy with more than a dozen elite divisions, and the hard-fought and bitter campaign with American and British forces lasted eighteen months.

The most important second front was opened on June 6, 1944, with the massive Allied landings in Normandy. Casualties were high, but careful planning and deception allowed the Allied invasion to gain a foothold in northern Europe, eventually leading to breakthrough of the German lines. A second landing in southern France also succeeded, aided by the resistance. By August, these Allied armies had liberated Paris and pushed into Belgium. In

STORMING "FORTRESS EUROPE." American troops landing on Omaha Beach June 6, 1944. In the three months that followed, the Allies poured more than 2 million men, almost a half million vehicles, and 4 million tons of supplies onto the Continent—a measure of how firmly the Germans were established.

the fall, the Germans managed to defeat a British airborne invasion in the Netherlands and an American thrust into the Rhineland forests before mounting a devastating attack in December 1944, in the Battle of the Bulge. The Allied lines nearly broke, but the American forces held long enough for a crushing counterattack. In April 1945, the Allies crossed the Rhine into Germany, and the last defenders of the German Reich were swiftly overwhelmed. This military success was helped by the fact that most Germans preferred to surrender to Americans or Britons than face the Russians to the east.

Those Soviet troops were approaching fast. The Russian army took Prague and Vienna, and by late April they reached the suburbs of Berlin. In the savage ten-day battle to take the German capital more than 100,000 Russians and Germans died. Adolf Hitler killed himself in a bunker beneath the Chancellery on April 30. On May 2, the heart of the city was captured, and the Soviets' red banner flew from the Brandenburg Gate. On May 7, the German high command signed a document of unconditional surrender. The war in Europe was over.

The War in the Pacific

The war in the Pacific ended four months later. The British pushed the Japanese out of Burma while the Germans were surrendering in the West, and soon after, Australian forces recaptured the Dutch East Indies. In the fall of 1944, the U.S. Navy had destroyed most of Japan's surface ships in the gulfs of the Philippine Islands, and American troops took

Manila house by house in bloody fighting. The remaining battles—amphibious assaults on a series of islands running toward the Japanese mainland—were just as brutal. Japanese pilots mounted suicide attacks on American ships while American marines and Japanese soldiers fought over

THE ATOM BOMB. A mushroom cloud hovers over Nagasaki after the city was bombed. Hiroshima was bombed three days earlier.

The Atomic Bomb and Its Implications

In July 1945, scientists associated with the Manhattan Project became involved in debates about how the atomic bomb could be deployed. Members of the Scientific Panel of the secretary of war's Interim Advisory Committee agreed that a bomb could be used militarily but disagreed about whether it could be used without prior warning and demonstration. Other groups of scientists secretly began to circulate petitions, such as the one reprinted here, in which they set out their views. The petitions never reached the president, but they raised issues that did emerge in the postwar period.

In the section of his memoirs reprinted here, President Harry S Truman sets out the views of other scientists on the secretary of war's advisory committee. He explains the logic of his decision to use the atomic bomb against Hiroshima (August 6, 1945) and Nagasaki (August 9, 1945) and the events as they unfolded.

A Petition to the President of the United States

July 17, 1945

A PETITION TO THE PRESIDENT OF THE UNITED STATES

We, the undersigned scientists, have been working in the field of atomic power. Until recently we have had to fear that the United States might be attacked by atomic bombs during this war and that her only defense might lie in a counterattack by the same means. Today, with the defeat of Germany, this danger is averted and we feel impelled to say what follows:

The war has to be brought speedily to a successful conclusion and attacks by atomic bombs may very well be an effective method of warfare. We feel, however, that such attacks on Japan could not be justified, at least not unless the terms which will be imposed after the war on Japan were made public in detail and Japan were given an opportunity to surrender. . . .

[I]f Japan still refused to surrender our nation might then, in certain circumstances, find itself forced to resort to the use of atomic bombs. Such a step, however, ought not to be made at any time without seriously considering the moral responsibilities which are involved.

The development of atomic power will provide the nations with new means of destruction. The atomic bombs at our disposal represent only the first step in this direction, and there is almost no limit to the destructive power which will become available in the course of their future development. Thus a nation which sets the precedent of using these newly liberated forces of nature for purposes of destruction may have to bear the responsibility of opening the door to an era of devastation on an unimaginable scale.

If after this war a situation is allowed to develop in the world which permits rival powers to be in uncontrolled possession of these new means of destruction, the cities of the United States as well as the cities of other nations will be in continuous danger of sudden annihilation. . . .

The added material strength which this lead [in the field of atomic power] gives to the United States brings with it the obligation of restraint and if we were to violate this obligation our moral position would be weakened in the eyes of the world and in our own eyes. It would then be more difficult for us to

live up to our responsibility of bringing the unloosened forces of destruction under control.

In view of the foregoing, we, the undersigned, respectfully petition: first, that you exercise your power as Commander-in-Chief, to rule that the United States shall not resort to the use of atomic bombs in this war unless the terms which will be imposed upon Japan have been made public in detail and Japan knowing these terms has refused to surrender; second, that in such an event the question of whether or not to use atomic bombs be decided by you in the light of the considerations presented in this petition as well as all the other moral responsibilities which are involved.

Source: Michael B. Stoff, Jonathan F. Fanton, and R. Hal Williams, eds., *The Manhattan Project: A Documentary Introduction to the Atomic Age* (New York: 2000), p. 173.

President Truman's Memoirs

I had realized, of course, that an atomic bomb explosion would inflict damage and casualties beyond imagination. On the other hand, the scientific advisers of the committee reported, "We can propose no technical demonstration likely to bring an end to the war; we see no acceptable alternative to direct military use." It was their conclusion that no technical demonstration they might propose, such as over a deserted island, would be likely to bring the war to an end. It had to be used against an enemy target.

The final decision of where and when to use the atomic bomb was up to me. Let there be no mistake about it. I regarded the bomb as a military weapon and never had any doubt that it should be used. The top military advisers to the President recommended its use, and when I talked to Churchill he unhesitatingly told me that he favored the use of the atomic bomb if it might aid to end the war.

In deciding to use this bomb I wanted to make sure that it would be used as a weapon of war in the manner prescribed by the laws of war. That meant that I wanted it dropped on a military target. I had told Stimson that the bomb should be dropped as nearly as possibly upon a war production center of prime military importance.

Stimson's staff had prepared a list of cities in Japan that might serve as targets. Kyoto, though favored by General Arnold as a center of military activity, was eliminated when Secretary Stimson pointed out that it was a cultural and religious shrine of the Japanese.

Four cities were finally recommended as targets: Hiroshima, Kokura, Niigata, and Nagasaki. They were listed in that order as targets for the first attack. The order of selection was in accordance with the military importance of these cities, but allowance would be given for weather conditions at the time of the bombing. Before the selected targets were approved as proper for military purposes, I personally went over them in detail with Stimson, Marshall, and Arnold, and we discussed the matter of timing and the final choice of the first target. . . .

On August 6, the fourth day of the journey home from Potsdam, came the historic news that shook the world. I was eating lunch with members of the *Augusta's* crew when Captain Frank Graham, White House Map Room watch officer, handed me the following message:

To the President from the
Secretary of War

Big bomb dropped on Hiroshima August 5 at 7:15 P.M. Washington time. First reports indicate complete success which was even more conspicuous than earlier test.

I was greatly moved. I telephoned Byrnes aboard ship to give him the news and then said to the group of sailors around me, "This is the greatest thing in history. It's time for us to get home."

Source: Harry S. Truman, *Memoirs*, vol. 1, *Year of Decisions* (Garden City, NY: 1955), pp. 419–21.

Questions for Analysis

1. To express their fears about how the atomic bomb would be used, scientists circulated petitions. Look at the outcomes the scientists proposed. Which came closest to subsequent events? Which was the most prudent? The most honest?

2. Is it appropriate for scientists to propose how new weapons should be used? Are they overreaching in trying to give advice in foreign affairs and military strategy? Or are they obligated to voice moral qualms?

every inch of the shell-blasted rocks in the Pacific. Okinawa fell to the Americans after eighty-two days of desperate fighting, giving the United States a foothold less than 500 miles from the Japanese home islands. The government in Tokyo called on its citizens to defend the nation against an invasion.

On July 26, the U.S., British, and Chinese governments jointly called on Japan to surrender or be destroyed. The United States had already been using long-range B-29 bombers in systematic attacks on Japanese cities, killing hundreds of thousands of Japanese civilians in firestorms produced by incendiary bombs. When the Japanese government refused to surrender, the United States decided to use its atomic bomb.

Many senior military and naval officers argued that the use of the bomb was not necessary, on the assumption that Japan was already beaten. Some of the scientists involved, who had done their part to defeat the Nazis, believed that using the bomb for political ends would set a deadly precedent. Harry Truman, who became president when Roosevelt died in April 1945, decided otherwise. On August 6, a single American plane dropped an atomic bomb on Hiroshima, obliterating 60 percent of the city. Three days later, the United States dropped a second bomb on Nagasaki. On August 14, Japan surrendered unconditionally.

The decision to use the bomb was extraordinary. It did not greatly alter the American plans for the destruction of Japan—in fact many more Japanese died in the earlier fire bombings than in the two atomic blasts. Yet the bomb was an entirely new kind of weapon, revealing a new and terrifying relationship between science and political power. The instant, total devastation of the blasts, and the lingering effects of cancerous radiation that could claim victims decades later was something terribly new. The world now had a weapon that could destroy not just cities and peoples, but humanity itself.

CONCLUSION

After the First World War, many Europeans awoke to find a world they no longer recognized. In 1945, many Europeans came out from shelters or began the long trips back to their homes, faced with a world that hardly existed at all. The products of industry—tanks, submarines, strategic bombing—had destroyed the structures of industrial society—factories, ports, and railroads. The tools of mass culture—fascist and communist appeals, patriotism proclaimed via radios and movie screens, mobilization of mass armies and industry—had been put to full use. In the after-

After You Read This Chapter

(S) Visit StudySpace for quizzes, additional review materials, and multimedia documents. **wwnorton.com/web/westernciv18**

REVIEWING THE OBJECTIVES

- The Second World War stemmed from the political and economic crises of the 1930s. What caused the war?
- British and French leaders in the 1930s hoped to avoid another war in Europe through diplomatic negotiation with Hitler. What were the consequences of these negotiations?
- The populations of nations occupied by the Germans faced a difficult set of choices. What were the consequences of occupation for European nations, and what possibilities existed for resistance?
- The mass murder of European Jews, homosexuals, and Gypsies reached a climax during the invasion of the Soviet Union, though the victims came from every corner of Europe. What efforts did this enormous project entail, and how did it come about?
- The Nazi regime and their allies eventually collapsed after costly defeats in both eastern and western Europe. Where and when did the major defeats take place, and what was their human cost?
- The Japanese government surrendered in August 1945 after the United States dropped two atomic bombs, on Hiroshima and Nagasaki. What events led to the decision to drop these bombs, and what were their consequences?

math, much of Europe lay destroyed and, as we will see, vulnerable to the rivalry of the postwar superpowers: the United States and the Soviet Union.

The two world wars profoundly affected Western empires. Nineteenth-century imperialism had made twentieth-century war a global matter. In both conflicts the warring nations had used the resources of empire to their fullest. Key campaigns, in North Africa, Burma, Ethiopia, and the Pacific, were fought in and over colonial territories. Hundreds of thousands of colonial troops—sepoys and Gurkhas from India and Nepal, Britain's King's African Rifles, French from Algeria and West Africa—served in armies on both sides of the conflict. After two massive mobilizations, many anticolonial leaders found renewed confidence in their own peoples' courage and resourcefulness, and they seized the opportunity of European weakness to press for independence. In many areas that had been under European or Japanese imperial control, from sections of China to Korea, Indochina, Indonesia, and Palestine—the end of the Second World War only paved the way for a new round of conflict. This time, the issue was when imperial control would be ended, and by whom.

The Second World War also carried on the Great War's legacy of massive killing. Historians estimate that nearly 50 million people died. The killing fields of the east took the highest tolls: 25 million Soviet lives. Of those, 8.5 million were in the military, and the rest civilians; 20 percent of the Polish population and nearly 90 percent of the Polish Jewish community; 1 million Yugoslavs, including militias of all sides; 4 million German soldiers and 500,000 German civilians, not including the hundreds of thousands of ethnic Germans who died while being deported west at the end of the war, in one of the many acts of ethnic cleansing that ran through the period. Even the United States, shielded from the full horrors of total war by two vast oceans, lost 292,000 soldiers in battle and more to accidents or disease.

Why was the war so murderous? The advanced technology of modern industrial war and the openly genocidal ambitions of the Nazis offer part of the answer. The global reach of the conflict offers another. Finally, the Second World War overlapped with, and eventually devolved into, a series of smaller, no less bitter conflicts: a civil war in Greece; conflicts among Orthodox, Catholics, and Muslims in Yugoslavia; and political battles for control of the French resistance. Even when those struggles claimed fewer lives, they left deep political scars. So did memories of the war. Hitler's empire could not have lasted as long as it did without active collaboration or passive acquiescence from many, a fact that produced bitterness and recrimination for years.

PEOPLE, IDEAS, AND EVENTS IN CONTEXT

- What was Hitler asking for at the **MUNICH CONFERENCE** of 1938, and what made many people in Europe think that **APPEASEMENT** was their best option?
- What was the **HITLER-STALIN PACT** of 1939?
- What was *BLITZKRIEG*, and what effect did it have on those who faced Hitler's invasions?
- What were Hitler's goals in **OPERATION BARBAROSSA**, the invasion of the Soviet Union in 1941? What were the consequences of the German defeat at **STALINGRAD**?
- What made the **SECOND WORLD WAR** a global war? Where were the main consequences of the war felt most keenly outside of Europe?
- What was the **MANHATTAN PROJECT**, and how did it affect the outcome of the Second World War?

THINKING ABOUT CONNECTIONS

- What long-term causes going back to the history of Europe in the nineteenth century might one point to in order to understand the outbreak of the Second World War? Can one link the story of this war with the history of European imperialism in the nineteenth century? With the successes and failures of movements for German national unification?
- What circumstances made the Second World War a global conflict?

Before
You
Read
This
Chapter

STORY LINES

- Postwar Europeans looked to rebuild their shattered continent in the shadow of a cold war between the United States and the Soviet Union. The new international order sharply curtailed the ability of European nations to act independently.

- After 1945, European imperial powers faced a challenge from movements for national independence in Africa, the Middle East, and Asia. By the early 1960s, almost all of Britain's and France's colonies had gained their independence.

- Western European nations increasingly turned toward political and economic cooperation, leading to unprecedented economic growth in the 1950s and 1960s. In Eastern Europe the socialist regimes of the Eastern bloc sought to chart a different path under Soviet sponsorship, achieving more modest growth in economies that emphasized heavy industries more than the manufacture of consumer goods.

CHRONOLOGY

1946–1964	Twenty French colonies, eleven British colonies, Belgian Congo, and Dutch Indonesia become independent nations
1947	Truman Doctrine
1948	Soviets create the Eastern bloc
1948	Marshall Plan
1949	Chinese Revolution
1949	Formation of NATO
1950–1953	Korean War
1953–1956	Revolts in East Germany, Poland, and Hungary
1955	Formation of Warsaw Pact
1957	Treaty of Rome creates the European Economic Community (EEC, the Common Market)
1961	Building of the Berlin Wall
1964–1975	U.S. Vietnam War

The Cold War World: Global Politics, Economic Recovery, and Cultural Change

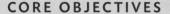

CORE OBJECTIVES

- **UNDERSTAND** the origins of the Cold War and the ways that the United States and the Soviet Union sought to influence the political and economic restructuring of Europe in the postwar period.

- **IDENTIFY** the policies that led to the economic integration of Western European nations in the postwar decades and the reasons for the rapid economic growth that accompanied this integration.

- **DESCRIBE** the process of decolonization that brought the colonial era in Africa and Asia to an end.

- **EXPLAIN** developments in European postwar culture, as intellectuals, writers, and artists reacted to the loss of European influence in the world and the ideological conflicts of the Cold War.

"The war ended the way a passage through a tunnel ends," wrote Heda Kovály, a Czech woman who survived the concentration camps. "From far away you could see the light ahead, a gleam that kept growing, and its brilliance seemed ever more dazzling to you huddled there in the dark the longer it took to reach it. But when at last the train burst out into the glorious sunshine, all you saw was a wasteland." The war left Europe a land of wreckage and confusion. Millions of refugees trekked hundreds or thousands of miles on foot to return to their homes while others were forcibly displaced from their lands. In some areas, housing was practically nonexistent, with no available means to build anew. Food remained in dangerously short supply; a year after the war, roughly 100 million people in Europe still lived on fewer than 1,500 calories per day. Families scraped vegetables from their gardens or traded smuggled goods on the black market. Governments continued to ration food, and without rationing, a large portion of the Continent's population would have starved. During the winter of 1945–46, many regions had little or no fuel for heat. What coal there was—less than half the prewar supply—could not be transported to the areas that needed it most. The brutality of international war, civil war, and occupation had divided countries against themselves, shredding relations among ethnic groups and fellow citizens. Ordinary people's intense relief at liberation often went hand in hand with recriminations over their neighbors' wartime betrayal, collaboration, or simple opportunism.

How does a nation, a region, or a civilization recover from a catastrophe on the scale of the Second World War? Nations had to do much more than deliver food and rebuild economic infrastructures. They had to restore—or create—government authority, functioning bureaucracies, and legitimate legal systems. They had to rebuild bonds of trust and civility between citizens, steering a course between demands for justice, on the one hand, and the overwhelming desire to bury memories of the past, on the other. On the contrary, rebuilding entailed a commitment to renewing democracy—to creating democratic institutions that could withstand threats such as those the West had experienced in the 1930s. Some aspects of this process were extraordinarily successful, more so than even the most optimistic forecaster might have thought possible in 1945. Others failed or were deferred until later in the century.

The war's devastating effects brought two dramatic changes in the international balance of power. The first change was the emergence of the so-called superpowers, the United States and the Soviet Union, and the swift development of a "cold war" between them. The Cold War divided Europe, with Eastern Europe occupied by Soviet troops, and Western Europe dominated by the military and economic presence of the United States. In both Western and Eastern Europe, the Cold War led to increased political and economic integration, resulting in the emergence of the European Common Market in the West and a socialist bloc dominated by the Soviet Union in the East. The second great change came with the dismantling of the European empires that had once stretched worldwide. The collapse of empires and the creation of newly emancipated nations raised the stakes in the Cold War and brought superpower rivalry to far-flung sections of the globe. Those events, which shaped the postwar recovery and necessarily created a new understanding of what "the West" meant, are the subject of this chapter.

THE COLD WAR AND A DIVIDED CONTINENT

No peace treaty ended the Second World War. Instead, as the war drew to a close, relations between the Allied powers began to fray over issues of power and influence in Central and Eastern Europe. After the war, they descended from mistrust to open conflict. The United States and Soviet Union rapidly formed the centers of two imperial blocs. Their rivalry, which came to be known as the Cold War, pitted against each other two military powers, two sets of state interests, and two ideologies: capitalism and communism. The Cold War's repercussions reached well beyond Europe, for anticolonial movements, sensing the weakness of European colonial powers, turned to the Soviets for help in their struggles for independence. The Cold War thus structured the peace, shaped international relations for four decades, and affected governments and peoples across the globe who depended on either of the superpowers.

The Iron Curtain

The Soviet Union had insisted during the wartime negotiations at Tehran (1943) and Yalta (1945) that it had a legitimate claim to control Eastern Europe, a claim that some Western

THE REMAINS OF DRESDEN, 1947. Dresden was devastated by a controversial Allied bombing in February 1945. Kurt Vonnegut dramatically portrayed its destruction and the aftermath in his novel *Slaughterhouse-Five.* ■ *How did the war's new strategies of aerial bombardment—culminating in the use of atomic weapons—change the customary division between combatants and noncombatant civilians?*

Legend:
- Allied occupation of Germany and Austria, 1945–1955
- Territory lost by Germany
- Territory gained by Soviet Union
- Postwar national boundaries, to 1989
- "Iron Curtain" to 1989
- 1945 Year Communist control of government was gained

EAST GERMANY inset:
French Sector · British Sector · U.S. Sector · Soviet Sector
WEST BERLIN · EAST BERLIN
Potsdam
Berlin Wall (1961–1989)
0   10 Miles
0   10 Kilometers

Map labels:
FINLAND · From Finland, 1940–1956 · NORWAY · Oslo · SWEDEN · Helsinki · Leningrad · Stockholm · ESTONIA To U.S.S.R., 1940 · LATVIA To U.S.S.R., 1940 · LITHUANIA To U.S.S.R., 1940 · NORTH SEA · BALTIC SEA · DENMARK · Copenhagen · Incorporated into U.S.S.R., 1945 · Gdansk (Danzig) · Incorporated into Poland, 1945 · WHITE RUSSIA · Brest · From Poland, 1940–1947 · NETHERLANDS · Amsterdam · U.S. Zone · Bremen · British Zone · Soviet Zone · Berlin · EAST GERMANY (1949) · Warsaw · POLAND (1947) · UKRAINE · From Czechoslovakia, 1945–1947 · Brussels · BELGIUM · Bonn · French Zone · WEST GERMANY · U.S. Zone · Prague · CZECHOSLOVAKIA (1948) · From Romania, 1940–1947 · LUXEMBOURG · Munich · U.S. Zone · Vienna · Soviet Zone · AUSTRIA British Zone · HUNGARY (1949) · Budapest · BESSARABIA · SWITZERLAND · Bern · French Zone · From Italy, 1945 · ROMANIA (1947) · CRIMEA · Milan · Yalta · BLACK SEA · YUGOSLAVIA (1945) · Bucharest · Danube R. · From Romania, 1940–1947 · ADRIATIC SEA · CORSICA (Fr.) · ITALY · Rome · BULGARIA (1946) · Sofia · Tirane · ALBANIA (1944) · Istanbul · SARDINIA (It.) · GREECE · TURKEY · Athens · SICILY (It.) · CRETE · CYPRUS · MEDITERRANEAN SEA

SOVIET UNION (1917)

0   200   400 Miles
0   200   400 Kilometers

EUROPE / AFRICA inset: Area of detail

TERRITORIAL CHANGES IN EUROPE AFTER THE SECOND WORLD WAR. At the end of the Second World War, the Soviet Union annexed territory in Eastern Europe to create a buffer between it and Western Europe. At the same time, the United States established a series of military alliances in Western Europe to stifle the spread of communism in Europe. ▪ *What Eastern European countries fell under Russian control?* ▪ *Where is Berlin located, and why did its location and control cause so much tension?* ▪ *How did these new territorial boundaries aggravate the tensions between the Soviet Union and the United States?*

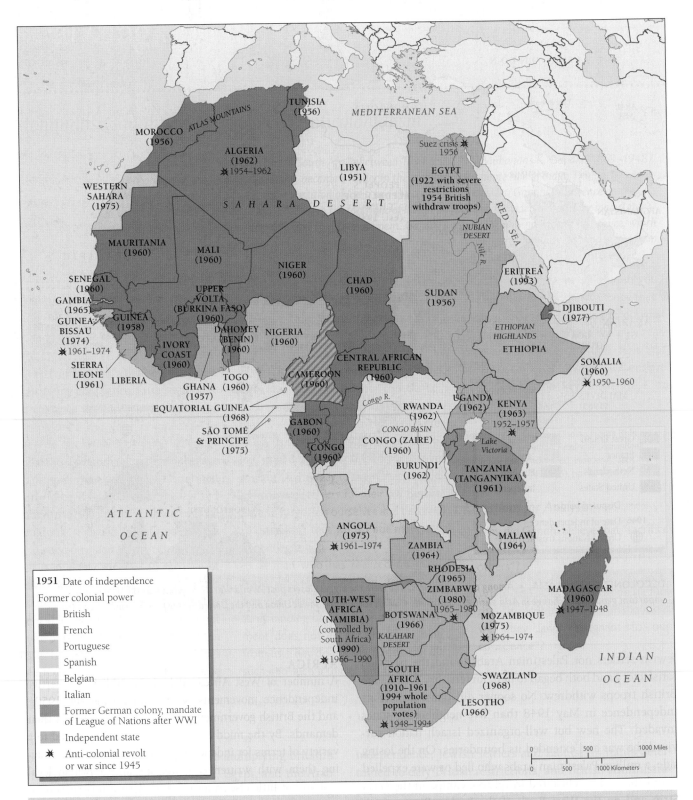

DECOLONIZATION OF AFRICA. ▪ *Who were the biggest imperial losers in the decolonization of Africa?* ▪ *By what decade had most African countries achieved their independence?* ▪ *What were the forces behind decolonization in Africa?*

its president, Kwame Nkrumah, became the first of several African leaders driven from office for corruption and autocratic behavior.

Belgium and France also withdrew from their holdings. By 1965, virtually all of the former African colonies had become independent, and virtually none of them possessed the means to redress losses from colonialism to make that independence work. As Belgian authorities raced out of the Congo in 1960, they left crumbling railways and fewer than two dozen indigenous people with college educations.

The process of decolonization was relatively peaceful—except where large populations of European settlers complicated European withdrawal. In the north, settler resistance made the French exit from Algeria wrenching and complex (discussed below). In the east, in Kenya, the majority Kikuyu population revolted against British rule and against a small group of settlers. The uprising, which came to be known as the Mau Mau rebellion, soon turned bloody. British troops fired freely at targets in rebel-occupied areas, sometimes killing civilians. Internment camps set up by colonial security forces became sites of atrocities that drew public investigations and condemnation by even the most conservative British politicians and army officers. In 1963, a decade after the rebellion began, the British conceded Kenyan independence.

In the late 1950s, the British prime minister Harold Macmillan endorsed independence for a number of Britain's African colonies as a response to powerful winds of change. In southern Africa, the exceptionally large and wealthy population of European settlers set their sails against those winds, a resistance that continued on for decades. These settlers, a mixture of English migrants and the Franco-Dutch Afrikaners who traced their arrival to the eighteenth century, controlled huge tracts of fertile farmland along with some of the most lucrative gold and diamond mines on earth. This was especially true in South Africa. There, during the late 1940s, Britain's Labour government set aside its deep dislike of Afrikaner racism in a fateful political bargain. In return for guarantees that South African gold would be used carefully to support Britain's global financial power, Britain tolerated the introduction of apartheid in South Africa. Even by other standards of segregation, apartheid was especially harsh. Under its terms, Africans, Indians, and colored persons of mixed descent lost all political rights. All the institutions of social life, including marriage and schools, were segregated. What was more, the government tried to block the dramatic social consequences of the expansion of mining and industrialization in general, especially African migration to cities and a new wave of labor militancy in the mines. Apartheid required Africans to live in designated "homelands," forbade them to travel without specific permits, and created elaborate government bureaus to manage the labor essential to the economy. The government also banned any political protest. These measures made Western powers uncomfortable with the segregationist regime, but white South Africans held on to American support by presenting themselves as a bulwark against communism.

To the north, in the territories of Rhodesia, the British government encouraged a large federation, controlled by white settlers but with the opportunity for majority rule in the future. By the early 1960s, however, the federation was on the verge of collapse; the majority-rule state of Malawi was allowed to exit the federation in 1964, and Rhodesia split on northern and southern lines. In the north, the premier relented and accepted majority government under the black populist Kenneth Kaunda. In the south, angry Afrikaners backed by 200,000 right-wing English migrants who had arrived since 1945 refused to accept majority rule. When the British government attempted to force their hand, the settlers unilaterally declared independence in 1965 and began a bloody civil war against southern Rhodesia's black population that lasted a half generation.

CRISIS IN SUEZ AND THE END OF AN ERA

For postwar Britain, empire was not only politically complicated but cost too much. Britain began to withdraw from naval and air bases around the world because they had become too expensive to maintain. The Labour government did try to maintain British power and prestige in the postwar world. In Malaya, British forces repressed a revolt by ethnic Chinese communists and then helped support the independent states of Singapore and Malaysia, maintaining British companies' and banks' ties with Malaysia's lucrative rubber and oil reserves. Labour also launched carefully targeted efforts at "colonial development" to tap local natural resources Britain hoped to sell on world markets. "Development," however, was underfunded and largely disregarded in favor of fulfilling Cold War commitments elsewhere. In the Middle East, the British government protected several oil-rich states with its military and helped overthrow a nationalist government in Iran to ensure that the oil states invested their money in British financial markets.

In Egypt, however, the British refused to yield a traditional point of imperial pride. In 1951, nationalists compelled the British to agree to withdraw their troops from Egyptian territory within three years. In 1952, a group of nationalist army officers deposed Egypt's King Farouk, who had close ties to Britain, and proclaimed a republic. Shortly after the final British withdrawal an Egyptian colonel, Gamal Abdel Nasser (1918–1970), became president of the country (1956–70). His first major public act as president was to nationalize the Suez Canal Company. So doing would help finance the construction of the Aswan Dam on the Nile, and both the dam and nationalizing the canal represented economic independence and Egyptian national pride. Nasser also helped develop the anticolonial ideology of pan-Arabism, proposing that Arab nationalists throughout the Islamic world should create an alliance of modern nations, no longer beholden to the West. Finally, Nasser was also willing to take aid and support from the Soviets to achieve that goal, which made the canal a Cold War issue.

Three nations found Nasser and his pan-Arab ideals threatening. Israel, surrounded on all sides by unfriendly neighbors, was looking for an opportunity to seize the strategic Sinai Peninsula and create a buffer against Egypt. France, already fighting a war against Algerian nationalists, hoped to destroy what it considered the Egyptian source of Arab nationalism. Britain depended on the canal as a route to its strategic bases and was stung by this blow to imperial dignity. Though the British were reluctant to intervene, they were urged on by their prime minister, Sir Anthony Eden; Eden had developed a deep personal hatred of Nasser. In the autumn of 1956, the three nations colluded in an attack on Egypt. Israel occupied the Sinai while British and French jets destroyed Egypt's air force on the ground. The former colonial powers landed troops at the mouth of the canal but lacked the resources to push on in strength toward Cairo. As a result the war left Nasser in power and made him a hero to the Egyptian public for holding the imperialists at bay. The attack was condemned around the world. The United States angrily called its allies' bluff, inflicting severe financial penalties on Britain and France. Both countries were forced to withdraw their expeditions. For policy makers in Great Britain and France, the failure at Suez marked the end of an era.

French Decolonization

In two particular cases, France's experience of decolonization was bloodier, more difficult, and more damaging to French prestige and domestic politics than any in Britain's experience, with the possible exception of Northern Ireland. The first was Indochina, where French efforts to restore imperial authority after losing it in the Second World War only resulted in military defeat and further humiliation. The second case, Algeria, became not only a violent colonial war but also a struggle with serious political ramifications at home.

THE FIRST VIETNAM WAR, 1946–1954

Indochina was one of France's last major imperial acquisitions in the nineteenth century. Here, as elsewhere, the two world wars had helped galvanize first nationalist and then, also, communist independence movements. In Indonesia, nationalist forces rebelled against Dutch efforts to restore colonialism, and the country became independent in 1949. In Indochina, the communist resistance became particularly effective under the leadership of Ho Chi Minh. Ho was French educated and, his expectations raised by the Wilsonian principles of self-determination, had hoped his country might win independence at Versailles in 1919 (see Chapter 24). He read Marx and Lenin and absorbed the Chinese communists' lessons about organizing peasants around social and agrarian as well as national issues. During the Second World War, Ho's movement fought first the Vichy government of the colony and later Japanese occupiers and provided intelligence reports for the Allies. In 1945, however, the United States and Britain repudiated their relationship with Ho's independence movement and allowed the French to reclaim their colonies throughout Southeast Asia. The Vietnamese communists, who were fierce nationalists as well as Marxists, renewed their guerrilla war against the French.

The fighting was protracted and bloody; France saw in it a chance to redeem its national pride. After one of France's most capable generals, Jean de Lattre de Tassigny, finally achieved a military advantage against the rebels in 1951, the French government might have decolonized on favorable terms. Instead, it decided to press on for total victory, sending troops deep into Vietnamese territory to root out the rebels. One major base was established in a valley bordering modern Laos, at a hamlet called Dien Bien Phu. Ringed by high mountains, this vulnerable spot became a base for thousands of elite French paratroopers and colonial soldiers from Algeria and West Africa—the best of France's troops. The rebels besieged the base. Tens of thousands of Vietnamese nationalist fighters hauled heavy artillery by hand up the mountainsides and bombarded the network of forts set up by the French. The siege lasted for months, becoming a protracted national crisis in France.

When Dien Bien Phu fell in May 1954, the French government began peace talks in Geneva. The Geneva Accords, drawn up by the French, Vietnamese politicians including the communists, the British, and the Americans, divided Indochina into three countries: Laos, Cambodia, and Vietnam, which was partitioned into two states. North Vietnam was taken over by Ho Chi Minh's party; South Vietnam by a succession of Western-supported politicians. Corruption, repression, and instability in the south, coupled with Ho

Analyzing Primary Sources

The Vietnam War: American Analysis of the French Situation

At the end of the Second World War, the French government sought to recoup its prestige and empire by reasserting control of the former colony of Indochina. The French faced fierce resistance from nationalist forces under the French-educated leader Ho Chi Minh. Within a few years, American advisers were beginning to shore up the faltering French army. Cold War ideology, anxiety about China and Korea, and a conviction that they could do what the French could not combined to draw the Americans more deeply into the war. In 1950, the Central Intelligence Agency drew up this analysis of the strategic situation.

or more than three years, an intense conflict has been in progress in Indochina in which nationalistic Vietnamese forces under the leadership of the Moscow-trained revolutionist, Ho Chi Minh, have opposed the reimposition of French authority. Within Vietnam . . . a precarious military balance exists between the French and their Vietnamese followers on the one hand and Ho's resistance forces on the other. Thus far, French progress toward both political and military objectives has been substantially less than is necessary to eliminate the threat to French tenure posed by the resistance.

The French position and Bao Dai's [emperor of Vietnam since 1926] prospects have recently been further weakened: politically by Chinese Communist and Soviet recognition of Ho Chi Minh, and militarily by the ability of the Chinese Communist forces to make military supplies available to Ho's forces. Unless the French and Bao Dai receive substantial outside assistance, this combined political and military pressure may accelerate a French withdrawal from all or most of Indochina which, previous to

the Chinese Communist and Soviet recognition of Ho, had been estimated as probably occurring within two years. . . .

The fighting in Indochina constitutes a progressive drain on French military resources which is weakening France as a partner in the Western alliance. If France is driven from Indochina, the resulting emergence of an indigenous Communist-oriented regime in Vietnam, in combination with the pressures which will be exerted by the new government of China and the Soviet Union, can be expected to cause adjacent Thailand and Burma to yield to this Communist advance. Under these conditions Malaya and Indonesia would also become highly vulnerable.

The French are trying to halt the present unfavorable trend by according certain aspects of sovereignty to Emperor Bao Dai. . . . The French political aim is to attract non-Communist nationalists from the leadership of Ho Chi Minh to that of Bao Dai.

Meanwhile, Soviet and Chinese Communist recognition of Ho's regime has made it clear that the Kremlin is now prepared to exert greater pressure to achieve its objective of installing a Communist regime in Indochina. France

alone is incapable of preventing such a development and can turn only to the US for assistance in thwarting this Communist strategy. Having already publicly proclaimed support of Bao Dai, the US is now faced with the choice of bolstering his weak and vulnerable position or of abandoning him and accepting the far-reaching consequences of Communist control of Indochina.

Source: National Archives, College Park, MD. Record Group 263 (Records of the Central Intelligence Agency), *Estimates of the Office of Research Evaluation, 1946–1950*, box 4.

Questions for Analysis

1. Explain how the author of this CIA report has used George Kennan's policy of containment. What would happen if the French military forces withdrew? Why was Southeast Asia such a hot spot in the decade following the Second World War?

2. Did the French or American military, just coming off a European theater of war, have any idea what it would be like to wage war in a place like Southeast Asia?

"DIEN-BIEN-PHU . . . THEY SACRIFICED THEMSELVES FOR LIBERTY." The sentiments expressed in this poster, which was intended to commemorate the French soldiers who died at Dien Bien Phu in May 1954, helped to deepen French commitments to colonial control in Algeria.

Chi Minh's nationalist desire to unite Vietnam, guaranteed that the war would continue. The U.S. government, which had provided military and financial aid to the French, began to send aid to the South Vietnamese regime. The Americans saw the conflict through the prism of the Cold War: their project was not to restore colonialism but to contain communism and prevent it from spreading through Southeast Asia. The limits of this policy would not become clear until the mid-1960s.

ALGERIA

Still reeling from the humiliation of Dien Bien Phu, France faced a complex colonial problem closer to home, in Algeria. Since the 1830s, the colony had evolved into a settler society of three social groups. First, in addition to a small class of French soldiers and administrators, there were also 1 million European settlers. They typically owned farms and vineyards near the major cities or formed the working-class and merchant communities inside those cities. All of them were citizens of the three administrative districts of Algeria, which were legally part of France. The community produced some of France's best-known writers and intellectuals: Albert Camus, Jacques Derrida, and Pierre Bourdieu, among others. In the small towns and villages of Algeria lived a second group of (largely Muslim) Berbers, whose long history of service in the French army entitled them to certain formal and informal privileges within the colony. Finally, there were millions of Muslim Arabs, some living in the desert south but most crowded into impoverished neighborhoods in the cities. The Arabs were the largest and most deprived group in Algerian society. Between the world wars the French government had offered small reforms to increase their rights and representation, and it had hoped to meld the three groups into a common Algerian society. Reforms came too late and were also undercut by European settlers anxious to maintain their privileges.

At the end of the Second World War, Algerian nationalists called on the Allies to recognize Algeria's independence in return for good service during the war. Public demonstrations became frequent and in several cases turned into attacks on settler-landowners. In one rural town, Setif, celebrations of the defeat of Germany flared into violence against settlers. French repression was harsh and immediate: security forces killed several thousand Arabs. After the war, the French government approved a provincial assembly for all of Algeria, elected by two pools of voters, one made up of settlers and mostly Berber Muslims, the other of Arabs. This very limited enfranchisement gave Arab Algerians no political power. The more important changes were economic. All of Algeria suffered in the difficulties after the war. Many Arab Algerians felt they had to emigrate; several hundred thousand went to work in France. While

COUNTERINSURGENCY IN ALGERIA. An Algerian POW imprisoned by the French in a cellar for animals during the Algerian War of Independence, 1961.

citizens of mainland France read their papers and frowned over the war in Indochina, the situation in Algeria grew more serious. By the middle of the 1950s, a younger generation of Arab activists, unhappy with the leadership of the moderates, had taken charge of a movement dedicated to independence by force. The National Liberation Front (FLN) was organized, which leaned toward socialism and demanded equal citizenship for all.

The war in Algeria became a war on three fronts. The first was a guerrilla war between the regular French Army and the FLN, fought in the mountains and deserts of the country. This war continued for years, a clear military defeat for the FLN but never a clear-cut victory for the French. The second war, fought out in Algeria's cities, began with an FLN campaign of bombing and terrorism. European civilians were killed, and the French administration retaliated with its own campaign. French paratroopers hunted down and destroyed the networks of FLN bombers. The information that allowed the French to break the FLN network was extracted through systematic torture conducted by French security forces. The torture became an international scandal, bringing waves of protest in France. This third front of the Algerian war divided France, brought down the government, and ushered de Gaulle back into power.

De Gaulle visited Algiers to wild cheering from settlers and declared that Algeria would always be French. After another year of violence, he and his advisers had changed their minds. By 1962, talks had produced a formula for independence: a referendum would be held, voted on by the whole population of Algeria. On July 1, 1962, the referendum passed by a landslide vote. Arab political groups and guerrillas from the FLN entered Algiers in triumph. Settlers and Berbers who had fought for the French army fled Algeria for France by the hundreds of thousands. Later, these refugees were joined in France by another influx of Arab economic migrants.

Algeria illustrated the dramatic domestic impact of decolonization. The war cut deep divides through French society, largely because the very identity of France seemed at stake. Withdrawing from Algeria meant reorienting French views of what it meant to be a modern power. De Gaulle summed up the trade-off in his memoirs: to stay in Algeria would "keep France politically, financially, and militarily bogged down in a bottomless quagmire when, in fact, she needed her hands free to bring about the domestic transformation necessitated by the twentieth century and to exercise her influence abroad unencumbered." In France and other imperial powers, the conclusions seemed clear. Traditional forms of colonial rule could not withstand the demands of postwar politics and culture; the leading European nations, once distinguished by their empires, would

THE STRUGGLE FOR NATIONAL INDEPENDENCE IN ALGERIA. Ben Cherif, a commander in the FLN, handcuffed in 1961. ■ *How might this struggle for independence against the French have shaped the generation of political leaders who took power after decolonization?*

have to look for new forms of influence. The domestic transformation of which de Gaulle spoke—recovery from the war, economic restructuring, and political renewal—had to take place on a radically changed global stage.

POSTWAR CULTURE AND THOUGHT

The postwar period brought a remarkable burst of cultural production. Writers and artists did not hesitate to take up big issues: freedom, civilization, and the human condition itself. The search for democratic renewal gave this literature urgency; the moral dilemmas of war, occupation, and resistance gave it resonance and popular appeal. The process of decolonization, too, forced the issues of race, culture, and colonialism to center stage in Western debates.

The Black Presence

The journal *Présence Africaine* ("*African Presence*"), founded in Paris in 1947, was only one in a chorus of new cultural voices. *Présence Africaine* published such writers as Aimé

Analyzing Primary Sources

Anticolonialism and Violence

Born in the French Caribbean colony of Martinique, Frantz Fanon (1925–1961) studied psychiatry in France before moving on to work in Algeria in the early 1950s. Fanon became a member of the Algerian revolutionary National Liberation Front (FLN) and an ardent advocate of decolonization. Black Skin, White Masks, *published in 1952 with a preface by Jean-Paul Sartre, was a study of the psychological effects of colonialism and racism on black culture and individuals.* The Wretched of the Earth *(1961) was a revolutionary manifesto, one of the most influential of the period. Fanon attacked nationalist leaders for their ambition and corruption. He believed that revolutionary change could come only from poor peasants, those who "have found no bone to gnaw in the colonial system." Diagnosed with leukemia, Fanon sought treatment in the Soviet Union and then in Washington, DC, where he died.*

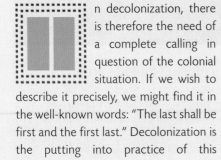n decolonization, there is therefore the need of a complete calling in question of the colonial situation. If we wish to describe it precisely, we might find it in the well-known words: "The last shall be first and the first last." Decolonization is the putting into practice of this sentence. . . .

The naked truth of decolonization evokes for us the searing bullets and bloodstained knives which emanate from it. For if the last shall be first, this will only come to pass after a murderous and decisive struggle between the two protagonists. That affirmed intention to place the last at the head of things, and to make them climb at a pace (too quickly, some say) the well-known steps which characterize an organized society, can only triumph if we use all means to turn the scale, including, of course, that of violence.

You do not turn any society, however primitive it may be, upside down with such a program if you have not decided from the very beginning, that is to say from the actual formation of that program, to overcome all the obstacles that you will come across in so doing. The native who decides to put the program into practice, and to become its moving force, is ready for violence at all time. From birth it is clear to him that this narrow world, strewn with prohibitions, can only be called in question by absolute violence.

Source: Frantz Fanon, *The Wretched of the Earth,* trans. Constance Farrington (New York: 1963), pp. 35–37.

Questions for Analysis

1. Why did Fanon believe that violence lay at the heart of both the colonial relationship and anticolonial movements?

2. What arguments would he offer to counter Gandhi?

Césaire (1913–2008), the surrealist poet from Martinique, and Léopold Senghor of Senegal (1906–2001). Césaire and Senghor were brilliant students, educated in the most elite French universities, and elected to the French National Assembly. Césaire became an important political figure in Martinique, a French Caribbean colony that became a department of France in 1946. In 1960, Senghor was elected the first president of Senegal. Both men, in important respects models of Frenchness, became the most influential exponents of *Négritude,* which could be translated as "black consciousness" or "black pride." Senghor wrote:

Assimilation was a failure. We could assimilate mathematics of the French language, but we could never strip off our black skins or root out black souls. And so we set out on a fervent quest for . . . our collective soul. Negritude is the whole complex of civilized values—cultural, economic, social and political—which characterize the black people.

Césaire's early work took its lead from surrealism and the exploration of consciousness. Later, his work became more political. *Discourse on Colonialism* (1950) was a powerful indictment of the material and spiritual squalor of colonialism, which, he argued, not only dehumanized colonial subjects but degraded the colonizers themselves.

Césaire's student Frantz Fanon (1925–1961), also from Martinique, went further. He argued that withdrawing into an insular black culture (as he interpreted Negritude) was not an effective response to racism. People of color, he believed, needed a theory of radical social change. Fanon trained in psychiatry and worked in Algeria, where he became a member of the National Liberation Front. In *Black Skin, White Masks* (1952), he examined the effects of colonialism and racism from the point of view of a radical psychiatrist. *The Wretched of the Earth* (1961) became one of the most influential revolutionary manifestos of the period. More than Césaire, and bluntly rejecting Gandhi's theories and practice, Fanon argued that violence was rooted in colonialism and, therefore, in anticolonial movements. But he also believed that many anticolonial leaders would be corrupted by their ambition and by collaboration with former colonial powers. Revolutionary change, he believed, could come only from poor peasants, or those who "have found no bone to gnaw in the colonial system."

How did these writers fit into postwar culture? Western intellectuals sought to revive humanism and democratic values after the atrocities of the Second World War. Fanon and others pointed out that the struggles over colonialism made that project more difficult; the violent repression of anticolonial movements in places such as Algeria seemed to be a relapse into brutality. They pointed to the ironies of Europe's "civilizing mission" and demanded a reevaluation of blackness as a central concept in Western culture. The

West's postwar recovery would entail eventually facing this challenge to the universal claims of its culture.

Existentialism

The French existentialist writers, most prominently Jean-Paul Sartre (*SAHR-truh*, 1905–1980) and Albert Camus (*KAM-oo*, 1913–1960), put the themes of individuality, commitment, and choice at center stage. The existentialists took themes from Nietzsche, Heidegger, and Kierkegaard, reworking them in the new context of war-torn Europe. Their starting point was that "existence precedes essence." In other words, meaning in life is not given but created. Thus, individuals were "condemned to be free" and to give their lives meaning by making choices and accepting responsibility. To deny one's freedom or responsibility was to act in "bad faith." War, collaboration and resistance, genocide, and the development of weapons of mass destruction all provided specific points of reference and gave these abstractions new meaning. The existentialists' writing was also clear and accessible, which contributed to their enormous popularity. Although Sartre wrote philosophical treatises, he also published plays and short stories. Camus's own experience in the resistance gave him tremendous moral authority—he became the symbol of a new generation. His novels—including *The Stranger* (1942), *The Plague* (1947), and *The Fall* (1956)—often revolved around metaphors for the war, showing that people were responsible for their own dilemmas and, through a series of antiheroes, exploring the limited ability of men and women to help each other.

Existentialist insights opened other doors. The existentialist approach to race, for instance, emphasized that no meaning inhered in skin color; instead, race derived meaning from a lived experience or situation. As Frantz Fanon wrote, white and black exist "only insofar as they create one another." The same approach could be applied to gender. In her famous introduction to *The Second Sex* (1949), Simone de Beauvoir (*duh bohv-WAHR*, 1908–1986) argued, "One is not born a woman, one becomes one." Women, like men, were condemned to be free. Beauvoir went on to ask why women seemed to accept their secondary status or why, in her words, they "dreamed the dreams of men." The scope and ambition of *The Second Sex* helped make it enormously influential; it was virtually encyclopedic, analyzing history, myth, biology, and psychology, bringing the insights of Marx and Freud to bear on the "woman question." Beauvoir's life also contributed to the book's high profile. A brilliant student from a strict middle-class background, she had a lifelong affair with Sartre but did not marry him,

SIMONE DE BEAUVOIR (1908–1986). A philosopher, novelist, memoirist, and path-breaking theorist of sex and gender, Beauvoir's work challenged widespread beliefs about femininity and womanhood.

leading many to romanticize her as a liberated and accomplished woman intellectual. She had little to do with feminism, however, until the late 1960s. When *The Second Sex* was published, it was associated with existentialism; only later would it become a key text of the women's movement (see Chapter 28).

Memory and Amnesia: The Aftermath of War

The theme of individual helplessness in the face of state power ran through countless works of the period, beginning, most famously, with George Orwell's *Animal Farm* (1946) and *1984* (1949). The American Joseph Heller's wildly popular *Catch-22* (1961) represented a form of popular existentialism, concerned with the absurdity of war and offering a biting commentary on regimentation and its toll on individual freedom. The Czech author Milan Kundera, who fled the repressive Czech government to live in Paris, eloquently captured the bittersweet efforts to resist senseless bureaucracy. Some writers expressed their despair by escaping into the absurd and fantastic. In Samuel Beckett's deeply pessimistic *Waiting for Godot* (1953, by an Irishman in French) and in the Briton Harold Pinter's *Caretaker*

THE COLD WAR IN EVERYDAY LIFE. A Soviet matchbook label, 1960, depicts a Soviet fist destroying a U.S. plane. Soviet nationalism had been a potent force since the Second World War. ■ *Could the Soviet leadership sustain this nationalist sentiment without an external threat?*

(1960) and *Homecoming* (1965), nothing happens. Characters speak in banalities, paralyzed by the absurdity of modern times.

Other authors ventured into the realms of hallucination, science fiction, and fantasy. The novels of the Americans William Burroughs and Kurt Vonnegut carry readers from interior fantasies to outer space. One of the most popular books of the period was *The Lord of the Rings* (1954–1955), written before and during the Second World War by the Briton J. R. R. Tolkien. Set in the fantasy world of Middle Earth, Professor Tolkien's tribute to the ancient Celtic and Scandinavian languages he studied and the power of human myths was seized on by a generation of young romantics who rebelled against postwar Western culture for their own reasons.

Questions of terror and dictatorship haunted social and political thought of the postwar era, and especially the work of émigrés from Europe. Representatives of the "Frankfurt school" of German Marxism, by wartime refugees in the United States, sought to understand how fascism and Nazism had taken root in Western culture and politics. Theodor Adorno joined Max Horkheimer in a series of essays, *Dialectic of Enlightenment* (1947), the best known of which indicted the "culture industry" for depoliticizing the masses and crippling democracy. Adorno also coauthored *The Authoritarian Personality* (1950), which used social surveys in an effort to discover how people become receptive to racism, prejudice, and dictatorship. Whatever the specific roots of German Nazism, the Frankfurt school suggested, there were also more general tendencies in modern societies that should give cause for concern.

Hannah Arendt (1906–1975), a Jewish refugee from Germany, was the first to propose that both Nazism and Stalinism should be understood as forms of a novel, twentieth-century form of government: totalitarianism (*The Origins of Totalitarianism,* 1951). Unlike earlier forms of tyranny or despotism, totalitarianism worked by mobilizing mass support. It used terror to crush resistance, break down political and social institutions, and atomize the public. Totalitarianism, Arendt argued, also forged new ideologies. Totalitarian regimes did not concern themselves with whether killing was justified by law; they justified camps and extermination by pointing to the objective laws of history or racial struggle. By unleashing destruction and eliminating entire populations, totalitarian politics made collective resistance virtually impossible. Arendt returned to the same theme in a provocative and disturbing essay on the trial of a Nazi leader, *Eichmann in Jerusalem* (1963). To many readers' distress, she pointedly refused to demonize Nazism. Instead, she explored what she termed "the banality of evil": how the rise of new forms of state power and

The War That Refuses to Be Forgotten

Heda Margolis Kovály was born in Prague and returned to her city after surviving the concentration camps. Like many refugees and survivors, she received an uncertain welcome home. In Czechoslovakia and elsewhere, the Nazi occupation left a legacy of bitterness and division that persisted for decades. Survivors reminded other Europeans of the war and made them defensive. Paradoxically, as Kovály shows, it was common to blame the victims for the war's troubles.

nd so ended that horrible long war that refuses to be forgotten. Life went on. It went on despite both the dead and the living, because this was a war that no one had quite survived. Something very important and precious had been killed by it or, perhaps, it had just died of horror, of starvation, or simply of disgust—who knows? We tried to bury it quickly, the earth settled over it, and we turned our backs on it impatiently. After all, our real life was now beginning and what to make of it was up to us.

People came crawling out of their hide-outs. They came back from the forests, from the prisons, and from the concentration camps, and all they could think was, "It's over; it's all over." . . . Some people came back silent, and some talked incessantly as though talking about a thing would make it vanish. . . . While some voices spoke of death and flames, of blood and gallows, in the background, a chorus of thousands repeated tirelessly, "You know, we also suffered. . . . [N]othing but

skimmed milk. . . . No butter on our bread. . . ."

Sometimes a bedraggled and barefoot concentration camp survivor plucked up his courage and knocked on the door of prewar friends to ask, "Excuse me, do you by any chance still have some of the stuff we left with you for safekeeping?" And the friends would say, "You must be mistaken, you didn't leave anything with us, but come in anyway!" And they would seat him in their parlor where his carpet lay on the floor and pour herb tea into antique cups that had belonged to his grandmother. . . . He would say to himself, "What does it matter? As long as we're alive? What does it matter?" . . .

It would also happen that a survivor might need a lawyer to retrieve lost documents and he would remember the name of one who had once represented large Jewish companies. He would go to see him and sit in an empire chair in a corner of an elegant waiting room, enjoying all that good taste and luxury, watching pretty secretaries rushing about. Until one of the pretty girls forgot to close a door behind her, and the

lawyer's sonorous voice would boom through the crack, "You would have thought we'd be rid of them finally, but no, they're impossible to kill off—not even Hitler could manage it. Every day there're more of them crawling back, like rats. . . ." And the survivor would quietly get up from his chair and slip out of the waiting room, this time not laughing. On his way down the stairs his eyes would mist over as if with the smoke of the furnaces at Auschwitz.

Source: Heda Margolis Kovály, *Under a Cruel Star: A Life in Prague 1941–1968*, trans. Franci Epstein and Helen Epstein with the author (Cambridge, MA: 1986), pp. 45–46.

Questions for Analysis

1. What did Kovály mean when she remarked that the Second World War was "a war that no one had quite survived"? Can such an argument be made about all wars? In what ways was the Second World War distinctive?

2. Kovály describes individual encounters. Do her stories illuminate larger social and cultural developments?

---

terror had created a world in which Nazis such as Adolf Eichmann could implement genocide as simply one more policy. The crisis of totalitarianism, Arendt argued, was the moral collapse of society, for it destroyed human feeling and the power of resistance in executioners and victims—"tormentors and the tormented"—alike.

Discussions of the war and its legacy, however, were limited. Some memoirs and novels dealing directly with the war and its brutal aftermath did reach a large international public: Jerzy Kosinski's novel about a boy in wartime Poland, *The Painted Bird*; Czesław Miłosz's memoir of intellectual collaboration in Eastern Europe, *The Captive* in the politics of their Eastern European allies in the 1940s and 1950s, ensuring the creation of hard-line governments in East Germany, Czechoslovakia, Poland, Hungary, and elsewhere in the Eastern bloc. In the United States, anti-communism became a powerful political force, shaping foreign policy and preparations for military confrontation with the Soviet Union to such an extent that President Eisenhower warned in his farewell address that a "military-industrial complex" had taken shape in the United States and that its "total influence—economic, political, even spiritual—is felt in every city, every statehouse, every office of the federal government."

In Western Europe, rebuilding the economy and creating a new political order in the aftermath of the Second World War meant accepting the new power and influence of the United States, but Europeans also searched for ways to create and express a European identity that would retain some independence and freedom of action. Led by the efforts of France and Germany, Western Europeans eventually found elements of this freedom in increasing integration and economic cooperation. In Eastern Europe, on the other hand, the political leadership found fewer opportunities for independent action and the threat of military intervention by the Soviet

After You Read This Chapter

Visit StudySpace for quizzes, additional review materials, and multimedia documents. **wwnorton.com/web/westernciv18**

REVIEWING THE OBJECTIVES

- The Cold War between the United States and the Soviet Union began as the Second World War ended. How did these two nations seek to influence the postwar political order in Europe?

- Postwar economic growth was accompanied by greater economic integration among Western European nations. What were the goals of those who sought to create the unified European market and which nations played key roles in its development?

- Between the late 1940s and the mid-1960s, almost all the European colonies in Asia and Africa demanded and received their independence, either peacefully or through armed conflict. What combination of events made Europeans less able to defend their colonial empires against the claims of nationalists who sought independence from Europe?

- Decolonization and the Cold War reinforced a sense that Europe's place in the world needed to be rethought. How did intellectuals, writers, and artists react to the loss of European influence in the world?

Union made any innovations or experimentation difficult or impossible.

The sense that Europeans were no longer in a position to act independently or exert their influence in other parts of the world was compounded by the loss of colonies abroad. Former European colonies in Africa and Asia became independent nations, and this loss of influence may have further encouraged the former European imperial powers in their attempts to lay the groundwork for a more integrated Europe. The consensus in the West about the new role that the state should take in economic planning, education, and ensuring social welfare helped lay the groundwork for a Europe that was dedicated to ensuring equal opportunities to its citizens. These commitments were driven by the search for stable forms of democratic government—the memories of the violent ideological conflicts of the 1920s and 1930s were still fresh, and the achievement of an integrated Western Europe (under U.S. sponsorship) on the hinge of Franco-German cooperation must be seen as one of the major victories of the postwar decades. The hard-won stability of this period was to be temporary, however, and beginning in the 1960s a new series of political conflicts and economic crises would test the limits of consensus in Cold War Europe.

PEOPLE, IDEAS, AND EVENTS IN CONTEXT

- When Allied leaders met to discuss the postwar order at **YALTA** and **POTSDAM** in 1945, what were the major issues they discussed?
- What were the goals of the U.S. **MARSHALL PLAN**? How did **JOSEPH STALIN** react to its implementation?
- What was the **TRUMAN DOCTRINE** and how was it related to the creation of **NATO**?
- How did the Soviet Union's successful explosion of an **ATOMIC BOMB** in 1949 change the dynamic of the **COLD WAR**?
- How did the political climate in the Soviet Union and Eastern Europe change under **NIKITA KHRUSHCHEV** during the Thaw that followed Stalin's death?
- What nations were key to the plans for the **EUROPEAN UNION**?
- Why was the decolonization of settler colonies in Africa such as Algeria, Kenya, and Rhodesia more violent than in other colonies on the continent?
- What was apartheid, and why was it adopted by the settler government in South Africa?

THINKING ABOUT CONNECTIONS

- Insofar as one can determine them from today's perspective, what were the long-term consequences of the Cold War for people in both Western and Eastern Europe?
- What challenges did the process of decolonization pose to those who believed that European traditions of democratic rule and individual rights—ideas associated with the Enlightenment and the French Revolution—were universal?

The film highlighted the contrast between rich and poor—the man's son enviously watches another's family enjoying huge plates of pasta—and between American glamour, represented by movie stars on the posters, and Italy's war-scarred poverty. Federico Fellini came out of the neorealist school and began his career writing for Rossellini. Fellini's break-out film *La Dolce Vita* (1959, starring Marcello Mastroianni) took Italian film to screens throughout Europe and the United States, and it also marked Fellini's transition to his signature surrealist and carnivalesque style, developed in *8½* (1963).

The French directors of the new wave continued to develop this unsentimental, naturalistic, and enigmatic social vision. New wave directors worked closely with each other, casting each other (and their wives and lovers) in their films, encouraged improvisation, and experimented with disjointed narrative. François Truffaut (1932–1984), *400 Blows* (1959) and *The Wild Child* (1969), and Jean-Luc Godard (1930–), *Breathless* (1959) and *Contempt* (1963, with Brigitte Bardot), are leading examples. *Closely Watched Trains* (1966) was the Czech director Jirí Menzel's (1938–) contribution to the new wave. The new wave raised the status of the director, insisting that the film's camera work and vision (rather than the writing) constituted the real art—part, again, of the new value accorded to the visual. France made other contributions to international film by sponsoring the Cannes Film Festival. The first Cannes Festival was held before the Second World War, but the city opened its gates again in 1946 under the banner of artistic internationalism. As one commentator put it, "There are many ways to advance the cause of peace. But the power . . . of cinema is greater than other forms of expression, for it directly and simultaneously touches the masses of the world." Placing itself at the center of an international film industry became part of France's ongoing recovery from the war, and Cannes became one of the world's largest markets for film.

HOLLYWOOD AND THE AMERICANIZATION OF CULTURE

The American film industry, however, had considerable advantages, and the devastating aftereffects of the Second World War in Europe allowed Hollywood to consolidate its earlier gains (see Chapter 27). The United States' huge domestic market gave Hollywood its biggest advantage. In 1946 an estimated hundred million Americans went to the movies every week. By the 1950s, Hollywood was making 500 films a year and counted for between 40 and 75 percent of films shown in Europe. The same period brought important innovations in filmmaking: the conversion to color and new optical formats, including widescreen. As far as their themes were concerned, some American directors moved in the same direction as the European neorealists. As one critic put it, they tried to "base fictional pictures on fact and, more importantly, to shoot them not in painted studio sets but in actual places."

The domestic politics of the Cold War weighed heavily on filmmaking in the United States. Between 1947 and 1951, the infamous House Un-American Activities Committee called before it hundreds of persons, investigating alleged sympathies with communism or association with any left-wing organization. Hundreds of actors, directors, and writers were blacklisted by the studios. At the same time, paradoxically, American censorship was breaking down, with dramatic consequences on screen. Since the early 1930s, the Motion Picture Production Code had refused to approve "scenes of passion" (including married couples sharing a bed), immorality and profanity (the code banned the words *virgin* and *cripes*), depictions of guns, details of crimes, suicide, or murder. Foreign films, however, came into the United States without the code's seal of approval. The state of New York tried to ban a film (*The Miracle*, directed by Rossellini and written by Fellini) as "sacrilegious," but in 1952 the Supreme Court ruled that film was protected by the First Amendment. A 1955 Otto Preminger movie in which Frank Sinatra played a heroin addict (*The Man with the Golden Arm*) was released despite the disapproval of the Production Code and went on to become a box-office success—a sign of changing mores. *Rebel without a Cause* (1955) made juvenile delinquency a

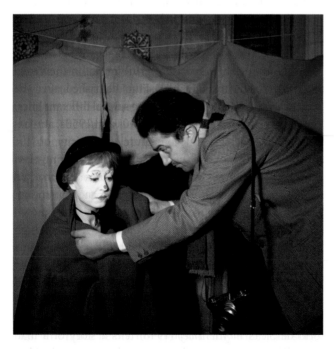

FEDERICO FELLINI ON THE SET OF *LA STRADA*, 1954. Fellini was an Italian neorealist filmmaker who sought to depict life as it was lived.

legitimate subject for film. By the 1960s, the Production Code had been scuttled. The extremely graphic violence at the end of Arthur Penn's *Bonnie and Clyde* (1967) marked the scope of the transformation.

Hollywood's expanding influence was but one instance of the "Americanization" of Western culture. Europeans had worried about the United States as a model since at least the 1920s; the United States seemed to be the center for the "production and organization of mass civilization." American films in the 1950s multiplied these worries. So did television, which by 1965 had found its way into 62 million homes in the United States, 13 million in Britain, 10 million in West Germany, and 5 million each in France and Italy and had an even more important impact on everyday life and sociability. The issues were not simply cultural; they included the power of American corporations, American business techniques, aggressive marketing, and American domination of global trade networks. Many concerns were raised, and sometimes they contradicted each other. Some observers believed that the United States and its cultural exports were materialistic, conformist, and complacent. Others considered Americans to be rebellious, lonely, and sexually unhappy. *Rebel without a Cause*, for instance, with James Dean as an alienated teenager in a dysfunctional family and with its scenes of knife fights and car races, provoked cries of outrage from German critics who deplored the permissiveness of American parents and expressed shock that middle-class children behaved like "hoodlums."

Is it helpful, though, to speak of the *Americanization* of culture? First, the term refers to many different processes.

JAMES DEAN IN *REBEL WITHOUT A CAUSE*. Films from the 1950s and 1960s contributed to the romanticization of automobiles, sexuality, and youthful rebellion.

U.S. industrialists openly sought greater economic influence and economic integration: opening markets to American goods, industry to American production techniques, and so on. The U.S. government also aimed to export American political values, above all anticommunism, via organizations such as Radio Free Europe. Yet the farthest-reaching American influences were conveyed, unintentionally, by music and film: images of rebellious teenagers, a society of abundance, cars and the romance of the road, tangled race relations, flirting working girls (who seemed less identifiably working-class than their European counterparts), or bantering couples. These images could not be completely controlled, and they had no single effect. Movies about young Americans might represent the romance of American power, they might represent a rebellion against that power. Second, *American* goods were put to different use in local cultures. Third, journalists, critics, and ordinary men and women tended to use *American* as an all-purpose label for various modern or mass culture developments that were more properly global, such as inexpensive electronics from Asia. As one historian puts it, America was less of a reality than an idea—and a contradictory one at that.

Gender Roles and Sexual Revolution

What some called the sexual revolution of the 1960s had several aspects. The first was less censorship, which we have already seen in film, and fewer taboos regarding discussion of sexuality in public. In the United States, the notorious Kinsey reports on male and female sexuality (in 1948 and 1953, respectively) made morality and sexual behavior front-page news. Alfred Kinsey was a zoologist turned social scientist, and the way in which he applied science and statistics to sex attracted considerable attention. An enthusiastic journalist in Europe reported that the massive numbers Kinsey compiled would, finally, reveal the "truth of sex." The truth, though, was elusive. At the very least Kinsey showed that moral codes and private behaviors did not line up neatly. For instance, 80 to 90 percent of the women he interviewed disapproved of premarital sex, but 50 percent of the women he interviewed had had it. *Time* magazine warned that publicizing disparities between beliefs and behavior might prove subversive—that women and men would decide there was "morality in numbers."

Across Europe and North America, however, young men and women seemed to be reaching rebellious conclusions on their own. As one Italian teenager said, defending her moral codes, "It is our elders who behave scandalously. . . . [W]omen were kept under lock and key, girls married to men who were twice their age. . . . [B]oys, even the very youngest, had total freedom and so queued up at the brothels." Teenage girls in Italy and France told researchers and reporters that taboos were not just old fashioned but damaging, that their mothers had kept them in the dark about matters as rudimentary as menstruation, leaving them unprepared for life.

Was the family crumbling? Transformations in agriculture and life in the countryside did mean that the peasant family was no longer the institution that governed birth, work, courtship, marriage, and death. Yet the family became newly important as the center of consumption, spending, and leisure time, for television took people (usually men) out of bars, cafes, and music halls. It became the focus of government attention in the form of family allowances, health care, and Cold War appeals to family values. People brought higher expectations to marriage, which raised rates of divorce, and they paid more attention to children, which brought smaller families. Despite a postwar spike in the birth rate that produced the "baby boom," over the long term, fertility declined, even in countries that outlawed contraception. The family assumed new meanings as its traditional structures of authority—namely paternal control over wives and children—eroded under the pressure of social change.

A second aspect of the revolution was the centrality of sex and eroticism to mass consumer culture. Magazines, which flourished in this period, offered advice on how to succeed in love and be attractive. Cultivating one's looks, including sexiness, fit with the new accent on consumption; indeed health and personal hygiene was the fastest rising category of family spending. Advertising, advice columns, TV, and film blurred boundaries between buying consumer goods, seeking personal fulfillment, and sexual desire. There was nothing new about appeals to eroticism. But the fact that sexuality was now widely considered a form of self-expression—perhaps even the core of oneself—was new to the twentieth century. These developments helped propel change, and they also made the sexual revolution prominent in the politics of the time.

The third aspect of the revolution came with legal and medical or scientific changes in contraception. Oral contraceptives, first approved for development in 1959, became mainstream in the next decade. The Pill did not have revolutionary effects on the birth rate, which was already falling. It marked dramatic change, however, because it was simple (though expensive) and could be used by women themselves. By 1975, two-thirds of British women between fifteen and forty-four said they were taking the Pill. Numbers like these marked a long, drawn-out end to centuries-old views that to discuss birth control was pornographic, an affront to religion, and an invitation to indulgence and promiscuity. By and large, Western countries legalized contraception in

the 1960s and abortion in the 1970s. In 1965, for instance, the U.S. Supreme Court struck down laws banning the use of contraception, though selling contraceptives remained illegal in Massachusetts until 1972. The Soviet Union legalized abortion in 1950, after banning it during most of Stalin's regime. Throughout Eastern Europe, abortion rates were extremely high. Why? Contraceptives proved as difficult to obtain as other consumer goods; men often refused to use them; and women—doubly burdened with long hours of work and housework and facing, in addition, chronic housing shortages—had little choice but to resort to abortion.

SECOND-WAVE FEMINISM. U.S. women celebrating the passage of the Equal Rights Amendment by the House of Representatives in 1970 beneath the Statue of Liberty. The bill did not pass the Senate and never became law. "Second wave" feminists distinguished themselves from the "first wave" of feminism in Europe and the Americas, which had focused on gaining voting rights in the nineteenth and early twentieth centuries. Second-wave feminists argued that votes for women had not ended pervasive gender discrimination. They demanded equal pay for equal work and challenged widespread expectations about the roles that women were expected to play in families and in the workplace.

Legal changes would not have occurred without the women's movements of the time. For nineteenth-century feminists, winning the right to vote was the most difficult practical and symbolic struggle (see Chapter 23). For the revived feminism of the 1960s and 1970s, the family, work, and sexuality—all put on the agenda by the social changes of the period—were central. Since the Second World War, the assumption that middle-class women belonged in the home had been challenged by the steadily rising demand for workers, especially in education and the service sector. Thus, many more married women and many more mothers were part of the labor force. Moreover, across the West young middle-class women, like men, were part of the rising number of university students. But in the United States, to take just one example, only 37 percent of women who enrolled in college in the 1950s finished their degrees, believing they should marry instead. As one of them explained, "We married what we wanted to be": doctor, professor, manager, and so on. Women found it difficult to get nonsecretarial jobs; received less pay for the same work; and, even when employed, had to rely on their husbands to establish credit.

The tension between rising expectations that stemmed from abundance, growth, and the emphasis on self-expression on the one hand and the reality of narrow horizons on the other created quiet waves of discontent. Betty Friedan's *The Feminine Mystique* (1963) brought much of this discontent into the open, contrasting the cultural myths of the fulfilled and happy housewife with the realities of economic inequality, hard work, and narrowed horizons. In 1949, Simone de Beauvoir had asked how Western culture (myth, literature, and psychology) had created an image of woman as the second, and lesser sex; Friedan, using a more journalistic style and writing at a time when social change had made readers more receptive to her ideas, showed how the media, the social sciences, and advertising at once exalted femininity and lowered women's expectations and possibilities. Friedan cofounded NOW (National Organization for Women) in 1966; smaller and often more radical women's movements multiplied across Europe in the following decades. For this generation of feminists, reproductive freedom was both a private matter and a basic right—a key to women's control over their lives. Outlawing contraception and abortion made women alone bear responsibility for the consequences of sweeping changes in Western sexual life. Such measures were ineffective as well as unjust, they argued. French feminists dramatized the point by publishing the names of 343 well-known women, including Beauvoir, who admitted to having had illegal abortions. A similar petition came out in Germany the following year and was followed by petitions from doctors and tens of thousands of supporters. In sum, the legal changes followed from political demands, and those in turn reflected a quiet or subterranean rebellion of many women (and men)—one with longer-term causes. Mass consumption, mass culture, and startlingly rapid transformations in public and private life were all intimately related.

SOCIAL MOVEMENTS DURING THE 1960s

The social unrest of the 1960s was international. Its roots lay in the political struggles and social transformations of the postwar period. Of these, the most important were anticolonial and civil rights movements. The successful anticolonial movements (see Chapter 27) reflected a growing racial consciousness and also helped encourage that consciousness. Newly independent African and Caribbean nations remained wary about revivals of colonialism and the continuing economic hegemony of Western Europe and America. Black and Asian immigration into those nations produced tension and frequent violence. In the West, particularly in the United States, people of color identified with these social and economic grievances.

The Civil Rights Movement

The emergence of new black nations in Africa and the Caribbean was paralleled by growing African American insurgency. The Second World War increased African American migration from the American South to northern cities, intensifying a drive for rights, dignity, and independence that began in the prewar era with organizations such as the National Association for the Advancement of Colored People and the National Urban League. By 1960, various civil rights groups, led by the Congress of Racial Equality (CORE), had started to organize boycotts and demonstrations directed at private businesses and public services that discriminated against blacks in the South. The preeminent figure in the Civil Rights Movement in the United States during the 1960s was Martin Luther King, Jr. (1929–1968). A Baptist minister, King embraced the philosophy of nonviolence promoted by the Indian social and political activist Mohandas K. Gandhi. King's personal participation in countless demonstrations, his willingness to go to jail for a cause that he believed to be just, and his ability as an orator to arouse both blacks and whites with his message led to

Competing Viewpoints

The "Woman Question" on Both Sides of the Atlantic

How did Western culture define femininity, and did women internalize those definitions? These questions were central to postwar feminist thought, and they were sharply posed in two classic texts: Simone de Beauvoir's The Second Sex *(1949) and Betty Friedan's* The Feminine Mystique *(1963). Beauvoir (1908–1986) started from the existentialist premise that humans were "condemned to be free" and to give their own lives meaning. Why, then, did women accept the limitations imposed on them and, in Beauvoir's words, "dream the dreams of men"? Although dense and philosophical,* The Second Sex *was read throughout the world. Betty Friedan's equally influential bestseller drew heavily on Beauvoir. Friedan sought the origins of the "feminine mystique," her term for the model of femininity promoted by experts, advertised in women's magazines, and seemingly accepted by middle-class housewives in the postwar United States. As Friedan points out in the excerpt here, the new postwar mystique was in many ways more conservative than prewar ideals had been, despite continuing social change, a greater range of careers opening up to women, the expansion of women's education, and so on. Friedan (1921–2006) cofounded the National Organization for Women in 1966 and served as its president until 1970.*

Simone de Beauvoir, *The Second Sex* (1949)

But first, what is a woman? . . . Everyone agrees there are females in the human species; today, as in the past, they make up about half of humanity; and yet we are told that "femininity is in jeopardy;" we are urged, "Be women, stay women, become women." . . . Although some women zealously strive to embody it, the model has never been patented. It is typically described in vague and shimmering terms borrowed from a clairvoyant's vocabulary. . . .

If the female function is not enough to define woman, and if we also reject the explanation of the "eternal feminine," but if we accept, even temporarily, that there are women on the earth, we then have to ask: what is a woman?

Merely stating the problem suggests an immediate answer to me. It is significant that I pose it. It would never occur to a man to write a book on the singular situation of males in humanity. If I want to define myself, I first have to say, "I am a woman;" all other assertions will arise from this basic truth. A man never begins by positing himself as an individual of a certain sex: that he is a man is obvious. The categories "masculine" and "feminine" appear as symmetrical in a formal way on town hall records or identification papers. The relation of the two sexes is not that of two electrical poles: the man represents both the positive and the neuter. . . . Woman is the negative, to such a point that any determination is imputed to her as a limitation, without reciprocity. . . . [A] man is in his right by virtue of being man; it is the woman who is in the wrong. . . . Woman has ovaries and a uterus; such are the particular conditions that lock her in her subjectivity; some even say she thinks with her hormones. Man vainly forgets that his anatomy also includes hormones and testicles. He grasps his body as a direct and normal link with the world that he believes he apprehends in all objectivity whereas he considers woman's body an obstacle, a prison, burdened by everything that particularises it. "The female is female by virtue of a certain *lack* of qualities," Aristotle said. "We should regard women's nature as suffering from natural defectiveness." And St. Thomas in his turn decreed that woman was an "incomplete man," an "incidental" being. This is what the Genesis story symbolises, where Eve appears as if drawn from Adam's "supernumerary" bone, in Bossuet's words. Humanity is male, and man defines woman, not in herself, but in relation to himself; she is not considered an autonomous being. . . . And she is nothing other than what man decides; she is thus called "the sex," meaning that the male sees her essentially as a sexed being; for him she is sex, so she is it in the absolute. She determines and differentiates herself in relation to man, and he does not in relation to her; she is the inessential in front of the essential. He is the Subject, he is the Absolute. She is the Other.

Source: Simone de Beauvoir, *The Second Sex*, trans. Constance Borde and Sheila Malovany-Chevallier (London: 2009), pp. 3–6.

Betty Friedan, *The Feminine Mystique* (1963)

In 1939, the heroines of women's magazine stories were not always young, but in a certain sense they were younger than their fictional counterparts today. They were young in the same way that the American hero has always been young: they were New Women, creating with a gay determined spirit a new identity for women—a life of their own. There was an aura about them of becoming, of moving into a future that was going to be different from the past. . . .

These stories may not have been great literature. But the identity of their heroines seemed to say something about the housewives who, then as now, read the women's magazines. These magazines were not written for career women. The New Woman heroines were the ideal of yesterday's housewives; they reflected the dreams, mirrored the yearning for identity and the sense of possibility that existed for women then. . . .

In 1949 . . . the feminine mystique began to spread through the land. . . .

The feminine mystique says that the highest value and the only commitment for women is the fulfillment of their own femininity. It says that the great mistake of Western culture, through most of its history, has been the undervaluation of this femininity. . . . The mistake, says the mystique, the root of women's troubles in the past, is that women envied men, women tried to be like men, instead of accepting their own nature, which can find fulfillment only in sexual passivity, male domination, and nurturing maternal love.

But the new image this mystique gives to American women is the old image: "Occupation: housewife." The new mystique makes the housewife-mothers, who never had a chance to be anything else, the model for all women; it presupposes that history has reached a final and glorious end in the here and now, as far as women are concerned. . . .

It is more than a strange paradox that as all professions are finally open to women in America, "career woman" has become a dirty word; that as higher edu-

cation becomes available to any woman with the capacity for it, education for women has become so suspect that more and more drop out of high school and college to marry and have babies; that as so many roles in modern society become theirs for the taking, women so insistently confine themselves to one role. Why . . . should she accept this new image which insists she is not a person but a "woman," by definition barred from the freedom of human existence and a voice in human destiny?

Source: Betty Friedan, *The Feminine Mystique* (New York: 2001), pp. 38, 40, 42–43, 67–68.

Questions for Analysis

1. Why does Beauvoir ask, "What is a woman?"

2. Why does Friedan think that a "feminine mystique" emerged after the Second World War?

---

his position as the most highly regarded—and most widely feared—defender of black rights. His inspiring career was tragically ended by assassination in 1968.

King and organizations such as CORE aspired to a fully integrated nation. Other charismatic and important black leaders sought complete independence from white society, fearing that integration would leave African Americans without the spiritual or material resources necessary for a community's pride, dignity, and autonomy. The most influential of the black nationalists was Malcolm X (1925–1965),

who assumed the "X" after having discarded his "white" surname (Little). For most of his adult life, Malcolm X, a spokesman for the Black Muslim movement, urged blacks to renew their commitment to their own heritage; to establish black businesses for economic autonomy; and to fortify economic, political, and psychological defenses against white domination. Like King, he was assassinated, in 1965 while addressing a rally in Harlem.

Civil rights laws passed under President Lyndon B. Johnson (1963–1969) in the 1960s did bring African

The Antiwar Movement

The United States' escalating war in Vietnam became a lightning rod for discontent. In 1961, President John F. Kennedy (1917–1963) promised to "bear any burden" necessary to fight communism and to ensure the victory of American models of representative government and free-market economics in the developing nations. Kennedy's plan entailed massive increases in foreign aid, much of it in weapons. It provided the impetus for humanitarian institutions such as the Peace Corps, intended to improve local conditions and show Americans' benevolence and good intentions. Bearing burdens, however, also meant fighting guerrillas who turned to the Soviets for aid. This involved covert interventions in Latin America, the Congo, and, most important, Vietnam.

By the time of Kennedy's death in 1963, nearly 15,000 American "advisers" were on the ground alongside South Vietnamese troops. Kennedy's successor, Lyndon Johnson, began the strategic bombing of North Vietnam and rapidly drew hundreds of thousands of American troops into combat in South Vietnam. The rebels in the south, known as the Viet Cong, were solidly entrenched, highly experienced guerrilla fighters, and were backed by the professional, well-equipped North Vietnamese army under Ho Chi Minh, who also received support from the Soviet Union. The South Vietnamese government resisted efforts at reform, losing popular support. Massive efforts by the United States produced only stalemate, mounting American casualties, and rising discontent.

Vietnam did much to cause the political turmoil of the 1960s in the United States. As Martin Luther King, Jr., pointed out, the war—which relied on a disproportionate number of black soldiers to conduct a war against a small nation of color—echoed and magnified racial inequality at home. Exasperated by troubles in the field, American planners continued to escalate military commitments, with no effect. Peace talks in Paris stalled while the death toll on all sides increased. The involuntary draft of young American men expanded and polarized the public. In 1968, criticism forced President Johnson to abandon his plans to run for a second term. Johnson's successor, Richard M. Nixon, who won a narrow victory on the basis of promises to end the war, expanded it instead. Student protests against the war frequently ended in violence. The government brought criminal conspiracy charges against Benjamin Spock, the nation's leading pediatrician, and William Sloane Coffin, the chaplain of Yale University, for encouraging young people to resist the draft. Avoiding the draft became so widespread that the system was changed in 1970. And from

MARTIN LUTHER KING, JR., 1964. The African American civil rights leader is welcomed in Oslo, Norway, on a trip to accept the Nobel Peace Prize. He would be assassinated four years later. ▪ *How might Europeans have viewed King's campaign?* ▪ *Would it affect their vision of the United States?*

Americans some measure of equality with regard to voting rights—and, to a much lesser degree, school desegregation. In other areas, such as housing and job opportunities, white racism continued. Economic development passed by many African American communities, and subsequent administrations pulled back from the innovative programs of the Johnson era.

These problems were not confined to the United States. West Indian, Indian, and Pakistani immigrants in Britain met with discrimination in jobs, housing, and everyday interaction with the authorities—producing frequent racial disturbances in major British cities. France witnessed hostility toward Algerian immigration, Germany toward the importation of Turkish labor. In Western Europe, as in the United States, struggles for racial and ethnic integration became central to the postcolonial world.

The Civil Rights Movement had enormous significance for the twentieth century, and it galvanized other movements as well. It dramatized as perhaps no other movement could the chasm between the egalitarian promises of American democracy and the real inequalities at the core of the American social and political life—a chasm that could be found in other Western nations as well. African American claims were morally and politically compelling, and the Civil Rights Movement sharpened others' criticisms of what they saw as a complacent, narrowly individualistic, materialist culture.

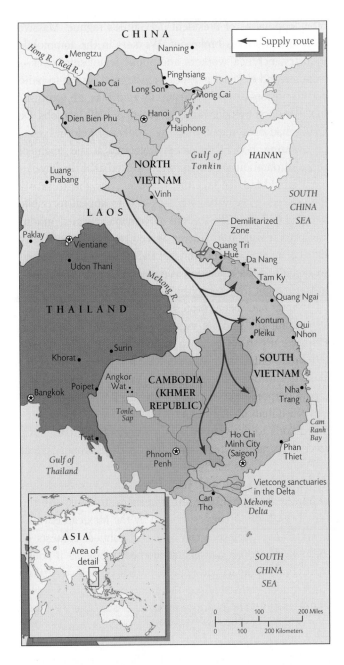

THE WAR IN VIETNAM AND SOUTHEAST ASIA. The 1954 Geneva Accords divided Vietnam at the seventeenth parallel. The north went to Ho Chi Minh, the communist leader, and the south was controlled by Ngo Dinh Diem, an ally of the United States. In 1956, South Vietnam refused to hold the elections mandated in the Geneva Accords. Ho Chi Minh mobilized a guerrilla army, the Viet Cong, and the Vietnam War began. ▪ *What other countries in this region were drawn into the war?* ▪ *How did the Viet Cong use the proximity of Cambodia and Laos to their strategic advantage?* ▪ *Why did the United States choose to get involved?*

generational consciousness heightened, in part, by the marketing of mass youth culture; and educational institutions unable to deal with rising numbers and expectations. In France, the number of students in high school rose from 400,000 in 1949 to 2 million in 1969; in universities, over the same period, enrollments skyrocketed, from 100,000 to 600,000. The same was true in Italy, Britain, and West Germany. Universities, which had been created to educate a small elite, found both their teaching staffs and their facilities overwhelmed. Lecture halls were packed, university bureaucracies did not respond to requests, and thousands of students took exams at the same time. More philosophically, students raised questions about the role and meaning of elite education in a democratic society and about the relationships among the university as a "knowledge factory," consumer culture, and neocolonial ventures such as the Vietnam War and—for the French—the Algerian wars. Conservative traditions made intellectual reform difficult. In addition, student demands for fewer restrictions on personal life—for instance, permission to have a member of the opposite sex in a dormitory room—provoked authoritarian reactions from university representatives. Waves of student protest were not confined to the United States and Western Europe. They swept across Poland and Czechoslovakia where students protested one-party bureaucratic rule, stifling intellectual life, and authoritarianism, and helped sustain networks of dissidents. By the mid-1960s, simmering anger in Eastern Europe had once again reached a dangerous point.

1968

The year 1968 was an extraordinary one, quite similar to 1848 with its wave of revolution (see Chapter 20). It was even more intensely international, a reflection of tightening global ties. International youth culture fostered a sense of collective identity. The new media relayed images of civil rights protests in the United States to Europe, and broadcast news footage of the Vietnam War on television screens

other countries' points of view, the Vietnam War became a spectacle: one in which the most powerful, wealthiest nation of the world seemed intent on destroying a land of poor peasants in the name of anticommunism, democracy, and freedom. The tarnished image of Western values stood at the center of 1960s protest movements in the United States and Western Europe.

The Student Movement

The student movement itself can be seen as a consequence of postwar developments: a growing cohort of young people with more time and wealth than in the past;

from West Virginia to West Germany. The wave of unrest shook both the Eastern and Western blocs. Protest movements assailed bureaucracy and the human costs of the Cold War: on the Soviet side, bureaucracy, authoritarianism, and indifference to civilians; on the Western side, bias and monopolies in the news media, the military-industrial complex, and American imperialism. The Soviet regime, as we have seen, responded with repression. In the United States and Western Europe, traditional political parties had little idea what to make of these new movements and those who participated in them. In both cases, events rapidly overwhelmed political systems.

PARIS

The most serious outbreak of student unrest in Europe came in Paris in the spring of 1968. The French Republic had been shaken by conflicts over the Algerian war in the early 1960s. Even more important, the economic boom had undermined the foundations of the regime and de Gaulle's traditional style of rule. French students at the University of Paris demanded reforms that would modernize their university. Protest first peaked at Nanterre, a new branch of the university built on a former air force depot. Nanterre was in a poor and poorly served neighborhood, starved for funds, and overcrowded with students. Petitions, demonstrations, and confrontations with university authorities traveled quickly from Nanterre to the Sorbonne, in central Paris. In the face of growing disorder, the University of Paris shut down—sending students into the streets and into uglier confrontations with the police. The police reacted with repression and violence, which startled onlookers and television audiences and backfired on the regime. Sympathy with the students' cause expanded rapidly, bringing in

THE PRESS IS POISON. Criticizing the official media was central to the politics of May 1968.

other opponents of President de Gaulle's regime. Massive trade-union strikes broke out. Workers in the automobile industry, technical workers, and public-sector employees—from gas and electricity utilities to the mail system to radio and television—went on strike. By mid-May, an astonishing 10 million French workers had walked off their jobs. De Gaulle had no sympathy for the students: "Reform, yes—bed wetting, no," he reportedly declared at the height of the confrontation. At one point, it looked as if the government would fall. The regime, however, was able to satisfy the strikers with wage increases and to appeal to public demand for order. The student movements, isolated, gradually petered out and students agreed to resume university life. The regime did recover, but the events of 1968 helped weaken de Gaulle's position as president and contributed to his retirement from office the following year.

There had been protest and rebelliousness in the 1950s, but the scale of events in 1968 was astonishing. Paris was not the only city to explode in 1968. Student protest broke out in West Berlin, targeting the government's close ties to the autocratic shah of Iran and the power of media corporations. Clashes with the police turned violent. In Italian cities, undergraduates staged several demonstrations to draw attention to university overcrowding. Twenty-six universities were closed. The London School of Economics was nearly shut down by protest. In Mexico City, a confrontation with the police ended with the deaths of hundreds of protesters, most of them students—on the eve of the 1968 Olympics, hosted by the Mexican government. Those Olympics reflected the political contests of the period: African nations threatened to boycott if South Africa, with its apartheid regime, participated. Two African American medalists raised their hands in a black power salute during an awards ceremony—and the Olympic Committee promptly sent them home. In Vietnam, the Viet Cong defied American claims to have turned the tide by launching a new offensive. The Tet offensive, named for the Vietnamese new year, brought the highest casualty rates to date in the Vietnam War and an explosion of protest. Antiwar demonstrations and student rebellions spread across the country. President Johnson, battered by the effects of Tet and already worn down by the war, chose not to run for reelection. The year 1968 also saw damage and trauma for the country's political future, because of the assassinations of Martin Luther King, Jr. (April 4, 1968) and presidential candidate Robert F. Kennedy (June 5, 1968). King's assassination was followed by a wave of rioting in more than fifty cities across the United States, followed in late summer by street battles between police and student protesters at the Democratic National Convention in Chicago. Some saw

1960s Politics: The Situationists

In 1957, a small group of European artists and writers formed a group called the Situationist International. The movement combined the artistic traditions of dada and surrealism with anarchism and Marxism. Unlike traditional Marxists, the situationists did not focus on the workplace. Instead, they developed a broad critique of everyday life, protesting the stifling of art, creativity, and imagination in contemporary society. They denounced the "tyranny" of consumer culture, which constantly invented new needs and desires to fuel consumption. Capitalism, they said, had "colonized" everyday life. The situationists' ideas and especially their unorthodox, surrealist style, became influential during the events of May 1968 in France. All around Paris students painted situationist slogans such as those printed here.

The social movements of 1968 cut across Cold War boundaries, attacking Western consumerism as well as Soviet authoritarianism. A group of students and situationists sent a telegram (second excerpt) to the Politburo of the Communist Party of the Soviet Union in May 1968.

Situationist Anticapitalism, 1968

OCCUPY THE FACTORIES

POWER TO THE
WORKERS COUNCILS

ABOLISH CLASS SOCIETY

DOWN WITH THE
SPECTACLE-COMMODITY SOCIETY

ABOLISH ALIENATION

ABOLISH THE UNIVERSITY

HUMANITY WON'T BE HAPPY
TILL THE LAST BUREAUCRAT
IS HUNG WITH THE GUTS
OF THE LAST CAPITALIST

DEATH TO THE COPS

FREE ALSO THE 4 GUYS
CONVICTED FOR LOOTING
DURING THE 6 MAY RIOT

—Occupation committee of the Autonomous
and Popular Sorbonne University

Situationist Anticommunist Slogans, 1968

17 MAY 1968 / To the Politburo of the Communist party of the USSR the Kremlin Moscow / Shake in your shoes bureaucrats. The international power of the workers councils will soon wipe you out. Humanity won't be happy till the last bureaucrat is hung with the guts of the last capitalist. Long live the struggle of the Kronstadt sailors and of the Makhnovshchina against Trotsky and Lenin. Long live the 1956 Councilist insurrection of Budapest • Down with the state • Long live revolutionary Marxism. Occupation committee of the Autonomous and Popular Sorbonne

Sources: "Slogans to Be Spread Now by Every Means," in *Situationist International Anthology*, ed. and trans. Ken Knabb (Berkeley, CA: 1981), pp. 334–45.

Questions for Analysis

1. Are there any common themes in these sets of slogans?

2. Why has 1968 often been called "the year of the barricades"?

A RUSSIAN TANK ATTACKED DUR
an end to Alexander Dubček's experi

images of women, and so on. T
up the issue of nuclear weapc
issue in Europe. Finally, the env
hold—concerned not only with
dwindling resources but also wi
tion and the kind of unrestrain
had given rise to the 1960s. O
Europe and the United States, vc
political parties became less re
multiplied; in this way, new so
became part of a very different p

ECONOMIC STAGN
PRICE OF SUCCESS

Economic as well as social proble
the 1970s and 1980s, but these p
By the middle of the 1960s, fo
man growth rate had slowed. I

the flowering of protest as another "springtime of peoples."
Others saw it as a long nightmare.

PRAGUE

The student movement in the United States and Western
Europe also took inspiration from one of the most significant challenges to Soviet authority since the Hungarian

revolt of 1956 (see Chapter 27): the "Prague spring" of
1968. The events began with the emergence of a liberal
communist government in Czechoslovakia, led by the Slovak Alexander Dubček (*DOOB-chehk*). Dubček had outma-
neuvered the more traditional, authoritarian party leaders.
He advocated "socialism with a human face"; he encouraged
debate within the party, academic and artistic freedom, and
less censorship. As was often the case, party members were

divided between proponent:
that reform would unleash re
ever, also gained support fro
dent organizations, the pres:
As in Western Europe and
movement overflowed into tr

In the Soviet Union, Kh
and the reins of Soviet power
secretary of the Communist |
servative than Khrushchev,
the West, and prone to defer
Soviet sphere of influence. 1
Dubček as a political eccentr
their fears. Most Eastern E
denounced Czech reformism
of support broke out in Pola
an end to one-party rule, less
judicial system. In addition,
and Nicolae Ceaușescu (*cho*
two of the more stubbornly
Eastern Europe—visited Du
activities looked as if they wer
Pact and Soviet security; they
tion in Vietnam as evidence
activities around the world.
democratize the Communist
meeting of members of the V
tanks and troops into Pragu
world watched as streams of
try and a repressive governm

creating safe areas for persecuted ethnic populations from all parties.

The crisis came to a head in the autumn of 1995. Sarajevo had been under siege for three years, but a series of mortar attacks on public marketplaces in Sarajevo produced fresh Western outrage and moved the United States to act. Already Croat forces and the Bosnian army had turned the war on the ground against the Serb militias, and now they were supported by a rolling wave of American air strikes. The American bombing, combined with a Croat-Bosnian offensive, forced the Bosnian Serbs to negotiate. Elite French troops supported by British artillery broke the siege of Sarajevo. Peace talks were held at Dayton, Ohio. The agreement divided Bosnia, with the majority of land in the hands of Muslims and Croats and a small, autonomous "Serb Republic" in areas that included land ethnically cleansed in 1992. Stability was restored, but three years of war had killed over 200,000 people.

The legacy of Bosnia flared into conflict again over Kosovo, the medieval homeland of the Orthodox Christian Serbs, now occupied by a largely Albanian, Muslim population. Milosevic accused the Albanians of plotting secession and of challenging the Serb presence in Kosovo. In the name of a "greater Serbia," Serb soldiers fought Albanian separatists rallying under the banner of "greater Albania." Both sides used terrorist tactics. Western nations were anxious lest the conflict might spread to the strategic, ethnically divided country of Macedonia and touch off a general Balkan conflict. Western political opinion was outraged, however, as Serbian forces used many of the same murderous tactics in Kosovo that they had employed earlier in Bosnia. Talks between Milosevic's government and the Albanian rebels were sponsored by the NATO powers but fell apart in early 1999. That failure was followed by a fresh wave of American-led bombing against Serbia itself, as well as against Serbian forces in Kosovo. A new round of ethnic cleansing drove hundreds of thousands of Albanians from their homes. Unwilling to fight a war on the ground in the mountainous, unforgiving terrain of the southern Balkans, the United States and its European allies concentrated on strategic attacks on bridges, power plants, factories, and Serbian military bases. The Russian government, bothered by this unilateral attack on fellow Slavs, nonetheless played an important part in brokering a cease-fire. Milosevic was forced to withdraw from Kosovo, leaving it in the hands of another force of armed NATO peacekeepers.

Finally, Serb-dominated Yugoslavia, worn by ten years of war and economic sanctions, turned against Milosevic's regime. Wars and corruption had destroyed Milosevic's credentials as a nationalist and populist. After he attempted to reject the results of a democratic election in 2000, his government fell to popular protests. He died in 2006, while being tried by a UN tribunal for war crimes.

As we gain perspective on the twentieth century, it is clear that the Yugoslavian wars of the 1990s were not an isolated instance of Balkan violence. The issues are thoroughly Western. The Balkans form one of the West's borderlands, where cultures influenced by Roman Catholicism, Eastern Orthodoxy, and Islam meet, overlap, and contend for political domination and influence. Since the nineteenth century, this region of enormous religious, cultural, and ethnic diversity has struggled with the implications of nationalism. We have seen how conflicts over the creation of new national states drawn

MASS FUNERAL IN KOSOVO, 1999. Ethnic Albanians bury victims of a Serbian massacre toward the end of Yugoslavia's ten years of fighting. ▪ *Although the nature of war has changed radically in the last hundred years, "ethnic cleansing" has remained remarkably constant and frequent in the modern period. What prevents states from taking effective action to prevent it?*

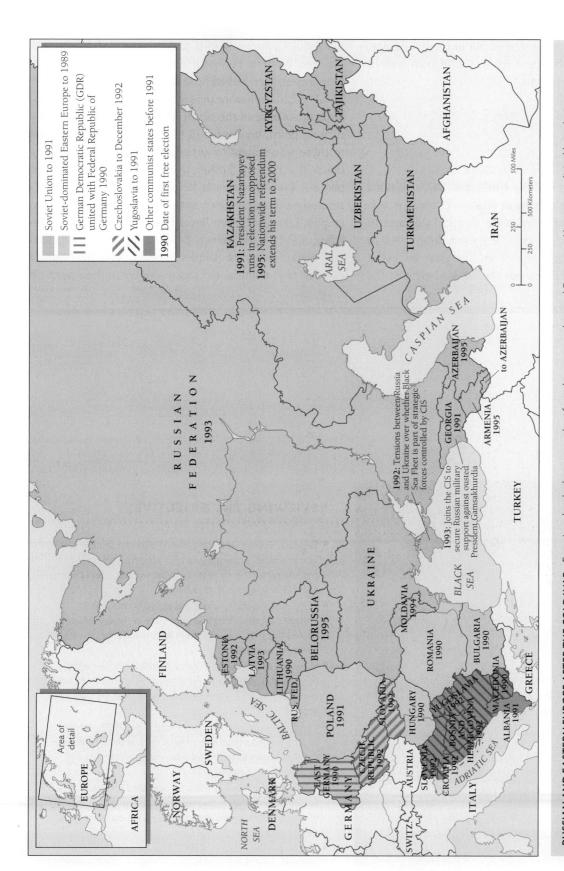

Legend:
- Soviet Union to 1991
- Soviet-dominated Eastern Europe to 1989
- German Democratic Republic (GDR) united with Federal Republic of Germany 1990
- Czechoslovakia to December 1992
- Yugoslavia to 1991
- Other communist states before 1991
- **1990** Date of first free election

KAZAKHSTAN
1991: President Nazarbayev runs in election unopposed
1995: Nationwide referendum extends his term to 2000

1992: Tensions between Russia and Ukraine over whether Black Sea Fleet is part of strategic forces controlled by CIS

1993: Joins the CIS to secure Russian military support against ousted President Gamsakhurdia

RUSSIAN AND EASTERN EUROPE AFTER THE COLD WAR. Examine closely the geography of southeastern and central Europe. ■ *How were political boundaries reorganized?* ■ *How did the collapse of the Soviet Union and the end of the Cold War allow for the reemergence of certain forces in the political landscape of Europe?* ■ *How were the boundaries of the Soviet Union reorganized after 1991?*

mostly on ethnic lines were worked out in Central Europe, with many instances of tragic violence. The Yugoslav wars fit into some of the same patterns.

CONCLUSION

The protest movements of the 1960s and 1970s revealed that postwar hopes for stability in Western Europe through economic development alone were shortsighted, and in any case, the astounding rates of growth from 1945 to 1968 could not be sustained forever. The great success of these first postwar decades was the establishment of the European Common Market and the spirit of cooperation between Western European nations that had only a few years before been locked in deadly conflict.

The Eastern European revolutions of 1989 and the subsequent collapse of the Soviet Union were a revolutionary turning point, however, and posed challenging questions to those who sought to guarantee stability by continuing down the path of further integration among European nations. Like the French Revolution of 1789, the 1989 revolutions brought down not only a regime but also an empire. Like the French Revolution, they gave way to violence, and like the French Revolution, they provided no easy consensus for the peoples who were left to reconstruct some form of political and social stability in their wake. In

After You Read This Chapter

 Visit StudySpace for quizzes, additional review materials, and multimedia documents. **wwnorton.com/web/westernciv18**

REVIEWING THE OBJECTIVES

- The success of economic rebuilding after the Second World War produced a new prosperity in Western Europe. What contributed to this success, and what were its effects on daily life and mass culture in Europe?
- The postwar decades witnessed an important shift in attitudes about women and their place in society. What caused this shift, and what were its consequences for European women?
- In Europe and the United States, significant movements of social and political protest emerged in the 1960s. What were the goals of these movements, and what did they accomplish?
- The postwar economic boom ended in the 1970s, leading to a prolonged period of economic contraction. What were the consequences of this recession for governments and populations in Europe?
- In the 1980s, Mikhail Gorbachev proposed reforms for the Soviet Union, reforms that failed to prevent the collapse of the Soviet bloc in Eastern Europe. What combination of events led to this collapse?
- The first post-Soviet decade in Europe was marked by political uncertainty, economic dislocation, and violence, with war in Yugoslavia and Chechnya. What circumstances made these years so difficult for Europeans?

the former Yugoslavia, in Slovakia, and in Russia itself, the uncertainty of the post-1989 years gave fresh impetus to energetic nationalist movements. Although militant nationalism might be a useful short-term political strategy for certain politicians, such nationalism is unlikely to create stability in Europe, however, because the broad population movements of the postwar years have continued unabated, and there is no part of Europe that possesses the ethnic or cultural homogeneity demanded by hard-line nationalists. Europe's long history is one of heterogeneity, and there is no reason to think that the future will be different in this respect.

Profound differences in wealth and economic capacity between Western and Eastern Europe were the most challenging hurdle to a stable integration of the newly independent nations of the post-Soviet empire. In the 1980s, it was possible to imagine that a relatively wealthy country like the Netherlands or Belgium might be willing to subsidize the integration of a less wealthy small country like Portugal into Europe. It has proved quite another task to convince the Dutch, the Belgians, or the Danes to help shoulder the burden for bringing large countries like Ukraine or Turkey into the European fold. Given this difficulty, can one say with confidence where Europe's outermost borders now lie? In the broader context of the global conflicts that emerged in the aftermath of the Cold War, Europe's boundaries and future remain both uncertain and linked to developments elsewhere in the world. This broader context and these global linkages are the subject of the last chapter of this book.

PEOPLE, IDEAS, AND EVENTS IN CONTEXT

- How did the wide availability of the **BIRTH CONTROL PILL** change public attitudes toward sex and sexuality in the 1960s?
- What made the **MASS CULTURE** of the postwar decades different from popular culture in previous historical eras?
- How did the struggles of the **CIVIL RIGHTS MOVEMENT** in the United States affect American efforts to promote democracy in Europe during the Cold War?
- What were the goals of **ALEXANDER DUBČEK**'s government in Czechoslovakia during the **PRAGUE SPRING**?
- How did the **1973 OPEC OIL EMBARGO** affect the economies of Eastern and Western Europe?
- How did **LECH WAŁĘSA** challenge the Polish government in the early 1980s?
- How did **MIKHAIL GORBACHEV** envision reforming the Soviet Union? What did he mean by *PERESTROIKA* and *GLASNOST*?
- What were the **VELVET REVOLUTIONS** of Central and Eastern Europe in 1989?
- What made **NATIONALISM IN YUGOSLAVIA** such a powerful force in Yugoslavia in the early 1990s, and what role did **SLOBODAN MILOSEVIC** play in the breakup of the Yugoslavian federation?

THINKING ABOUT CONNECTIONS

- The wave of protest and cultural discontent that spread throughout Europe in the 1960s encompassed both Western and Eastern Europe, in spite of the divisions imposed by the Cold War. Can one detect an echo of the revolutions of 1848 in the protests of 1968? What common concerns can one detect? What is different?
- Many observers were surprised by the resurgence of nationalism in Eastern Europe in the aftermath of the collapse of the Soviet Union. Can one compare the situation in Yugoslavia after 1989 to circumstances in that part of the world in the late nineteenth century, as Ottoman power waned and the Russian and Austrian Empires competed for influence in the region?

Before
You
Read
This
Chapter

A World without Walls: Globalization and the West

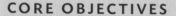

CORE OBJECTIVES

- **DEFINE** *globalization* and understand what is new about current patterns of interconnection in the world as well as the continuities that can be seen with earlier periods of global connection.

- **EXPLAIN** the continued relevance of the colonial past in shaping the politics, economy, and society of independent states in Asia and Africa and the nature of their ongoing relationships to the societies and states of Europe and North America.

- **UNDERSTAND** the global connections that link societies in other parts of the world to the events and persistent conflicts in the Middle East.

n the twenty-first century, the world has reentered a period in which basic assumptions about the role of nation-states, the roots of prosperity, and the boundaries of cultures are changing fast. We say *reentered* because, as we have seen, a disconcerting sense of seismic and little-understood change has been central to Western culture during several different historical periods. The Industrial Revolution of the nineteenth century is an example, and just as *industrial revolution*, a term coined in the early nineteenth century, seemed to capture contemporaries' perceptions of changes in their own time, so *globalization* seems to capture ours. Globalization is not new, but our acute consciousness of it is.

We know, intuitively, what globalization means: the Internet, protests against the World Trade Organization (WTO), outsourcing of jobs and services, Walmart in Mexico, the dismantling of the Berlin Wall. All of these are powerful images of larger, enormously significant developments. The Internet represents the stunning transformation of global communication, the media, and forms of knowledge. The Berlin Wall once stood for a divided Cold War world; its fall marked a dramatic reconfiguration of international relations, an end to the ideological

As far as the history of human rights is concerned, perhaps the most important development of the nineteenth century was the rise of nationalism and nation-states. Rights, and political movements claiming them, became increasingly inseparable from nationhood. "What is a country . . . but the place in which our demands for individual rights are most secure?" asked the Italian nationalist Giuseppe Mazzini. For nineteenth-century Italians, Germans, Serbs, and Poles and for twentieth-century Indians, Vietnamese, and Algerians—to name just a few—fighting for national independence was the way to secure the rights of citizens. National sovereignty, once achieved, was tightly woven into the fabric of politics and international relations and would not be easily relinquished.

The world wars marked a turning point. The First World War, an unprecedented global conflict, almost inevitably fostered dreams of global peace under the auspices of international organizations. The Peace of Paris aimed for more than a territorial settlement: with the League of Nations it tried, tentatively, to establish an organization that would transcend the power of individual nations and uphold the (ill-defined) principles of "civilization." (Despite this commitment, the League bowed to British and American objections to a statement condemning racial discrimination.) The experiment failed: the fragile League was swept aside by the surge of extreme nationalism and aggression in the 1930s. The shock and revulsion at the atrocities of the war that followed, however, brought forth more decisive efforts. The Second World War's aftermath saw the establishment of the United Nations, an International Court of Justice at the Hague (Netherlands), and the UN's High Commission on Human Rights. Unlike anything attempted after the First World War, the Commission on Human Rights set out to establish the rights of individuals—against the nation-state.

This Universal Declaration of Human Rights, published by the High Commission in 1948, became the touchstone of our modern notion of human rights. It was very much a product of its time. Its authors included Eleanor Roosevelt and the French jurist René Cassin, who had been wounded in the First World War (and held his intestines together during a nearly 400-mile train ride to medical treatment), lost his family in the Holocaust, and had seen his nation collaborate with the Nazis. The High Commission argued that the war and the "barbarous acts which have outraged the conscience of mankind," showed that no state should have absolute power over its citizens. The Universal Declaration prohibited torture, cruel punishment, and slavery. A separate convention, also passed in 1948, dealt with the newly defined crime of genocide. The Universal Declaration of 1948 built on earlier declarations that universal-ized the rights to legal equality, freedom of religion and speech, and the right to participate in government. Finally, it reflected the postwar period's effort to put democracy on a more solid footing by establishing *social* rights—to education, work, a "just and favorable remuneration," a "standard of living," and social security, among others.

Few nations were willing to ratify the Universal Declaration of Human Rights. For decades after the war, its idealistic principles could not be reconciled with British and French colonialism, American racial segregation, or Soviet dictatorship. For as long as wars to end colonialism continued, declarations of universal principles rang hollow. (Mahatma Gandhi, asked to comment on Western civilization, replied that he thought it was a "good idea.") For as long as the Cold War persisted, human rights seemed only a thinly veiled weapon in the sparring between the superpowers. Thus decolonization and, later, the end of the Cold War began to enhance the legitimacy and luster of human rights. International institutions set up after the Second World War matured, gaining expertise and stature. Global communications and media dramatically expanded the membership and influence of organizations that, like Amnesty International (founded in 1961), operated outside the economic or political boundaries of the nation-state. Memories of the Second World War, distorted or buried by the Cold War, continue to return, and the force of those memories helped drive the creation of International Criminal Tribunals for Yugoslavia and Rwanda in 1993. Finally, as one historian points out, at a time when many feel vulnerable to the forces of globalization, human rights offers a way of talking about rights, goods, and protections (environmental, for example) that the nation-state cannot—or can no longer—provide.

It is nevertheless the case that the troubled era that began with the 9/11 attacks on the United States in 2001 has seen many challenges to the notion of universal human rights. Terrorism, no matter what the ideology of the perpetrator, is a fundamental violation of every human's right to safety and security. In their zeal to punish terrorists, meanwhile, many nations in the world have tacitly turned away from the emerging international legal structures that attempted to defend the rights of all individuals everywhere. The struggle that the United States and its allies waged against al Qaeda and Taliban leadership has raised difficult questions about the tactics used, which included torture, indefinite detention without trial, and the use of pilotless drones to kill suspected militant leaders in distant countries. The use of drone technologies make it easier to avoid U.S. casualties in operations against a dangerous enemy, but many in the United States and abroad have expressed concerns about the government's right to identify, target, and execute individuals, including in some cases U.S. citizens, based on criteria that are never subject to independent legal review. Public opinion in the United States remains strongly in favor of such tactics, but in recent years public anger in Afghanistan and Pakistan has focused on cases of mistaken identity and the deaths of family members and bystanders in drone attacks. Even within the U.S. government and military, some have expressed concern that these methods could be counterproductive.

As the U.S. and European governments pursue their interests abroad, debates about the use of military power in other parts of the world and the form that this power takes have become pressing concerns, and the issues turn on questions that have been a central part of the liberal democratic political tradition since it emerged in opposition to monarchist forms of government in the seventeenth century. How should a nation determine the balance between individual freedoms and national security? What forms of force or violence can the state legitimately use against its enemies at home or abroad? What kinds of information about its citizenry should a government be allowed to keep? Are the terrorist threats that democratic regimes routinely face today so serious that they justify the suspension of internationally recognized human rights? No easy answers to these questions exist—but the answers that governments and societies in Europe and the United States give to them will shape how people everywhere will perceive the legitimacy of the democratic political institutions that they claim to represent.

EUROPE AND THE UNITED STATES IN THE TWENTY-FIRST CENTURY

As the first decade of the twenty-first century drew to a close, the initial confidence that Europeans felt in the aftermath of the revolutions of 1989 seemed badly shaken. The process of European integration, which had contributed so much to the political stability of Europe in the decades after the Second World War, seemed to have reached its limits in the East. Although a few independent nations that were formerly a part of the Soviet Union, such as Ukraine, might be interested in joining the European Union, it is unlikely that Russia would be comfortable with this realignment toward the West. Even the future membership of Turkey, an official candidate for entry into the EU since 1999 and an associate member of the European Union since 1963, remains uncertain because of growing discomfort in many European nations about admitting a historically Muslim nation into Europe. Turkey is a modern industrial nation that has been governed by a secular government since the 1920s, participated in the Marshall Plan after the Second World War, was a member of the Council of Europe in 1949, and became a member of NATO in 1952. A 2010 poll carried out in five European countries nevertheless found that 52 percent of respondents were opposed to Turkish membership in the European Union and only 41 percent in favor.

In the economic realm, the global financial crisis of 2007–2010 caused many in Europe and North America to rethink the central assumptions of late-twentieth-century neoliberalism, especially the belief that markets were by definition self-regulating. The crisis had its origins in a classic bubble in global housing prices, which encouraged banks to make ever-riskier bets in the real estate market while also experimenting with the sale of complicated securities whose risk became difficult to gauge with accuracy. When housing prices fell, many key banks in different parts of the world found themselves unable to state clearly the value of their plummeting investments tied to real estate. Since nobody knew how much money the largest financial institutions had, banks simply stopped lending money to one another, and in the resulting liquidity crisis many businesses failed and trillions of dollars of consumer savings were wiped out. Massive government bailouts of the largest banks with taxpayer money were required to stabilize the global financial system, and popular resentment against the financial industry stimulated many nations to consider widespread reform and government regulation of banks as a result.

Contemporary debates about political integration in Europe or the benefits of free-market capitalism are closely connected with the developments that followed the end of the Cold War in the early 1990s and the period of economic globalization that followed, but they can also be seen as a continuation of debates within the traditions of political and economic liberalism that go back to the eighteenth century. In its classic formulation as put forth by liberal theorists such as Adam Smith, political and economic liberties were best defended in a nation that possessed a small and limited government. The closely related traditions of social democracy that developed in Europe in the nineteenth and twentieth century, on the other hand, arose out of a concern that limited governments in the classic liberal mold could not do enough to remedy the inequalities that emerged from modern industrial societies, and the result was the creation of welfare state institutions that aimed to use the power of the state to maintain a base level of social and economic equality. This tension between the goals of liberty and equality is a constant one within the liberal tradition, and the different trajectories of Europe and the United States in the twentieth century reflect the respective priorities of successive governments in both places.

Many Europeans, therefore, watched the election of Barack Obama in the United States in 2008 with great interest. Since the election of Ronald Reagan in 1980, the divergences between governments in the United States and Europe in their attitudes toward the role that the state might play in remedying social problems had become even more acute. With few exceptions, European governments were much more willing to use the power of the state to assist the unemployed or the aged, to support families, and to provide subsidies for education, public transportation, and national programs for health care. As we have seen, this consensus emerged in part because of a belief that the economic dislocations of the 1920s and 1930s had led directly to the emergence of destabilizing and antidemocratic extremist political movements. In the United States, on the other hand, widespread discontent with attempts by the Johnson administration in the 1960s to use the power of the federal government to end racial segregation and address broad problems such as urban poverty and environmental pollution contributed to a conservative backlash in the 1980s and 1990s. Throughout those years, conservatives in the United States called for an end to welfare programs, repeal of environmental regulations, and less government oversight in the marketplace.

Obama's election in 2008, following on the heels of the financial meltdown earlier the same year, seemed to mark a turning point of sorts in American politics, as his pragmatic campaign was predicated on a claim that government itself was not the problem facing industrial democracies at the outset of the twenty-first century. The Obama administration's ambitious plan to overhaul the health care system faced stiff opposition from many quarters, but a compromise package succeeded in passing the Congress and was signed into law in 2010. Obama's reelection in 2012 has led to the implementation of the law's first measures. The fierceness of the health care debate—which revolved around questions about the power of the state, the responsibilities of elected governments, the nature of the public good, and the balance between liberty and equality—should not obscure the fact that partisans on both sides of these controversies are using a vocabulary and a set of references that are part of the same liberal democratic political traditions that emerged in Europe and North America in the previous two centuries.

If Obama's two-term presidency has given some hope to those who see an important role for the state in solving persistent social and economic problems, the situation in Europe in the aftermath of the 2008 financial crisis has been less comforting. The European welfare state model inherited from the post–Second World War decades was based on a combination of Marshall Plan investment, European economic integration, and cooperation among representatives of labor, employers, and the state. Trade unions agreed to wage moderation in exchange for social protections from the state. Business leaders agreed to higher taxes for social protections in exchange for labor peace. Govern-

ment officials convinced their electorates to pay higher taxes in exchange for social protections such as universal health care, unemployment, and old age pensions.

This system worked well as long as the economy kept growing. When the economy flattened out beginning in the 1970s, however, businesses reduced their investments, unemployment went up, workers expressed discontent with their former restraint on wages, and European states had less revenue for social protection. In the 1980s and 1990s, European governments resorted to deficit spending to protect their welfare programs, and this system worked well enough as long as the banks that were lending the governments money were confident that they would be repaid. Faith in this system led to the creation of the eurozone as a single currency area in 2002.

After the financial crisis of 2008, however, the delicate balance in Europe between banks and governments in Europe began to crumble. European banks that were already fragile from losses in the real estate bubble demanded extraordinarily high interest rates before they would loan money to governments that were in financial trouble. The crisis was most acute in Greece, Spain, Italy, Ireland, and Portugal, where government debt reached threatening levels. So far, the solution has been for the stronger economies in the eurozone to bail out the weaker economies by providing emergency funds. To receive them, however, the indebted governments are forced to accept steep cuts in state spending, which are deeply unpopular with their populations. The ensuing political crisis has caused some to think that the eurozone might not survive in its present form and that some countries might be forced out or choose to leave of their own will. If that happens, it will mark a significant turning point in the history of European integration, which has provided a template for thinking about the European future since the years after the Second World War.

THE ARAB SPRING OF 2011

The dramatic events that began in Tunisia in December 2010 brought a wave of protest and popular insurrection to much of the Arab Middle East, overthrowing powerful dictators and presidents for life in Tunisia, Egypt, and Libya. The speed of these momentous changes surprised people living in these countries as much as they astonished foreign observers—many had long assumed that political change, when it came to these regimes, would proceed at a glacial pace. Zine al-Abidine Ben Ali of Tunisia, Hosni Mubarak of Egypt, and Muammar Qadhafi of Libya had governed for decades. Ben Ali and Mubarak were establishment figures in the international world, regularly meet-

Past and Present

The Arab Spring in Historical Perspective

With the collapse of the Berlin Wall in 1989 a relatively recent memory, many people in Europe and North America sought to compare the recent protests in the Middle East against authoritarian governments to these European events. Comparisons with 1968 (see left, the Prague Spring), 1989, or 1848 may be instructive, but it is also likely that the forms of democracy that protesters in Tunisia, Egypt (see right, protesters in Tahrir Square, Cairo), and most recently, Turkey, are striving to create will reflect their own values, rather than conform to political models borrowed from elsewhere.

 Watch related author interview on StudySpace
wwnorton.com/web/westernciv18

ing with European leaders and U.S. presidents who were among their most loyal supporters. How had this happened so suddenly? Did it mean that a wave of democratic revolution was sweeping through the Middle East?

To explain these events, many observers in Europe and the United States looked for explanations from their own histories. Some people suggested that these revolts were comparable to the movements to overthrow the dictatorial regimes of Eastern Europe that culminated in the fall of the Berlin Wall in 1989 and the collapse of the Soviet Union in 1991. The very name "Arab Spring" recalled the Prague Spring of 1968 when young people in Czechoslovakia attempted, and ultimately failed, to create a different and more democratic form of socialism in that country. Others feared that these revolts might turn out like the Tiananmen Square protests in China of 1989, which ended up in a violent repression of a democratic movement. The continued civil war in Syria is a haunting reminder of the reality of this possibility.

All of these comparisons might be instructive, but they also reveal something significant about the way that many people think about movements for democratic revolutions: there is a tendency to assume that movements for democracy all want the same thing. History shows that it is usually much more complicated than that. Great coalitions can be assembled at a moment of crisis to challenge established regimes, but success brings on new challenges. As the protests in the Middle East and North Africa unfolded in 2011, observers frequently noted how new technologies such as cell phones and new social media such as Facebook and Twitter allowed people to make their voices heard in a new way and to coordinate mass actions almost instantaneously. It remains to be seen, however, what the lasting accomplishments of this movement for change will be. How can this unity be maintained when it comes to building a new political system, a new and different society?

Prior to 2011, many people in the United States, in Europe, and in the Middle East itself had been filled with

Grafton, Anthony, and Lisa Jardine. *From Humanism to the Humanities: Education and the Liberal Arts in Fifteenth- and Sixteenth-Century Europe.* London, 1986. An account that presents Renaissance humanism as the elitist cultural program of a self-interested group of pedagogues.

Grendler, Paul, ed. *Encyclopedia of the Renaissance.* New York, 1999. A valuable reference work.

Jardine, Lisa. *Worldly Goods.* London, 1996. A revisionist account that emphasizes the acquisitive materialism of Italian Renaissance society and culture.

Kanter, Laurence, Hilliard T. Goldfarb, and James Hankins. *Botticelli's Witness: Changing Style in a Changing Florence.* Boston, 1997. This catalog for an exhibition of Botticelli's works, at the Gardner Museum in Boston, offers an excellent introduction to the painter and his world.

King, Margaret L. *Women of the Renaissance.* Chicago, 1991. Deals with women in all walks of life and in a variety of roles.

Kristeller, Paul O. *Renaissance Thought: The Classic, Scholastic, and Humanistic Strains.* New York, 1961. Very helpful in defining the main trends of Renaissance thought.

Machiavelli, Niccolò. *The Discourses* and *The Prince.* Many editions. These two books must be read together if one is to understand Machiavelli's political ideas properly.

Mallett, Michael and Christine Shaw. *The Italian Wars, 1494–1559: War, State, and Society in Early Modern Europe.* Boston, 2012. Argues that the endemic warfare of this period within Italy revolutionized European military tactics and technologies.

Mann, Charles. *C. 1491: New Revelations of the Americas Before Columbus.* New York, 2006.

———. *1493: Uncovering the New World Columbus Created.* New York, 2012. Written for a popular audience, these are also engaging and well-informed syntheses of historical research.

Martines, Lauro. *Power and Imagination: City-States in Renaissance Italy.* New York, 1979. Insightful account of the connections among politics, society, culture, and art.

More, Thomas. *Utopia.* Many editions.

Olson, Roberta, *Italian Renaissance Sculpture.* New York, 1992. The most accessible introduction to the subject.

Parker, Geoffrey. *The Military Revolution: Military Innovation and the Rise of the West (1500–1800).* 2d ed. Cambridge and New York, 1996. A work of fundamental importance for understanding the global dominance achieved by early modern Europeans.

Perkins, Leeman L. *Music in the Age of the Renaissance.* New York, 1999. A massive new study that needs to be read in conjunction with Reese.

Phillips, J. R. S. *The Medieval Expansion of Europe.* 2d ed. Oxford, 1998. An outstanding study of the thirteenth- and fourteenth-century background to the fifteenth-century expansion of Europe. Important synthetic treatment of European relations with the Mongols, China, Africa, and North America. The second edition includes a new introduction and a bibliographical essay; the text is the same as in the first edition (1988).

Phillips, William D., Jr., and Carla R. Phillips. *The Worlds of Christopher Columbus.* Cambridge and New York, 1991. The first book to read on Columbus: accessible, engaging, and scholarly. Then read Fernández-Armesto's biography.

Rabelais, François. *Gargantua and Pantagruel.* Trans. J. M. Cohen. Baltimore, MD, 1955. A robust modern translation.

Reese, Gustave. *Music in the Renaissance,* rev. ed. New York, 1959. A great book; still authoritative, despite the more recent work by Perkins, which supplements but does not replace it.

Rice, Eugene F., Jr., and Anthony Grafton. *The Foundations of Early Modern Europe, 1460–1559,* 2d ed. New York, 1994. The best textbook account of its period.

Rowland, Ingrid D. *The Culture of the High Renaissance: Ancients and Moderns in Sixteenth-Century Rome.* Cambridge and New York, 2000. Beautifully written examination of the social, intellectual, and economic foundations of the Renaissance in Rome.

Russell, Peter. *Prince Henry "The Navigator": A Life.* New Haven, CT, 2000. A masterly biography by a great historian who has spent a lifetime on the subject. The only book one now needs to read on Prince Henry.

Scammell, Geoffrey V. *The First Imperial Age: European Overseas Expansion, 1400–1715.* London, 1989. A useful introductory survey, with a particular focus on English and French colonization.

CHAPTER 13

Bainton, Roland. *Erasmus of Christendom.* New York, 1969. Still the best biography in English of the Dutch reformer and intellectual.

Benedict, Philip. *Christ's Churches Purely Reformed: A Social History of Calvinism.* New Haven, CT, 2002. A wide-ranging recent survey of Calvinism in both western and eastern Europe.

Bossy, John. *Christianity in the West, 1400–1700.* Oxford and New York, 1985. A brilliant, challenging picture of the changes that took place in Christian piety and practice as a result of the sixteenth-century reformations.

Bouwsma, William J. *John Calvin: A Sixteenth-Century Portrait.* Oxford and New York, 1988. The best biography of the magisterial reformer.

Dixon, C. Scott, ed. *The German Reformation: The Essential Readings.* Oxford, 1999. A collection of important recent articles.

Duffy, Eamon. *The Stripping of the Altars: Traditional Religion in England, c. 1400–c. 1550.* A brilliant study of religious exchange at the parish level.

———. *The Voices of Morebath: Reformation and Rebellion in an English Village.* New Haven, 2003. How the crises of this period affected and are reflected in the history of a single parish.

Hart, D. G. *Calvinism: A History.* New Haven, 2013. A new survey of this leading Protestant movement from its beginnings to the present day.

John Calvin: Selections from His Writings, ed. John Dillenberger. Garden City, NY, 1971. A judicious selection, drawn mainly from Calvin's *Institutes.*

Koslofksy, Craig. *The Reformation of the Dead: Death and Ritual in Early Modern Germany.* Basingstoke, 2000. How essential rituals and responses to death were reshaped in this period.

Loyola, Ignatius. *Personal Writings.* Trans. by Joseph A. Munitiz and Philip Endean. London and New York, 1996. An excellent collection that includes Loyola's autobiography, his spiritual diary, and some of his letters, as well as his *Spiritual Exercises.*

Luebke, David, ed. *The Counter-Reformation: The Essential Readings*. Oxford, 1999. A collection of nine important recent essays.

MacCulloch, Diarmaid. *Reformation: Europe's House Divided, 1490–1700*. London and New York, 2003. A definitive new survey; the best single-volume history of its subject in a generation.

Martin Luther: Selections from His Writings, ed. John Dillenberger. Garden City, NY, 1961. The standard selection, especially good on Luther's theological ideas.

McGrath, Alister E. *Reformation Thought: An Introduction*. Oxford, 1993. A useful explanation, accessible to non-Christians, of the theological ideas of the major Protestant reformers.

Mullett, Michael A. *The Catholic Reformation*. London, 2000. A sympathetic survey of Catholicism from the mid-sixteenth to the eighteenth century that presents the mid-sixteenth-century Council of Trent as a continuation of earlier reform efforts.

Murray, Linda. *High Renaissance and Mannerism*. London, 1985. The place to begin a study of fifteenth- and sixteenth-century Italian art.

Oberman, Heiko A. *Luther: Man between God and the Devil*. Trans. by Eileen Walliser-Schwarzbart. New Haven, CT, 1989. A biography stressing Luther's preoccupations with sin, death, and the devil.

O'Malley, John W. *The First Jesuits*. Cambridge, MA, 1993. A scholarly account of the origins and early years of the Society of Jesus.

———. *Trent and All That: Renaming Catholicism in the Early Modern Era*. Cambridge, MA, 2000. Short, lively, and with a full bibliography.

———. *Trent: What Happened at the Council*. Cambridge, MA, 2012. A clear and comprehensive narrative of the Church council that gave birth to the modern Catholic Church.

Pettegree, Andrew, ed. *The Reformation World*. New York, 2000. An exhaustive multi-author work representing the most recent thinking about the Reformation.

Pelikan, Jaroslav. *Reformation of Church and Dogma, 1300–1700*. Vol. 4 of *A History of Christian Dogma*. Chicago, 1984. A masterful synthesis of Reformation theology in its late-medieval context.

Roper, Lyndal. *The Holy Household: Women and Morals in Reformation Augsburg*. Oxford, 1989. A pathbreaking study of Protestantism's effects on a single town, with special attention to its impact on attitudes toward women, the family, and marriage.

Shagan, Ethan H. *Popular Politics and the English Reformation*. Cambridge, 2002. Argues that the English Reformation reflects an ongoing process of negotiation, resistance, and response.

Tracy, James D. *Europe's Reformations, 1450–1650*. 2d ed. Lanham, MD, 2006. An outstanding survey, especially strong on Dutch and Swiss developments, but excellent throughout.

Williams, George H. *The Radical Reformation*. 3d ed. Kirksville, MO, 1992. Originally published in 1962, this is still the best book on Anabaptism and its offshoots.

CHAPTER 14

Bonney, Richard. *The European Dynastic States, 1494–1660*. Oxford and New York, 1991. An excellent survey of continental Europe during the "long" sixteenth century.

Briggs, Robin. *Early Modern France, 1560–1715*, 2d ed. Oxford and New York, 1997. Updated and authoritative, with new bibliographies.

———. *Witches and Neighbors: The Social and Cultural Context of European Witchcraft*. New York, 1996. An influential recent account of Continental witchcraft.

Cervantes, Miguel de. *Don Quixote*. Trans. Edith Grossman. New York, 2003. A splendid new translation.

Clarke, Stuart. *Thinking with Demons: The Idea of Witchcraft in Early Modern Europe*. Oxford and New York, 1999. By placing demonology into the context of sixteenth- and seventeenth-century intellectual history, Clarke makes sense of it in new and exciting ways.

Cochrane, Eric, Charles M. Gray, and Mark A. Kishlansky. *Early Modern Europe: Crisis of Authority*. Chicago, 1987. An outstanding source collection from the University of Chicago Readings in Western Civilization series.

Elliot, J. H. *The Old World and the New, 1492–1650*. Cambridge, 1992 repr. A brilliant and brief set of essays on the ways that the discovery of the Americas challenged European perspectives on the world and themselves.

———. *Empires of the Atlantic World: Britain and Spain in America, 1492–1830*. An illuminating comparative study. New Haven, 2007.

Hibbard, Howard. *Bernini*. Baltimore, MD, 1965. The basic study in English of this central figure of Baroque artistic activity.

Hirst, Derek. *England in Conflict, 1603–1660: Kingdom, Community, Commonwealth*. Oxford and New York, 1999. A complete revision of the author's *Authority and Conflict* (1986), this is an up-to-date and balanced account of a period that has been a historical battleground over the past twenty years.

Hobbes, Thomas. *Leviathan*. Ed. Richard Tuck. 2d ed. Cambridge and New York, 1996. The most recent edition, containing the entirety of *Leviathan*, not just the first two parts.

Holt, Mack P. *The French Wars of Religion, 1562–1629*. Cambridge and New York, 1995. A clear account of a confusing time.

Kors, Alan Charles, and Edward Peters. *Witchcraft in Europe, 400–1700: A Documentary History*, 2d ed. Philadelphia, 2000. A superb collection of documents, significantly expanded in the second edition, with up-to-date commentary.

Kingdon, Robert. *Myths about the St. Bartholomew's Day Massacres, 1572–1576*. Cambridge, MA, 1988. A detailed account of this pivotal moment in the history of France.

Levack, Brian P. *The Witch-Hunt in Early Modern Europe*, 2d ed. London and New York, 1995. The best account of the persecution of suspected witches; coverage extends from Europe in 1450 to America in 1750.

Levin, Carole. *The Heart and Stomach of a King: Elizabeth I and the Politics of Sex and Power*. Philadelphia, PA, 1994. A provocative argument for the importance of Elizabeth's gender for understanding her reign.

Limm, Peter, ed. *The Thirty Years' War*. London, 1984. An outstanding short survey, followed by a selection of primary-source documents.

Lynch, John. *Spain, 1516–1598: From Nation-State to World Empire*. Oxford and Cambridge, MA, 1991. The best book in English on Spain at the pinnacle of its sixteenth-century power.

MacCaffrey, Wallace. *Elizabeth I*. New York, 1993. An outstanding traditional biography by an excellent scholar.

Martin, Colin, and Geoffrey Parker. *The Spanish Armada*. London, 1988. Incorporates recent discoveries from undersea archaeology with more traditional historical sources.

Mattingly, Garrett. *The Armada*. Boston, 1959. A great narrative history that reads like a novel; for more recent work, however, see Martin and Parker.

McGregor, Neil. *Shakespeare's Restless World*. London, 2013. Based on an acclaimed BBC Radio program, this book illuminates Shakespeare's life, times, and plays with reference to specific objects in the British Museum.

Newson, Linda A. and Susie Minchin. *From Capture to Sale: The Portuguese Slave Trade to Spanish South America in the Early Seventeenth Century*. London, 2007. Makes use of slave traders' own rich archives to track the process of human trafficking.

Parker, Geoffrey. *The Dutch Revolt*, 2d ed. Ithaca, NY, 1989. The standard survey in English on the revolt of the Netherlands.

———. *Philip II*. Boston, 1978. A fine biography by an expert in both the Spanish and the Dutch sources.

———, ed. *The Thirty Years' War*, rev. ed. London and New York, 1987. A wide-ranging collection of essays by scholarly experts.

Pascal, Blaise. *Pensées* (French-English edition). Ed. H. F. Stewart. London, 1950.

Pestana, Carla. *Protestant Empire: Religion and the Making of the British Atlantic World*. Philadelphia, 2010. How the Reformation helped to drive British imperial expansion.

Roberts, Michael. *Gustavus Adolphus and the Rise of Sweden*. London, 1973. Still the authoritative English-language account.

Russell, Conrad. *The Causes of the English Civil War*. Oxford, 1990. A penetrating and provocative analysis by one of the leading "revisionist" historians of the period.

Schmidt, Benjamin. *Innocence Abroad: The Dutch Imagination and the New World, 1570–1670*. Cambridge, 2006. A cultural history of Europeans' encounter with the Americas that highlights the perspective and experience of Dutch merchants, colonists, and artists.

Tracy, James D. *Holland under Habsburg Rule, 1506–1566: The Formation of a Body Politic*. Berkeley and Los Angeles, CA, 1990. A political history and analysis of the formative years of the Dutch state.

Kishlansky, Mark A. *A Monarchy Transformed: Britain, 1603–1714*. London, 1996. An excellent survey that takes seriously its claims to be a "British" rather than merely an "English" history.

Klein, Herbert S. *The Atlantic Slave Trade*. Cambridge and New York, 1999. An accessible survey by a leading quantitative historian.

Lewis, William Roger, gen. ed. *The Oxford History of the British Empire*. Vol. I: *The Origins of Empire: British Overseas Enterprise to the Close of the Seventeenth Century*, ed. Nicholas Canny. Vol. II: *The Eighteenth Century*, ed. Peter J. Marshall. Oxford and New York, 1998. A definitive, multiauthor account.

Locke, John. *Two Treatises of Government*. Ed. Peter Laslett. Rev. ed. Cambridge and New York, 1963. Laslett has revolutionized our understanding of the historical and ideological context of Locke's political writings.

Massie, Robert. *Peter the Great, His Life and World*. New York, 1980. Prize-winning and readable narrative account of the Russian tsar's life.

Monod, Paul K. *The Power of Kings: Monarchy and Religion in Europe, 1589–1715*. New Haven, CT, 1999. A study of the seventeenth century's declining confidence in the divinity of kings.

Quataert, Donald. *The Ottoman Empire, 1700–1822*. Cambridge and New York, 2000. Well balanced and intended to be read by students.

Riasanovsky, Nicholas V., and Steinberg, Mark D. *A History of Russia*. 7th ed. Oxford and New York, 2005. Far and away the best single-volume textbook on Russian history: balanced, comprehensive, intelligent, and with full bibliographies.

Saint-Simon, Louis. *Historical Memoirs*. Many editions. The classic source for life at Louis XIV's Versailles.

Snyder, Timothy, *The Reconstruction of Nations: Poland, Ukraine, Lithuania, Belarus, 1569–1999*. New Haven, CT, 2004. Essential account of nation-building and state-collapse in Eastern Europe with significant relevance to the region's contemporary situation.

Thomas, Hugh. *The Slave Trade: The History of the Atlantic Slave Trade, 1440–1870*. London and New York, 1997. A survey notable for its breadth and depth of coverage and for its attractive prose style.

Tracy, James D. *The Rise of Merchant Empires: Long-Distance Trade in the Early Modern World, 1350–1750*. Cambridge and New York, 1990. Important collection of essays by leading authorities.

White, Richard. *The Middle Ground: Indians, Empires and Republics in the Great Lakes Region, 1650–1815*. Cambridge, UK, 1991. A path-breaking account of interactions between Europeans and Native Americans during the colonial period.

CHAPTER 15

Beik, William. *A Social and Cultural History of Early Modern France*. Cambridge, UK, 2009. A broad synthesis of French history from the end of the Middle Ages to the French Revolution, by one of the world's foremost authorities on absolutism.

Clark, Christopher, *Iron Kingdom: The Rise and Downfall of Prussia, 1600–1947*. Cambridge, MA, 2009. A definitive account of Prussian history over nearly four centuries.

Jones, Colin. *The Great Nation: France From Louis XV to Napoleon*. New York, 2002. An excellent and readable scholarly account that argues that the France of Louis XV in the eighteenth century was even more dominant than the kingdom of Louis XIV in the preceding century.

CHAPTER 16

Biagioli, Mario. *Galileo, Courtier*. Chicago, 1993. Emphasizes the importance of patronage and court politics in Galileo's science and career.

Cohen, I. B. *The Birth of a New Physics*. New York, 1985. Emphasizes the mathematical nature of the revolution; unmatched at making the mathematics understandable.

Daston, Lorraine, and Elizabeth Lunbeck, eds. *Histories of Scientific Observation*. Chicago, IL, 2011. Field-defining collection of essays on the history of scientific observation from the seventeenth to the twentieth centuries.

Daston, Lorraine. *Wonders and the Order of Nature, 1150–1750*. Cambridge, MA, 2001. Erudite sweeping account of the history of science in the early modern period, emphasizing the natural philosopher's awe and wonder at the marvelous, the unfamiliar, and the counter-intuitive.

Dear, Peter. *Revolutionizing the Sciences: European Knowledge and Its Ambitions, 1500–1700*. Princeton, NJ, 2001. Among the best short histories.

Drake, Stillman. *Discoveries and Opinions of Galileo*. Garden City, NY, 1957. The classic translation of Galileo's most important papers by his most admiring modern biographer.

Feingold, Mardechai, *The Newtonian Moment: Isaac Newton and the Making of Modern Culture*. New York, 2004. An engaging essay on the dissemination of Newton's thought, with excellent visual material.

Gaukroger, Stephen. *Descartes: An Intellectual Biography*. Oxford, 1995. Detailed and sympathetic study of the philosopher.

Gleick, James. *Isaac Newton*. New York, 2003. A vivid and well-documented brief biography.

Grafton, Anthony. *New Worlds, Ancient Texts: The Power of Tradition and the Shock of Discovery*. Cambridge, MA, 1992. Accessible essay by one of the leading scholars of early modern European thought.

Jacob, Margaret. *Scientific Culture and the Making of the Industrial West*. Oxford, 1997. A concise examination of the connections between developments in science and the Industrial Revolution.

Kuhn, Thomas. *The Structure of Scientific Revolutions*. Chicago, 1962. A classic and much-debated study of how scientific thought changes.

Pagden, Anthony, *European Encounters with the New World*. New Haven, CT, and London, 1993. Subtle and detailed on how European intellectuals thought about the lands they saw for the first time.

Scheibinger, Londa. *The Mind Has No Sex? Women in the Origins of Modern Science*. Cambridge, MA, 1989. A lively and important recovery of the lost role played by women mathematicians and experimenters.

Shapin, Steven. *The Scientific Revolution*. Chicago, 1996. Engaging, accessible, and brief—organized thematically.

Shapin, Steven, and Simon Schaffer. *Leviathan and the Air Pump*. Princeton, NJ, 1985. A modern classic, on one of the most famous philosophical conflicts in seventeenth-century science.

Stephenson, Bruce. *The Music of the Heavens: Kepler's Harmonic Astronomy*. Princeton, NJ, 1994. An engaging and important explanation of Kepler's otherworldly perspective.

Thoren, Victor. *The Lord of Uraniburg: A Biography of Tycho Brahe*. Cambridge, 1990. A vivid reconstruction of the scientific revolution's most flamboyant astronomer.

Westfall, Richard. *The Construction of Modern Science*. Cambridge, 1977.

———. *Never at Rest: A Biography of Isaac Newton*. Cambridge, 1980. The standard work.

Wilson, Catherine. *The Invisible World: Early Modern Philosophy and the Invention of the Microscope*. Princeton, NJ, 1995. An important study of how the "microcosmic" world revealed by technology reshaped scientific philosophy and practice.

Zinsser, Judith P. *La Dame d'Esprit: A Biography of the Marquise Du Châtelet*. New York, 2006. An excellent cultural history. To be issued in paper as *Emilie du Châtelet: Daring Genius of the Enlightenment* (2007).

CHAPTER 17

Baker, Keith. *Condorcet: From Natural Philosophy to Social Mathematics*. Chicago, 1975. An important reinterpretation of Condorcet as a social scientist.

Blum, Carol. *Rousseau and the Republic of Virtue: The Language of Politics in the French Revolution*. Ithaca and London, 1986. Fascinating account of how eighteenth-century readers interpreted Rousseau.

Buchan, James. *The Authentic Adam Smith: His Life and Ideas*. New York, 2006.

Calhoun, Craig, ed. *Habermas and the Public Sphere*. Cambridge, MA, 1992. Calhoun's introduction is a good starting point for Habermas's argument.

Cassirer, E. *The Philosophy of the Enlightenment*. Princeton, NJ, 1951.

Chartier, Roger. *The Cultural Origins of the French Revolution*. Durham, NC, 1991. Looks at topics from religion to violence in everyday life and culture.

Darnton, Robert. *The Business of Enlightenment: A Publishing History of the* Encyclopédie, *1775–1800*. Cambridge, MA, 1979. Darnton's work on the Enlightenment offers a fascinating blend of intellectual, social, and economic history. See his other books as well: *The Literary Underground of the Old Regime* (Cambridge, MA, 1982); *The Great Cat Massacre and Other Episodes in French Cultural History* (New York, 1984); and *The Forbidden Best Sellers of Revolutionary France* (New York and London, 1996).

Davis, David Brion. *The Problem of Slavery in Western Culture*. New York, 1988. A Pulitzer Prize–winning examination of a central issue as well as a brilliant analysis of different strands of Enlightenment thought.

Gay, Peter. *The Enlightenment: An Interpretation*. Vol. 1, *The Rise of Modern Paganism*. Vol. 2, *The Science of Freedom*. New York, 1966–1969. Combines an overview with an interpretation. Emphasizes the *philosophes'* sense of identification with the classical world and takes a generally positive view of their accomplishments. Includes extensive annotated bibliographies.

Gray, Peter. *Mozart*. New York, 1999. Brilliant short study.

Goodman, Dena. *The Republic of Letters: A Cultural History of the French Enlightenment*. Ithaca, NY, 1994. Important in its attention to the role of literary women.

Hazard, Paul. *The European Mind: The Critical Years (1680–1715)*. New Haven, CT, 1953. A basic and indispensable account of the changing climate of opinion that preceded the Enlightenment.

Hunt, Lynn, Margaret C. Jacob, and Wijnand Mijnhardt. *The Book That Changed Europe: Picart and Bernard's Religious Ceremonies of the World*. Cambridge, MA, 2010. Lively study of a book on global religions that came out of the fertile world of the Dutch Enlightenment in the eighteenth century.

Israel, Jonathan Irvine. *Radical Enlightenment: Philosophy and the Making of Modernity, 1650–1750*. New York, 2001. Massive and erudite, a fresh look at the international movement of ideas.

———. *Enlightenment Contested: Philosophy, Modernity, and the Emancipation of Man, 1670–1752*. New York, 2006. Massive and erudite, a fresh look at the international movement of ideas.

Munck, Thomas. *The Enlightenment: A Comparative Social History 1721–1794*. London, 2000. An excellent recent survey, especially good on social history.

Outram, Dorinda. *The Enlightenment*. Cambridge, 1995. An excellent short introduction and a good example of new historical approaches.

Pagden, Anthony. *The Enlightenment: And Why It Still Matters*. New York, 2013. Spirited history of the Enlightenment and a defense of its continued relevance.

Porter, Roy. *The Creation of the Modern World: The Untold Story of the British Enlightenment*. New York, 2000.

Sapiro, Virginia. *A Vindication of Political Virtue: The Political Theory of Mary Wollstonecraft*. Chicago, 1992. A subtle and intelligent analysis for more advanced readers.

Shklar, Judith. *Men and Citizens: A Study of Rousseau's Social Theory*. London, 1969.

———. *Montesquieu*. Oxford, 1987. Shklar's studies are brilliant and accessible.

Taylor, Barbara. *Mary Wollstonecraft and the Feminist Imagination*. Cambridge and New York, 2003. Fascinating study that sets Wollstonecraft in the radical circles of eighteenth-century England.

Taylor, Barbara and Sarah Knott, eds. *Women, Gender, and Enlightenment*. New York, 2007. Multi-author collection examining the significance of sex, gender, and politics across a wide swath of the Enlightenment world, from Europe to the American colonies.

Venturi, Franco. *The End of the Old Regime in Europe, 1768–1776: The First Crisis*. Trans. R. Burr Litchfield. Princeton, NJ, 1989.

———. *The End of the Old Regime in Europe, 1776–1789*. Princeton, NJ, 1991. Both detailed and wide-ranging, particularly important on international developments.

Watt, Ian P. *The Rise of the Novel*. London, 1957. The basic work on the innovative qualities of the novel in eighteenth-century England.

Wolff, Larry. *Inventing Eastern Europe: The Map of Civilization on the Mind of the Enlightenment*. Stanford, CA, 1994. The place of Eastern Europe in the imagination of Enlightenment thinkers interested in the origins and destiny of the civilizing process.

CHAPTER 18

Applewhite, Harriet B., and Darline G. Levy, eds. *Women and Politics in the Age of the Democratic Revolution*. Ann Arbor, MI, 1990. Essays on France, Britain, the Netherlands, and the United States.

Bell, David A. *The First Total War: Napoleon's Europe and the Birth of Warfare as We Know It*. Boston and New York, 2007. Lively and concise study of the "cataclysmic intensification" of warfare.

Blackburn, Robin. *The Overthrow of Colonial Slavery*. London and New York, 1988. A longer view of slavery and its abolition.

Blanning, T. C. W. *The French Revolutionary Wars, 1787–1802*. Oxford, 1996. On the revolution and war.

Blum, Carol. *Rousseau and the Republic of Virtue: The Language of Politics in the French Revolution*. Ithaca, NY, 1986. Excellent on how Rousseau was read by the revolutionaries.

Cobb, Richard. *The People's Armies*. New Haven, CT, 1987. Brilliant and detailed analysis of the popular militias.

Cole, Juan. *Napoleon's Egypt: Invading the Middle East*. New York, 2007. Readable history by a scholar familiar with sources in Arabic as well as European languages.

Connelly, Owen. *The French Revolution and Napoleonic Era*. 3rd ed. New York, 2000. Accessible, lively, one-volume survey.

Darnton, Robert, *The Forbidden Best-Sellers of Pre-Revolutionary France*. New York, 1995. One of Darnton's many imaginative studies of subversive opinion and books on the eve of the revolution.

Desan, Suzanne. *The Family on Trial in Revolutionary France*. Berkeley, CA, 2006. Persuasive study of the ways that women in France were able to take advantage of the revolution and defend their interests in debates about marriage, divorce, parenthood, and the care of children.

Desan, Suzanne, Lynn Hunt, and William Max Nelson, eds. *The French Revolution in Global Perspective*. Ithaca, NY, 2013. Multi-author exploration of the French Revolution's global resonance.

Doyle, William. *Origins of the French Revolution*. New York, 1988. A revisionist historian surveys recent research on the political and social origins of the revolution and identifies a new consensus.

———. *Oxford History of the French Revolution*. New York, 1989.

Dubois, Laurent. *Avengers of the New World. The Story of the Haitian Revolution*. Cambridge, MA, 2004. Now the best and most accessible study.

———, and John D. Garrigus. *Slave Revolution in the Caribbean, 1789–1804: A Brief History with Documents*. New York, 2006. A particularly good collection.

Englund, Steven. *Napoleon, A Political Life*. Cambridge, MA, 2004. Prize-winning biography, both dramatic and insightful.

Forrest, Alan. *The French Revolution and the Poor*. New York, 1981. A moving and detailed social history of the poor, who fared little better under revolutionary governments than under the Old Regime.

Furet, Francois. *Revolutionary France, 1770–1880*. Trans. Antonia Nerill. Cambridge, MA, 1992. Overview by the leading revisionist.

Hunt, Lynn. *The French Revolution and Human Rights*. Boston, 1996. A collection of documents.

———. *Politics, Culture, and Class in the French Revolution*. Berkeley, CA, 1984. An analysis of the new culture of democracy and republicanism.

Hunt, Lynn, and Jack R. Censer. *Liberty, Equality, Fraternity: Exploring the French Revolution*. University Park, PA, 2001. Two leading historians of the revolution have written a lively, accessible study, with excellent documents and visual material.

Landes, Joan B. *Women and the Public Sphere in the Age of the French Revolution*. Ithaca, NY, 1988. On gender and politics.

Lefebvre, Georges. *The Coming of the French Revolution*. Princeton, NJ, 1947. The classic Marxist analysis.

Lewis, G., and C. Lucas. *Beyond the Terror: Essays in French Regional and Social History, 1794–1815*. New York, 1983. Shifts focus to the understudied period after the Terror.

O'Brien, Connor Cruise. *The Great Melody: A Thematic Biography of Edmund Burke*. Chicago, 1992. Passionate, partisan, and brilliant study of Burke's thoughts about Ireland, India, America, and France.

Palmer, R. R. *The Age of the Democratic Revolution: A Political History of Europe and America, 1760–1800.* 2 vols. Princeton, NJ, 1964. Impressive for its scope; places the French Revolution in the larger context of a worldwide revolutionary movement.

————, and Isser Woloch. *Twelve Who Ruled: The Year of the Terror in the French Revolution.* Princeton, NJ, 2005. The terrific collective biography of the Committee of Public Safety, now updated.

Schama, Simon. *Citizens: A Chronicle of the French Revolution.* New York, 1989. Particularly good on art, culture, and politics.

Scott, Joan. *Only Paradoxes to Offer: French Feminists and the Rights of Man.* Cambridge, MA, 1997. A history of feminist engagement with a revolutionary ideology that promised universal liberties while simultaneously excluding women from citizenship.

Soboul, Albert. *The Sans-Culottes: The Popular Movement and Revolutionary Government, 1793–1794.* Garden City, NY, 1972. Dated, but a classic.

Sutherland, D. M. G. *France, 1789–1815: Revolution and Counter-revolution.* Oxford, 1986. An important synthesis of work on the revolution, especially in social history.

Tocqueville, Alexis de. *The Old Regime and the French Revolution.* Garden City, NY, 1955. Originally written in 1856, this remains a provocative analysis of the revolution's legacy.

Trouillot, Michel Rolph. *Silencing the Past.* Boston, 1995. Essays on the Haitian revolution.

Woloch, Isser. *The New Regime: Transformations of the French Civic Order, 1789–1820.* New York, 1994. The fate of revolutionary civic reform.

Woolf, Stuart. *Napoleon's Integration of Europe.* New York, 1991. Technical but very thorough.

CHAPTER 19

Bridenthal, Renate, Claudia Koonz, and Susan Stuard, eds. *Becoming Visible: Women in European History.* 2d ed. Boston, 1987. Excellent, wide-ranging introduction.

Briggs, Asa. *Victorian Cities.* New York, 1963. A survey of British cities, stressing middle-class attitudes toward the new urban environment.

Chevalier, Louis. *Laboring Classes and Dangerous Classes during the First Half of the Nineteenth Century.* New York, 1973. An important, though controversial, account of crime, class, and middle-class perceptions of life in Paris.

Cipolla, Carlo M., ed. *The Industrial Revolution, 1700–1914.* New York, 1976. A collection of essays that emphasizes the wide range of industrializing experiences in Europe.

Clark, Anna. *The Struggle for the Breeches: Gender and the Making of the British Working Class.* Berkeley, CA, 1997. Examines the process of class formation during the industrial revolution in Britain through the lens of gender.

Cott, Nancy. *The Bonds of Womanhood: "Woman's Sphere" in New England, 1780–1935.* New Haven, CT, and London, 1977. One of the most influential studies of the paradoxes of domesticity.

Davidoff, Leonore, and Catherine Hall. *Family Fortunes: Men and Women of the English Middle Class, 1780–1850.* Chicago, 1985. A

brilliant and detailed study of the lives and ambitions of several English families.

Ferguson, Niall. "The European Economy, 1815–1914." In *The Nineteenth Century,* ed. T. C. W. Blanning. Oxford and New York, 2000. A very useful short essay.

Gay, Peter. *The Bourgeois Experience: Victoria to Freud.* New York, 1984. A multivolume, path-breaking study of middle-class life in all its dimensions.

————. *Schnitzler's Century: The Making of Middle-Class Culture, 1815–1914.* New York and London, 2002. A synthesis of some of the arguments presented in *The Bourgeois Experience.*

Hellerstein, Erna, Leslie Hume, and Karen Offen, eds. *Victorian Women: A Documentary Account.* Stanford, CA, 1981. Good collection of documents, with excellent introductory essays.

Hobsbawm, Eric J. *The Age of Revolution, 1789–1848.* London, 1962.

————, and George Rudé. *Captain Swing: A Social History of the Great English Agricultural Uprising of 1830.* New York, 1975. Analyzes rural protest and politics.

Horn, Jeff. *The Path Not Taken: French Industrialization in the Age of Revolution, 1750–1830.* Cambridge, 2006. Argues that industrialization in France succeeded in ways that other historians have not appreciated, and was much more than a failed attempt to imitate the British model.

Jones, Eric. *The European Miracle: Environments, Economies and Geopolitics in the History of Europe and Asia.* Cambridge, 2003. Argues that the Industrial Revolution is best understood as a European phenomenon.

Kemp, Tom. *Industrialization in Nineteenth-Century Europe.* London, 1985. Good general study.

Kindelberger, Charles. *A Financial History of Western Europe.* London, 1984. Emphasis on finance.

Landes, David S. *The Unbound Prometheus: Technological Change and Industrial Development in Western Europe from 1750 to the Present.* London, 1969. Excellent and thorough on technological change and its social and economic context.

McNeill, J. R. *Something New under the Sun: An Environmental History of the Twentieth-Century World.* New York and London, 2000. Short section on the nineteenth century.

Mokyr, Joel. *The Lever of Riches: Technological Creativity and Economic Progress.* New York, 1992. A world history, from antiquity through the nineteenth century

O'Gráda, Cormac. *Black '47 and Beyond: The Great Irish Famine.* Princeton, NJ, 1999.

————. *The Great Irish Famine.* Cambridge, 1989. A fascinating and recent assessment of scholarship on the famine.

Kenneth Pomeranz. *The Great Divergence: China, Europe, and the Making of the Modern World Economy.* Princeton, NJ, 2000. Path-breaking global history of the Industrial Revolution that argues that Europe was not as different from other parts of the world as scholars have previously thought.

Rendall, Jane. *The Origins of Modern Feminism: Women in Britain, France and the United States, 1780–1860.* New York, 1984. Helpful overview.

Rose, Sonya O. *Limited Livelihoods: Gender and Class in Nineteenth-Century England.* Berkeley, CA, 1992. On the intersection of culture and economics.

Sabean, David Warren. *Property, Production, and Family Neckarhausen, 1700–1870*. New York, 1990. Brilliant and very detailed study of gender roles and family.

Sabel, Charles, and Jonathan Zeitlin. "Historical Alternatives to Mass Production." *Past and Present* 108 (August 1985): 133–176. On the many forms of modern industry.

Schivelbusch, Wolfgang. *Disenchanted Night: The Instrialization of Light in the Nineteenth Century*. Berkeley, CA, 1988.

———. *The Railway Journey*. Berkeley, 1986. Schivelbusch's imaginative studies are among the best ways to understand how the transformations of the nineteenth century changed daily experiences.

Thompson, E. P. *The Making of the English Working Class*. London, 1963. Shows how the French and Industrial Revolutions fostered the growth of working-class consciousness. A brilliant and important work.

Tilly, Louise, and Joan Scott. *Women, Work and the Family*. New York, 1978. Now the classic study.

Valenze, Deborah. *The First Industrial Woman*. New York, 1995. Excellent and readable on industrialization and economic change in general.

Williams, Raymond. *Keywords: A Vocabulary of Culture and Society*. New York, 1976. Brilliant and indispensable for students of culture, and now updated as *New Keywords: A Revised Vocabulary of Culture and Society* (2005), by Lawrence Grossberg and Meaghan Morris.

Zeldin, Theodore. *France, 1848–1945*, 2 vols. Oxford, 1973–1977. Eclectic and wide-ranging social history.

CHAPTER 20

Anderson, Benedict. *Imagined Communities: Reflections on the Origin and Spread of Nationalism*. London, 1983. The most influential recent study of the subject, highly recommended for further reading.

Barzun, Jacques. *Classic, Romantic, and Modern*. Chicago, 1943. An enduring and penetrating mid-twentieth-century defense of the Romantic sensibility by a humane and influential cultural historian.

Berlin, Isaiah. *Karl Marx: His Life and Environment*. 4th ed. New York, 1996. An excellent short account.

Briggs, Asa. *The Age of Improvement, 1783–1867*. New York, 1979. A survey of England from 1780 to 1870, particularly strong on Victorian attitudes.

Colley, Linda. *Britons: Forging the Nation, 1707–1837*. New Haven, CT, 1992. An important analysis of Britain's emerging national consciousness in the eighteenth and early nineteenth centuries.

Furet, François. *Revolutionary France, 1770–1880*. New York, 1970. An excellent and fresh overview by one of the preeminent historians of the revolution of 1789.

Gilbert, Sandra M., and Susan Gubar. *The Madwoman in the Attic: The Woman Writer and the Nineteenth-Century Literary Imagination*. New Haven, CT, and London, 1970. A study of the history of women writers and on examination of women writers as historians of their time.

Kramer, Lloyd. *Nationalism: Political Cultures in Europe and America, 1775–1865*. London, 1998. Excellent recent overview.

Langer, William. *Political and Social Upheaval, 1832–1851*. New York, 1969. Long the standard and still the most comprehensive survey.

Laven, David, and Lucy Riall. *Napoleon's Legacy: Problems of Government in Restoration Europe*. London, 2002. A recent collection of essays.

Levinger, Matthew. *Enlightened Nationalism: The Transformation of Prussian Political Culture 1806–1848*. New York, 2000. A nuanced study of Prussian conservatism, with implications for the rest of Europe.

Macfie, A. L. *Orientalism*. London, 2002. Introductory but very clear.

Merriman, John M., ed. *1830 in France*. New York, 1975. Emphasizes the nature of revolution and examines events outside Paris.

Pinkney, David. *The French Revolution of 1830*. Princeton, NJ, 1972. A reinterpretation, now the best history of the revolution.

Porter, Roy, and Mikulas Teich, eds. *Romanticism in National Context*. Cambridge, 1988.

Raeff, Marc. *The Decembrist Movement*. New York, 1966. A study of the Russian uprising with documents.

Sahlins, Peter. *Forest Rites: The War of the Demoiselles in Nineteenth-Century France*. Cambridge, MA, 1994. A fascinating study of relations among peasant communities, the forests, and the state.

Said, Edward W. *Orientalism*. New York, 1979. A brilliant and biting study of the imaginative hold of the Orient on European intellectuals.

Saville, John. *1848: The British State and the Chartist Movement*. New York, 1987. A detailed account of the movement's limited successes and ultimate failure.

Schroeder, Paul. *The Transformation of European Politics, 1763–1848*. Oxford and New York, 1994. For those interested in international relations and diplomacy; massively researched and a fresh look at the period. Especially good on the Congress of Vienna.

Sewell, William H. *Work and Revolution in France: The Language of Labor from the Old Regime to 1848*. Cambridge, 1980. A very influential study of French radicalism and its larger implications.

Smith, Bonnie. *The Gender of History: Men, Women, and Historical Practice*. Cambridge, MA, 1998. On Romanticism and the historical imagination.

Sperber, Jonathan. *Karl Marx: A Nineteenth-Century Life*. New York, 2013. A detailed biography examining Marx's public and private engagements, setting him in the context of his time.

Wordsworth, Jonathan, Michael C. Jaye, and Robert Woof. *William Wordsworth and the Age of English Romanticism*. New Brunswick, NJ, 1987. Wide ranging and beautifully illustrated, a good picture of the age.

CHAPTER 21

Agulhon, Maurice. *The Republican Experiment, 1848–1852*. New York, 1983. A full treatment of the revolution in France.

Beales, Derek. *The Risorgimento and the Unification of Italy.* New York, 1971. Objective, concise survey of Italian unification.

Blackbourn, David. *The Long Nineteenth Century: A History of Germany, 1780–1918.* New York, 1998.

Blackbourn, David, and Geoff Eley. *The Peculiarities of German History: Bourgeois Society and Politics in Nineteenth-Century Germany.* Oxford, 1984. Critical essays on the course of German history during the age of national unification and after.

Blackburn, Robin. *The Overthrow of Colonial Slavery.* London, 1988. Brilliant and detailed overview of the social history of slavery and antislavery movements.

Brophy, James M. *Capitalism, Politics, and Railroads in Prussia, 1830–1870.* Columbus, Ohio, 1998. Important, clear, and helpful.

Coppa, Frank. *The Origins of the Italian Wars of Independence.* London, 1992. Lively narrative.

Craig, Gordon. *Germany, 1866–1945.* New York, 1978. An excellent and thorough synthesis.

Davis, David Brian. *Inhuman Bondage: The Rise and Fall of Slavery in the New World.* New York, 2006. As one reviewer aptly puts it, "A gracefully fashioned masterpiece."

Deak, Istvan. *The Lawful Revolution: Louis Kossuth and the Hungarians, 1848–1849.* New York, 1979. The best on the subject.

Eyck, Erich. *Bismarck and the German Empire.* 3d ed. London, 1968. The best one-volume study of Bismarck.

Hamerow, Theodore S. *The Birth of a New Europe: State and Society in the Nineteenth Century.* Chapel Hill, NC, 1983. A discussion of political and social change, and their relationship to industrialization and the increase in state power.

———. *The Social Foundations of German Unification, 1858–1871.* 2 vols. Princeton, NJ, 1969–1972. Concentrates on economic factors that determined the solution to the unification question. An impressive synthesis.

Higonnet, Patrice. *Paris: Capital of the World.* London, 2002. Fascinating and imaginative study of Paris as "capital of the nineteenth century."

Hobsbawm, Eric J. *The Age of Capital, 1848–1875.* London, 1975. Among the best introductions.

———. *Nations and Nationalism since 1870: Programme, Myth, Reality.* 2d ed. Cambridge, 1992. A clear, concise analysis of the historical and cultural manifestations of nationalism.

Howard, Michael. *The Franco-Prussian War.* New York, 1981. The war's effect on society.

Hutchinson, John, and Anthony Smith, eds. *Nationalism.* New York, 1994. A collection of articles, not particularly historical, but with the merit of discussing non-European nationalisms.

Johnson, Susan. *Roaring Camp.* New York, 2000. A history of one mining camp in California and a micro-history of the larger forces changing the West and the world.

Kolchin, Peter. *Unfree Labor: American Slavery and Russian Serfdom.* Cambridge, MA, 1987. Pioneering comparative study.

Mack Smith, Denis. *Cavour and Garibaldi.* New York, 1968.

———. *The Making of Italy, 1796–1870.* New York, 1968. A narrative with documents.

McPherson, James. *Battle Cry of Freedom: The Civil War Era.* New York, 1988. Universally acclaimed and prize-winning book on the politics of slavery and the conflicts entailed in nation building in mid-nineteenth-century United States.

Pflanze, Otto. *Bismarck and the Development of Germany.* 2d ed. 3 vols. Princeton, NJ, 1990. Extremely detailed analysis of Bismarck's aims and policies.

Pinkney, David. *Napoleon III and the Rebuilding of Paris.* Princeton, NJ, 1972. An interesting account of the creation of modern Paris during the Second Empire.

Robertson, Priscilla. *Revolutions of 1848: A Social History.* Princeton, NJ, 1952. Old-fashioned narrative, but very readable.

Sammons, Jeffrey L. *Heinrich Heine: A Modern Biography.* Princeton, NJ, 1979. An excellent historical biography as well as a study of culture and politics.

Scott, Rebecca J. *Degrees of Freedom: Louisiana and Cuba after Slavery.* Cambridge, MA, 2008. Brings the lives of slaves and their owners to life during the era of emancipation in a comparative history that places the southern United States in the context of the Atlantic world.

Sheehan, James J. *German Liberalism in the Nineteenth Century.* Chicago, 1978. Fresh and important synthesis.

Sperber, Jonathan. *The European Revolutions, 1848–1851.* Cambridge, 2005. An excellent synthesis and the best one-volume treatment of the 1848 revolutions, describing the reasons for their failure.

———. *Rhineland Radicals: The Democratic Movement and the Revolution of 1848–1849.* Princeton, NJ, 1993. A detailed study of Germany, by the author of an overview of the revolutions of 1848.

Stearns, Peter N. *1848: The Revolutionary Tide in Europe.* New York, 1974. Stresses the social background of the revolutions.

Zeldin, Theodore. *The Political System of Napoleon III.* New York, 1958. Compact and readable, by one of the major scholars of the period.

CHAPTER 22

Achebe, Chinua. *Things Fall Apart.* Expanded edition with notes. Portsmouth, NH, 1996. An annotated edition of the now classic novel about colonial Africa.

Adas, Michael. *Machines as the Measure of Man: Science, Technology, and Ideologies of Western Dominance.* Ithaca, NY, and London, 1989. An important study of Europeans' changing perceptions of themselves and others during the period of industrialization.

Bayly, C. A. *Indian Society and the Making of the British Empire.* Cambridge, 1988. A good introduction, and one that bridges eighteenth- and nineteenth-century imperialisms.

Burbank, Jane, and Frederick Cooper. *Empires in World History: Power and the Politics of Difference.* Princeton, NJ, 2010. Powerful synthesis that sets European empires in the broader context of world history.

Burton, Antoinette. *Burdens of History: British Feminists, Indian Women, and Imperial Culture, 1865–1915.* Chapel Hill, NC, 1994. On the ways in which women and feminists came to support British imperialism.

Cain, P. J., and A. G. Hopkins. *British Imperialism, 1688–2000.* London, 2002. One of the most influential studies. Excellent overview and exceptionally good on economics.

Chakrabarty, Dipesh. *Provincializing Europe: Postcolonial Thought and Historical Difference.* Princeton, 2000. Sophisticated theoretical challenge to European narratives of social and political progress.

Clancy Smith, Julia, and Frances Gouda. *Domesticating the Empire: Race, Gender, and Family Life in French and Dutch Colonialism.* Charlottesville, VA, and London, 1998. A particularly good collection of essays that both breaks new historical ground and is accessible to nonspecialists. Essays cover daily life and private life in new colonial cultures.

Cohn, Bernard S. *Colonialism and its Forms of Knowledge.* Princeton, 1996. Argues that new forms of cultural knowledge were essential to the project of British imperialism in India.

Conklin, Alice. *A Mission to Civilize: The Republican idea of Empire in France and West Africa, 1895–1930.* Stanford, CA, 1997. One of the best studies of how the French reconciled imperialism with their vision of the Republic.

Cooper, Frederick. *Colonialism in Question: Theory, Knowledge, History.* Berkeley, 2005. Crucial collection of path-breaking essays on the history of colonialism.

Cooper, Frederick, and Ann Laura Stoler. *Tensions of Empire: Colonial Cultures in a Bourgeois World.* Berkeley, CA, 1997. New approaches, combining anthropology and history, with an excellent bibliography.

Darwin, John. *The Empire Project: The Rise and Fall of the British World System.* Cambridge, 2009.

Headrick, Daniel R. *The Tools of Empire: Technology and European Imperialism in the Nineteenth Century.* Oxford, 1981. A study of the relationship between technological innovation and imperialism.

Hobsbawm, Eric. *The Age of Empire, 1875–1914.* New York, 1987. Surveys the European scene at a time of apparent stability and real decline.

Hochschild, Adam. *King Leopold's Ghost: A Story of Greed, Terror, and Heroism in Colonial Africa.* Boston, 1998. Reads like a great novel.

Hull, Isabell. *Absolute Destruction: Military Culture and the Practices of War in Imperial Germany.* Ithaca, 2005. A study of the German military and its role in imperial expansion in Africa, arguing that the experience was crucial in shaping the institution as it entered the twentieth century.

Lorcin, Patricia. *Imperial Identities: Stereotyping, Prejudice and Race in Colonial Algeria.* New York, 1999.

Louis, William Roger. *The Oxford History of the British Empire.* 5 vols. Oxford, 1998. Excellent and wide-ranging collection of the latest research.

Metcalf, Thomas. *Ideologies of the Raj.* Cambridge, 1995.

Pakenham, Thomas. *The Scramble for Africa, 1876–1912.* London, 1991. A well-written narrative of the European scramble for Africa in the late nineteenth century.

Prochaska, David. *Making Algeria French: Colonialism in Bône, 1870–1920.* Cambridge, 1990. One of the few social histories of European settlement in Algeria in English.

Robinson, Ronald, and J. Gallagher. *Africa and the Victorians: The Official Mind of Imperialism.* London, 1961. A classic.

Said, Edward. *Culture and Imperialism.* New York, 1993. A collection of brilliant, sometimes controversial, essays.

Sangari, Kumkum, and Sudesh Vaid. *Recasting Women: Essays in Colonial History.* New Delhi, 1989. A collection of essays on women in India.

Schneer, Jonathan. *London 1900: The Imperial Metropolis.* New Haven, CT, 1999. Excellent study of the empire—and opposition to empire—in the metropole.

Spence, Jonathan. *The Search for Modern China.* New York, 1990. An excellent and readable introduction to modern Chinese history.

CHAPTER 23

Berghahn, Volker. *Imperial Germany, 1871–1914: Economy, Society, Culture, and Politics.* Providence, 1994. Inclusive history that seeks to go beyond standard political accounts.

Berlanstein, Lenard. *The Working People of Paris, 1871–1914.* Baltimore, MD, 1984. A social history of the workplace and its impact on working men and women.

Blackbourn, David. *The Long Nineteenth Century: A History of Germany, 1780–1918.* New York, 1998. Among the best surveys of German society and politics.

Bowler, Peter J. *Evolution: The History of an Idea.* Berkeley, CA, 1984. One of the author's several excellent studies of evolution of Darwinism.

Burns, Michael. *Dreyfus: A Family Affair.* New York, 1992. Follows the story Dreyfus through the next generations.

Clark, T. J. *The Painting of Modern Life: Paris in the Art of Manet and His Followers.* New York, 1985. Argues for seeing impressionism as a critique of French society.

Eley, Geoff. *Forging Democracy.* Oxford, 2002. Wide-ranging and multinational account of European radicalism from 1848 to the present.

Engelstein, Laura. *Slavophile Empire: Imperial Russia's Illiberal Path.* Ithaca, 2009. An examination of Russia's political culture before World War 1, with an eye toward later evolution in the twentieth century.

Frank, Stephen. *Crime, Cultural Conflict, and Justice in Rural Russia, 1856–1914.* Berkeley, CA, 1999. A revealing study of social relations from the ground up.

Gay, Peter. *The Bourgeois Experience: Victoria to Freud,* 5 vols. New York, 1984–2000. Imaginative and brilliant study of private life and middle class culture.

———. *Freud: A Life of Our Time.* New York, 1988. Beautifully written and lucid about difficult concepts; now the best biography.

Harris, Ruth. *Dreyfus: Politics, Emotion, and the Scandal of the Century.* London, 2011. A reassessment of the politics of the Dreyfus affair, with a eye toward its resonance in the culture as a whole.

Herbert, Robert L. *Impressionism: Art, Leisure, and Parisian Society.* New Haven, CT, 1988. An accessible and important study of the impressionists and the world they painted.

Hughes, H. Stuart. *Consciousness and Society.* New York, 1958. A classic study on late-nineteenth-century European thought.

Jelavich, Peter. *Munich and Theatrical Modernism: Politics, Playwriting, and Performance, 1890–1914.* Cambridge, MA, 1985. On modernism as a revolt against nineteenth-century conventions.

Jones, Gareth Stedman. *Outcast London*. Oxford, 1971. Studies the breakdown in class relationships during the second half of the nineteenth century.

Joyce, Patrick. *Visions of the People: Industrial England and the Question of Class, 1848–1914*. New York, 1991. A social history of the workplace.

Kelly, Alfred. *The German Worker: Autobiographies from the Age of Industrialization*. Berkeley, CA, 1987. Excerpts from workers' autobiographies provide fresh perspective on labor history.

Kern, Stephen. *The Culture of Time and Space*. Cambridge, MA, 1983. A cultural history of the late nineteenth century.

Lidtke, Vernon. *The Alternative Culture: Socialist Labor in Imperial Germany*. New York, 1985. A probing study of working-class culture.

Marrus, Michael Robert. *The Politics of Assimilation: A Study of the French Jewish Community at the Time of the Dreyfus Affair*. Oxford, 1971. Excellent social history.

Micale, Mark S. *Approaching Hysteria: Disease and Its Interpretations*. Princeton, NJ, 1995. Important study of the history of psychiatry before Freud.

Rupp, Leila J. *Worlds of Women: The Making of an International Women's Movement*. Princeton, NJ, 1997.

Schivelbusch, Wolfgang. *Disenchanted Night: The Industrialization of Light in the Nineteenth Century*. Berkeley, CA, 1995. Imaginative study of how electricity transformed everyday life.

Schorske, Carl E. *Fin-de-Siècle Vienna: Politics and Culture*. New York, 1980. Classic account of avant-garde art, music, and intellectual culture set against the background of mass politics in the Austrian capital.

Schwartz, Vanessa. *Spectacular Realities: Early Mass Culture in Fin-de-Siècle Paris*. Berkeley, 1998. Innovative approach to the emergence of mass culture in modern France.

Showalter, Elaine. *The Female Malady: Women, Madness, and English Culture, 1890–1980*. New York, 1985. Brilliant and readable on Darwin, Freud, gender, and the First World War.

Silverman, Deborah L. *Art Nouveau in Fin-de-Siècle France: Politics, Psychology, and Style*. Berkeley, CA, 1989. A study of the relationship between psychological and artistic change.

Smith, Bonnie. *Changing Lives: Women in European History since 1700*. New York, 1988. A useful overview of European women's history.

Stern, Fritz. *The Politics of Cultural Despair: A Study of the Rise of the Germanic Ideology*. Berkeley, 1974. Classic account of the rise of nationalist and populist politics in German-speaking lands of central Europe before World War I.

Tickner, Lisa. *The Spectacle of Women: Imagery of the Suffrage Campaign, 1907–14*. Chicago, 1988. A very engaging study of British suffragism.

Verner, Andrew. *The Crisis of Russian Autocracy: Nicholas II and the 1905 Revolution*. Princeton, NJ, 1990. A detailed study of this important event.

Vital, David. *A People Apart: A Political History of the Jews in Europe, 1789-1939*. Oxford and New York, 1999. Comprehensive and extremely helpful.

Walkowitz, Judith. *City of Dreadful Delight: Narratives of Sexual Danger in Late-Victorian London*. Chicago, 1992. Cultural history of the English capital at the end of the nineteenth century.

Weber, Eugen. *Peasants into Frenchmen: The Modernization of Rural France, 1870–1914*. Stanford, CA, 1976. A study of how France's peasantry was assimilated into the Third Republic.

Wehler, Hans-Ulrich. *The German Empire, 1871–1918*. Dover, 1997. Standard account by respected German historian.

CHAPTER 24

Aksakal, Mustapha. *The Ottoman Road to War in 1914: The Ottoman Empire and the First World War*. Cambridge, 2009. A compelling look at Ottoman involvement in the First World War.

Bourke, Joanna. *Dismembering the Male: Men's Bodies, Britain, and the Great War*. Chicago, 1996. A cultural history of the war's effects on male bodies and codes of masculinity.

Chickering, Roger. *Imperial Germany and the Great War, 1914–1918*. New York, 1998. An excellent synthesis.

Clark, Christopher. *The Sleepwalkers: How Europe Went to War in 1914*. New York, 2013. Comprehensive reassessment of the war's origins.

Eksteins, Modris. *Rites of Spring: The Great War and the Birth of the Modern Age*. New York, 1989. Fascinating, though impressionistic, on war, art, and culture.

Ferguson, Niall. *The Pity of War*. London, 1998. A fresh look at the war, including strategic issues, international relations, and economics.

Ferro, Marc. *The Great War, 1914–1918*. London, 1973. Very concise overview.

Figes, Orlando. *A People's Tragedy: A History of the Russian Revolution*. New York, 1997. Excellent, detailed narrative.

Fischer, Fritz. *War of Illusions*. New York, 1975. Deals with Germany within the context of internal social and economic trends.

Fitzpatrick, Sheila. *The Russian Revolution, 1917–1932*. New York and Oxford, 1982. Concise overview.

Fussell, Paul. *The Great War and Modern Memory*. New York, 1975. A brilliant examination of British intellectuals' attitudes toward the war.

Hynes, Samuel. *A War Imagined: The First World War and English Culture*. New York, 1991. The war as perceived on the home front.

Jelavich, Barbara. *History of the Balkans: Twentieth Century*. New York, 1983. Useful for an understanding of the continuing conflict in eastern Europe.

Joll, James. *The Origins of the First World War*. London, 1984. Comprehensive and very useful.

Keegan, John. *The First World War*. London, 1998. The best overall military history.

Macmillan, Margaret, and Richard Holbrooke. *Paris 1919: Six Months That Changed the World*. New York, 2003. Fascinating fresh look at the peace conference.

Mazower, Mark. *Dark Continent: Europe's Twentieth Century*. New York, 1999. An excellent survey, particularly good on nations and minorities in the Balkans and eastern Europe.

Rabinowitch, Alexander. *The Bolsheviks Come to Power*. New York, 1976. A well-researched and carefully documented account.

Roberts, Mary Louise. *Civilization without Sexes: Reconstructing Gender in Postwar France, 1917–1927*. Chicago, 1994. A prize-winning study of the issues raised by the "new woman."

Schivelbusch, Wolfgang. *The Culture of Defeat: On National Trauma, Mourning, and Recovery.* New York, 2001. Fascinating if impressionistic comparative study.

Smith, Leonard. *Between Mutiny and Obedience: The Case of the French Fifth Infantry Division during World War I.* Princeton, NJ, 1994. An account of mutiny and the reasons behind it.

Stevenson, David. *Cataclysm: The First World War as Political Tragedy.* New York, 2003. Detailed and comprehensive, now one of the best single-volume studies.

Stites, Richard. *Revolutionary Dreams: Utopian Visions and Experimental Life in the Russian Revolution.* New York, 1989. The influence of utopian thinking on the revolution.

Suny, Ronald Grigor, Fatma Muge Gocek, and Norman Naimark, eds. *A Question of Genocide: Armenians and Turks at the End of the Ottoman Empire.* Oxford, 2011. Multi-author work offering a comprehensive summary of research on the Armenian genocide.

Williams, John. *The Home Fronts: Britain, France and Germany, 1914–1918.* London, 1972. A survey of life away from the battlefield and the impact of the war on domestic life.

Winter, Jay. *Sites of Memory, Sites of Mourning: The Great War in European Cultural History.* Cambridge, 1998. An essential reference on the legacy of World War I in European cultural history.

Winter, Jay and Jean-Louis Robert. *Capital Cities at War: Paris, London, Berlin, 1914–1919.* Cambridge, 1997 (vol. 1), 2007 (vol. 2). Multi-author work on the demographic, social, and cultural effects of the war on civilian populations of three European capitals.

CHAPTER 25

Bosworth, R. J. B. *Mussolini's Italy: Life under the Fascist Dictatorship, 1915–1945.* New York, 2007. Comprehensive account of "everyday" fascism in Italy.

Conquest, Robert. *The Great Terror: A Reassessment.* New York, 1990. One of the first histories of the Terror, should be read in conjunction with others in this list.

Crew, David F., ed. *Nazism and German Society, 1933–1945.* New York, 1994. An excellent and accessible collection of essays.

de Grazia, Victoria. *How Fascism Ruled Women: Italy, 1922–1945.* Berkeley, 1993. The contradictions between fascism's vision of modernity and its commitment to patriarchal instutions, seen from the point of view of Italian women.

Figes, Orlando. *Peasant Russia Civil War: The Volga Countryside in Revolution, 1917–1921.* Oxford, 1989. Detailed and sophisticated but readable. Study of the region from the eve of the revolution through the civil war.

Fitzpatrick, Shelia. *Everyday Stalinism: Ordinary Life in Extraordinary Times: Soviet Russia in the 1930s.* Oxford and New York, 1999. Gripping on how ordinary people dealt with famine, repression, and chaos.

Friedlander, Saul. *Nazi Germany and the Jews: The Years of Persecution. 1933–1939.* Rev. ed. New York, 2007. Excellent; the first of a two-volume study.

Gay, Peter. *Weimar Culture.* New York, 1968. Concise and elegant overview.

Getty, J. Arch, and Oleg V. Naumov. *The Road to Terror: Stalin and the Self-Destruction of the Bolsheviks, 1932–1939.* New Haven, CT, 1999. Combines analysis with documents made public for the first time.

Goldman, Wendy Z. *Women, the State, and Revolution: Soviet Family Policy and Social Life, 1917–1936.* New York, 1993. On the Bolshevik attempts to transform gender and family.

Kershaw, Ian. *Hitler.* 2 vols: *1889–1936 Hubris,* New York, 1999; *1936–1945: Nemesis,* New York, 2001. The best biography: insightful about politics, culture, and society as well as the man.

———. *The Hitler Myth: Image and Reality in the Third Reich.* New York, 1987. Brilliant study of how Nazi propagandists sold the myth of the Fuhrer and why many Germans bought it.

Klemperer, Victor. *I Will Bear Witness: A Diary of the Nazi Years, 1933–1941.* New York, 1999. *I Will Bear Witness: A Diary of the Nazi Years, 1942–1945.* New York, 2001. Certain to be a classic.

Lewin, Moshe. *The Making of the Soviet System: Essays in the Social History of Interwar Russia.* New York, 1985. One of the best to offer a view from below.

Maier, Charles. *Recasting Bourgeois Europe.* Princeton, 1975. Now classic account of the political and social adjustments made between state and society in the interwar years throughout Europe.

McDermott, Kevin. *Stalin: Revolutionary in an Era of War.* Basingstoke, UK, and New York, 2006. Useful, short, and recent.

Montefior, Simon Sebag. *Stalin: The Court of the Red Tsar.* London, 2004. On the relations among the top Bolsheviks, an interesting personal portrait. Takes you inside the inner circle.

Orwell, George. *The Road to Wigan Pier.* London, 1937. On unemployment and life in the coal mining districts of England, by one of the great British writers of the twentieth century.

———. *Homage to Catalonia.* London, 1938. A firsthand account of the Spanish Civil War.

Payne, Stanley G., *A History of Fascism, 1914–1945.* Madison, WI, 1996. Thorough account of the origins and evolution of fascism in Europe through the end of World War II.

Paxton, Robert O. *The Anatomy of Fascism.* New York, 2004. Excellent introduction to a complex subject by a foremost historian of twentieth century Europe.

Peukert, Detlev. *The Weimar Republic.* New York, 1993. Useful and concise history of Weimar by respected German historian of the period.

Rentschler, Eric. *The Ministry of Illusion: Nazi Cinema and Its Afterlife.* Cambridge, MA, 1996. For the more advanced student.

Service, Robert. *Stalin: A Biography.* London, 2004. Updates Tucker.

Suny, Ronald Grigor. *The Revenge of the Past: Nationalism, Revolution, and the Collapse of the Soviet Union.* Stanford, CA, 1993. Path-breaking study of the issues of nationalism and ethnicity form the revolution to the end of the Soviet Union.

Tucker, Robert C. *Stalin as Revolutionary, 1879–1929.* New York, 1973.

———. *Stalin in Power: The Revolution from Above, 1928–1941.* New York, 1990. With *Stalin as Revolutionary* emphasizes Stalin's purpose and method and sets him in the tradition of Russian dictators.

Weitz, Eric D. *Weimar Germany: Promise and Tragedy.* Princeton, NJ, 2009. A valuable and thorough account that ties together the complex connections between Weimar culture and politics in this transformational period.

CHAPTER 26

The U.S. Holocaust Memorial Museum has an extraordinary collection of articles, photographs, and maps. See www.ushmm.org.

Bartov, Omer. *Hitler's Army: Soldiers, Nazis, and War in the Third Reich*. New York, 1991. A Study of the radicalization of the German army on the Russian front.

Braithwaite, Rodric. *Moscow. 1941: A City and Its People at War*. London, 2006. Readable account of one of the turning points of the war.

Browning, Christopher R. *The Path to Genocide: Essays on Launching the Final Solution*. Cambridge, 1992. Discusses changing interpretations and case studies. See also the author's *Ordinary Men: Reserve Police Battalion 101 and the Final Solution in Poland*.

Burrin, Philippe. *France under the Germans: Collaboration and Compromise*. New York, 1996. Comprehensive on occupation and collaboration.

Carr, Raymond. *The Spanish Tragedy: The Civil War in Perspective*. London, 1977. A thoughtful introduction to the Spanish Civil War and the evolution of Franco's Spain.

Davies, Norman. *Heart of Europe: The Past in Poland's Present*. Oxford, 2001. Revised edition of a classic account of Poland's place in European history, with special attention to the second half of the twentieth century.

Dawidowicz, Lucy S. *The War against the Jews, 1933–1945*. New York, 1975. A full account of the Holocaust.

Divine, Robert A. *Roosevelt and World War II*. Baltimore, MD, 1969. A diplomatic history.

Djilas, Milovan. *Wartime*. New York, 1977. An insider's account of the partisans' fighting in Yugoslavia and a good example of civil war within the war.

Fritzsche, Peter. *Life and Death in the Third Reich*. Cambridge, MA, 2009. A compelling account of the appeal of Nazi ideology and the extent to which it was embraced by ordinary people in Germany.

Gellately, Robert, and Ben Kiernan, eds. *The Specter of Genocide: Mass Murder in Historical Perspective*. New York, 2003. A particularly thoughtful collection of essays.

Graham, Helen. *The Spanish Civil War: A Very Short Introduction*. Oxford and New York, 2005. Excellent and very concise, based on the author's new interpretation in the more detailed *The Spanish Republic at War, 1936–1939*. Cambridge, 2002.

Hilberg, Raul. *The Destruction of the European Jews*. 2nd ed. 3 vols. New York, 1985. An excellent treatment of the Holocaust, its origins, and its consequences.

Hitchcock, William I. *The Bitter Road to Freedom: A New History of the Liberation of Europe*. New York, 2008. The story of Europe's liberation from Hitler's control, seen from the point of view of civilian populations.

Kedward, Roderick. *In Search of the Maquis: Rural Resistance in Southern France, 1942–1944*. Oxford, 1993. An engaging study of French guerilla resistance.

Keegan, John. *The Second World War*. New York, 1990. By one of the great military historians of our time.

Marrus, Michael R. *The Holocaust in History*. Hanover, NH, 1987. Thoughtful analysis of central issues.

Mawdsley, Evan. *Thunder in the East: The Nazi-Soviet War, 1941–1945*. New York, 2005.

Megargee, Geoffrey. *War of Annihilation: Combat and Genocide on the Eastern War, 1941*. Lanham, MD, 2006. Represents some of the new historical work on the eastern front.

Merridale, Catherine. *Ivan's War: Life and Death in the Red Army, 1939–1945*. New York, 2006. Raised many questions and insights.

Michel, Henri. *The Shadow War: The European Resistance, 1939–1945*. New York, 1972. Compelling reading.

Milward, Alan S. *War, Economy, and Society, 1939–1945*. Berkeley, CA, 1977. On the economic impact of the war and the strategic impact of the economy.

Noakes, Jeremy, and Geoffrey Pridham. *Nazism: A History in Documents and Eyewitness Accounts, 1919–1945*. New York, 1975. An excellent combination of analysis and documentation.

Overy, Richard. *Russia's War*. New York, 1998. A very readable account that accompanies the PBS series by the same title.

———. *Why the Allies Won*. New York, 1995. Excellent analysis; succint.

Paxton, Robert O. *Vichy France: Old Guard and New Order, 1940–1944*. New York, 1982. Brilliant on collaboration and Vichy's National Revolution.

Roberts, Mary Louise. *What Soldiers Do: Sex and the American GI in World War II France*. Chicago, 2013. Critical reappraisal of how sex between GIs and civilians became an issue for French and U.S. military personnel after the D-Day invasion.

Snyder, Timothy. *Bloodlands: Europe between Hitler and Stalin*. New York, 2010. Thorough and penetrating account of the methods and motives of Hitler's and Stalin's regimes.

Stoff, Michael B. *The Manhattan Project: A Documentary Introduction to the Atomic Age*. New York, 1991. Political, scientific, and historical; excellent documents and commentary.

Weinberg, Gerhard L. *A World At Arms: A Global History of World War II*. Cambridge, 2005. Second edition of a comprehensive and respected global account of the Second World War.

Wilkinson, James D. *The Intellectual Resistance in Europe*. Cambridge, MA, 1981. A comparative study of the movement throughout Europe.

CHAPTER 27

Aron, Raymond. *The Imperial Republic: The United States and the World, 1945–1973*. Lanham, MD, 1974. An early analysis by a leading French political theorist.

Carter, Erica. *How German Is She? Postwar West German Reconstruction and the Consuming Woman*. Ann Arbor, MI, 1997. A thoughtful examination of gender and the reconstruction of the family in West Germany during the 1950s.

Clayton, Anthony. *The Wars of French Decolonization*. London, 1994. Good survey.

Connelly, Matthew. *A Diplomatic Revolution: Algeria's Fight for Independence and the Origins of the Post–Cold War Era*. New York and Oxford, 2003. An international history.

Cooper, Frederick, and Ann Laura Stoler, eds. *Tensions of Empire: Colonial Cultures in a Bourgeois World.* Berkeley, CA, 1997. Collection of new essays, among the best.

Darwin, John. *Britain and Decolonization: The Retreat from Empire in the Postwar World.* New York, 1988. Best overall survey.

Deák, István, Jan T. Gross, and Tony Judt, eds. *The Politics of Retribution in Europe: World War II and Its Aftermath.* Princeton, NJ, 2000. Collection focusing on the attempt to come to terms with the Second World War in Eastern and Western Europe.

Farmer, Sarah. *Martyred Village: Commemorating the 1944 Massacre at Oradour-sur-Glane.* Berkeley, CA, 1999. Gripping story of French attempts to come to terms with collaboration and complicity in atrocities.

Holland, R. F. *European Decolonization 1918–1981: An Introductory Survey.* New York, 1985. Sprightly narrative and analysis.

Jarausch, Konrad Hugo, ed. *Dictatorship as Experience: Towards a Socio-Cultural History of the GDR.* Trans. Eve Duffy. New York, 1999. Surveys recent research on the former East Germany.

Judt, Tony. *The Burden of Responsibility: Blum, Camus, and the French Twentieth Century.* Chicago and London, 1998. Also on French intellectuals.

———. *A Grand Illusion? An Essay on Europe.* New York, 1996. Short and brilliant.

———. *Past Imperfect: French Intellectuals, 1944–1956.* Berkeley, CA, 1992. Very readable, on French intellectuals, who loomed large during this period.

———. *Postwar: A History of Europe Since 1945.* London, 2005. Detailed, comprehensive, and ground breaking, this single volume surpasses any other account of the entire postwar period.

Koven, Seth, and Sonya Michel. *Mothers of a New World: Maternalist Politics and the Origins of Welfare States.* New York, 1993. Excellent essays on the long history of welfare politics.

LaFeber, Walter. *America, Russia, and the Cold War.* New York, 1967. A classic, now in its ninth edition.

Large, David Clay. *Berlin.* New York, 2000. Accessible and engaging.

Leffler, Melvyn P. *A Preponderance of Power: National Security, the Truman Administration, and the Cold War.* Stanford, CA, 1992. Solid political study.

Louis, William Roger. *The Ends of British Imperialism: The Scramble for Empire, Suez, and Decolonization.* London, 2006. Comprehensive and wide ranging.

Macey, David. *Frantz Fanon.* New York, 2000. Comprehensive recent biography.

Medvedev, Roy. *Khrushchev.* New York, 1983. A perceptive biography of the Soviet leader by a Soviet historian.

Milward, Alan S. *The Reconstruction of Western Europe, 1945–1951.* Berkeley, CA, 1984. A good discussion of the "economic miracle."

Moeller, Robert G. *War Stories: The Search for a Usable Past in the Federal Republic of Germany.* Berkeley, CA, 2001. Revealing analyses of postwar culture and politics.

Reynolds, David. *One World Divisible: A Global History Since 1945.* New York, 2000. Fresh approach, comprehensive, and very readable survey.

Rousso, Henri. *The Vichy Syndrome: History and Memory in France since 1944.* Cambridge, MA, 1991. First in a series of books by one of the preeminent French historians.

Schissler, Hanna, ed. *The Miracle Years: A Cultural History of West Germany, 1949–1968.* Princeton, NJ, 2001. The cultural effects of the economic miracle.

Schneider, Peter. *The Wall Jumper: A Berlin Story.* Chicago, 1998. A fascinating novel about life in divided Berlin.

Shepard, Todd. *The Invention of Decolonization: The Algerian War and the Remaking of France.* Ithaca, NY, 2006. Excellent and original: a study of the deeply wrenching war's many ramifications.

Shipway, Martin. *Decolonization and Its Impact: A Comparative Approach to the End of the Colonial Empires.* Malden, MA, 2008. Accessible account emphasizing the unintended consequences of decolonization.

Trachtenberg, Mark. *A Constructed Peace: The Making of the European Settlement, 1945–1963.* Princeton, NJ, 1999. A detailed study of international relations that moves beyond the Cold War framework.

Tessler, Mark. *A History of the Israeli-Palestinian Conflict.* 2nd ed. Bloomington, IN, 2009. Updated edition of the definitive account from the 1990s.

Westad, Odd Arne. *The Global Cold War.* New York, 2005. An international history that sees the roots of the world's present conflict in the history of the Cold War.

Wilder, Gary. *The French Imperial Nation-State: Negritude and Colonial Humanism between the Two World Wars.* Chicago, 2005. Fascinating new study of the Negritude thinkers in their context.

Yergin, Daniel. *Shattered Peace: The Origins of the Cold War.* New York, 1977. Rev. ed. 1990. Dramatic and readable.

Young, Marilyn B. *The Vietnam Wars, 1945–1990.* New York, 1991. Excellent account of the different stages of the war and its repercussions.

CHAPTER 28

Bailey, Beth. *From Front Porch to Back Seat: Courtship in Twentieth-Century America.* Baltimore, MD, 1988. Good historical perspective on the sexual revolution.

Beschloss, Michael, and Strobe Talbott. *At the Highest Levels: The Inside Story of the End of the Cold War.* Boston, 1993. An analysis of the relationship between presidents Gorbachev and George H. W. Bush and their determination to ignore hard-liners.

Brown, Archie. *The Gorbachev Factor.* Oxford and New York, 1996. One of the first serious studies of Gorbachev, by an Oxford scholar of politics.

Caute, David. *The Year of the Barricades: A Journey through 1968.* New York, 1988. A well-written global history of 1968.

Charney, Leo, and Vanessa R. Schwartz, eds. *Cinema and the Invention of Modern Life.* Berkeley, CA, 1995. Collection of essays.

Dallin, Alexander, and Gail Lapidus. *The Soviet System: From Crisis to Collapse.* Boulder, CO, 1995.

de Grazia, Victoria. *Irresistable Empire: America's Advance through Twentieth-Century Europe.* Cambridge, MA, 2006. Thorough exploration of the history of consumer culture in Europe and its links to relations with the United States.

Echols, Alice. *Daring to Be Bad: Radical Feminism in America, 1967–1975.* Minneapolis, Minn., 1989. Good narrative and analysis.

Eley, Geoff. *Forging Democracy: The History of the Left in Europe, 1850–2000.* Oxford and New York, 2002. Among its other qualities, one of the best historical perspectives on the 1960s.

Fink, Carole, Phillipp Gassert, and Detlef Junker, eds. *1968: The World Transformed.* Cambridge, 1998. A transatlantic history of 1968.

Fulbrook, Mary, ed. *Europe since 1945* (The Short Oxford History of Europe). Oxford, 2001. Particularly good articles on economics and political economy. Structural analysis.

Garton Ash, Timothy. *In Europe's Name: Germany and the Divided Continent.* New York, 1993. An analysis of the effect of German reunification on the future of Europe.

Glenny, Misha. *The Balkans, 1804–1999: Nationalism, War and the Great Powers.* London, 1999. Good account by a journalist who covered the fighting.

Horowitz, Daniel. *Betty Friedan and the Making of the Feminine Mystique: The American Left, the Cold War, and Modern Feminism.* Amherst, MA, 1998. A reconsideration.

Hosking, Geoffrey. *The Awakening of the Soviet Union.* Cambridge, MA, 1990. The factors that led to the end of the Soviet era.

Hughes, H. Stuart. *Sophisticated Rebels: The Political Culture of European Dissent, 1968–1987.* Cambridge, MA, 1990. The nature of dissent on both sides of the disintegrating Iron Curtain in the years 1988–1989.

Hulsberg, Werner. *The German Greens: A Social and Political Profile.* New York, 1988. The origins, politics, and impact of environmental politics.

Jarausch, Konrad. *The Rush to German Unity.* New York, 1994. The problems of reunification analyzed.

Judah, Tim. *The Serbs: History, Myth, and the Destruction of Yugoslavia.* New Haven, CT, 1997. Overview of Serbian history by journalist who covered the war.

Kaplan, Robert D. *Balkan Ghosts: A Journey through History.* New York, 1993. More a political travelogue than a history, but very readable.

Kotkin, Stephen. *Armegeddon Averted: The Soviet Collapse, 1970–2000.* Oxford, 2001. Excellent short account.

Kurlansky, Mark. *1968: The Year that Rocked the World.* New York, 2005. An accessible introduction for nonspecialists.

Lewin, Moshe. *The Gorbachev Phenomenon.* Expanded ed. Berkeley, CA, 1991. Written as a firsthand account, tracing the roots of Gorbachev's successes and failures.

Lieven, Anatol. *Chechnya, Tomb of Russia Power.* New Haven, CT, and London, 1998. Longer view of the region, by a journalist.

Maier, Charles S. *Dissolution: The Crisis of Communism and the End of East Germany.* Princeton, NJ, 1997. Detailed and sophisticated.

Mann, Michael. *The Dark Side of Democracy: Explaining Ethnic Cleansing.* New York, 2005. Brilliant essay on different episodes from Armenia to Rwanda.

Marwick, Arthur. *The Sixties.* Oxford and New York, 1998. An international history.

Pells, Richard. *Not Like Us: How Europeans Have Loved, Hated, and Transformed American Culture since World War II.* New York, 1997. From the point of view of an American historian.

Poiger, Uta G. *Jazz, Rock, and Rebels: Cold War Politics and American Culture in a Divided Germany.* Berkeley, CA, 2000. Pioneering cultural history.

Sheehan, Neil. *A Bright Shining Lie: John Paul Vann and America in Vietnam.* New York, 1988. A study of the war and its escalation through one of the U.S. Army's field advisers.

Strayer, Robert. *Why Did the Soviet Union Collapse? Understanding Historical Change.* Armonk, NY, and London, 1998. A good introduction, with bibliography.

Suri, Jeremi. *Power and Protest.* New ed. Cambridge, MA, 2005. One of the best of the new global histories of the 1960s, looking at relations between social movements and international relations.

Wright, Patrick. *On Living in an Old Country: The National Past in Contemporary Britain.* New York, 1986. The culture of Britain in the 1980s.

CHAPTER 29

Bowen, John R. *Why the French Don't Like Headscarves: Islam, the State, and Public Space.* Princeton, NJ, 2008. An ethnographic account of this volatile debate in France.

Coetzee, J. M. *Waiting for the Barbarians.* London, 1980. A searing critique of apartheid-era South Africa by a leading Afrikaner novelist.

Epstein, Helen. *The Invisible Cure: Africa, the West, and the Fight Against AIDS.* New York, 2007. One of the best recent studies.

Frieden, Jeffrey H. *Global Capitalism: Its Rise and Fall in the Twentieth Century.* New York, 2007. Broad-ranging history for the advanced student.

Geyer, Michael, and Charles Bright. "World History in a Global Age." *American Historical Review* (October 1995). An excellent short discussion.

Glendon, Mary Ann. *A World Made New: Eleanor Roosevelt and the Universal Declaration of Human Rights.* New York, 2001. A fascinating study of the High Commission in its time by a legal scholar.

Harvey, David. *A Brief History of Neoliberalism.* New York, 2007, A critical account of the history of neoliberalism that encompasses the U.S., Europe, and Asia.

Held, David, et al. *Global Transformations: Politics, Economics, and Culture.* Stanford, CA, 1999. Major survey of the globalization of culture, finance, criminality, and politics.

Hopkins, A. G., ed. *Globalization in World History.* New York, 2002. Excellent introduction, written by one of the first historians to engage the issue.

Hunt, Lynn. *Inventing Human Rights: A History.* New York, 2007. A short study of the continuities and paradoxes in the West's human rights tradition, by one of the foremost historians of the French Revolution. On 1776, 1789, and 1948.

Keddie, Nikki. *Modern Iran: Roots and Results of Revolution.* New Haven, CT, 2003. A revised edition of her major study of Iran's 1979 revolution, with added perspective on Iran's Islamic government.

Lacqueur, Walter. *The Age of Terrorism.* Boston, 1987. An important study of the first wave of post-1960s terrorism.

Landes, David. *The Wealth and Poverty of Nations: Why Some Are So Rich and Some So Poor*. New York, 1998. Leading economic historian's account of globalization's effects on the international economy.

Lewis, Bernard. *The Crisis of Islam: Holy War and Unholy Terror*. New York, 2003. Conservative scholar of the Arab world discussing the political crises that fueled terrorism.

Mckeown, Adam. "Global Migration, 1846–1940." *Journal of World History* 15.2 (2004). Includes references to more work on the subject.

McNeill, J. R. *Something New under the Sun: An Environmental History of the Twentieth-Century World*. New York and London, 2000. Fascinating new approach to environmental history.

Merlini, Cesare, and Olivier Roy, eds. *Arab Society in Revolt: The West's Mediterranean Challenge*. Washington DC, 2012. A multi-author attempt to understand the Arab Spring of 2011

Novick, Peter. *The Holocaust in American Life*. Boston, 1999.

Power, Samantha. *The Problem from Hell: America in the Age of Genocide*. A prize-winning survey of the entire twentieth century, its genocides, and the different human rights movements that responded to them.

Reynolds, David. *One World Divisible: A Global History since 1945*. New York and London, 2000. Excellent study of the different dimensions of globalization.

Roy, Olivier. *Globalized Islam: The Search for a New Ummah*. New York, 2006. Examines changes in religious belief and practice as Islam has spread from its historic centers in the Middle East to other areas of the world, including Europe and North America.

Scott, Joan. *The Politics of the Veil*. Princeton, NJ, 2010. A leading feminist scholar analyzes the debate about the veil and the Islamic headscarf in Europe.

Shilts, Randy. *And the Band Played On: Politics, People, and the AIDS Epidemic*. New York, 1987. An impassioned attack on the individuals and governments that failed to come to grips with the early spread of the disease.

Shlaim, Avi. *The Iron Wall: Israel and the Arab World*. New York, 2000. Leading Israeli historian on the evolution of Israel's defensive foreign policy.

Stiglitz, Joseph E. *Globalization and Its Discontents*. New York, 2002. A recent and important consideration of contemporary globalization's character and the conflicts it creates, particularly over commerce and culture.

———. *Freefall: America, Free Markets, and the Sinking of the World Economy*. New York, 2010. Nobel-prize-winning economist gives account of the financial crisis of 2008.

Turkle, Sherry. *Life on the Screen: Identity in the Age of the Internet*. New York, 1995. An important early study of Web culture and the fluid possibilities of electronic communication.

Winter, Jay. *Dreams of Peace and Freedom: Utopian Moments in the Twentieth Century*. New Haven, CT, 2006. One of the leading historians of war and atrocity turns here to twentieth-century hopes for peace and human rights.

1973 OPEC oil embargo Some leaders in the Arab-dominated Organization of the Petroleum Exporting Countries (OPEC) wanted to use oil as a weapon against the West in the Arab-Israeli conflict. After the 1972 Arab-Israeli war, OPEC instituted an oil embargo against Western powers. The embargo increased the price of oil and sparked spiraling inflation and economic troubles in Western nations, triggering in turn a cycle of dangerous recession that lasted nearly a decade. In response, Western governments began viewing the Middle Eastern oil regions as areas of strategic importance.

Abbasid Caliphate (750–930) The Abbasid family claimed to be descendants of Muhammad, and in 750 they successfully led a rebellion against the Umayyads, seizing control of Muslim territories in Arabia, Persia, North Africa, and the Near East. The Abbasids modeled their behavior and administration on that of the Persian princes and their rule on that of the Persian Empire, establishing a new capital at Baghdad.

Peter Abelard (1079–1142) Highly influential philosopher, theologian, and teacher, often considered the founder of the University of Paris.

absolutism Form of government in which one body, usually the monarch, controls the right to make war, tax, judge, and coin money. The term was often used to refer to the state monarchies in seventeenth- and eighteenth-century Europe. In other countries the end of feudalism is often associated with the legal abolition of serfdom, as in Russia in 1861.

abstract expressionism The mid-twentieth-century school of art based in New York that included Jackson Pollock, Willem de Kooning, and Franz Kline. It emphasized form, color, gesture, and feeling instead of figurative subjects.

Academy of Sciences This French institute of scientific inquiry was founded in 1666 by Louis XIV. France's statesmen exerted control over the academy and sought to share in the rewards of any discoveries its members made.

Aeneas Mythical founder of Rome, Aeneas was a refugee from the city of Troy whose adventures were described by the poet Virgil in the *Aeneid,* which mimicked the oral epics of Homer.

Aetolian and Achaean Leagues These two alliances among Greek poleis formed during the Hellenistic period in opposition to the Antigonids of Macedonia. Unlike the earlier defensive alliances of the classic period, each league represented a real attempt to form a political federation.

African National Congress (ANC) Multiracial organization founded in 1912 whose goal was to end racial discrimination in South Africa.

Afrikaners Descendants of the original Dutch settlers of South Africa; formerly referred to as Boers.

agricultural revolution Numerous agricultural revolutions have occurred in the history of Western civilizations. One of the most significant began in the tenth century C.E., and increased the amount of land under cultivation as well as the productivity of the land. This revolution was made possible through the use of new technology, an increase in global temperatures, and more efficient methods of cultivation.

AIDS Acquired Immunodeficiency Syndrome. AIDS first appeared in the 1970s and has developed into a global health catastrophe; it is spreading most quickly in developing nations in Africa and Asia.

Akhenaten (r. 1352–1336 B.C.E.) Pharaoh whose attempt to promote the worship of the sun god, Aten, ultimately weakened his dynasty's position in Egypt.

Alexander the Great (356–323 B.C.E.) The Macedonian king whose conquests of the Persian Empire and Egypt created a new Hellenistic world.

Tsar Alexander II (1818–1881) After the Crimean War, Tsar Alexander embarked on a program of reform and modernization, which included the emancipation of the serfs. A radical assassin killed him in 1881.

Alexius Comnenus (1057–1118) This Byzantine emperor requested Pope Urban II's help in raising an army to recapture Anatolia from the Seljuk Turks. Instead, Pope Urban II called for knights to go to the Holy Land and liberate it from its Muslim captors, which launched the First Crusade.

Algerian War (1954–1962) The war between France and Algerians seeking independence. Led by the National Liberation Front (FLN), guerrillas fought the French army in the mountains and desert of Algeria. The FLN also initiated a campaign of bombing and terrorism in Algerian cities that led French soldiers to torture many Algerians, attracting world attention and international scandal.

Dante Alighieri (c. 1265–1321) Florentine poet and intellectual whose *Divine Comedy* was a pioneering work in the Italian vernacular and a vehicle for political and religious critique.

Allied Powers The First World War coalition of Great Britain, Ireland, Belgium, France, Italy, Russia, Portugal, Greece, Serbia, Montenegro, Albania, and Romania.

al Qaeda The radical Islamic organization founded in the late 1980s by former mujahidin who had fought against the Soviet Union in Afghanistan. Al Qaeda carried out the 9/11 terrorist attacks and is responsible as well for attacks in Africa, Southeast Asia, Europe, and the Middle East.

Ambrose (c. 340–397) One of the early "fathers" of the Church, he helped to define the relationship between the sacred authority of bishops and other Church leaders and the secular authority of worldly rulers. He believed that secular rulers were a part of the Church and therefore subject to it.

Americanization The fear of many Europeans, since the 1920s, that U.S. cultural products, such as film, television, and music, exerted too much influence. Many of the criticisms centered on America's emphasis on mass production and organization. The fears about Americanization were not limited to culture. They extended to corporations, business techniques, global trade, and marketing.

Americas The name given to the two great landmasses of the New World, derived from the name of the Italian geographer Amerigo Vespucci. In 1492, Christopher Columbus reached the Bahamas and the island of Hispaniola, which began an era of Spanish conquest in North and South America. Originally, the Spanish sought a route to Asia. Instead they discovered two continents whose wealth they decided to exploit. They were especially interested in gold and silver, which they either stole from indigenous peoples or mined using indigenous peoples as labor. Silver became Spain's most lucrative export from the New World.

Amnesty International Nongovernmental organization formed in 1961 to defend "prisoners of conscience"—those detained for their beliefs, color, sex, ethnic origin, language, or religion.

Anabaptists Protestant movement that emerged in Switzerland in 1521; its adherents insisted that only adults could be baptized Christians.

anarchists In the nineteenth century, they were a political movement with the aim of establishing small-scale, localized, and self-sufficient democratic communities that could guarantee a maximum of individual sovereignty. Renouncing parties, unions and any form of modern mass organization, the anarchists fell back on the tradition of conspiratorial violence.

Anti–Corn Law League This organization successfully lobbied Parliament to repeal Britain's Corn Laws in 1846. The Corn Laws of 1815 had protected British landowners and farmers from foreign competition by establishing high tariffs, which kept bread prices artificially high for British consumers. The league saw these laws as unfair protection of the aristocracy and pushed for their repeal in the name of free trade.

anti-Semitism Anti-Semitism refers to hostility toward Jewish people. Religious forms of anti-Semitism have a long history in Europe, but in the nineteenth century anti-Semitism emerged as a potent ideology for mobilizing new constituencies in the era of mass politics. Playing on popular conspiracy theories about alleged Jewish influence in society, anti-Semites effectively rallied large bodies of supporters in France during the Dreyfus Affair, and then again during the rise of National Socialism in Germany after the First World War. The Holocaust would not have been possible without the acquiescence or cooperation of many thousands of people who shared anti-Semitic views.

apartheid The racial segregation policy of the Afrikaner-dominated South African government. Legislated in 1948 by the Afrikaner National Party, it existed in South Africa for many decades.

appeasement The policy pursued by Western governments in the face of German, Italian, and Japanese aggression leading up to the Second World War. The policy, which attempted to accommodate and negotiate peace with the aggressive nations, was based on the belief that another global war like the First World War was unimaginable, a belief that Germany and its allies had been mistreated by the terms of the Treaty of Versailles, and a fear that fascist Germany and its allies protected the West from the spread of Soviet communism.

Thomas Aquinas (1225–1274) Dominican friar and theologian whose systematic approach to Christian doctrine was influenced by Aristotle.

Arab-Israeli conflict Between the founding of the state of Israel in 1948 and the present, a series of wars has been fought between Israel and neighboring Arab nations: the war of 1948 when Israel defeated attempts by Egypt, Jordon, Iraq, Syria, and Lebanon to prevent the creation of the new state; the 1956 war between Israel and Egypt over the Sinai peninsula; the 1967 war, when Israel gained control of additional land in the Golan Heights, the West Bank, the Gaza strip, and in the Sinai; and the Yom Kippur War of 1973, when Israel once again fought with forces from Egypt and Syria. A particularly difficult issue in all of these conflicts has been the situation of the 950,000 Palestinian refugees made homeless by the first war in 1948 and the movement of Israeli settlers into the occupied territories (outside of Israel's original borders). In the late 1970s, peace talks between Israel and Egypt inspired some hope of peace, but an ongoing cycle of violence between Palestinians and the Israeli military have made a final settlement elusive.

Arab nationalism During the period of decolonization, secular forms of Arab nationalism, or pan-Arabism, found a wide following in many countries of the Middle East, especially in Egypt, Syria, and Iraq.

Arianism A variety of Christianity condemned as a heresy by the Roman Church, it derives from the teaching of a fourth-century priest called Arius, who rejected the idea that Jesus could be the divine equal of God.

aristocracy From the Greek word meaning "rule of the best." By 1000 B.C.E., the accumulated wealth of successful traders in Greece had created a new type of social class, which was based on wealth rather than warfare or birth. These men saw their wealth as a reflection of their superior qualities and aspired to emulate the heroes of old.

Aristotle (384–322 B.C.E.) A student of Plato, his philosophy was based on the rational analysis of the material world. In contrast to his teacher, he stressed the rigorous investigation of real phenomena, rather than the development of universal ethics. He was, in turn, the teacher of Alexander the Great.

Asiatic Society A cultural organization founded in 1784 by British Orientalists who lauded native culture but believed in colonial rule.

Assyrians A Semitic-speaking people that moved into northern Mesopotamia around 2400 B.C.E.

Athens Athens emerged as the Greek polis with the most markedly democratic form of government through a series of political struggles during the sixth century B.C.E. After its key role in the defeat of two invading Persian forces, Athens became the preeminent naval power of ancient Greece and the exemplar of Greek culture. But it antagonized many other poleis, and became embroiled in a war with Sparta and her allies in 431 B.C.E. Called the Peloponnesian War, this bloody conflict lasted until Athens was defeated in 404 B.C.E.

atomic bomb In 1945, the United States dropped atomic bombs on Hiroshima and Nagasaki in Japan, ending the Second World War. In 1949, the Soviet Union tested its first atomic bomb, and in 1953 both superpowers demonstrated their new hydrogen bombs. Strategically, the nuclearization of warfare polarized the world. Countries without nuclear weapons found it difficult to avoid joining either the Soviet or American military pacts. Over time, countries split into two groups: the superpowers with enormous military budgets and those countries that relied on agreements and international law. The nuclearization of warfare also encouraged "proxy wars" between clients of superpowers. Culturally, the hydrogen bomb came to symbolize the age and both humanity's power and vulnerability.

Augustine (c. 354–397) One of the most influential theologians of all time, Augustine described his conversion to Christianity in his autobiographical *Confessions* and articulated a new Christian worldview in *The City of God*, among other works.

Augustus (63 B.C.E.–14 C.E.) Born Gaius Octavius, this grandnephew and adopted son of Julius Caesar came to power in 27 B.C.E. His reign signals the end of the Roman Republic and the beginning of the Principate, the period when Rome was dominated by autocratic emperors.

Auschwitz-Birkenau The Nazi concentration camp in Poland that was designed to systematically murder Jews and Gypsies. Between 1942 and 1944 over 1 million people were killed in Auschwitz-Birkenau.

Austro-Hungarian Empire The dual monarchy established by the Habsburg family in 1867; it collapsed at the end of the First World War.

authoritarianism A centralized and dictatorial form of government, proclaimed by its adherents to be superior to parliamentary democracy. Authoritarian governments claim to be above the law, do not respect individual rights, and do not tolerate political opposition. Authoritarian regimes that have developed a central ideology such as fascism or communism are sometimes termed "totalitarian."

Avignon A city in southeastern France that became the seat of the papacy between 1305 and 1377, a period known as the "Babylonian Captivity" of the Roman Church.

Aztecs An indigenous people of central Mexico; their empire was conquered by Spanish conquistadors in the sixteenth century.

baby boom (1950s) The post–Second World War upswing in U.S. birth rates; it reversed a century of decline.

Babylon An ancient city between the Tigris and Euphrates Rivers, which became the capital of Hammurabi's empire in the eighteenth century B.C.E. and continued to be an important administrative and commercial capital under many subsequent imperial powers, including the Neo-Assyrians, Chaldeans, Persians, and Romans. It was here that Alexander the Great died in 323 B.C.E.

Babylonian captivity Refers both to the Jews' exile in Babylon during the sixth century B.C.E. and the period from 1309 to 1378, when papal authority was subjugated to the French crown and the papal court was moved from Rome to the French city of Avignon.

Francis Bacon (1561–1626) British philosopher and scientist who pioneered the scientific method and inductive reasoning. In other words, he argued that thinkers should amass many observations and then draw general conclusions or propose theories on the basis of these data.

balance of powers The principle that no country should be powerful enough to destabilize international relations. Starting in the seventeenth century, this goal of maintaining balance influenced diplomacy in western and central Europe for two centuries until the system collapsed with the onset of the First World War.

Balfour Declaration A letter dated November 2, 1917, by Lord Arthur J. Balfour, British foreign secretary, that promised a homeland for the Jews in Palestine.

Laura Bassi (1711–1778) She was accepted into the Academy of Science in Bologna for her work in mathematics, which made her one of the few women to be accepted into a scientific academy in the seventeenth century.

Bastille The Bastille was a royal fortress and prison in Paris. In June 1789, a revolutionary crowd attacked the Bastille to show support for the newly created National Assembly. The fall of the Bastille was the first instance of the people's role in revolutionary change in France.

Bay of Pigs (1961) The unsuccessful invasion of Cuba by Cuban exiles, supported by the U.S. government. The rebels intended to incite an insurrection in Cuba and overthrow the communist regime of Fidel Castro.

Cesare Beccaria (1738–1794) An influential writer during the Enlightenment who advocated for legal reforms. He believed that the only legitimate rationale for punishments was to maintain social order and to prevent other crimes. He argued for the greatest possible leniency compatible with deterrence and opposed torture and the death penalty.

Beer Hall Putsch (1923) An early attempt by the Nazi party to seize power in Munich; Adolf Hitler was imprisoned for a year after the incident.

Benedict of Nursia (c. 480–c. 547) Benedict's rule for monks formed the basis of western monasticism and is still observed in monasteries all over the world.

Benedictine Monasticism This form of monasticism was developed by Benedict of Nursia. Its followers adhere to a defined cycle of daily prayers, lessons, communal worship, and manual labor.

Berlin airlift (1948) The transport of vital supplies to West Berlin by air, primarily under U.S. auspices, in response to a blockade of the city that had been instituted by the Soviet Union to force the Allies to abandon West Berlin.

Berlin Conference (1884) At this conference, the leading colonial powers met and established ground rules for the partition of Africa by European nations. By 1914, 90 percent of African territory was under European control. The Berlin Conference ceded control of the Congo region to a private company run by King Leopold II of Belgium. They agreed to make the Congo valleys open to free trade and commerce, to end the slave trade in the region, and to establish a Congo Free State. In reality, King Leopold II's company established a regime that was so brutal in its treatment of local populations that an international scandal forced the Belgian state to take over the colony in 1908.

Berlin Wall The wall built in 1961 by East German Communists to prevent citizens of East Germany from fleeing to West Germany; it was torn down in 1989.

birth control pill This oral contraceptive became widely available in the mid-1960s. For the first time, women had a simple method of birth control that they could take themselves.

Otto von Bismarck (1815–1898) The prime minister of Prussia and later the first chancellor of a unified Germany, Bismarck was the architect of German unification and helped to consolidate the new nation's economic and military power.

Black Death The epidemic of bubonic plague that ravaged Europe, Asia, and North Africa in the fourteenth century, killing one third to one half of the population.

Black Jacobins A nickname for the rebels in Saint-Domingue, including Toussaint L'Ouverture, a former slave who in 1791 led the slaves of this French colony in the largest and most successful slave insurrection.

Blackshirts The troops of Mussolini's fascist regime; the squads received money from Italian landowners to attack socialist leaders.

Black Tuesday (October 29, 1929) The day on which the U.S. stock market crashed, plunging U.S. and international trading systems into crisis and leading the world into the "Great Depression."

William Blake (1757–1827) Romantic writer who criticized industrial society and factories. He championed the imagination and poetic vision, seeing both as transcending the limits of the material world.

Blitzkrieg The German "lightning war" strategy used during the Second World War; the Germans invaded Poland, France, Russia, and other countries with fast-moving and well-coordinated attacks using aircraft, tanks and other armored vehicles, followed by infantry.

Bloody Sunday On January 22, 1905, the Russian tsar's guards killed 130 demonstrators who were protesting the tsar's mistreatment of workers and the middle class.

Giovanni Boccaccio (1313–1375) Florentine author best known for his *Decameron*, a collection of prose tales about sex, adventure, and trickery written in the Italian vernacular after the Black Death.

Jean Bodin (1530–1596) A French political philosopher whose *Six Books of the Commonwealth* advanced a theory of absolute sovereignty, on the grounds that the state's paramount duty is to maintain order and that monarchs should therefore exercise unlimited power.

Boer War (1898–1902) Conflict between British and ethnically European Afrikaners in South Africa, with terrible casualties on both sides.

Boethius (c. 480–524) Member of a prominent Roman family, he sought to preserve aspects of ancient learning by compiling a series of handbooks and anthologies appropriate for Christian readers. His translations of Greek philosophy provided a crucial link between classical Greek thought and the early intellectual culture of Christianity.

Bolsheviks Former members of the Russian Social Democratic Party who advocated the destruction of capitalist political and economic institutions and started the Russian Revolution. In 1918, the Bolsheviks changed their name to the Russian Communist Party. Prominent Bolsheviks included Vladimir Lenin and Josef Stalin. Leon Trotsky joined the Bolsheviks late but became a prominent leader in the early years of the Russian Revolution.

Napoleon Bonaparte (1769–1821) Corsican-born French general who seized power and ruled as dictator from 1799 to 1814. After the successful conquest of much of Europe, he was defeated by Russian and Prussian forces and died in exile.

Boniface VIII During his pontificate (1294–1303), repeated claims to papal authority were challenged by King Philip IV of France. When Boniface died in 1309 (at the hands of Philip's thugs), the French king moved the papal court from Rome to the French city of Avignon, where it remained until 1378.

Sandro Botticelli (1445–1510) An Italian painter devoted to the blending of classical and Christian motifs by using ideas associated with the pagan past to illuminate sacred stories.

bourgeoisie Term for the middle class, derived from the French word for a town-dweller, *bourgeois*.

Boxer Rebellion (1899–1900) Chinese peasant movement that opposed foreign influence, especially that of Christian missionaries; it was finally put down after the Boxers were defeated by a foreign army composed mostly of Japanese, Russian, British, French, and American soldiers.

Tycho Brahe (1546–1601) Danish astronomer who believed that the careful study of the heavens would unlock the secrets of the universe. For over twenty years, he charted the movements of significant objects in the night sky, compiling the finest set of astronomical data in Europe.

British Commonwealth of Nations Formed in 1926, the Commonwealth conferred "dominion status" on Britain's white settler colonies in Canada, Australia, and New Zealand.

Bronze Age (3200–1200 B.C.E.) The name given to the era characterized by the discovery of techniques for smelting bronze (an alloy of copper and tin), which was then the strongest known metal.

Brownshirts Troops of young German men who dedicated themselves to the Nazi cause in the early 1930s by holding street marches, mass rallies, and confrontations. They engaged in beatings of Jews and anyone who opposed the Nazis.

Lord Byron (1788–1824) Writer and poet whose life helped give the Romantics their reputation as rebels against conformity. He was known for his love affairs, his defense of working-class movements, and his passionate engagement in politics, which led to his death in the war for Greek independence.

Byzantium The name of a small settlement located at the mouth of the Black Sea and at the crossroads between Europe and Asia, it was chosen by Constantine as the site for his new imperial capital of Constantinople in 324. Modern historians use this name to refer to the eastern Roman Empire that persisted in this region until 1453, but the inhabitants of that empire referred to themselves as Romans.

Julius Caesar (100–44 B.C.E.) The Roman general who conquered the Gauls, invaded Britain, and expanded Rome's territory in Asia Minor. He became the dictator of Rome in 46 B.C.E. His assassination led to the rise of his grandnephew and adopted son, Gaius Octavius Caesar, who ruled the Roman Empire as Caesar Augustus.

caliphs Islamic rulers who claim descent from the prophet Muhammad.

John Calvin (1509–1564) French-born theologian and reformer whose radical form of Protestantism was adopted in many Swiss cities, notably Geneva.

Canary Islands Islands off the western coast of Africa that were colonized by Portugal and Spain in the mid-fifteenth century, after which they became bases for further expeditions around the African coast and across the Atlantic.

Carbonari An underground organization that opposed the Concert of Europe's restoration of monarchies. They held influence in southern Europe during the 1820s, especially in Italy.

Carolingian Derived from the Latin name Carolus (Charles), this term refers to the Frankish dynasty that began with the rise to power of Charlemagne's grandfather, Charles Martel (688–741). At its height under Charlemagne (Charles the Great), the dynasty controlled what is now France, Germany, northern Italy, Catalonia, and portions of central Europe. The Carolingian Empire collapsed under the combined weight of Viking raids, economic disintegration, and the growing power of local lords.

Carolingian Renaissance A cultural and intellectual flowering that took place around the court of Charlemagne in the late eighth and early ninth centuries.

Carthage The great maritime empire that grew out of Phoenician trading colonies in North Africa and rivaled the power of Rome. Its wars with Rome, collectively known as the Punic Wars, ended in its destruction in 146 B.C.E.

Cassidorus (c. 490–c. 583) Member of an old senatorial family, he was largely responsible for introducing classical learning into the monastic curriculum and for turning monasteries into centers for the collection, preservation, and transmission of knowledge. His *Institutes*, an influential handbook of classical literature for Christian readers, was intended as a preface to more intensive study of theology and the Bible.

Catholic Church The "universal" (catholic) church based in Rome, which was redefined in the sixteenth century, when the Counter-Reformation resulted in the rebirth of the Catholic faith at the Council of Trent.

Margaret Cavendish (1623–1673) English natural philosopher who developed her own speculative natural philosophy. She used this philosophy to critique those who excluded her from scientific debate.

Camillo Benso di Cavour (1810–1861) Prime minister of Piedmont-Sardinia and founder of the Italian Liberal party; he played a key role in the movement for Italian unification under the Piedmontese king, Victor Emmanuel II.

Central Powers The First World War alliance between Germany, Austria-Hungary, Bulgaria, and Turkey.

Charlemagne (742–814) As king of the Franks (767–813), Charles "the Great" consolidated much of western Europe under his rule. In 800, he was crowned emperor by the pope in Rome, establishing a problematic precedent that would have wide-ranging consequences for western Europe's relationship with the eastern Roman Empire in Byzantium and for the relationship between the papacy and secular rulers.

Charles I (1625–1649) The second Stuart king of England, Charles attempted to rule without the support of Parliament, sparking a controversy that erupted into civil war in 1642. The king's forces were ultimately defeated and Charles himself was executed by act of Parliament, the first time in history that a reigning king was legally deposed and executed by his own government.

Charles II of England Nominally King of England, Ireland, and Scotland after his father Charles I's execution in 1649, Charles II lived in exile until he was restored to the throne in 1660. Influenced by his cousin, King Louis XIV of France, he presided over an opulent royal court until his death in 1685.

Chartists A working-class movement in Britain that called for reform of the British political system during the 1840s. They were supporters of the "People's Charter," which had six demands: universal white male suffrage, secret ballots, an end to property qualifications as a condition of public office, annual parliamentary elections, salaries for members of the House of Commons, and equal electoral districts.

Geoffrey Chaucer (1340–1400) English poet whose collection of versified stories, *The Canterbury Tales*, features characters from a variety of different classes.

Christine de Pisan (c. 1364–c. 1431) Born in Italy, Christine spent her adult life attached to the French court and, after her husband's death, became the first laywoman to earn her living by writing. She is the author of treatises in warfare and chivalry as well as of books and pamphlets that challenge long-standing misogynistic claims.

Church of England Founded by Henry VIII in the 1530s, as a consequence of his break with the authority of the Roman pope.

Winston Churchill (1874–1965) British prime minister who led the country during the Second World War. He also coined the phrase "Iron Curtain" in a speech at Westminster College in 1946.

Cicero (106–43 B.C.E.) Influential Roman senator, orator, Stoic philosopher, and prose stylist. His published writings still form the basis of the instruction in classical Latin grammar and usage.

Cincinnatus (519–c. 430 B.C.E.) A legendary citizen-farmer of Rome who reluctantly accepted an appointment as dictator. After defeating Rome's enemies, he allegedly left his political office and returned to his farm.

Civil Constitution of the Clergy Issued by the French National Assembly in 1790, the Civil Constitution of the Clergy decreed that all bishops and priests should be subject to the authority of the state. Their salaries were to be paid out of the public treasury, and they were required to swear allegiance to the new state, making it clear they served France rather than Rome. The Assembly's aim was to make the Catholic Church of France a truly national and civil institution.

civilizing mission An argument made by Europeans to justify colonial expansion in the nineteenth century. Supporters of this idea believed that Europeans had a duty to impose western ideas of economic and political progress on the indigenous peoples they ruled over in their colonies. In practice, the colonial powers often found that ambitious plans to impose European practices on colonial subjects led to unrest that threatened the stability of colonial rule, and by the early twentieth century most colonial powers were more cautious in their plans for political or cultural transformation.

Civil Rights Movement The Second World War increased African American migration from the American South to northern cities, intensifying a drive for rights, dignity, and independence. By 1960, civil rights groups had started organizing boycotts and demonstrations directed at discrimination against blacks in the South. During the 1960s, civil rights laws passed under President Lyndon B. Johnson did bring African Americans some equality with regard to voting rights and, to a much lesser degree, school desegregation. However, racism continued in areas such as housing, job opportunities, and the economic development of African American communities.

Civil War (1861–1865) Conflict between the northern and southern states of America that cost over 600,000 lives; this struggle led to the abolition of slavery in the United States.

classical learning The study of ancient Greek and Latin texts. After Christianity became the only legal religion of the Roman Empire, scholars needed to find a way to make classical learning applicable to a Christian way of life. Christian monks played a significant role in resolving this problem by reinterpreting the classics for a Christian audience.

Cluny A powerful Benedictine monastery founded in 910 whose enormous wealth and prestige would derive from its independence from secular authorities as well as from its wide network of daughter houses (priories).

Cold War (1945–1991) Ideological, political, and economic conflict in which the USSR and Eastern Europe opposed the United States and Western Europe in the decades after the Second World War. The Cold War's origins lay in the breakup of the wartime alliance between the United States and the Soviet Union in 1945 and resulted in a division of Europe into two spheres: the West, commited to market capitalism, and the East, which sought to build Socialist republics in areas under Soviet Control. The Cold War ended with the collapse of the Soviet Union in 1991.

collectivization Stalin's plan for nationalizing agricultural production, begun in 1929. Twenty-five million peasants were forced to give up their land and join 250,000 large collective farms. Many who resisted were deported to labor camps in the Far East, and Stalin's government cut off food rations to those areas most marked by resistance to collectivization. In the ensuing man-made famines, millions of people starved to death.

Columbian Exchange The widespread exchange of peoples, plants, animals, diseases, goods, and culture between the African and Eurasian landmass (on the one hand) and the region that encompasses the Americas, Australia, and the Pacific Islands (on the other); precipitated by voyage of Columbus in 1492.

Christopher Columbus (1451–1506) A Genoese sailor who persuaded King Ferdinand and Queen Isabella of Spain to fund his expedition across the Atlantic, with the purpose of discovering a new trade route to Asia. His miscalculations landed him in the Bahamas and the island of Hispaniola in 1492.

Commercial Revolution A period of economic development in Europe lasting from c. 1500–c.1800. Advances in agriculture and handicraft production, combined with the expansion of trade networks in the Atlantic world, brought new wealth and new kinds of commercial activity to Europe. The commercial revolution prepared the way for the industrial revolution of the 1800s.

Committee of Public Safety Political body during the French Revolution that was controlled by the Jacobins, who defended the revolution by executing thousands during the Reign of Terror (September 1793–July 1794).

commune A community of individuals who have banded together in a sworn association, with the aim of establishing their independence and setting up their own form of representative government. Many medieval towns originally founded by lords or monasteries gained their independence through such methods.

The Communist Manifesto Radical pamphlet by Karl Marx (1818–1883) that predicted the downfall of the capitalist system and its replacement by a classless egalitarian society. Marx believed that this revolution would be accomplished by workers (the proletariat).

Compromise of 1867 Agreement between the Habsburgs and the peoples living in Hungarian parts of the empire that the Habsburg state would be officially known as the Austro-Hungarian Empire.

Concert of Europe (1814–1815) The body of diplomatic agreements designed primarily by Austrian minister Klemens von Metternich between 1814 and 1848 and supported by other European powers until 1914. Its goal was to maintain a balance of power on the Continent and to prevent destabilizing social and political change in Europe.

conciliarism A doctrine developed in the thirteenth and fourteenth centuries to counter the growing power of the papacy, conciliarism holds that papal authority should be subject to a council of the Church at large. Conciliarists emerged as a dominant force after the Council of Constance (1414–1418) but were eventually outmatched by a rejuvenated papacy.

Congress of Vienna (1814–1815) International conference to reorganize Europe after the downfall of Napoleon and the French Revolution. European monarchies restored the Bourbon family to the French throne, agreed to respect each other's borders and to cooperate in guarding against future revolutions and war.

conquistador Spanish term for "conqueror," applied to the mercenaries and adventurers who campaigned against indigenous peoples in central and southern America.

Conservatives In the nineteenth century, conservatives aimed to legitimize and solidify the monarchy's authority and the hierarchical social order. They believed that change had to be slow, incremental, and managed so that the structures of authority were strengthened and not weakened.

Constantine (275–337) The first emperor of Rome to convert to Christianity, Constantine came to power in 312. In 324, he founded a new imperial capital, Constantinople, on the site of a maritime settlement known as Byzantium.

Constantinople Founded by the emperor Constantine on the site of a village called Byzantium, Constantinople became the new capital of the Roman Empire in 324 and continued to be the seat of imperial power after its capture by the Ottoman Turks in 1453. It is now known as Istanbul.

contract theory of government A theory of government written by Englishman John Locke (1632–1704) which posits that government authority was both contractual and conditional; therefore, if a government has abused its given authority, society had the right to dissolve it and create another.

Nicholas Copernicus (1473–1543) Polish astronomer who advanced the idea that the earth moved around the sun.

cosmopolitanism Stemming from the Greek word meaning "universal city," the culture characteristic of the Hellenistic world challenged and transformed the more narrow worldview of the Greek polis.

cotton gin Invented by Eli Whitney in 1793, this device mechanized the process of separating cotton seeds from the cotton fiber, which sped up the production of cotton and reduced its price. This change made slavery profitable in the United States.

Council of Constance (1417–1420) A meeting of clergy and theologians in an effort to resolve the Great Schism within the Roman Church. The council deposed all rival papal candidates and elected a new pope, Martin V, but it also adopted the doctrine of conciliarism, which holds that the supreme authority within the Church rests with a representative general council and not with the pope. However, Martin V himself was an opponent of this doctrine and refused to be bound by it.

Council of Trent The name given to a series of meetings held in the Italian city of Trent (Trento) between 1545 and 1563, when leaders of the Roman Church reaffirmed Catholic doctrine and instituted internal reforms.

Counter-Reformation The movement to counter the Protestant Reformation, initiated by the Catholic Church at the Council of Trent in 1545.

coup d'état French term for the overthrow of an established government by a group of conspirators, usually with military support.

Crimean War (1854–1856) War waged by Russia against Great Britain and France. Spurred by Russia's encroachment on Ottoman territories, the conflict revealed Russia's military weakness when Russian forces fell to British and French troops.

Cuban missile crisis (1962) Diplomatic standoff between the United States and the Soviet Union that was provoked by the Soviet Union's attempt to base nuclear missiles in Cuba; it brought the world closer to nuclear war than ever before or since.

Cuius regio, eius religio A Latin phrase meaning "as the ruler, so the religion." Adopted as a part of the settlement of the Peace of Augsburg in 1555, it meant that those principalities ruled by Lutherans would have Lutheranism as their official religion and those ruled by Catholics must practice Catholicism.

cult of domesticity Concept associated with Victorian England that idealized women as nurturing wives and mothers.

cult of the Virgin The beliefs and practices associated with the veneration of Mary, the mother of Jesus, which became increasingly popular in the twelfth century.

cuneiform An early writing system that began to develop in Mesopotamia in the fourth millennium B.C.E. By 3100 B.C.E., its distinctive markings were impressed on clay tablets using a wedge-shaped stylus.

Cyrus the Great (c. 585–529 B.C.E.) As architect of the Persian Empire, Cyrus extended his dominion over a vast territory stretching from the Persian Gulf to the Mediterranean and incorporating the ancient civilizations of Mesopotamia. His successors ruled this Persian Empire as "Great Kings."

Darius (521–486 B.C.E.) The Persian emperor whose conflict with Aristagoras, the Greek ruler of Miletus, ignited the Persian Wars. In 490 B.C.E., Darius sent a large army to punish the Athenians for their intervention in Persian imperial affairs, but this force was defeated by Athenian hoplites on the plain of Marathon.

Charles Darwin (1809–1882) British naturalist who wrote *On the Origin of Species* and developed the theory of natural selection to explain the evolution of organisms.

D-Day (June 6, 1944) Date of the Allied invasion of Normandy, under General Dwight Eisenhower, to liberate Western Europe from German occupation.

Decembrists Russian army officers who were influenced by events in France and formed secret societies that espoused liberal governance. They were put down by Nicholas I in December 1825.

Declaration of Independence (1776) Historic document stating the principles of government on which the United States was founded.

Declaration of the Rights of Man and of the Citizen (1789) French charter of liberties formulated by the National Assembly during the French Revolution. The seventeen articles later became the preamble to the new constitution, which the assembly finished in 1791.

democracy In ancient Greece, this form of government allowed a class of propertied male citizens to participate in the governance of their polis; but excluded women, slaves, and citizens without property from the political process. As a result, the ruling class amounted to only a small percentage of the entire population.

René Descartes (1596–1650) French philosopher and mathematician who emphasized the use of deductive reasoning.

Denis Diderot (1713–1784) French philosophe and author who was the guiding force behind the publication of the first encyclopedia. His *Encyclopedia* showed how reason could be applied to nearly all realms of thought and aimed to be a compendium of all human knowledge.

Dien Bien Phu (1954) Defining battle in the war between French colonialists and the Viet Minh that secured North Vietnam for Ho Chi Minh and his army and left the south to form its own government, to be supported by France and the United States.

Diet of Worms The select council of the Church that convened in the German city of Worms and condemned Martin Luther on a charge of heresy in 1521.

Diocletian (245–316) As emperor of Rome from 284 to 305, Diocletian recognized that the empire could not be governed by one man in one place. His solution was to divide the empire into four parts, each with its own imperial ruler, but he himself remained the dominant ruler of the resulting tetrarchy (rule of four). He also initiated the Great Persecution, a time when many Christians became martyrs to their faith.

Directory (1795–1799) Executive committee that governed after the fall of Robespierre and held control until the coup of Napoleon Bonaparte.

Discourse on Method Philosophical treatise by René Descartes (1596–1650) proposing that the path to knowledge was through logical deduction, beginning with one's own self: "I think, therefore I am."

Dominican Order Also called the Order of Preachers, it was founded by Dominic of Osma (1170–1221), a Castilian preacher and theologian, and approved by Innocent III in 1216. The order was dedicated to the rooting out of heresy and the conversion of Jews and Muslims. Many of its members held teaching positions in European universities and contributed to the development of medieval philosophy and theology. Others became the leading administrators of the Inquisition.

Dominion in the British Commonwealth Canadian promise to maintain their fealty to the British crown, even after their independence in 1867; later applied to Australia and New Zealand.

Dreyfus Affair The 1894 French scandal surrounding accusations that a Jewish captain, Alfred Dreyfus, sold military secrets to the Germans. Convicted, Dreyfus was sentenced to solitary confinement for life. However, after public outcry, it was revealed that the trial documents were forgeries, and Dreyfus was pardoned after a second trial in 1899. In 1906, he was fully exonerated and reinstated in the army. The affair revealed the depths of popular anti-Semitism in France.

Alexander Dubček (1921–1992) Communist leader of the Czechoslovakian government who advocated for "socialism with a human face." He encouraged debate within the party, academic and artistic freedom, and less censorship, which led to the "Prague spring" of 1968. People in other parts of Eastern Europe began to demonstrate in support of Dubček and demand their own reforms. When Dubček tried to democratize the Communist party and did not attend a meeting of the Warsaw Pact, the Soviets sent tanks and troops into Prague and ousted Dubček and his allies.

Duma The Russian parliament, created in response to the revolution of 1905.

Dunkirk The French port on the English Channel where the British and French forces retreated after sustaining heavy losses against the German military. Between May 27 and June 4, 1940, the Royal Navy evacuated over 300,000 troops using commercial and pleasure boats.

Eastern Front Battlefront between Berlin and Moscow during the First and Second World Wars..

East India Company (1600–1858) British charter company created to outperform Portuguese and Spanish traders in the Far East; in the eighteenth century the company became, in effect, the ruler of a large part of India. There was also a Dutch East India Company.

Edict of Nantes (1598) Issued by Henry IV of France in an effort to end religious violence. The edict declared France to be a Catholic country but tolerated some forms of Protestant worship.

Edward I of England King of England from 1272 to his death in 1307, Edward presided over the creation of new legal and bureaucratic institutions in his realm, violently subjugated the Welsh, and attempted to colonize Scotland. He expelled English Jews from his domain in 1290.

Eleanor of Aquitaine (1122–1204) Ruler of the wealthy province of Aquitaine and wife of Louis VII of France, Eleanor had her marriage annulled in order to marry the young count of Anjou, Henry Plantagenet, who became King Henry of England a year later. Mother of two future kings of England, she was an important patron of the arts.

Elizabeth I (1533–1603) Protestant daughter of Henry VIII and his second wife, Anne Boleyn, Elizabeth succeeded her sister Mary as the second queen regnant of England (1558–1603).

emancipation of the serfs (1861) The abolition of serfdom was central to Tsar Alexander II's program of modernization and reform, but it produced a limited amount of change. Former serfs now had legal rights. However, farm land was granted to the village communes instead of to individuals. The land was of poor quality and the former serfs had to pay for it in installments to the village commune.

emperor Originally the term for any conquering commander of the Roman army whose victories merited celebration in an official triumph. After Augustus seized power in 27 B.C.E., it was the title born by the sole ruler of the Roman Empire.

empire A centralized political entity consolidated through the conquest and colonization of other nations or peoples in order to benefit the ruler and/or his homeland.

Enabling Act (1933) Emergency act passed by the Reichstag (German parliament) that helped transform Hitler from Germany's chancellor, or prime minister, into a dictator, following the suspicious burning of the Reichstag building and a suspension of civil liberties.

enclosure Long process of privatizing what had been public agricultural land in eighteenth-century Britain; it helped to stimulate the development of commercial agriculture and forced many people in rural areas to seek work in cities during the early stages of industrialization.

The Encyclopedia Joint venture of French philosophe writers, led by Denis Diderot (1713–1784), which proposed to summarize all modern knowledge in a multivolume illustrated work with over 70,000 articles.

Friedrich Engels (1820–1895) German social and political philosopher who collaborated with Karl Marx on many publications.

English Civil War (1642–1649) Conflicts between the English Parliament and King Charles I erupted into civil war, which ended in the defeat of the royalists and the execution of Charles on charges of treason against the crown. A short time later, Parliament's hereditary House of Lords was abolished and England was declared a Commonwealth.

English Navigation Act of 1651 Act stipulating that only English ships could carry goods between the mother country and its colonies.

Enlightenment Intellectual movement in eighteenth-century Europe, that believed in human betterment through the application of reason to solve social, economic, and political problems.

Epicureanism A philosophical position articulated by Epicurus of Athens (c. 342–270 B.C.E.), who rejected the idea of an ordered universe governed by divine forces; instead, he emphasized individual agency and proposed that the highest good is the pursuit of pleasure.

Desiderius Erasmus (c. 1469–1536) Dutch-born scholar, social commentator, and Catholic humanist whose new translation of the Bible influenced the theology of Martin Luther.

Estates-General The representative body of the three estates in France. In 1789, King Louis XVI summoned the Estates-General to meet for the first time since 1614 because it seemed to be the only solution to France's worsening economic crisis and financial chaos.

Etruscans Settlers of the Italian peninsula who dominated the region from the late Bronze Age until the rise of the Roman Republic in the sixth century B.C.E.

Euclid Hellenistic mathematician whose *Elements of Geometry* forms the basis of modern geometry.

eugenics A Greek term, meaning "good birth," referring to the project of "breeding" a superior human race. It was popularly championed by scientists, politicians, and social critics in the late nineteenth and early twentieth centuries.

European Common Market (1957) The Treaty of Rome created the European Economic Community (EEC), or Common Market. The original members were France, West Germany, Italy, Belgium, Holland, and Luxembourg. The EEC sought to abolish trade barriers between its members and it pledged itself to common external tariffs, the free movement of labor and capital among the member nations, and uniform wage structures and social security systems to create similar working conditions in all member countries.

European Union (EU) Successor organization to the European Economic Community or European Common Market, formed by the Maastricht Treaty, which took effect in 1993. Currently twenty-eight member states compose the EU, which has a governing council, an international court, and a parliament. Over time, member states of the EU have relinquished some of their sovereignty, and cooperation has evolved into a community with a single currency, the euro.

Exclusion Act of 1882 U.S. congressional act prohibiting nearly all immigration from China to the United States; fueled by animosity toward Chinese workers in the American West.

existentialism Philosophical movement that arose out of the Second World War and emphasized the absurdity of human condition. Led by Jean-Paul Sartre and Albert Camus, existentialists encouraged humans to take responsibility for their own decisions and dilemmas.

expulsion of the Jews European rulers began to expel their Jewish subjects from their kingdoms beginning in the 1280s, mostly due to their inability to repay the money they had extorted from Jewish money-lenders but also as a result of escalating anti-Semitism in the wake of the Crusades, Jews were also expelled from the Rhineland in the fourteenth century and from Spain in 1492.

fascism The doctrine founded by Benito Mussolini, which emphasized three main ideas: statism ("nothing above the state, nothing outside the state, nothing against the state"), nationalism, and militarism. Its name derives from the Latin *fasces*, a symbol of Roman imperial power adopted by Mussolini.

Fashoda Incident (1898) Disagreements between the French and the British over land claims in North Africa led to a standoff between armies of the two nations at the Sudanese town of Fashoda. The crisis was solved diplomatically. France ceded southern Sudan to Britain in exchange for a stop to further expansion by the British.

The Feminine Mystique Groundbreaking book by feminist Betty Friedan (b. 1921), which tried to define *femininity* and explored how women internalized those definitions.

Franz Ferdinand (1863–1914) Archduke of Austria and heir to the Austro-Hungarian Empire; his assassination led to the beginning of the First World War.

Ferdinand (1452–1516) **and Isabella** (1451–1504) In 1469, Ferdinand of Aragon married the heiress to Castile, Isabella. Their union allowed them to pursue several ambitious policies, including the conquest of Granada, the last Muslim principality in Spain, and the expulsion of Spain's large Jewish community. In 1492, Isabella granted three ships to Christopher Columbus of Genoa (Italy), who went on to claim portions of the New World for Spain.

Fertile Crescent An area of fertile land in what is now Syria, Israel, Turkey, eastern Iraq, and western Iran that was able to sustain settlements due to its wetter climate and abundant natural food resources. Some of the earliest known civilizations emerged there between 9000 and 4500 B.C.E.

feudalism A problematic modern term that attempts to explain the diffusion of power in medieval Europe, and the many different kinds of political, social, and economic relationships that were forged through the giving and receiving of fiefs (*feoda*). But because it is anachronistic and inadequate, this term has been rejected by most historians of the medieval period.

First Crusade (1095–1099) Launched by Pope Urban II in response to a request from the Byzantine emperor Alexius Comnenus, who had asked for a small contingent of knights to assist him in fighting Turkish forces in Anatolia; Urban instead directed the crusaders' energies toward the Holy Land and the recapture of Jerusalem, promising those who took the cross (*crux*) that they would merit eternal salvation if they died in the attempt. This crusade prompted attacks against

Jews throughout Europe and resulted in six subsequent—and unsuccessful—military campaigns.

First World War A total war from August 1914 to November 1918, involving the armies of Britain, France, and Russia (the Allies) against Germany, Austria-Hungary, and the Ottoman Empire (the Central Powers). Italy joined the Allies in 1915, and the United States joined them in 1917, helping to tip the balance in favor of the Allies, who also drew upon the populations and raw materials of their colonial possessions. Also known as the Great War.

Five Pillars of Islam The Muslim teaching that salvation is only assured through observance of five basic precepts: submission to God's will as described in the teachings of Muhammad, frequent prayer, ritual fasting, the giving of alms, and an annual pilgrimage to Mecca (the Hajj).

Five-Year Plan Soviet effort launched under Stalin in 1928 to replace the market with a state-owned and state-managed economy in order to promote rapid economic development over a five-year period and thereby "catch and overtake" the leading capitalist countries. The First Five-Year Plan was followed by the Second Five-Year Plan (1933–1937) and so on, until the collapse of the Soviet Union in 1991.

fly shuttle Invented by John Kay in 1733, this device sped up the process of weaving.

Fourteen Points President Woodrow Wilson proposed these points as the foundation on which to build peace in the world after the First World War. They called for an end to secret treaties, "open covenants, openly arrived at," freedom of the seas, the removal of international tariffs, the reduction of arms, the "self-determination of peoples," and the establishment of a League of Nations to settle international conflicts.

Franciscan Order Also known as the Order of the Friars Minor. The earliest Franciscans were followers of Francis of Assisi (1182–1226) and strove, like him, to imitate the life and example of Jesus. The order was formally established by Pope Innocent III in 1209. Its special mission was the care and instruction of the urban poor.

Frankfurt Parliament (1848–1849) Failed attempt to create a unified Germany under constitutional principles. In 1849, the assembly offered the crown of the new German nation to Frederick William IV of Prussia, but he refused the offer and suppressed a brief protest. The delegates went home disillusioned.

Frederick the Great (1712–1786) Prussian ruler (1740–1786) who engaged the nobility in maintaining a strong military and bureaucracy and led Prussian armies to notable military victories. He also encouraged Enlightenment rationalism and artistic endeavors.

French Revolution of 1789 In 1788, a severe financial crisis forced the French monarchy to convene an assembly known as the Estates General, representing the three estates of the realm: the clergy, the nobility, and the commons (known as the Third Estate). When the Estates General met in 1789, representatives of the Third Estate demanded major constitutional changes, and when the king and his government proved uncooperative, the Third Estate broke with the other two estates and renamed themselves the National Assembly, demanding a written constitution. The position of the National Assembly was confirmed by a popular uprising in Paris and the king was forced to accept the transformation of France into a constitutional monarchy. This constitutional phase of the revolution lasted until 1972, when the pressures of foreign invasion and the emergence of a more radical revolutionary movement caused the collapse of the monarchy and the establishment of a Republic in France.

French Revolution of 1830 The French popular revolt against Charles X's July Ordinances of 1830, which dissolved the French Chamber of Deputies and restricted suffrage to exclude almost everyone except the nobility. After several days of violence, Charles abdicated the throne and was replaced by a constitutional monarch, Louis Philippe.

French Revolution of 1848 Revolution overthrowing Louis-Philippe in February, 1848, leading to the formation of the Second Republic (1848–1852). Initially enjoying broad support from both the middle classes and laborers in Paris, the new government became more conservative after elections in which the French peasantry participated for the first time. A workers' revolt was violently repressed in June, 1848, and in December 1848, Napoleon Bonaparte's nephew, Louis-Napoleon Bonaparte, was elected president. In 1852, Louis-Napoleon declared himself emperor and abolished the republic.

Sigmund Freud (1856–1939) The Austrian physician who founded the discipline of psychoanalysis and suggested that human behavior was largely motivated by unconscious and irrational forces.

Galileo Galilei (1564–1642) Italian physicist and inventor; the implications of his ideas raised the ire of the Catholic Church, and he was forced to retract most of his findings.

Gallipoli (1915) In the First World War, a combined force of French, British, Australian and New Zealand troops tried to invade the Gallipoli Peninsula, in the first large-scale amphibious attack in history, and seize it from the Turks. After seven months of fighting, the Allies had lost 200,000 soldiers. Defeated, they withdrew.

Mohandas K. (Mahatma) Gandhi (1869–1948) The Indian leader who advocated nonviolent noncooperation to protest colonial rule and helped win home rule for India in 1947.

Giuseppe Garibaldi (1807–1882) Italian revolutionary leader who led the fight to free Sicily and Naples from the Habsburg Empire; the lands were then peaceably annexed by Sardinia to produce a unified Italy.

Gaul The region of the Roman Empire that was home to the Celtic people of that name, comprising modern France, Belgium, and western Germany.

Geneva Peace Conference (1954) International conference to restore peace in Korea and Indochina. The chief participants were the United States, the Soviet Union, Great Britain, France, the People's Republic of China, North Korea, South Korea, Vietnam, the Viet Minh party, Laos, and Cambodia. The conference resulted in the division of North and South Vietnam.

Genoa Maritime city on Italy's northwestern coast, the Genoese were active in trading ventures along the Silk Road and in the establishment of trading colonies in the Mediterranean. They were also involved in the world of finance and backed the commercial ventures of other powers, especially Spain's.

German Democratic Republic Nation founded from the Soviet zone of occupation of Germany after the Second World War; also known as East Germany.

German Social Democratic party Founded in 1875, it was the most powerful socialist party in Europe before 1917.

Gilgamesh Sumerian ruler of the city of Uruk around 2700 B.C.E., Gilgamesh became the hero of one of the world's oldest epics, which circulated orally for nearly a millennium before being written down.

Giotto (c. 1266–1337) Florentine painter and architect who is often considered a forerunner of the Renaissance.

glasnost Introduced by Soviet leader Mikhail Gorbachev in June 1987, *glasnost* was one of the five major policies that constituted *perestroika*. Often translated into English as "openness," it called for transparency in Soviet government and institutional activities by reducing censorship in mass media and lifting significant bans on the political, intellectual, and cultural lives of Soviet civilians.

globalization The term used to describe political, social, and economic networks that span the globe. These global exchanges are not limited by nation-states and in recent decades are associated with new technologies, such as the Internet. Globalization is not new, however, as human cultures and economies have been in contact with one another for centuries.

Glorious Revolution The overthrow of King James II of England and the installation of his Protestant daughter, Mary Stuart, and her husband, William of Orange, to the throne in 1688 and 1689. It is widely regarded as the founding moment in the development of a constitutional monarchy in Britain, while also establishing a more favorable climate for the economic and political growth of the English commercial classes.

Gold Coast Name that European mariners and merchants gave to that part of West Equatorial Africa from which gold and slaves were exported. Originally controlled by the Portuguese, this area later became the British colony of the Gold Coast.

Mikhail Gorbachev (1931–) Soviet leader who attempted to reform the Soviet Union through his programs of glasnost and perestroika in the late 1980s. He encouraged open discussions in other countries in the Soviet bloc, which helped inspire the velvet revolutions throughout Eastern Europe. Eventually the political, social, and economic upheaval he had unleashed would lead to the breakup of the Soviet Union.

Gothic style A type of graceful architecture emerging in twelfth- and thirteenth-century England and France. The style is characterized by pointed arches, delicate decoration, and large windows.

Olympe de Gouges (1748–1793) French political radical and feminist whose *Declaration of the Rights of Woman* demanded an equal place for women in France.

Great Depression Global economic crisis following the U.S. stock market crash on October 29, 1929, and ending with the onset of the Second World War.

Great Famine A period of terrible hunger and deprivation in Europe that peaked between 1315 and 1317, caused by a cooling of the climate and by the exhaustion of over-farming. It is estimated to have reduced the population of Europe by 10 to 15 percent.

Great Fear (1789) Following the outbreak of revolution in Paris, fear spread throughout the French countryside, as rumors circulated that armies of brigands or royal troops were coming. The peasants and villagers organized into militias, while others attacked and burned the manor houses in order to destroy the records of manorial dues.

Great Schism (1378–1417) Also known as the Great Western Schism, to distinguish it from the longstanding rupture between the Greek East and Latin West. During the schism, the Roman Church was divided between two (and, ultimately, three) competing popes. Each pope claimed to be legitimate and each denounced the heresy of the others.

Great Terror (1936–1938) The systematic murder of nearly a million people and the deportation of another million and a half to labor camps by Stalin's regime in an attempt to consolidate power and remove perceived enemies.

Greek East After the founding of Constantinople, the eastern Greek-speaking half of the Roman Empire grew more populous, prosperous and central to imperial policy. Its inhabitants considered themselves to be the true heirs of Rome, and their own Orthodox Church to be the true manifestation of Jesus's ministry.

Greek independence Nationalists in Greece revolted against the Ottoman Empire and fought a war that ended in Greek independence in 1827. They received crucial help from British, French, and Russian troops as well as widespread sympathy throughout Europe.

Pope Gregory I (r. 590–604) Also known as Gregory the Great, he was the first bishop of Rome to successfully negotiate a more universal role for the papacy. His political and theological agenda widened the rift between the western Latin (Catholic) Church and the eastern Greek (Orthodox) Church in Byzantium. He also articulated the Church's official position on the status of Jews, promoted affective approaches to religious worship, encouraged the Benedictine monastic movement, and sponsored missionary expeditions.

Guernica The Basque town bombed by German planes in April 1937 during the Spanish Civil War. It is also the subject of Pablo Picasso's famous painting from the same year.

guilds Professional organizations in commercial towns that regulated business and safeguarded the privileges of those practicing a particular craft. Often identical to confraternities ("brotherhoods").

Gulag The vast system of forced labor camps under the Soviet regime; it originated in 1919 in a small monastery near the Arctic Circle and spread throughout the Soviet Union. Penal labor was required of both ordinary criminals and those accused of political crimes. Tens of millions of people were sent to the camps between 1928 and 1953; the exact figure is unknown.

Gulf War (1991) Armed conflict between Iraq and a coalition of thirty-two nations, including the United States, Britain, Egypt, France, and Saudi Arabia. The seeds of the war were planted with Iraq's invasion of Kuwait on August 2, 1990.

Johannes Gutenberg European inventor of the printing press, his shop in Mainz produced the first printed book—a Bible—between the years 1453 and 1455.

Habsburg Dynasty A powerful European dynasty which came to power in the eleventh century in a region now part of Switzerland. Early generations of Habsburgs consolidated their control over neighboring German-speaking lands; through strategic marriages with other royal lines, later rulers eventually controlled a substantial part of Europe—including much of central Europe, the Netherlands, and even Spain and all its colonies for a time. In practice, the Holy Roman Emperor chosen from a member of the Habsburg lineage. By the latter half of the seventeenth century, the Austrian Habsburg Empire was made of up nearly 300 nominally autonomous dynastic kingdoms, principalities, duchies, and archbishoprics.

Hagia Sophia The enormous church dedicated to "Holy Wisdom," built in Constantinople at the behest of the emperor Justinian in the sixth century C.E. When Constantinople fell to Ottoman forces in 1453, it became an important mosque.

Haitian Revolution (1802–1804) In 1802, Napoleon sought to reassert French control of Saint-Domingue, but stiff resistance and yellow fever crushed the French army. In 1804, Jean-Jacques Dessalines, a general in the army of former slaves, declared the independent state of Haiti. (See **slave revolt in Saint-Domingue**.)

Hajj The annual pilgrimage to Mecca; an obligation for Muslims.

Hammurabi Ruler of Babylon from 1792 to 1750 B.C.E., Hammurabi issued a collection of laws that were greatly influential in the Near East and which constitute the world's oldest surviving law code.

Harlem Renaissance Cultural movement in the 1920s that was based in Harlem, a part of New York City with a large African American population. The movement gave voice to black novelists, poets, painters, and musicians, many of whom used their art to protest racial subordination.

Hatshepsut (1479–1458 C.E.) As a pharaoh during the New Kingdom, she launched several successful military campaigns and extended trade and diplomacy. She was an ambitious builder who probably constructed the first tomb in the Valley of the Kings. Though she never pretended to be a man, she was routinely portrayed with a masculine figure and a ceremonial beard.

Hebrews Originally a pastoral people divided among several tribes, they were briefly united under the rule of David and his son, Solomon, who promoted the worship of a single god, Yahweh, and constructed the first temple at the new capital city of Jerusalem. After Solomon's death, the Hebrew tribes were divided between the two kingdoms of Israel and Judah, which were eventually conquered by the Neo-Assyrian and Chaldean empires. It was in captivity that the Hebrews came to define themselves through worship of Yahweh and to develop a religion, Judaism, that could exist outside of Judea. They were liberated by the Persian king Cyrus the Great in 539 B.C.E.

Hellenistic art The art of the Hellenistic period bridged the tastes, ideals, and customs of classical Greece and those that would be more characteristic of Rome. The Romans strove to emulate Hellenistic city planning and civic culture and thereby exported Hellenistic culture to their own far-flung colonies in western Europe.

Hellenistic culture The "Greek-like" culture that dominated the ancient world in the wake of Alexander's conquests.

Hellenistic kingdoms Following the death of Alexander the Great, his vast empire was divided into three separate states: Ptolemaic Egypt (under the rule of the general Ptolemy and his successors), Seleucid Asia (ruled by the general Seleucus and his heirs) and Antigonid Greece (governed by Antigonus of Macedonia). Each state maintained its independence, but the shared characteristics of Greco-Macedonian rule and a shared Greek culture and heritage bound them together in a united cosmopolitan world.

Hellenistic world The various Western civilizations of antiquity that were loosely united by shared Greek language and culture, especially around the eastern Mediterranean.

Heloise (c. 1090–1164) One of the foremost scholars of her time, she became the pupil and the wife of the philosopher and teacher Peter Abelard. In later life, she was the founder of a new religious order for women.

Henry IV of Germany King of Germany and Holy Roman Emperor from 1056—when he ascended the throne at the age of six years old—until his death in 1106. Henry's reign was first weakened by conflict with the Saxon nobility and later marked by the Investiture Controversy with Pope Gregory VII.

Henry VIII (1491–1547) King of England from 1509 until his death, Henry rejected the authority of the Roman Church in 1534 when the pope refused to annul his marriage to his queen, Catherine of Aragon; he became the founder of the Church of England.

Henry of Navarre (1553–1610) Crowned King Henry IV of France, he renounced his Protestantism but granted limited toleration for Huguenots (French Protestants) by the Edict of Nantes in 1598.

Prince Henry the Navigator (1394–1460) A member of the Portuguese royal family, Henry encouraged the exploration and conquest of western Africa and the trade in gold and slaves.

hieroglyphs The writing system of ancient Egypt, based on a complicated series of pictorial symbols. It fell out of use when Egypt was absorbed into the Roman Empire and was only deciphered after the discovery of the Rosetta Stone in the early nineteenth century.

Hildegard of Bingen (1098–1179) A powerful abbess, theologian, scientist, musician, and visionary who claimed to receive regular revelations from God. Although highly influential in her own day, she was never officially canonized by the Church, in part because her strong personality no longer matched the changing ideal of female piety.

Hiroshima Japanese port devastated by an atomic bomb on August 6, 1945.

Adolf Hitler (1889–1945) The author of *Mein Kampf* and leader of the Nazis who became chancellor of Germany in 1933. Hitler and his Nazi regime started the Second World War and orchestrated the systematic murder of over 5 million Jews.

Hitler-Stalin Pact (1939) Treaty between Stalin and Hitler, which promised Stalin a share of Poland, Finland, the Baltic States, and Bessarabia in the event of a German invasion of Poland, which began shortly thereafter, on September 1, 1939.

HIV epidemic The first cases of HIV-AIDS appeared in the late 1970s. As HIV-AIDS became a global crisis, international organizations recognized the need for an early, swift, and comprehensive response to future outbreaks of disease.

Thomas Hobbes (1588–1679) English political philosopher whose *Leviathan* argued that any form of government capable of protecting its subjects' lives and property might act as an all-powerful sovereign. This government should be allowed to trample over both liberty and property for the sake of its own survival and that of his subjects. For in his natural state, Hobbes argued, man was like "a wolf" toward other men.

Holy Roman Empire The loosely allied collection of lands in central and western Europe ruled by the kings of Germany (and later Austria) from the twelfth century until 1806. Its origins are usually identified with the empire of Charlemagne, the Frankish king who was crowned emperor of Rome by the pope in 800.

homage A ceremony in which an individual becomes the "man" (French: *homme*) of a lord.

Homer (fl. eighth century B.C.E.) A Greek rhapsode ("weaver" of stories) credited with merging centuries of poetic tradition in the epics known as the *Iliad* and the *Odyssey*.

hoplite A Greek foot-soldier armed with a spear or short sword and protected by a large round shield (*hoplon*). In battle, hoplites stood shoulder to shoulder in a close formation called a phalanx.

Huguenots French Protestants who endured severe persecution in the sixteenth and seventeenth centuries.

humanism A program of study associated with the movement known as the Renaissance, humanism aimed to replace the scholastic emphasis on logic and philosophy with the study of ancient languages, literature, history, and ethics.

human rights The belief that all people have the right to legal equality, freedom of religion and speech, and the right to participate in government. Human rights laws prohibit torture, cruel punishment, and slavery.

David Hume (1711–1776) Scottish writer who applied Newton's method of scientific inquiry and skepticism to the study of morality, the mind, and government.

Hundred Years' War (1337–1453) A series of wars between England and France, fought mostly on French soil and prompted by the territorial and political claims of English monarchs.

Jan Hus (c. 1373–1415) A Czech reformer who adopted many of the teachings of the English theologian John Wycliffe, and who also demanded that the laity be allowed to receive both the consecrated bread and wine of the Eucharist. The Council of Constance burned him at the stake for heresy. In response, his supporters, the Hussites, revolted against the Church.

Saddam Hussein (1937–2006) The former dictator of Iraq who invaded Iran in 1980 and started the eight-year-long Iran-Iraq War; invaded Kuwait in 1990, which led to the Gulf War of 1991; and was overthrown when the United States invaded Iraq in 2003. Involved in Iraqi politics since the mid-1960s, Hussein became the official head of state in 1979.

Iconoclast Controversy (717–787) A serious and often violent theological debate that raged in Byzantium after Emperor Leo III ordered the destruction of religious art on the grounds that any image representing a divine or holy personage is prone to promote idol worship and blasphemy. Iconoclast means "breaker of icons." Those who supported the veneration of icons were called iconodules, "adherents of icons."

Il-khanate Mongol-founded dynasty in thirteenth-century Persia.

Indian National Congress Formed in 1885, this Indian political party worked to achieve Indian independence from British colonial control. The Congress was led by Ghandi in the 1920s and 1930s.

Indian Rebellion of 1857 The uprising began near Delhi, when the military disciplined a regiment of Indian soldiers employed by the British for refusing to use rifle cartridges greased with pork fat—unacceptable to either Hindus or Muslims. Rebels attacked law courts and burned tax rolls, protesting debt and corruption. The mutiny spread through large areas of northwest India before being violently suppressed by British troops.

Indo-Europeans A group of people speaking variations of the same language who moved into the Near East and Mediterranean region shortly after 2000 B.C.E.

indulgences Grants exempting Catholic Christians from the performance of penance, either in life or after death. The abusive trade in indulgences was a major catalyst of the Protestant Reformation.

Incas The highly centralized South American empire that was toppled by the Spanish conquistador Francisco Pizarro in 1533.

Innocent III (1160/61–1216) As pope, he wanted to unify all of Christendom under papal hegemony. He furthered this goal at the Fourth Lateran Council of 1215, which defined one of the Church's dogmas as the acknowledgment of papal supremacy. The council also took an unprecedented interest in the religious education and habits of every Christian.

Inquisition Tribunal of the Roman Church that aims to enforce religious orthodoxy and conformity.

International Monetary Fund (IMF) Established in 1945 to ensure international cooperation regarding currency exchange and monetary policy, the IMF is a specialized agency of the United Nations.

Investiture Conflict The name given to a series of debates over the limitations of spiritual and secular power in Europe during the eleventh and early twelfth century, it came to a head when Pope Gregory VII and Emperor Henry IV of Germany both claimed the right to appoint and invest bishops with the regalia of office. After years of diplomatic and military hostility, it was partially settled by the Concordat of Worms in 1122.

Irish potato famine Period of agricultural blight from 1845 to 1849 whose devastating results produced widespread starvation and led to mass immigration to America.

Iron Curtain Term coined by Winston Churchill in 1946 to refer to the borders of Eastern European nations that lay within the zone of Soviet control.

Italian invasion of Ethiopia (1896) Italy invaded Ethiopia, which was the last major independent African kingdom. Menelik II, the Ethiopian emperor, soundly defeated them.

Ivan the Great (1440–1505) Russian ruler who annexed neighboring territories and consolidated his empire's position as a European power.

Jacobins Radical French political group during the French Revolution that took power after 1792, executed the French king, and sought to remake French culture.

Jacquerie Violent 1358 peasant uprising in northern France, incited by disease, war, and taxes.

James I (1566–1625) Monarch who ruled Scotland as James VI, and who succeeded Elizabeth I as king of England in 1603. He oversaw the English vernacular translation of the Bible known by his name.

James II of England King of England, Ireland, and Scotland from 1685–88 whose commitment to absolutism and Catholic zealotry led to his exile to France in the Glorious Revolution of 1688.

Janissaries Corps of enslaved soldiers recruited as children from the Christian provinces of the Ottoman Empire and brought up to display intense personal loyalty to the Ottoman sultan, who used these forces to curb local autonomy and as his personal bodyguards.

Jerome (c. 340–420) One of the early "fathers" of the Church, he translated the Bible from Hebrew and Greek into a popular form of Latin—hence the name by which this translation is known: the Vulgate, or "vulgar" (popular), Bible.

Jesuits The religious order formally known as the Society of Jesus, founded in 1540 by Ignatius Loyola to combat the spread of Protestantism. The Jesuits would become active in politics, education, and missionary work.

Jesus (c. 4 B.C.E.–c. 30 C.E.) A Jewish preacher and teacher in the rural areas of Galilee and Judea who was arrested for seditious political activity, tried, and crucified by the Romans. After his execution, his followers claimed that he had been resurrected from the dead and taken up into heaven. They began to teach that Jesus had been the divine representative of God, the Messiah foretold by ancient Hebrew prophets, and that he had suffered for the sins of humanity and would return to judge all the world's inhabitants at the end of time.

Joan of Arc (c. 1412–1431) A peasant girl from the province of Lorraine who claimed to have been commanded by God to lead French forces against the English occupying army during the Hundred Years' War. Successful in her efforts, she was betrayed by the French king and handed over to the English, who condemned her to death for heresy. Her reputation underwent a process of rehabilitation, but she was not officially canonized as a saint until 1920.

Judaism The religion of the Hebrews as it developed in the centuries after the establishment of the Hebrew kingdoms under David and Solomon, especially during the period of Babylonian Captivity.

Justinian (527–565) Emperor of Rome who unsuccessfully attempted to reunite the eastern and western portions of the empire. Also known for his important codification of Roman law, in the *Corpus Juris Civilis*.

Justinian's Code of Roman Law Formally known as the *Corpus Juris Civilis* or "body of civil law," this compendium consisted of a systematic compilation of imperial statutes, the writings of Rome's great legal authorities, a textbook of legal principles, and the legislation of Justinian and his immediate successors. As the most authoritative collection of Roman law, it formed the basis of canon law (the legal system of the Roman Church) and became essential to the developing legal traditions of every European state as well as of many countries around the world.

Das Kapital (Capital) The 1867 book by Karl Marx that outlined the theory behind historical materialism and attacked the socioeconomic inequities of capitalism.

Johannes Kepler (1571–1630) Mathematician and astronomer who elaborated on and corrected Copernicus's theory and is chiefly remembered for his discovery of the three laws of planetary motion that bear his name.

Keynesian Revolution Postdepression economic ideas developed by the British economist John Maynard Keynes, wherein the state took a greater role in managing the economy, stimulating it by increasing the money supply and creating jobs.

KGB Soviet political police and spy agency, first formed as the Cheka not long after the Bolshevik coup in October 1917. It grew to more than 750,000 operatives with military rank by the 1980s.

Genghis Khan (c. 1167–1227) "Oceanic Ruler," the title adopted by the Mongol chieftain Temujin, founder of a dynasty that conquered much of southern Asia.

Khanate The major political unit of the vast Mongol Empire. There were four Khanates, including the Yuan Empire in China, forged by Chingiz Khan's grandson Kubilai in the thirteenth century.

Ruhollah Khomeini (1902–1989) Iranian Shi'ite religious leader who led the revolution in Iran after the abdication of the shah in 1979. His government allowed some limited economic and political populism combined with strict constructions of Islamic law, restrictions on women's public life, and the prohibition of ideas or activities linked to Western influence.

Nikita Khrushchev (1894–1971) Leader of the Soviet Union during the Cuban missile crisis, Khrushchev came to power after Stalin's death in 1953. His reforms and criticisms of the excesses of the Stalin regime led to his fall from power in 1964.

Kremlin Once synonymous with the Soviet government, it refers to Moscow's walled city center and the palace originally built by Ivan the Great.

Kristallnacht Organized attack by Nazis and their supporters on the Jews of Germany following the assassination of a German embassy official by a Jewish man in Paris. Throughout Germany, thousands of stores, schools, cemeteries and synagogues were attacked on November 9, 1938. Dozens of people were killed, and tens of thousands of Jews were arrested and held in camps, where many were tortured and killed in the ensuing months.

Labour party Founded in Britain in 1900, this party represented workers and was based on socialist principles.

Latin West After the founding of Constantinople, the western Latin-speaking half of the Roman Empire became poorer and more peripheral, but it also fostered the emergence of new barbarian kingdoms. At the same time, the Roman pope claimed to have inherited both the authority of Jesus and the essential elements of Roman imperial authority.

League of Nations International organization founded after the First World War to solve international disputes through arbitration; it was dissolved in 1946 and its assets were transferred to the United Nations.

Leonardo da Vinci (1452–1519) Florentine inventor, sculptor, architect, and painter whose breadth of interests typifies the ideal of "the Renaissance man."

Vladimir Lenin (1870–1924) Leader of the Bolshevik Revolution in Russia (1917) and the first leader of the Soviet Union.

Leviathan A book by Thomas Hobbes (1588–1679) that recommended a ruler have unrestricted power.

liberalism Political and social theory that judges the effectiveness of a government in terms of its ability to protect individual rights. Liberals support representative forms of government, free trade, and freedom of speech and religion. In the economic realm, liberals believe that individuals should be free to engage in commercial or business activities without interference from the state or their community.

lithograph Art form that involves putting writing or design on stone and producing printed impressions.

John Locke (1632–1704) English philosopher and political theorist known for his contributions to liberalism. Locke had great faith in human reason and believed that just societies were those that infringed the least on the natural rights and freedoms of individuals. This led him to assert that a government's legitimacy depended on the consent of the governed, a view that had a profound effect on the authors of the United States' Declaration of Independence.

Louis IX of France King of France from 1226 to his death on Crusade in 1270, Louis was famous for his piety and for his close attention to the administration of law and justice in his realm. He was officially canonized as Saint Louis in 1297.

Louis XIV (1638–1715) Called the "Sun King," he was known for his success at strengthening the institutions of the French absolutist state.

Louis XVI (1754–1793) Well-meaning but ineffectual king of France, finally deposed and executed during the French Revolution.

Ignatius Loyola (1491–1556) Founder of the Society of Jesus (commonly known as the Jesuits), whose members vowed to serve God through poverty, chastity, and missionary work. He abandoned his first career as a mercenary after reading an account of Christ's life written in his native Spanish.

Lucretia According to Roman legend, Lucretia was a virtuous Roman wife who was raped by the son of Rome's last king and who virtuously committed suicide in order to avoid bringing shame on her family.

Luftwaffe Literally "air weapon," this is the name of the German air force, which was founded during the First World War, disbanded in 1945, and reestablished when West Germany joined NATO in 1950.

Lusitania The British passenger liner that was sunk by a German U-boat (submarine) on May 7, 1915. Public outrage over the sinking contributed to the U.S. decision to enter the First World War.

Martin Luther (1483–1546) A German monk and professor of theology whose critique of the papacy launched the Protestant Reformation.

ma'at The Egyptian term for the serene order of the universe, with which the individual soul (*ka*) must remain in harmony. The power of the pharaoh was linked to *ma'at*, insofar as it ensured the prosperity of the kingdom. After the upheavals of the First Intermediate Period, the perception of the pharaoh's relationship with ma'at was revealed to be conditional, something that had to be earned.

Niccolò Machiavelli (1469–1527) As the author of *The Prince* and the *Discourses on Livy*, he looked to the Roman past for paradigms of greatness while at the same time hoping to win the patronage of contemporary rulers who would restore Italy's political independence.

Magna Carta The "Great Charter" of 1215, enacted during the reign of King John of England and designed to limit his powers. Regarded now as a landmark in the development of constitutional government. In its own time, its purpose was to restore the power of great lords.

Magyar nationalism Lajos Kossuth led this national movement in the Hungarian region of the Habsburg Empire, calling for national independence for Hungary in 1848. With the support of Russia, the Habsburg army crushed the movement and all other revolutionary activities in the empire. Kossuth fled into exile.

Moses Maimonides (c. 1137–1204) Jewish scholar, physician, and scriptural commentator whose *Mishneh Torah* is a fundamental exposition of Jewish law.

Thomas Malthus (1766–1834) British political economist who believed that populations inevitably grew faster than the available food supply. Societies that could not control their population growth would be checked only by famine, disease, poverty, and infant malnutrition. He argued that governments could not alleviate poverty. Instead, the poor had to exercise "moral restraint," postpone marriage, and have fewer children.

Nelson Mandela (b. 1918) The South African opponent of apartheid who led the African National Congress and was imprisoned from 1962 until 1990. After his release from prison, he worked with Prime Minister Frederik Willem De Klerk to establish majority rule. Mandela became the first black president of South Africa in 1994.

Manhattan Project The secret U.S. government research project to develop the first nuclear bomb. The vast project involved dozens of sites across the United States, including New Mexico, Tennessee, Illinois, California, Utah, and Washington. The first test of a nuclear bomb was near Alamogordo, New Mexico on July 16, 1945.

manors Common farmland worked collectively by the inhabitants of entire villages, sometimes on their own initiative, sometimes at the behest of a lord.

Mao Zedong (1893–1976) The leader of the Chinese Revolution who defeated the Nationalists in 1949 and established the Communist regime in China.

Marne A major battle of the First World War in September 1914, which halted the German invasion of France and led to protracted trench warfare on the Western Front.

Marshall Plan Economic aid package given to Europe by the United States after the Second World War to promote reconstruction and economic development and to secure the countries from a feared communist takeover.

Karl Marx (1818–1883) German philosopher and economist who believed that a revolution of the working classes would overthrow the capitalist order and create a classless society. Author of *Das Kapital* and *The Communist Manifesto*.

Marxists Followers of the socialist political economist Karl Marx who called for workers everywhere to unite and create an independent political force. Marxists believed that industrialization produced an inevitable struggle between laborers and the class of capitalist property owners, and that this struggle would culminate in a revolution that would abolish private property and establish a society committed to social equality.

Mary See **cult of the Virgin**.

Mary I (1516–1558) Catholic daughter of Henry VIII and his first wife, Catherine of Aragon, Mary Tudor was the first queen regnant of England. Her attempts to reinstitute Catholicism in England met with limited success, and after her early death she was labeled "Bloody Mary" by the Protestant supporters of her half sister and successor, Elizabeth I.

mass culture The spread of literacy and public education in the nineteenth century created a new audience for print entertainment and a new class of entrepreneurs in the media to cater to this audience. The invention of radio, film, and television in the twentieth century carried this development to another level, as millions of consumers were now accessible to the producers of news, information, and entertainment. The rise of this "mass culture" has been celebrated as an expression of popular tastes but also criticized as a vehicle for the manipulation of populations through clever and seductive propaganda.

Mayans Native American peoples whose culturally and politically sophisticated empire encompassed lands in present-day Mexico and Guatemala.

Giuseppe Mazzini (1805–1872) Founder of Young Italy and an ideological leader of the Italian nationalist movement.

Mecca Center of an important commercial network of the Arabian Peninsula and birthplace of the prophet Muhammad. It is now considered the holiest site in the Islamic world.

Medici A powerful dynasty of Florentine bankers and politicians whose ancestors were originally apothecaries ("medics").

Meiji Empire Empire created under the leadership of Mutsuhito, emperor of Japan from 1868 until 1912. During the Meiji period Japan became a world industrial and naval power.

Mensheviks Within the Russian Social Democratic Party, the Mensheviks advocated slow changes and a gradual move toward socialism, in contrast with the Bolsheviks, who wanted to push for a proletarian revolution. Mensheviks believed that a proletarian revolution in Russia was premature and that the country needed to complete its capitalist development first.

mercantilism A theory and policy for directing the economy of monarchical states between 1600 and 1800 based on the assumption that wealth and power depended on a favorable balance of trade (more exports and fewer imports) and the accumulation of precious metals. Mercantilists advocated forms of economic protectionism to promote domestic production.

Maria Sybilla Merian (1647–1717) A scientific illustrator and an important early entomologist. She conducted research on two continents and published the well-received *Metamorphosis of the Insects of Surinam*.

Merovingian A Frankish dynasty that claimed descent from a legendary ancestor called Merovic, the Merovingians were the only powerful family to establish a lasting kingdom in western Europe during the fifth and sixth centuries.

Mesopotamia The "land between the Tigris and the Euphrates rivers," Tigris and Euphrates where the civilization of Sumer, the first urban society, flourished.

Klemens von Metternich (1773–1859) Austrian foreign minister whose primary goals were to bolster the legitimacy of monarchies and, after the defeat of Napoleon, to prevent another large-scale war in Europe. At the Congress of Vienna, he opposed social and political change and wanted to check Russian and French expansion.

Michelangelo Buonarroti (1475–1564) A virtuoso Florentine sculptor, painter, and poet who spent much of his career in the service of the papacy. He is best known for the decoration of the Sistine Chapel and for his monumental sculptures.

Middle Kingdom of Egypt (2055–1650 B.C.E.) The period following the First Intermediate Period of dynastic warfare, which ended with the reassertion of pharonic rule under Mentuhotep II.

Miletus A Greek polis and Persian colony on the Ionian coast of Asia Minor. Influenced by the cultures of Mesopotamia, Egypt, and Lydia, it produced several of the ancient world's first scientists and sophists. Thereafter, a political conflict between the ruler of Miletus, Aristagoras, and the Persian Emperor, Darius, sparked the Persian Wars with Greece.

John Stuart Mill (1806–1873) English liberal philosopher whose faith in human reason led him to support a broad variety of civic and political freedoms for men and women, including the right to vote and the right to free speech.

Slobodan Milosevic (1941–2006) The Serbian nationalist politician who became president of Serbia and whose policies during the Balkan wars of the early 1990s led to the deaths of thousands of Croatians, Bosnian Muslims, Albanians, and Kosovars. After leaving office in 2000, he was arrested and tried for war crimes at the International Court in The Hague. The trial ended before a verdict with his death in 2006.

Minoan Crete A sea empire based at Knossos on the Greek island of Crete and named for the legendary King Minos. The Minoans dominated the Aegean for much of the second millennium B.C.E.

Modernism There were several different modernist movements in art and literature, but they shared three key characteristics. First, they had a sense that the world had radically changed and that this change should be embraced. Second, they believed that traditional aesthetic values and assumptions about creativity were ill-suited to the present. Third, they developed a new conception of what art could do that emphasized expression over representation and insisted on the value of novelty, experimentation, and creative freedom.

Mongols A nomadic people from the steppes of Central Asia who were united under the ruler Genghis Khan. His conquest of China was continued by his grandson Kubilai and his great-grandson son Ogedei, whose army also seized southern Russia and then moved through Hungary and through Poland toward eastern Germany. The Mongol armies withdrew from eastern Europe after the death of Ogedei, but his descendants continued to rule his vast empire for another half century.

Michel de Montaigne (1533–1592) French philosopher and social commentator, best known for his *Essays*.

Montesquieu (1689–1755) An Enlightenment philosophe whose most influential work was *The Spirit of Laws*. In this work, he analyzed the structures that shaped law and categorized governments into three types: republics, monarchies, and despotisms. His ideas about the separation of powers among the executive, the legislative, and the judicial branches of government influenced the authors of the U.S. Constitution.

Thomas More (1478–1535) Christian humanist, English statesman, and author of *Utopia*. In 1529, he was appointed lord chancellor of England but resigned because he opposed King Henry VIII's plans to establish a national church under royal control. He was eventually executed for refusing to take an oath acknowledging Henry to be the head of the Church of England and has since been canonized by the Catholic Church.

mos maiorum Literally translated as "the code of the elders" or "the custom of ancestors." This unwritten code governed the lives of Romans under the Republic and stressed the importance of showing reverence to ancestral tradition. It was sacrosanct and essential to Roman identity, and an important influence on Roman culture, law, and religion.

Wolfgang Amadeus Mozart (1756–1791) Austrian composer, famous at a young age as a concert musician and later celebrated as a prolific composer of instrumental music and operas that are seen as the apogee of the Classical style in music.

Muhammad (570–632 C.E.) The founder of Islam, regarded as God's last and greatest prophet by his followers.

Munich Conference (1938) Hitler met with the leaders of Britain, France, and Italy and negotiated an agreement that gave Germany a major slice of Czechoslovakia. British prime minister Chamberlain believed that the agreement would bring peace to Europe. Instead, Germany invaded and seized the rest of Czechoslovakia.

Muscovy The duchy centered on Moscow whose dukes saw themselves as heirs to the Roman Empire. In the early fourteenth century, Moscow was under the control of the Mongol Khanate. After the collapse of the Khanate, the Muscovite grand duke, Ivan III, conquered all the Russian principalities between Moscow and the border of Poland-Lithuania, and then Lithuania itself. By the time of his death, Ivan had established Muscovy as a dominant power.

Muslim learning and culture The Crusades brought the Latin West in contact with the Islamic world, which impacted European culture in myriad ways. Europeans adapted Arabic numerals and mathematical concepts as well as Arabic and Persian words. Through Arabic translations, Western scholars gained access to Greek learning, which had a profound influence on Christian theology. European scholars also learned from the Islamic world's accomplishments in medicine and science.

Benito Mussolini (1883–1945) The Italian founder of the Fascist party who came to power in Italy in 1922 and allied himself with Hitler and the Nazis during the Second World War.

Mycenaean Greece (1600–1200 B.C.E.) The term used to describe the civilization of Greece in the late Bronze Age, when territorial kingdoms like Mycenae formed around a king, a warrior caste, and a palace bureaucracy.

Nagasaki Second Japanese city on which the United States dropped an atomic bomb. The attack took place on August 9, 1945; the Japanese surrendered shortly thereafter, ending the Second World War.

Napoleon III (1808–1873) Nephew of Napoleon Bonaparte, Napoleon III was elected president of the French Second Republic in 1848 and made himself emperor of France in 1852. During his reign (1852–70), he rebuilt the French capital of Paris. Defeated in the France-Prussian War of 1870, he went into exile.

Napoleonic Code Legal code drafted by Napoleon in 1804 and based on Justinian's *Corpus Iuris Civilis*. It distilled different legal traditions to create one uniform law. The code confirmed the abolition of feudal privileges of all kinds and set the conditions for exercising property rights.

Napoleon's military campaigns In 1805, the Russians, Prussians, Austrians, Swedes, and British attempted to contain Napoleon, but he defeated them. Out of his victories, Napoleon created a new empire and affiliated states. In 1808, he invaded Spain, but fierce resistance prevented Napoleon from achieving a complete victory. In 1812, Napoleon invaded Russia, and his army was decimated as it retreated from Moscow during the winter. After the Russian campaign, the united European powers defeated Napoleon and forced him into exile. He escaped and reassumed command of his army, but the European powers defeated him for the final time at the Battle of Waterloo.

Gamal Abdel Nasser (1918–1970) Former president of Egypt and the most prominent spokesman for secular pan-Arabism. He became a target for Islamist critics, such as Sayyid Qutb and the Muslim Brotherhood, angered by the Western-influenced policies of his regime.

National Assembly of France Governing body of France that succeeded the Estates General in 1789 during the French Revolution. It was composed of, and defined by, the delegates of the Third Estate.

National Association for the Advancement of Colored People (NAACP) Founded in 1910, this U.S. civil rights organization was dedicated to ending inequality and segregation for black Americans.

National Convention The governing body of France from September 1792 to October 1795. It declared France a republic and then tried and executed the French king. The Convention also confiscated the property of the enemies of the revolution, instituted a policy of de-Christianization, changed marriage and inheritance laws, abolished slavery in its colonies, placed a cap on the price of necessities, and ended the compensation of nobles for their lost privileges.

nationalism Movement to unify a country under one government based on perceptions of the population's common history, customs, and social traditions.

nationalism in Yugoslavia In the 1990s, Slobodan Milosevic and his allies reignited Serbian nationalism in the former Yugoslavia, which led non-Serb republics in Croatia and Slovenia to seek independence. The country erupted into war, with the worst violence taking place in Bosnia, a multi-ethnic region with Serb, Croatian and Bosnian Muslim populations. European diplomats proved powerless to stop attempts by Croatian and Serbian military and paramilitary forces to claim territory through ethnic cleansing and violent intimidation. Atrocities were committed on all sides, but pro-Serb forces were responsible for the most deaths.

NATO The North Atlantic Treaty Organization, a 1949 military agreement among the United States, Canada, Great Britain, and eight Western European nations, which declared that an armed attack against any one of the members would be regarded as an attack against all. Created during the Cold War in the face of the Soviet Union's control of Eastern Europe, NATO continues to exist today and the membership of twenty-eight states includes former members of the Warsaw Pact as well as Albania and Turkey.

Nazi party Founded in the early 1920s, the National Socialist German Workers' Party (NSDAP) gained control over Germany under the leadership of Adolf Hitler in 1933 and continued in power until Germany was defeated in 1945.

Nazism The political movement in Germany led by Adolf Hitler, which advocated a violent anti-Semitic, anti-Marxist, pan-German ideology.

Neo-Assyrian Empire (883–859 B.C.E.–612–605 B.C.E.) Assurnasirpal II laid the foundations of the Neo-Assyrian Empire through military campaigns against neighboring peoples. Eventually, the empire stretched from the Mediterranean Sea to western Iran. A military dictatorship governed the empire through its army, which it used to frighten and oppress both its subjects and its enemies. The empire's ideology was based on waging holy war in the name of its principal god, Assur, and the exaction of tribute through terror.

Neoliberalism Neoliberals believe that free markets, profit incentives, and restraints on both budget deficits and social welfare programs are the best guarantee of individual liberties. Beginning in the 1980s, neoliberal theory was used to structure the policy of financial institutions like the International Monetary Fund and the World Bank, which turned away from interventionist policies in favor of market-driven models of economic development.

Neolithic Revolution The "New" Stone Age, which began around 11,000 B.C.E., saw new technological and social developments, including managed food production, the beginnings of permanent settlements, and the rapid intensification of trade.

Neoplatonism A school of thought based on the teachings of Plato and prevalent in the Roman Empire, which had a profound effect on the formation of Christian theology. Neoplatonists argued that nature is a book written by its creator to reveal the ways of God to humanity. Convinced that God's perfection must be reflected in nature, neoplatonists searched for the ideal and perfect structures that they believed must lie behind the "shadows" of the everyday world.

New Deal President Franklin Delano Roosevelt's package of government reforms that were enacted during the depression of the 1930s to provide jobs for the unemployed, social welfare programs for the poor, and security to the financial markets.

New Economic Policy In 1921, the Bolsheviks abandoned war communism in favor of the New Economic Policy (NEP). Under NEP, the state still controlled all major industry and financial concerns, while individuals could own private property, trade freely within limits, and farm their own land for their own benefit. Fixed taxes replaced grain requisition. The policy successfully helped Soviet agriculture recover from the civil war but was later abandoned in favor of collectivization.

Isaac Newton (1642–1727) One of the foremost scientists of all time, Newton was an English mathematician and physicist; he is noted for his development of calculus, work on the properties of light, and theory of gravitation.

Tsar Nicholas II (1868–1918) The last Russian tsar, who abdicated the throne in 1917. He and his family were executed by the Bolsheviks on July 17, 1918.

Friedrich Nietzsche (1844–1900) The German philosopher who denied the possibility of knowing absolute "truth" or "reality," since all knowledge comes filtered through linguistic, scientific, or artistic systems of representation. He also criticized Judeo-Christian morality for instilling a repressive conformity that drained civilization of its vitality.

nongovernmental organizations (NGOs) Private organizations like the Red Cross that play a large role in international affairs.

Novum Organum Work by English statesman and scientist Francis Bacon (1561–1626) that advanced a philosophy of study through observation.

October Days (1789) The high price of bread and the rumor that the king was unwilling to cooperate with the assembly caused the women who worked in Paris's large central market to march to Versailles along with their supporters to address the king. Not satisfied with their initial reception, they broke through the palace gates and called for the king to return to Paris from Versailles, which he did the following day.

Old Kingdom of Egypt (c. 2686–2160 B.C.E.) During this time, the pharaohs controlled a powerful and centralized bureaucratic state whose vast human and material resources are exemplified by the pyramids of Giza. This period came to an end as the pharaoh's authority collapsed, leading to a period of dynastic warfare and localized rule.

OPEC (Organization of the Petroleum Exporting Countries) Organization created in 1960 by oil-producing countries in the Middle East, South America, and Africa to regulate the production and pricing of crude oil.

Operation Barbarossa The codename for Hitler's invasion of the Soviet Union in 1941.

Opium Wars (1839–1842) War fought between the British and Qing China to protect British trade in opium; resulted in the ceding of Hong Kong to the British.

Oracle at Delphi The most important shrine in ancient Greece. The priestess of Apollo who attended the shrine was believed to have the power to predict the future.

Ottoman Empire (c.1300–1923) During the thirteenth century, the Ottoman dynasty established itself as leader of the Turks. From the fourteenth to sixteenth centuries, they conquered Anatolia, Armenia, Syria, and North Africa as well as parts of southeastern Europe, the Crimea, and areas along the Red Sea. Portions of the Ottoman Empire persisted up to the time of the First World War, but it was dismantled in the years following it.

Reza Pahlavi (1919–1980) The Western-friendly shah of Iran who was installed during a 1953 coup supported by Britain and the United States. After a lengthy economic downturn, public unrest, and personal illness, he retired from public life under popular pressure in 1979.

Pan-African Conference 1900 assembly in London that sought to draw attention to the sovereignty of African people and their mistreatment by colonial powers.

Panhellenism The "all Greek" culture that allowed ancient Greek colonies to maintain a connection to their homeland and to each other through their shared language and heritage. These colonies also exported their culture into new areas and created new Greek-speaking enclaves, which permanently changed the cultural geography of the Mediterranean world.

pan-Slavism Cultural movement that sought to unite native Slavic peoples within the Russian and Habsburg Empires under Russian leadership.

Partition of India (1947) At independence, British India was partitioned into the nations of India and Pakistan. The majority of the population in India was Hindu and the majority of the population in Pakistan was Muslim. The process of partition brought brutal religious and ethnic warfare. More than 1 million Hindus and Muslims died and 12 million became refugees.

Blaise Pascal (1623–1662) A Catholic philosopher who wanted to establish the truth of Christianity by appealing simultaneously to intellect and emotion. In his *Pensées*, he argued that faith alone can resolve the world's contradictions and that his own awe in the face of evil and uncertainty must be evidence of God's existence.

Paul of Tarsus Originally known as Saul, Paul was a Greek-speaking Jew and Roman citizen who underwent a miraculous conversion experience and became the most important proponent of Christianity in the 50s and 60s C.E.

Pax Romana (27 B.C.E.–180 C.E.) Literally translated as "the Roman Peace." During this time, the Roman world enjoyed an unprecedented period of peace and political stability.

Peace of Augsburg A settlement negotiated in 1555 among factions within the Holy Roman Empire, it formulated the principle *cuius regio, eius religio*, "he who rules, his religion": meaning that the inhabitants of any given territory should follow the religion of its ruler, whether Catholic or Protestant.

Peace of Paris The 1919 Paris Peace Conference established the terms to end the First World War. Great Britain, France, Italy, and the United States signed five treaties with each of the defeated nations: Germany, Austria, Hungary, Turkey, and Bulgaria. The settlement is notable for the territory that Germany had to give up, including large parts of Prussia to the new state of Poland, and Alsace and Lorraine to France; the disarming of

Germany; and the "war guilt" provision, which required Germany and its allies to pay massive reparations to the victors.

Peace of Westphalia (1648) An agreement reached at the end of the Thirty Years' War that altered the political map of Europe. France emerged as the predominant power on the Continent, while the Austrian Habsburgs had to surrender all the territories they had gained and could no longer use the office of the Holy Roman Emperor to dominate central Europe. Spain was marginalized and Germany became a volatile combination of Protestant and Catholic principalities.

Pearl Harbor The American naval base in Hawaii that was bombed by the Japanese on December 7, 1941, bringing the United States into the Second World War.

peasantry Term used in continental Europe to refer to rural populations that lived from agriculture. Some peasants were free and could own land. Serfs were peasants who were legally bound to the land and subject to the authority of the local lord.

Peloponnesian War The name given to the series of wars fought between Sparta (on the Greek Peloponnesus) and Athens from 431 B.C.E. to 404 B.C.E., and which ended in the defeat of Athens and the loss of her imperial power.

perestroika Introduced by Soviet leader Mikhail Gorbachev in June 1987, *perestroika* was the name given to economic and political reforms begun earlier in his tenure. It restructured the state bureaucracy, reduced the privileges of the political elite, and instituted a shift from the centrally planned economy to a mixed economy, combining planning with the operation of market forces.

Periclean Athens Following his election as *strategos* in 461 B.C.E., Pericles pushed through political reforms in Athens, which gave poorer citizens greater influence in politics. He promoted Athenians' sense of superiority through ambitious public works projects and lavish festivals to honor the gods, thus ensuring his continual reelection. But eventually, Athens' growing arrogance and aggression alienated it from the rest of the Greek world.

Pericles (c. 495–429) Athenian politician who occupied the office of strategos for thirty years and who presided over a series of civic reforms, building campaigns, and imperialist initiatives.

Persian Empire Consolidated by Cyrus the Great in 559, this empire eventually stretched from the Persian Gulf to the Mediterranean and also encompassed Egypt. Persian rulers were able to hold this empire together through a policy of tolerance and a mixture of local and centralized governance. This imperial model of government would be adopted by many future empires.

Persian Wars (490–479 B.C.E.) In 501 B.C.E., a political conflict between the Greek ruler of Miletus, Aristagoras, and the Persian Emperor, Darius, sparked the first of the Persian Wars when Darius sent an army to punish Athens for its intervention on the side of the Greeks. Despite being heavily outnumbered, Athenian hoplites defeated the Persian army at the plain of Marathon. In 480 B.C.E., Darius's son Xerxes invaded Greece but was defeated at sea and on land by combined Greek forces under the leadership of Athens and Sparta.

Peter the Great (1672–1725) Energetic tsar who transformed Russia into a leading European country by centralizing government, modernizing the army, creating a navy, and reforming education and the economy.

Francesco Petrarca (Petrarch) (1304–1374) Italian scholar who revived interest in classical writing styles and was famed for his vernacular love sonnets.

pharaoh A term meaning "household" which became the title borne by the rulers of ancient Egypt. The pharaoh was regarded as the divine representative of the gods and the embodiment of Egypt itself. The powerful and centralized bureaucratic state ruled by the pharaohs was more stable and longlived than any another civilization in world history, lasting (with few interruptions) for approximately 3,000 years.

Pharisees A group of Jewish teachers and preachers who emerged in the third century B.C.E. They insisted that all of Yahweh's (God's) commandments were binding on all Jews.

Philip II (382–336 B.C.E.) King of Macedonia and father of Alexander, he consolidated the southern Balkans and the Greek city-states under Macedonian domination.

Philip II of Spain King of Spain from 1556–98 and briefly King of England and Ireland during his marriage to Queen Mary I of England. As a staunch Catholic, Philip responded with military might to the desecration of Catholic churches in the Spanish Netherlands in the 1560s. When commercial conflict with England escalated, Philip sent the Spanish Armada to conquer England in 1588, but it was largely destroyed by stormy weather.

Philip II Augustus (1165–1223) The first French ruler to use the title "king of France" rather than "king of the French." After he captured Normandy and its adjacent territories from the English, he built an effective system of local administration, which recognized regional diversity while promoting centralized royal control. This administrative pattern would characterize French government until the French Revolution.

Philip IV of France King of France from 1285 until his death, Philip's conflict with Pope Boniface VIII led to the transfer of the papal court to Avignon from 1309 to 1378.

Philistines Descendants of the Sea Peoples who fled to the region that now bears their name, Palestine, after their defeat at the hands of the pharaoh Ramses III. They dominated their neighbors, the Hebrews, who used writing as an effective means of discrediting them (the Philistines themselves did not leave a written record to contest the Hebrews' views).

philosophe During the Enlightenment, this word referred to a person whose reflections were unhampered by the constraints of religion or dogma.

Phoenicians A Semitic people known for their trade in exotic purple dyes and other luxury goods, they originally settled in present-day Lebanon around 1200 B.C.E. and from there established commercial colonies throughout the Mediterranean, notably Carthage.

Plato (429–349 B.C.E.) A student of Socrates, Plato dedicated his life to transmitting his teacher's legacy through the writing of dialogues on philosophical subjects, in which Socrates himself plays the major role. The longest and most famous of these, known as the *Republic*, describes an idealized polis governed by a superior group of individuals chosen for their natural attributes of intelligence and character, who rule as "philosopher-kings."

Plotinus (204–270 C.E.) A Neoplatonist philosopher who taught that everything in existence has its ultimate source in the divine, and that the highest goal of life should be the mystic reunion of the soul with this divine source, something that can be achieved through contemplation and asceticism. This outlook blended with that of early Christianity and was instrumental in the spread of that religion within the Roman Empire.

poleis One of the major political innovations of the ancient Greeks was the *polis*, or city-state (plural *poleis*). These independent social and political entities began to emerge in the ninth century B.C.E., organized around an urban center and fostering markets, meeting places, and religious worship; frequently, poleis also controlled some surrounding territory.

Marco Polo (1254–1324) Venetian merchant who traveled through Asia for twenty years and published his observations in a widely read memoir.

population growth In the nineteenth century, Europe experienced a dramatic population growth. During this period, the spread of rural manufacturing allowed men and women to begin marrying younger and raising families earlier, which increased the size of the average family. As the population grew, the portion of young and fertile people also increased, which reinforced the population growth. By 1900, population growth was strongest in Britain and Germany, and slower in France.

portolan charts Also known as *portolani*, these special charts were invented by medieval mariners during the fourteenth century and were used to map locations of ports and sea routes, while also taking note of prevailing winds and other conditions at sea.

Potsdam (1945) At this conference, Truman, Churchill and Stalin met to discuss their options at the conclusion of the Second World War, including making territorial changes to Germany and its allies and the question of war reparations.

Prague spring A period of political liberalization in Czechoslovakia between January and August 1968 that was initiated by Alexander Dubček, the Czech leader. This period of expanding freedom and openness in this Eastern bloc nation ended on August 20, when the USSR and Warsaw Pact countries invaded with 200,000 troops and 5,000 tanks.

pre-Socratics A group of philosophers in the Greek city of Miletus, who raised questions about humans' relationship with the natural world and the gods and who formulated rational theories to explain the physical universe they observed. Their name reflects the fact that they flourished prior to the lifetime of Socrates.

price revolution An unprecedented inflation in prices in the latter half of the sixteenth century, resulting in part from the enormous influx of silver bullion from Spanish America.

principate Modern term for the centuries of autocratic rule by the successors of Augustus, who seized power in 27 B.C.E. and styled himself *princeps* or Rome's "first man." See **Roman Republic**.

printing press Introduced in Europe by Johannes Gutenberg of Mainz in 1453–55, this new technology quickly revolutionized communication and played a significant role in political, religious, and intellectual revolutions.

Protestantism The name given to the many dissenting varieties of Christianity that emerged during the Reformation in sixteenth-century western Europe. While Protestant beliefs and practices differed widely, all were united in their rejection of papal authority and the dogmas of the Roman Catholic Church.

provisional government After the collapse of the Russian monarchy, leaders in the Duma organized this government and hoped to establish a democratic system under constitutional rule. They also refused to concede military defeat, and it was impossible to institute domestic reforms and fight a war at the same time. As conditions worsened, the Bolsheviks gained support. In October 1917, they attacked the provisional government and seized control.

Claudius Ptolomeus, called Ptolemy (c. 85–165 C.E.) A Greek-speaking geographer and astronomer active in Roman Alexandria, he rejected the findings of previous Hellenistic scientists in favor of the erroneous theories of Aristotle, publishing highly influential treatises that promulgated these errors and suppressed (for example) the accurate findings of Aristarchus (who had discovered the Heliocentric universe) and Erathosthenes (who had calculated the circumference of the earth).

Ptolemaic system Ptolemy of Alexandria promoted Aristotle's understanding of cosmology. In this system, the heavens orbit the earth in an organized hierarchy of spheres, and the earth and the heavens are made of different matter and subject to different laws of motion. A prime mover produces the motion of the celestial bodies.

Ptolemy (c. 367–c. 284 B.C.E.) One of Alexander the Great's trusted generals (and possibly his half brother), he became pharaoh of Egypt and founded a new dynasty that lasted until that kingdom's absorption into the Roman Empire in 30 B.C.E.

public sphere Between the official realm of state activities and the private realm of the household and individual, lies the "public sphere." The public sphere has a political dimension—it is the space of debate, discussion, and expressions of popular opinion. It also has an economic dimension—it is where business is conducted, where commercial transactions take place, where people enter into contracts, search for work, or hire employees.

Punic Wars (264–146 B.C.E.) Three periods of warfare between Rome and Carthage, two maritime empires who struggled for dominance of the Mediterranean. Rome emerged as the victor, destroyed the city of Carthage and took control of Sicily, North Africa and Hispania (Spain).

pyramid Constructed during the third millennium B.C.E., these structures were monuments to the power and divinity of the pharaohs entombed inside them.

Qur'an (often Koran) Islam's holy scriptures, comprised of the prophecies revealed to Muhammad and redacted during and after his death.

Raphael (Raffaelo Sanzio) (1483–1520) Italian painter active in Rome, his works include *The School of Athens*.

realism Artistic and literary style which sought to portray common situations as they would appear in reality.

Realpolitik Political strategy based on advancing power for its own sake.

reason The human capacity to solve problems and discover truth in ways that can be verified intellectually. Philosophers distinguish the knowledge gained from reason from the teachings of instinct, imagination, and faith, which are verified according to different criteria.

Reformation Religious and political movement in sixteenth-century Europe that led to a break between dissenting forms of Christianity and the Roman Catholic Church; notable figures include Martin Luther and John Calvin.

Reich A term for the German state. The First Reich corresponded to the Holy Roman Empire (9th c.–1806), the Second Reich was from 1871 to 1919, and the Third Reich lasted from 1933 through May 1945.

Renaissance From the French word meaning "rebirth," this term came to be used in the nineteenth century to describe the artistic, intellectual, and cultural movement that emerged in Italy after 1300 and that sought to recover and emulate the heritage of the classical past.

Restoration period (1815–1848) European movement after the defeat of Napoleon to restore Europe to its pre–French Revolution status and to prevent the spread of revolutionary or liberal political movements.

Cardinal Richelieu (1585–1642) First minister to King Louis XIII, he is considered by many to have ruled France in all but name, centralizing political power and suppressing dissent.

Roman army Under the Republic, the Roman army was made up of citizen-soldiers who were required to serve in wartime. As Rome's empire grew, the need for more fighting men led to the extension of citizenship rights and, eventually, to the development of a vast, professional, standing army that numbered as many as 300,000 by the middle of the third century B.C.E. By that time, however, citizens were not themselves required to serve, and many legions were made up of paid conscripts and foreign mercenaries.

Roman citizenship The rights and responsibilities of Rome's citizens were gradually extended to the free (male) inhabitants of other Italian provinces and later to most provinces in the Roman world. In contrast to slaves and non-Romans, Romans had the right to be tried in an imperial court and could not be legally subjected to torture.

Roman Republic The Romans traced the founding of their republic to the overthrow of their last king and the establishment of a unique form of constitutional government, in which the power of the aristocracy (embodied by the Senate) was checked by the executive rule of two elected consuls and the collective will of the people. For hundreds of years, this balance of power provided the Republic with a measure of political stability and prevented any single individual or clique from gaining too much power.

Romanticism Beginning in Germany and England in the late eighteenth century and continuing up to the end of the nineteenth century, Romanticism was a movement in art, music, and literature that countered the rationalism of the Enlightenment by placing greater value on human emotions and the power of nature to stimulate creativity.

Jean-Jacques Rousseau (1712–1778) Philosopher and radical political theorist whose *Social Contract* attacked privilege and inequality. One of the primary principles of Rousseau's political philosophy is that politics and morality should not be separated.

Royal Society This British society's goal was to pursue collective research. Members would conduct experiments, record the results, and share them with their peers, who would study the methods, reproduce the experiment, and assess the results. The arrangement gave English scientists a sense of common purpose as well as a system to reach a consensus on facts.

Russian Revolution of 1905 After Russia's defeat in the Russo-Japanese War, Russians began clamoring for political reforms. Protests grew over the course of 1905, and the autocracy lost control of entire towns and regions as workers went on strike, soldiers mutinied, and peasants revolted. Forced to yield, Tsar Nicholas II issued the October Manifesto, which pledged individual liberties and provided for the election of a parliament (called the Duma). The most radical of the revolutionary groups were put down with force, and the pace of political change remained very slow in the aftermath of the revolution.

Russo-Japanese War (1904–1905) Japanese and Russian expansion collided in Mongolia and Manchuria. Russia was humiliated after the Japanese navy sunk its fleet, which helped provoke a revolt in Russia and led to an American-brokered peace treaty.

sacrament A sacred rite. In the Catholic tradition, the administration of the sacraments is considered necessary for salvation.

Saint Bartholomew's Day Massacre The mass murder of French Protestants (Huguenots) instigated by Queen Catherine de' Medici of France and carried out by Catholics. It began in Paris on 24 August 1572 and spread to other parts of France, continuing into October of that year. More than 70,000 people were killed.

salons Informal gatherings of intellectuals and aristocrats that allowed discourse about Enlightenment ideas.

Sappho (c. 620–c. 550 B.C.E.) One of the most celebrated Greek poets, she was revered as "the Tenth Muse" and emulated by many male poets. Ironically, though, only two of her poems survive intact, and the rest must be pieced together from fragments quoted by later poets.

Sargon the Great (r. 2334–2279 B.C.E.) The Akkadian ruler who consolidated power in Mesopotamia.

SARS epidemic (2003) The successful containment of severe acute respiratory syndrome (SARS) is an example of how international health organizations can effectively work together to recognize and respond to a disease outbreak. The disease itself, however, is a reminder of the dangers that exist in a globalized economy with a high degree of mobility in both populations and goods.

Schlieffen Plan Devised by German general Alfred von Schlieffen in 1905 to avoid the dilemma of a two-front war against France and Russia. The Schlieffen Plan required that Germany attack France first through Belgium and secure a quick victory before wheeling to the east to meet the slower armies of the Russians on the Eastern Front. The Schlieffen Plan was put into operation on August 2, 1914, at the outset of the First World War.

scientific revolution of antiquity The Hellenistic period was the most brilliant age in the history of science before the seventeenth century C.E. Aristarchus of Samos posited the existence of a heliocentric universe. Eratosthenes of Alexandria accurately calculated the circumference of the earth. Archimedes turned physics into its own branch of experimental science. Hellenistic anatomists became the first to practice human dissection, which improved their understanding of human physiology. Ironically, most of these discoveries were suppressed by pseudo-scientists who flourished under the Roman Empire during the second century C.E., notably Claudus Ptolomeus Ptolemy) and Aelius Galenus (Galen).

second industrial revolution The technological developments in the last third of the nineteenth century, which included new techniques for refining and producing steel; increased availability of electricity for industrial, commercial, and domestic use; advances in chemical manufacturing; and the creation of the internal combustion engine.

Second World War Worldwide war that began in September 1939 in Europe, and even earlier in Asia (the Japanese invasion of Manchuria began in 1931), pitting Britain, the United States, and the Soviet Union (the Allies) against Nazi Germany, Italy, and Japan (the Axis). The war ended in 1945 with Germany and Japan's defeat.

Seleucus (d. 280 B.C.E.) The Macedonian general who ruled the Persian heartland of Alexander the Great's empire.

Semitic The Semitic language family has the longest recorded history of any linguistic group and is the root for most languages of the Middle and Near East. Ancient Semitic languages include those of the ancient Babylonians and Assyrians, Phoenician, the classical form of Hebrew, early dialects of Aramaic, and the classical Arabic of the Qu'ran.

Sepoy Mutiny of 1857 See **Indian Rebellion of 1857**.

serfdom Peasant labor. Unlike slaves, serfs are "attached" to the land they work, and are not supposed to be sold apart from that land.

William Shakespeare (1564–1616) An English playwright who flourished during the reigns of Elizabeth I and James I, Shakespeare received a basic education in his hometown of Stratford-upon-Avon and worked in London as an actor before achieving success as a dramatist and poet.

Shi'ites An often-persecuted minority within Islam, Shi'ites believe that only descendants of Muhammad's successor Ali and his wife Fatimah (Muhammad's daughter) can have any authority over the Muslim community. Today, Shi'ites constitute the ruling party in Iran and are numerous in Iraq but otherwise comprise only 10 percent of Muslims worldwide.

Abbé Sieyès (1748–1836) In 1789, he wrote the pamphlet "What is the Third Estate?" in which he posed fundamental questions about the rights of the Third Estate and helped provoke its secession from the Estates-General. He was a leader at the Tennis Court Oath, but he later helped Napoleon seize power.

Sinn Féin The Irish revolutionary organization that formed in 1900 to fight for Irish independence.

Sino-Japanese War (1894–1895) Conflict over the control of Korea in which China was forced to cede the province of Taiwan to Japan.

slave revolt in Saint-Domingue (1791–1804) In September of 1791, the largest slave rebellion in history broke out in Saint-Domingue, an important French colony in the Caribbean. In 1794, the revolutionary government in France abolished slavery in the colonies, though this act was essentially only recognizing the liberty that the slaves had seized by their own actions. Napoleon reestablished slavery in the French Caribbean in 1802, but failed in his attempt to reconquer Saint-Domingue. Armies commanded by former slaves succeeded in winning independence for a new nation, Haiti, in 1804, making the revolt in Saint-Domingue the first successful slave revolt in history.

slavery The practice of subjugating people to a life of bondage, and of selling or trading these unfree people. For most of human history, slavery had no racial or ethnic basis, and was widely practiced by all cultures and civilizations. Anyone could become a slave, for example, by being captured in war or by being sold for the payment of a debt. It was only in the fifteenth century, with the growth of the African slave trade, that slavery came to be associated with particular races and peoples.

Adam Smith (1723–1790) Scottish economist and liberal philosopher who proposed that competition between self-interested individuals led naturally to a healthy economy. He became famous for his influential book, *The Wealth of Nations* (1776).

Social Darwinism Belief that Charles Darwin's theory of natural selection (evolution) was applicable to human societies and justified the right of the ruling classes or countries to dominate the weak.

social democracy The belief that democracy and social welfare go hand in hand and that diminishing the sharp inequalities of class society is crucial to fortifying democratic culture.

socialism Political ideology that calls for a classless society with collective ownership of all property.

Society of Jesus See **Jesuits**.

Socrates (469–399 B.C.E.) The Athenian philosopher and teacher who promoted the careful examination of all inherited opinions and assumptions on the grounds that "the unexamined life is not worth living." A veteran of the Peloponnesian War, he was tried and condemned by his fellow citizens for engaging in allegedly seditious activities and was executed in 399 B.C.E. His most influential pupils were the philosopher Plato and the historian and social commentator Xenophon.

Solon (d. 559 B.C.E.) Elected archon in 594 B.C.E., this Athenian aristocrat enacted a series of political and economic reforms that formed the basis of Athenian democracy.

Somme (1916) During this battle of the First World War, Allied forces attempted to take entrenched German positions from July to mid-November of 1916. Neither side was able to make any real gains despite massive casualties: 500,000 Germans, 400,000 British, and 200,000 French.

Soviet bloc International alliance that included the East European countries of the Warsaw Pact as well as the Soviet Union; it also came to include Cuba.

soviets Local councils elected by workers and soldiers in Russia. Socialists started organizing these councils in 1905, and the Petrograd soviet in the capital emerged as one of the centers of power after the Russian monarchy collapsed in 1917 in the midst of World War I. The soviets became increasingly powerful and pressed for social reform, the redistribution of land, and called for Russian withdrawal from the war effort.

Spanish-American War (1898) War between the United States and Spain in Cuba, Puerto Rico, and the Philippines. It ended with a treaty in which the United States took over the Philippines, Guam, and Puerto Rico; Cuba won partial independence.

Spanish Armada Supposedly invincible fleet of warships sent against England by Philip II of Spain in 1588 but vanquished by the English fleet and bad weather in the English Channel.

Sparta Around 650 B.C.E., after the suppression of a slave revolt, Spartan rulers militarized their society in order to prevent future rebellions and to protect Sparta's superior position in Greece, orienting their society toward the maintenance of their army. Sparta briefly joined forces with Athens and other poleis in the second war with Persia in 480–479 B.C.E., but these two rivals ultimately fell out again in 431 B.C.E. when Sparta and her Peloponnesian allies went to war against Athens and her allies. This bloody conflict lasted until Athens was defeated in 404 B.C.E., after Sparta received military aid from the Persians.

Spartiate A full citizen of Sparta, hence a professional soldier of the hoplite phalanx.

spinning jenny Invention of James Hargreaves (c. 1720–1774) that revolutionized the British textile industry by allowing a worker to spin much more thread than was possible on a hand spinner.

SS (Schutzstaffel) Formed in 1925 to serve as Hitler's personal security force and to guard Nazi party (NSDAP) meetings, the SS grew into a large militarized organization that became notorious for their participation in carrying out Nazi policies.

Joseph Stalin (1879–1953) The Bolshevik leader who succeeded Lenin as the leader of the Soviet Union and ruled until his death in 1953.

Stalingrad (1942–1943) The turning point on the Eastern Front during the Second World War came when the German army tried to take the city of Stalingrad in an effort to break the back of Soviet industry. The German and Soviet armies fought a bitter battle, in which more than a half million German, Italian, and Romanian soldiers were killed and the Soviets suffered over a million casualties. The German army surrendered after over five months of fighting. After Stalingrad, the Soviet army launched a series of attacks that pushed the Germans back.

Stoicism An ancient philosophy derived from the teachings of Zeno of Athens (fl. c. 300) and widely influential within the Roman Empire; it also impacted the development of Christianity. Stoics believe in the essential orderliness of the cosmos, and that everything that occurs happens for the best. Since everything is determined in accordance with rational purpose, no individual is master of his or her fate, and the only agency that human beings have consists in their responses to good fortune or adversity.

Sumerians The ancient inhabitants of southern Mesopotamia (modern Iraq and Kuwait) whose sophisticated civilization emerged around 4000 B.C.E.

Sunnis Proponents of Islam's customary religious practices (*sunna*) as they developed under the first two caliphs to succeed Muhammad, his father-in-law Abu-Bakr and his disciple Umar.

Sunni orthodoxy is dominant within Islam but is opposed by the Shi'ites (from the Arabic word *shi'a,* "faction").

syndicalists A nineteenth-century political movement that embraced a strategy of strikes and sabotage by workers. Their hope was that a general strike of all workers would bring down the capitalist state and replace it with workers' syndicates or trade associations. Their refusal to participate in politics limited their ability to command a wide influence.

tabula rasa Term used by John Locke (1632–1704) to describe man's mind before he acquired ideas as a result of experience; Latin for "clean slate."

Tennis Court Oath (1789) Oath taken by representatives of the Third Estate in June 1789, in which they pledged to form a National Assembly and write a constitution limiting the powers of the king.

Reign of Terror (1793–1794) Campaign at the height of the French Revolution in which violence, including systematic executions of opponents of the revolution, was used to purge France of its "enemies" and to extend the revolution beyond its borders; radicals executed as many as 40,000 persons who were judged enemies of the state.

Tetrarchy The result of Diocletian's political reforms of the late third century C.E., which divided the Roman Empire into four quadrants.

Theban Hegemony The term describing the period when the polis of Thebes dominated the Greek mainland, which reached its height after 371 B.C.E., under leadership of the Theban general Epaminondas. It was in Thebes that the future King Philip II of Macedon spent his youth, and it was the defeat of Thebes and Athens at the hands of Philip and Alexander—at the Battle of Chaeronea in 338—that Macedonian hegemony was forcefully asserted.

theory of evolution Darwin's theory that linked biology to history. Darwin believed that competition between different organisms and struggle with the environment were fundamental and unavoidable facts of life. In this struggle, those individuals who were better adapted to their environment survived, whereas the weak perished. This produced a "natural selection," or favoring of certain adaptive traits over time, leading to a gradual evolution of different species.

Third Estate The population of France under the Old Regime was divided into three estates, corporate bodies that determined an individual's rights or obligations under royal law. The nobility constituted the First Estate, the clergy the Second, and the commoners (the vast bulk of the population) made up the Third Estate.

Third Reich The German state from 1933 to 1945 under Adolf Hitler and the Nazi party.

Third World nations—mostly in Asia, Latin America, and Africa—that are not highly industrialized.

Thirty Years' War (1618–1648) Beginning as a conflict between Protestants and Catholics in Germany, this series of skirmishes escalated into a general European war fought on German soil by armies from Sweden, France, and the Holy Roman Empire.

Timur the Lame (1336–1405) Also known as Tamerlane, he was the last ruler of the Mongol Khans' Asian empire.

Marshal Tito (1892–1980) The Yugoslavian communist and resistance leader who became the leader of Yugoslavia and fought to keep his government independent of the Soviet Union. In response, the Soviet Union expelled Yugoslavia from the communist countries' economic and military pacts.

towns Centers for markets and administration. Towns existed in a symbiotic relationship with the countryside. They provided markets for surplus food from outlying farms as well as producing manufactured goods. In the Middle Ages, towns tended to grow up around a castle or monastery which afforded protection.

transatlantic triangle The trading of African slaves by European colonists to address labor shortages in the Americas and the Caribbean. Slaves were treated like cargo, loaded onto ships and sold in exchange for molasses, tobacco, rum, and other precious commodities.

Treaty of Brest-Litovsk (1918) Separate peace between imperial Germany and the new Bolshevik regime in Russia. The treaty acknowledged the German victory on the Eastern Front and withdrew Russia from the war.

Treaty of Utrecht (1713) Resolution to the War of Spanish Succession that reestablished a balance of power in Europe, to the benefit of Britain and in ways that disadvantaged Spain, Holland, and France.

Treaty of Versailles Signed on June 28, 1919, this peace settlement ended the First World War and required Germany to surrender a large part of its most valuable territories and to pay huge reparations to the Allies.

trench warfare Weapons such as barbed wire and the machine gun gave tremendous advantage to defensive positions in World War I, leading to prolonged battles between entrenched armies in fixed positions. The trenches eventually consisted of 25,000 miles of holes and ditches that stretched across the Western Front in northern France, from the Atlantic coast to the Swiss border during the First World War. On the eastern front, the large expanse of territories made trench warfare less significant.

triangular trade The eighteenth-century commercial Atlantic shipping pattern that took rum from New England to Africa, traded it for slaves taken to the West Indies, and brought sugar back to New England to be processed into rum.

Triple Entente Alliance developed before the First World War that eventually included Britain, France, and Russia.

Truman Doctrine (1947) Declaration promising U.S. economic and military intervention to counter any attempt by the Soviet Union to expand its influence. Often cited as a key moment in the origins of the Cold War.

tsar Russian word for "emperor," derived from the Latin *caesar* and similar to the German *kaiser,* it was the title claimed by the rulers of medieval Muscovy and of the later Russian Empire.

Ubaid culture An early civilization that flourished in Mesopotamia between 5500 and 4000 B.C.E., it was characterized by large village settlements and temple complexes: a precursor to the more urban civilization of the Sumerians.

Umayyad Caliphate (661–930) The Umayyad family resisted the authority of the first two caliphs who succeeded Muhammad but eventually placed a member of their own family in that position of power. The Umayyad Caliphate ruled the Islamic world from 661 to 750, modeling their administration on that of the Roman Empire. But after a rebellion led by the rival Abbasid family, the power of the Umayyad Caliphate was confined to their territories in al-Andalus (Spain).

Universal Declaration of Human Rights (1948) United Nations declaration that laid out the rights to which all human beings were entitled.

University of Paris The reputation of Peter Abelard and his students attracted many intellectuals to Paris in the twelfth century, some of whom began offering instruction to aspiring scholars. By 1200, this loose association of teachers had formed themselves into a *universitas*, or corporation. They began collaborating in the higher academic study of the liberal arts with a special emphasis on theology.

Pope Urban II (1042?–1099) Instigator of the First Crusade (1096–1099), who promised that anyone who fought or died in the service of the Church would receive absolution from sin.

urban populations During the nineteenth century, urban populations in Europe increased sixfold. For the most part, urban areas had medieval infrastructures, which new populations and industries overwhelmed. As a result, many European cities became overcrowded and unhealthy.

Utopia Title of a semi-satirical social critique by the English statesman Sir Thomas More (1478–1535); the word derives from the Greek "best place" or "no place."

Lorenzo Valla (1407–1457) One of the first practitioners of scientific philology (the historical study of language), Valla's analysis of the so-called Donation of Constantine showed that the document could not possibly have been written in the fourth century C.E., but must have been forged centuries later.

vassal A person who pledges to be loyal and subservient to a lord in exchange for land, income, or protection.

velvet revolutions The peaceful political revolutions throughout Eastern Europe in 1989.

Verdun (1916) This battle between German and French forces lasted for ten months during the First World War. The Germans saw the battle as a chance to break French morale through a war of attrition, and the French believed the battle to be a symbol of France's strength. In the end, over 400,000 lives were lost and the German offensive failed.

Versailles Conference (1919) Peace conference between the victors of the First World War; resulted in the Treaty of Versailles, which forced Germany to pay reparations and to give up its colonies to the victors.

Queen Victoria (1819–1901) Influential monarch who reigned from 1837 until her death; she presided over the expansion of the British Empire as well as the evolution of English politics and social and economic reforms.

Viet Cong Vietnamese communist group formed in 1954; committed to overthrowing the government of South Vietnam and reunifying North and South Vietnam.

Vikings (800–1000) The collapse of the Abbasid Caliphate disrupted Scandinavian commercial networks and turned traders into raiders (the word *viking* describes the activity of raiding). These raids often escalated into invasions that contributed to the collapse of the Carolingian Empire, resulted in the devastation of settled territories, and ended with the establishment of Viking colonies. By the tenth century, Vikings controlled areas of eastern England, Scotland, the islands of Ireland, Iceland, Greenland, and parts of northern France. They had also established the beginnings of the kingdom that became Russia and made exploratory voyages to North America, founding a settlement at Newfoundland (Canada).

A Vindication of the Rights of Woman Noted work of Mary Wollstonecraft (1759–1797), English republican who applied Enlightenment political ideas to issues of gender.

Virgil (70–19 B.C.E.) An influential Roman poet who wrote under the patronage of the emperor Augustus. His *Aeneid* mimicked the ancient Greek epics of Homer and told the mythical tale of Rome's founding by the Trojan refugee Aeneas.

Visigoths The tribes of "west" Goths who sacked Rome in 410 C.E. and later established a kingdom in the Roman province of Hispania (Spain).

Voltaire Pseudonym of French philosopher and satirist François Marie Arouet (1694–1778), who championed the cause of human dignity against state and Church oppression. Noted deist and author of *Candide*.

Lech Wałęsa (1943–) Leader of the Polish labor movement Solidarity, which organized a series of strikes across Poland in 1980. They protested working conditions, shortages, and high prices. Above all, they demanded an independent labor union. Solidarity's leaders were imprisoned and the union banned, but they launched a new series of strikes in 1988, which led to the legalization of Solidarity and open elections.

war communism The Russian civil war forced the Bolsheviks to take a more radical economic stance. They requisitioned grain from the peasantry and outlawed private trade in consumer goods as "speculation." They also militarized production facilities and abolished money.

Wars of the Roses Fifteenth-century civil conflict between the English dynastic houses of Lancaster and York, each of which was symbolized by the heraldic device of a rose (red and white, respectively). It was ultimately resolved by the accession of the Lancastrian king Henry VII, who married Elizabeth of York.

Warsaw Pact (1955–1991) Military alliance between the USSR and other communist states that was established as a response to the creation of the NATO alliance.

The Wealth of Nations 1776 treatise by Adam Smith, whose laissez-faire ideas predicted the economic boom of the Industrial Revolution.

Weimar Republic The government of Germany between 1919 and the rise of Hitler and the Nazi party.

Western Front Military front that stretched from the English Channel through Belgium and France to the Alps during the First World War.

Whites Refers to the "counterrevolutionaries" of the Bolshevik Revolution (1918–1921) who fought the Bolsheviks (the "Reds"); included former supporters of the tsar, Social Democrats, and large independent peasant armies.

William the Conqueror (1027–1087) Duke of Normandy who laid claim to the throne of England in 1066, defeating the

Anglo-Saxon King Harold at the Battle of Hastings. He and his Norman followers imposed imperial rule in England through a brutal campaign of military conquest, surveillance, and the suppression of the indigenous Anglo-Saxon language.

William of Ockham (d. 1349) An English philosopher and Franciscan friar, he denied that human reason could prove fundamental theological truths, such as the existence of God: he argued that there is no necessary connection between the observable laws of nature and the unknowable essence of divinity. His theories, derived from the work of earlier scholastics, form the basis of the scientific method.

Woodrow Wilson (1856–1924) U.S. president who requested and received a declaration of war from Congress so that America could enter the First World War. After the war, his prominent role in the Paris Peace Conference signaled the rise of the United States as a world power. He also proposed the Fourteen Points, which influenced the peace negotiations.

Maria Winkelmann (1670–1720) German astronomer who worked with her husband in his observatory. Despite discovering a comet and preparing calendars for the Berlin Academy of Sciences, the academy would not let her take her husband's place within the body after he died.

witch craze The rash of persecutions that took place in both Catholic and Protestant countries of early modern Europe and their colonies, facilitated by secular governments and religious authorities.

women's associations Because European women were excluded from the workings of parliamentary and mass politics, some women formed organizations to press for political and civil rights. Some groups focused on establishing educational opportunities for women while others campaigned energetically for the vote.

William Wordsworth (1770–1850) Romantic writer whose central themes were nature, simplicity, and feeling. He considered nature to be man's most trustworthy teacher and source of sublime power that nourished the human soul.

World Bank International agency established in 1944 to provide economic assistance to war-torn nations and countries in need of economic development.

John Wycliffe (c. 1330–1384) A professor of theology at the University of Oxford, Wycliffe urged the English king to confiscate ecclesiastical wealth and to replace corrupt priests and bishops with men who would live according to the apostolic standards of poverty and piety. He advocated direct access to the scriptures and promoted an English translation of the Bible. His teachings played an important role in the Peasants' Revolt of

1381 and inspired the still more radical initiatives of a group known as Lollards.

Xerxes (519?–465 B.C.E.) Xerxes succeeded his father, Darius, as Great King of Persia. Seeking to avenge his father's shame and eradicate any future threats to Persian hegemony, he launched his own invasion of Greece in 480 B.C.E. An allied Greek army defeated his forces in 479 B.C.E.

Yalta Accords Meeting among President Franklin D. Roosevelt, Prime Minister Winston Churchill, and Premier Joseph Stalin that occurred in the Crimea in 1945 shortly before the end of the Second World War to plan for the postwar order.

Young Turks The 1908 Turkish reformist movement that aimed to modernize the Ottoman Empire, restore parliamentary rule, and depose Sultan Abdul Hamid II.

ziggurats Temples constructed under the Dynasty of Ur in what is now Iraq, beginning around 2100 B.C.E.

Zionism A political movement dating to the end of the nineteenth century holding that the Jewish people constitute a nation and are entitled to a national homeland. Zionists rejected a policy of Jewish assimilation and advocated the reestablishment of a Jewish homeland in Palestine.

Zollverein In 1834, Prussia started a customs union, which established free trade among the German states and a uniform tariff against the rest of the world. By the 1840s, the union included almost all of the German states except German Austria. It is considered an important precedent for the political unification of Germany, which was completed in 1870 under Prussian leadership.

Zoroastrianism One of the three major universal faiths of the ancient world, alongside Judaism and Christianity, it was derived from the teachings of the Persian Zoroaster around 600 B.C.E. Zoroaster redefined religion as an ethical practice common to all, rather than as a set of rituals and superstitions that cause divisions among people. Zoroastrianism teaches that there is one supreme god in the universe, Ahura-Mazda (Wise Lord) but that his goodness will be constantly assailed by the forces of evil until the arrival of a final "judgment day." Proponents of this faith should therefore help good to triumph over evil by leading a good life, and by performing acts of compassion and charity. Zoroastrianism exercised a profound influence over many early Christians, including Augustine.

Ulrich Zwingli (1484–1531) A former priest from the Swiss city of Zurich, Zwingli joined Luther and Calvin in attacking the authority of the Roman Catholic Church.

Leon B. Alberti: "On the Family" from *The Family in Renaissance Florence*, trans./ed. by Renée Neu Watkins (University of South Carolina Press, 1969), pp. 208–213. Reprinted by permission of the translator.

Aristophanes: 300 words from *Lysistrata and Other Plays* by Aristophanes, translated with an introduction by Alan H. Sommerstein (Penguin Classics, 1973). Copyright © Alan H. Sommerstein, 1973. Reproduced by permission of Penguin Books Ltd.

Arrian: 300 words from *The Campaigns of Alexander* by Arrian, translated by Aubrey de Sélincourt, revised with an introduction and notes by J.R. Hamilton (Penguin Classics 1958, Revised edition 1971). Copyright © the Estate of Aubrey de Sélincourt, 1958. Introduction and Notes copyright © J.R. Hamilton, 1971. Reproduced by permission of Penguin Books Ltd.

Nels Bailkey (ed.): From Bailkey, *Readings in Ancient History*, 5th Edition. © 1996 Wadsworth, a part of Cengage Learning, Inc. Reproduced by permission. www.cengage.com/permissions.

Armand Bellee (ed.): *Cahiers de plaintes & doleances des paroisses de la province du Maine pour les Etats-generaux de 1789*, 4 vols. (Le Mans: Monnoyer, 1881-92), 2: 578–82. Translated by the American Social History Project, "Liberty, Equality, Fraternity: Exploring the French Revolution" by Jack R. Censer and Lynn Hunt. Reprinted by permission.

Bernard of Angers: "Miracles of Saint Foy" from *Readings in Medieval History*, 2nd Edition, edited by Patrick J. Geary (Toronto, Ont: University of Toronto Press, 2003). Copyright © 2003. Reprinted by permission of the publisher.

Henry Bettenson (ed.): "Obedience as a Jesuit Hallmark" from *Documents of the Christian Church*, 2nd Edition. Copyright © 1967, Oxford University Press. Reprinted by permission of Oxford University Press.

Gabriel Biel: "Execrabilis." Reprinted by permission of the publisher from *Defensorium Obedientiae Apostolicae Et Alia Documenta* by Gabriel Biel, edited and translated by Heiko A. Oberman, Daniel E. Zerfoss and William J. Courtenay, pp. 224–227, Cambridge, Mass.: The Belknap Press of Harvard University Press, Copyright © 1968 by the President and Fellows of Harvard College.

Jose Bove: *The World Is Not for Sale: Farmers Against Junk Food*, pp. 3–13, © Verso, 2001. Reprinted by permission of the publisher.

Walter Bower: "A Declaration of Scottish Independence," from *Scotichronicon*, Volume 7, by Walter Bower. Edited by B. Scott and D. E. R. Watt. Copyright © 1996 Aberdeen University Press. Reprinted with permission.

Boyer, Baker & Kirshner (eds): "Declaration of the Rights of Man and of the Citizen", "Napoleon's Letter to Prince Eugene" and "Circular Letter to Sovereigns" from *University of Chicago Readings in Western Civilization, Vol. 7*, pp. 238–239; 419–420; 426–427, Copyright © 1987 by The University of Chicago. Reprinted by permission of The University of Chicago Press.

Anna Comnena: 340 words from *The Alexiad of Anna Comnena*, translated by E.R.A. Sewter (Penguin Classics, 1969). Copyright © E.R.A. Sewter, 1969. Reproduced by permission of Penguin Books Ltd.

James Cracraft: "Alexander II's Decree Emancipating the Serfs, 1861," *Major Problems in the History of Imperial Russia*. Copyright © 1994 by D.C. Heath and Company.

David Brion Davis: From *Encyclopédie*, Vol. 16, Neuchâtel, 1765, p. 532 as cited in David Brion Davis, *The Problem of Slavery in Western Culture*. (Ithaca, N.Y.: Cornell University Press, 1966), p. 416. Copyright © 1966 by David Brion Davis. Reprinted by permission.

Simone de Beauvoir: From *The Second Sex* by Simone de Beauvoir, translated by Constance Borde & Sheila Malovany-Chevalier, published by Jonathan Cape, translation copyright © 2009 by Constance Borde and Sheila Malovany-Chevalier, Introduction copyright © 2010 by Judith Thurman. Reprinted by permission of Alfred A. Knopf, a division of Random House, Inc. and The Random House Group Ltd.

Geoffrey de Charny: From *The Book of Chivalry of Geoffrey de Charny: Text, Context, and Translation*, translated by Richard W. Kaeuper and Elspeth Kennedy, pp. 99. Copyright © 1996 University of Pennsylvania Press. Reprinted with permission.

Marie de France: "Equitan" in The Lais of Marie de France, translated by Gllyn S. Burgess and Kieth Burgess. Pp. 56–57. Copyright © 1985. Reproduced by permission of Penguin Books Ltd.

Bartolome de las Casas: 500 words from *A Short Account of the Destruction of the Indies* by Bartolome de las Casas, edited and translated by Nigel Griffin, introduction by Anthony Pagden (Penguin Classics, 1992). Translation and Notes copyright © Nigel Griffin, 1992. Introduction copyright © Anthony Pagden 1992. Reproduced by permission of Penguin Books Ltd.

Michel de Montaigne: From *Montaigne: Selections from the Essays*, translated and edited by Donald M. Frame (Harlan Davidson, Inc., 1973), pp. 34–38. Reprinted by permission of Harlan Davidson, Inc.

Alexis de Tocqueville: From *Recollections: The French Revolution of 1848*; trans. George Lawrence, ed. J.P. Mayer, pp. 436–437. Copyright © 1987 by Transaction Publishers. Reprinted by permission of the publisher.

Rene Descartes: From *A Discourse on the Method of Correctly Conducting One's Reason*, trans. Ian Maclean. Copyright © Ian Maclean 2006. Reprinted by permission of Oxford University Press.

Armand J. du Plessis: "Cardinal Richelieu on the Common People of France," pp. 31–32 from Hill, Henry Bertram, *The Political Testament of Cardinal Richelieu*. © 1961 by the Board of Regents of the University of Wisconsin System. Reprinted by permission of The University of Wisconsin Press.

Ecumenical Councils: "Epitome of the Definition of the Iconoclastic Conciliabulum" from *A Select Library of Nicene and Post-Nicene Fathers of the Christian Church, Vol. XIV*, eds. Schaff & Wace (Grand Rapids, MI: Wm. B. Eerdmans Publishing Company, 1955), pp. 543–544.

Frantz Fanon: Excerpt from *The Wretched of the Earth* by Frantz Fanon, copyright © 1963 by *Présence Africaine*. Used by permission of Grove/Atlantic, Inc.

Robert Filmer: "Observations upon Aristotle's Politiques" (1652), in *Divine Right and Democracy: An Anthology of Political Writing in Stuart England*, edited by David Wootton. Pp 110–18. Copyright © 1986. Reproduced by permission of Penguin Books Ltd.

Gregory L. Freeze (ed.): From *From Supplication to Revolution: A Documentary Social History of Imperial Russia*. Copyright © 1988, Oxford University Press, Inc. Reprinted by permission of Oxford University Press.

Betty Friedan: From *The Feminine Mystique* by Betty Friedan. Copyright © 1983, 1974, 1973, 1963 by Betty Friedan. Used by permission of Victor Gollancz, an imprint of The Orion Publishing Group, London and W.W. Norton & Company, Inc.

Galileo Galilei: From *Discoveries and Opinions of Galileo* by Galileo Galilei, translated by Stillman Drake, copyright © 1957 by Stillman Drake. Used by permission of Doubleday, a division of Random House, Inc.

Mohandas K. Gandhi: From *Hind Swaraj* or *Indian Home Rule* by M.K. Gandhi, p. 56, Ahmedabad: Navajivan Trust, 1946. Reprinted by permission of the publisher.

Pierre Gassendi: From *The Selected Works of Pierre Gassendi*, Edited by Craig B. Brush. (New York: Johnson Reprint Corporation, 1972) pp. 334–336. Reprinted with permission.

Joseph Goebbels: "Why are we enemies of the Jews?" from Snyder, Louis, *Documents of German History*. Copyright © 1958 by Rutgers, the State University. Reprinted by permission of Rutgers University Press.

Homer: *Iliad*, translated by Stanley Lombardo, selections from pp. 115–118. Copyright © 1997 by Hackett Publishing Company, Inc. Reprinted by permission of Hackett Publishing Company, Inc. All rights reserved.

Rosemary Horrox (ed.): From *The Black Death*, by Horrox (Trans., Ed.), 1994, Manchester University Press, Manchester, UK. Reprinted with permission.

Juvenal: 224 words from *The Sixteen Satires* by Juvenal, translated by Peter Green (Penguin Classics 1967, Revised edition 1974). Copyright © Peter Green 1967, 1974. Reproduced by permission of Penguin Books Ltd.

Nikita Khrushchev: "Report to the Communist Party Congress (1961)" from *Current Soviet Policies IV*, eds. Charlotte Saikowski and Leo Gruliow, from the translations of the Current Digest of the Soviet Press. Joint Committee on Slavic Studies, 1962, pp. 42–45. Reprinted by permission of the Current Digest of the Soviet Press.

Maureen Gallery Kovacs (trans.): Excerpts from *The Epic of Gilgamesh*, with an Introduction and Notes by Kovacs, Maureen Gallery, translator. Copyright © 1985, 1989 by the Board of Trustees of the Leland Stanford Junior University. All rights reserved. Used with the permission of Stanford University Press, www.sup.org.

Heda Margolius Kovály: *Under a Cruel Star: A Life in Prague 1941–1968*. Translated from the Czech by Franci Epstein and Helen Epstein with the author. (Cambridge, Mass.: Plunkett Lake Press, 1986), pp. 45–46.

Fritz Lang: "The Future of the Feature Film in Germany" from *The Weimar Republic Sourcebook*, edited by Anton Kaes, Martin Jay, and Edward Dimendberg (Berkeley: University of California Press, 1959), pp. 622–623. © 1994 by the Regents of the University of California. Reprinted by permission of the University of California Press.

Carolyne Larrington: "The Condemnation of Joan of Arc by the University of Paris" from *Women and Writing in Medieval Europe*, Carolyne Larrington, Copyright © 1995 Routledge. Reproduced by permission of Taylor & Francis Books UK.

Art Resource, NY; **p. 504:** Photo © Philip Mould Ltd, London / The Bridgeman Art Library; **p. 507:** The Art Archive/Musee du Chateau de Versailles/Dagli Orti; **p. 509:** Interfoto / Alamy; **p. 510:** Bildarchiv Preussischer Kulturbesitz / Art Resource, NY; **p. 511:** Lebrecht Authors; **p. 513:** Courtesy Dr. Alexander Boguslawski, Professor of Russian Studies, Rollins College.

Chapter 16: p. 518: Cellarius, Andreas/The Bridgeman Art Library; **p. 521:** Jeffrey Coolidge/Getty Images; **p. 522 (left):** Private Collection/The Bridgeman Art Library; **p. 522 (right):** © Peter Ginter/Science Faction/Corbis; **p. 523:** Erich Lessing/Art Resource, NY; **p. 525:** Stapleton Collection/Corbis; **p. 526 (left):** The Granger Collection, NY; **p. 526 (right):** Wikimedia Commons; **p. 528:** Erich Lessing/Art Resource, NY; **p. 530:** John P. McCaskey cropped by Smartse/Wikimedia Commons; **p. 531:** Rene Descartes, L'homme de René Descartes, et la formation du foetus . . . Paris: Compagnie des Libraires, 1729/"Courtesy of Historical Collections & Services, Claude Moore Health Sciences Library, University of Virginia;" **p. 535:** Wikimedia Commons; **p. 538:** Plate 20 from Metamorphosis Insectorum (1705) by Maria Sybilla Merian (1647–1717). ©The Natural History Museum, London / The Image Works; **p. 539 (right):** Bettmann/Corbis; **p. 539 (left):** Newton, Sir Isaac (1642-1727) / © Courtesy of the Warden and Scholars of New College, Oxford / The Bridgeman Art Library; **p. 540:** Bodleian Library; **p. 543:** Giraudon/Art Resource, NY.

Chapter 17: p. 546: Bridgeman Art Library; **p. 548:** Elizabeth Nesbitt Room Chapbook Collection/Information Sciences Library/University of Pittsburgh; **p. 551:** © Ali Meyer/CORBIS; **p. 552:** The New York Public Library / Art Resource, NY; **p. 553:** Bibliotheque Nationale, Paris, France/ Lauros / Giraudon/ The Bridgeman Art Library; **p. 554:** Erich Lessing / Art Resource, NY; **p. 555:** Giraudon / Bridgeman; **p. 556:** Historisches Museum der Stadt Wien; **p. 557:** Moritz Daniel Oppenheim, "Lavater and Lessing Visit Moses Mendelssohn." In the permanent collections, Judah L. Magnes Museum. Photo: Ben Ailes; **p. 561:** Stapletib Collection/Corbis **p. 562 (left):** Sir Joshua Reynolds/Omai of the Friendly Isles/ nla.pic-an5600097/ National Library of Australia; **p. 562 (right):** William Hodges/ King of Otaheite//National Library of Australia; **p. 563:** Francesco Bartolozzi/A view of the inside of a house in the island of Ulietea, with the representation of a dance to the music of the country/nla. pic-an9184905/National Library of Australia; **p. 565 (top):** Bibliotheque Nationale, Paris, France / Bridgeman Art Library, Flammarion; **p. 565 (bottom):** © Tate Gallery, London/Art Resource, NY; **p. 570:** Bridgeman Art Library; **p. 571:** Bettmann/Corbis; **p. 573 (left):** The Granger Collection, New York; **p. 573 (right):** Bluberries/iStock Photo; **p. 575 (left):** Scala / Art Resource, NY; **p. 575: (right):** akg-images; **p. 577:** The Granger Collection, New York.

Chapter 18: p. 580: Erich Lessing / Art Resource, NY; **p. 584 (left):** AKG-Images; **p. 584 (right):** The Art Archive / Musée Carnavalet Paris / Marc Charmet; **p. 585:** Giraudon / The Bridgeman Art Library; **p. 587:** Chateau de Versailles, France / The Bridgeman Art Library; **p. 589:** Musee de la Ville de Paris, Musee Carnavalet, Paris, France / Giraudon / The Bridgeman Art Library; **p. 590:** Musee de la Revolution Francaise, Vizille, France / The Bridgeman

Art Library; **p. 596:** Bibliotheque Nationale, Paris, France / The Bridgeman Art Library; **p. 597:** Erich Lessing / Art Resource, NY; **p. 598:** Bettmann/Corbis; **p. 599:** Scala/White Images / Art Resource, NY; **p. 602 (left):** Risma Archivo / Alamy; **p. 602 (right):** The Art Archive; **p. 603 (left):** Musee de la Ville de Paris, Musee Carnavalet, Paris, France/ Lauros / Giraudon/ The Bridgeman Art Library; **p. 603 (right):** Courtesy of the Warden and Scholars of New College, Oxford / The Bridgeman Art Library; **p. 607 (left):** The Gallery Collection/Corbis; **p. 607 (right):** Wikimedia Commons; **p. 608:** Erich Lessing/Art Resource, NY; **p. 609:** © The Trustees of the British Museum / Art Resource, NY; **p. 612 (left):** The Granger Collection, New York; **p. 612 (right):** © Thorsten Strasas/Demotix/Corbis; **p. 613:** © Gianni Dagli Orti/CORBIS.

Chapter 19: p. 616: National Gallery, London / Art Resource, NY; **p. 619:** Peak District National Park; **p. 621:** Stefano Bianchetti/Corbis; **p. 622:** SSPL via Getty Images; **p. 623 (left):** The National Archives of the UK; **p. 623 (right):** The Granger Collection, New York; **p. 624 (top):** Snark / Art Resource, NY; **p. 624 (bottom):** Hulton-Deutsch Collection/Corbis; **p. 625:** Hulton-Deutsch Collection/Corbis; **p. 628:** Wikimedia Commons; **p. 631:** Hulton Deutsch Collection/Corbis; **p. 632:** HIP-Archive / Topham/ The Image Works; **p. 633:** HIP-Archive / Topham/ The Image Works; **p. 634 (left):** © Heritage Images/Corbis; **p. 634 (right):** © ACE STOCK LIMITED / Alamy; **p. 636 (left):** Fotomas / Topham / The Image Works; **p. 363 (right):** Mary Evans / The Image Works; **p. 640:** Geoffrey Clements /Corbis; **p. 641:** Constantin Guys/Wikipedia; **p. 642:** Giraudon / Art Resource, NY; **p. 643:** North Wind / Nancy Carter\North Wind Picture Archives; **p. 647:** The Granger Collection, NY; **p. 649:** The Granger Collection, NY.

Chapter 20: p. 652: Erich Lessing / Art Resource, NY; **p. 657:** Private Collection / Bridgeman Art Library, Archives Charmet; **p. 659:** Photo RMN, Paris; **p. 661:** Erich Lessing / Art Resource, NY; **p. 662:** Reproduced by the Gracious Permission of Her Majesty the Queen; **p. 665:** © The Trustees of the British Museum; **p. 661:** Michael Nicholson/Corbis; **p. 671 (left):** akg-images; **p. 671 (right):** Time & Life Pictures/Getty Images; **p. 672 (top):** The Stapleton Collection / The Bridgeman Art Library; **p. 672 (bottom):** Bettmann/Corbis; **p. 678:** Bettmann/Corbis; **p. 679 (left):** Portrait of Mary Shelley (1797-1851) at the Age of Nineteen, c.1816 (litho) by English School (19th century), Russell-Cotes Art Gallery and Museum, Bournemouth, UK / Bridgeman Art Library; **p. 679 (right):** Illustration from 'Frankenstein' by Mary Shelley (1797-1851) (engraving) (b/w photo) by English School (19th century), Private Collection / Bridgeman Art Library; **p. 681:** Archivo Iconografico S.A./Corbis; **p. 682:** Wikimedia Commons; **p. 683 (top):** Wikimedia Commons; **p. 683 (bottom):** Wikimedia Commons.

Chapter 21: p. 686: Erich Lessing/Art Resource, NY; **p. 692:** Gianni Dagli Orti / The Art Archive at Art Resource, NY; **p. 693 (top):** Erich Lessing / Art Resource, NY; **p. 693 (bottom):** Bildarchiv Preussischer Kulturbesitz / Art Resource, NY; **p. 695 (left):** ullstein bild/ The Granger Collection, New York; **p. 695 (right):** Image Source; **p. 697:** Bildarchiv Preussischer Kulturbesitz / Art Resource, NY; **p. 698 (left):** Bildarchiv Preussischer Kulturbesitz / Art Resource,

NY; **p. 698 (right)**: Corbis; **p. 700**: Imagno/Getty Images; **p. 704 (top)**: Rischgitz/Getty Images; **p. 704 (bottom)**: Scala/Art Resource, NY; **p. 706**: Charles E. Rotkin / Corbis; **p. 707**: Hulton-Deutsch Collection / Corbis; **p. 708**: Scala/Art Resource, NY; **p. 710**: Ann Ronan Picture Library / HIP / The Image Works; **p. 712**: Deutsches Historisches Museum; **p. 713 (left)**: Bildarchiv Preussischer Kulturbesitz / Art Resource, NY; **p. 713 (right)**: Bildarchiv Preussischer Kulturbesitz / Art Resource, NY; **p. 716**: Bettmann / Corbis; **p. 721**: Louie Psihoyos/Corbis; **p. 723 (top)**: Corbis; **p. 723 (bottom)**: Foto Marburg / Art Resource, NY; **p. 724**: Bettmann/Corbis.

Chapter 22: p. 726: The Granger Collection, New York; **p. 728**: Bibliotheque des Arts Decoratifs, Paris, France / Archives Charmet / The Bridgeman Art Library; **p. 732 (left)**: Ken and Jenny Jacobson Orientalist Photography Collection/Research Library, The Getty Research Institute, Los Angeles (2008.R.3); **p. 732 (right)**: Hulton Archive/Getty Images; **p. 733 (left)**: Bettmann/Corbis; **p. 733 (right)**: Punchcartoons.com; **p. 737 (left)**: The Granger Collection, New York/The Granger Collection; **p. 737 (right)**: © Janine Wiedel Photolibrary/Alamy; **p. 738**: AKG-images; **p. 741 (top)**: Oriental and India Office Collections, The British Library/Art Resource, NY; **p. 741 (bottom)**: Bettmann/Corbis; **p. 743**: Wikimedia Commons; **p. 744**: Hulton-Deutsch/Corbis; **p. 746 (left)**: Wikimedia Commons; **p. 746 (right)**: Hulton Archive/Getty Images; **p. 747 (left)**: North Wind Picture Archives; **p. 747 (right)**: Image Courtesy of The Advertising Archives; **p. 750**: Matthew Fontaine Maury, *New Complete Geography* (New York: University Publishing Company, 1906); **p. 754 (top)**: 1999 National Gallery of Art, Washington D.C.; **p. 754 (left)**: 1999 National Gallery of Art, Washington D.C.; **p. 754 (center)**: 1999 National Gallery of Art, Washington D.C.; **p. 754 (right)**: 1999 National Gallery of Art, Washington D.C.; **p. 755**: Bettmann/Corbis; **p. 757**: Bridgeman Art Library; **p. 758**: The Ohio State University Billy Ireland Cartoon Library & Museum.

Chapter 23: p. 760: AKG-images; **p. 763**: AKG-images; **p. 766**: Bildarchiv Preussischer Kulturbesitz / Art Resource, NY; **p. 769**: Hulton-Deutsch Collection / Corbis; **p. 770**: Austrian Archives/Corbis; **p. 771**: Leemage/Getty; **p. 772 (top)**: The Hulton Deutsch Collection/Corbis; **p. 772 (bottom)**: The Hulton Deutsch Collection/Corbis; **p. 773 (top)**: Library of Congress; **p. 773 (bottom)**: Bettmann/Corbis; **p. 774**: The Hulton Deutsch Collection/Corbis; **p. 779 (left)**: The Granger Collection, New York; **p. 779 (center)**: Charles Leandre (1862-1930) Private Collection/ The Bridgeman Art Library Nationality; **p. 779 (right)**: Rue des Archives / The Granger Collection , New York; **p. 780**: Bettmann/Corbis; **p. 783 (left)**: Universal History Archive/UIG; **p. 783 (right)**: © Charles Platiau/Reuters/Corbis; **p. 784**: Hulton-Deutsch Collection/CORBIS; **p. 786**: Staatliche Museen zu Berlin-Preußisher Kulturbesitz; **p. 789**: From *An Autobiography: Herbert Spencer, 1904*; **p. 792**: Bettmann/Corbis; **p. 793**: © Bettmann/Corbis; **p. 794**: *Black Lines*, December 1913. Oil on canvas, 51 x 51 5/8 inches. Solomon R. Guggenheim Museum, Solomon R. Guggenheim Founding Collection, Gift, Solomon R. Guggenheim. 37.241. Vasily Kandinsky © 2007 Artists Rights Society (ARS), New York/ADAGP, Paris; **p. 795 (left)**: Erich Lessing / Art Resource, NY; **p. 795 (right)**: Scala / Art Resource, NY.

Chapter 24: p. 798: The Art Archive / Imperial War Museum; **p. 803**: Staatliche Museen zu Berlin-Preußisher Kulturbesitz; **p. 807**: Bettmann/Corbis; **p. 808 (left)**: Swim Ink 2, LLC/Corbis; **p. 808 (right)**: Swim Ink 2, LLC/Corbis; **p. 809 (left)**: Hoover Institution, Stanford University; **p. 809 (right)**: Wikimedia Commons; **p. 810 (left)**: Bundesarchiv; **p. 810 (right)**: Bundesarchiv; **p. 811 (left)**: Hulton-Deutsch Collection/Corbis; **p. 811 (right)**: © Bettmann/CORBIS; **p. 812**: Trustees of the Imperial War Museum, London; **p. 813**: Hulton-Deutsch Collection / Corbis; **p. 814 (top)**: Wikimedia Commons; **p. 814 (left)**: Bundesarchiv; **p. 814 (right)**: Bundesarchiv; **p. 817**: Bettmann/Corbis; **p. 819 (left)**: Corbis; **p. 819 (right)**: Bundesarchiv; **p. 822**: Bildarchiv Preussischer Kulturbesitz; **p. 823**: Private Collection / Ken Walsh / The Bridgeman Art Library; **p. 824**: Bettmann/Corbis; **p. 826**: Hulton-Deutsch Collection/Corbis; **p. 827**: Bettmann/Corbis; **p. 828**: Bettmann/Corbis; **p. 830 (left)**: Bettmann/Corbis; **p. 830 (right)**: © Wally McNamee/Corbis; **p. 831**: National Archives.

Chapter 25: p. 836: Erich Lessing / Art Resource, NY, © VAGA; **p. 838**: 2013 Artists Rights Society (ARS), New York/VG Bild-Kunst, Bonn; **p. 839**: Picture History; **p. 842**: © 2013 Estate of Gustav Klutsis/Artists Rights Society (ARS), New York; **p. 844**: Courtesy of Schickler-Lafaille Collection; **p. 845**: Hoover Institution, Stanford University; **p. 848**: Hoover Institution, Stanford University; **p. 851**: Brown Brothers; **p. 852**: © Underwood & Underwood/Corbis; **p. 853**: Hulton-Deutsch Collection/Corbis; **p. 855 (left)**: © Daily Mail/Rex/Alamy; **p. 855 (right)**: Giorgio Cosulich/Getty Images; **p. 856**: AKG Images; **p. 860**: Hulton-Deutsch Collection/Corbis; **p. 862**: Arthur Rothstein/Corbis; **p. 863**: © 2013 Man Ray Trust/Artists Rights Society (ARS), NY/ADAGP, Paris/Succession Marcel Duchamp, CNAC/MNAM/Dist. Réunion des Musées Nationaux/Art Resource, NY; **p. 864**: The Museum of Modern Art, New York. Photograph courtesy the Museum of Modern Art, New York/Art Resource, NY. © 2013 Artists Rights Society (ARS), New York/VG Bild-Kunst, Bonn; **p. 866 (left)**: Topham / The Image Works; **p. 866 (right)**: The Kobal Collection; **p. 867**: Photo by William Vanderson/Fox Photos/Getty Images; **p. 868 (top)**: Musee National d'Art Moderne, Centre Georges Pompidou, Paris, France. Photo CNAC/MNAM/Dist. RMN/Art Resource, NY; **p. 868 (bottom)**: Granger Collection.

Chapter 26: p. 872: Giraudon/Art Resource, NY. © 2013 Estate of Pablo Picasso/Artists Rights Society (ARS), New York; **p. 876 (left)**: © Bettmann/CORBIS; **p. 876 (right)**: The Southworth Collecion, The Mandeville Special Collections Library of UC San Diego; **p. 877**: Giraudon/Art Resource, NY. © 2013 Estate of Pablo Picasso/Artists Rights Society (ARS), New York; **p. 879**: © Hulton-Deutsch Collection/CORBIS; **p. 881**: The Granger Collection, NYC; **p. 882**: Bettmann/Corbis; **p. 883**: Hulton-Deutsch Collection/Corbis; **p. 885**: Bettmann/Corbis; **p. 888**: Hoover Institution, Stanford University; **p. 890**: AP Photo; **p. 894 (top)**: akg-images / ullstein bild; **p. 894 (bottom)**: Yevgeny Khaldei; **p. 898**: Yad Vashem Archives; **p. 899**: Yad Vashem Archives; **p. 901 (left)**: © Photoshot; **p. 901 (right)**: © Egon Steiner/dpa/Corbis; **p. 902**: Public Record Office Image Library, National Archives, UK; **p. 904 (top)**: Corbis; **p. 904 (bottom)**: National Archives; **p. 905 (top)**: Library of Congress; **p. 905 (bottom)**: Library of Congress.

Index

Page numbers in *italics* refer to illustrations, maps, and tables.

United States, 577
  and Americanization of mass culture,
    867–68
  Arab-Israeli conflict and, 931, 995
  atomic bomb developed by, 865, 903, 906–7,
    908
  Balkans conflict and (1990s), 978
  Chinese Revolution and, 927
  civil rights movement in, 957–60, 962
  Civil War in, 688, 717–21, 721
  in cold war, 909, 912, 914, 916–17, 942–45,
    943, 947, 964
  cotton industry in, 631
  film industry of, 866
  in First World War, 807, 810, 810, 821, 826,
    828, 828, 834
  after First World War, 838, 839, 860–63
  global economics and, 924
  Great Depression in, 861–63, 862, 875
  health care reform in, 1010
  immigration to, 633
  imperialism of, 729, 739, 745, 758–59
  industrialization of, 720
  in Industrial Revolution, 621, 631
  Iranian hostage crisis and, 1001
  in Iraq War of 2003, 1005
  in Korean War, 927–28, 964
  as major power, 723
  Manifest Destiny doctrine of, 717
  nation-building in, 716–17
  in NATO, 917
  New Deal in, 862–63
  nineteenth century expansion of, 717, 720
  in Persian Gulf War, 1001
  racism in, 957–60, 1010
  radio industry in, 865
  Roman Empire compared with, 174–77
  in Second World War, 883–87, 888, 902,
    908
  September 11, 2001 terrorist attacks in,
    1004–5, 1005, 1008
  "sexual revolution" in, 955–57
  slavery in, 613, 664, 688, 716–17
  in Spanish-American War (1898), 758–59
  steel industry in, 762, 766
  Suez crisis and (1956), 934
  in twenty-first century, 1009–10
  Versailles Treaty and, 875
  Vietnam War and, 934–36, 960–61, 964
  in war with Mexico, 688, 717
  women's movement in, 956–57, 956
  women's suffrage in, 818
Universal Declaration of Human Rights, 1008
universalism, 67, 70, 133
universities:
  degrees granted by, 311, 321
  Lutheran Reformation and, 430
  medieval, 311, 312, 313–14, 321
  1960s student movements and, 961–65
  see also specific universities
Universum Film AG (UFA), 866–67
Ur, 10, 16, 16, 17, 18
ʾUrabi Pasha, 728
Urban II, Pope (r. 1088–1099), 271–74,
  294
Urban VI, Pope (r. 1378–1389), 380
Urban VIII, Pope (r. 1623–1644), 529

urban growth, in early modern England, 637
urbanization:
  in eighteenth-century Europe, 550
  in High Middle Ages, 255–59, 256
  in Industrial Revolution, 637–39, 637
  see also cities
Ure, Andrew, 626
Ur-Nammu, king of Ur, 18
Urraca, queen of Léon-Castile (c. 1080–1126),
  316
Ursuline order, 448
Uruk, 9, 9
Uruk Period (4300–2900 B.C.E.), 9–10
Ustasha (Croatian fascists), 890, 892
Uthman, caliph, 225
utilitarianism, 669, 706
Utnapishtim, 40
Utopia (More), 404
utopianism, 404, 671, 795
Utrecht, Treaty of (1713), 506–7, 507, 508, 515,
  573, 655

Vaculík, Ludvík, 966
Valentinian II, Roman emperor, 200
Valerian, Roman emperor (253–260), 191
Valla, Lorenzo (1407–1457), 370, 404
Valley of the Kings, 45
Valois dynasty, 348, 348
Vandals, 200–201, 202, 213
van der Meulen, Adam Franz, 495
van der Straet, Jan (1523–1605), 416
van der Weyden, Roger (c. 1400–1464), 363,
  365, 365
Van Dyck, Anthony, 476
Van Gogh, Vincent (1853–1890), 795
vassals, 261
Vatican City, 298
Vatican Council, Second, 448
Velázquez, Diego (1599–1660), 484–85, 485
"velvet revolutions" of 1989, 969, 974, 976
Venetia, 699, 700, 704, 708, 711
Venetian School, 397–99
Venezuela, 656
Venice, 256, 257, 270, 275, 316, 329, 331, 378,
  406, 412, 492
  colonizing by, 331
  Fourth Crusades and, 296–97
  government of, 501
  Renaissance painting in, 397–99
  siege of, 704
Ventris, Michael, 50
Venus (deity), 152, 153
Venus (planet), 535
Verdi, Giuseppe (1813–1901), 641
Verdun, battle of (1916), 811–12
Versailles, palace at, 493, 494, 495, 515, 588,
  589
Versailles, Treaty of (1919), 829–30, 853, 857,
  871, 879
  German protest against, 853, 878
  mandates created by, 831, 874, 875
  provisions of, 831
  reparations required in, 831, 853, 875
  Second World War and, 874–75
  war-guilt provision of, 831, 875
Vespucci, Amerigo (1454–1512), 415,
  521

Vichy France, 883, 885, 888, 934
  Holocaust and, 898–99
Victor Emmanuel II, king of Italy (1820–1878),
  707, 708, 710
Victor Emmanuel III, king of Italy (1869–
  1947), 851
Victoria, queen of England (1819–1901), 646,
  647, 735
Vienna, 507, 509
  Congress of (1814), 654–56, 655, 660, 661,
    693
  as intellectual and cultural center, 715
  and Revolutions of 1848, 699, 700, 700
Viet Cong, 960, 962
Vietnam, 744
Vietnam, Democratic Republic of (North
  Vietnam), 934, 960
Vietnam, Republic of (South Vietnam), 934,
  960
Vietnam War (1964–1975), 960–61, 961, 964
  antiwar movement and, 960–61, 964
  Tet offensive in, 962
Vietnam War, first (1946–1954), 934–36
View of London with Saint Paul's Cathedral in the
  Distance (Crome), 640
View of the Inside of a House in the Island of
  Ulietea, 563
View of Toledo (El Greco), 484
Vikings, 241–43, 242, 248–50, 249, 253, 255,
  263, 269, 333, 336–37, 415
villages:
  agricultural surpluses and, 7, 8
  emergence of, 4, 7
  handcrafts and, 8
  pottery and, 7
  religion and, 8
  social stratification and, 8
  trade and, 8
  and transition to sedentary communities, 8
  see also cities
Villa of the Mysteries, 159
Vindication of the Rights of Woman, A
  (Wollstonecraft), 567, 590
Vinland, 333, 336–37
Virgil (70–19 B.C.E.), 140, 146, 169, 205, 308,
  340, 366, 366, 402
Virginia, 467
  slave rebellion in, 665
  tobacco plantations in, 477
Virginia Company, 455
Virgin of the Rocks, The (Leonardo), 396, 397
Visigoths, 201, 213, 224, 228, 232
Vitruvius (fl. c. 60–15 B.C.E.), 401
Vladimir, prince of Kiev, 270
Vladivostok, 716
Voice of the People, Voice of God (Grosz), 868
Volkswagen, 923, 950, 965
Voltaire (1694–1778), 539, 541–42, 547–48,
  551, 553–54, 553, 556, 559, 571, 584–85
Von Holst, Theodore, 679
Vonnegut, Kurt (1922–2007), 912, 940
von Ribbentrop, Joachim (1893–1946), 874
Vulgate Bible, 203, 446, 446

Wagner, Otto (1841–1918), 864
Wagner, Richard (1813–1883), 315
Wagram, battle of (1809), 608

casualties in, 800, 806, 807, 812, *827*, 829, 832, 838
causes of, 725, 800–803
"cult of the offensive" in, 811
decline of democracy after, 838
domestic conflicts during, 816–17
Eastern Front in, 806
economic upheaval in, 817–22, *822*, 834
German surrender in, 828
home front in, 817–22
legacy of, 800, 832–34, 871
"lost generation" of, 832, 863
nationalism after, 835, 837–38
from 1914–1916, *814*
from 1917–1918, *815*
peace treaties after, 829–31
propaganda in, 808–9, *808*, *809*, 819
Russian military failures in, 806, 824–26
Russian surrender in, 826
Schlieffen Plan in, 803, 806, *806*
science and technology after, 864–65
Second World War compared with, 874
stalemate in, 807, 810, 813
strikes in, 822
submarine warfare in, 807, 810, *810*, 821, 828
territorial changes after, *833*
as total war, 817, 828–29
treaties following, 840
trench warfare in, 806, 810–13
U.S. entry into, 807, 828
as war of empires, 829
weapons introduced in, 810–13, *810*, *811*, 812–13, 828–29, *828*
Western Front in, 803–6, 807, 810–13, *812*
women and, 707, 817–18, *819*, 820, 821
World War, Second (1939–1945), 759, 800, 846, 872–909, 911–12
aerial warfare in, 874, 881–83, 903, 908
Allied blockade in, 875
anti-communism and, 878, 888, 890
appeasement policy before, 876–78
atomic bomb in, 874, 903, *905*, 906–7, 908
atrocities against civilians in, 1008
Blitzkrieg warfare in, 874, 881, 904
casualties in, 909
causes of, 873–76
culture and thought after, 937–42
D-Day invasion in, 904, *904*
Dunkirk evacuation in, 882
Eastern Front in, 887–88, 890, 903–4, *905*
end of, 905–8
in Europe, *884*
European integration after, 1008

fall of France in, 881–83
First World War compared with, 874
First World War peace settlement and, 874, 876–78
as global war, 883–87
Holocaust in, *see* Holocaust
home front in, 903
imperialism and, 909
legacy of, 908, 909, 911–12, *913*, 937–42, 947–48
Lend-Lease program in, 883
mass culture after, 951–52
Middle East in aftermath of, 929–31
nationalism and, 873, 876
onset of, 881–83
Pacific Theater of, 883, *886*, 908
Pearl Harbor attack in, 885–86, *885*
phony war in, 882
prisoners of war in, *904*
psychological cost of, 940–42
as racial war, 887, 888, 890–902, *895*, *900*
resistance movements in, 890, 901, 903, 909
submarine warfare in, 885
as total war, 902–3
Western Front in, 904–5
women in, 902, *902*
Worms:
Concordat of (VOHRMS) (1122), 268
Diet of (1521), 430–32
Wretched of the Earth, The (Fanon), 938, 939
Wright, Frank Lloyd (1867–1959), 864
writing, 73
Carolingian, 240, *240*
cuneiform, 10, *10*, 41, 48
demotic, 27
Egyptian, 25–28, *27*
hieratic, 27, *27*
hieroglyphic, 27–28, *27*
Islamic, 226, *226*
of Levites, 70
Linear A, 50
Linear B, 50, *51*, 52, 76
Minoan, 50, 52
of numerals, 276, 278
origins of, 9–10
Phoenician, 55, *56*
as political tool, 18, 22
see also alphabets
WTO (World Trade Organization), 983, 990
Württemburg, 656, 711
Würzburg, witch hunts in, 481
Wyclif, John (c. 1330–1384), 357, 383–84, *385*, 426

Xavier, Saint Francis (1506–1552), 448
Xenophanes of Colophon, 92–93
Xenophon (430–354 B.C.E.), 80, 111, *113*, 114, 115, 119, 148
Xerxes I, king of Persia (486–465 B.C.E.), 66, 95–96, *96*, 97
Ximenez de Cisneros, Cardinal Francisco (1436–1517), 445

Yad Vashem (Holocaust archive), 899
Yahweh, 58, 69–73, 182
cult of, 58–59, 69, 71
Yalta Conference (1944), 912
Yeltsin, Boris (1931–), 972–73
Yersinia pestis, 353
Yes and No (Abelard), 309–11
York Castle, *260*
Yorktown, battle of (1781), 577
Young Italy, 701
Young Turks, 786
youth culture, 951–52
Ypres, battles of (1915, 1917), 810, *811*, 812, *813*
Yugoslavia, 815, 827, 831, 849, 876, 887, 890, 902, 904, 909, 915, 948, 964, 972, 974–75, 1008
civil war in former republics of, 974–78
communists ousted in, 972

Zaire (Congo), 730, 745–47, 933, 993–94
Zama, battle of, 155
Zambia, 746
Zara, Fourth Crusade and, 297
Zarathustra (Zoroaster) (c. 628–c. 551 B.C.E.), 66–67
Zawahiri, Ayman al-, 1004
Zealots, 182
Zeno, Roman emperor (474–91), 201
Zeno of Citium (c. 335–c. 263 B.C.E.), 133
Zetkin, Clara (1857–1933), 771
Zeus, 52, 124, 139, *140*, 152
Zhirinovsky, Vladimir, 973
ziggurats, *17*, 18
Zimbabwe (Rhodesia), 746–47, *746*, 933
Zimmerman, Arthur (1864–1940), 828
Zionism, 776–78, 832
Balfour Declaration and, 816, 929–31
Zola, Émile (1840–1902), 767, 775
Zollverein (customs union), 694
Zoroastrianism, 40, 66–69, 73, 134, 180, 192, 211
Zürich, 435
Zwingli, Ulrich (1484–1531), 435
Zwinglianism, 435